REFRAMING RHETORICAL HISTORY

REFRAMING RHETORICAL HISTORY

Cases,
Theories,
and
Methodologies

EDITED BY

Kathleen J. Turner

and

Jason Edward Black

THE UNIVERSITY OF ALABAMA PRESS
TUSCALOOSA

The University of Alabama Press
Tuscaloosa, Alabama 35487-0380
uapress.ua.edu

Typeface: Scala Pro / Scala Sans Pro

Cover design: David Nees

Cataloging-in-Publication data is available from the Library of Congress.
ISBN: 978-0-8173-6050-4
E-ISBN: 978-0-8173-9359-5

Dedicated with deep love and appreciation
to Jennifer Berg Black and Raymond Sprague

Contents

Preface

Kathleen J. Turner

More than two decades ago, the University of Alabama Press published *Doing Rhetorical History* following a productive conference in 1995 on "Rhetoric, History, and Critical Interpretation: The Recovery of the Historical-Critical Praxis" at the Greenspun School of Communication at the University of Nevada–Las Vegas. To our surprise and delight, the volume has come to be a staple in many graduate programs, inspired a range of insightful research, and garnered an entry in the *International Encyclopedia of Communication*. We are heartened by how many scholars, both emerging and veteran, embraced what I called "the challenge and the promise" of rhetorical history, offering "an understanding of rhetoric as a process rather than simply as a product."[1] Studies since that time have ranged from sex and education to South African reconciliation, from queering rhetorical history to Barack Obama, from photos of rural poverty to American Indian activism.[2] Rhetorical scholars have indeed worked to counter the observation that "history is one of the few resources Americans haven't fully exploited."[3]

On an individual level, the volume introduced me in 2004 to Jason Edward Black, a doctoral student at the time, whose insight, acumen, and exuberance infused me with a sense of wonder. When Dan Waterman of the University of Alabama Press encouraged me to consider a second edition, I knew that Jason would be the perfect partner. Jason, in fact, came up with the idea of making this a second *volume*, leaving the first to stand on its own while adding the voices of new scholars on a range of new topics.

We began the process of the volume before you with a seminar at the National Communication Association (NCA) convention in Salt Lake City in 2018 on the twentieth anniversary of *Doing Rhetorical History*. The seminar attracted a delicious range of scholars, from graduate students to senior faculty. An open call for additional submissions rounded out the entries that are included here in *Reframing Rhetorical History*.

With this second volume, Jason and I hope to continue what Robert Terrill terms the "menacing" quality of the first book, menacing in its challenge to those who consider rhetorical history to be "scholars and the dead" communing in "musty archives" in "a stultifying way that blurs the boundaries between lifeworld and crypt."[4] The vibrancy, vitality, and vividness of these sixteen essays indeed menace such stodgy stereotypes. May you enjoy reading them as much as we have enjoyed working with these fine scholars.

Notes

1. Kathleen J. Turner, "Introduction: Rhetorical History as Social Construction," in Turner, *Doing Rhetorical History*, 13, 2.

2. Robin E. Jensen, "Sexual Polysemy: The Discursive Ground of Talk about Sex and Education in U.S. History," *Communication, Culture and Critique* 1, no. 4 (December 2008): 396–415, https://doi.org/10.1111/j.1753–9137.2008.00032.x; Erik Doxtader, "Making Rhetorical History in a Time of Transition: The Occasion, Constitution, and Representation of South African Reconciliation," *Rhetoric & Public Affairs* 4, no. 2 (2001): 223–60; Charles E. Morris III, "Context's Critic, Invisible Traditions, and Queering Rhetorical History," *Quarterly Journal of Speech* 101, no. 1 (2015): 225–43, https://doi.org/10.1080/00335630.2015.995926; John M. Murphy, "Barack Obama and Rhetorical History," *Quarterly Journal of Speech* 101, no. 1 (2015): 213–24, https://doi.org/10.1080/00335630.2015 .995927; Cara A. Finnegan, "What Is This a Picture Of? Some Thoughts on Images and Archives." *Rhetoric & Public Affairs* 9 no. 1 (2006): 116–23; John Sanchez and Mary E. Stuckey, "The Rhetoric of American Indian Activism in the 1960s and 1970s," *Communication Quarterly*, 48, no. 2 (2000): 120–36, https://doi.org /10.1080/01463370009385586.

3. Edward Connery Lathem, ed., *Bernard Bailyn on the Teaching and Writing of History* (Hanover, NH: University Press of New England, 1994), 12, cited in Turner, "Introduction," 15.

4. Robert E. Terrill, "Ways of Rhetorical History," *Review of Communication* 3, no. 3 (July 2003): 298.

Acknowledgments

We remain grateful to the authors included in the first volume. Their lucidity, creativity, and eloquence have inspired scholars for more than two decades. That inspiration will continue for decades to come.

Kudos to the University of Alabama Press for patiently waiting for the germ of an idea for this volume to come to fruition. We are all grateful to the two anonymous readers who gave the project its initial thumbs-up despite the burdens of COVID; to the press's board for its enthusiastic endorsement; to Dan Waterman, who has proven to be a patient, meticulous, conscientious, and wonderfully understanding editor; to Joanna Jacobs, who shepherded the project through production; and to Susan Harris, whose eagle-eyed copyediting saved us from many a potential embarrassment.

Shawn J. Parry-Giles and J. Michael Hogan thank the archivists at the Kansas Historical Society in Topeka, Kansas.

Christopher J. Oldenburg and Adrienne E. Hacker Daniels offer sincere gratitude to Marc Daniels, founder of the Weed Out Hate Initiative, who, in the course of his world travels, edified them on the history of King's 1964 visit to East Berlin and the contemporaneous King-Code project.

Madison A. Krall is grateful to her peers in Robin E. Jensen's Rhetoric of Science graduate seminar and to attendees of the 2019 Rhetoric Society of America (RSA) Institute "Medical Rhetoric in the Archives" seminar for their helpful feedback concerning the development of this chapter. This project was also made possible thanks to archival assistance from Jeffrey Flannery at the Library of Congress and the financial support granted by an RSA Institute Graduate Development Award.

Roseann M. Mandziuk expresses gratitude for the generous insights into earlier version of this chapter from colleagues at the 2018 International Society for the Study of Argumentation Conference and from the participants in the Returning to Rhetorical History Seminar at the 2018 NCA convention.

Daniel P. Overton thanks Dave Tell for his early encouragement of this project.

Margaret Franz expresses gratitude to the participants in the NCA seminar on Returning to Rhetorical History, and to Chris Lundberg, Kumi Silva, Eric King Watts, and Tim Barouch, whose guidance helped polish this chapter.

Andrew D. Barnes thanks Eric Fife in the School of Communication at James Madison University for allocating resources to attend the NCA seminar on Returning to Rhetorical History and for several research trips to the John F. Kennedy Presidential Library and Museum. Conversations with Nicole R. Barnes sharpened the argument, and Stephen J. Heidt helped to clarify his reading of National Security Archives.

Christina L. Moss thanks her research assistant, Catherine Eakin, for her help with this project.

Finally, each and every one of us thanks the spouses, partners, significant others, children, friends, pets, and associates who have lived through this process with us. We are overjoyed with this continuation of a grand rhetorical history!

Introduction

The *Doing* and *Reframing* of Rhetorical History

Jason Edward Black

In the foundational 1998 edited volume *Doing Rhetorical History: Concepts and Cases* (also published by the University of Alabama Press), Kathleen J. Turner characterizes rhetorical history as akin to assembling a jigsaw puzzle, with three distinct challenges: there is no picture on the box top, the puzzle does not have a discrete number of pieces that can be used to complete the picture in any intended way, and the pieces themselves are "rather more amoebas, changing shape and significance depending on the context in which they are placed."[1] Many of the complications related to performing such scholarship speaks to the ways that rhetoric, particularly the body of discourse deemed *history* and the discursive study of such considered *historical*, is a "process rather than simply a product."[2] Questions about how to approach rhetorical history through cases, theories, and methodologies—an enterprise that is at once protean and plural, yet also situated and systematic—became the imprimatur of *Doing Rhetorical History* at the dawn of rhetorical study in the twenty-first century.

Over twenty years later, the puzzles actuated in *Doing Rhetorical History* remain. During the two intervening decades, developments in historical research, engaged scholarship, academic interventionism, topical diversity and inclusivity, interdisciplinary theories, multidisciplinary methods, and cultural practices have kindled familiar questions about the process and purpose of rhetorical history and have generated new inquiries into the efficacy and ends of such study. As we continue moving deeper into the century, now in its third decade, and as the role of rhetorical sensibility and sensitivity intensifies in and among our many publics—especially in the service of understanding our society's complicated sociopolitical pasts and presents—the mysteries of rhetorical history abound. Rejecting the "images of musty archives where scholars and the dead commune in a stultifying way that blurs the boundaries between lifeworld and crypt," this scholarship continues to promise "richly researched and nuanced" analyses.[3] As a result of these academic and public changes, *Reframing Rhetorical History: Cases, Theories, and Methodologies* presents new and innovative scholarship that reassesses both *history as rhetoric* and *rhetorical history* as practice.

The Thoroughfares of Rhetorical History

There is a long and complex *history* to rhetorical history in the field, but there remains neither space nor bandwidth here to mark all of the milestones with any sense of comprehensive justice. *Historians* of rhetorical history have offered us some richly detailed and poignantly insightful narratives of the past one hundred years in rhetorical history.[4] But there are some moments within rhetorical history's past that ought to be mentioned, if only briefly.

To begin, we know in our field that rhetorical history originated within a tradition of platform oratory, discovering through Aristotelian "available means of persuasion" the aims and tactics, motives and effects, and purposes and legacies of mostly canonical speeches of white male leadership. These speeches were examined in situated context, with rhetorical biography and thick, historical detail driving the bulk of study. Early on in the field, nearly at the twentieth century's halfway point, Ernest Wrage expanded what this study of rhetoric could do and could be. In his foundational 1947 essay, "Public Address: A Study in Social and Intellectual History," Wrage suggests both that ideas, perhaps what we later deemed "ideologies," could be discovered through textual analysis in context and that the discourse itself could influence those ideas and ideologies. He wrote then that "social and intellectual history" was "an index to the history of man's [sic] values and goals, his hopes and fears, his aspirations and negations."[5] With Wrage's early take—combined with Edwin Black's watershed tome on rhetorical criticism as a burgeoning method accounting for changes in US sociopolitical culture, Karlyn Kohrs Campbell's critically provocative work on expanding what discourse can be and how the role of the rhetorician-as-social-actor could function, and the ascension of social movement studies necessitated by "the rhetoric of the streets" of 1960s and 1970s America—the field of rhetorical history began to turn.[6]

The scope of rhetorical history widened as the on-the-ground politics of US communities demanded a shift in discourse's role from merely describing texts in their neat and discrete universes to actually unveiling and challenging power through both vivifying resistive voices and sanctioning intervention by critics as rhetors in and of themselves.[7]

The canon, while still existent, was complemented more and more by diverse (albeit additive) studies of marginalized and colonial histories and activist responses and decoloniality; different discursive forms beyond platform oratory, too, found their way into the field. According to Shawn Parry-Giles and J. Michael Hogan, the field began to diversify in topic, method, and approach. They argue, "Studies in public address now encompass a broader range of voices and a greater variety of written and mass mediated texts, including advertisements, autobiographies, cartoons, films, manifestoes, memorials, photographs, television and print news. . . . In addition, public address scholars have embraced a variety of new critical vocabularies and methodologies, ranging from genre and social movement studies to an 'ideological turn' emphasizing issues of race, gender, sexuality, and class. . . . In search of 'lessons of history' relevant to today's political issues, these scholars find important parallels between the past and the present."[8]

To be sure, the link between past and present ultimately punctuates this volume and has goaded over time the study and practice of rhetorical history. Moreover, we know, too, that rhetorical history veers slightly away from rhetorical criticism and public address studies, which typically engage intrinsic analyses of rhetorical artifact or practice within larger contexts of ideas, ideologies, and sociopolitical landscapes. In *Doing Rhetorical History*, Turner asserts that "broadly speaking, whereas rhetorical criticism seeks to understand the message in context, rhetorical history seeks to understand the context through the messages that reflect and construct that context."[9] Rhetorical history thus flips the balance of text/context to help elucidate grander senses of cultural terrain and ideological geography, all while centering rhetorical text itself. Such a process harkens to what Stephen Lucas calls "textual context." He notes that "once one begins to attend to linguistic context, the lines between text and context, between intrinsic and extrinsic analysis, begin to blur. But there is yet another kind of context—textual context—which obliterates those lines altogether."[10]

The intricacies of this relationship in rhetorical studies served as a key focus for two journals' special issues—one in 1990 edited by John Angus Campbell for the *Western Journal of Communication* and the other edited by Charles E. Morris III and Jeffrey Allen Bennett in 2016 for the *Review of Communication*—dedicated, in part, to the intricacies of this relationship in rhetorical studies.[11]

It does seem that scholars of rhetorical history can agree on one concept: that the constructivism of history is a living, constitutive, and contestable matrix of meaning within evolving zeitgeists; its processual nature proscribes singular understandings and solitary textual products. For as Turner concludes in her 1998 introduction, "rhetorical history as social construction includes both the ways in which rhetorical processes have constructed social reality at particular times and in particular contexts and the nature of the study of history as an essentially rhetorical process."[12]

Given the practice-as-process riff, it is unsurprising that rhetorical history is not yet finished nor will it ever be as a sociopolitical force in the world or in terms of academic study. It commands cultural expansion, and we in the field demand that it do so and do so with responsible aplomb, reflexive genuineness, and unbridled collaboration dedicated to justice—not merely diversities and pluralities of topic, approach, and politic. We do have to be careful with the notion of expansion. As Matthew deTar argues in the present volume, "as scholars in rhetorical studies explore difference, race, non-Western cases, and transnational movements, it is imperative to be critical of the form this expansion takes, since expansion . . . is now nearly synonymous with colonialism." Indeed, rhetorical history ought not continue the "additive" forms of addressing voices outside the canon; such voices are, rather, *inside* the heart of contemporary cultures and deserve not just respect and understanding but also revered agency. Thus, rather than seeking additive changes to rhetorical history—those changes that would contribute to colonial ownership and saviorship—the practice needs to take on *transformative* power. We have seen transformative politics gaining strength in the larger rhetorical studies field. Such scholars as Sara Baugh-Harris, Bernadette Marie Calafell, Karma R. Chavez, Lisa Corrigan, Jessica Enoch, Lisa Flores, Martin Law, Ersula Ore, Darrel Wanzer-Serrano, Karrieann Soto Vega, Eric King Watts, and many, many worthy others have moved histories of rhetoric into productive spaces of justice. Readers would be wise to access the *Quarterly Journal of Speech*'s 2019 special section on #RhetoricSoWhite and the 2018 special section of *Communication and Critical/Cultural Studies* on "Race and Rhetoric" for inspiration.[13]

In the end, the past twenty years of rhetorical history scholarship have stretched and improved our understanding of rhetorical study thanks to dedicated innovation on the part of those in the field. One such early innovator, Karlyn Kohrs Campbell, reminds us of the deliciousness—for better or bitter—of the rhetorical history enterprise. She writes that there are no particular "methods other than the recurring patterns that inhere in and constitute our language . . . and cohere into complex symbolic works that amaze, delight, and sometimes horrify us. Our critical task is to possess those riches."[14] *Reframing Rhetorical History* celebrates these riches by spotlighting new directions forward.

Reframing in Focus

Overall, this book attends to a number of subjects that have become not just hot buttons in rhetorical history and in rhetorical scholarship over the past two decades but rather have entrenched themselves as staples, as veritable anchors within the field's continued study of rhetoric and history. Such topics include digital rhetoric, public memory, race and ethnicity, gender dynamics, sexualities (orientation, identity, expression), religion and spirituality, dis/abilities, health and well-being rhetoric, the rhetoric of science and environmentalism, class and regionalism, transnationalism and globalization, partisan politics, social justice and movement cases, scholarly intervention, space and place in rhetorical history, rhetorical field methods, archival methods and archival politics, rhetorical performance, identities and subjectivities, and colonialism and decoloniality.[15] Building from our rhetorical-historical pasts, *Reframing Rhetorical History* is organized into four sections: Digital Humanities and Culture; Identities, Cultures, and Archives; Approaches to Nationalism and Transnationalism; and Metahistories and Pedagogies.

Part I: Digital Humanities and Culture

The first section introduces innovations in methods and cases involving twenty-first century technologies. Goaded by the digital turn beyond traditional uses of the internet, these chapters address the profundity, utility, and limitations of data science, digital archiving, and social media in both gathering rhetorical-historical texts and analyzing them as a method. These cases do not just "add technology and stir" in terms of merely finding traditional rhetoric in untraditional venues. Rather, the chapters activate technology as a rhetorical force, centering digital tools as theoretical craft and critical space.

Joe Edward Hatfield's chapter, "#leelah alcorn: Trans*-ing Rhetorical History in the Digital Humanities Lab," examines the suicide of transgender teenager Leelah Alcorn and the ways users of the social media platform Tumblr circulated Alcorn's suicide letter, which culminated in a large-scale, youth-led digital memorialization effort. Conceptualized as a historical event, Alcorn's suicide and its dissemination as rhetorical invention challenges traditional methodological procedures for doing rhetorical history. Whereas rhetorical historians once prioritized printed texts from the past, the rise of contemporary digital social media culture presses rhetorical historians to consider history as it unfolds in real time and across a range of networked contexts. Toward these ends, Hatfield engages Reaper, a new tool designed to algorithmically facilitate the process of webscraping data from social media platforms. Hatfield's essay shows how in an age of digital humanities, protocols for historical-rhetorical research shift at the levels of method (from humanist to algorithmic) and analysis (from close to distant reading).

In their contribution, "Rhetorical History, the Public Humanities, and the Exoduster Movement," Shawn J. Parry-Giles and J. Michael Hogan argue that rhetoricians' skills in recovering, authenticating, contextualizing, and interpreting artifacts uniquely position them to bring the American democratic experience of the past into the present. They challenge rhetorical historians to step up efforts to digitally archive significant rhetorical artifacts, especially those from historically underrepresented groups. Here, Parry-Giles and Hogan reflect on the place of rhetorical history in the public and digital humanities. By turning to their twenty-year work in national-scale digital humanities projects in the field, they elaborate how rhetorical history enhances the public humanities initiative. They do so by tracing the development of two digital humanities efforts—the Voices of Democracy and Recovering Democracy Archive projects—and by investigating a case study involving the recovery, digitization, and analysis of documents from the Exoduster movement archive. The chapter specifically examines how pro-Exodusters and anti-Exodusters rhetorically navigated their relationship in light of the patterns of racial migration and the politics of free Black sojourners within the last quarter of the nineteenth century.

Next, Christopher J. Oldenburg and Adrienne E. Hacker Daniels incorporate historical, rhetorical, theological, spiritual, and digital lenses to challenge the concepts of "wall politics" in an East Berlin sermon given by the Rev. Martin Luther King Jr. in 1964. Their chapter, "Martin Luther King Jr. in East Berlin: Prophetic History and the Convergence of Codes from the Sermonic to the King-Code," examines the rhetorical history of King's sermon as it functioned to catalyze over half a century of work in Judeo-Christian consubstantiality, reconciliation, and unification. They specifically analyze the diachronic progeny of King's "East Berlin Address," manifested in the form of a contemporaneous intercultural and pedagogical project aptly titled the King-Code. The King-Code is a multimedia educational program that centers around King's 1964 visit to both sides of the then-divided Berlin. Oldenburg and Daniels unpack the digital efficacy of the King-Code project, particularly how it utilizes QR (quick response) code technology as a present window into the past.

Finally, in "Visually Based Rhetorical History: The *Sola Vidēre* Principle in Christian Nationalist Videos," Philip Perdue explores how the ideology of Christian nationalism recast itself during the culture war years by addressing audiences in the idiom of academic historiography. He shows how this idiom finds expression in matters of visuality and style and how "believing" audiences have come to accept the historical claims of Christian nationalists in large measure because textbooks, educational videos, and commercial products adopt generic markers that "look" like history. Perdue's chapter offers a close rhetorical analysis of a series of digitally animated educational videos called Learn Our History. He argues that the videos simulate the experience of directly eyewitnessing events that resolves interpretive challenges for audiences who believe in a Christian nationalist rendition of American history. Digital technologies here help us understand how unmediated witnessing is central to the visual rhetoric of Christian nationalist historiography.

Part II: Identities, Cultures, and Archives

The second section addresses subject positionality in terms of (mostly) race and gender within the contexts of critical race theory, gendered health rhetoric, race-based public memory, and classism/sectionalism. The unifying connection among these pieces positioned in diversity as a frame is that they explore fresh perspectives of/on archives, maneuvering the archives from dusty, stagnant repositories of power-laden and dominant ideas to living and breathing bodies of resistive agency as well.

In "Doing Rhetorical History with Ralph Ellison: Meta-Archival Meditations on the Present, via the Past," Bryan Crable contends that our thinking of Black writer and activist Ralph Ellison as simply a novelist is far too limiting. Rather, he argues that Ellison made significant contributions to the theorizing, not just dramatizing, of race in America. Crable's chapter therefore illustrates the power of scholarship in rhetorical history in two ways. First, he does so by shifting our methodological gaze from the archival to what he calls the meta-archival, a process of constituting an archive from an already archived collection of materials. Second, he draws upon this meta-archival engagement to reclaim Ellison's body of work, both novels and nonfiction alike, for the critical-rhetorical theorizing of race. Ostensibly, Crable presents Ellison as playing with the past in order to reconceptualize a vital issue of his (and our) present: white supremacy. This contribution engages the methodological implications of the meta-archive and extends our conception of Ellison's effort to connect the rhetorical and historical to specifically challenge rhetorical processes centered on matters of race that maintain American social order.

Moving toward rhetorical histories of science and feminism, Madison A. Krall's "Negotiating Public Scientific Regulatory Controversies: Dr. Frances O. Kelsey's Productive Postponement of Thalidomide in the United States" investigates a relatively unknown pharmacologist credited for saving the United States from the thalidomide catastrophe that had global impact in the late 1950s and early 1960s. Krall revisits the communications between Dr. Frances O. Kelsey and the pharmaceutical company Richardson-Merrell regarding their Federal Drug Administration application for the drug thalidomide. Krall argues that Kelsey's consistent and calculated responses to Richardson-Merrell embodied an epistemological filibuster, demonstrating the productive potential of appeals to scientific (un)certainty that prompted regulatory policy implementation. Extending a new understanding of scientific *controversia*, Krall traces three tactics unique to a rhetorical history involving drug regulation: the situating of scientific proof as primary, the reinforcement of historical regulatory norms, and the prioritization of public safety.

In "'To Wake Up the Latent Powers': The Rhetoric of Henry McNeal Turner and the Legacy of the Israel AME Lyceum," Andre E. Johnson assesses the role and rhetoric of Henry McNeal Turner in the founding and creation of the Israel AME Church Lyceum in the 1860s. Understanding that rhetorical history can also function as a rhetorical project and drawing from "cultural-making rhetorical practices," this chapter moves beyond a rhetorical-historical study of Black leadership alone to instead center the rhetoric of a larger learned Black community in the United States that talked publicly *about* the lyceum. In so doing, Johnson contends that Black lyceum participants not only wanted to display their artistry in public address or debate but also that writers who reported on the lyceum had as their aim a pedagogical function that helped shape their primarily Black audience into informed citizens.

Attending to public memory, Roseann M. Mandziuk's chapter, "Crucial Intersections: Public Memories and/as Rhetorical History," explores how rhetorical history that grounds the materiality of place gets lost in the tumult of time and in the tempests of scholarly study. At the intersection of public memory and rhetoric, she argues, we often forget to explore the historical path through which a monument or memorial entered into the public and came to occupy space in the material landscape. The persistence of Confederate memorials, as well as opposition to them, provides a significant illustration of this missing dimension in our public memory studies. Mandziuk specifically unpacks the rhetoric of the United Daughters of the Confederacy (UDC) for how the group represents a provocative intersection of gender politics, ideology, and rhetorical history that goes far beyond the materiality of any single disputed memorial. She concludes that a "dig" through the archives to understand how the UDC formed, came to prominence, and exerted such public influence is essential to understanding the material presence/absence of these monuments in public memory.

Part III: Approaches to Nationalism and Transnationalism

Reframing Rhetorical History's third section explores ideologies related to US and international cultures. This collection of chapters explores nationalistic fervor and fragility in cases of colonial states, citizenship, legal imperialism, the construction and use of a national hero, ways to examine presidential messages abroad, and remembering and forgetting past mechanisms of control as a paradigm for supporting or resisting (respectively) contemporary ideologies related to nationalism and transnationalism.

In "Decolonizing Rhetorical History," Matthew deTar moves us away from a singular focus on US history and politics and toward global cases, diverse forms of rhetorical practice, and non-Greek traditions of persuasion. Given the increased study of global rhetorical practices, he asks: How does a globalized rhetorical study avoid becoming a simple proliferation of cases? That is, does a globalized rhetorical study involve only the "rhetorical study of historical events" in new places, or must it also revise the methods and concepts of the "rhetorical tradition" used to study these cases? Here, deTar contends that globalized rhetorical study must reimagine the methods of rhetorical history for all cases—including US public address—in a way that can speak diversely (rather than uniformly) about different forms of situated symbolic action. By building on postcolonial scholarship that destabilizes presumptions of canonical, Eurocentric academic paradigms, rhetorical history can mine its own tradition for concepts that destabilize its foundations and presumptions. This chapter focuses specifically on the classical concept of "figure" and focuses on the term "minority" in Turkish political speech, a rhetorical trope that contains both descriptive and figural qualities, to indicate the limits of some formal, Western definitions of individual rhetorical staples such as metonymy.

Drawing on circulation as a concept, Chandra A. Maldonado's "Forgetting or Remembering the Nation? Amnesic Rhetoric and Circulation of the Past" interrogates the connection between the rhetorical values inscribed in the act of preserving the memory of Theodore Roosevelt in commemorative practices and the resurfacing of hegemonic masculinity in contemporary political culture. Through a rhetorical analysis of the

Roosevelt Memorial on Roosevelt Island in Washington, DC, she introduces the concept of circulation as amnesia in order to frame the role of the visitor's experience as a vital aspect of rhetorical agency in the circulation of the manifest-masculinity narrative. This is done not through the material features of the memorial itself but instead through the participation and embodiment of the visitor. In addition to accessing circulation, Maldonado introduces an argument for the critical application of ethnographic participation while studying the diffusion of visual discourse to better articulate how and to what extent commemorative sites/artifacts participate as cogs within overarching networks responsible for the making and movement of memory.

In "The Greatest Hero of the Great War: Alvin C. York as a Rhetorical Construction," Daniel P. Overton examines the narrative of a World War I hero as fashioned by George Pattullo, a writer for the *Saturday Evening Post*. Overton argues that Pattullo crafted his narrative rendering of Alvin York, the hero, as a historical fiction to meet the ideological needs of the *Post*-reading public. In particular, the chapter illustrates how Pattullo's account of York "constrained" two critical components of York's story—the role of other soldiers aiding York and the extent of York's conscientious objection to the First World War—suggesting how this formulation of history advanced "a particular interpretation" for particular ends. A study in rhetorical-historical recovery, Overton's analysis of Pattullo's *Post* article sheds light on the concept of rhetorical liberties, amalgamations of the American Western myth, and the virtues of civil religion and heroic characterology.

Blending nationalism and nativist fervor, Margaret Franz's contribution, "Writing the Sovereign Citizen in Cold War Era Expatriation Law: A Rhetorical History of Yaser Hamdi's Settlement Agreement (2004)," illuminates why birthright citizenship (as declared by the Fourteenth Amendment) has been so controversial and why the interpretation of the amendment has changed so drastically over time. Moreover, it attends to what struggles over birthright citizenship tell us about national belonging and democratic culture. The field of rhetorical history has been dominated by theoretically grounded studies that portray citizenship as an ideal type of civic discourse and as the primary identity of actors in public culture. Yet, this framing deters us from adequately addressing citizenship complications because it scripts the Athenian citizen and republican citizen as necessary for democracy. In doing so, rhetorical historians have tended to see citizenship as a static concept. Viewing citizenship through the lens of social construction, however, helps scholars map how citizenship as a concept has been articulated throughout history in multiple domains of public life, how and why it has changed, and how these changes may have played out in political contexts. Franz explores methodologies for studying citizenship within the social imaginary.

Andrew D. Barnes's contribution, "The Frankfurt Anecdote and Rhetorical History: Toward a Method for Reading National Security Archives," starts with Turner's 1998 claim that the purpose of rhetorical history is understanding "the context through messages that reflect and construct that context."[16] He explores how John F. Kennedy's Frankfurt address problematizes this purpose because the speech lacks a situational antecedent and concomitantly its speech-writing archive offers scant evidence for building a contextual case. As a result of these complications, Barnes expanded research into the national security files at the Kennedy Library and to the Department of State archives in order to recover the text/context relationship of the Frankfurt address. In the process, he developed a method for scholars to pursue presidential addresses on foreign soil when lacking the evidence that typically substantiates claims of significance or grounds an analysis of the relationship between text and context. After recovering and explicating this vital part of Kennedy's corpus, Barnes concludes with a discussion of how reading foreign policy rhetoric as tactical, as opposed to strategic, expands critical interrogation of the text/context relationship with implications for international relations.

Part IV: Metahistories and Pedagogies

This volume's final section, Metahistories and Pedagogies, seeks creative ways to approach the frame of metarhetorical history given what we now know, some two decades following *Doing Rhetorical History*. The first two chapters in this section address *writing about* rhetorical history, and the final chapter addresses *teaching about* rhetorical history. Cases here aim to retrieve lost rhetorical-historical documents, to examine emphases and omissions in an area of rhetorical history, and to work the study of rhetorical history into our contemporary classrooms. Together, these contributions provide a heuristic way of moving the study and teaching of rhetorical history forward.

Lisbeth A. Lipari's contribution, "Reading the Logos in Hebrew: A Provocation for Rethinking through Rhetorical History," evaluates the constituent attributes of evidence and narrative to challenge the ways ancient Greek texts tend to be read as self-contained literature wholly separate from the archaic Mediterranean culture. First, in the case of the pre-Socratics, scholars grapple with complex evidentiary questions: There are simply no surviving intact original texts, and most scholarship on this period depends on renderings by much later philosophers. A second set of questions relate to narrative, particularly issues of periodization, temporal punctuation, and cultural scale. Contrary to the conventional view of the pre-Socratics as "revolutionary," Lipari demonstrates the value of reading the few surviving texts in light of their predecessors in eighth to sixth century BCE Hebrew prophetic texts. Lipari concludes that we need to examine "well-documented forms of cultural exchange that have long characterized the East Mediterranean region"—an approach that uses rhetorical history to infuse an appreciation of cultural dispersion, interconnection, and circulation into our interpretations.

Southern rhetoric is arguably the first established regional context in the rhetorical studies discipline. Christina L. Moss's "A Rhetorical History of Southern Rhetoric" follows the historical evolution of southern oratory and rhetoric, and how it is and is not examined within the domain of rhetorical history. Moss focuses special attention on how definitions attached to southern rhetoric have included and excluded vital aspects of what makes the South *southern*. The consequence of these exclusions is a rhetorical regionalism oddly limited by its own history. Moss resolves this complex regional amnesia of sorts by offering new definitions and perceptions of southern rhetoric, while connecting its relevance to larger pathways of rhetorical histories in the contexts of regionalism, sectionalism, geopolitical identity, and cultural lifeways.

Finally, Sean Patrick O'Rourke and Melody Lehn bring rhetorical history to the contemporary rhetorical studies classroom. Their chapter, "Knowledge, Rhetorical History, and Undergraduate Scholars: Reimagining Liberal Education," suggests that two critical components of rhetorical education, undergraduate research and rhetorical history, have for too long stood apart. Working from the conviction that undergraduate students can conduct original research and make significant contributions to humanities scholarship, they propose a way forward that joins the work of undergraduate scholars, archival research, and rhetorical history. O'Rourke and Lehn offer guideposts to vivifying rhetorical history in our classrooms, such as refining how knowledge occurs when students read and respond to published scholarship and helping students recover archival work that discovers, preserves, and provides general access to lost or corrupted rhetorical texts.

Reframing Rhetorical History

The time is ripe with kairos for a follow-up to *Doing Rhetorical History*, a volume that was in 1998, and continues to be, influential as a text that to date has been cited as a source over three hundred times in books, peer-reviewed articles, book chapters, theses, and dissertations. And, of course, the tome has been a useful fount of rhetorical-historical methodologies for graduate-level courses in rhetorical studies, public address, and contemporary rhetorical theory. It is highly probable that any rhetorician educated during the past twenty years will report that they have read this book and, likely, that it changed their perspective on working within rhetorical studies. We hope that *Reframing Rhetorical History* will add to that legacy.

Much has happened in the two decades since *Doing Rhetorical History* was published in terms of public cultures that draw on historical precedent, digital methodologies, in situ field methods, and historical indexicality, not to mention crucial political, social, and cultural moments that have affected the contexts of rhetorical history. To wit, consider the 2016 election and its critical aftermath, the vibrancy of Black Lives Matters and antiracist activism, the sturdy #MeToo movement, the high-water mark of the *Obergefell v. Hodges* ruling on marriage equality and other safeguards for LGBTQIA rights, growing pro-DACA and new immigration interventions, the uptick of Women's Marches, increased student activism in the wake of mass gun violence, the calls to action of decolonial Indigenous and Latinx campaigns, the ascension of dis/abilities activism, and the strengthening of transgender rights initiatives, to name just a few. Such contemporary cases and terrain require historical anchorage as a prerequisite to contemporary intervention. As Campbell reminds us, "although much remains to be done in studies of language in US culture, our critical work is weakest where our linguistic competence and cultural knowledge are limited."[17] Without question, our field's approaches to said rhetorical history deserve some updating. *Reframing Rhetorical History* aspires to actuate an ethos of innovation, appraisal, and creative design.

Notes

1. Kathleen J. Turner, "Introduction: Rhetorical History as Social Construction," in Turner, *Doing Rhetorical History*, 10.

2. Turner, "Introduction," 2.

3. Robert E. Terrill, "Ways of Rhetorical History," *Review of Communication* 3, no. 3 (2003): 298–99.

4. See Michelle Ballif, "Introduction," in *Theorizing Histories of Rhetoric*, ed. Michelle Ballif (Carbondale: Southern Illinois University Press, 2013), 1–7; Sharon Crowley, "Afterword: A Reminiscence," in *Theorizing Histories of Rhetoric*, 190–98; Martin J. Medhurst, "The History of Public Address as an Academic

Study," in Parry-Giles and Hogan, *Handbook of Rhetoric and Public Address*, 19–66; Shawn Parry-Giles and J. Michael Hogan, "Introduction: The Study of Rhetoric and Public Address" in Parry-Giles and Hogan, *Handbook of Rhetoric and Public Address*, 1–16; David Zarefsky, "Four Senses of Rhetorical History," in Turner, *Doing Rhetorical History*, 19–32.

5. Ernest J. Wrage, "Public Address: A Study in Social and Intellectual History," *Quarterly Journal of Speech* 33, no. 4 (1947): 451.

6. Edwin Black, *Rhetorical Criticism: A Study in Method* (Madison: University of Wisconsin Press, 1965); Karlyn Kohrs Campbell, "'Conventional Wisdom'—'Traditional' Form: A Rejoinder," *Quarterly Journal of Speech* 58, no. 4 (1972): 451–54; Karlyn Kohrs Campbell, "The Rhetoric of Women's Liberation: An Oxymoron," *Quarterly Journal of Speech* 59, no. 1 (1973): 74–86; Robert S. Cathcart, "Movements: Confrontation as Rhetorical Form," *Southern Speech Communication Journal* 43, no. 3 (1978): 233–47; Michael Calvin McGee, "'Social Movement': Phenomenon or Meaning?," *Central States Speech Journal* 31, no. 4 (1980): 233–44; Robert L. Scott and Donald K. Smith, "The Rhetoric of Confrontation," *Quarterly Journal of Speech* 55, no. 1 (1969): 1–8; Malcolm O. Sillars, "Defining Movements Rhetorically: Casting the Widest Net," *Southern Speech Communication Journal* 46, no. 1 (1980): 17–32; and Herbert W. Simons, "Requirements, Problems, and Strategies: A Theory of Persuasion for Social Movements," *Quarterly Journal of Speech* 56, no. 1 (1970): 1–11.

7. Our commitments to justice regarding gender, gender identity, and gender expression lead us to use the plural pronoun throughout this volume.

8. Parry-Giles and Hogan, "Introduction," 3.

9. Turner, "Introduction," 2.

10. Stephen E. Lucas, "The Renaissance of Public Address: Text and Context in Rhetorical Criticism," *Quarterly Journal of Speech* 74, no. 2 (1988): 249.

11. John Angus Campbell, "Special Issue on Rhetorical Criticism," *Western Journal of Communication* 54, no. 3 (1990): 249–376; and Charles E. Morris III and Jeffrey Allen Bennett, eds., "Special Issue: Rhetorical Criticism's Multitudes," *Review of Communication*, 16, no. 1 (2016): 1–107.

12. Turner, "Introduction," 2.

13. Sara Baugh-Harris and Darrel Wanzer-Serrano, "Against Canon: Engaging the Imperative of Race in Rhetoric," *Communication and Critical/Cultural Studies* 15, no. 4 (2018): 337–42; Bernadette Marie Calafell, *Monstrosity, Performance, and Race in Contemporary Culture* (New York: Peter Lang, 2015); Karma R. Chávez, "Beyond Inclusion: Rethinking Rhetoric's Historical Narrative," *Quarterly Journal of Speech* 101, no. 1 (2015): 162–72; Jessica Enoch, "Releasing Hold: Feminist Historiography without the Tradition," in *Theorizing Histories of Rhetoric*, 58–73; Lisa A. Flores, "Between Abundance and Marginalization: The Imperative of Racial Rhetorical Criticism," *Review of Communication* 16, no. 1

(2016): 4–24; Martin Law and Lisa M. Corrigan, "On White-Speak and Gatekeeping: or, What Good Are the Greeks?" *Communication and Critical/Cultural Studies* 15, no. 4 (2018): 326–30; Karrieann Soto Vega and Karma R. Chávez, "Latinx Rhetoric and Intersectionality in Racial Rhetorical Criticism," *Communication and Critical/Cultural Studies* 15, no. 4 (2018): 319–25; Eric King Watts, "'Voice' and 'Voicelessness' in Rhetorical Studies," *Quarterly Journal of Speech* 87, no. 2 (2001): 179–96; Darrel Wanzer-Serrano, "Rhetoric's Race/ist Problems," *Quarterly Journal of Speech* 105, no. 4 (2019): 465–76 and the remainder of this issue's essays; and Matthew Houdek, "The Imperative of Race for Rhetorical Studies: Toward Divesting from Disciplinary and Institutionalized Whiteness—Special Forum on Race and Rhetoric," *Communication and Critical/Cultural Studies* 15, no. 4 (2018): 292–99 and the remainder of this issue's essays.

14. Karlyn Kohrs Campbell, "Rhetorical Criticism 2009: A Study in Method," in Parry-Giles and Hogan, *Handbook of Rhetoric and Public Address*, 101.

15. See Ballif, "Introduction," 1–7, for more contemporary studies in rhetorical history.

16. Turner, "Introduction," 2.

17. Campbell, "Rhetorical Criticism 2009," 91–92.

I

DIGITAL HUMANITIES AND CULTURE

1

#leelah alcorn

Trans*-ing Rhetorical History in the Digital Humanities Lab

Joe Edward Hatfield

I n late December 2014, sometime before stepping in the path of a semitrailer and ending her life at the age of seventeen, Leelah Alcorn queued her suicide letter to posthumously post to her public Tumblr account. In the letter, Alcorn made her identity as a trans woman known to the world and recounted her tumultuous home life, including details of her mother's unwillingness to allow her to undergo gender confirmation therapy and surgery. Alcorn also remembered her forced participation in sessions with, in her words, "christian therapists (who were all very biased)." Alcorn wrote hopelessly of the ordeal, stating, "I never actually got the therapy I needed to cure me of my depression. I only got more christians telling me that I was selfish and wrong and that I should look to God for help." Over two hundred thousand Tumblr users shared the suicide letter across the platform prior to the website removing Alcorn's account at the request of her parents.

Despite the disappearance of the account, Tumblr users continued to circulate the suicide letter and newly produced content in remembrance of Alcorn under such hashtags as #leelah alcorn, #her name was leelah, and others.[1] These efforts culminated in a viral digital memorialization effort across the platform that quickly bled into the broader public sphere. By April 2015, Pres. Barack Obama endorsed calls for legislation banning conversion therapy nationwide, what was then unofficially designated Leelah's Law. The extraordinary circumstances surrounding Alcorn's suicide rose to such a level of prominence that the trailblazing trans historian Susan Stryker judged it worthy of documentation in the second edition of the influential *Transgender History*.[2]

Presently, representations of Alcorn function as palimpsests for remembering the still persistent tragedy of trans youth suicide. Public memories of Alcorn act as synecdochic rhetorics for the triangulated crises of religious conversion therapy, transphobic/homophobic bullying, and anti-LGBTQ attitudes within the US familial sphere. However, the proliferation of Alcorn's memory came at the expense of others who died under similar circumstances but did not capture mainstream public attention in the same way as she did. In the ten-month period following Alcorn's death, at least thirteen more trans teenagers died by suicide across the United States, including Melonie Rose (nineteen years old, died February 11, 2015), Zander Mahaffey (fifteen years old, died February 15, 2015), Ash Haffner (sixteen years old, died February 26, 2015), Sage David (age unconfirmed, died March 2, 2015), Taylor Wells (eighteen years old, died March 15, 2015), Blake Brockington (eighteen years old, died March 23, 2015), Ezra Page (fifteen years old, died March 28, 2015), Taylor Alesana (sixteen years old, died April 2, 2015), Sam Taub (fifteen years old, died April 9, 2015), Cameron Langrell (fifteen years old, died May 1, 2015), Kyler Prescott (fourteen years old, died May 18, 2015), Skylar Marcus Lee (sixteen years old, died September 28, 2015), and Emmett Castle (fourteen years old, died October 7, 2015).[3]

Continued coverage of the circumstances surrounding Alcorn's death largely overshadowed the deaths of the individuals just named, even though many aspects of their suicides paralleled those of Alcorn's. Mahaffey, for example, also scheduled a letter to post to his public Tumblr account after his suicide in Austell, Georgia. Similarly, Brockington expressed his despair on Tumblr prior to walking into incoming traffic. Wells, too, was a frequent Tumblr user. And, like Alcorn, Rose's family chose to memorialize her with the name they assigned to her at birth, as well as to bury her in masculine attire, despite her objections to both during her lifetime. But perhaps because Alcorn died first—and no doubt due to her identity as a white, middle-class, trans woman—she became a more palatable token of visibility for the causes and effects of trans suicide. As some commentators have remarked, Alcorn's transformation into a celebrity supported the continued erasure of a large number of trans people of color who die regularly and violently at disproportionate rates in the United States. Evan Mitchell Schares suggests that public performances of white grief buttressed Alcorn's memory, while perpetuating Black and brown queer and trans lives as ungrievable.[4]

In this chapter, I conceptualize the network of remembrance constellated by #leelah alcorn as an event in rhetorical history, with focused attention directed toward the racialized, gendered, and classed ghosts caught in its vertices. This performance of rhetorical historiography follows C. Riley Snorton and Jin Haritaworn's interrogation of what they name a "transnormative subject," whose mainstream recognition in public culture conceals a convergence and complicity with racist politics and norms of visibility.[5] I heed Charles E. Morris III's career-long insistence that rhetorical scholars do more to uncover the underlying, sometimes submerged, or purposefully excised "invisible contexts" that queerly constitute dominant readings of rhetoric and public address.[6] My investigation is necessarily hauntological, as I dwell with the absences that make #leelah alcorn possible in an earnest effort to realize Lisa Flores's call for a more robust "racial rhetorical criticism."[7] Consequently, I denaturalize Alcorn's status as a trans icon by showing how her visibility pulls attention away from the effects of violence and suicide on trans youth who are not identifiably white, feminine presenting, and/or middle to upper class.[8]

Rather than a physical archive, I locate my study within the physical and virtual parameters of the digital humanities (DH) lab, where I experimented with computational software to forward a historical portraiture of Alcorn's suicide that exposed the crucial invisibilities made captive by its unfolding on Tumblr from 2014 to 2018. In an era marked by an increasingly digital culture, scholars allied with the humanities have begun utilizing digital methods to conduct historical research and build multimedia histories. These DH practitioners are, to quote Anne Burdick and colleagues, animated by "the conviction that computational tools have the potential to transform the content, scope, methodologies, and audience of humanistic inquiry."[9] Indeed, the emergent encounter between DH and rhetorical studies has already started to alter the methodological trajectory of rhetorical history. For instance, Jessica Enoch and David Gold explain how rhetorical historians have combined their unique analytics with digital tools and methods to build original, interactive, and highly visual projects that present rhetorical history in digital modes, overcoming some of the limitations of traditional print scholarship.[10] In recognizing the data comprising #leelah alcorn as historical rhetoric, I seek to further extend rhetorical history, advocating on behalf of its potential as a methodology for extracting, collecting, recontextualizing, and preserving historically significant data from digital platforms.

Treating #leelah alcorn as historical rhetoric thus offers rhetorical historians a renewed understanding of rhetorical history in a conjunctural moment marked by the persistent rise of digital rhetorical forms and the interrelated decline of the logics of print literacy that have undergirded humanistic disciplines like rhetorical studies for centuries. Emphasizing the constant state of transition of rhetorical analytics, corresponding to their shifting technological and cultural contexts of possibility, I advance a metamethodological thesis on the *trans-ness* of rhetorical history. By *trans-*, I do not mean a stable category of human identity, although trans people certainly provide the crucial frame of reference from which to derive any de-essentialized sense of the prefix. The hyphenated trans-, in the words of Susan Stryker, Paisley Currah, and Lisa Jean Moore, "remains open-ended and resists premature foreclosure by attachment to any single suffix." [11] Trans-, in this sense, functions as a verb—as in *trans-ing*—a queer move across seemingly fixed binaries, bodies, and borders. Stryker's capacious definition of *transgender* captures the art of trans-ing as "the movement across a socially imposed boundary away from an unchosen starting place, rather than any particular destination or mode of transition."[12] Trans-ing names the existential phenomenon of boundary transgression set to the temporal rhythm of the future. I adopt this usage of trans-ing to describe the adaptive ethos of a rhetorical history that embraces its indeterminability and its capacity to at any moment undo established, normative figurations of the rhetorical historian.

In the DH lab, rhetorical history is not characterized by closure; rather, it is revealed as open-ended and replete with possibility. With each new technological update, more opportunities for methodological experimentation come to fruition, opening up possibilities for rhetorical historians to improvise with emergent digital modalities in their research. In this way, rhetorical history is quite transitory, as it constantly changes and threatens to unsettle the ontological security of established modes of scholarly identity. Put differently, when considered in relation to its technological conditions of possibility, rhetorical history is undergirded by its irreducible *trans*-ness*. As Marquis Bey writes on the particularity of the prefix, "trans* is elsewhere, not here, because here is known, ontologically discernable and circumscribable."[13] Like Bey, I prefer the asterisk in trans* due to its star-like shape, reminding us that "the beginning was, in fact, trans*—because in the beginning stars floating without laws set into motion that originary trans*-ness, the fundamental openness of our world."[14] For the duration of this chapter, I implicate myself within the trans* futurity of rhetorical history by modeling one way in which the convergence of digital media technologies and rhetorical historical methodology carves out pathways for addressing new forms and exigencies wrought by the unfurling digital epoch. I aim to demonstrate that rhetorical history can, should, and will transform in tandem with the flows of technological and cultural change, and that rhetorical historians can help determine the future of rhetorical history by experimenting with computational methods of research in the context of the DH lab.

Digital Archival Queer

Rhetorical scholars have long recognized the historical qualities of their research and have consistently used the designator "rhetorical history" as a point from which to rethink relations between methodology and scholarly identity in rhetorical studies. After the Wingspread and Pheasant Run conferences of 1970, a new generation of rhetorical scholars began expanding the object domain of rhetoric. In so doing, they effectively ended the routinized neo-Aristotelian analysis of historically significant speeches made by "great" (i.e., dead, white, and once powerful) men by shifting their criticisms toward the broader symbolic terrain of social movements, mass media, and public culture. In a 1981 *Quarterly Journal of Speech* article, Stephen E. Lucas observes a growing "schism" in rhetorical studies with critics of the "new rhetoric" positioned on one side and traditional rhetorical historians on the other.[15] Lucas points out the flawed arbitrariness of the history/criticism divide, arguing that actually all rhetorical criticism was history, since all criticism was a reflection on past events, and that all rhetorical history was criticism involving the subjective evaluation of evidence.[16] Later recounting the development of this schism, David Zarefsky conceded Lucas's point, noting, "For the most part, the distinctions among history, criticism, and theory in rhetorical studies are unnecessary and without foundation."[17] Zarefsky concluded that strict partitions among history, criticism, and theory ultimately served to territorialize rhetorical studies in self-defeating ways.

Yet, even in the years since the publication of Zarefsky's chapter in *Doing Rhetorical History*, certain distinguishing stereotypes remain attached to rhetorical history as a methodology. In a review of the collection, Robert E. Terrill puts it this way: "The book offers little comfort to those for whom 'rhetorical history' conjures images of musty archives where scholars and the dead commune in a stultifying way that blurs the boundaries between lifeworld and the crypt."[18] Terrill astutely observes the synonymous relationship rhetorical history shares with archival research, which still remains largely intact. Within the first quarter of the twenty-first century, Terrill's ironic characterization of rhetorical history as a stultifying dance with the dead would quickly become the topic of a field-wide fever, launching a robust metamethodological conversation on the literal *doing* of rhetorical history that some like myself contend *Doing Rhetorical History* aided in kick-starting. Today, two decades after the publication of the collection, methodological dialogues on rhetorical history and archives continue to captivate the minds of established and emerging rhetorical scholars alike.

Across several journal articles, edited collections, and monographs, rhetorical scholars have thought deeply about the rhetoric and politics of archives and have invented socially engaged rhetorical methodologies designed to facilitate the archival research process.[19] Of particular relevance to the context of #leelah alcorn is Morris's figuration of the "archival queer," a rhetorical historian who recognizes that "a significant portion of that [LGBTQ] history is housed in straight archives and circulated in straight collections" and who responds by seeking out these materials and crafting rhetorical historiographies that recontextualize their queerness using inventive reading strategies attuned toward absences, slippages, inuendoes, and other rhetorical forms many might discount as mere happenstance.[20] Archival queers are also driven by an impending sense of urgency. They know all too well that queer materials are vulnerable, subject to redaction, and prone to vanishing under the rule of institutions that mobilize the certainly nonobjective ideology of objectivity to render them too inconsequential or distasteful to be worthy of preservation.

On December 3, 2018, nearly four years after Alcorn's suicide, Tumblr officials announced their intention to ban pornography from their platform after child pornography appeared on the website. Beginning December 17, 2018, algorithms would remove existing pornographic content from the platform, simultaneously banishing entire communities built around the sharing of sexually explicit still images, GIFs, and videos. Upon learning this news, I was immediately reminded of Alessandra Mondin's study of communities who forged kinship networks by circulating feminist, queer, and BDSM pornography on Tumblr.[21] Jacob Engelberg and Gary Needham aver that the communal curation and sharing of sexually explicit images and video on Tumblr constituted the website as a connective hub for a large number of networked queer archives. As they elegantly describe such activity, "the labour involved in organizing and curating Tumblr's queer porn microblogs, which often took place over several years and with daily updates, must also be understood as a type of queer archival practice. . . . Archiving as practised through Tumblr is queered through mutable, multiple, illegitimate, and non-traditional methods of selection and curation."[22]

Of course, under Tumblr's new rules, many communities formed through sex would no longer be welcome, and I knew some, and I predicted *most*, queer users of the platform would soon lose their accounts and/or major segments of their data in the wake of Tumblr's antiporn crusade. Even before the popularity of digital media technologies, efforts to "clean up" alternative cultural spaces, driven by neoliberal political ideals of privatization, efficiency, and profitability, have historically devastated the queer enclaves that tend to thrive within them. In an imaginative analysis of New York City's Times Square before and after the Times Square Development Project, Samuel R. Delany demonstrates how efforts to expel sex and pornography from the area resulted in the displacement of marginalized communities, particularly queer ones and others considered "deviant," who were able to make a living and survive together in the seedy establishments along Forty-Second Street.[23] Aware of the devastating effects of gentrification on queer and trans networks within urban locales, I was troubled by the possibility that #leelah alcorn, a hashtag I once helped to circulate during my days as an avid Tumblr user not too long ago, could begin disappearing in the aftermath of an algorithmic raid driven by a sex panic.

Although once a relatively obscure hub fueled by the circulation of quirky memes and populated by a primarily teenage/young adult demographic, by the time of its antiporn announcement, Tumblr had become, in the words of Morris, a quintessentially "straight archive."[24] The first major blow to the platform was its billion-dollar acquisition by Yahoo in 2013, which sent cracks through Tumblr's cool, underground facade and caused a large portion of its original users to flee in droves. Around the same time of this exodus, Tumblr fell victim to what *New York Times* editorialist Kara Swisher identifies as many of the problems afflicting the internet presently: "What plagues the internet today hit Tumblr hard and early. There were the inevitable copyright problems and spam and security problems and product problems. And the content itself, which started as edgy, got rather gnarly, from self-harm sites to neo-Nazis to what really tanked Tumblr: sex."[25]

Faced with a child pornography scandal and having been newly purchased by Verizon as part of its nearly $5 billion acquisition of Yahoo, Tumblr officials were ready to discard all of its pornographic content without much regard for the differences between that which united a major segment of its users and the small minority of illegal imagery they had failed to ensure was never uploaded to the platform in the first place. By banning pornography, many commentators predicted Tumblr's ultimate demise, including Nathalie Graham, who recalled that in the wake of the ban, "everyone on my Tumblr dashboard was posting their goodbyes."[26] Logging into my Tumblr account for the first time in at least a year, I, too, sensed the collective adieu, especially with the flood of references to the impending "Tumblr apocalypse" flooding my screen.[27] Through Tumblr, I began to view all digital social media platforms as less like permanent archival environments and more like spaces where ephemeral acts only temporarily materialize in digitized form and often against institutional logics.[28] These acts of transmission— everyday, embodied, transitory, ritualized, vernacular, marginalized, and subterranean—Diana Taylor assigns to the cultural "repertoire," a term signifying unofficial, archiveless, sometimes nonarchivable knowledge forms.[29] As a repertoire of rhetorics on trans suicide hosted on a corporatized social media platform, the fragments connected via #leelah alcorn beckoned to my archival queer sensibility, calling me to save them from deletion.

Late on the night of December 3, 2018, I utilized the webscraping software Reaper to collect just over thirteen thousand individual Tumblr posts circulated within the network #leelah alcorn. Reaper, an open-access software created by developers at the University of Queensland, allows researchers to easily collect data from major social media networks such as Tumblr, Facebook, Instagram, and Reddit. In the case of Tumblr, Reaper requires an API key.[30] The API key authenticates access to Tumblr's public data, as well as the name of an existing blog or hashtag hosted on the platform, which enables the extraction or "scraping" of the data from the site. I knew that #leelah alcorn was the primary hashtag through which memories of Alcorn circulated, and I used this label to collect over thirteen thousand unique tagged posts. Almost instantly, Reaper produced a 55 MB .csv file, which sorted each post into columns of metadata, including the username of its original poster, its URL, all of its hashtags, and links to images contained within the post, among other information. With this dataset, I felt as if I had salvaged something significant. What was required now was a rhetorical historiography that not only examined this repertoire and confirmed its existence in print scholarship but one that also intervened in the immediate context of its production and dissemination by preserving it for future generations of rhetorical scholars and possibly other nonacademic publics. Such a rhetorical history would enact Kathleen J. Turner's observation that history is always a socially constructed rhetoric involving subjective selection of the past by people with varied personal experiences and interests.[31] An archival queer partiality would shape my analysis of the data collection and lay bare the historical importance of #leelah alcorn for trans rhetorical history.

Rhetorical History and the DH Lab

Whereas many digital rhetorical history projects entail the digitization and curation of once nondigital objects, I am invested in (re)archiving historically significant digital data that originated online, particularly that which is stored within digital social media contexts and remains vulnerable to top-down policies of its platform. Moreover, I advocate for a more concerted effort on the part of rhetorical historians to traverse the internet while viewing it as a vast zone of scattered memories documenting both the extraordinary and the mundane rhetorical happenings of everyday life, as well as a repository for creating, uploading, sharing, and hosting this data and preserving it for the future. In the context of internet research, the infusion of DH and rhetorical history transforms the methodology of rhetorical historiography, challenging the rhetorical historian to perform as historical analyst while also acting as data collector and archivist. This digital rhetorical history necessitates a reworking of the field's methodological imagination by shifting what rhetorical historians do and how they do it.

In tandem with the rise in DH scholarship has come a greater interest and investment in labs within the humanities. Amy E. Earhart observes that a growing number of DH practitioners have started appropriating the lab model from the fields of design, art, and, most prominently, the sciences. Labs are spaces where DH practitioners collaborate across disciplines and experiment with the different technologies in the service of research oriented toward the manipulation and modeling of objects traditionally associated with the humanities, such as literary texts or historical documents. Instead of fetishizing the veneer of scientific infrastructures, Earhart warns that DH practitioners should "tailor the existing science laboratory model to meet best practices in the digital humanities."[32] The DH lab offers an opportunity for infusing a unique, ethically informed, humanistic orientation toward historical research with the structures and practices traditionally associated with the sciences. Practitioners can use their bodies to implement this fusion by imagining the DH lab as an everyday practice of space making rather than as a stagnant physical location that merely contains DH research. These efforts should seek to avoid reproducing the pitfalls commonly associated with scientific labs, like their uncritical formation around the myth of objectivity or their frequent lack of diverse representation. For a rhetorical historian such as myself, the DH lab provides a material, metaphorical, virtual, and physical realm of possibility—as well as an interdisciplinary space of collaboration and practice-based hypothesis testing—for performing digital rhetorical historiographies that alter how rhetorical scholars imagine and enact the future of rhetorical history.

Such transformative reimaginings of rhetorical history would do much to destabilize available scholarly identities in rhetorical studies by loosening the lines dividing rhetorical history, criticism, and theory, as well as reconfiguring rhetorical history beyond its textual roots in print culture. In the DH lab, we become historians, critics, theorists, participant-observers, archivists, and algorithmic subjects all at once, oscillating between textual and digital modalities of reading and doing. In this project specifically, I experimented with what early trans and digital studies scholar Sandy Stone calls "prosthetic communication," by considering the various ways humans collaborate with nonhuman beings and technologies to produce knowledge.[33] Stone states that with the intensification of "cyberspace" comes emergent behaviors and the potential for "new social forms that arise in a circumstance in which *body, meet, place,* and even *space* mean something quite different than our accustomed understanding."[34] Rhetorical history transmogrifies within the DH lab. Firm boundaries between humans and nonhumans disintegrate, trans*-ing, as it were, the humanist as the dominant occupiable subject position in historical rhetorical research.

With their capacity to enmesh bodies and technologies, humans and nonhumans, laboratories teem with trans* possibility. In a live performance piece turned academic essay, Stryker draws at times uncomfortable parallels between her "transsexual" body and the lab-produced body of Frankenstein's monster.[35] Stryker declares: "The transsexual body is an unnatural body. It is the product of medical science. It is a technological construction. It is flesh torn apart and sewn together again in a shape other than that in which it was born."[36] Digital rhetorical history shares an affinity with Frankenstein's monster, as it, too, emerges from a lab and, by its design, is engineered in order to animate life beyond its expiration date. Moreover, digital rhetorical history is a "technological construction" or a grotesque amalgamation of bodies, texts, data, technologies, and affects rolled into an assemblage of the past meant to produce effects long after its spatiotemporal point of invention. For Stryker, the link between the trans body and the monster is one to relish as a catalyst for unbridled political rage that dismantles fixed categories, normative foundations, and hegemonic borders—from gender to the very notion of the human itself.

The posthumanist ambience of the DH lab is perhaps no better pronounced than in its capacity to queer the most irrefutably static of human metaphysical categories: life and death. While rhetorical historians have always challenged the life/death threshold by stirring up the past and setting it loose into the present, digital media technologies in the DH lab intensify this aspect of the research process by shoring up ghosts and moving them at viral speeds across a host of digital networks and screens. Digital rhetorical histories crack open historical artifacts like that of #leelah alcorn, enabling its contents to spill out and haunt but never permitting them to settle. Jacques Derrida, Avery Gordon, and several others have ruminated on the politics of hauntology, claiming that how and why one recognizes and responds to ghosts is a resolutely ethical matter.[37] Hauntings also require extrarational and, at times, irrational reading strategies that attend at once to the past and present, looking beyond the empirical and toward the underbelly of the epistemologically or ontologically sensible.

In the DH lab, rhetorical historians can invent digital historical methodologies capable of traversing the incongruous ontology of history, with its slopes and craters, where some objects may never appear as real as others because what they represent vibrates resistantly against the intelligible. I assert that, at its best, the DH lab offers rhetorical historians a chance to dwell with rhetorical history's trans*-ness or what Bey posits as a "para-ontological" force that, like Blackness, is "only tangentially, and ultimately arbitrarily, related to bodies said to be black or transgender."[38] Trans*, a moving intensity and "a besidedness to ontology,"[39] precedes and exceeds the human, the nonhuman animal, and legibility itself; it indexes a lawlessness that "though pointed at by bodies that identify as Black and/or trans*, precede and provide the foundational conditions for those fugitive identificatory demarcations."[40] When digital rhetorical historians consciously move toward trans*-ness in their research, they risk becoming swallowed by the centrifugal pull of the abyss. They venture toward that which lies outside the center yet makes the center form and toward that which is unarchivable by virtue of its situatedness outside of official history. In doing so, digital rhetorical historians also endanger themselves by closing in on objects that by their nature reconstitute the object of study in rhetorical history and, by extension, uproot any firm sense of oneself as a rhetorical historian.

Visualizing the Ghosts of Ecological Rhetorical Agency

To clarify, "the" DH lab does not refer to any single standardized infrastructure. Rather, as I have referenced it so far, the DH lab encapsulates a full range of practices enacted by scholars invested in better understanding what digital tools and methods can do in the service of existing humanistic research protocols or how they might even transform humanistic inquiry beyond its textual roots in print culture. The DH lab, like DH itself, is in process, always ongoing and undergoing a series of constant changes corresponding to a broader and rapidly changing cultural and technological context. Given that every DH project is unique, and requires different perspectives and techniques, there must be at least as many DH labs as there are DH projects. To be perfectly clear, then, what I am *not* outlining for the rest of this chapter is a prescriptive method that other scholars may simply duplicate in their own research, as part of what I think makes a DH lab a *humanities* lab is the embodied positionalities of the researchers who constitute it through their partial analytic perspectives.[41] Henceforth, I provide a brief glimpse into my own process of inventing a digital rhetorical history of #leelah alcorn so as to reveal what else rhetorical history can be and do through its encounter with digital media technologies. The DH lab I constructed to facilitate the scraping, visualization, and preservation of #leelah alcorn materializes as a result of a specific set of concerns, both political and theoretical, reflecting my position as an archival queer whose rhetorical historiography is oriented toward the oft taken-for-granted illegibility of trans*. It is also one informed by what Lisa Blackman names "data hauntology," as it recognizes from the outset that data conceals as much as it reveals, and it accordingly orients toward both presences *and* absences.[42] As I have suggested elsewhere, such exigencies as the one produced by the suicide of Leelah Alcorn circulate as sensations, becoming sensationalized and then constituting rhetorical ecologies made up of bodies, technologies, texts, and other modalities of rhetorical and affective transmission.[43] Viral sensations of exigence can extend a kairotic moment beyond its spatiotemporal point of emergence and assemble bodies into networks oriented toward queer world making; however, these collective efforts run the risk of an intense sensationalism that can make absent—or better yet, *ghostly*—those exigencies that become submerged within its orbit. Hence, I designed my lab as a space to pursue these ghosts, particularly those marginalized due to their identities, whose absences within #leelah alcorn revealed how the dominant exigency of trans youth suicide is plagued by representational disparities.

Additionally, I engineered my lab in a way that facilitated my own goal to deepen, extend, challenge, and *trans** existing rhetorical knowledges, especially those I played a role in generating. If the circulation of Alcorn's memory through #leelah alcorn sensationally fueled the production of an extended kairotic moment that transformed unpredictably into the future, then how can my scholarly labor within the DH lab assist in shifting the future course of the kairotic moment by seeking out its gendered and racialized ghosts? And how can digital tools and methods enable me to compose a rhetorical history of the materialization of Alcorn's suicide on Tumblr that visually uncovers how these invisibilities haunt her memory's circulation? These questions can be at least partially answered with recourse to existing rhetorical scholars invested in and developing digital rhetorical methodologies. Laurie Gries argues that rhetorical scholars should be more daring in their research by experimenting with data visualization techniques to render visible often abstract and sometimes unfathomable processes of viral circulation.[44] Taking a cue from Gries, I expand on my previous research where I analyzed the efforts of those who generated the archival accumulation through #leelah alcorn. There, I state, "Today the archive continues to be held together by the connective affordances of hashtags."[45] I then assert that the hashtags signified the rhetorical labors of the bodies of those who participated in the viral circulation of Alcorn's memory. While I do not think this claim is inaccurate, I am willing to admit it is founded on a certain degree of speculation, as I did not do much to empirically verify its validity. Beyond simply preserving #leelah alcorn, I want to use this data as evidence to validate previous claims I have made about the collective rhetorical agency of those who circulated the hashtag. My objective is to visually illuminate the absences lost within but nevertheless still crucial to the rhetorical formation of the network on Tumblr.

Navigating #leelah alcorn was no small task because the network itself was massive. During the period spanning December 30, 2014 (the date when word of Alcorn's suicide became public) and December 3, 2018 (the night I utilized Reaper to scrape all data posted to Tumblr under #leelah alcorn), Tumblr hosted 13,055 unique posts featuring #leelah alcorn. I used OpenRefine to "wrangle" or "scrub" the data. OpenRefine is a standalone desktop application for manipulating large quantities of data, which is especially useful for data stored in spreadsheet formats such as a .csv file. OpenRefine helped me determine that 49,161 other hashtags were circulated along with those 13,055 posts. I then entered these hashtags in a Microsoft Excel file, where I deleted all duplicate values and found that of those 49,161 hashtags 12,081 were unique. Including #leelah alcorn, 12,082 total hashtags circulated to form the network dedicated to propelling Alcorn's memory beyond its point of origination.

To visualize this network, I employed Gephi, an open-source network analysis and data visualization software popular among many DH practitioners. Gephi is a powerful platform for transforming complex datasets into diagrams that render relationships between and among datapoints visually intelligible. With the help of Miriam Posner's detailed instruction on how to make use of Gephi in the service of network analysis in DH,[46] I turned 12,082 hashtags into a list of *nodes*, or a list of individual actors or vertices within the network. In order to ensure anonymity of the Tumblr user, I then used the UUID (universally unique identifier) provided by Reaper for each Tumblr blog to craft a list of *edges*, or the relationships connecting each of the nodes to one another. After, I used existing tools within Gephi to size and color each node by degree of frequency, as well as the layout "OpenOrd"—an algorithm best equipped to represent a network as large as #leelah alcorn—to further refine and enhance the visual legibility of the network. Finally, I generated a PDF of the network, but due to its size, I did not make the individual names of each node visible. The result was a dense and ultimately unreadable network; however, I felt I was finally able to visually verify the enormous scale of #leelah alcorn and the kairotic moment it sparked on Tumblr.[47] Unfortunately, this network visualization is simply too massive to be reproduced in print here; however, one can access the images I describe by visiting the Open Science Framework project wiki page.[48]

But how did I discover the absences haunting this network? I entered the hashtags into a new Excel file and used the pivot table function to sort the hashtags by frequency of use. As I scrolled through them, I noticed the forty-third most circulated hashtag was #his name was zander, a reference to Zander Mahaffey, the previously mentioned fifteen-year-old trans man who like Alcorn queued his suicide letter to post on Tumblr before dying by suicide in February 2015. I also spotted #black lives matter, the one hundred thirty-first most frequently used hashtag. These hashtags signaled to me hidden elements of gender and race within the structure of the network, which prompted me to code the top one thousand hashtags into four categories based on whether they were (1) predominantly gendered, (2) predominantly racialized, (3) predominantly gendered *and* racialized, or (4) none. Further confirming my hypothesis that aspects of gender and race haunted the network through their obscurity, of the 1,000 hashtags, I found that 16 were predominantly gendered, 17 were predominantly racialized, 3 were predominantly gendered and racialized, and 964 were neither gendered nor racialized. Hashtags in the category of "none" included those like #suicide, #RIP, and #love, among many others. While certainly an imperfect system based in my own perceptions as to what hashtags could be considered differentially gendered and/or racialized, I predicted I would be able to better visualize how certain ghosts figured within this ecology once I understood who and what these ghosts were.

Most of the gendered hashtags revolved around three trans teenage men, Zander Mahaffey, Damien Shrum, and Ash Haffner (table 1). Like the rest of the trans teenagers who died by suicide in 2015, Mahaffey did not receive as much attention as Alcorn. Some, including myself, have guessed the reason for Mahaffey's obscurity was his entrance into a cultural zeitgeist that has historically privileged the visibility of trans women over trans men. The same likely applies to Shrum and Haffner. Their absence should be startling when one considers that, according to the findings of one major study, 51 percent of trans men attempt suicide during their adolescences, which is the largest suicide attempt rate among trans youth populations.[49]

Table 1. Gendered Hashtags Found within the Top One Thousand Most Frequently Shared Hashtags in #leelah alcorn

GENDERED	TOTAL NUMBER OF SHARES
#his name was zander	143
#ftm	118
#zander mahaffey	94
#zander	57
#rip zander	28
#hisnamewaszander	17
#trans men	14
#zander nicholas mahaffey	13
#damien	12
#his name was Damien	11
#damien shrum	9
#trans man	7
#trans male	6
#ash haffner	6
#his name is Damien	5
#trans boys	4

The racialized hashtags (table 2) seemed to overwhelmingly reflect the overlapping context of #blacklivesmatter, which at this time was still relatively new. Black youth victims of police violence appear, including Trayvon Martin, Tamir Rice, and Antonio Martin, the latter of whom died just five days before Alcorn. Melonie Rose is the only teenage trans woman of color who died by suicide to be featured in the top one thousand hashtags circulated along with #leelah alcorn. Her submerged position, indicated by #melonie rose and #her name was melonie, demonstrates that despite a growing cultural awareness of the link between identity and violence in contemporary youth culture, little to no attention has moved toward the disproportionate number of trans women of color who commit suicide or are murdered in the United States each year. This disparity is also highlighted by the numerous queer and trans of color commentators who questioned why Alcorn so quickly resonated with mainstream media outlets and became the overnight face of antiqueer and antitrans violence. As Asam Ahmad writes, "at a time when Black and racialized trans women are most at risk of dying from transphobic

Table 2. Racialized Hashtags Found within the Top One Thousand Most Frequently Shared Hashtags in #leelah alcorn.

RACIALIZED	TOTAL NUMBER OF SHARES
#black lives matter	44
#michael brown	43
#tamir rice	41
#blacklivesmatter	38
#all lives matter	22
#police brutality	16
#transgender lives matter	12
#antonio martin	12
#trayvon martin	10
#alllivesmatter	7
#melonie rose	5
#lgbt lives matter	5
#trans women of color	4
#muslim lives matter	4
#race	4
#her name was Melonie	4
#furgeson [sic]	4

violence in America, turning a young white trans woman into the face of trans death in this country is a particularly insidious form of 'unintentional' racism if it means ignoring and continuing to erase the violence that trans women of color face."[50]

Although comparatively few in number, the gendered and racialized hashtags (table 3) illustrate the emergence of the rhetoric of intersectionality, pointing toward an awareness of the various ways in which vectors of race, gender, class, sexuality, and other identity markers come together amid a complex matrix of power within #leelah alcorn. Blake Brockington is the only teenage trans man of color who died by suicide featured in the top one thousand hashtags circulated along with #leelah alcorn.

With this information, I sought to reveal these ghostly nodes in the #leelah alcorn network. I did so by first splitting the event of the network's unfolding into five manageable slices, assembling data from (1) December 30, 2014, (2) December 31, 2014, (3) January–June 2015, (4) July–December 2015, and (5) 2016–2018 into separate, legible visualizations. I chose to cordon this network into these particular timespans in

Table 3. Gendered and Racialized Hashtags Found within the Top One Thousand Most Frequently Shared Hashtags in #leelah alcorn.

GENDERED + RACIALIZED	TOTAL NUMBER OF SHARES
#blake Brockington	23
#intersectionality	5
#intersectional feminism	4

order to better visualize how activity within the hashtag peaked within the first half year of its emergence and has since greatly decreased in the months and years after Alcorn's suicide. Respectively, each network contained 2,306; 5,289; 6,059; 596; and 626 unique nodes (hashtags). Once again, I color-coded nodes by their frequency in degree utilizing existing settings in Gephi. I then chose the layout "Fruchterman Reingold" to visualize the network as a spherical shape with #leelah alcorn at its center. Finally, I enlarged the nodes from my list of gendered and/or racialized hashtags, so that they were the same size as the largest node in the visualization, #leelah alcorn.

The visualization of the network for December 30, 2018, situates #leelah alcorn at the center outlined by a semitransparent blue box.[51] On the outer edges lie the gendered and racialized hashtags, many of which are clustered together, indicating they originate from commonly shared posts by people likely invested in similar issues. What is made visually clear here is that #leelah alcorn is a centrifugal force by which the gendered and racialized hashtags become cast toward the margins.

The visualization of the January–June 2015 network again situates #leelah alcorn at the center.[52] However, in this network, many of the gendered and racialized hashtags appear closer to the middle of the network, revealing that users circulated these hashtags quite often during this period. By removing the edges in this particular visual, I aimed to more clearly represent how these hashtags formed within the network.

With fewer nodes and fewer edges connecting them, the visualization of the 2016–2018 network is less dense than most of the other networks preceding it.[53] The image attests to the waning popularity of #leelah alcorn in the years since Alcorn's actual death; yet it also reminds us of the continual presence of gendered and racialized absences on its outskirts, even in its more mature form. As one can deduce based on the visual evidence presented, gender and race differentials played a consistent role in the construction of Alcorn's memory within this specific rhetorical ecology, verifying the claims of scholars and commentators who surmised the centering of Alcorn's memory in discourses of trans suicide further marginalized already oppressed identities who also suffer the deleterious effects of an antitrans social economy. A digital rhetorical history of #leelah alcorn such as the one I have proposed seeks out these ghosts so as to give them a moment of overdue recognition, as well as to ponder what our responsibilities are as rhetorical historians in recontextualizing digital memories of the past for future generations.

Conclusion

Queer and trans histories have always been vulnerable and prone to vanishing. This chapter demonstrates how the same continues to be true in an increasingly digital world, even as our cultural memory is circulated and stored online at inhuman rates. For queer and trans rhetorical historians in particular, I point out how the changing character of queer and trans archives amid the rise of the digital era creates new opportunities to invent methodologies for collecting endangered, historically significant material from the internet and to transform such material into something that can serve the interests of the marginalized communities who most stand to benefit from its preservation. In this respect, I share with Bonnie Ruberg, Jason Boyd, and James Howe the perspective that "digital tools have the unique capacity to make visible the histories of queer representation and issues affecting queer communities."[54]

I advocate on behalf of the convergence of DH and rhetorical historical methodology so as to keep pace with evolving cultural and technological contexts of humanities research. I contend that rhetorical historians can and should envision their scholarly enterprise anew in a culture driven by the digital circulation of information. I argue that rhetorical historians can use digital media technologies to build digital rhetorical histories that do more than simply analyze online objects by directly intervening in the contexts of their circulation. In other words, we can look toward DH as a site from which to envision ourselves as critical curators, thus taking seriously the value of digital methods for collecting and preserving born-digital histories that remain all too precarious under the surveillance of institutional platform politics and the logics of algorithmic culture.

Throughout this chapter, I offer a description of the specific practices through which I actualized one iteration of a DH lab tailored to facilitate the research process. My aim in doing so is to provide rhetorical historians a view of what I will wager is the future of rhetorical history. My intention is not to recommend a fully replicable method that will be useful across every context. Against the positivist impulse to simply use digital methods and tools in objectively representing reality, I engaged network data visualization techniques to begin manipulating a rhetorical history of #leelah alcorn that highlighted the injustices mired in this particular rhetorical ecology. As more archival queers and other DH-invested rhetorical historians turn toward digital social media culture as a rich field site for gathering vulnerable culturally significant rhetorical artifacts, they should continue to invent practice-based methodologies in their own DH labs, while concurrently mobilizing the generative insights of rhetorical studies in the production of critically contextualized digital scholarship that showcases the politics of the past and its relevance for the present and impending future. Toward these ends, we should also consider the constraints of printed text when pursuing publication options for this type of scholarship. Briefly imagine how your impression of #leelah alcorn would have changed if you could have experienced this piece of rhetorical history through the multisensory interactivity of a web page rather than the visuality of this largely alphabetic chapter. Beyond this book, open-access, online publications of rhetorical history present rhetorical historians another avenue from which to contribute to the broader multidisciplinary field of DH, while also extending an as-of-yet chartered future for further revealing the trans*-ness of rhetorical history as an ever-changing methodological project.

Notes

1. Tumblr hashtags may include a space between words.

2. Susan Stryker, *Transgender History: The Roots of Today's Revolution*, 2nd ed. (New York: Seal Press, 2017), 200–201.

3. These thirteen teenagers represent those *accounted-for* trans youth who died by suicide during the period of February 11, 2015, to October 7, 2015. Because trans death rates, particularly the rate of death for trans youth, cannot be verified in the United States due to the possible concealment of trans identities by family members and others, there is no way of knowing exactly how many trans people have died, whether by suicide or other means, after Leelah Alcorn. To gather even an approximate sense of this information, one must turn to nonofficial sources, such as those organized and disseminated by journalists and activists. I obtained this information from an article published by a source for trans news, *Planet Transgender*. See Nillin Dennison, "14-Year-Old Emmett Castle is 19th Reported Trans Death by Suicide This Year," *Planet Transgender*, October 9, 2015, https://planettransgender.com.

4. Evan Mitchell Schares, "The Suicide of Leelah Alcorn: Whiteness in the Cultural Wake of Dying Queers," *QED: A Journal in GLBTQ Worldmaking* 6, no. 1 (2019): 9.

5. C. Riley Snorton and Jin Haritaworn, "Trans Necropolitics: A Transnational

Reflection on Violence, Death, and the Trans of Color Afterlife," in *Transgender Studies Reader 2*, ed. Susan Stryker and Aren Z. Aizura (New York: Routledge, 2013), 67.

6. Charles E. Morris III, "Contextual Twilight/Critical Liminality: J. M. Barrie's Courage at St. Andrews, 1922," *Quarterly Journal of Speech* 82, no. 3 (1996): 207–27.

7. Lisa A. Flores, "Between Abundance and Marginalization: The Imperative of Racial Rhetorical Criticism," *Review of Communication* 16, no. 1 (2016): 5.

8. For more rhetorical analysis on the potentially harmful repercussions of trans iconicity, see GPat Patterson and Leland G. Spencer, "Toward Trans Rhetorical Agency: A Critical Analysis of Trans Topics in Rhetoric and Composition and Communication Scholarship," *Peitho: Journal of the Coalition of Feminist Scholars in the History of Rhetoric & Composition* 22, no. 4 (2020), https://cfshrc.org.

9. Anne Burdick, Johanna Drucker, Peter Lunenfeld, Todd Presner, and Jeffrey Schnapp, "Digital Humanities Fundamentals," in *Digital Humanities*, ed. Anne Burdick, Johanna Drucker, Peter Lunenfeld, Todd Presner, and Jeffrey Schnapp (Cambridge, MA: Massachusetts Institute of Technology Press, 2016), 123.

10. Jessica Enoch and David Gold, "Introduction: Seizing the Methodological Moment: The Digital Humanities and Historiography in Rhetoric and Composition," *College English* 76, no. 2 (2013): 106.

11. Susan Stryker, Paisley Currah, and Lisa Jean Moore, "Introduction: Trans-, Trans, or Transgender?" *Women's Studies Quarterly* 36, no. 4 (2008): 11.

12. Stryker, *Transgender History*, 1.

13. Marquis Bey, "The Trans*-Ness of Blackness, the Blackness of Trans*-Ness," *TSQ: Transgender Studies Quarterly* 4, no. 2 (2017): 285.

14. Bey, "The Trans*-Ness," 284.

15. Stephen E. Lucas, "The Schism in Rhetorical Scholarship," *Quarterly Journal of Speech* 67, no. 1 (1981): 17. For more detail regarding the "new rhetoric" and its emergence during this particular time period, see Carole Blair, "'We Are All Just Prisoners Here of Our Own Device': Rhetoric in Speech Communication after Wingspread," in *Making and Unmaking the Prospects of Rhetoric: Selected Papers From the 1996 Rhetoric Society of America Conference*, ed. Theresa Enos (Manwah, NJ: Lawrence Erlbaum Associates, 1997), 29–36.

16. Lucas, "The Schism in Rhetorical Scholarship," 17.

17. David Zarefsky, "Four Senses of Rhetorical History," in Turner, *Doing Rhetorical History*, 20.

18. Robert E. Terrill, "Ways of Rhetorical History," *Review of Communication* 3, no. 3 (July 2003): 298.

19. Many works examine rhetoric and archives. For some of the more prominent examples, see Charles E. Morris III, "The Archival Turn in Rhetorical

Studies; or, The Archive's (Re)turn," *Rhetoric & Public Affairs* 9, no. 1 (2006): 113–15;. Barbara Biesecker, "Of Historicity, Rhetoric: The Archive as Scene of Invention," *Rhetoric & Public Affairs* 9, no. 1 (2006): 124–31; Mary E. Stuckey, "Presidential Secrecy: Keeping Archives Open," *Rhetoric & Public Affairs* 9, no. 1 (Spring 2006): 138–44; Charles E. Morris III, "Archival Queer," *Rhetoric & Public Affairs* 9, no. 1 (Spring 2006): 145–51; Cheryl Glenn and Jessica Enoch, "Drama in the Archives: Rereading Methods, Rewriting History," *College Composition and Communication* 61, no. 2 (2009): 321–42; Matthew Houdek, "The Rhetorical Force of 'Global Archival Memory': (Re)Situating Archives along the Global Memoryscape," *Journal of International and Intercultural Communication* 9, no. 3 (2016): 204–21; E. Cram, "Archival Ambience and Sensory Memory: Generating Queer Intimacies in the Settler Colonial Archive," *Communication and Critical/ Cultural Studies* 13, no. 2 (2016): 109–29; K. J. Rawson, "The Rhetorical Power of Archival Description: Classifying Images of Gender Transgression," *Rhetoric Society Quarterly* 48, no. 4 (2018): 327–51.

20. Morris, "Archival Queer," 147.

21. Alessandra Mondin, "'Tumblr Mostly, Great Empowering Images:' Blogging, Reblogging, and Scrolling Feminist, Queer, and BDSM Desires," *Journal of Gender Studies* 26, no. 3 (2017): 282–92.

22. Jacob Engelberg and Gary Needham, "Purging the Queer Archive: Tumblr's Counterhegemonic Pornographies," *Porn Studies* 6, no. 3 (2019): 352.

23. Samuel R. Delany, *Times Square Red, Times Square Blue* (New York: New York University Press, 1999).

24. Morris, "Archival Queer," 147.

25. Kara Swisher, "Who Killed Tumblr? We All Did," *New York Times* (New York), August 14, 2019, https://www.nytimes.com.

26. Nathalie Graham, "Tumblr is Dead: The Internet Could Be Next," *Stranger*, December 17, 2018, https://www.thestranger.com.

27. For more scholarly insight on the demise of Tumblr, see Paul Byron, "'How Could You Write Your Name Below That?' The Queer Life and Death of Tumblr," *Porn Studies* 6, no. 3 (2019): 336–49.

28. My suggestion here acknowledges yet also resists tendencies to conceive of the Internet itself as an archive. Whereas Viktor Mayer-Schönberger claims that the digital age makes it harder for humans to forget, I contend that institutional platforms like Tumblr can easily induce forgetting by removing large swaths of information generated by its users. See Viktor Mayer-Schönberger, *Delete: The Virtue of Forgetting in the Digital Age* (Princeton, NJ: Princeton University Press, 2009).

29. Diana Taylor, *The Archive and the Repertoire: Performing Cultural Memory in the Americas* (Durham, NC: Duke University Press, 2003), 20.

30. Although most often used by designers and engineers, anyone can

acquire an API key from Tumblr. For more information, see https://www.tumblr.com/docs/en/api/v2.

31. Kathleen J. Turner, "Introduction: Rhetorical History as Social Construction," in Turner, *Doing Rhetorical History*, 8.

32. Amy E. Earhart, "The Digital Humanities as a Laboratory," in *Humanities and the Digital*, ed. David Theo Goldberg and Patrik Svensson (Boston: Massachusetts Institute of Technology Press, 2015), 396.

33. Allucquére Rosanne (Sandy) Stone, *The War of Desire and Technology at the Close of the Mechanical Age* (Cambridge: Massachusetts Institute of Technology Press, 1995), 37.

34. Stone, *War of Desire and Technology*.

35. Susan Stryker, "My Words to Victor Frankenstein above the Village of Chamounix: Performing Transgender Rage," *GLQ: A Journal of Lesbian and Gay Studies* 1, no. 3 (1994): 238.

36. Stryker, "My Words to Victor Frankenstein," 238.

37. See Jacques Derrida, *Specters of Marx: The State of the Debt, the Work of Mourning, & the New International*, trans. Peggy Kamuf (New York: Routledge, 1994); Avery Gordon, *Ghostly Matters: Haunting and the Sociological Imagination* (Minneapolis: University of Minnesota Press, 2008).

38. Bey, "Trans*-ness of Blackness," 276.

39. Bey, "Trans*-ness of Blackness," 278.

40. Bey, "Trans*-ness of Blackness," 278.

41. In the DH lab, researchers should acknowledge their embodied "situated knowledges" and use them as heuristics from which to generate novel rhetorical research. See Donna Haraway, "Situated Knowledges: The Science Question in Feminism and the Privilege of Partial Perspective," *Feminist Studies* 14, no. 3 (1988): 595.

42. Lisa Blackman, *Haunted Data: Affect, Transmedia, Weird Science* (London: Bloomsbury, 2019), 17.

43. See Joe Edward Hatfield, "The Queer Kairotic: Digital Transgender Suicide Memories and Ecological Rhetorical Agency," *Rhetoric Society Quarterly* 49, no. 1 (2019): 25–48.

44. Laurie Gries, "Mapping Obama Hope: A Data Visualization Project for Visual Rhetorics," *Kairos: A Journal of Rhetoric, Technology, and Pedagogy* 21, no. 2 (2017), http://kairos.technorhetoric.net.

45. Hatfield, "Queer Kairotic," 38.

46. See Miriam Posner, "Creating a Network Graph with Gephi," accessed August 20, 2019, http://miriamposner.com/dh101f15/index.php/creating-a-network-graph-with-gephi/. See also http://web.archive.org/web/20190821000552/http://miriamposner.com/dh101f15/index.php/creating-a-network-graph-with-gephi/.

47. To view a visualization of the network #leelah alcorn, including 12,081 other unique hashtags circulated from 2014 through 2018, see https://doi.org/10 .17605/OSF.IO/V7BTS; once there, click on the "Wiki" tab and scroll to figure 1.

48. To view the aforementioned Open Science Framework project wiki page, see https://doi.org/10.17605/OSF.IO/V7BTS.

49. Russell B. Toomey, Amy K. Syvertson, and Maura Shramko, "Transgender Adolescent Behavior," *Pediatrics* 142, no. 4 (2018): 1–8.

50. Asam Ahmad, "Useful Martyrs and Invisible Deaths," *{Young}ist*, January 22, 2015, https://youngist.github.io/clean-blog/useful-martyrs-invisible -deaths#.XcMhW5NKhN0.

51. To view a visualization of the network #leelah alcorn, including 2,035 other unique hashtags circulated on December 30, 2014, see https://doi.org/10 .17605/OSF.IO/V7BTS. Click on the "Wiki" tab and scroll to figure 2.

52. To view a partial visualization of the network #leelah alcorn, including 6,058 other unique hashtags circulated from January to June 2015, see https:// doi.org/10.17605/OSF.IO/V7BTS. Click on the "Wiki" tab and scroll to figure 3.

53. To view a partial visualization of the network #leelah alcorn, including 625 other unique hashtags circulated from 2016 to 2018, see https://doi .org/10.17605/OSF.IO/V7BTS. Click on the "Wiki" tab and scroll to figure 4.

54. Bonnie Ruberg, Jason Boyd, and James Howe, "Toward a Queer Digital Humanities" in *Bodies of Information: Intersectional Feminism and the Digital Humanities*, ed. Elizabeth Losh and Jacqueline Wernimont (Minneapolis: University of Minnesota Press, 2018), 108. Beyond DH, I also join a more general, large, interdisciplinary consortium of queer and trans scholars who have sought to design and apply methodologies informed by queer and trans theoretical orientations. For a sampling of scholarship on queer methods, see William P. Banks, Matthew B. Cox, and Caroline Dadas, eds., *Re/Orienting Writing Studies: Queer Methods, Queer Projects* (Logan: Utah State University Press, 2019); and Amin Ghaziani and Matt Brim, ed., *Imagining Queer Methods* (New York: New York University Press, 2019).

2

Rhetorical History, the Public Humanities, and the Exoduster Movement

Shawn J. Parry-Giles and J. Michael Hogan

In a 2018 statement on its Action Network site, the Modern Language Association (MLA) urged scholars to join the "public humanities movement," an effort to demonstrate the "democratic value of an informed citizenry."[1] Scholars of rhetorical history are well positioned to contribute to this effort, as we have long been involved with civic learning and engagement.[2] Our skills in recovering, authenticating, contextualizing, and interpreting rhetorical artifacts uniquely position us to connect the American democratic experience of the past to the present.[3] By also embracing the digital turn in the humanities,[4] we are now poised to extend our reach beyond the classroom and disciplinary venues to audiences worldwide.

Rhetorical historians treat public discourse as integral to civic life, often turning to history and archives to deepen our understanding of rhetorical artifacts.[5] Some of us theorize, reasoning inductively from case studies grounded in political practice to rhetorical generalizations. Others focus on change over time, identifying key rhetorical "moments" in political or social movements or charting the evolution of influential ideas.[6] Studying political rhetoric both diachronically and synchronically,[7] rhetorical historians look to the past to better understand contemporary political controversies, including the deep-seated fissures that impede productive deliberation and reify social injustices. We study both rhetorics of power and rhetorics of dissent, shedding light on the complexities of political progress and the challenges of resistance. Above all, we value robust speech and uphold an ideal of ethical, "good faith" deliberations as we recover, analyze, and ultimately judge the rhetoric of political actors.

The digital age has invigorated the public humanities, as more rhetorical resources have become available online. Rhetorical historians benefit from the digital turn because of the rich resources available to us without expensive trips to the archives. But we are also equipped to enhance the recovery and preservation efforts of the public and digital humanities by contributing online, open-source materials to the rich mosaic of artifacts that make up the rhetorical history of the United States.

In championing the study of public rhetoric, rhetorical historians traditionally have turned to the study of speeches as a mode of historical and civic education. Reviving the classical tradition, American rhetoricians in the first half of the twentieth century published textbooks and collections of "great speeches" explicitly designed to prepare students for citizenship.[8] In the latter half of the century, the canon of great speeches expanded to include a broader range of voices, reflecting the impact of women's movements, civil rights movements, LGBTQ movements, and other movements for social change.[9] As we recover, interpret, and digitally archive an even greater diversity of rhetorical artifacts (e.g., broadsides, pamphlets, manifestos, photographs, poems, podcasts, and memorials), we not only expand the diversity of the texts we study but also take more seriously a variety of vernacular voices that suggest new models of civic engagement. By providing more online, open-source access to the rich mosaic of voices and artifacts that make up the rhetorical history of the United States, we help to transform civic education for the digital age.

Rhetorical historians have led the way in the new public humanities movement with the Voices of Democracy (VOD) project, an online archive of historically significant speeches and related educational materials. Now a companion website, the Recovering Democracy Archive (RDA): Speech Recovery Project, is expanding the diversity of speeches available online with a new digital archive of lesser-known but still important speeches. To ensure the continued expansion of the speeches recovered, preserved, and studied, both projects invite submissions from scholars, students, and the wider public.

In this chapter, we begin by showcasing the contributions of these two digital initiatives to the new public humanities movement. We then explore a case study in textual recovery and digital preservation that illustrates some of the challenges, processes, and benefits involved in extending our recovery efforts beyond the speeches of well-known movement leaders to more obscure figures whose voices are in danger of being lost to history. In this case study, we focus on the Exoduster movement, which was made up of formerly enslaved people who left the South in search a new homeland in the post-Reconstruction era.[10] Our case study thus brings to life the political agency of the most politically oppressed, as recently freed peoples organized and moved North in search of freedom and equality. At the same time, we show why that choice was so difficult: opposed by such prominent Black leaders as Frederick Douglass, the Exoduster movement urged freed Black people to move to unfamiliar lands with uncertain futures. The fact that so many did so testifies to their unwillingness to submit to continued injustices in the states that had enslaved them. Yet their migration also demonstrates the reach of racism in America beyond the South, as many Exodusters ended up in impoverished, segregated communities rather than in the land of freedom and opportunity they had imagined.

Voices of Democracy: A Digital Innovator

In 2002, the former chair of the National Endowment for the Humanities (NEH), Bruce Cole, coined the phrase "Our American Amnesia" to describe the lack of understanding, particularly among young people, of our nation's past, its founding principles, and its democratic traditions.[11] Established in 2005 with a major NEH grant, the VOD project responded to Cole's call for initiatives to combat that amnesia by creating an online curriculum resource for studying great speeches and debates in US history. Recognized in 2013 as among the best online educational resources by the website EDSITEment!,[12] VOD is now widely used by teachers. It also attracts a broad public audience, averaging more than a thousand unique visitors a day from more than fifty countries worldwide. With a view toward "reinvigorating the humanistic study of US oratory," VOD was a pioneer in the public and digital humanities movement, showing how rhetorical history could be used "to foster understanding of the nation's principles and history and promote civic engagement among scholars, teachers, and students."[13]

Like the speech anthologies of an earlier era, VOD features many of the "Top 100 Speeches of the Twentieth Century," as identified in a 1999 survey of rhetorical scholars.[14] Yet, going beyond most traditional print anthologies, it includes complete, unabridged, and authenticated speech texts, along with full-length scholarly essays analyzing each speech. The "curriculum unit" built around each speech also includes a collection of teaching-learning materials and a list of suggested resources, including print, audio-visual, and online items. Organized around seven perennial themes in American rhetorical history, including "War and Peace," "Civil Rights," and "Social and Economic Justice," the site now boasts more than eighty curriculum units, along with a growing collection of lesson plans for middle school and high school teachers.

VOD also goes beyond the speech anthologies of an earlier era by placing more emphasis on the *diversity* of our nation's heritage, traditions, and history. VOD includes many speeches by well-known political figures, such as Abraham Lincoln and Hillary Clinton, but it also gives voice to those pushing back against "ascriptive" visions of "citizenship,"[15] such as Mabel Vernon, a suffrage activist overshadowed by her more famous ally, Alice Paul, and Ella Baker, a civil rights activist who also has been largely overlooked.[16] As salient as statements by powerful political leaders, these speeches are part of America's rhetorical heritage, and by studying them, students can develop "the necessary skills of a democratic public: how to listen, how to argue, and how to deliberate."[17] Studying these speeches also broadens our theoretical understandings of rhetoric, as the rhetoric of social protest has inspired rhetorical scholars to develop theoretical alternatives to the neoclassicism that prevailed in traditional rhetorical criticism.[18]

There is more recovery work to do of course.[19] Since its genesis, our country and our communities have been shaped by the known and the unknown who used their words to foment or forestall political change. As rhetorical historians, we are positioned to pursue and preserve the speeches of lesser-known politicians and political activists. Recovering, preserving, and making those sorts of speeches more widely available is the mission of VOD's new companion site, the RDA.

The Recovering Democracy Archives

Like other twenty-first-century digital humanities initiatives,[20] RDA brings the work of rhetorical historians to a broader public, showcasing how a diversity of individuals—the people and their leaders—deliberated over issues that continue to resonate today.[21] Before photographs fade, audio and videotapes disintegrate, and textual artifacts fray, RDA works to expand public access to these rhetorical resources with a new digital archive of lesser-known but still important speeches. The website features more obscure speeches by such powerful leaders as Theodore Roosevelt, as well as speeches by activists who have challenged the barriers that restrict equitable participation in civic life, including César Chávez, Paul Robeson, and Marie Wilson.[22] Envisioned, created, and launched by PhD students and faculty in rhetoric at the University of Maryland, the site already has posted more than twenty speeches, including speeches by advocates of gender and racial equity, LGBTQ rights, labor justice, and Native American rights, among other causes.[23]

Although the project began as a speech recovery project, we have expanded the archives to include photographs from the relevant historical contexts along with digitized audio and video versions of the speeches when available. Among the speeches included is one by Harry Burn, a swing voter in the Tennessee state legislature's debate over ratifying the woman suffrage amendment. Because of a letter from his mother, Burn unexpectedly broke a tie in the Tennessee House of Representatives, famously making Tennessee the last state needed to ratify the Nineteenth Amendment.[24] Similarly, we have learned more about George Gillette, a tribal leader compelled to sign away the land rights of three Native American nations so that the Garrison Dam in North Dakota could be built in 1948. Photographs located in the National Archives and Records Administration's collection provide a striking visual accompaniment to Gillette's address, as they show him openly weeping as the agreement was signed.[25] And through digitized audio of a speech by Dorothy Pitman Hughes, an African American woman who traveled around the country with Gloria Steinem advocating women's rights, we can hear the boos and jeers directed at the two of them as they braved a hostile audience of cadets at the US Naval Academy in 1972.[26]

RDA researchers have forged important collaborations with local and national archives that can serve as a model for other rhetorical historians interested in the public humanities. Through such efforts, we can engage graduate and undergraduate students in archival research as part of their rhetorical education. RDA researchers already have worked with a variety of archives across the country to recover the speeches on the project website, including the Arab American National Museum, the Calvin M. McClung Historical Collection, the Library of Congress, and the Social Welfare History Archives. On the Maryland campus, RDA is now partnering with the George Meany Memorial AFL-CIO Archive to help recover, transcribe, digitize, authenticate, and contextualize speeches from their holdings.[27] This archive alone contains more than 1,200 speech files, thousands of photographs, and hundreds of audio and videotapes of speeches from important labor leaders, including Samuel Gompers, John L. Lewis, and Mary Harris "Mother" Jones. These archives also include speeches by civil rights leaders who both challenged and collaborated with labor leaders, including César Chávez, A. Philip Randolph, and Nancy Wohlforth.[28] Their holdings also help connect the activism of African American leaders like Frederick Douglass to the fight for labor justice in the Reconstruction era and beyond.

As more archives digitize their collections, there will be a growing need for students trained in rhetorical history to bring those resources to the attention of broader publics and utilize their rhetorical expertise to analyze and elucidate the significance of those artifacts. To illustrate how rhetorical historians might both benefit from and contribute to the missions of the public and digital humanities, we now turn to a case study in textual recovery and analysis: the Exoduster movement in post-Reconstruction America. Thanks to the efforts of state and local archivists who have worked to recover, digitize, and post online many primary texts,[29] we are now in a better position to assess the movement's significance in its own day and to understand the rhetorical practices that reified white supremacy and the segregationist practices of the postwar era.

The Exodusters: The Rhetorical Antecedents

The Exoduster movement amalgamates much of the debate over the meaning of US citizenship in both the eighteenth and nineteenth centuries and beyond. To understand the Exoduster movement is to comprehend the roots of a white-dominated nation grappling with persons of color within its borders. Federal and state governments routinely resorted to controlling diverse peoples through enslavement, colonization, segregation, relocation, imprisonment, and extermination.[30] Freed Black folks had a difficult choice to make—to assimilate or separate—as there was no clear pathway to self-determination, safety, and solvency.[31] Exodusters chose to enact their freedom by moving out of the South to a land of greater promise. As rhetorical historians studying this case, we need to consider the conditions of the past (rhetorical antecedents), present (rhetorical strategies and structures), and future (rhetorical legacies) that help us make meaning and develop judgments about these political acts.

Understanding the Exodusters' choice to migrate begins with attending to the debates within antebellum America over what to do with freed Black people.[32] While most Northerners opposed slavery, they still objected to welcoming African Americans into their communities.[33] Some of the nation's foremost white leaders (e.g., Thomas Jefferson, Henry Clay, and Abraham Lincoln) strategized a back-to-Africa campaign (to "Liberia") decades before Marcus Garvey advocated such a move in the early twentieth century. Such efforts were cast as "benevolent" efforts to return free Black people to their ancestral homeland and avoid the dilemma of integrating populations.[34] For those freed Black Americans remaining in the country, states worked to restrict their mobility by requiring "travel permits" to exit and reenter the state.[35] Their physical movements were "consistently met with resistance," violence, and even death.[36]

Such repressive conditions, even in the North, led some African American leaders to organize their own emigration efforts to escape the injustices facing them in pre–Civil War America.[37] Although both efforts supported keeping the populations separate, "emigration" offered freed Black people "self-determination," while "colonization" amounted to "compulsion" and "coerced movement" against their will.[38] Emigrationist Martin Robison Delany called colonization a "hideous thing," the "offspring of slavery," even as he gave a full-throated defense for emigration to Latin America and the Caribbean, where he imagined that Black people might "enjoy real freedom" and "equality of rights."[39]

Well before the Exodusters made their fateful decision to migrate north and west, African Americans used their feet to defy acts of unimaginable cruelty and tyranny. The most rebellious enslaved people plotted escape routes to secure their own freedom. The "exodus" metaphor became a common way for the formerly enslaved to constitute "a sense of peoplehood" through a common oppression and a "common history and destiny." Such racial "solidarity" formed the foundation of "Black Nationalism," along with the belief that freed Black people needed to assume "the responsibility for liberating themselves" in their pursuit of "racial uplift."[40] Scholar Rogers Smith suggests that this idea of "political peoplehood" typically involves a "bottom-up" vision of identity, where "supporters" express a "willing[ness]" to submit "allegiance to . . . associations and their leaders" in pursuit of the "'good life.'" The people involved are at once endowed with "agency," but they also commonly defer authority to leaders.[41] The symbolism of the exodus for the emancipated enslaved citizens reinforced the importance of authority figures leading the people out of slavery and oppression to freedom and justice.[42]

Together, free Black people, both the leaders and the people, needed to determine how best to enact their own freedoms. But would they "consent" to living under the hegemony of the southern Confederacy,[43] hoping to secure their due rights in time? Or would they leave their homes behind in search of a land that promised greater protections of their civil rights? As newly minted citizens with constitutional rights, freed Black people were presumably granted their rights of consent under the "social contract."[44] Yet the Exoduster debate provides a stark reminder of the *paradox of consent* that freed Black individuals faced in the postwar years when neither choice—to stay or to move—produced genuine protection of their constitutional rights. Many African American leaders, themselves escaped from slavery, constituted competing images of consent for the newly emancipated, rehearsing past rhetorical patterns that reappeared in future battles over segregation and integration.[45]

Frederick Douglass: The Anti-Exoduster

Frederick Douglass is known as one of the most influential abolitionists demanding equal rights for African Americans in the pre- and postslavery eras.[46] Lesser known is his involvement in debates with other civil rights leaders over whether freed Black people should remain in the South and demand equal rights or emigrate north and west in search of true freedom.[47] Douglass opposed the Exoduster movement from the start. The RDA project contributes to a more comprehensive understanding of Douglass's rhetorical and political life by recovering one of his anti-Exoduster speeches, along with a published "address" from a group of movement members. Together these documents help us understand the divisions that opened up in the aftermath of emancipation as African Americans faced difficult decisions over how to fight back against the recalibration of white supremacy.[48]

As Republican promises of freedom went unfilled in the Reconstruction era, Douglass weighed in on the Exoduster debate in September 1879. In a statement read by another attendee before the American Social Science Association convention in Saratoga Springs, New York,[49] Douglass set the scene by describing the grim conditions freed Black people faced following emancipation, an emancipation that southerners launched a "death struggle . . . to prevent." Douglass conceded that emancipation had not really freed African Americans, as they faced "violence and intimidation," "poverty," a lack of "justice," and a "virtually closed" jury system.[50]

Yet Douglass drew different lessons from these dismal postwar realities than the Exodusters, who cited these same exigencies to justify migration. After his own escape to freedom, Douglass had earned a reputation for impatient demands,[51] but now, he took a more moderate, even "assimilationist" approach as he condemned freed Black people for wanting to leave the South.[52] Douglass defined the mass exodus as an act of "surrender," acting "by flight, rather than right," and making "freedom . . . depend upon migration rather than protection."[53] Around the same time, Douglass delivered a speech at the Centennial M.E. Church in Baltimore where he recounted the number of failed attempts to emigrate in years past that resulted in many dying of "starvation." He predicted that "in less than a year," they would be "handing around the hat" to help the Exodusters "return" to their southern homes. He ultimately called on the Exodusters to "stay home" and "demand fair wages from the 'old master class.'"[54]

Foreshadowing Booker T. Washington,[55] Douglass defended "manual labor" as the pathway to true liberation for freed Black populations. He seemingly enjoyed the irony of "southern men," acknowledging that there was "nothing more powerful than the naked iron arm" of the African American man, a "humiliating fact," Douglass mused, for southern planters whose future depended on the labor of "the despised and hated." His reasoning reflected the slavery-era commonplace that no other race could handle the harsh and backbreaking conditions of southern farming. An African American plantation worker, he boasted, "walks, labors, or sleeps in the sunlight unharmed," and "slavery was based on a knowledge of this fact." But now African Americans could seemingly use that "fact" to their own advantage. "His labor made him a slave," Douglass reasoned, but now, "his labor can . . . make him free, comfortable and independent."[56] In short, Douglass envisioned a class of formerly enslaved people forging their path to equal citizenship in the South through their blood, toil, and sweat.[57]

Almost immediately members of his own community pushed back.[58] William S. McFeely notes that for the first time in his life, Douglass was "hissed and shouted down by Black audiences." Many felt his "compassion was failing him" and so "was his intellectual grasp of a new problem."[59] Writers from the *Colored Citizen*, an African American newspaper in Topeka, Kansas, taunted "Uncle Fred" to "come out" and "stop dodging behind the stump." They demeaned his anti-Exoduster stance as "exceedingly thin" and a "poor excuse" for condemning those for leaving a life of "suffering" and poverty at the hands of former slave owners.[60] In response, then, the Exodusters rejected Douglass's southern vision and imagined a future where they could put their labor to use for themselves rather than former slave owners.

The Exodusters

The Exoduster case epitomizes the challenges and rewards of the public and digital humanities. Local and state archives have pieced together a patchwork of primary sources from across the South and Midwest that allow us to track the triumphs and tragedies of the Exodusters. By digitizing these texts, the Kansas Historical Society and other archival repositories have preserved the raw materials needed to tell the story of the Exodusters. But it remains for rhetorical historians and other scholars to synthesize and interpret those archival "fragments" and draw out the "lessons of history" for our students and a broader public.[61]

After a life of bondage, thousands of freed Black folks made the hard choice to pull up stakes and move their families, by foot, horseback, buggy, or train, hundreds of miles to states like Kansas, Missouri, and Indiana.[62] They were persuaded to leave their homes by a new group of leaders, themselves formerly enslaved, bent on defying the South's iron grip over their lives and pursuing a life of freedom in a new land. If Kansas kept slavery from its borders, they reasoned, it provided the best hope of providing a safe haven for those victimized by slavery in the South.[63] The Exoduster leaders spoke out in their planning meetings and conferences, but their words were more commonly recorded and preserved in broadsides, newspaper editorials, and advertisements, where they made their pitch for African Americans to leave the South.[64] They devoted considerable effort to countering Douglass and condemning others bent on stopping them, including white plantation owners trying to block their escape.

The Exoduster movement owed much to a small group of leaders who sought to instill freed Black people with a new sense of political agency, the agency needed to break free of the chains of slavery. Benjamin "Pap" Singleton emerged as one of those leaders. As a "carpenter and coffin maker," Singleton seemed an unlikely movement leader. He escaped slavery and repeatedly challenged the South's racist practices. Before the war, he provided support for the Underground Railroad. After the war, he stepped forward to convince Black southerners to leave their homeland in search for a new life, and he also served as an informal archivist of the movement by creating a scrapbook (now digitized) chronicling the movement.[65] Singleton and other Exoduster leaders built their case for migration, in part, on the same rhetorical ground as earlier emigrationists: their prospects in the South were grim, for the region had made "a mockery" out of the ideal of "Liberty."[66]

Typical of this dark motif was from a group of eight Exodusters, including Singleton, published in 1879 in the *Commonwealth*, a newspaper in Topeka, Kansas. According to the authors, "nothing but desolation" remained for African Americans in the South; they faced a life without "justice."[67] The Exodusters also painted an idyllic portrait of the alternative, with images of Kansas with "rolling prairie[s]," enriched with "stone and water," "wood . . . [and] coal."[68] Although they recognized the decision to migrate might be "imprudent for some," they argued that there was no alternative "to better our own condition." For some, the choice boiled down to the lesser of "two evils." Accusing white southern planters of defrauding Black laborers "out of [the] fruits of [their] labor," the Exodusters seemed confident that the labor of African Americans was at least "worth as much in the North, East, and West as in the South."[69]

In responding to critics like Douglass, Singleton took direct aim at the elitism of those African American leaders opposed to the exodus. In a statement published in the Nashville press in August 1877, Singleton called out Douglass and other critics of the movement: "I am now compelled to say something to our leading men of our race that sit in high places and get their living off of our poor laboring classes and then point fingers of scorn at us for calling together a meeting for our future wellbeing. . . . Such men as these should not be leaders of our race any longer."[70]

In organizing what they called "The Colored Convention," Stokely Walton joined Singleton and other leaders who sought to mobilize freed

Black people to join their exodus out of the South to forge their own independent and self-sustaining communities. They made their pitch by stressing the importance of enabling the "colored race to become a people"—a people that ultimately could become "one of the nations of the earth."[71]

The press coverage of the Exoduster campaign reflects the circulation of their ideas at the time of their mass migration. An illustration in *Harper's Weekly* from May 1, 1880, for example, juxtaposed the "Old Style" and "New Style" of life for Black people in America. The "Old Style" shows the archetypal image of someone who escaped slavery, wearing rags, crouching in a swamp in the dark of night, and hiding from the posse seeking to recapture him against his consent. The illustration of the "New Style," in contrast, features well-dressed African Americans traveling together in the light of day with their suitcases and purses. They smile and engage with one another against the backdrop of a cityscape. Billowing smoke appears in the background, suggesting they had just exited a train en route to their new homes. People are jubilant and hugging, conjuring up new images of an emancipated community enjoying their "freedom of movement," their newfound wealth, and their future opportunities.[72]

Exodusters chose to remain Americans, but they also chose to separate themselves from white southerners for self-preservation and survival.[73] And they made that choice in the face of growing threats from southern plantation owners, who went into a "panic" over losing their "cheap labor."[74] Reminiscent of the conditions of slavery, many Exodusters escaped in the dark of night to avoid the threats and violence of white plantation owners and their sympathizers. To disrupt the movement, white mobs beat and lynched Exoduster leaders and those trying to escape the southern juggernaut.[75] Thousands of formerly enslaved people took the risk of moving and starting over, although exact numbers are difficult to pin down. We do know that some twenty separate African American communities were established outside of the South in the postwar period.[76] One of those communities, named after a famous African American who escaped slavery, was Nicodemus, Kansas, located in the northwest part of the state. Nicodemus proved one of the more successful Exoduster communities,[77] attracting a few thousand to the city by circulating pamphlets like the one from July 2, 1877, promising land "rather rolling and . . . most pleasing to the human eye," filled with a "soil"—"rich, black, and sandy loam."[78] Community members also built some three hundred homes for the new arrivals and bought some "twenty thousand acres of land." They even formed a public school system, educating themselves by teaching one another how to read and write.[79] As Charlotte Hinger observes, Nicodemus gained "a national reputation" for showing that "African Americans . . . could do all the things whites had done."[80]

Nicodemus survives to this day, but other Exodusters struggled in their new destinations or stopped short in St. Louis or other communities en route to Kansas. Still others perished during the journey itself, never getting a chance to start a "better life." Those who made it to Kansas were typically malnourished, ill, and penniless, which seriously restricted their ability to forge their own futures.[81] Segregated neighborhoods also popped up in urban areas like Kansas City and Topeka, while both white and Black benevolent societies helped clothe and feed these "refugees." Although the support derived predominantly from philanthropic groups, a few high-level political leaders made pleas for aid and organized support for them, especially in Kansas.[82]

Eventually, the local governments in cities like St. Louis, Kansas City, and Topeka segregated the Exodusters into permanent enclaves. The Exodusters thus traded slavery for segregation, which was codified into law by the "separate but equal" doctrine of *Plessy v. Ferguson* (1896).[83] The segregated schools in Kansas ultimately became the focus of the landmark decision of *Brown v. Topeka Board of Education* (1954) that struck down the "separate but equal" doctrine.[84] This decision had roots going back to the 1890s, when a local church created the first African American kindergarten west of the Mississippi in a neighborhood of Topeka called Tennessee Town.[85] Elisha Scott, a graduate of that kindergarten, grew up to become a heralded civil rights attorney for the NAACP. Scott's two sons, John and Charles, would later litigate the Topeka portion of the *Brown vs. Topeka Board of Education* lawsuit.[86] Thus, the legacy of the Exodusters in Kansas illustrates both the successes and the frustrations of the movement. By moving west, they were able to educate their children, and some of those children made history. They also met with segregationist policies that re-created de jure acts of exclusion and discrimination. That Topeka, Kansas, served as the battleground for *Brown* owes much to the Exodusters' tenacity and the segregationist legacy they confronted.

The Rhetorical Legacies of the Exodusters

Rhetorical historians are most concerned with the politics animating our case studies and the historical and rhetorical antecedents that helped shape them. To deepen the study of rhetorical history, we must continue to seek out voices from our past. These voices expand the inventional resources that we bring to life in our scholarship and classrooms and contribute to the public and digital humanities. In the process, we attend to the rhetorical resonances of our historical cases by tracing the circulation of arguments and ideologies into the present day.[87] And we intervene in contemporary politics from the perspective of the past, historicizing rhetorics of oppression and resistance that shape the contemporary political landscape. On the Voices of Democracy site, for example, we ask authors to conclude each critical essay with reflections on a speech's "legacy and relevance to ongoing social and/or political controversies and debates."[88]

Exodusters provide a case study in rhetorical agency and political consent, as newly emancipated people debated and advocated for different responses to the rearticulation of white supremacy after the Civil War. In the era of Jim Crow, freed Black individuals were forced to choose the lesser of two evils: submit to continued injustices in the states that had enslaved them or flee to an uncertain and challenging future in unfamiliar lands. As it turned out, few had the economic resources to thrive in their new homes, and as the "separate but equal" doctrine took hold, many were cordoned off in segregated and impoverished neighborhoods.[89]

The interplay among integration, segregation, and separatism has continued to haunt American politics since the nation's founding. Segregated schools like those in Topeka's Tennessee Town resulted in inferior educational systems that continued to undermine the civil rights of African Americans. Civil rights advances, like the *Brown* decision and the Civil Rights Act of 1964, invariably produced backlashes and resistance from white citizens.[90] In addition, African Americans have struggled throughout US history for equal opportunity in the workplace, a goal that has never been realized because of discrimination practiced both by employers and by labor unions like the AFL-CIO.[91]

Today, we see renewed debates over how to manage the diversity of people within US borders. The federal government has stirred a national debate over the use of detention centers and makeshift jails in often deplorable conditions to detain those lacking documentation and those seeking asylum.[92] Candidates in the 2020 presidential campaign stepped back in time to debate the effectiveness of busing to integrate the public schools in the 1960s and 1970s, an issue that remains controversial more than sixty years after *Brown* and more than one hundred years after Tennessee Town's first kindergarten class matriculated. Whether to force integration or be satisfied with segregated and often substandard educational systems remains an unresolved dilemma,[93] as do the experiences that too many African Americans face with racial profiling by police, racial biases by the courts, racial inequities by employers, and any number of other issues affecting African American communities in the United States.[94]

In spite of entrenched oppressions, however, the Exodusters also passed down a legacy of African American self-determination, mobilization, and freedom that they inherited from their abolitionist forebearers. The movement inspired a wave of "Black populism" that influenced national politics at the turn of the twentieth century,[95] and labor activism among African Americans had a significant impact in their new home states. The Exodusters and other Black emigrants to the North and Midwest also changed the demographic landscape of many states, establishing an influential political base in many urban areas. Marcus Garvey and others carried the torch of Black Nationalism through his "back to Africa movement" in the early twentieth century, and that legacy persisted into the 1960s and beyond in the emigrationist and Black Nationalist ideas of Malcolm X, the Black Power movement, and others.[96]

In order to understand contemporary racial strife, we need to trace the historical roots of both oppression and resistance in US history. We cannot understand this struggle without committing to a robust recovery and study of rhetorical resources needed to read the past into the present. We need to grasp the complexities of power and the rhetorical strategies of those who have led the ongoing struggle for equality and justice. By recovering, preserving, digitizing, and interpreting these voices of resistance, we gain political inspiration and rhetorical guidance from those who, against all odds, asserted their own political agency, stood up to oppression and violence, and pursued their own vision of a more perfect union. The structures and ideologies of racism persist to this day. By studying the rhetorical tug and pull between the forces of political progress and backlash, we can help both our students and the broader public better understand the complicated racial politics of our country.

Notes

1. "Going Public: Humanities Beyond the Classroom," MLA: Action Network, September 25, 2018, https://action.mla.org.

2. Gerard A. Hauser, "Rhetorical Democracy and Civic Engagement," in *Rhetorical Democracy: Discursive Practices of Civic Engagement*, ed. Gerard A. Hauser and Amy Grim (New York: Routledge, 2004), 1.

3. Kathleen J. Turner, "Introduction: Rhetorical History as Social Construction," in Turner, *Doing Rhetorical History*, 2–8; David Zarefsky, "Four Senses of Rhetorical History," in Turner, *Doing Rhetorical History*, 25–32; Davis W. Houck, "Textual Recovery, Textual Discovery: Returning to Our Past, Imagining Our

Future," in Parry-Giles and Hogan, *Handbook of Rhetoric and Public Address*, 114–17; Robert N. Gaines, "The Processes and Challenges of Textual Authentication," in Parry-Giles and Hogan, *Handbook of Rhetoric and Public Address*, 138–39.

4. Douglas Eyman, *Digital Rhetoric: Theory, Method, and Practice* (Ann Arbor: University of Michigan Press, 2015), 1–2.

5. Debra Hawhee and Crista J. Olson, "Pan-Historiography: The Challenges of Writing History across Time and Space," in *Theorizing Histories of Rhetoric*, ed. Michelle Ballif (Carbondale: Southern Illinois University Press, 2013), 98–101. Hawhee and Olson make the important point that "parallels . . . cannot be drawn" across archives, necessitating the need to treat each archive as distinct and idiosyncratic in its holdings and its politics.

6. Ernest J. Wrage, "Public Address: A Study in Social and Intellectual History," *Quarterly Journal of Speech* 33, no. 4 (1947): 451–57.

7. That is, we study both how language functions across particular historical contexts at a given moment in time (synchronically) and how language changes over time (diachronically). See Michael Calvin McGee, "The 'Ideograph': A Link between Rhetoric and Ideology," *Quarterly Journal of Speech* 66, no. 1 (1980): 5.

8. Chief among those articulating this rationale for the study of speech and great speeches was William Norwood Brigance, who imagined speech as a discipline that could lay claim to that "great body of rhetorical or oratorical literature" that defined our national identity and civic traditions. See W. Norwood Brigance, "Whither Research?" *Quarterly Journal of Speech* 19, no. 4 (1933): 556; and Martin J. Medhurst, "The History of Public Address as an Academic Study," in Parry-Giles and Hogan, *Handbook of Rhetoric and Public Address*, 37.

9. See, for example, John C. Hammerback and Richard J. Jensen, "History and Culture as Rhetorical Constraints: Cesar Chavez's Letter from Delano," in Turner, *Doing Rhetorical History*, 212–16; Richard J. Jensen and John C. Hammerback, *The Words of César Chávez* (College Station: Texas A&M University Press, 2002), xi–xii; Jason Edward Black and Charles E. Morris III, eds., *An Archive of Hope: Harvey Milk's Speeches and Writings* (Berkeley: University of California Press, 2013), xi; Karlyn Kohrs Campbell, *Key Texts of the Early Feminists*, vol. 2 of *Man Cannot Speak for Her* (Westport, CT: Praeger Press, 1989); Davis W. Houck and David E. Dixon, ed., *Women and the Civil Rights Movement, 1954–1965* (Jackson: University Press of Mississippi, 2009), xviii–xix.

10. Kansas Historical Society, "Exodusters," Kansapedia, Topeka, updated October 2019, https://www.kshs.org/kansapedia.

11. Bruce Cole, "Our American Amnesia," *Wall Street Journal*, June 11, 2002, https://www.wsj.com/articles/SB102375410062692040.

12. EDSITEment! The Best of the Humanities on the Web, https://edsitement.neh.gov/.

13. Voices of Democracy: The US Oratory Project, https://voicesofdemocracy.umd.edu/.

14. See Stephen E. Lucas and Martin J. Medhurst, eds., *Words of a Century: The Top 100 American Speeches, 1900–1999* (New York: Oxford University Press, 2009), xvii–xviii.

15. Rogers M. Smith, *Civic Ideals: Conflicting Visions of Citizenship in US History* (New Haven, CT: Yale University Press, 1997), 5–6.

16. See, for example, Lauren Hunter, "Abraham Lincoln, 'Speech of Hon. Abraham Lincoln at Cooper Institute,' New York City, New York, February 27, 1860," *Voices of Democracy* 13 (2018): 1–12, http://voicesofdemocracy.umd.edu; Heather Brook Adams, "Eleanor Roosevelt, 'Address by Mrs. Franklin D. Roosevelt—The Chicago Civil Liberties Committee,' March 14, 1940," *Voices of Democracy* 4 (2009): 60–82, https://voicesofdemocracy.umd.edu; Cheryl R. Jorgensen-Earp, "Mable Vernon, 'The Picketing Campaign Nears Victory,' National Advisory Council Conference, December 7, 1917," *Voices of Democracy* 2 (2007): 1–25, https://voicesofdemocracy.umd.edu; Nikki Orth, "Ella Baker, 'Address at the Hattiesburg Freedom Day Rally,' January 12, 1964," *Voices of Democracy* 11 (2016): 25–43, http://voicesofdemocracy.umd.edu.

17. Kevin Mattson, *Creating a Democratic Public: The Struggle for Urban Participatory Democracy during the Progressive Era* (University Park: Pennsylvania State University Press, 1998), 45.

18. For a collection of influential work in the rhetoric of social protest, see Charles E. Morris III and Stephen Howard Browne, eds., *Readings in the Rhetoric of Social Protest*, 3rd ed. (State College, PA: Strata Publishing, 2013).

19. Davis W. Houck distinguishes between textual "recovery" and "discovery." He conceives of "recovery" as confirming "that a speech already deemed significant does, in fact, exist." He defines "discovery" as not knowing that a text existed prior to the scholar locating it. In most cases, the primary texts we address in this chapter and with the Recovering Democracy Archives reflect what Houck defines as recovery since these texts have been discovered by others and are part of archival holdings but have not widely circulated. Rhetorical histories and digital humanities can help make such texts more accessible. See Houck, "Textual Recovery, Textual Discovery," 114.

20. See, for example, University of Kansas, The Emmett Till Memory Project, Humanities for All, 2015, https://humanitiesforall.org; North Carolina State University, The Virtual Martin Luther King, Jr. Project, accessed June 20, 2019, https://vmlk.chass.ncsu.edu/; and University of Maryland, African American History, Culture and Digital Humanities, https://aadhum.umd.edu/.

21. François Hartog, *Regimes of Historicity: Presentism and Experiences of Time*, trans. Saskia Brown (New York: Columbia University Press, 2017), xv. See also Zarefsky, "Four Senses of Rhetorical History," 31.

22. Hagar Attia, "Unit on Theodore Roosevelt, 'Law and Order in Egypt,' Cairo, Egypt, March 28, 1910," Recovering Democracy Archives: Speech Recovery Project, https://recoveringdemocracyarchives.umd.edu/; Randall Fowler, "Unit

on Paul Robeson, 'Forge Negro-Labor and Unity for Peace,' Chicago, IL, June 10, 1950," Recovering Democracy Archives, https://recoveringdemocracyarchives .umd.edu; Lauren Hunter et al., "Unit on César Chávez, 'César Chávez at Graham Hall,' St. Louis, MO, February 1, 1973," https://recoveringdemocracyarchives .umd.edu/rda-unit/speech-at-graham-memorial-chapel-washington-st-louis-university; Skye de Saint Felix, "Unit on Marie Watson, 'A Voice from the Eastern Shore,' Hyattsville, MD, November 5, 1945," Recovering Democracy Archives, https://recoveringdemocracyarchives.umd.edu.

23. University of Maryland, Recovering Democracy Archives: Speech Recovery Project, https://recoveringdemocracyarchives.umd.edu/. See a list of those most involved in the founding of RDA at https://recoveringdemocracyarchives .umd.edu/about/.

24. William Howell, "Unit on Harry T. Burn, 'The New Citizenship,' Knoxville, TN, September 20, 1921," Recovering Democracy Archives, https://recovering democracyarchives.umd.edu.

25. Naette Lee and Lauren Hunter, "Unit on George Gillette, 'The Garrison Dam Agreement Signing,' Fort Berthold, ND, May 21, 1948," Recovering Democracy Archives, https://recoveringdemocracyarchives.umd.edu.

26. Alyson Farzad Phillips, "Unit on Gloria Steinem and Dorothy Pitman Hughes, 'Speech to Naval Academy,' Annapolis, MD, May 4, 1972," Recovering Democracy Archives, https://recoveringdemocracyarchives.umd.edu.

27. Fowler, "Unit on Paul Robeson"; Hunter et al., "Unit on César Chávez."

28. University of Maryland, George Meany Memorial AFL-CIO Archive, updated July 2021, https://www.lib.umd.edu. We are working with the Meany Archive to digitize speeches on audiotapes. The archive contains behind-the-scenes documents on the United Farm Workers and the AFL-CIO (e.g., letters and minutes), and some of the speeches are saved on audiotapes that are so fragile that experts must digitize them.

29. See Digital Public Library of America, the Kansas City Public Library, the Kansas Historical Society, the Missouri History Museum, the Tennessee State Library, and many other state and local archives. See, for example: "Pap Singleton: To Kansas," PBS Learning Media, 2002, https://mpt.pbslearningme-dia.org; Virginia Center for Digital History, Miller Center of Public Affairs, Reshaping the Nation and the Emergence of Modern America: 1877 to 1930s, University of Virginia, Charlottesville, 2005, http://www.vcdh.virginia.edu/solguide/VUS08/vus08a01.html.

30. Richard Rothstein, *The Color of Law: A Forgotten History of How Our Government Segregated America* (New York: Liveright Publishing, 2017), vii–xii.

31. Chandra Manning, *Troubled Refuge: Struggling for Freedom in the Civil War* (New York: Vintage Books, 2017), 285–87; Heather Cox Richardson, *West from Appomattox: The Reconstruction of America after the Civil War* (New Haven,

CT: Yale University Press, 2007), 78–94; William Loren Katz, *The Black West: A Documentary and Pictorial History of the African American Role in the Westward Expansion of the United States* (New York: Touchstone Book, 1996), 170.

32. Richard W. Leeman, "Fighting for Freedom Again: African American Reform Rhetoric in the Late Nineteenth Century," in *The Rhetoric of Nineteenth-Century Reform*, vol. 5, ed. Martha S. Watson and Thomas R. Burkholder (East Lansing: Michigan State University Press, 2008), 2.

33. Paul Goodman, *Of One Blood: Abolitionism and the Origins of Racial Equality* (Berkeley: University of California Press, 1998), 6–7.

34. Bjørn F. Stillion Southard, *Peculiar Rhetoric: Slavery, Freedom, and the African Colonization Movement* (Jackson: University Press of Mississippi, 2019), 3–17. See also Dean E. Robinson, *Black Nationalism in American Politics and Thought* (Cambridge: Cambridge University Press, 2001), 8–9. Such solutions mirror the Indian Removal Act of 1830. See Jason Edward Black, *American Indians and the Rhetoric of Removal and Allotment* (Jackson: University Press of Mississippi, 2015), 4–6.

35. Martha S. Jones, *Birthright Citizens: A History of Race and Rights in Antebellum America* (Cambridge: Cambridge University Press, 2018), 92.

36. Manning, *Troubled Refuge*, 285.

37. Wilson Jeremiah Moses, *The Golden Age of Black Nationalism, 1850–1925* (New York: Oxford University Press, 1978), 54. Moses suggests Douglass lived in a nice house with fifteen acres on a hill in DC.

38. Jones, *Birthright Citizens*, 37–38; Matthew Salafia, *Slavery's Borderland: Freedom and Bondage along the Ohio River* (Philadelphia: University of Pennsylvania Press, 2013), 186; Phillip W. Magness and Sebastian N. Page, *Colonization after Emancipation: Lincoln and the Movement for Black Resettlement* (Columbia: University of Missouri Press, 2011), 1, 6.

39. Martin Robison Delany, *The Condition, Elevation, Emigration, and Destiny of the Colored People of the United States: Politically Considered* (Philadelphia, PA: self-published, 1852), 35, 179, 191, https://archive.org/details /conditionelevati00dela_0. See also Dexter B. Gordon, *Black Identity: Rhetoric, Ideology, and Nineteenth-Century Black Nationalism* (Carbondale: Southern Illinois University Press, 2003), 131. Because the Naturalization Act of 1790 made clear the country was created for "free white person[s]," many Black people believed the Constitution offered no protection as a "proslavery document." See 1790 Naturalization Act, US House of Representatives and Senate, lst Cong., 2d sess., 1 stat 103, March 26, 1790, http://library.uwb.edu/Static/USimmigration/1790 _naturalization_act.html.

40. Eddie S. Glaude Jr., *Exodus! Religion, Race, and Nation in Early Nineteenth-Century Black America* (Chicago: University of Chicago Press, 2000), 3–4, 6, 10, 15, 17, 35. Among others, David Walker epitomized Black Nationalist

thought by condemning the United States for its slavery practices ("does not the blood of our fathers and of us . . . cry aloud to the Lord . . . against you") and urging African Americans to act morally responsible in self-determining their own future ("let the aim of your labours . . . be the dissemination of education and religion"). See David Walker, *David Walker's Appeal to the Coloured Citizens of the World*, ed. Peter P. Hinks (University Park: Pennsylvania State University Press, 2002), 8, 32.

41. Rogers M. Smith, *Political Peoplehood: The Roles of Values, Interests, and Identities* (Chicago: University of Chicago Press, 2015), 2–3, 42–44, 121–23.

42. Exodusters saw their "emigration" west as a biblical mission away from their existence as a "stranger in a strange land." Like the Israelites escaping Egypt, they believed God would lead them out of southern enslavement to a safer place that repudiated slavery and promised free labor and equal justice for all. See Nell Irvin Painter, *Exodusters: Black Migration to Kansas after Reconstruction* (New York: W. W. Norton, 1986), 195–96.

43. Gillian Brown, *The Consent of the Governed: The Lockean Legacy in Early American Culture* (Cambridge, MA: Harvard University Press, 2001), 15.

44. Mark Hulliung, *The Social Contract in America: From the Revolution to the Present Age* (Lawrence: University Press of Kansas, 2007), 1–2, 6.

45. To gain an understanding of the "constitutive rhetorics," see James Jasinski and Jennifer R. Mercieca, "Analyzing Constitutive Rhetorics: The Virginia and Kentucky Resolutions and the 'Principles of '98,'" in Parry-Giles and Hogan, *Handbook of Rhetoric and Public Address*, 313–41.

46. David B. Chesebrough, *Frederick Douglass: Oratory from Slavery* (Westport, CT: Greenwood Press, 1998), 17, 44. See also Frederick Douglass, "Address of the Colored National Convention to the People of the United States," *Proceedings of the Colored National Convention*, Rochester, New York, July 6, 1853, 11.

47. William S. McFeely, *Frederick Douglass* (New York: W. W. Norton, 1991), 299.

48. Shawn J. Parry-Giles, "Unit on Frederick Douglass, 'The Southern Exodus,' May 4, 1879, Baltimore, MD," Recovering Democracy Archives, https://recoveringdemocracyarchives.umd.edu/rda-unit/the-southern-exodus. This unit includes the following supplemental "address" from M. Watson Overton, D. B. Garrett, Thos. J. Watts, G. W. Smith, White Marshall, Benj. Singleton, W. A. Sizemore, and A. D. Defrantz, "An Address: From the Colored People," *Commonwealth*, June 18, 1879, Topeka, KS, in Benjamin Singleton, Benjamin "Pap" Singleton Scrapbook, 25, n.d., Kansas Historical Society, Topeka, http://www.kansasmemory.org/item/211642/page/30.

49. McFeely, *Frederick Douglass*, 301.

50. Frederick Douglass, "Southern Questions: The Negro Exodus from the Gulf States," American Social Science Association, Saratoga Springs, NY,

September 12, 1879, *Journal of Social Science* 11 (May 1880): 3, 4, 8. Douglass did not attend the conference.

51. Harold Holzer, ed., *Lincoln as I Know Him* (Chapel Hill, NC: Algonquin Books, 2009), 208.

52. Leeman, "Fighting for Freedom Again," 3.

53. Douglass, "Southern Questions," 14.

54. Frederick Douglass, "The Southern Exodus," *Baltimore American*, May 5, 1879, 1; Douglass, "Fred. Douglass on Whites and Blacks: His Opposition to Colored Exodus from the South," *Baltimore Sun*, May 5, 1879, 1. The *Baltimore American* and the *Baltimore Sun* both published portions of the May 4, 1879, speech. John W. Blassingame and John R. McKivigan authenticated a speech text that integrates versions from both newspaper texts. See "The South Knows Us: An Address Delivered in Baltimore, Maryland," May 4, 1879, in *The Frederick Douglass Papers, Series One: Speeches, Debates, and Interviews*, vol. 4, *1864–1880*, ed. John W. Blassingame and John R. McKivigan (New Haven, CT: Yale University Press, 1991), 496–503.

55. Booker T. Washington, "Address by Booker T. Washington, Principal Tuskegee Normal and Industrial Institute, Tuskegee, Alabama, at Opening of Atlanta Exposition," September 18, 1895, Library of Congress, https://memory.loc.gov/mss/mssmisc/ody/ody0605/0605001v.jpg.

56. Douglass, "Southern Questions," 2–3.

57. Waldo E. Martin Jr., *The Mind of Frederick Douglass* (Chapel Hill: University of North Carolina Press, 1984), 76–77.

58. Some felt Douglass had sold out his own people to expand the electoral influence of African Americans in the South. See "Report of the Minority," *Report and Testimony of the Select Committee of the United States Senate to Investigate the Causes of the Removal of the Negroes from the Southern States to the Northern States*, part 1 (Washington, DC: Government Printing Office, 1880), ix.

59. See "Going Down," Topeka (KS) *Colored Citizen*, May 10, 1879; McFeely, *Frederick Douglass*, 300–304. Douglass was not alone in his emigration opposition. Edmund Kelly also spoke against the Exoduster movement in a broadside entitled *The Great Exodous of the Colored People from the South to the West*, American Broadsides and Ephemera, Series 1, no. 13897 (Washington, DC: np, 1879), 1.

60. "Going Down." See also *Colored Citizen*, Library of Congress, https://www.loc.gov/item/sn83040558/.

61. Michael Calvin McGee, "Text, Context, and the Fragmentation of Contemporary Culture," *Western Journal of Communication* 54, no. 3 (Summer 1990): 287.

62. Bryan M. Jack, *The St. Louis African American Community and the Exodusters* (Columbia: University of Missouri Press, 2007), 193.

63. Richard Sheridan, "From Slavery in Missouri to Freedom in Kansas: The Influx of Black Fugitives and Contrabands into Kansas, 1854–1865," in *Kansas*

and the West: New Perspectives, ed. Rita Napier (Lawrence: University Press of Kansas, 2003), 164–68; Jack, *St. Louis African American Community*, 2–5; Charlotte Hinger, *Nicodemus: Post-Reconstruction Politics and Racial Justice in Western Kansas* (Norman: University of Oklahoma Press, 2016), 3; Katz, *Black West*, 170.

64. Although some of the Exoduster documents are available only by traveling to the archives, the archivists at the Kansas Historical Society (KHS) have committed to digitizing a wealth of holdings they have collected over decades of recovery work. Our archival research involved studying the digitized texts and traveling to the KHS to review supporting documents not digitized. We recognize that we have accessed an incomplete record of the movement's rhetorical activities and a record that shows Kansas's reaction to the Exoduster migration in a favorable light. Many of the documents saved reflect the reactions of local and state leaders as well as the religious organizations to the migration. Even when Exoduster speeches were available, the biographies of the speakers are at best spotty because they did not attract the level of attention that speakers like Douglass did. That more of the Exoduster papers were not salvaged may well reflect the "politics of the archives" and the lack of commitment to saving the papers of marginalized communities as the movement commenced. See "Forum: The Politics of Archival Research," *Rhetoric & Public Affairs* 9, no. 1 (Spring 2006): 113–51.

65. Painter, *Exodusters*, 108–9. Singleton donated his scrapbook to the Kansas Historical Society on March 26, 1889. Others added to his scrapbook from approximately 1889 to 1950. See Michael Church, "Benjamin Singleton's Scrapbook," *Kansas Memory* (blog), Kansas Memory, March 20, 2009, https://www.kansasmemory.org/blog/post/63836394.

66. Overton et al., "An Address," in Singleton Scrapbook, http://www.kansasmemory.org/item/211642/page/30.

67. Overton et al., "An Address," in Singleton Scrapbook, http://www.kansasmemory.org/item/211642/page/30.

68. Benjamin Singleton, Flier—"Ho For Sunny Kansas," Benjamin "Pap" Singleton Scrapbook, Insert, n.d., Kansas Historical Society, Topeka, KS, http://www.kansasmemory.org/item/211642/page/75.

69. Overton et al., "An Address," in Singleton Scrapbook, http://www.kansasmemory.org/item/211642/page/30.

70. "Benjamin Singleton's Rebut," in Singleton Scrapbook, 24, nd, http://www.kansasmemory.org/item/211642/page/29.

71. "The Colored Convention," in Singleton Scrapbook, 24, nd, http://www.kansasmemory.org/item/211642/page/29. The convention likely took place in Nashville in 1875; yet the article that Singleton inserted into his scrapbook only references Tennessee without identifying a specific date or location. These arguments mirrored the tenets of Black Nationalism as a force for Black "liberation"

and "empowerment'" See Katz, *Black West*, 170; Robert Carr, *Black Nationalism in the New World: Reading the African-American and West Indian Experience* (Durham, NC: Duke University Press, 2002), 25–27; Moses, *Golden Age of Black Nationalism*, 55; and Robinson, *Black Nationalism*, 8–9.

72. "The Negro Exodus: The Old Style and the New," *Harper's Weekly*, May 1, 1880, Digital Public Library of America, https://dp.la. See Jack, *St. Louis African American Community*, 114. Women were also central to such migration efforts, as mothers, worried about the safety of their children, put pressure on their families to leave the South. See Katz, *Black West*, 183.

73. See "Declaration of Colored Citizens," in Singleton Scrapbook, 25, nd, http://www.kansasmemory.org/item/211642/page/15. See also James M. Campbell, "African Americans in Southern Cities," in *Reconstruction: People and Perspectives*, ed. James M. Campbell and Rebecca J. Fraser (Santa Barbara, CA: ABC-CLIO, 2008), 57. Campbell wrongly reports that the migration movements faltered by the end of the Civil War until Marcus Garvey initiated his "Back to Africa" movement.

74. Katz, *Black West*, 170.

75. Painter, *Exodusters*, 292.

76. Cedric J. Robinson, *Forgeries of Memory and Meaning: Blacks and the Regimes of Race in American Theater and Film before World War II* (Chapel Hill: University of North Carolina Press, 2007), 149.

77. See introduction to Hinger, *Nicodemus*; Quintard Taylor, *In Search of the Racial Frontier: African Americans in the American West: 1528–1990* (New York: W. W. Norton, 1998), 139. Nicodemus was also a biblical figure addressed in John as a "ruler of the Jews" that Jesus, the story suggests, said could be "born again." See Darcey Steinke, *The Gospel According to John* (New York: Grove Press, 1999), 6.

78. "To the Colored Citizens of the United States," Nicodemus, Graham County, KS, July 2, 1877, Kansas Memory, Kansas Historical Society, https://www.kansasmemory.org/item/208456.

79. Katz, *Black West*, 175, 182.

80. Hinger, *Nicodemus*, 8–9.

81. Robert G. Athearn, *In Search of Canaan: Black Migration to Kansas, 1879–1880* (Lawrence: Regents Press of Kansas, 1978), 243–63; Katz, *Black West*, 175.

82. Athearn, *In Search of Canaan*, 259–79; Painter, *Exodusters*, 225–33. Similar issues occurred with the Exodusters in St. Louis. See Jack, *St. Louis African American Community*, 159. The Republican governor of Kansas—John P. St. John, an 1884 presidential candidate—formed the Kansas Freedman's Relief Association with other Kansas political leaders, including the secretary of state, treasurer, attorney general, and judges. See "Office of the Kansas Freedman Relief Association," June 26, 1879, in Singleton Scrapbook, Insert, nd, Kansas Historical

Society, Topeka, http://www.kansasmemory.org/item/211642/page/55, http://www.kansasmemory.org/item/211642/page/56, http://www.kansasmemory.org/item/211642/page/57.

83. Plessy v. Ferguson, 163 US 537 (1896); Steve Luxenberg, *Separate: The Story of* Plessy v. Ferguson, *and America's Journey from Slavery to Segregation* (New York: W. W. Norton, 2019), xviii–xix.

84. "Tennessee Town History: From Freedom to the Future," Tennessee Town Neighborhood Improvement Association, History, updated March 14, 2019, https://tenntownnia.weebly.com/history.html; Sherrita Camp, *African American Topeka* (Charleston, SC: Arcadia Publishing, 2013), 44–45, 97; Brown v. Board of Educ., 347 US 483 (1954), https://www.loc.gov/item/usrep347483.

85. Judith Lynne McConnell and Blythe F. Hinitz, "In Their Words: A Living History of the Brown Decisions," *Educational Studies* 37, no. 1 (2005): 77–78. Many of the Exodusters were from Tennessee. The Central Congregational Church represented the sponsoring church.

86. "Tennessee Town History"; Sherrita Camp, *African American Topeka* (Charleston, SC: Arcadia Publishing, 2013), 44–45, 97; Brown v. Board of Educ., 347 US 483 (1954), https://www.loc.gov/item/usrep347483.

87. For more on how rhetorical critics investigate the "circulation" of arguments and ideologies, see the special forum, Mary E. Stuckey, ed., "Forum on Rhetorical Circulation," in *Rhetoric & Public Affairs* 15, no. 4 (Winter 2012): 609–94.

88. "For Contributors: Guidelines for Preparing Manuscripts," Voices of Democracy, http://voicesofdemocracy.umd.edu.

89. See Blair L. M. Kelley's discussion of Black Americans' resistance to *Plessy v. Ferguson* in *Right to Ride: Streetcar Boycotts and African American Citizenship in the Era of* Plessy v. Ferguson (Chapel Hill: University of North Carolina Press, 2010), 12–13.

90. Martha Minow, *"Brown"'s Wake: Legacies of America's Educational Landmark* (New York: Oxford, 2010), 6–9; Matthew D. Lassiter, *The Silent Majority: Suburban Politics in the Sunbelt South* (Princeton, NJ: Princeton University Press, 2006), 308–10.

91. Paul D. Moreno, *Black Americans and Organized Labor: A New History* (Baton Rouge: Louisiana State University Press, 2006), 1–36; Beth Tompkins Bates, *Pullman Porters and the Rise of Protest Politics in Black America, 1925–1945* (Chapel Hill: University of North Carolina Press, 2001), 38.

92. Susan Cornwell and Imani Moise, "As Migrants Languish in Border Facilities, U.S. Congress Struggles to Finalize Military Aid," *Reuters*, June 26, 2019, https://www.reuters.com.

93. Rothstein, *Color of Law*, xii–xv. See also Elaine Godfrey and Adam Harris, "The 10 Presidential Candidates Who Support Busing," *Atlantic*, July 10,

2019, https://www.theatlantic.com; Dana Goldstein and Anemona Hartocollis, "'Separatist Programs for Separate Communities': California School District Agrees to Desegregate," *New York Times*, August 9, 2019, https://www.nytimes.com/2019/08/09/us/sausalito-school-segregation.html.

94. P. R. Lockhart, "At NAACP Convention, 2020 Democrats Criticize Trump's Record on Race," *Vox*, July 24, 2019, https://www.vox.com/identities/2019/7/24/20726568/naacp-democratic-primary-2020-donald-trump-racism.

95. Laura Grattan, *Populism's Power: Radical Grassroots Democracy in America* (Oxford: Oxford University Press, 2016), 78.

96. Melanye T. Price, *Dreaming Blackness: Black Nationalism and African American Public Opinion* (New York: New York University Press, 2009), 21, 35–36.

3

Martin Luther King Jr. in East Berlin

Prophetic History and the Convergence of Codes from the
Sermonic to the King-Code

Christopher J. Oldenburg and Adrienne E. Hacker Daniels

On January 20, 2019, in an interview with the television news program *Face the Nation*, Vice Pres. Michael Pence compared Pres. Donald Trump's proposal to strengthen the national security of the United States with a border wall to the civil rights work of Martin Luther King Jr. Admittedly, King did speak to the meaning of a wall on September 13, 1964, at the Marienkirche (St. Mary's Church) in East Berlin. However, for King a wall did not embody a venerated ideal that promulgated democracy but rather one that vilified democratic ideals and vitiated human rights. Pence's profane interpolation prompted us to examine the rhetorical history of King's sermon "East or West, God's Children" as it functioned as the impetus for over half a century of work in Germany that fostered intercultural unification. King's message called for Christian consubstantiality, reconciliation, and unification through a prefigured, transhistorical sacred typology, or sermonic code beginning with Moses and the Exodus narrative and culminating with Jesus Christ's crucifixion and resurrection. King connected this sacred typology with an "eschatological hope" for the German people.[1] Appealing to such a code engendered the first fault line in the Berlin Wall by extolling the virtues of, and the necessary faith for, achieving racial and religious harmony.

This religious harmony is instantiated in the tenets of J. Vernon Jensen's characteristics for ethical communication. The communicative connections among dissimilar faiths belie their differences. Of Jensen's six tenets, the three most germane to this project are (1) wisdom is revealed by sages "through holy or venerated documents," (2) in making teaching more accessible and comprehensible, the tenets are "embedded in a narrative form," and (3) "a sense of intimate linkage between the divine or sage communicator and the human communicatee" is required in ethical communication.[2]

Through a historical and rhetorical analysis of "East or West, God's Children," we argue King's sermon can be read as a speech code inviting his oppressed East German audience to see themselves as part of the trans-historical concatenation that is the Judeo-Christian prophetic tradition.[3] In doing so, King enacted an inductive argument by allusive analogy that situates East Berliners in this sacred temporality of God's providence. We support this claim primarily by an examination of the interanimation of King's text and context, focusing specifically on his inventive imagery of the Berlin Wall as a political symbol of division, captivity, isolation, and despair that will ultimately be vanquished by unity in a common faith.

Because rhetorical history can be understood as "a process rather than simply a product,"[4] our chapter concludes by examining the diachronic progeny of King's East Berlin sermon manifested in the form of a contemporaneous intercultural and pedagogical project aptly titled the King-Code. Started in 2013, the King-Code is a multimedia educational youth program that centers around Dr. Martin Luther King Jr.'s 1964 visit to both sides of the then-divided Berlin. The King-Code project comprises high school students from two Berlin public high schools (Rosa-Luxemburg Gymnasium in Pankow and the Ernst-Reuter-School in Wedding) located in different boroughs.[5] Rosa-Luxemburg Gymnasium enrolls more upper-middle-class students while Ernst-Reuter, located in a multicultural district, has more working-class students. The students work together to retrace King's historic visit, elided from both American and German history books, through the construction of what they call a "virtual historical tram."[6] We examine the work students are doing as they return to King's rhetorical history and how his dream is kept alive in Germany today through this unique pedagogical project. The King-Code project uses a QR code as its primary logo that functions as a "multimodal act" for documenting their work,[7] sharing the lessons they have learned while advancing the cause of Martin Luther King Jr.

The King-Code project is less about unmasking the symbolic structures of domination abiding in ideological signifying systems. It is more about illuminating how multimodal, pedagogical, and intercultural discourses that are committed to returning to the rhetorical history of King's emancipatory message of unity and love serve to challenge the actual political systems of division and oppression directly through an interrogation and interaction with history itself. Student decoders not only interact with the physical landmarks imbued within the public memory of King's 1964 visit, they also analyze historical artifacts, archival materials, interviews with eyewitnesses, and other evidentiary materials. Via a virtual site with QR code technology, publics can access their cumulative and interdependent rhetorical and historical work. As a hermeneutic guide, students learn and teach this history, discuss the sustained impact it had on the peaceful reunification of Germany, and communicate its relevance for intercultural understanding today. Their mission "aims to bring together young people of different backgrounds and different schools, reduce prejudices, and encourage them to work together to promote the city and society in order to live the dream of King!"[8]

The convergence of King's 1964 East Berlin sermon and the contemporaneous King-Code project demonstrate what E. Culpepper Clark and Raymie McKerrow, in *Doing Rhetorical History*, call the "ontic relationship between rhetoric and its construction of history as a narrative told—only to be retold anew in a future that year by year recedes before us."[9] Thus, this enterprise, ostensibly anachronistic, actually performs an atavistic function for the reappearance of rhetorical history.

King's Codes: Sermonic and Pedagogical

King's historic sermon and the contemporary intercultural and pedagogical project aimed at learning from King's visit to Berlin pivot on reading these texts and contexts as both sermonic and multimodal semiotic codes. First, a word on how we intend to employ the polysemous term *code* is in order. We define code as a sociocultural agreed-upon framework of meaning, a rhetorical interaction between encoder and decoder that coordinates language (or any symbol system, including visual images and sites of spatiotemporal significance) to its purpose.[10] For Gerry Philipsen, a speech code is "a system of socially constructed symbols and meanings, premises, and rules, pertaining to communicative conduct."[11] In several respects, the Judaic notion of code is an embodiment of King's sermonic rhetoric as well as the pedagogical King-Code, scaffolded with this interplay between the sacred and the secular. The Hebrew word for code, *tsofen* (which is also the word for cipher), is here less of an encoding enterprise than a decoding enterprise, manifest in the work of the teachers and students pursuing the mission of King-Code.

Concomitantly, the term *sermonic* is equally equivocal and has been interpreted more broadly by contemporary rhetoricians Kenneth Burke, Chaïm Perelman, and Richard Weaver as a counterstatement to authoritative scientism.[12] For the purposes of this chapter, we define sermonic more granularly with a focus on King's rhetorical purpose. Sermonic, then, as Carolyn Calloway-Thomas and John Louis Lucaites explicate, refers to a form of religious exhortation in which an orator or prophet illuminates and, at times, admonishes a congregation to comprehend the values of their collective, religious community and act in accordance with those principles.[13] Calloway-Thomas and Lucaites argue King's virtuosity as an orator and moral leader, par excellence, is owed to the sermonic virtue of his rhetoric.

Heuristically deepening the Calloway-Thomas and Lucaites sermonic taxonomy, particularly the elements of "identifying and defining core communal values" and "performing of communal existence," we argue that these rhetorical functions of the sermonic effectuated in King's East Berlin homily align with the chief aims of prophetic rhetoric.[14] According to both Burke's and Weaver's hortatory nature of language, humans employ a religious language (morally coded discourse that motivates action) as a heuristic for language itself. Weaver argues that language is sermonic and thereby predicated on culturally coded meanings, including "a scheme of values," that reinforce communal existence and spur collective action.[15] Burke refers to these coded communal urgings as the "thou shalt not[s]."[16] Likewise, as Calloway-Thomas and Lucaites see it, the sermonic function of discourse occurs whenever prescriptions about the relationship between communal values and collective action are enacted, for example, in efforts by prophetic rhetors to reform injustices and inspire hope.

Such enactments have powerful purchase for prophetic rhetors such as King whose sermonic persuasion weaves together both sacred and secular ideals. The Roman orator Cicero, appropriating from the metaphysical poet Lucretius, reminds us that the word *religio* means "to bind together."[17] These situated codes or, in more theological language, "covenants," are foundational (re)articulations of the prophet's moral vision of which an audience needs to be reminded and toward which they need to be redirected.

A Brief Chronology of King's Historic Visit

Not only is "East or West, God's Children," rarely invoked in historical or rhetorical scholarship, but King's visit to a then-divided Germany from September 12 to September 14, 1964, is only sporadically alluded to as a noteworthy and significant point on the timeline of his life.[18] Ironically, when gaining acquaintance with the sermon, the reasons for King's trip to Berlin, and ultimately the consequentialism of the sermon at the Marienkirche in East Berlin, one would be hard pressed to wholly dismiss the extraordinary confluence of events that took place on Sunday, September 13, 1964. And these events left a profound and arguably indelible mark on the study of rhetorical history. For King's message was one of transcendence, demonstrating not only that the struggle for equality, freedom, and justice was not unique to America but also that such a vision was bound up in the single garment of global destiny. His rhetoric engendered a synergy in which America, Germany, and the world were invited to be persuaded by a sermonic rhetoric of unity, reconciliation, peace, and hope. In other words, King's message went beyond the Berlin Wall to surpass and surmount local "wall politics" and other human-made divisions.

How did this momentous trip come into being? Willy Brandt, the mayor of West Berlin, invited King to speak as part of a cultural festival at the Berlin Philharmonic Hall, part of which involved a memorial service for Pres. John F. Kennedy. Recall that Kennedy had visited Berlin the prior year, delivering one of his most moving and memorable speeches on June 26, 1963, just months before his assassination on November 22 of that year.[19] King's Marienkirche sermon has been compared to Kennedy's "Ich Bin Ein Berliner" speech—with its inspired message of hope directed to the citizenry of East Berlin, who, in the summer of 1961, became cut off from their West Berlin neighbors.[20] The physical and political division commenced on August 13 with the construction of the Berlin Wall,[21] a monolith seen as an abominable edifice to the Cold War and characterized by Benjamin Dreschel as a "political media icon."[22] Clayborne Carson, director of the Martin Luther King Jr. Research and Education Institute, commented that "it was a big deal. It was major. In fact, some people compared it to Kennedy's visit to Berlin";[23] some argue the sermon was tantamount to Kennedy's "pledge of solidarity."[24]

The early hours of September 13 began a journey fraught with both peril and amazement. After King's paean to President Kennedy, a cataclysmic event turned the day grim. King learned that when Michael Meyer, a twenty-one-year-old East German professional jockey, attempted an escape, he was shot multiple times. In his successful rescue of Meyer, American soldier Sgt. Hans Puhl threw a smoke bomb, shouted to the German Democratic Republic border guards, "Let the boy go, or I'll shoot," and then spirited Meyer over the wall to safety.[25] Distraught by what had transpired at the Berlin Wall, King visited the site in the Kreuzberg district where Meyer was shot, spoke with residents of 42 Stallschreiberstraße, and bore witness to the apartment's windows and facade riddled with bullet holes. So moved by what Meyer endured, King visited him at the Urban Hospital. In fact, King's visit to Meyer was shrouded in secrecy because any transparency about his destination might have led to King being blocked from visiting East Berlin.[26]

At three o'clock, King attended the Tag der Kirchen (Day of Churches) and delivered a sermon at the Waldbühne amphitheater to an audience of twenty thousand attendees. In tandem with Brandt's invitation, Heinrich Grüber extended an invitation for King to speak in East Berlin at the Marienkirche where Gruber had been a pastor. A former concentration camp prisoner, opponent of Nazism, and pacifist now living in West Berlin, Grüber wrote to King articulating the equivalency between the German travails and those of Black people: "During the time of Hitler, I was often ashamed of being a German, as today I am ashamed of being white. I am grateful to you, dear brother, and to all who stand with you in this fight for justice, which you are conducting in the spirit of Jesus Christ."[27] The centerpiece of King's visit came in the evening at the Marienkirche.

"East or West, God's Children," Summary

After pleasantries and expressions of delectation at the opportunity to share in Christian fellowship with his East Berlin audience, King identified with the whole of Germany through the familiarity of his namesake and its historic significance for the German people and the Protestant Reformation. Such an allusion to Martin Luther, the "Great Reformer," functioned as a synecdoche that appealed to national and Christian unity. A central appeal to unification and reconciliation on the shared foundation of Judeo-Christian values embedded in what we will call King's sermonic code became the crux of his message. King exclaimed, "We are all one in Christ Jesus, for in Christ there is no East, no West, no North, no South, but one great fellowship of love throughout the whole, wide world."[28] King invited the segregated audience of the East German people to learn from the ways in which God's destiny for the civil rights movement in the United States may have applied to their particular situation and thereby demonstrated that the fight for racial and religious harmony was truly a global struggle. This purpose was furthered primarily through a transhistorical prophetic rhetoric that invited the East German people to see themselves in solidarity with the Israelites of Egypt and Babylon as well as African Americans—in short, as part of the biblical epic of salvation history. He clearly argued that regardless of man-made divisions (pointedly, the Berlin Wall), the Christian faith as predicated on unity under "one God, one faith, and one baptism" underwrites the common humanity of both African Americans and East Germans, an "inescapable destiny that binds us together."[29]

According to Michael S. Bruner, Kennedy used the imagery of the divisive Berlin Wall as a rhetorical strategy to emphasize political consubstantiality between East Berliners and the West in his famous 1963 "Ich Bin Ein Berliner" speech.[30] Moreover, Bruner notes that Reagan, too, in his 1987 "Mr. Gorbachev, Tear Down This Wall" speech, employed the wall as a rhetorical resource. However, Reagan's use was a more pious means by which to vituperate the spiritual poverty engendered by the totalitarian ideology responsible for the wall's construction.[31]

King established his consubstantiality with his audience via appeals to history and a global Judeo-Christian unity predicated on a common faith and the prophetic saga of salvation. Nevertheless, King did not shy away from acknowledging differences and divisions, for reconciliation and identification are based upon the precepts of division.[32] King provided evidence for the success of this prophetic vision through an application and recapitulation of the civil rights movement in America. As King had done many times before, he clearly framed his movement's narrative by the Exodus typology.[33] Additionally, King drew theological parallels to familiar New Testament and Gospel passages on reconciliation and Christ's ministry and enumerated exemplars of "God's action in our midst."[34]

Next, in keeping with biblical parallels, King cast African Americans and East Berliners as the Israelites of Exodus. Here, King inventively transported auditors through this sweeping scriptural narrative history, starting with fleeing "the Egypt of slavery," traversing through the "'wilderness' of segregation" to "the mountain looking into the 'promised land' of . . . integrated living," and finally culminating in a faith that "there can be no resurrection without crucifixion," thereby affirming "Jesus Christ's victory over the world, whether it be an Eastern world or a Western world."[35] The dynamics of King's transhistorical retelling of salvation can be further elucidated through an understanding of the prophetic tradition. We now turn to an examination of King's sermonic code and prophetic rhetoric in "East or West, God's Children."

King's Sermonic Code and Convening Prophetic Voices

King's sermonic discourse merges both the symbolic and the moral meanings of the term *code*. Thus, speech codes are inherently sermonic in their efforts to unify audiences around shared values and a common faith. Moreover, speech code theory recognizes that shared meanings and values, and their impact on how humans understand and coordinate actions with others, are endemic to a culture itself. This knowledge is a robust inventional resource for rhetorical action. For King, these core communal values were the Judeo-Christian ideals of unity, freedom, nonviolence, social justice, reconciliation, and redemption. The prophetic power of King's sermonic rhetoric resides in its capacity to coordinate Judeo-Christian religious speech codes and prophetic intertextuality with the plight of an audience of oppressed people.[36]

In a reflection on King's speech at Marienkirche and the audience's collective response to his inspired message, Alcoyne Scott observed, "It was the power of his message, and it was also couched in very clear Christian terminology. This was clearly a man of faith with a profound belief in humanity and in reconciliation. He believed it, and you felt it. And for people in this audience, who really saw no future for themselves because the Cold War was hot (no one even imagined a point in time that it would ever end), for him to talk about hope was electrifying."[37]

However, as on point as this perception is, Paul Kengor provides a heuristic augmentation to Scott's firsthand account in saying, "Actually, make that Judeo-Christian terminology."[38] And the Judaic (including Old Testament) motifs and allusions irrefutably support Kengor's revision to Scott's account. In fact, given the relationship that King cultivated with Rabbi Abraham Joshua Heschel that predated King's trip to West and East Berlin by approximately one and a half years, the incorporation of these interfaith motifs is neither surprising nor extraneous in the least.

King and Heschel are arguably the two major prophetic voices of the twentieth century, certainly within the purview of the civil rights and antiwar movements. As Susannah Heschel observes, "For both, the prophets were central to nearly all of their speeches and writings."[39] Their camaraderie as kindred spirits from different faith traditions commenced at the Chicago Conference on Religion and Race, January 14–17, 1963, conceived as a milestone religious commemoration of the Emancipation Proclamation centennial.[40] An organizational memorandum from the conference stipulated that Heschel would provide "the prophetic inspirational statement."[41] This unprecedented ecumenical conference purported to be "a candid discussion of race relations."[42]

As we demonstrate, King's sermon in East Berlin is a key rhetorical moment in the eternal progression that is the prophetic tradition. Prefigured by Moses and the Exodus typology, King's retelling of this biblical literature elegantly glides through history, harmonizing with Daniel, Ezekiel, and St. Paul, and coming full circle with Jesus Christ's crucifixion and resurrection. As Keith Miller argues, King's use of the prophetic hermeneutic of the Exodus as reiterated by Second Isaiah in "I Have a Dream" afforded a "triple equation: Hebrews in Egypt equal Hebrews in Babylon equal African Americans in the US. King grounds his hope in the same God who eliminated Hebrew bondage in Egypt and Hebrew captivity and exile in Babylon, and who would therefore end captivity/segregation/exile of African Americans."[43]

We argue that to this analysis, in "East or West, God's Children" a fourth equation can be added to the calculus of King's prophetic drama of hope to include the East German people. Miller contends that King implied prophets like Moses, Daniel, Ezekiel, Isaiah, Amos,[44] and he himself held fast to the belief that "although the world is badly skewed and sinful, the magnificent drama of the Exodus continues unabated, offering hope to all oppressed people."[45] Thus, King's speech constructed his East Berlin audience as a second persona similar to the hermeneutic work Miller argues King accomplished in his use of Second Isaiah.

The literary theorist Northrop Frye, appropriating from the British bard William Blake, characterizes the Bible as "The Great Code."[46] King routinely appealed to specific narratives and prophets, using this "Great Code" as a hermeneutic. The prophet Moses and his role in the Exodus story became one of King's paradigmatic tropes precisely for the political, rhetorical, and moral work it performs. Gary Selby, who has an excellent expatiation of King's use of the Exodus narrative, refers to it as a "rhetoric of freedom," enthymematically packaged in that "ancient religious drama" that animates "a symbolic context in which his hearers could experience their present circumstances, representing their campaign for racial [political and religious] justice as the enactment of a modern day Exodus."[47] Selby even characterizes King's stylistic configuring as "'code' references to the Exodus."[48] In other words, King's Exodus allusion functions as part and parcel of his broader sermonic code. And, as Selby quite rightly points out, African American preachers and orators have long relied on the Exodus story as a rhetorical strategy in the struggle for racial justice. In King's instance, how might the Exodus narrative play in East Berlin?

The Exodus typology is fitting for King's East Berlin context: the ignoble Berlin Wall engenders metonymic and metaphorical signification for the draconian Egyptians who enslaved the Israelites, making their lives bitter with hard service in mortar and bricks.[49] The East German people were, too, a people of mortar and brick, or as Angela Merkel characterized them, "concrete and steel,"[50] a people confined to a European Gehenna.[51] Profoundly aware of the Berlin Wall's signification, King employed it as a conceptual metaphor and a concrete structure. King characterized the wall as "a symbol of the divisions of men on the face of the earth. For here on either side of the wall are God's children, and no man-made barrier can obliterate that fact. Whether it be East or West, men and women search for meaning, hope for fulfillment, yearn for faith in something beyond themselves, and cry desperately for love and community to support them in this pilgrim journey."[52]

The reference to "God's children" echoes God's act of salvation from Egypt as told by the prophet Hosea: "When Israel was a child, I loved him, and out of Egypt I called my son."[53] A key component of the mise-en-scène at King's Marienkirche sermon included a rendition of the spiritual "Go Down Moses," sung by the church choir immediately after King's opening words of salutation, "My dear Christian friends of East Berlin." The spiritual's provenance is Exodus 5:1: "And afterward Moses and Aaron came, and said unto Pharaoh: 'Thus saith the Lord, the God of Israel: Let my people go, that they may hold a feast unto me in the wilderness.'"[54]

After having cultivated Judeo-Christian identification with his East Berlin audience, King then repudiated all odious obstructions and appealed to a transcendent coessentiality achieved through unity in humanity, suffering, faith, and redemption. King declared that "regardless of the barriers of race, creed, ideology, or nationality, there is an escapable destiny which binds us together. There is a common humanity which makes us sensitive to the suffering of one another. And for many of us, there is one Lord, one faith, and one baptism which binds us in a common history, a common calling, and a common hope for salvation of the world."[55]

With the skill of a bravura orator, King continued to conflate text and context by metaphorically exploiting the material, impeding presence of the wall to dramatically foreground the rhetorical situation of his East Berlin sermon. Clearly, the corrective to these "barriers," King argued, was a collective understanding of the common suffering and inescapable destiny of his audience, a shared history and future that binds all oppressed people. This initial characterization of King's context provides support for our addition of a fourth equation to Miller's formula of transcendent redemption that thereby yokes the Hebrews of Exodus with the East German people of the twentieth century. Moreover, unity, temporal continuity, and consubstantiality of Judeo-Christian identity are reached with the anaphoric phrase "one Lord, one faith, one baptism, which binds us in a common history, a common calling, and a common hope for the salvation of the world."[56] Beyond repetitive unison, King's twin set of triadic parataxis also conflates the temporality of the Old and New Testament and extends salvation history to include King's present context. The belief in one Lord is a common religious tenet to both Jews and Christians, a common calling, and serves as a constitutive allegiance to a faith tradition. One baptism (which began in the New Testament with the prophet John the Baptist) becomes a common teleological hope or, as Andre LaCocque and Paul Ricoeur put it, "the perpetual futurity of Redemption."[57]

King's prophetic intertextuality continued with an allusive analogy to Daniel and the Babylonian captivity. Recall Daniel was a visionary and interpreter of dreams, perhaps best known for his escape from the lion's den. More salient to our analysis, Daniel was a consummate de-cryptor in his interpretation of the "coded message" written on a Babylonian wall, portending ominous events.[58] King exclaimed, "We have found ourselves literally 'thrown to the lions' in the arena of life."[59] Daniel's is a story of faith and perseverance, a faith that King reminded his audience "has enabled us to face death, . . . has given us a way when there seem to be no way."[60] Although an Old Testament narrative, the reference "thrown to the lions" also suggests the Roman persecution of Christians, whereby punishment was meted out by the ghastly practice of *damnatio ad bestias*, exposing Christians to beasts in the arena. The subsequent phrase "in the arena of life" would engender a particular painful resonance with East Berliners by recalling the wall actually surrounded Berlin and immured inhabitants in a ringlike enclosure to make it impossible to escape to West Berlin. As an eyewitness to King's sermon, Gesine Schuppan observed that the audience responded "because we felt so trapped and thought we are so cut off here. And that's I think why all these people came to hear someone who spoke of nonviolence, who spoke of his faith, who spoke of freedom and who spoke of justice."[61] Schuppan's testament to this watershed moment in German history was captured by the King-Code students in the significant interviewing portion of the project.

A third prophetic voice animated in King's sermonic text is that of Ezekiel when King stated, "We have been as a 'valley of dry bones,'"[62] a biblical allusion to the spiritual demise and revival of the Israelites during the Babylonian captivity. As Miller points out, this biblical motif became the impetus for a ubiquitous sermon expounded by early African American preachers and homilists titled "Dry Bones in the Valley."[63] King interpolated it here as a genuflection to that pious tradition but also to truss his East Berlin audience to this sacred typology of Hebrew prophecy. Moreover, the imagery of the valley, cleaved out with massive walls of rock on either side, presents a painful place of desolation, isolation, and desiccation of faith and hope—not unlike the Berlin Wall.

Another significant stage in King's redemptive history is the New Testament. This sacrosanct setting thereby provides the *antistrophos* or antitype to the Old Testament types (people or events in sacred history that adumbrate people or events in the New Testament, e.g., Moses as a type for Christ) and also links "Judeo" with "Christian" as in the common parlance, "Judeo-Christian tradition." This context is recognized by King's references to the Gospels and quoting epistolary passages from the apostle Paul, with whose rhetorical style King was intimately familiar and, according to Malinda Snow, imitated.[64]

Similar to Paul addressing Corinthians, Romans, Galatians, and Ephesians, King preached for unity over separation and division through reconciliation in Christ. Avowing a passage from Paul's Letter to the Ephesians, King encouraged the people of Germany to "unite all things in him, things of heaven, and things on earth."[65] Snow argues that Paul is the preacher/prophet par excellence for King to emulate, and this mimesis is most apropos considering Paul's commitment to the "destruction of barriers" and opposition to "division or separation and all social institutions, including jails, segregated churches,"[66] and, we would add, exiled nationalities. Thus, it is no surprise that King would echo Paul's pleas for unity in East Berlin with the divisive wall as a dramatic and ubiquitous political backdrop. In point of fact, King proceeded to be even more contextually explicit by quoting Ephesians 2:14 where, through Paul's words, King equated reconciliation in Christ with ineluctably "breaking down the dividing walls of hostility."[67]

King's peroration reaffirmed faith in the covenant promised to both Jews and Christians, an active faith articulated and enacted by a prophetic history of redemptive deliverance; it began with Moses, traversed through the New Testament to Christ, and arrived at King's present moment. Albert J. Raboteau observes the typological parallel between Moses and Jesus within slave religion; Miller later expands the parallel by arguing for a linkage between Egyptian bondage and the crucifixion and analogized the Promised Land with Easter.[68] This elegance is most illustrative in the verses of the following slave spiritual:

> Jesus Christ, He died for me,
> Way down in Egypt Land
> Jesus Christ, He set me free,
> Way down in Egypt Land.[69]

King concluded his sermon by elaborating on the inexorable and instrumental faith that brought him to East Berlin, a faith that would bring about the unity necessary for "marching on to freedom land" for the Eastern and Western worlds of Germany. He proclaimed:

> This is the faith which has kept us going. This is a faith
> which has enabled us to face death. This is the faith which
> has given us a way when there seemed to be no way. This is
> a faith that lets us face our daily crucifixions, in knowledge
> that God's world is changed through resurrection, and there
> can be no resurrection without crucifixion. This is the faith
> I commend to you Christians here in Berlin. A living, active,

massive faith that affirms the victory of Jesus Christ over the world, whether it be an Eastern world or a Western world.

With this faith, we will be able to hew out of the mountain of despair, a stone of hope. With this faith, we will be able to transform the jangling discords of the nations into a beautiful symphony of brotherhood. With this faith, we will be able to work together, to pray together, to struggle together, to suffer together, to stand up for freedom together, knowing that we will be free one day.[70]

Stylistically, the scheme of anaphora with "this is the faith" serves as a prelude to the second passage, which integrates anaphora and epistrophe. The passage in its entirety exemplifies a tetracolon, where the last clause, "to stand up for freedom together," is inclusive of not only the action (hew, transform, work, pray, struggle) but the action's raison d'être. In comporting with understanding the speech from a Judeo-Christian perspective, the focus on "faith" in these passages resonates with significant theological and etymological connotations. King stated that the prerequisite of "faith" is a sine qua non for a salubrious result: to "be free one day." These action verbs are of particular import as connective tissue to faith. The Hebrew word for faith, *emunah*, shares the same Hebrew root for artisan, artist, and craftsman. In explaining how one acquires emunah, chabad.org explains that the "artisan is called in Hebrew an 'uman'—because he has practiced his craft repeatedly until it becomes natural for him. So too, Emunah grows taller and deeper as you accustom yourself to see all the phenomena of life as manifestations of the Creator's presence and glory. All the more so is Emunah enriched by being tested and withstanding those tests; and by making sacrifices in life for the sake of your Emunah."[71]

Prefigured by the prophetic tradition that King had hitherto narrated, the repetition of faith's incipience moved King's East Berlin audience to affirm that they, too, shared in the telos of this predetermined salvation narrative, to "be free one day." Most plausibly, it is freedom, considering that "this faith" King preached about was a prophetic faith couched in the language of Isaiah and the archetypal metaphors of mountains and valleys.[72]

After King situated his East Berlin audience in the prophetic tradition, he emphasized "this faith's" percussive instrumentality. It was not a static faith. In his penultimate paragraph, King reprised several tropes from his iconic "I Have a Dream Speech" the year before. However, in the context of East Berlin and the wall, they evoked a more sublime vivacity and compulsion.

Reframing Rhetorical History via King-Code

As part of the ongoing commemoration of King's trip to Berlin, Clayborne Carson noted that in 2014 "several Berlin schoolteachers have encouraged their students to contribute to a 'KING-CODE' website retracing King's activities in Berlin."[73] As discussed above, in this pedagogically innovative project pupils from two schools are returning to

Figure 1. QR King-Code. Courtesy of www.king-code.de. Used with permission.

this rhetorical history, elided from both American and German history books, through the construction of what they call a "virtual historical tram."[74] Teacher and coarchitect of the project Daniel Schmöcker notes that students "collect documents, have working groups, [and] . . . look at sites under a magnifying glass [to] discover the history."[75] Students treat King's history as a mystery, where the narrative plot invites them to crack the code. They collect clues, evidence, and eyewitness accounts, espouse theories, and record, store, and share personal emotional reflections via a digital website accessed by QR code technology (figure 1). Conceived by Schmöcker, a teacher of art and religion at the Rosa-Luxemburg-Gymnasium in Pankow, and Saraya Gomis, a teacher of history and world studies at the Ernst Reuter secondary school in Wedding, the King-Code project employs QR code technology to create a digital-pedagogical platform for doing and ultimately reframing rhetorical history.

In examining the reconstruction of King's historic visit, it is interesting how a multimodal social semiotic QR code aids in investigating, promulgating, and articulating this rhetorical history. QR codes are small, pixelated designs that are rapidly readable through an application when scanned in any direction by a tablet or smartphone. The most common storehouses of QR-related content are website addresses or URLs, displayed when the code is scanned. Helen Nissenbaum views technology like QR codes as a high-capacity, high-density two-dimensional symbol that stores data. Such technology as QR codes, she writes, "are a socio-technical system": not a stand-alone physical device but connected with an interdependent nexus of complex telecommunication networks that are contingent on "a host of social, political, and economic arrangements."[76]

Moreover, its two-dimensional symbolicity seamlessly and simultaneously processes the physical past and digital present, the diachronic and the synchronic. The QR code strikes us as an eminently suitable and instrumental technology for reframing rhetorical history. QR code technology allows for audiences to experience spatiotemporal renegotiation through their direct sensory contact with present-day sites, amplified by a digitally enhanced historical interaction illuminated on a smart phone in the palm of their hands. King-Code's strategic use of QR code technology functions as a protean portal, opening students and viewers to the educational and inventional world of experiencing rhetorical history. King-Code permits participants to step into the mythos of King's historic visit and return forever transformed by self-discovery and the yearning to enact King's righteous vision in their own time.

The diversity, curiosity, and inquisitiveness on the part of student participants leads them on a quest to understand and illumine Martin Luther King Jr.'s historic visit to East Berlin. Part sleuth, part historian, part documentarian, part rhetorician, part storyteller, and even part diagnostician, each student traces the clues through the venues King visited, the words he spoke, and the accounts of those who bore witness to these few historic days. It chronicles the German students' investigation of King's visit and vision through a synthesis of material site explorations and digital site creations. The physical landmarks invite subjective, semiotic, and metonymic readings, but further interpretations and recontextualizations can be gleaned through the interactive QR code, linking to website data via what we might call "hypertransits," where the material site and the virtual site work together to consummate the narrative of King's historic visit and what that means for the present-day viewer. Under the banner "Discover the history—Discover the city—Discover your life," the King-Code website also offers actual guided walking and biking tours.[77] A King tour can be arranged by mail or by phone.[78]

The King-Code website is not a static site but an interactive, multimodal experience where the QR code enlivens this history through an engagement with documents, audio clips, and short films. Through engaging with individuals who provide eyewitness accounts, students learn about the import of this rhetorical history. One of the most stunning experiences for the students involved their interview with Georg Meusel, who founded the King Center for Nonviolence and Moral Courage at Werdau in Saxony. Meusel learned that the sextant of Marienkirche discovered an audio tape of King's sermon. A visibly emotional Meusel played the sermon for the students on a reel-to-reel tape recorder, demonstrating that rhetorical history survives and thrives with both old and state-of-the art technology.[79] Albeit rudimentary, this audio technology plays an integral role in preserving King's words through his voice.

Moreover, Gesine Schuppan, who was seventeen years old at the time, observed that King "was a very authentic man to my mind. As a person and as a preacher, [he] brought together faith and politics in a very bold way."[80] Another student disclosed that before tracing King's visit, "I wasn't really aware how much racism there is."[81] And in the spirit of King's own civil rights movement and its aim to eviscerate racism, another student avowed, "We the youth have to write history."[82]

Still another astonishing moment for students in retracing King's history was meeting Michael Meyer, the East German man who had been shot attempting to escape East Germany. Alia, a Wedding student who talked with Meyer, shared that "there was this moment when we realized that it is a true story, that he did not just make it up: he really went through this."[83] As if galvanized by the aura of King's presence emanating from Meyer, Ester, another student from Wedding, declared, "It was like, well, as if I was connected to him." Whether the student was explicitly expressing a personal connection with Meyer or King is moot. The experience in its 360-degree historic (re)turn certainly impacted and moved her in a profound way. As narrator of the King-Code documentary, Peter Kloeppel, puts it, it helped her understand that one has to "learn about oneself through history."[84]

Additionally, the King-Code project orients viewers and participants through various multimediated "inroads." One such display involves an exhibition of King-Code traveling panels that tours Germany and Austria, stopping at such venues as churches, schools, and universities that express the most interest in the project.[85] One of the more innovative convergences expanding the website and the exhibition is the Berlin-based, free-downloadable and educational Actionbound app, accessed by a different QR code (figure 2). Beginning in February 2017, King-Code interfaced its King exhibition with this Actionbound app. Developed for teenagers and adults, this forty-five-minute, multiplayer, trivia-style game of questions and answers includes six stages, seventeen quizzes, and four missions all related to King's 1964 visit and the larger history of civil rights.[86] After selecting a specific stage, players earn points while they learn about and interact with this significant history.

Sociologist Joshua Meyrowitz remarks that "the walls of the mightiest fortress no longer define a truly segregated social setting if a camera, a microphone, or even a telephone is present."[87] Meyrowitz's commentary encourages the King-Code students, whose reframing of rhetorical history confronts the Cold War and its vestiges of persecution. Semiotically, QR codes invite readers/viewers/tourists to experience the narrative history through retracing, and thereby reliving, the action and events of King's visit through his experience. Such a project may prove to be an effective strategy for breaking down those literal and material walls still standing, those exacerbated by an alt-Right, anti-immigrant rhetoric that destroys the possibility for intercultural and interfaith dialogue. True to the meaning of this project, Schmöcker articulates the educational goal of King-Code as one that cultivates a discernment between truth and falsity in utilizing original or primary documents, artifacts, eyewitness accounts, and the built environment—the physical environment in which all this history takes place.[88]

Figure 2. Actionbound App. Courtesy of Actionbound. Used with permission.

Conclusion

Our analysis and explication of King's codes, both sermonic and peda-gogical, reveal a tertiary relationship in reframing rhetorical history. First, we highlight King's own return to the rhetorical history of the pro-phetic tradition drawing on the Exodus typology and its foreshadowed resonance in Christ and the New Testament as a fitting response to his rhetorical situation in East Berlin in 1964. Secondly, the King-Code stu-dents return to the rhetorical history of that context as a way to address the intercultural exigencies of their own day. And finally, we as rhetorical analysts now return to all three of these rhetorical histories and present these interdependent narratives as our own rhetorical-critical code for rhetoricians, scholars of King, history, religion, and interfaith studies to decode facilely and be edified by our unique and reflective contribution in returning to rhetorical history.

In a 1963 speech at the National Conference on Religion and Race, "A Challenge to the Churches and Synagogues," King extolled America's contributions to the "built" environment: "America has brought the nation and the world to an awe-inspiring threshold of the future. Through our scientific and technological genius we have built mighty bridges to span the seas and skyscraping buildings to kiss the skies."[89]

In contrast to the positive connotations of the horizontality of the bridge and the verticality of the skyscraper, King excoriated the wall and its meaning as a profane dimension of the built environment, conceived neither as mighty nor as empowering. Whether the Berlin Wall or a contested virtually continuous wall along the southern border of the United States, a wall is not a sacrament of the cultivation of love and dignity but rather a desecration and profanity that typifies hate, degradation, and humiliation. This trek through the rhetorical history of King-Code's contemporaneous work unlocks and magnifies the discrepancy of Vice President Pence's attempt to marshal King's remarks in support of a wall on the southern border of the United States. History should compel us to navigate back to our moral compass.

As coarchitects of the King-Code, Schmöcker and Gomis are wholly aligned with German chancellor Angela Merkel's deleterious characterization of walls during her commencement address at Harvard University on May 30, 2019. She shared her very personal journey from the early years of her life on the East Berlin side of a divided city: "I grew up in East Germany in the GDR, at a time when that part of my homeland was not free, in a dictatorship. People were oppressed and monitored by the state. Political opponents were persecuted. The government of the GDR was afraid that the people would run away to freedom. And that's why the Berlin Wall was built."[90] Merkel continued, "The Berlin Wall limited my possibilities. It was literally in my way." But then Merkel reflected on the life-changing events that transpired three decades before her address, in 1989, with the fall of the Berlin Wall. She acknowledged, with regret, that in 2019 walls of manifold manifestations existed as "walls in the mind, walls of ignorance and narrowmindedness. They exist between members of a family as well as between social groups, between those of different skin color, peoples, religions. I would like us to break down these walls— walls that repeatedly prevent us from communicating about the world in which we want to live together."[91]

Merkel exhorted the Harvard University graduating class with the conditional aspirational statement: "But if we tear down the walls that restrict us, if we open the door and embrace new beginnings, then everything is possible." King's sermonic discourse reminds us of our own obligations to cultivate those aspirations, eloquently resonating in Merkel's address, and to rebuke the demagoguery and policies of those whose intentions are to destroy dreams and inhibit freedom. In the precarious times in which we live, the fifty-fifth anniversary of Martin Luther King Jr.'s historic visit to East Berlin admonishes us to heed his prophetic words.

As Chancellor Merkel said in the Chapel of Reconciliation, in Berlin during the commemoration of the thirtieth anniversary of the fall of the Berlin Wall, "No wall that keeps people apart and restricts their freedom is so tall or so wide that it cannot be breached."[92] Building physical walls as edifices that restrict freedom ought not be celebrated, but strengthening edifying principles that promote, as Merkel stated, "freedom, democracy, equality, rule of law, [and] human rights"[93] should be vigilantly pursued and defended. The fifty-fifth anniversary of Martin Luther King Jr.'s historic visit to East Berlin and the thirtieth anniversary of the Fall of the Berlin Wall compel us in these precarious times to heed these prophetic words.

Notes

1. Walther Eichrodt, "Is Typology Exegesis an Appropriate Method?" trans. James Barr, in *Essays on Old Testament Hermeneutics*, ed. Claus Westermann (New York: John Knox, 1979), 234.

2. J. Vernon Jensen, *Ethical Issues in the Communication Process* (Mahawah, NJ: Lawrence Erlbaum, 1997), 20–21.

3. Our use of the term prophetic is grounded more in the tradition of reform rhetoric and, yet, shares a genuflective semblance to James Darsey's prophetic rhetoric, a radical version that he acknowledges "exhibit[s] similarities with the discursive tradition of the Old Testament prophets . . . [that calls for] a sense of mission and a desire to bring the practice of the people into accord with a sacred principle." See James Darsey, *The Prophetic Tradition and Radical Rhetoric in America* (New York: New York University Press, 1997), 16. Because we view King's sermonic rhetoric in East Berlin as reform, and not necessarily radical, prophetic rhetoric, our perspective also diverges from Darsey's supposition that prophetic rhetoric is extremist and vitiates traditional discursive functions by accentuating division over unity (20). Given King's rhetorical deftness, sense of decorum, and dream of a "beloved community," as our analysis reveals, it seems rhetorically defective that King would emphasize division while speaking to an East German audience and trope the Berlin Wall in the venial ways he did.

4. Kathleen J. Turner, "Introduction: Rhetorical History as Social Construction," in Turner, *Doing Rhetorical History*, 2.

5. Daniel Schmöcker and Saraya Gomis, "King-Code ein multimediales Schul-Jugenprojekt," accessed October 9, 2019, https://king-code.de/homeen.htm.

6. All student quotations and testimony from eyewitnesses are taken from Andreas Kuno Richter, dir., *Der King-Code: Martin Luther King Jr. in Berlin* (Hamburg, Ger.: Eikon Nord, 2014), English version DVD.

7. The term "multimodal act" is used by Theo van Leeuwen in the subsection "Social Semiotics" of his entry "Rhetoric and Semiotics," in *Oxford Handbook of Rhetorical Studies*, ed. Michael J. MacDonald (Oxford: Oxford University Press, 2017), 680.

8. Schmöcker and Gomis, "King-Code."

9. E. Culpepper Clark and Raymie E. McKerrow, "The Rhetorical Construction of History," in Turner, *Doing Rhetorical History*, 46.

10. For more on a discussion of *code* in the field of semiotics, see chapter 3, "Implications of Codes," in Scott Simpkins, *Literary Semiotics: A Critical Approach* (Lanham, MD: Lexington Books, 2001), 33–56.

11. Gerry Philipsen, "Speech Codes," in *Developing Communication Theories*, ed. Gerry Philipsen and Terrance L. Albrecht (Albany: State University of New York, 1977), 126.

12. See Kenneth Burke, *Language as Symbolic Action: Essays in Life, Literature, and Method* (Berkeley: University of California Press, 1966); Chaïm Perelman, "Rhetoric and Philosophy," *Philosophy and Rhetoric* 1, no. 1 (1968): 15–24; Richard Weaver, "Language Is Sermonic," in *Language Is Sermonic*, ed Richard L. Johannesen, Rennard Strickland, and Ralph T. Eubanks (Baton Rouge: Louisiana State University Press, 1970), 201–25.

13. Carolyn Calloway-Thomas and John Louis Lucaites, eds., *Martin Luther King Jr. and the Sermonic Power of Public Discourse* (Tuscaloosa: University of Alabama Press, 1993), 3.

14. Calloway-Thomas and Lucaites, *Martin Luther King Jr.*, 3–4.

15. Weaver, "Language Is Sermonic," 201.

16. Burke, *Language as Symbolic Action*, 10.

17. Cicero, *De Natura Deorum Libri Tres*, edited by Joseph B. Mayor and J. H. Swainson (Cambridge: Cambridge University Press, 2010), 2, 186.

18. Richter, *Der King-Code*; Maria Hohn and Martin Klimke, *A Breath of Freedom: The Civil Rights Struggle, African American GIs, and Germany* (New York: Palgrave, 2010); Jason Sokol, *The Heavens Might Crack* (New York: Basic Books, 2018); Taylor Branch, *Pillar of Fire* (New York: Simon & Schuster, 1998), 483; Schmöcker and Gomis, "King-Code"; "Remembering Martin Luther King's Visit to Berlin," November 9, 2014, https://www.dw.com/en/remembering-martin-luther-kings-visit-to-berlin/a-17907455; Olivia B. Waxman, "What Martin Luther King Jr. Said about Walls during His 1964 Visit to Berlin," *Time* January 28, 2019, https://time.com; Trichita M Chestnut, "'. . . There Is No East, No

West . . .' Dr. Martin Luther King, Jr. Visits Cold War Berlin," October 7, 2014, https://rediscovering-black-history.blogs.archives.gov; Lars-Broder Keil, "When Martin Luther King Jr. Spoke to East Berlin," *Daily Dose*, January 18, 2016, https://www.ozy.com; German Way and More, Notable People, "Martin Luther King Jr. in Berlin," https://www.german-way.com; "MLK: 1964 Berlin Locations Tour, "German Way and More," nd, https://www.german-way.com/notable-people/featured-bios/martin-luther-king-jr-in-berlin/mlk-1964-berlin-locations-photo-tour/.

19. See Waxman, "What Martin Luther King Jr. Said."

20. For the comparison of King's speech to JFK's: Paul Kengor, "Martin Luther King and the Berlin Wall," *Washington Post*, October 30, 2014, https://www.washingtonpost.com/opinions/martin-luther-king-and-the-berlin-wall/2014/10/30/b72c90aa-48ad-11e4-b72e-d60a9229cc10_story.html?noredirect=on&utm_term=.34f2058a795a.

21. See "Remembering Martin Luther King's Visit."

22. Benjamin Drechsel, "The Berlin Wall from Visual Perspective: Comments on the Construction of a Political Media Icon," *Visual Communication* 9, no. 1 (2010): 4.

23. Clayborne Carson, quoted in Waxman, "What Martin Luther King Jr. Said."

24. "Remembering Martin Luther King's Visit."

25. Richter, *Der King-Code.*

26. Richter, *Der King-Code.*

27. Heinrich Grüber, quoted in Waxman, "What Martin Luther King Jr. Said."

28. Martin Luther King Jr., "Sermon 'God's Children,' East Berlin." September 13, 1964. Inside the Cold War, Kings Sermon in East Berlin. 2015. http://insidethecoldwar.org/.

29. King, "Sermon 'God's Children.'"

30. Michael S. Bruner, "Symbolic Uses of the Berlin Wall, 1961–1989," *Communication Quarterly* 37, no. 4. (1989): 322–24.

31. Bruner, "Symbolic Uses of the Berlin Wall," 325.

32. See Kenneth Burke, *A Rhetoric of Motives* (Berkeley: University of California Press, 1969), 25.

33. Michael Walzer argues that the Exodus narrative is a broad revolutionary strategy endemic to the history of political theory and "part of the cultural consciousness of the West." Eddie S. Glaude Jr. supports Walzer's assertions and contends that such discourse served as the basis for claims to nationhood born out of the Black convention movements of the early nineteenth century. See Walzer, *Exodus and Revolution* (New York: Basic Books, 1985), 7; and Glaude, *Exodus! Religion, Race, and Nation in Early Nineteenth-Century Black America* (Chicago: University of

Chicago Press, 2000), 111. See also James H. Smylie, "On Jesus, Pharaohs, and the Chosen People: Martin Luther King as Biblical Interpreter and Humanist," *Interpretation* 24, no. 1 (1970): 74–91; Malinda Snow, "Martin Luther King's 'Letter from Birmingham Jail' as Pauline Epistle," *Quarterly Journal of Speech* 71, no. 3 (1985): 318–34; Keith D. Miller, *Voices of Deliverance: The Language of Martin Luther King, Jr., and Its Sources* (Athens: University of Georgia Press, 1998); Keith D. Miller, "Alabama as Egypt: Martin Luther King, Jr. and the Religion of Slaves," in Calloway-Thomas and Lucaites, *Martin Luther King Jr.,* 18–32; Thomas Rosteck, "Narrative in Martin Luther King's 'I've Been to the Mountaintop,'" *Southern Communication Journal* 58, no. 1 (1992): 22–32; Susannah Heschel, "Theological Affinities in the Writings of Heschel and King," in *Black Zion: African American Religious Encounters with Judaism,* eds. Yvonne Chireau and Nathaniel Deutsch (London: Oxford University Press, 2000), 168–86; Michael Osborn, "The Last Mountaintop of Martin Luther King Jr.," in Calloway-Thomas and Lucaites, *Martin Luther King Jr.,* 147–61; Gary S. Selby, "Framing Social Protest: The Exodus Narrative in Martin Luther King's Montgomery Bus Boycott Rhetoric," *Journal of Communication and Religion* 24, no. 1 (2001): 68–93.

34. King, "Sermon 'God's Children.'"

35. King, "Sermon 'God's Children.'"

36. For more on King's prophetic rhetoric, see Andre Johnson and Anthony J. Stone Jr., "'The Most Dangerous Negro in America': Rhetoric, Race, and the Prophetic Pessimism of Martin Luther King Jr.," *Journal of Communication & Religion* 41:1 (2018): 8–22; Keith D. Miller, "Second Isaiah Lands in Washington, DC: Martin Luther King, Jr.'s 'I Have a Dream' as Biblical Narrative and Biblical Hermeneutic," *Rhetoric Review* 26, no. 4 (2007): 405–24; Mark Vail, "The 'Integrative' Rhetoric of Martin Luther King Jr.'s 'I Have a Dream' Speech," *Rhetoric & Public Affairs* 9, no. 1 (2006): 53–55; Christopher Lynch, "Reaffirmation of God's Anointed Prophet: The Chiasm in Martin Luther King's Mountaintop Speech," *Howard Journal of Communications* 6 (1995): 12–31; David Bobbitt and Harold Mixon, "Prophecy and Apocalypse in the Rhetoric of Martin Luther King, Jr." *Journal of Communication & Religion* 17, no. 1 (1994): 27–38; Keith Miller, "Alabama as Egypt," 18–32; Abraham Joshua Heschel, *The Prophets* (Peabody MA: Hendrickson Publishing, 2007).

37. Sr. Alcoyne Scott, quoted in Hohn and Klimke, *Breath of Freedom,* 102.

38. Kengor, "Martin Luther King."

39. Susannah Heschel, "A Friendship in the Prophetic Tradition: Abraham Joshua Heschel and Martin Luther King, Jr.," *Telos* 182 (2018): 73.

40. Taylor Branch, *At Canaan's Edge* (New York: Simon & Schuster, 1998), 21; Susannah Heschel, introduction to *Moral Grandeur and Spiritual Audacity* (New York: Farrar Straus Giroux, 1996), xxiii; Mathew Ahmann, preface to *Race: Challenge to Religion* (Chicago: Henry Regnery, 1963), x; Patricia Bizzell, "Rabbi

Abraham Joshua Heschel, 'Religion and Race' (14 January 1963)," *Voices of Democracy*, vol. 1 (2006): 1–14, https://voicesofdemocracy.umd.edu.

41. Edward K. Kaplan, *Spiritual Radical: Abraham Joshua Heschel in America, 1940–1972* (New Haven, CT: Yale University Press, 2007), 215.

42. Kaplan, *Spiritual Radical*, 215.

43. Miller "Second Isaiah," 415.

44. In addition to Moses, the greatest of Hebrew prophets, Isaiah, Ezekiel, Jeremiah, and the twelve minor prophets (of which Amos is one) make up the Latter Books of the Prophets. Daniel is depicted as an "exilic prophet" and characterized by his wisdom and as a *tzadik*, or righteous person. See R. J. Zwi Weblowsky and Geoffrey Wigoder, eds., *The Oxford Dictionary of the Jewish Religion* (Oxford: Oxford University Press, 1997), 549, 186.

45. Miller, "Second Isaiah," 419, 414, 417.

46. Northrop Frye, *The Great Code: The Bible and Literature* (New York: Harcourt Brace Jovanovich, 1982), xiii.

47. Gary S. Selby, *Martin Luther King and the Rhetoric of Freedom: The Exodus Narrative in America's Struggle for Civil Rights* (Waco, TX: Baylor University Press, 2008), 10, 15, and all of chapter 2.

48. Selby, *Martin Luther King*, 105.

49. Exodus 1:11–14, *Good News Bible: Catholic Study Edition* (New York: Sadlier, 1979); Exodus 1:13–14, *The Pentateuch and Haftorahs*, 2nd ed., ed. Dr. J. H. Hertz, C. H. (London: Soncino Press 1993), 208.

50. Angela Merkel, Commencement Address, Harvard University, May 30, 2019, American Rhetoric Online Speech Bank, https://americanrhetoric.com. Metonymy works through interpretive associations, or as Burke sees it through reductions, relationships, and connections (*A Grammar of Motives* [Berkeley: University of California Press, 1969], 509). We argue that King's intent in using the Berlin Wall as a metonymy was to invite his East German audience to establish an ancestral linkage, a historic and biblical relationship, with the ancient Israelites through shared trauma that was visually present in the very material of that which enslaved them, bricks and mortar, concrete and steel. The metonymies, "bricks and mortar" and "the wall," are more than simple contested symbols. To describe the ancient Israelites and the East Germans as "people of brick and mortar" or of "concrete and steel" (as Merkel did) is a relational reference to the very edifice that oppresses them. To us these are clearly metonymies, precisely because "the wall" (and its properties—bricks and mortar—and here one might argue this is representative, as in synecdoche, a subspecies of metonymy) is another way to speak of oppression and the Exodus narrative. In augmenting the metonymic-synecdochic connections, in addition to its use to bind stone and brick, mortar is also utilized as material to bind concrete. Burke's discussion of these tropes clarifies our example: "Language develops by metaphorical extension, in borrowing words from the

realm of the corporeal, visible, tangible and applying them by analogy to the realm of the incorporeal, invisible, intangible; and finally, poets regain the original relation, in reverse, by a 'metaphorical extension' back from the intangible into a tangible equivalent (the first 'carrying-over' from the material to the spiritual being compensated by a second 'carrying-over' from the spiritual back into the material)" (506). To concretize this point, Burke further argues that synecdoche can mean the "material for the thing made (which brings us nearer to metonymy). . . . All such conversions imply an integral relationship, relationship of convertibility, between the two terms" (507–8).

51. Gehenna or Geihinnom is the valley outside the western wall of Jerusalem mentioned in the Bible, a site at which some kings of Judah ostensibly burned their children as a sacrifice. It is therefore widely considered the antithesis of the Garden of Eden. See R. J. Zwi Weblowsky and Geoffrey Wigoder, eds., *The Oxford Dictionary of the Jewish Religion* (Oxford: Oxford University Press, 1997), 266–67.

52. King, "Sermon 'God's Children.'"

53. Hosea 11:1–7, *Good News Bible*.

54. Exodus 5:1, *Good News Bible*.

55. King, "Sermon 'God's Children.'"

56. King, "Sermon 'God's Children.'"

57. Andre LaCocque and Paul Ricoeur, *Thinking Biblically: Exegetical and Hermeneutical Studies*, trans. David Pellauer (Chicago: University of Chicago Press, 1998), 67.

58. Avrohom Bergstein, "Daniel the Prophet of the Bible, His Life and Accomplishments," https://www.chabad.org.

59. King, "Sermon 'God's Children.'"

60. King, "Sermon 'God's Children.'"

61. Richter, *Der King-Code*.

62. Richter, *Der King-Code*.

63. Miller, "Alabama as Egypt," 22.

64. See Snow, "Martin Luther King's 'Letter,'" 318–34.

65. King, "Sermon 'God's Children.'"

66. Snow, "Martin Luther King's 'Letter,'" 330.

67. Ephesians 2:14, *Good News Bible*.

68. See Albert J. Raboteau, *Slave Religion: The 'Invisible Institution' in the Antebellum South* (New York: Ohio University Press, 1978), 311–12; Miller, "Alabama as Egypt," 20; and Miller, "Second Isaiah," 408.

69. See John Lovell, *Black Song: The Forge and the Flame* (New York: Macmillan, 1972), 234.

70. King, "Sermon 'God's Children.'"

71. Tzvi Freeman, "What Is Emunah?," accessed March 18, 2018, https://www.chabad.org.

72. Aside from seeing mountains and valleys as part of the light/dark family of archetypal metaphors, Michael Osborn suggests that the Exodus out of bondage motif for King was an "archetypal experience." See Michael Osborn, *Michael Osborn on Metaphor and Style* (East Lansing: Michigan State University Press, 2018), 67–68, 280–81, 193n47.

73. King Institute, "Commemorating the 50th Anniversary of King's Berlin Trip," Martin Luther King, Jr. Research and Education Institute, Stanford University, October 6, 2014, https://kinginstitute.stanford.edu.

74. Richter, *Der King-Code.*

75. Richter, *Der King-Code.*

76. Helen Nissenbaum, *Privacy in Context: Technology, Policy, and the Integrity of Social Life* (Stanford, CA: Stanford University Press, 2010), 5.

77. Schmöcker and Gomis, "King-Code."

78. Daniel Schmöcker, e-mail message to author, October 9, 2019.

79. Richter, *Der King-Code.*

80. Richter, *Der King-Code.*

81. Richter, *Der King-Code.*

82. Richter, *Der King-Code.*

83. Richter, *Der King-Code.*

84. Richter, *Der King-Code.*

85. Schmöcker, e-mail message to author, October 9, 2019. In 2020, King-Code planned for the exhibition to visit Bayreuth, Braunschweig, and Dortmund, but the COVID-19 pandemic derailed those plans. As of June 27, 2021, the King-Code website did not show revised tour dates under its King Tour or News tabs.

86. See Schmöcker and Gomis, "King-Code."

87. Joshua Meyrowitz, *No Sense of Place: The Impact of Electronic Media on Social Behavior* (Oxford: Oxford University Press, 1985), viii.

88. Schmöcker, e-mail message to author, October 9, 2019.

89. Martin Luther King, Jr., "A Challenge to the Churches and Synagogues," in *Race: Challenge to Religion*, ed. Mathew Ahmann (Chicago: Henry Regnery, 1963), 155.

90. Merkel, "Commencement Address."

91. Merkel, "Commencement Address."

92. "Remembrance, Commemoration, Celebrations," (German) Federal Government, November 9, 2019, https://www.bundesregierung.de/breg-en/news/30-jahre-mauerfall-1690550.

93. Bianca Britton, "Germany Marks 30 Years Since the Fall of the Berlin Wall," November 9, 2019, https://www.cnn.

4

Visually Based Rhetorical History

The *Sola Vidēre* Principle in Christian Nationalist Videos

Philip Perdue

In the spring of 2011, Maureen Costello, the director of Teaching Tolerance at the Southern Poverty Law Center, accused Fox News personality Mike Huckabee of peddling "kiddie-propaganda." She was referring to a new educational product called Learn Our History, a series of digitally animated cartoon videos that promises to teach important lessons of American history to young students who might otherwise be turned off by what its creators termed "boring textbooks" and "dry lectures."[1] As one of Learn Our History's cofounders and public promoters, Huckabee argued that cartoons, unlike cumbersome textbooks and homework assignments, provide a "fun and engaging" medium for getting adolescents interested in learning about American history. In contrast, Costello urges readers to see Learn Our History as manipulative agit-prop in cartoon clothing. She warns that it was designed to "indoctrinate youngsters" by promoting "a very specific and political worldview associated with right-wing conservative politics." She questions the scholarly integrity of the video series as well, noting that a staff without academic qualifications had produced an educational product that bore "no correlation to either educational standards or vetted curriculum." Costello even questions whether the visual qualities of cartoon videos could promote serious historical thinking, thereby seeming to dismiss visual media as an illegitimate, physiologically gratifying, but intellectually stunted form of education about history. Instead of "teaching more history by engaging kids with the serious and challenging problems of our past," she writes, "Huckabee thinks the solution is to brainwash kids into thinking that history is entertainment meant to make them feel good."[2]

Costello's critique is sympathetic to the view that serious historical education should require students to think, question, and make inferences based on textual evidence. But the political tenor of her charges against Huckabee also indicates a concern that Learn Our History portrays America's past from a Christian nationalist perspective. Consistent with Huckabee's style of political conservatism, the Learn Our History series is premised on "the crucial role that God has played in America's founding and development," and as such, it advances a vision of American identity in which "all of our rights and freedom come directly from God, not the government."[3] In this way, Learn Our History recirculates a sprawling historiographic discourse designed to reconstruct a picture of the past where whiteness and Christianity occupy dominant positions in the country's social, political, and legal institutions.[4] This depiction of the past continues to shape American public consciousness. More than half of Americans profess to believe that either the United States always has been and currently is a Christian nation or that it used to be but is no longer.[5] These numbers offer some context for the rhetorical significance of Christian nationalist historiography. By packaging a theological perspective in the idiom of academic history, the central theological claim of Christian nationalism—that the United States is, in its history and identity, an outgrowth of the Christian religion—has been made to look like history.[6]

Understood as a "rhetorical use of the past in the construction especially of political arguments,"[7] Christian nationalist historiography invites opposition from those who discourage the way advocates of right-wing nationalism have appropriated American history.[8] Usually the debate between advocates and skeptics of Christian nationhood revolves around competing interpretations of founding documents, political speeches, court rulings, and other kinds of textual evidence.[9] But the contest to shape national identity through historiographic means also encompasses visual rhetorical strategies. We know that collective memories and national identities in particular result in and from an amalgamation of imagery and imagination. Paintings of idyllic landscapes and famous battles, portraits of national heroes, widely circulated photographs, public monuments, national emblems and icons, historical movies and television, and other kinds of pictorial formation establish visual contours for the national body. Christian nationalist depictions of American history are mediated in many of these same ways. Advocates of Christian nationhood marshal textual evidence and construct verbal arguments, to be sure, while commercial literature and media that package these arguments, and that make them available to the broader public, often feature a visual rhetorical style based on the patterned articulation of Christian symbolism and American iconography.[10] Christian nationalist media outlets encompass propositional beliefs about history, while their public legibility is tethered to a strategically composed visual rhetoric. Learn Our

History is but one nodal point in this broader symbolic network. Its application of digitally animated motion pictures illustrates how reframing rhetorical history can be augmented by directing critical attention to the visual rhetoric of history.

Rhetorical History and the Visual

By focusing on the pictorial mediation of history in particular, this study continues the work of those who, by the close of the twentieth century, had reinforced the groundwork upon which today's scholars take both "the rhetoric *of* history" and "rhetoric *as* history" as axiomatic, along with "history's socially constructed meaning and its fluidity."[11] And yet for many of those same scholars, when it came to demonstrating the rhetorically constructed nature of historical discourse and the ways in which rhetoric shaped the outcomes of history, in most cases the "proof" was in the verbiage. Hence James Jasinski's remark, offered without controversy, that "language has become the lingua franca of the humanities."[12] E. Culpepper Clark and Raymie McKerrow note as well that rhetoricians are drawn to history as a subject of critique because "history emerges from the world of ordinary language." Because "its meanings are so observably negotiated," as they put it, history is "by its very nature an *argument*."[13] Accordingly, each one of the studies in *Doing Rhetorical History* focuses on linguistic rhetoric.[14] Still, even among a series of discussions that proceed on the textual analysis of historical discourse, there are clear moments that gesture toward widening conceptualizations of discursivity and toward the rich variety of communicative modes through which history is made and remade.[15] Analysis that focuses on cases where historical knowledge is mediated primarily through pictorial imagery thus extends that gesture toward multimodality.

Rhetorical history has always been multimodal, in fact. The visual rhetoric of Christian nationalism illustrates what has long been recognized, if not widely emphasized, about the close relationship between historical discourse and visual experience generally. We routinely use such phrases as "a picture of the past" when referring to the product of historical research, and even the historian's methods have been explained in terms of pictorial composition.[16] In *How to Write History*, the second-century writer Lucian encourages the use of *enargeia*, or vivid language that could help the reader "actually see what is being described," invoking the enduring bond between word and image by suggesting that the one could imitate the other.[17] Oddly then, even though vivid depiction is a bar historians still try to clear, history as a modern academic discipline has resisted embracing its kinship to pictures and visual illustration.[18]

Historians, artists, and publishers faced difficulty striking a balance between historical writing and the visual arts, with writers and artists both jockeying to plant their trade "at the dramatic center of the historical enterprise."[19] Pictures are powerful teaching tools, however, and in the decades following the World Wars we have seen them used with increasing regularity in K-12 textbooks and learning materials designed for use in historical education.[20] Along the way, defenders of written histories have warned against displacing the expository primer with more visually appealing texts, calling for substance over style, serious reading over quick sales.[21] But historical education's visual turn is altogether consistent with its aim to depict the past in ways that develop a civic consciousness and that help audiences to see themselves as part of a national story.[22] Knowing their task requires stimulating the imagination, educators in history increasingly replace the old gray tome with inviting multimodal texts, and they embrace sophisticated visual pedagogies that make the past come alive.[23]

Learn Our History

It may have been inevitable, then, that the era of multimedia educational materials in history would venture into digital animation. Digital animation is a powerful platform for reconstructing history because it can make virtually any image or series of images possible. Given how pictures and visual illustrations can help audiences encounter vivid depictions of the past, conferring concrete form on bygone figures and events, the advent of digital motion picture technology represents a significant development in both the production and analysis of rhetorical history. Not only can "one give visible form to abstract ideas and improbable dreams," as media theorist Robert Stam says of animation technology, but one also can set those improbable dreams into motion, breathing life into them, eliminating the synchronic limitations of the still image.[24] Digital animation produces new kinds of spectatorship, too, as audiences have no expectation that animated depictions ought to coordinate with empirical reality. This agreement between audience and animation makes the case of Learn Our History especially compelling, since it is one where digitally produced images can collapse past and present in a way that draws spectators into the story and positions them as immediate coparticipants in past events. Each Learn Our History episode features this same virtual reproduction of immediate access to the past. I want to turn to a few examples that illustrate the point and then assess what they reveal about the importance of visual experience in authorizing the historiography of Christian nationalism.

The Learn Our History video series stars five young teenagers from the present who set out to learn about American history by circumventing the scholastic traditions of textbook, schoolteacher, and the brick-and-mortar classroom. When dusty old books and a bumbling history teacher fail to generate compelling explanations to questions about history, the teenagers use a time machine to teleport themselves instantly to any period and location they choose. Time travel allows the teenagers to be physically present at any time and place while events of history unfold before them. Recurrent depictions of present-day actors who have immediate access to the past serve not just as a clever narrative device. They also furnish the sense of immediate, firsthand access to the past and therefore undergird the stated rationale for why Learn Our History's depiction of the past can be trusted.

Take, for example, the opening montage for each episode. After a quick sequence designed to give the backstory about how their time machine was built, Addison, one of the time-traveling teens, tells viewers that she and her friends get to see the past for themselves. The suggestion, of course, is that their immediate historiographic encounters give them a front-row perspective that pedagogically and epistemologically surpasses conventional scholastic methods. Sitting alone in an empty classroom, Addison is depicted looking into the camera as she explains to viewers how she and her friends "travel together to learn the truth about the past." An uncommonly large history textbook sits unopened on the desk in front of her. "What we see and hear," she says, as if speaking into the camera, "isn't always the same as what we read in books or see on TV." Textbooks and news reporting sometimes get it wrong, as do the academic experts. While undoubtedly true to some extent, this claim positions the series as a more reliable alternative to other forms of media. "So what?" Addison continues. "We know the truth, and that's good enough for us!"[25] As she speaks, different scenes flash across the screen showing the five characters present at key historical locations, visually reiterating her claim that they are there to see for themselves what really happened.

With the help of teleportation technology, Addison and her friends time travel to a variety of key chapters in American history. They go to New England and Pennsylvania to witness colonists mobilizing for war against the British. They make their way to the beaches of Hawaii where they view the bombing of Pearl Harbor. They watch Christopher Columbus as he makes his "great discovery," observe the Lincoln-Douglas debates, and participate in the first Thanksgiving. They watch the wall crumble at East Berlin, and they go to Manhattan to watch airplanes crash into the World Trade Center. On and on they go in more than forty episodes.[26] In each one, the five time-traveling teenagers meet and interact with such iconic American figures as George Washington, Abraham Lincoln, and Dwight D. Eisenhower. As they listen to primary sources say their piece, the teenage characters are privy to evidence that no secondary account can provide. In these encounters, viewing audiences witness virtual oral histories that displace the need for interpretive debate. Such encounters are presented as methodologically and pedagogically superior to conventional research practices. They are depictions of an experiential pedagogy where students of history learn by seeing events happen right before their eyes, including the speeches and orations of famous Americans.

Depictions of immediate access are noteworthy not only because they rehearse a kind of methodological and pedagogical ideal but also because viewers who watch these stories are positioned as coparticipants in the characters' experience of direct relationality.[27] Consider, for example, a scene from *9/11 and the War on Terror*. In this episode, the five teenagers travel back in time to observe the September 2001 attack on the Pentagon in Arlington, Virginia. It shows the five characters arriving on the scene, just in time, only moments after the explosion. While the characters watch the smoke billow out from the building, viewers are positioned behind them, looking on just over their shoulders. They can be seen bearing witness to the event, and the viewing audiences become witnesses in turn. The viewers observe students of history experiencing a moment of direct observation, once again without the mediation of textbook, classroom, or teacher, as if having only their senses to guide them.

This same viewing structure appears again and again throughout the Learn Our History series. In *The Declaration of Independence*, the animated characters huddle together outside a red brick building looking through a ground-level window. As the DVD insert for the episode explains, "the time travelers go back in time to *see* how the Second Continental Congress passed the Declaration of Independence."[28] They watch through the window as the framers inside give their orations and have their debates. A chyron indicates the date and location as Philadelphia 1776, and like the scene from Arlington, the video's audience once again is positioned just over the shoulders of ostensible direct eyewitnesses to the proceedings of the Second Continental Congress. Audiences thus share a direct line of sight onto the discussions and deliberations that shaped the drafting of the Declaration of Independence. Later in the episode, the animated characters speak directly with the most famous founders. Thomas Jefferson, John Adams, and Benjamin Franklin each tell the students about their experiences. Viewing audiences, too, participate in this confirmational structure that scene after scene, and episode after episode, makes available. By watching the videos, viewers travel back in time virtually and are present on location as the important events of American history unfold right before their eyes.

Sola Vidēre and the Power of Visual Rhetorical History

Learn Our History authorizes the epistemological authority of Christian nationalist historiography by positioning spectators in virtual representations of immediate access to, and participation in, the events of history. The physiological experience of seeing for oneself is fundamental to the way Christian nationalism reconstructs the past because the rhetoric of eyewitnessing provides a strong insulation against interpretive challenges. Commitment to the authority of individual experience is rooted in an interpretive structure shaping the Reformation-era belief that one can bypass interpretive authority and instead encounter divine revelation directly through immediate contact with the Word. This belief found expression in the Protestant doctrine *sola scriptura*, which roughly translated means "by scripture alone." Its purpose was to displace Roman Catholic authority in matters of scriptural interpretation. Protestant reformers emphasized sola, or only, not to establish a singularity (for there were five solas) but rather to establish a definitive hierarchy across different modes of religious experience and practice.[29] By the same token, the Latinate *sola vidēre* (by seeing alone) furnishes rhetorical theorists with a conceptual device that accounts for a media hierarchy and mode of spectatorship that is being constructed across the Learn Our History video series. Much like the old Protestant belief that the words of scripture provide direct, "unmediated" access to divine revelation, sola vidēre equips the spectator with a claim on direct experience with the truth about history by denying the mediated conditions of that history. This orientation overlooks, or looks past, the ways in which the physical experience of observation is historically and culturally constructed.[30] From this vantage, the act of seeing, in the physical experience of witnessing through one's sensory capacities, equips the viewer with a firsthand observational account not subject to empirical refutation and therefore unassailable.

Meanwhile, just as the sola vidēre principle reinstantiates a Protestant commitment to the authority of individual conscience, it also is informed by a Protestant perspective on what visual forms are and what they should do. For this reason, the sola vidēre principle is present in different ways and degrees across a longer tradition of Protestant visual rhetoric. Early modern Protestantism, like earlier iconoclastic groups, often is remembered as having an ambivalent, if not altogether hostile, relationship to visual display.[31] Such characterizations are consistent with Protestant elevation of the Word as the only undiluted and unembellished source of revelation. Yet, while it is true that Protestant logocentrism correlated with strong resistance to Roman Catholic opulence in matters of ritual and display, it was not due to a blanket opposition to visual representation. Rather, it was because Protestants *revered* the power of shapes and symbols to focus the attention. They were convinced that Roman Catholic visual practices, in their magnificent architecture and ornate works of art, represented excessive and careless manipulation of forms. Catholic forms of representation consequently distracted individuals from focusing on the unadorned truths of scripture. Protestants therefore distinguished naturally occurring forms—which reflected the divine order—from the carnal manipulation of visual shapes.[32] Later, with the aid of Industrial Age print and mass media technologies, Protestants would go on to pioneer the pedagogical application of visual images, convinced that pictures could be used as teaching aids in moral and civic education.[33] By the time conservative Protestants entered the commercial textbook market in the mid-1970s, they would build on this centuries-long foundation that insisted on the right and proper use of visual images. In almost every case, this meant using visual illustration to corroborate and teach truths based on the Word. Now in the twenty-first century, this winding tradition of moral and civic education through visual media continues to evolve in the form of digitally animated motion pictures.

In addition to the Protestant valuation of the proper use of images, sola vidēre is rooted in an epistemology of common sense. Visuality in the context of Protestant Christianity emphasizes interpretive and creative restraint, looking to strip away embellishment and elaboration. Such an approach found its philosophical counterpart in the early modernism of the seventeenth and eighteenth centuries, when individuals were encouraged to stop relying on institutional authority and instead to trust that the truths of a divine order were available to them directly through the world of the senses. This meant accepting sensory impression as the one direct avenue to truth. As the modern era progressed, faith in unmediated sensory experience was encased in a philosophical discourse of common sense. Historian George Marsden marks the "anti-elitist" school of eighteenth-century Scottish empiricism as one of the most rigorous formulations of commonsense philosophy. For the empiricists, Marsden writes, "the human mind was so constructed that we can know the real world directly." Unlike rationalist philosophers, who were criticized for interposing ideas between the real world and the human mind, such commonsense realists as David Hume maintained that through their senses, people experience the world *exactly as it is*. Because the "common sense of mankind," according to Marsden, "whether of the man behind the plow or the man behind the desk, was the surest guide to truth," commonsense realism provided a philosophical basis for the democratizing impulses of the new American nation.[34] Not only does Learn Our History grow out of a visual pedagogical tradition, then, it also reanimates an iteration of commonsense epistemology that places the powers of individual observation at the apex of credibility. The commonsense approach to knowing asserts an equivalence between the actual experience of observation and the epistemological claim that one can make to knowing for one's self. Direct observation of empirical reality is in this way inoculated against theoretical counterarguments or conflicting historical explanations. The historical record is, according to the sola vidēre principle, something that is corroborated not by leveraging data and argument but by the petition of self-evidence.

There is a remarkable scene in a Learn Our History episode called *The Civil War: Brother against Brother* that illustrates how sola vidēre not only informs but encourages a visual rhetoric of common sense.[35] Daliah, a Black teenage girl who is one of the time-traveling characters, gets kidnapped by a Confederate soldier after she and her friends have been caught observing a Civil War battle. (It is one of the many scenes in the series where watching events happen gets the teenagers in trouble, since as eyewitnesses they become participants in the scene and therefore know too much). The kidnapper, a white supporter of the Confederacy, assumes the young Daliah is a fugitive slave. He demands his right, under Confederate law, to seize her and send her back. Her friends look on as the white man overpowers Daliah and takes her away.

Later in the episode, after a long search, Daliah's friends look through the brush to see her alone, off in the distance, wearing a slave's clothing and busily hanging laundry behind a quaint, Southern cabin. The scene is pastoral. She is shown surrounded by lush vegetation and chirping birds. Trying to avoid being seen by plantation masters, Daliah's friends sneak up closer and ask if she is okay. "Yeah, I'm okay," she says with bright eyes and a reassuring smile. Now living as a slave, Daliah shows no sign of distress. She offers no remarks on her enslavement but instead updates her friends on the state of the war, narrating based on what she has learned while toiling on the plantation. Suddenly, her friends see that now is the opportune moment to rescue their kidnapped friend from slavery and mount their escape. But Daliah hesitates. "I don't think I can go yet," she says. Still mindful that no one there on the plantation knows she is a time traveler, she explains that escaping now would introduce a wrinkle into the Civil War record, and they must not alter the course of events that already have happened. So Daliah volunteers to wait on the rescue and to stay instead willingly where she will remain a slave. Quickly, she is congratulated by a white gentleman bystander who has befriended the five teenagers. The man commends Daliah's decision to stay on the plantation, calling her "one brave woman" and then declaring, "I salute you!" Daliah does not respond with words but is shown beaming with happiness at the affirmation.

Daliah thus sees the slave's plight from the perspective of immediate experience. The lesson she draws is that slavery on a nineteenth-century plantation really was not all that bad. The plantation is where she belongs, as enslavement in this scenario is just a minor inconvenience when compared to the danger of revising the historical record. Her bravery depends on submitting to the truth of history and retaining her role as a submissive and obedient slave. Most importantly, Daliah gains this perspective on the dangers of historical revision not by reading any books or attending any classes in school but by having experienced enslavement firsthand. The historical record is fixed, and yielding to its truth is common sense.

Computer-Generated Imagery and Visual Form

In addition to recurrent depictions of firsthand spectatorship, the sola vidēre principle is evident in the rudimentary style of animation that distinguishes the Learn Our History series. The series may promise a gateway to "the truth about the past," but just as its depictions of immediate historiographic encounter rebel against the interpretive methodologies of academic experts, so too does its crude animation style rebel against the rendering capabilities of computer-generated imagery (CGI). Appearances of stylistic deviation or even deficiency matter because audiences may be socialized to expect that certain kinds of visual distortions result from creativity and ingenuity instead of an absence of artistic interest or concern. Miles Klee addresses this problem of the expectations of audiences, noting that poorly drawn comics in particular face what he calls "the Picasso problem." That is, we can allow for figures to be drawn grossly out of proportion or shape, as Picasso famously enjoyed doing, but as observers we might expect that such proportionalities are made deliberately. We prefer, in many cases, that badly drawn pictures "show subliminal assurance" of artistic intentionality or control. "The aesthetic wrongness" of a picture "can't be due to laziness or hackery. It has to be innovation."[36]

Cartoons usually simplify their subject matter in ways that are deliberately "wrong," of course. Cartoonish representations can even be construed categorically as a kind of rudimentary or "elementary" mode of depiction. It is a mode that revels in its own fabrication by flattening forms in two dimensions, establishing hard, "unnatural" boundaries around physical objects or integrating bright, playful color schemes.[37] Thus, cartoon images are given wide liberties when it comes to radical or even "comical" deviations in such elements as form, value, texture, shape, and depth. At the same time, given the aid of magnificent processing speed and power, CGI can render enhanced fantastical worlds that are, in their clarity, color, sharpness, and intensity, more vivid than mundane, day-to-day observational experience. According to Lev Manovich, who theorizes on the relationship between film and ontology, synthetic images now are capable of being almost "too real." CGI is sharper and more richly defined than images we encounter through the eye or the camera lens. Producers, therefore, often have to degrade the quality of animated imagery as a way to keep it from standing out against other photographic representations. CGI breaks through the material limitations of photography and film in this sense because its visual representations are *not* beholden to the material constraints of the camera lens. The irony, of course, is how such representational liberties allow computer animation to extend the old Platonic problem of making what is not real *seem* real. CGI is for this reason a tool of choice for those who want to get us as close as possible to a synthetic reality populated by fantastical worlds otherwise inaccessible through the camera lens. For all of its advancements, the photographic image is bound by the play of light on a surface, whereas the "fake visual reality" of CGI, as Manovich puts it, is not "an inferior representation of our reality, but a realistic representation of a different reality."[38] CGI constantly is being pushed in the direction of mediated experience that can mimic the sensory impressions of "real life." This makes computational technology well-suited for the purposes of historical education in the twenty-first century because it can bring audiences closer to the experience of seeing past figures and events *as if* they were witnessing them firsthand.

Learn Our History is an odd case, then, because its claim to historiographic realism is belied not just by its fictive mode of depiction but by recurrent evidence that its artists downgraded the obligation to demonstrate competency with the CGI platform. The crude style of animation suggests few assurances of artistic control in matters of design and presentation. Across the Learn Our History episodes, human forms and physical settings are rendered in a style that is aesthetically uninspiring in its representation of shapes, textures, and proportionality. Deficiencies in the form and execution of human characters are prominent, as characters have misshapen frames and oddly deformed limbs, and they move about and contort in stiff, robotic ways, like wooden dolls.[39] Physiognomic features are effectively indistinguishable across all secondary characters, and each speaking character repeats only a limited range of stilted oratorical gestures. Pictorial compositions consistently exhibit a rudimentary kind of flatness, such that each one of the Learn Our History videos, in the view of this analyst, comes up short in terms of its visual appeal. When compared to almost any other commercially available animated picture, Learn Our History appears amateurish from start to finish.

And yet, the flattened, cut-rate imagery that distinguishes Learn Our History's visual style is not incidental but central to its rhetorical purpose of authorizing the Christian nationalist view of American history. Poorly rendered digital imagery announces what is apparent, that Learn Our History is not pulling one over on its audience, as if the gang of time travelers is a group of "real" people who "really" saw the founders debate and who "really" tried to rescue their friend from a Southern plantation. The Second Continental Congress and the Civil War are, to be sure, "undeniable in their occurrence."[40] But according to the sola vidēre principle, such occurrences need not be reproduced, or reanimated, in a "convincing" manner. They only need to be made accessible in the form of a historiographic encounter. Since the firsthand encounter establishes the grounds for understanding, the encounter between individual and occurrence needs to be reanimated. The conceit of the Learn Our History series, then, is that it supplies the historiographic encounter that, in its structural claim to immediacy, justifies a corresponding claim to clear historical understanding. Thus, the encounter is what needs to be depicted, over and over, and the representational accuracy of that depiction is negligible against the reinforcing effect of its repetition.

Visualizing Rhetorical History

One of the more familiar arguments used by advocates of Christian nationalist history is that today's professional historians are "revisionists" who set out to change the facts about American history through a standard of "political correctness."[41] The corrective offered by Learn Our History is to examine historical evidence "objectively," thereby letting the truth of history reveal itself plainly. Like Scottish realists who insist on the self-evidence of the observable world, a historiography of Christian nationalism denies the requirement of interpretive judgment by saying: "Not what I want to believe but what 'nature' or 'what is the case' requires me to believe!"[42] Against a critical historiography that asks how the contingencies of time and place condition perceptions of "what is the case," Learn Our History's visual rhetoric closes the gap between "what is the case" and the authority of individual experience. That visual rhetoric plainly reveals the nation's Christian character. It makes the truth about America's past obvious, and it justifies belief in the immediacy of self-evidence. This commonsense perspective on historical interpretation finds expression in words written by Richard Lee, editor of *The American Patriot's Bible*, a volume that illustrates passages of scripture with scenes from American history: "American history is *vividly clear* that a faith in God and a reverence for the Bible provided the basis for the founding of our nation. . . . *Anyone who examines* the original writings, personal correspondence, biographies, and public statements of the individuals who were instrumental in the founding of America *will find* an abundance of quotations *showing* the profound extent to which their thinking and lives were influenced by a Christian worldview."[43]

In a critique of the Christian America thesis, John Wilsey explains that the kind of commonsense philosophy expressed by Lee underwrites an "evangelical hermeneutical method." According to Wilsey, the evangelical hermeneutical method is historiographic. It is premised on a belief that "the Founders of the American nation clearly expressed their original intent in their writings, and that America has deviated from it. The assumption undergirding this tenet is that the original intent of the Founders can be accurately discerned in the first place."[44] Following William Moyer's description of evangelical hermeneutics as "the Logos paradigm," Wilsey notes that Christian nationalism treats documents of the Founders in the same way that evangelical Christians interpret scripture: as clear, unambiguous evidence of authorial intent.[45] This partly explains why Christian nationalist writers point to intentionality as observable factual evidence. David Barton, author of a book called *Original Intent* and prominent advocate for Christian nationalism, encourages the Logos paradigm: "Because the portrayal of history so affects current policy, some groups have found it advantageous to their political agenda to distort historical facts intentionally. Those particularly adept at this are termed 'revisionists.' . . . There is an unhealthy tendency in many current books on the Founders . . . to cite predominantly contemporary 'authorities' speaking *about* the Founders rather than citing the Founders' own words. Such evidence is termed 'hearsay' and would never stand up in a court of law. *Original Intent*, however, has pursued the practice of 'best evidence': it lets the Founders speak for themselves in accordance with the legal rules of evidence."[46]

These remarks illustrate how Christian nationalism denies the interpretive process with a rhetoric of self-evidence and neutral observation of facts. Christian nationalism views history as a terrain of plainly established facts directly accessible by the faculty of observation. Such attitudes are serviceable equipment for fending off interpretive difficulties. They help to prevent what Patrick Hutton calls those "alternate pathways into history" that may reveal "unsuspected worlds" and complicate "the appreciation of our heritage."[47]

Learn Our History's visual rhetoric reinforces the association between spectatorship and epistemology not by the presentation of facts but by the visual depiction of a historiographic idealism. Each episode re-creates familiar chapters of American history in a visual format designed to attract young viewers by dispensing with both the textbook format and the school classroom. It draws viewers into the events of the past by positioning them alongside fictional characters who witness history directly, thereby formulating a visual pedagogy of unmediated spectatorship. Viewers learn that observing the past serves as a reliable way to understand their nation's history. A twenty-first-century reframing of rhetorical history therefore should attend more broadly to the ways in which history is made and remade in a variety of symbolic modalities, including pictorial images, graphic designs, and practices of spectatorship made possible by the application of emergent media technologies. Here, I conceptualize a particular practice of spectatorship, one based on individual experience and the authority of the senses, as the sola vidēre principle of Christian nationalist historiography. Its central function is to displace the authority of outside interpretation and instead elevate the experience of individual contact with truth as the only reliable standard or metric by which a depiction might be called "convincing." Each episode in the Learn Our History series shows, again and again, that historical reality is plainly observable to anyone willing to trust common sense over the sophisticated interpretations and explanations of outside experts.

In this way, the historiography of Christian nationalism is not so much a matter of faith as it is a matter of face value. Seen this way, both the depictions of eyewitnessing experiences and the austere visual style of the episodes perform a visual rhetorical strategy for encompassing a situation. Whether in the flattening of time and space or in the hastily rendered gestures of speaking figures, artistic designs are stylized responses that fulfill specific needs and desires for its audience.[48] In the same way that characteristics of form, shape, rigidity, and pliancy serve rhetorical purposes in language, the same elements in visual modalities also make available a coordinate range of social and psychological responses. Surely, there is an implicit recognition in Costello's warnings with which we begin this discussion, that in something as seemingly banal as a cartoon about history there are designs to furnish a perspective on questions about the national character. During a time when the Christian nationalist perspective is asserting itself in the United States, it is therefore useful to remember that the politics of national identity reformation usually revolve around a particular way of looking at the past.

Notes

1. Learn Our History, About Us, 2015, http://learnourhistory.com.

2. Maureen Costello, "Meet Mike Hucksterbee," HuffPost, May 14, 2011, https://www.huffpost.com/entry/meet-mike-hucksterbee_b_861905.

3. Learn Our History, *One Nation Under God*, DVD (Glendale Heights, IL, 2013).

4. Andrew L. Whitehead, Samuel L. Perry, and Joseph O. Baker, "Make America Christian Again: Christian Nationalism and Voting for Donald Trump in the 2016 Presidential Election," *Sociology of Religion* 79, no. 2 (2018): 1–25.

5. Baylor Religion Survey, "American Values, Mental Health, and Using Technology in the Age of Trump," September 2017 (Waco, TX: Baylor University).

6. This picture of the past grafts Christianity onto American identity, and it gets promoted by other prominent Christian nationalist advocates such as David Barton, Richard Lee, and Robert Jeffress. See David Barton, *Original Intent: The Courts, the Constitution & Religion* (Aledo, TX: WallBuilder Press, 2000); Richard Lee, ed., *The American Patriot's Bible: The Word of God and the Shaping of America* (Nashville, TN: Thomas Nelson, 2011); Dr. Robert Jeffress, *America Is a Christian Nation*, DVD, Pathway to Victory (Virginia Beach, VA: CBN, 2019).

7. Bruce E. Gronbeck, "The Rhetorics of the Past: History, Argument, and Collective Memory," in Turner, *Doing Rhetorical History*, 47.

8. Critics of Christian nationalist historiography include Mark A. Noll, George M. Marsden, and Nathan O. Hatch, *The Search for Christian America* (Colorado Springs: Helmers & Howard, 1989); Gregory A. Boyd, *The Myth of a Christian Nation: How the Quest for Political Power Is Destroying the Church* (Grand Rapids, MI: Zondervan, 2005); John Fea, *Was America Founded as a Christian Nation? A Historical Introduction* (Louisville, KY: Westminster John Knox Press, 2011); Steven K. Green, *Inventing a Christian America: The Myth of the Religious Founding* (New York: Oxford University Press, 2015).

9. The verbal-argumentative wing of the debate is exemplified in works such as Barton, *Original Intent*, and Fea, *Was America Founded*. Barton's work is critiqued in a chapter called "The Amateur Christian Historian" by Randall

J. Stephens and Karl Giberson, *The Anointed: Evangelical Truth in a Secular Age* (Cambridge, MA: Belknap Press of Harvard University Press, 2011).

10. See for example the website for Freedom Sunday, an annual celebration of America's Christian identity hosted by First Baptist Dallas, where Robert Jeffress is pastor: https://web.archive.org/web/20190807223603/http://www.first dallas.org/freedomsunday/.

11. E. Culpepper Clark and Raymie E. McKerrow, "The Rhetorical Construction of History," in Turner, *Doing Rhetorical History*, 34, 33.

12. James Jasinski, "A Constitutive Framework for Rhetorical Historiography: Toward an Understanding of the Discursive (Re)Constitution of 'Constitution' in *The Federalist Papers*," in Turner, *Doing Rhetorical History*, 73.

13. Clark and McKerrow, "Rhetorical Construction of History," 35.

14. Whether it is the internal documents of Kennedy's administration, key concepts in *The Federalist Papers*, inaugural addresses, policy proposals and responses, or a letter published in *Christian Century* and the *National Catholic Reporter*, subject matter taken up across the first volume reflect the utility, if not the predominance, of a verbal framework for the rhetorical analysis of history.

15. Although she does not develop the study in the volume, Kathleen J. Turner references her work on pictorial images, describing that work as an effort "to construct a rhetorical history of images of women in comic strips across a century." See Kathleen J. Turner, "Introduction: Rhetorical History as Social Construction," in Turner, *Doing Rhetorical History*, 12.

16. Turner suggests that constructing a convincing account of the past "is like putting together pieces of a jigsaw puzzle—only more complicated" (Turner, "Introduction," 10).

17. Quoted in Thomas O. Sloane, ed., *Encyclopedia of Rhetoric* (New York: Oxford University Press, 2001), 340.

18. Peter Burke, *Eyewitnessing: The Uses of Images as Historical Evidence* (Ithaca, NY: Cornell University Press, 2008). Gregory M. Pfitzer maps out a revealing account of the struggle over visual images and illustrations in *Picturing the Past: Illustrated Histories and the American Imagination, 1840–1900* (Washington, DC: Smithsonian Institution Press, 2002).

19. Pfitzer, *Picturing the Past*, 29.

20. Matthew T. Downey, "Pictures as Teaching Aids: Using the Pictures in History Textbooks," *Social Education* 44, no. 2 (January 1980): 93–100; Louis P. Masur, "'Pictures Have Now Become a Necessity': The Use of Images in American History Textbooks," *Journal of American History* 84, no. 4 (March 1, 1998): 1409–24; James A. LaSpina, *The Visual Turn and the Transformation of the Textbook* (Mahwah, NJ: Routledge, 1998).

21. See Lynne V. Cheney, "The End of History," *Historian* 57, no. 2 (1995): 454–56; Lynne V. Cheney, "The End of History, Part II," *Wall Street Journal*, April

1, 2015, sec. Opinion, http://www.wsj.com/articles/lynne-cheney-the-end-of
-history-part-ii-1427929675. Some have treated the distinction in terms of "academic" versus "popular" history. Stylistic variations across these two categories
may have informed Gronbeck's assumption that what academic historians write
and what general audiences read constitute "clearly separable discursive practices." Academic historians write "in increasingly arcane and specialized ways,"
he goes on to say, while "the books your mother and mine ordered from the book
club or checked out of the local library . . . have almost no connection whatsoever
with academic histories." The gap between academic and popular history may
be smaller than these remarks imply, however, as evidenced by commercially
marketed K–12 history curricula, which address audiences in an academic idiom
while also exhibiting many of the popularizing (which is to say stylistic) conventions displayed at the book club and local library. See Gronbeck, "Rhetorics of
the Past," 49.

22. On the use of visual images for civic education, see James Leith,
"Ephemera: Civic Education through Images," in *Revolution in Print: The Press
in France, 1775–1800*, ed. Robert Darnton and Daniel Roche (Berkeley: Univ
of California Press, 1989), 270–89; and Lester C. Olson, *Emblems of American
Community in the Revolutionary Era: A Study in Rhetorical Iconology* (Washing-
ton, DC: Smithsonian Institution Press, 1991). On history as civic education, see
Robert Lerner, Althea K. Nagai, and Stanley Rothman, *Molding the Good Citizen:
The Politics of High School History Texts* (Westport, CT: Praeger, 1995); Keith C.
Barton and Linda S. Levstik, *Teaching History for the Common Good* (New York:
Routledge, 2013); Organization of American Historians, "History, Democracy,
and Citizenship: The Debate over History's Role in Teaching Citizenship and
Patriotism," April 1, 2004, http://www.oah.org.

23. Downey, "Pictures as Teaching Aids," 93–100; Masur, "'Pictures Have
Now Become a Necessity,'" 1409–24; Theo van Leeuwen, "The Schoolbook as a
Multimodal Text," *Internationale Schulbuchforschung* 14, no. 1 (1992): 35–58.

24. Robert Stam, *Film Theory: An Introduction* (Malden, MA: Blackwell,
2000), 314.

25. All episodes include this opening montage. The episodes can be found at
the Our Lessons section of the Learn Our History website, https://learnourhistory
.com.

26. DVD cover jacket designs for each episode can be seen at http://lear-
nourhistory.com/our-lessons.html.

27. Theories of spectator positioning encompass a range of possibilities. In
a discussion of the different senses of "position," Nick Browne describes a few
scenarios. One derives from being "placed by the camera in a certain fictional
position with respect to the depicted action"; another occurs when "we see from
what we might take to be the eye of the character, [so] we are invited to occupy

the place allied to the place he holds." Spectator positioning is not always so straightforward, but these characterizations encapsulate, more or less, what I have in mind when I invoke the notion of viewers being positioned by Learn Our History videos. See Nick Browne, "The Spectator-in-the-Text: The Rhetoric of *Stagecoach*," in *Film Theory and Criticism: Introductory Readings*, ed. Leo Braudy and Marshall Cohen, 7th ed. (New York: Oxford University Press, 2009), 133.

28. Learn Our History, *The Declaration of Independence*, DVD (Glendale Heights, IL, 2011) (emphasis added).

29. Bruce Atkinson, "The Seven Solas: Toward Reconciling Evangelical and Anglo-Catholic Perspectives," *Virtue Online*, December 31, 2009, https://virtue-online.org/seven-solas-toward-reconciling-evangelical-and-anglo-catholic-perspectives.

30. The cultural constructedness of visual perception is addressed at length by E. H. Gombrich, *Art and Illusion: A Study in the Psychology of Pictorial Representation*, A. W. Mellon Lectures in the Fine Arts (Washington, DC: National Gallery of Art, 1956).

31. Sergiusz Michalski, *Reformation and the Visual Arts : The Protestant Image Question in Western and Eastern Europe* (London: Routledge, 2013).

32. Ann Kibbey, *The Interpretation of Material Shapes in Puritanism: A Study of Rhetoric, Prejudice, and Violence* (London: Cambridge University Press, 1986).

33. David Morgan, *Protestants and Pictures: Religion, Visual Culture, and the Age of American Mass Production* (New York: Oxford University Press, 1999).

34. George M. Marsden, *Fundamentalism and American Culture*, 2nd ed (New York: Oxford University Press, 2006), 14–15.

35. Learn Our History, *The Civil War: Brother against Brother*, DVD (Glendale Heights, IL, 2013).

36. Miles Klee, "A Note to Badly Drawn Webcomics Everywhere," *Bad Art* (blog), March 1, 2018.

37. For a demonstration of cartoon reduction and simplification, see Scott McCloud, *Understanding Comics: The Invisible Art* (New York: HarperPerennial, 1994).

38. Lev Manovich, "Synthetic Realism and Its Discontents," in *Film Theory and Criticism: Introductory Readings*, ed. Leo Braudy and Marshall Cohen, 7th ed. (London: Oxford University Press, 2009), 790.

39. I want to be careful not to impose a regime of body normativity onto the analysis. The aim here is not to call for idealized representations of the human form. Mindful that aesthetic judgments are historically conditioned and always serve partial interests, I am reserving a space to formulate critical evaluations about the quality of craftsmanship on display in the object of analysis.

40. Clark and McKerrow, "Rhetorical Construction of History," 36.

41. See Scott Thurman, dir., *The Revisionaries*, DVD (New York: Kino International, 2012).

42. Wayne C. Booth, *Modern Dogma and the Rhetoric of Assent* (Chicago: University of Chicago Press, 1974), 13.

43. Lee, *American Patriot's Bible*, I-1, I-9 (emphases added).

44. John D. Wilsey, *One Nation under God? An Evangelical Critique of Christian America* (Eugene, OR: Pickwick Publications, 2011), 61.

45. William Andrew Moyer III, "Battle for the City on the Hill: Evangelical Interpretations of American History 1960–1996," PhD diss., George Washington University, 1998, 290–339.

46. Barton, *Original Intent*, 8.

47. Patrick H. Hutton, *History as an Art of Memory* (Hanover, NH: University Press of New England, 1993), xvi.

48. Kenneth Burke, *The Philosophy of Literary Form: Studies in Symbolic Action*, 3d ed. (Berkeley: University of California Press, 1974), 1.

II
IDENTITIES, CULTURES, AND ARCHIVES

5

Doing Rhetorical History with Ralph Ellison

Meta-Archival Meditations on the Present, via the Past

Bryan Crable

Today, Ralph Ellison is best known as the author of the 1953 award-winning novel *Invisible Man,* which almost instantly catapulted him into the pantheon of twentieth-century literary giants.[1] Given the invitations, lectureships, honorary degrees, and critical acclaim that followed the novel's publication, one could justly concur with Timothy Parrish that "Ellison, within his lifetime, became the first 'canonical' black *American* author."[2] This remarkable achievement in the realm of fiction, though, has led most readers to equate Ellison's career with this single text—and we in rhetoric (at least in communication) have correspondingly relegated him to the journals, books, and conferences devoted to the study of literature and literary criticism.

Yet, in this chapter I argue that thinking of Ellison as a novelist is actually far too limiting. Ellison made significant contributions to the *analysis,* not just the *depiction,* of race in America—and, indeed, his fiction and nonfiction have much to offer our field's current engagement with this vital topic.[3] To be clear, however, I do not seek to "replicat[e] problematic add and stir practices," simply to append a Black name to our (historically white) disciplinary list.[4] Instead, I would challenge us to acknowledge Ellison as a rhetorical theorist of race, since his writings offer transformative insight into twenty-first-century white supremacy. This interpretation of Ellison requires us to first recognize him as an intellectual who was, through his writings from 1950 onward, *doing rhetorical history.*

As John Murphy points out, "The relationship between rhetoric and history has animated . . . debates in this field since its earliest days."[5] However, this relationship was transformed by Kathleen J. Turner's germinal 1998 collection, *Doing Rhetorical History,* which sought to both define the nature of rhetorical history and outline its importance to scholarship in our discipline—to, as Turner explains, demonstrate that "rhetorical history offers insights that are central to the study of communication and unavailable through other approaches."[6] It is clear that, over twenty years after Turner's collection first appeared, "rhetorical history continues to influence theoretical and critical work," and the scholarship inspired by Turner's call takes many forms: "the historical study of rhetorical events, the analysis of history as management of serial rhetorical problems, the critique of collective memory, a powerful means of intellectual history, or the privileging of archival work."[7]

At its most basic level, my reading of Ellison reflects the concerns of rhetorical history in this last sense: it was prompted by and necessitated archival work. However, beyond its roots in the archives, this chapter illustrates and extends the power of scholarship in rhetorical history in two ways. First, drawing upon Ellison's studies of ritual, it shifts our methodological gaze from the archival to what I call the *meta-archival*. By this term, I want to suggest the possibility of constituting an archive from an already archived collection of materials; more specifically, my archival research within Ellison's manuscripts suggests that *Ellison himself was an (unrecognized) archivist of whiteness*. Second, as part of this meta-archival engagement with Ellison, this chapter seeks to reclaim his body of work, and its meditations on the historical, for the critical rhetorical theorizing of race; simply put, I see Ellison as playing with the past in order to reconceptualize a vital issue of his (and our) present: white supremacy.

From the Archive to the Meta-Archive

As is often the case with archival research, this project on Ellison, rhetorical history, and whiteness took shape by accident. No tidy narrative here, just a simple confession: I had originally aimed at something quite different. Interested in Ellison's education in myth and ritual, I sought deeper insight into Ellison's reading of Lord Raglan's best-known work, *The Hero*.[8] Since Ellison credited Raglan's treatment of the archetypal "mythic hero"[9] with inspiring aspects of *Invisible Man*,[9] I wanted to study the copy in Ellison's personal library, housed in the Library of Congress's Rare Book and Special Collections Division.[10] I hoped that Ellison's annotations within it would open a window into the composition of his first novel but was instead surprised (and, initially, disappointed) to discover that it contained few markings—and, further, that those that *were* present had very little to do with Raglan's conception of the "mythic hero."[11]

In light of this discovery (and, honestly, desperate to salvage the project), I tried a different approach and looked more closely at the other volumes Ellison owned on myth and ritual, at least the ones preserved by the Library of Congress. Given the number of books in this collection, I focused my attention on those by or about the Cambridge Ritualists, the "myth and ritual school" widely acknowledged as the theoretical foundation of and inspiration for Raglan's book.[12] Upon examination of Ellison's copies of these works, I realized that he had studied Jane Ellen Harrison's Ritualist masterpiece, *Themis: A Study of the Social Origins of Greek Religion*, much more closely than previous scholarship had recognized,[13] and certainly more carefully than the Raglan book.[14] Further, I began to recognize that the annotations within Harrison's book overlapped in important ways with Ellison's notations within *The Hero*. In short, the archival evidence suggested to me that it made more sense to read Ellison, and Raglan, through Harrison than Ellison through Raglan.

Prompted to explore these intersections further, I followed an archival visit to the Jane Harrison Collection at the University of Cambridge[15] by immersing myself in the Ralph Ellison Papers, also housed at the Library of Congress.[16] While working with these unpublished letters, manuscripts, and notebooks, I became increasingly convinced that Harrison's text shed new light upon them: within Ellison's papers lie indications that *he was himself an archivist*—that he, simply put, spent thirty-plus years constructing an archive of white supremacy, articulating the American past to his present. As a result, I came to realize that my archival work had shifted to *meta*-archival work, an attempt to reconstruct Ellison's own archive, and its distinct organizing principle, from within his already cataloged papers. This argument, I believe, has important (and, to this point, underexplored) implications for scholarship in rhetorical history. Yet, before developing these, it is important to first outline the arguments regarding time and ritual that Ellison encountered in his studies of Harrison and Raglan—the arguments that ultimately led me to recognize the meta-archival dimensions of Ellison's collected papers.

Jane Ellen Harrison and the Historical

She is not now as widely known as, for example, J. G. Frazer, but Jane Harrison was one of the most renowned classicists of the late nineteenth and early twentieth centuries and the prime intellectual and personal force behind the Cambridge Ritualists, a group of scholarly collaborators who drew in innovative ways on the "comparative anthropological study of 'primitive' religion" in order to trace "the origins of Greek drama."[17] Although Harrison's earliest writings were widely praised by classicists, her publication of *Themis* in 1912 was rather controversial because "it was, in its sociological-anthropological orientation, radically out of sympathy with the dominant textual-mindedness of classical scholarship."[18] Particularly troubling to classicists was *Themis*'s tracing of the origins of drama to the ritual of the "Eniautos-Daimon," a term Harrison invented; claiming that the neologism "grew on my hands from sheer necessity,"[19] she defines the Eniautos-Daimon as the ancestor of the mythic hero as well as the Olympian god. It is not, she says, a term referencing a particular, distinct individual, whether human or divine, but "the representation of the life of the group and the life of nature."[20]

To grasp the importance of Harrison's use of this term, we must turn to her unconventional emphasis upon history, in two distinct senses. First, typical studies of myth and ritual focus on the legendary heroes from the stories of Homer and Hesiod, the figures from distant history whose trials brought renown, reward, and poetic memorialization. However, Harrison focuses her attention not on the Homeric Greeks but much earlier, on the archaic communities that were their predecessors. Her studies led her to insist that a myth is not the story, however stylized and embellished, of a particular individual from a particular point in the past. Instead, in wonderfully rhetorical fashion, she argues that myth "is the spoken correlative of the acted rite, the thing done; it is τὸ λεγόμενον as contrasted with or rather as related to τὸ δρώμενον,"[21] that is, myth is the "thing spoken" in conjunction with the ritual "thing done" during a religious ceremony. For archaic Greek communities, according to Harrison, religious practice was a vital performance incorporating and uniting word and deed: a sacred, prescribed set of actions accompanied by a sacred, prescribed verbal script.[22]

Harrison emphasizes that these are not the sacrificial rituals described by Homer or Hesiod, since, she argues, archaic culture and consciousness "knows no god; it creates sanctities but not divinities."[23] Since individual deities had not yet been identified and catalogued by these archaic Greeks, their characteristic religious ceremony was the *sacrament*, not the sacrificial gift to the gods; it was a communal gathering and distribution of power through speech and action, designed to accomplish "the magical inducement of fresh life, for man, for other animals and for plants."[24] Here lies the importance of the Eniautos-Daimon; this term, again, refers not to a particular individual, but to "an office, defined by its functions and capable of being filled by a series of representatives."[25] The Eniautos-Daimon is, Harrison argues, at the heart of pretheological, sacramental ceremony because it is "the product, the projection, the representation of collective emotion."[26] Those filling the ritual office of the Eniautos-Daimon are invested with the shared emotion of the group; the Eniautos-Daimon collects and stores this vital communal charge and subsequently serves as a channel for its redistribution. Through sacramental ritual, contact is created between this power-charged functionary and the collective; this contact (or "communication") releases the Eniautos-Daimon's accumulated power and distributes it to the community.

Because, as Harrison notes, "eating is not the only means of communicating, though perhaps it is among the most effective," she identifies the paradigmatic sacramental ritual as the communal feast of flesh.[27] Although typically (mis)described as a gift-sacrifice, Harrison emphasizes that this ritual form originally reflected a pretheological form of religion—that is, one not premised upon the existence of distinct gods in need of propitiation. As a result, she argues that, in this feast, "the bull is not a gift to Zeus, but a vehicle of [power] for distribution among the people. In him is concentrated as it were the life of the year: he is the incarnate ideal of the year; his life begins with the sowing, is cherished through the winter, and when it comes to full maturity in the early summer dies to live again in the people."[28]

This passage captures the essential ritual role of the Eniautos-Daimon; the "daimon of the year," as she summarizes, "lives and works for his people; he does more, he dies for them."[29] Through the consumption of the daimon—in this case, a bull—the power stored in this ritual office is shared with, communicated to, the people of the community.

Although we typically assume that these rites center on the killing of the animal consumed, these ceremonies of death and dismemberment, Harrison emphasizes, invariably involve a *rebirth*; following the dismemberment, the ritual daimon is born again, restored to life. She insists that we miss the nature and function of the ceremony if we attend only to the kill, since the ceremony is only truly complete once the daimon's resurrection has been announced. In fact, she contends that this rebirth is the true focus of the ceremony, not the daimon's death.[30] In other words, according to Harrison, "the Year-daimon in the form of a Bull lived his year-long life that he might die, and died that he might live again."[31] Here lies the vital function carried out by sacramental ritual and by the daimon as functionary: this process, by channeling the power of the universe, effectively *renews the world*, assures the passing of one year to the next, and thereby ensures the "permanent life of the group."[32] In sacramental ceremonies like the feast of flesh, the daimon's death-that-is-not, the drama of death and resurrection, accomplishes critical communal work; although the individual serving as daimon is consumed in and through the ritual, the transferring of power to the collective ensures the *preservation* of both community and ceremonial office. Sacramental ritual, that is, renders both immortal, in the sense of *perpetually reborn*. The figure of the Eniautos-Daimon thus contains "the whole world-process of decay, death, renewal."[33]

This emphasis on rebirth and renewal originally motivated Harrison's invention of the term *Eniautos-Daimon*. She explains that she ultimately rejected the more anglicized term *year-spirit* (or even *year-daimon*) because *year* is too closely associated with our linear, literate, rational conception of time: "To us 'year' means something definitely chronological, a precise segment as it were of spatialized time; whereas *Eniautos*, as contrasted with *etos*, means a *period* in the etymological sense, a cycle of waxing and waning."[34] In the ritual context of archaic Greece, she claims, time was not measured in or conceptualized as a line but treated as a *circle*, and a circle that must be continually retraced, even *completed*, through communal religious activity focused on the ritual office of the daimon. This cyclicality is embodied in the Eniautos-Daimon, whose function, Harrison says, is "to give food and increase to man *and make the year go round*";[35] this nonlinear, participative view of time, the driving force behind sacramentalism, has simply been obscured by our commitment to the "modern notion of non-recurrent evolution."[36]

As Harrison points out, "Our year with its four seasons is a sun-year," but "primitive man would not base his calendar on solstices and equinoxes which are only observed late; his year would be based not on astronomy, but on the seasons of his food-supply."[37] In other words, Harrison sees in archaic Greece a mode of time reckoning based upon the Earth, with its recurrent processes of growth, decay, death, and rebirth—processes specifically mirrored in, and symbolically controlled through, the ritual office of the daimon. However, the irruption of early Greek rationalism, with its emphasis upon linearity, observation, and clear distinctions, Harrison writes, produced not only a new form of religion but also a decisive shift in the conception of time. Once Greek culture fell under the spell of early rationalism, the archaic, ritual conception of time as a circle eternally traced and retraced through proper ceremonial enactment lost its significance: "To Olympian theology, in its ignorance and ineptitude, 'recurrent' had come to spell 'fruitless'; the way of life [i.e., time as an endless circle] was envisaged as an immutable sterility and therefore rejected."[38] In this way, Harrison contends that we see, in Greek history, the process by which "one mode of time-reckoning supersedes another."[39] With the birth of rationalism, the cyclical mode of time-reckoning characteristic of sacramentalism was replaced by the conception of time as an endless, unidirectional, measurable succession of seconds, minutes, hours, days, months, and years.

As Ellison's annotations within *The Hero* attest, Raglan recognized the importance of Harrison's discussion of the archaic "view of time as a ritual circle," or "'a view of Time as a vast circle in which the pattern of the individual life and of the course of history was a recurring cyclic process."[40] Ellison marked a long series of passages where Raglan cites a Harrison-influenced text to underscore the contrast between the linear and ritual conceptions of time: "Time is, in our experience, a stream of events descending from the unknown mists of beginning and running in a continuous flow down the future into the unknown; to the men of classical ages the actual life is the result of a recurrent beginning and has its source in the religious feast. . . . Not only the future needed creation, the past too had to be renewed . . . to retain its reality. The eternity of life lay not in the fact that it had once begun, but solely in the fact that it was constantly being begun."[41]

Extending and elaborating upon Harrison's arguments, this passage from Raglan emphasizes that the ritual conception of time entails a very different relationship to the past, to *history*. Within sacramentalism, and its characteristic form of time reckoning, the vitality, even *reality*, of the past depends upon action in the present; the past is not the distant ancestor of the present moment but something "constantly being begun," something perpetually restored, regenerated in the present. This means, as Raglan's text suggests, that ritual action in the present "not only condenses and renews the past, but in true earnest creates it over and over again."[42]

Those of an empirical cast of mind, especially in fields such as anthropology, history, and classical studies, have rather harshly rejected the argument presented above and Harrison's work as a whole. Ironically, central to this rejection is disbelief in the historical accuracy of Harrison's account, the plausibility of the direct line she draws from extant texts and textual fragments to particular rituals sacred to archaic communities.[43] Yet, I suggest, Ellison took a different perspective on Harrison's argument: he recognized the importance of Harrison's statement that sacramental forms of ritual are incredibly tenacious and "may long survive" the form of social life that birthed them.[44] Indeed, she insists that "sacraments show no sign of dying, but rather of renewed life and vigour. This need not surprise us. . . . The oldest things lie deepest and live longest,"[45] and, I believe, this inspired Ellison to create an archive of his own, tracking the continuing presence of sacramental rituals of white supremacy in his own twentieth-century America.

Excavating Ritual Time: Ellison's Meta-Archival Work

In the years since the original publication of *Doing Rhetorical History*, rhetorical scholars have recognized the need to attend not simply to the contents of an archive but to the archive itself as exerting a substantial symbolic and material force on the production and circulation of meaning and knowledge.[46] As Charles Morris eloquently summarizes, "the archive significantly influences what we are able to study, to say, and to teach about rhetorical history, and what we do, as rhetors, with its holdings in our scholarship, in our classrooms, and in the streets. The archive, therefore, should rightly be understood not as a passive receptacle for historical documents and their 'truths,' or a benign research space, but rather as a dynamic site of rhetorical power."[47] To this important claim, I propose a complementary dimension of the archive for rhetorical historians to consider, what I term the possibility of an archive *within* the archive, the discovery that transforms the critic's methodology from the archival to the *meta*-archival.

The recognition of this meta-archival dimension, of course, necessarily emerges from more traditional archival research processes, as it did in my own studies of Ellison. For the first ten-plus years of my engagement with Ellison's collected papers, I attended to the kinds of materials familiar to scholars in rhetorical history: draft manuscripts, notebooks, unpublished correspondences, press clippings, autobiographical musings, and collections of photographs.[48] After discovering Ellison's connection to Harrison, however, I began to pay attention to another portion of the collection, one I had, up to that point, largely ignored: a number of boxes identified as Ellison's "Reference File" by the Library of Congress. The finding aid describes these as "printed matter, primarily newspaper and magazine clippings, on topics of interest to Ellison, such as jazz, blues, photography, art, and prominent individuals."[49] Initially, since I was not engaged, at least principally, in biographical research, I treated these as tangential to my own Ellisonian interests and mentally set them aside; however, my studies of Ellison and the Ritualists led me to recognize how serious an omission that had been.

As the finding aid indicates, the folders in these boxes most often contain magazine articles (cut from such outlets as *LIFE*, the *Saturday Evening Post*, and *Time*) and newspaper articles (most often cut from the *New York Times* or *New York Post*). These are occasionally mixed with other kinds of materials, such as flyers, pamphlets, or posters; interestingly, the items in these reference files are rarely annotated in any detail, although they still bear the traces of the man who collected them. Many include dates in the margins, written in Ellison's own hand, and a few have arrows or other notations indicating which story on the ripped-out page had captured his attention. More importantly, the folders are arranged by subject matter, and the categories appear to have been created by Ellison himself; for example, he added "Africa" in pencil at the top of a page from a 1958 issue of *Time*, which is collected within the folder "Africa, 1943–1989."[50] Some of these categories, as the Library of Congress suggests, correspond to Ellison's interests or hobbies, as with the folder of materials on "Audio equipment and technology."[51] However, I would point out that many more reflect his preoccupation with matters of race in American culture (significantly, a topic *not* highlighted in the finding aid), and, further, these particular files most often span not simply a number of years but a number of *decades*. For example, this portion of the archive contains a folder he labeled "Discrimination," which includes materials as early as 1940 and as late as 1984; similarly, the contents of the folder "Ku Klux Klan" span nearly fifty years, from 1948 to 1993, and the folder on "Civil Rights" covers three decades, 1958 to 1988.

On first working through this portion of the Ellison collection, I approached it in straightforward fashion: as a set of resources he had amassed for use in his fiction, first *Invisible Man*, and subsequently the forty-year project resulting in a posthumously published second novel, *Three Days Before the Shooting . . . .*[52] In short, I read these clippings as the Library of Congress asked me to: as items that he found interesting, inspiring, or worth preserving, which he felt would fund his fictional efforts. After awakening to Harrison's influence on Ellison's thought, however, I began to recognize the limitations of treating Ellison as a kind of aesthetically driven "coupon clipper." After all, some of these folders were on subjects that decidedly do *not* appear in his fiction, as with "Africa," "Caribbean Countries," "Black Panthers," or "Chicago, Ill." Moreover, other folders contain clippings that appear to comment on each other; for example, the contents of the folder on the assassination of Black American activist Harry T. Moore and his wife in 1951 juxtapose the *New York Post*'s coverage of the bombers with a two-page story and photo from the *Post* on a police officer's killing of a Black man, entitled "Cop Kills Maniac in Rooftop Battle."[53]

At this point, my methodology shifted from the archival to the meta-archival. Instead of taking these at face value, as items that simply struck Ellison's fancy, I began to recognize the *intellectual project* that they constituted: that I was faced with a curated archive of materials on race in America, reflecting and arranged according to a particular, Ritualist-influenced perspective. That is, I began to recognize an organizing principle at work in these folders, one that articulated and illuminated their contents in important ways. This principle first came into focus when I realized that these folders do not simply contain materials spanning decades; it is also the case that, within these folders, Ellison collected evidence of the *recurring patterns* of whiteness in American culture, evidence of white supremacy "constantly being begun."

For example, the two folders titled "African-American studies, 1917, 1940–1994, n.d." include a series of items that repeat themes from the Moynihan Report and its troubling depiction of the "pathological" Black American family. The cyclicality of ritual time that Harrison emphasizes emerged when I compared a September 1965 essay from the *New Yorker* that focuses on the "failure of the Negro male" and "breakdown" of the Black family[54] to a November 1983 clipping from the *New York Times* titled "Breakup of Black Family Imperils Gains of Decades" and to another story from the *Times* in May 1984, titled "Black Men, Welfare, and Jobs."[55] Similarly, I noted the Harrisonian pattern evident within his folder on "Civil Rights," which contains newspaper coverage of civil rights leaders demanding action from the president in January 1959, March 1965, December 1972, and September 1982.[56] Finally, I saw the signs of time as a circle eternally traced and retraced in Ellison's "Ku Klux Klan" folder. Significantly, the folder contains not only material spanning several decades but also, in the Southern Poverty Law Center's 1982 special report, *The Ku Klux Klan: A History of Racism and Violence,* an interesting meditation from Julian Bond: "I turn on my television set and see reports of robed figures again handing out hate literature on the town square, I read in my newspaper of crosses again burned in folks' yards, and it seems as if we were back in the Sixties."[57] Although just a sample of the material in Ellison's "Reference Files," I contend that such patterns point to Ellison's interest in the repetition and resurgence of whiteness, signs not of unwelcome intrusions from or reminders of a distant past but signs of ritual processes at work that complete the cycle of life, death, and renewal that continue to ensure the whiteness of American culture and the permanence of white supremacy. However, grasping the significance of this point requires a return to Ellison, Harrison, and the nature of the historical.

"Keep America White Again"

In a letter to his close friend Stanley Edgar Hyman (who had introduced Ellison to *Themis*), Ellison commented that "the core of folklore, myth and ritual, is with us always—if only we get the rational mud out of our eyes and see the prerational fleece."[58] Following his reading of *Themis* and the Ritualists, I suggest that Ellison began to explore the implications of this claim by distinguishing two senses of history: history as recollection of the distant past and history as that which is perpetually, ritually re-created in the present. Ellison describes most Americans as accepting the first of these, what he calls the "sentimental" or "innocent" view of history,[59] which is organized according to the rational, linear conception of time. Our eyes fill with "rational mud," Ellison suggests, as we apply our modern conception of time as "non-recurrent evolution" and thereby approach the historical as that which has been superseded, as, in its simplest sense, that which is *past*. History, in this view, is *not* the present but instead provides a starting point from which we can measure our progress as a nation.

However, Ellison draws our attention to what this view of history overlooks: the sacramentalism, with its characteristic mode of time reckoning, that continues to display "life and vigour" in contemporary social life. Here, he was guided by Harrison's emphasis on this "mode of time-reckoning" as both distinct from and prior to the "innocent," rational view of time that we have inherited from early Greek rationalism; we mistakenly accept the linearity of time as given and thereby overlook the enduring power of sacramentalism and its relevance for our conception of history. Further, as Ellison's own archival collections demonstrate, Harrison's alternate conception of time—the ritual, cyclical conception—not only yields another understanding of the historical but also offers a much more complex understanding of the persistence of white supremacy within American culture.

Ellison offers provocative meditations on this point in a 1964 review of Howard Zinn's book *The Southern Mystique*—interestingly, the only one of Ellison's published essays to explicitly cite Harrison. Reflecting upon a resurgence of anti-Black sentiment and violence, Ellison comments that "American history is caught again in the excruciating process of executing a spiral—that is, in returning at a later point in time to an earlier point in historical space—and the point of maximum tortuosity is once again the South."[60] Yet, he goes beyond this rather familiar refrain to offer a sacramental interpretation of this recurring pattern: "While our history is characterized by a swift and tightly telescoped continuity, our *consciousness* of history is typically discontinuous. Like quiescent organisms in the blood, our unresolved issues persist, but with our attention turned to other concerns we come to regard the eruption of boils and chancres that mark their presence with our well-known 'American innocence.'"[61]

Here, Ellison's stress on a "tightly telescoped continuity" recalls Harrison's emphasis on time as eternal recurrence, ensured by proper ceremonial performance. In other words, he tells us that these "eruptions" should not be read as interruptions in a linear sequence of distinct temporal moments, as anomalies in an otherwise progressive movement forward. He argues instead that these "boils and chancres" testify to the cyclicality of time, that they are better read as ritual events whereby the past is renewed and given new life in the present. In this way, I believe that Ellison's essay calls us to *attend differently to the historical*, to reject a sentimental or "innocent" view of the past, and instead concentrate in Harrisonian fashion on the present-day processes renewing the reality of the past. In other words, Ellison cautions against treating public eruptions of white supremacist violence according to the linear, rational conception of time and, thus, of history; if white supremacy remains alive and well in American culture, that is because, as Harrison's work suggests, its permanence is recurrently reassured through the performance of sacramental rituals centered on Blackness.

In the 2019 film by Jim Jarmusch, *The Dead Don't Die*, Steve Buscemi's character is shown wearing a red baseball cap with the slogan, written in white, "Keep America White Again." Given the satirical bent of Jarmusch's film, this hat has been read as a rather ham-fisted critique of the Trump era. Those on the Left see it as "an indictment of Trump-voter mentality—witless, awful, unabashed."[62] Conservatives reject the hat's critique but read its message similarly: "That MAWA cap reveals Jarmusch's failed humor. . . . MAWA not only defames the Make America Great Again (MAGA) movement, it mischaracterizes national dissatisfaction and virtue-signals to hipster filmgoers that Jarmusch is on their ill-considered side."[63] I contend that both responses too easily dismiss the significance of Buscemi's hat; I argue that, beyond broad political caricature, this slogan correctly captures Ellison's insight into the ritualistic nature of white supremacy and its relationship to American history. That is, I read this hat as the perfect expression of Ellison's Harrisonian studies of ritual, history, and white supremacy—the logic embodied in his meta-archive of race in America and in his writings.

Treating the past as a marker from which present-day progress can be measured, Ellison suggests, we might simply express shock and dismay at the present-day violence of whiteness and offer verbal handwringing over its seemingly unthinkable "return." Such a position is clearly satirized in Buscemi's hat, with not only its casual racism but also its apparently incoherent treatment of the nature of time: how can we "keep" something "again"? As an expression of our "well-known 'American innocence,'" this might be our immediate response, but Ellison would have argued that such a move effectively severs the longstanding American investment in white supremacy from any connection to current events. In his words, it renders history discontinuous from the present. To claim that America has (or should have) progressed "beyond" its white supremacist history treats the recurrent as the once occurrent, to impose a view of time as "non-recurrent evolution" upon events that suggest a different mode of temporality. And correcting this, for Ellison, requires a Harrisonian analysis.

By refusing to apply the rational, "discontinuous" approach to the historical, Ellison instead emphasizes that the past is not something that the present is "beyond" but instead *a product of ritual action, something perpetually reborn in the present*. That is, drawing on Harrison, Ellison argues that the white past of American culture is itself renewed in the present through action centered on the Black body; by creating means of contacting and communing with the power of Blackness, whiteness's reality is perpetually reassured. The power derived from contact with the power-charged Black Eniautos-Daimon flows back into the white community, ritually ensuring its preservation, protection, and renewal. History, for Ellison, is therefore characterized by a "tight and telescoping continuity" because of the persistence of American *ritual processes tied to race*; these continue to secure the reality of the past even as they purport to be of a moment distinct from it. White supremacy, as a consequence, is America's past because the present continually, sacramentally reaffirms its reality: ritual enables us to, quite seriously, *keep America white again*. This is why, Ellison argues, we regularly experience a present-day "return" to a moment that is an "earlier point in historical space." In place of the discontinuous, linear, nonrecurrent approach to American history, Ellison substitutes a Harrisonian recognition of the communal drive to perennially preserve American racial order through correct, and repeated, ritual reenactment, the drive to continually resecure America's white past through a connection to the power the white community has vested in Blackness. Ellison drew on Harrison's work to highlight this different sense of the historical, one rooted in the ritual conception of time as cyclical and as controlled through sacrament.

Ellison's clippings from magazines and newspapers suggest his attention to the role of the Black American as daimon, as the power-charged focus of sacramental ritual, themes that also recurred in his writings of the 1950s onward. As in the *New York Post* article cited above, which contained breathless descriptions of the Black "maniac" whose superhuman strength and endurance could only be stopped by a police officer's bullet, Ellison's essays emphasize that "it is almost impossible for many whites to consider questions of sex, women, economic opportunity, the national identity, historic change, social justice—even the 'criminality' implicit in the broadening of freedom itself—without summoning malignant images of black men into consciousness."[64] Nearly thirty years after writing those words, as he collected materials on an "eruption" of white supremacism, Ellison again points out that, for whites, "blackness is a sign of satanic evil given human form. It is the dark consubstantial shadow which symbolizes all that its opponents reject in social change and in democracy."[65] By creating contact with this power-charged figure, American sacramental rituals, like those described by Harrison, are deeply functional; through the vehicle of the Black Eniautos-Daimon, vast stores of power are channeled back into the white community. These processes ritually ensure the renewal and preservation of white supremacy, and are even felt by whites to renew *the entirety of existence*, because "not only [are] the stability of social order and the health of business seen as depending upon white dominance, but the sanctity of the moral order as well."[66]

Although a full consideration of this point requires a book-length treatment,[67] I believe that Ellison, from 1950 onward, made a clear case for the complex and vital connection of the rhetorical and historical and of the historic and enduring consequentiality of the rhetorical processes, centered on Blackness, that maintain the American (white) social order. Ellison recognized that the sacramental *process* was the vital heart of Harrison's book: the need to secure and renew the life of the community, the solidity of its past, through correct speech and action. Further, he recognized the power of these insights for engaging matters of race in American culture; as Michael Germana writes, Ellison was keenly attuned to "the connection between coercive racial and temporal constructs."[68] Or, as Ellison wryly warns in *Invisible Man*: "Beware of those who speak of the *spiral* of history; they are preparing a boomerang. Keep a steel helmet handy."[69]

I would press matters even further, however, to highlight a deeper connection between Ellison and *rhetorical* history. Ellison's work embodies both dimensions of Turner's description of rhetorical history as social construction: "both 1) the ways in which rhetorical processes have constructed social reality at particular times and in particular contexts and 2) the nature of the study of history as an essentially rhetorical process."[70] Here, we see the impact of Harrison's studies of archaic Greece on Ellison's analysis of American history and culture. By drawing on Harrison, Ellison was able to excavate the rhetorical processes that fund (and have historically funded) our discourses and practices of race and that regularly result in the eruption of racial violence—that is, through his encounter with Jane Harrison, Ellison was doing rhetorical history in order to better think about his present moment and the possibilities of disrupting the perennial, present-day renewal of its (white) past. Reflecting Moya Ann Ball's powerful argument that "doing rhetorical history generates theoretical as well as historical knowledge,"[71] this reading of Ellison not only deepens our insight into his body of work but also into the rhetorical processes ensuring the survival of white supremacy, thereby continuing an endeavor that Ellison began over seventy years ago. By following Ellison's conceptual insights into ritual and the historical, we can not only continue to build upon his own (meta-archival) record but also generate the kind of insight necessary to disrupt twenty-first century—tenacious, consequential, sacramental—rituals of race.

Notes

1. Arnold Rampersad, *Ralph Ellison: A Biography* (New York: Vintage, 2008), 3–4.

2. Timothy Parrish, *Ralph Ellison and the Genius of America* (Amherst: University of Massachusetts Press, 2012), 2 (emphasis in the original).

3. See, for example, the forum "Special Issue: #RhetoricSoWhite," *Quarterly Journal of Speech* 105, no. 4 (2019): 465–507.

4. Lisa A. Flores, "Towards an Insistent and Transformative Rhetorical Criticism," *Communication and Critical/Cultural Studies* 15, no. 4 (2018): 351.

5. John M. Murphy, "Barack Obama and Rhetorical History," *Quarterly Journal of Speech* 101, no. 1 (2015): 214.

6. Kathleen J. Turner, "Introduction: Rhetorical History as Social Construction," in Turner, *Doing Rhetorical History*, 2.

7. Murphy, "Barack Obama," 214.

8. Lord Raglan, *The Hero: A Study in Tradition, Myth, and Drama* (London: Methuen, 1936).

9. Ralph Ellison, *The Collected Essays of Ralph Ellison*, ed. John F. Callahan (New York: Modern Library, 1995), 76, 218, 524; David L. Carson, "Ralph Ellison: Twenty Years After," in *Conversations with Ralph Ellison*, ed. Maryemma Graham and Amritjit Singh (Jackson, MS: University Press of Mississippi, 1995), 195–96.

10. For details on this collection, consult https://www.loc.gov/rr/rarebook /coll/ellison.html.

11. For a more comprehensive treatment of the annotations within Ellison's copy of *The Hero*, see Bryan Crable, "'Who Invents Rituals?': Ralph Ellison Reads Lord Raglan," *Literature of the Americas*, 5 (2018): 27–42, https://doi .org/10.22455/2541-7894-2018-5-27-42.

12. Stanley Edgar Hyman, "Myth, Ritual, and Nonsense," *Kenyon Review*, 11, no. 3 (1949): 463–66.

13. Although the literature has consistently recognized Ellison's connection to Raglan, to my knowledge Barbara Foley is the only other scholar to include Harrison in treatment of Ellison's studies of myth and ritual—and although full consideration of this point lies outside the bounds of this essay, even Foley, I believe, fails to recognize the full impact of *Themis* on Ellison's life and work. See

Barbara Foley, *Wrestling with the Left: The Making of Ralph Ellison's* Invisible Man (Durham, NC: Duke University Press, 2010), 84–86.

14. Unlike *The Hero,* Ellison's copy of *Themis* bears witness to multiple, and more thorough, readings; its annotations are in pencil, green ink, and black ink and are much more extensive than in the Raglan. For more on Ellison's reading of Harrison, the project that generated the argument presented in this chapter, see Bryan Crable, "From Sacrifice to Sacraments: Ralph Ellison's Appropriation of Jane Ellen Harrison's *Themis,*" in *Global Ralph Ellison: Transnational Aesthetics and Politics,* ed. Tessa Roynon and Marc C. Connner (Oxford: Peter Lang Press, 2021).

15. For details on this collection, consult https://archiveshub.jisc.ac.uk/search /archives/178cb5b9–91be-32a9–91f9-a5131003cd77.

16. For details on this collection, consult https://lccn.loc.gov/mm96083111.

17. Robert Ackerman, *The Myth and Ritual School: J. G. Frazer and the Cambridge Ritualists* (New York: Routledge, 2002), xi.

18. Ackerman, *Myth and Ritual School,* 161. Not surprisingly, this meant that the Ritualists' reputation actually was stronger outside of classical studies; indeed, their work was especially influential in the field of literary criticism.

19. Jane Ellen Harrison, *Themis: A Study of the Social Origins of Greek Religion,* 2nd ed. (Cambridge: Cambridge University Press, 1927), xvii.

20. Harrison, *Themis,* xix.

21. Harrison, *Themis,* 328.

22. Indeed, according to Harrison, only when myths are removed from this communal, ritual context can they begin to take on a more aesthetic, literary life (or, more rhetorically, that the words can be separated from actions, and treated as self-sufficient).

23. Harrison, *Themis,* xvi.

24. Harrison, *Themis,* xvi.

25. Harrison, *Themis,* 259. Ellison marked this passage extensively.

26. Harrison, *Themis,* 260. Ellison annotated this section of text.

27. Harrison, *Themis,* 137.

28. Harrison, *Themis,* 154.

29. Harrison, *Themis,* 467.

30. Harrison, *Themis,* 245.

31. Harrison, *Themis,* 467.

32. Harrison, *Themis,* xiv.

33. Harrison, *Themis,* xvii.

34. Harrison, *Themis,* xvii.

35. Harrison, *Themis,* 467. Emphasis added.

36. Harrison, *Themis,* xvii.

37. Harrison, *Themis,* 184.

38. Harrison, *Themis*, 530.

39. Harrison, *Themis*, 237. Ellison marked this phrase and the passage around it.

40. Raglan, *The Hero*, 160. Raglan here quotes from a collection of essays devoted to the "myth and ritual" position. Ellison underlined this phrase and drew a line in the margin across the entirety of this paragraph.

41. Raglan, *The Hero*, 158–59. Raglan here quotes from a Ritualist-inspired study of Norse myths. Ellison drew long lines next to these passages in the text. For Harrison and Raglan, of course, this would apply to archaic communities, not those of the classical age.

42. Raglan, *The Hero*, 159.

43. Thus, scholars rejecting, say, Harrison's interpretation of a textual fragment as originating from an archaic ritual of initiation in archaic Cretan communities thereby rejected the entirety of her argument. See, for example, Joseph E. Fontenrose, *The Ritual Theory of Myth* (Berkeley: University of California Press, 1966), 29–34.

44. Harrison, *Themis*, xvi.

45. Harrison, *Themis*, 134.

46. See, for example, Jennifer Clary-Lemon, "Archival Research Processes: A Case for Material Methods," *Rhetoric Review* 33, no. 4 (2014): 381–402.

47. Charles E. Morris III, "The Archival Turn in Rhetorical Studies; or, The Archive's Rhetorical (Re)turn," *Rhetoric & Public Affairs* 9, no. 1 (2006): 115.

48. Over the course of a decade, I engaged his archival materials in order to reconstruct his deep intellectual and personal relationship to Kenneth Burke. See Bryan Crable, *Ralph Ellison and Kenneth Burke: At the Roots of the Racial Divide* (Charlottesville: University of Virginia Press, 2012).

49. Ralph Ellison, Papers, Finding Aid, Library of Congress, accessed November 11, 2019, https://findingaids.loc.gov/db/search/xq/searchMfer02.xq?_id=loc.mss.eadmss.ms002008&_faSection=overview&_faSubsection=did&_dmdid=.

50. Box I: 179, F. 3, Ellison Papers, Manuscript Division, Library of Congress, Washington, DC. Ellison's literary executor, John Callahan, indicated in a personal correspondence that the categories were, *at the very least*, guided by the titles Ellison added to the materials he collected. However, Ellison was strongly influenced by his friendship with Stanley Edgar Hyman, and Hyman maintained a meticulous, organized, catalogued set of files until his death in 1970. In one of his first letters to Ellison, for example, Hyman wrote, "I have followed your stuff eagerly for quite a while, and thought your story, Mister Toussan, so good that I have it filed away in a little folder marked 'Ellison, Ralph'" (Stanley Edgar Hyman to Ralph Ellison, June 24, 1942, Box I: 51, F. 14, Ellison Papers). I would therefore find it quite natural that Ellison would emulate his close friend's practices and that his own files would involve a similarly formal system of categorization.

51. Ellison was well-known as an audiophile, even designing and installing hi-fi stereo equipment for his friends Stanley Edgar Hyman and Shirley Jackson. See, for example, Stanley Edgar Hyman to Ralph Ellison, November 10, 1959, Box I: 51, F. 14, Ellison Papers.

52. For more on Ellison's work on a second novel, see Adam Bradley, *Ralph Ellison in Progress: From* Invisible Man *to* Three Days Before the Shooting... (New Haven: Yale University Press, 2010).

53. Box I: 199, F. 8, Ellison Papers.

54. Box I: 179, F. 6, Ellison Papers.

55. Box I: 179, F. 7, Ellison Papers. I would point out these same themes widely circulated again in June 2015, with the fiftieth anniversary of the report.

56. Box I: 200, F. 4, Ellison Papers. These same themes, of course, appeared in coverage of the Trump presidency.

57. Box I: 203, F. 3, Ellison Papers. I think it significant that these same themes widely circulated again in August 2017, following the violent, white supremacist incidents in Charlottesville's "Unite the Right" rally.

58. Ralph Ellison to Stanley Edgar Hyman, August 16, 1948, Box 6, F. 30, Stanley Edgar Hyman Papers, Manuscript Division, Library of Congress, Washington, DC.

59. Ellison to Hyman, August 16, 1948.

60. Ellison, *Collected Essays*, 563. Note the similarity to Bond's language in the SPLC report twenty years later.

61. Ellison, *Collected Essays*, 563.

62. Richard Lawson, "Cannes Kicks Off with a Zombie Comedy for the Trump Age," review of *The Dead Don't Die*, by Jim Jarmusch, *Vanity Fair*, May 15, 2019, https://www.vanityfair.com/hollywood/2019/05/the-dead-dont-die-movie-review-jim-jarmusch-cannes.

63. Armond White, "*The Dead Don't Die*: Climate-Change Comedy for the Alexandria Ocasio-Cortez Era," review of *The Dead Don't Die*, by Jim Jarmusch, *National Review*, June 14, 2019, https://www.nationalreview.com. As Billie Murray pointed out to me, White actually misidentifies the slogan, substituting "Make" for "Keep"—which erases both Jarmusch's joke and the connection to Ellison's Harrisonian view of history. It is also worth noting that White is often characterized as a "troll" for reasons that have little or nothing to do with his politics and more to do with his penchant for kneejerk contrarian takes on films. As Edirin Oputu puts it, White has "spent his career cultivating a critical voice so caustic and contentious that even Roger Ebert felt compelled to label him a 'troll.'" In 2014, White was expelled from the New York Film Critics Circle (an action that the group had never before taken in its then-seventy-nine-year history) after White heckled the director Steve McQueen as he was receiving an award. White denied doing this, but many attendees at the awards dinner confirmed

that he did. Edirin Oputu, "Contrarian Critic: Armond White's Expulsion From the New York Film Critics Circle Is Unfortunate, but Not Unexpected," *Columbia Journalism Review*, January 17, 2014, https://archives.cjr.org/critical_eye/contrarian_critic.php; Owen Gleiberman, "Why Armond White Got Kicked Out of the New York Film Critics Circle," *Entertainment Weekly*, January 13, 2014, https://ew.com/article/2014/01/13/armond-white-kicked-out-of-ny-critics/.

64. Ellison, *Collected Essays*, 102.

65. Ellison, *Collected Essays*, 641.

66. Ellison, *Collected Essays*, 639.

67. See my forthcoming volume: Bryan Crable, *White Sacraments: Race, Rhetoric, Blackness* (Columbus: Ohio State University Press).

68. Michael Germana, *Ralph Ellison, Temporal Technologist* (New York: Oxford University Press, 2018), 127.

69. Ralph Ellison, *Invisible Man* (New York: Vintage Books, 1980), 6.

70. Turner, Introduction, 2.

71. Moya Ann Ball, "Theoretical Implications of Doing Rhetorical History," in Turner, *Doing Rhetorical History*, 70.

6

Negotiating Public Scientific Regulatory Controversies

Dr. Frances O. Kelsey's Productive Postponement of Thalidomide in the United States

Madison A. Krall

The thalidomide disaster has been called one of the most horrifying technological tragedies of the twentieth century. Much like its catastrophic counterpart, the 1912 sinking of the *Titanic*, the thalidomide tragedy is a reflection of the dangers of modernizing technology and medicine and of the consequences that result from selfishness and putting too much trust in the safety of new technological advancements.[1] First commonly prescribed as a sedative, thalidomide eventually became used as a way for pregnant women to ward off nausea and reduce morning sickness. Yet the drug would take a serious toll on families in forty-six countries throughout the globe, affecting an estimated 275,500 babies across only a five-year span.[2] Many of those afflicted were stillborn, miscarried in their mothers' wombs, the victims of infanticide upon birth, or born with internal injuries and/or severe physical abnormalities. The drug caused such external physical deformities as an absence of legs, wherein children were born with just toes connected to their hips; or with no arms, an effect that has historically been likened to short flippers because the hands are attached directly to the shoulders.[3] Despite the worldwide horrors created by thalidomide from the 1950s through the early 1960s, only forty or so cases of infants affected by thalidomide who survived past childhood were reported in the United States.[4] The person who ensured that no more than this relatively small number of thalidomide-affected births would occur in the United States was Food and Drug Administration (FDA) medical officer Dr. Frances Oldham Kelsey.

Newly commissioned at the FDA in Washington, DC, in September 1960, Kelsey faced pharmaceutical company Richardson-Merrell's four-volume application for approval of the drug thalidomide, or Kevadon, as her second case. Richardson-Merrell assumed that Kevadon would go to market quickly because it had been sold as an over-the-counter drug for a few years in parts of Europe. However, the lack of "well-designed, well-executed studies" presented in the clinical reports led Kelsey to suspect issues associated with the drug,[5] so she consistently postponed the application's approval by citing such problems as an incomplete submission. The importance of this delaying tactic cannot be overstated: federal guidelines in 1960 stated that a new drug need not receive approval in order to be marketed to the public if it passed a sixty-day marker without being reviewed by a medical officer such as Kelsey. Between September 12, 1960, and March 8, 1962, Kelsey documented fifty-one exchanges with Richardson-Merrell, requiring the drug company to resubmit their application for Kevadon six times to delay its trajectory.[6] Kelsey stood her ground against approving the Kevadon application, employing a range of rhetorical strategies to reject the application despite the harassment she endured from Richardson-Merrell's scientists. Finally, the confirmation from Germany that thalidomide caused birth defects led Richardson-Merrell to withdraw its application.

Today, scholars credit Kelsey with catalyzing the FDA's drastic overhaul of drug regulation during the latter half of the twentieth century. This overhaul included raising standards for drug licensing, standards still enforced today. Clearly Kelsey was and is a key figure in US regulatory safety; yet questions remain about how Kelsey resisted Richardson-Merrell's aggressive advances for so long and how the nuances of this public controversy over scientific regulation led to such significant changes at both the technical and the public levels of drug regulation and drug legislation in the United States. Here, I demonstrate how Kelsey's communications with the drug company Richardson-Merrell— handwritten drafts, typed drafts, final official records, and telephone memoranda—embody what Marcus Paroske identifies as an "epistemological filibuster."[7] In what follows, I situate these rhetorical mechanisms of the epistemological filibuster within the expansive study of scientific and regulatory controversies and contribute to the "definitional contours" of these terms to explicate the nuances of what I label a public scientific regulatory controversy.[8] Given the contextualization of the thalidomide disaster as a technological and medical catastrophe, and Kelsey's rhetorical engagement with Richardson-Merrell within that context, I consider throughout my analysis the historical and contemporary implications of identifying these mechanisms and their role for engaging with scientific uncertainty in the overlapping spaces of the technical and public spheres.

Public Scientific Regulatory Controversy

Nathan Crick and Joseph Gabriel define *scientific controversies* as "disputes about knowledge that arise when technical authority intersects with public interests within salient political exigencies" that can be articulated in epistemological, educational, and juridical terms.[9] Research on scientific controversies has primarily focused on interactions between scientists and members of the broader public, what Celeste M. Condit, John Lynch, and Emily Winderman call public-science interactions. These authors also suggest that when scholars from history, philosophy, and sociology study "pseudo-controversies," they focus on the production of uncertainty, whereas rhetoricians instead address the production of controversy.[10] Few studies in the rhetoric of science have assessed how the context of a scientific controversy and the textual evidence creating it work together.

Existing research on public scientific controversies in general includes a focus on the origins of public scientific controversies and the benefits of articulating the differing ways that scientific discourses confront varied audiences.[11] For instance, Crick and Gabriel propose that "public scientific controversies necessitate attention both to the dramatic aspects of communication and to the constitutive function of citizen participation and experience, alongside those of experts, within the deliberative process."[12] They provide a reminder that public scientific controversies require an acceptance of the dynamics of rhetoric for the audiences engaged in the controversy and a realization that objective policies are not the only markers of success.

Moreover, a traditional scientific controversy might be viewed differently when it enters the realm of the public. Lawrence Prelli, for example, considers how scientific research might rhetorically be contrived as legitimate for and among nonscientific audiences.[13] When conceiving of public discourses and the role scientific controversies play in them, according to Ron Von Burg, "the side that best represents the tropes of disinterestedness and skepticism . . . typically prevails."[14] In this sense, then, public scientific controversies can be understood as merely those technical controversies that are introduced to the public realm.

Public scientific controversies have also enabled scholars to advance theory regarding the phenomenon of the *manufactured* scientific controversy.[15] Leah Ceccarelli explains that manufactured controversies are a special variation of public scientific controversy characterized by a strategic distortion of communication that corrodes the democratic process.[16] The first tell-tale sign that a public scientific controversy is of the manufactured variety is the claim of a scientific debate around an issue despite clear scientific consensus in the technical sphere. In this context, Ceccarelli suggests that, because there is no controversy among scientists about the science itself, the second sign of manufacturing is its invention in an effort "to achieve certain political goals like delaying the enactment of regulatory public policy, or forcing the teaching of alternatives to the dominant scientific paradigm in public schools."[17] Such scholars as Marlia E. Banning, Paroske, and Rachel Avon Whidden evidence the utility of a manufactured scientific controversy and speak to how the rhetorics of these controversies are understood in relation to the public sphere.[18] In contrast, in this project I engage the permeability of both spheres to introduce the nexus where scientific and regulatory controversies meet.

Josh Boyd contends that "when a regulatory agency and its prescribed technical standards are added to a science-based controversy, a *regulatory* controversy occurs."[19] He focuses in particular on the communicative practices betwixt the argumentative spheres of science and public. Similarly, Lisa B. Keränen assesses "spheres of argument" in the B-06 lumpectomy controversy as she analyzes the argumentative demarcation of borders between the public and technical spheres.[20] While Boyd and Keränen offer two rich opportunities for seeing the way technical and public arguments might be shaped within a science-based controversy, work building from these contentions demands further consideration of the rhetorical encounters defining the relationship between a regulatory controversy and a true scientific controversy. I introduce these rhetorical parameters for a public scientific regulatory controversy in the case of Dr. Kelsey and her creation and maintenance of Paroske's epistemological filibuster.

Epistemological Filibuster

One of the key means by which regulatory and scientific controversies unfold is by way of the epistemological filibuster, but scholarship has yet to delineate the mechanisms involved in its rhetorical construction. For Paroske, an epistemological filibuster occurs when "one side in a science policy controversy exploits uncertainty over how thoroughly to deliberate as a means to preclude the resolution of that issue in government action."[21] Past usages of the concept demonstrate the importance of deconstructing it to determine the rhetorical mechanisms that work to sustain it, as I offer in my analysis below.

Many scholars take up Paroske's notion of the epistemological filibuster, admiring its international focus and recommending future research to engage the strategy in productive ways.[22] Other scholars recommend that both science communicators and scientists be aware of existing creative rhetorical strategies that are useful in overcoming science deniers, using Paroske's epistemological filibuster as one such rhetorically creative device.[23]

Scholars have used the epistemological filibuster to explore such topics as scientism and Manichean idioms[24] and the public rhetoric that develops during controversies regarding scientific discoveries and claims.[25] Kenneth C. Walker, for instance, uses it to examine the discourse of uncertainties in his study of the ozone hole controversy,[26] and John Joseph Rief identifies it in an argument to explicate uncertainty's role in the "ongoing contestation, negotiation, and study" of the "obesity" problem/controversy.[27] Similarly, Kenny Walker and Lynda Walsh use Paroske's concept to explore how "industry representatives and other critics of scientific authority leverage scientific uncertainty to delay policy action" in order to examine Rachel Carson's use of scientific uncertainty in *Silent Spring*.[28] Murphy also uses the concept with *Silent Spring* to discuss the "troubling history of interested parties exploiting uncertainty to postpone policy change" in scientific controversies and manufactured controversies.[29]

Here, I examine how a member of the scientific community employed the epistemological filibuster in a historically rich public scientific regulatory controversy. Similar to Tobiason's work, I investigate not only the role of uncertainty but also the rhetorical ways in which the epistemological filibuster was implemented and effectively sustained.[30]

Evidencing Productive Postponement

Kelsey's rhetorical appeals and mechanisms demonstrate the productive potential of the epistemological filibuster for navigating a public controversy over scientific regulation and for understanding the role of the "public" scientist in technical spheres of argument.[31] Further, I speak to the value of rhetorical history by demonstrating how, as Zarefsky offers, "a better understanding of an unusual situation"—such as the prevention of a thalidomide catastrophe in the United States—contributes to both rhetorical theory and general regulatory and scientific knowledge about the rhetoric of science.[32]

The epistemological filibuster used by Kelsey worked to "indefinitely delay action by forcing a search for the kind of indubitable evidence" that Richardson-Merrell could never provide.[33] In manuscripts from my archival research at the Library of Congress and secondary sources that feature pieces of Kelsey's interactions with Richardson-Merrell, her writings enacted this epistemological filibuster via three strategic tactics: (1)

centering scientific uncertainty first and foremost, (2) reinforcing normative appeals wherein present FDA standards were maintained, and (3) highlighting difficulties that might become societally problematic at a public level.

Richardson-Merrell submitted the Kevadon application to the FDA on September 8, 1960. When the drug application arrived on Kelsey's desk, thalidomide had been on the market throughout the globe for almost three years with a positive track record. Consequently, executives at Richardson-Merrell felt "cocky" about the drug's release and planned a huge campaign in the United States seven months later.[34] The campaign glorified thalidomide, recommending it for anxiety affiliated with a vast number of conditions including anorexia, cancer, emotional instability, kidney disease, marital discord, nightmares, tuberculosis, and nausea and vomiting.

Despite being a brand-new medical officer at the FDA, Kelsey's experience taught her how to approach highly praised drugs. From her work as an editorial assistant for the American Medical Association, Kelsey had encountered drug testimonials from doctors "who came to be known as well-paid hacks for the pharmaceutical industry." Kelsey viewed Kevadon as such a case, despite supervisors telling her the thalidomide application would be an easy one because the sedative was presumably safe given its sales in Europe. After her first written response to the Kevadon application in 1960, Kelsey proceeded to have fifty-one documented exchanges with Richardson-Merrell about the drug, with 1962 marking the close of her official FDA communications with the company.[35] During this time, she sustained an epistemological filibuster in the US public scientific regulatory controversy surrounding thalidomide through three rhetorical tactics analogous to centering scientific uncertainty, identifying with FDA standards and using them to new ends, and extending the case to consider broader and seemingly supplemental implications.

Centering Scientific Uncertainty: The Desires and Demands of Scientific Proof

One of Kelsey's primary arguments against Richardson-Merrell centered on the many gaps and shortcomings in their application for the drug Kevadon. According to Brynner and Stephens, Kelsey felt discouraged by both the "brazen inadequacy of the test data submitted" to the FDA by Richardson-Merrell and also the application's "scientific sloppiness." Buttressed by these frustrations, Dr. Kelsey prioritized in her messages the need for improved data and better scientific proof surrounding thalidomide's ability to effectively achieve what the pharmaceutical company claimed it could *safely* achieve.[36] In the majority of her responses to the pharmaceutical company, for example, the need for "science" or, more specifically, the need for clinical data grounded in science appeared front and center. "Science" often acts metonymically for "credibility, for legitimate knowledge, for reliable and useful predictions" and "for a trustable reality." Recognizing science's authority, Kelsey rightly demanded scientific evidence from her adversary, along with its "epistemic seal of approval."[37] Throughout her responses to Richardson-Merrell, Kelsey embodied the idea that "science is practically useful but useless" when offered as evidence without the prerequisite data, facts, and figures needed to support the company's claims of scientific efficacy.[38] In support of this, she both highlighted the areas of the application lacking in scientific authority and asked for information that would address the scientific uncertainty presented in the original application.

The first interaction wherein Kelsey centered uncertainty and pointed out the lack of scientific proof in the Kevadon application occurred regarding chronic toxicity studies surrounding thalidomide and its impact on humans versus rats. The material presented in the application stated that humans who took thalidomide lapsed into a deep sleep, but the rats did not. This finding surprised Kelsey who thought, perhaps, that the rats did not absorb the thalidomide at all. She demanded, therefore, that the company support their claim that the rats absorbed the thalidomide into their bloodstream and that it did not merely go through them. Given the implications presented by this case, Kelsey questioned the presentation of the clinical trials and animal studies she had in front of her. Thus, she told Richardson-Merrell that at the current time "no evaluation can be made of the safety of the drug when used for a prolonged period of time."[39] In this circumstance, the lack of scientific evidence in the clinical trial with the rats proved enough for Dr. Kelsey to inform the company that at present she could not even *evaluate* the safety of the drug for human consumption, particularly when it concerned prolonged use. She delayed action by forcing the company to conduct more animal studies, clinical trials that *should* ultimately provide scientific evidence for the company's claims about thalidomide's effects on human beings and rats. She needed *better* scientific data and *more* scientific data to move forward with her evaluation of the drug application.

Kelsey further prioritized drawing attention to the lack of scientific evidence provided by Richardson-Merrell in her response on May 5, 1961. At this point, the pharmaceutical company shifted away from focusing on the clinical trials with rats, instead turning their attention for approval of the drug based on its effectiveness as a barbiturate that could be used for hypnotic use. While this information would later prove important to Kelsey and her appeals against approving the drug, she was more concerned with the effects of these barbiturates and her new knowledge—accidentally garnered from a letter in the *British Medical Journal*[40]—presenting thalidomide as the possible causal factor in several incidences of the condition called peripheral neuritis occurring in adults in Europe. After again signaling her dissatisfaction with the poor quality of the evidence presented by Richardson-Merrell refuting these reports of peripheral neuritis, Kelsey declared that she needed scientific proof before she would move forward with the application. In seeking out a more comprehensive account of past studies, she purported that "in particular the application does not include complete reports of animal studies nor sufficiently extensive, complete, and adequate clinical studies to permit an evaluation of the toxic effects of the drug which have been manifested by reports of cases of peripheral neuritis. On the present evidence we cannot regard Kevadon tablets as safe in the sense that its usefulness as a sedative hypnotic outweighs the toxic effects indicated by the cases of peripheral neuritis."[41]

She highlighted the uncertainty from lacking clinical studies, or lacking accounts of the studies and reports, which allowed her to maintain her stance that the Kevadon tablets had not been proven safe for public consumption. Consistent with Roger Pielke's foundational definition of scientific uncertainty as "a situation with more than one outcome consistent with our understanding," and with Walker and Walsh's application of the scientific uncertainty topos,[42] Kelsey clearly isolated the uncertainty of the science provided by Richardson-Merrell, doing so strategically to further destabilize the thalidomide application's potential movement forward. Therefore, in observing the scientific uncertainty surrounding thalidomide, Kelsey warranted her request for more scientific proof, delaying the drug's status, further upsetting Richardson-Merrell, and clearly embodying the status of an epistemological filibuster in a controversy such as this one.

On May 11, 1961, Kelsey required even more significant answers to mitigate the scientific uncertainty already at the forefront of her mind. In a typed rough draft of her notes from a meeting on that date among herself, Drs. R. G. Smith and J. Archer of the FDA, and Dr. Joseph Murray of Richardson-Merrell, she acknowledged three main points necessitating more information before anything could be done to expedite the clearance of Kevadon. The following notable points evoke the scientific uncertainty central to her claims: (1) "Neuropathology and neurophysiological and pharmacologic studies with long-term animal experiments,"

(2) "Details of their recent studies with labeled Kevadon," and (3) "Up-to-date report on work by Lester to establish the validity of his proposed assay procedure with EEG studies."[43] Kelsey outlined clear standards for the scientific proof that one might expect to come from these studies across this timeline that she employed as a warrant for her continued resistance to the pressures of Richardson-Merrell. In a June 8, 1961, memo of a telephone interview she wrote that she inquired "about blood level studies"; and in another telephone memo from July 27, 1961, she documented a previous reminder to Dr. Murray that the FDA had "asked for human absorption data." Kelsey grounded her epistemological fili-buster with Richardson-Merrell in a centering of scientific uncertainty that succeeded to productively halt, time and time again, any forward movement—and ultimately approval—of the Kevadon application.

Normative Appeals: The Maintenance and Rearticulation of FDA Standards

When Kelsey first saw the Kevadon application in 1960, the FDA and its medical officers had little leverage in changing drug-testing methods: "Agency officials were not expected to pass judgment on the clinical value or effectiveness of new medicines, making it difficult for them to challenge what they viewed as shoddy testing methods."[44] Despite these circumstances, wherein Kelsey had little power to effect change in drug-testing methodologies or "demand adherence to specific testing regimens,"[45] she and her colleagues referred to the one option working in their favor to put the Kevadon application on hold. Under the existing 1938 statute, the Food, Drug, and Cosmetic Act, a New Drug Application would automatically receive approval after 60 days unless the FDA specifically reviewed and disapproved the application or unless the effective date happened to receive a postponement "up to a maximum of 180 days."[46] Despite the clear gaps and weaknesses in the original application, Kelsey did not have grounds to permanently reject it, so she requested data and then she did something unusual: "She waited until the fifty-eighth day after the submission before declaring the application incomplete, and thus ineligible for submission—as if the application had never been submitted at all. That meant it would have to be resubmitted, giving her a further sixty days in which to ponder the application—and perhaps, to wait for any problems to be reported from Europe."[47]

Kelsey's "holding" of the application evidences her application of then-current FDA standards to effectively create a new sixty-day deadline wherein FDA review would only be initiated after the agency received the company's response with "supplementary laboratory and clinical findings."[48] Kelsey thus exercised power by engaging a regulatory loop-hole that held the thalidomide application for sixty days. To be sure, this delaying action was well within Kelsey's authority. She, along with her colleagues, used their technical communication to create a fresh sixty-day deadline for the FDA that Richardson-Merrell could only inaugurate with more research findings. This sharp-witted postponement sustained her epistemological filibuster. Kelsey created her own power out of the federal regulatory discourse set in place to strip her of any true authority to fight against companies like Richardson-Merrell by demanding they complete rigorous and controlled clinical drug tests.

Kelsey also engaged other discursive historical norms tied to her employer's standards that permitted a delay for the Kevadon application and increased the length of this particular scientific regulatory controversy. By demarcating her role as a medical officer with regulatory responsibilities against the expectations and responsibilities of Richardson-Merrell, she maintained FDA standards and her job and productively put the Kevadon application on hold. In her May 5, 1961, letter to Richardson-Merrell, Kelsey argued, "In the consideration of an application for a new drug, the burden of proof that the drug causes side-effects does not lie with this Administration [the FDA]. The burden of proof that the drug is safe—which must include adequate studies of all the manifestations of toxicity which medical or clinical experience suggest—lies with the applicant."[49]

In delineating the difference between her job in reviewing final data and a pharmaceutical company's responsibility for conducting studies on new drugs, Kelsey was "restating her institutional neutrality and disinterestedness" to the effect of further delay.[50] For Von Burg, when exploring scientific controversies within public discourses, often the group positioning "the tropes of disinterestedness and skepticism" come out on top.[51] Her job itself, and the FDA's expectation of neutrality, gave Kelsey a different type of authoritative power to position herself "on top" and against Richardson-Merrell's attempts to market thalidomide. The pharmaceutical company became the responsible applicant expected to meet the FDA's demands and to provide scientific evidence before the application could progress. Kelsey endeavored to do the bare minimum expected of her as an FDA medical officer as a way to deprive Richardson-Merrell of the laissez-faire administrative attitude they desired. By meeting the professionalization standards established by the FDA, Kelsey's normative appeals for "more" proof of safety deliberately established a resetting of the Kevadon application and continued Kelsey's epistemological filibuster.

Kelsey also used her regulatory role and normative appeals to her advantage to prevent the expedited approval of Kevadon by using Richardson-Merrell's own strategic attempts at approving the drug under a different guise against them. In their efforts to get the application passed more quickly they intended to acknowledge on the Kevadon label warnings that the drug might cause nerve damage. The company hoped, as of February 23, 1961, that this decision would help them get approval for an over-the-counter selling of the sedative. Despite pressures from Richardson-Merrell in the moment for an oral commitment that the inclusion of a warning might be enough to gain her approval, Kelsey harnessed both her past knowledge of drugs and a modeling of FDA standards for the approval of prescribed and over-the-counter drugs. In her dissent, she noted that Kevadon was *not* "an indispensable, life-saving drug, but a sedative, and therefore should not be marketed unless it were free of serious side effects."[52] Again, because the drug was now being peddled as a sedative and not a life-saving drug, Kelsey used her regulatory role to enforce FDA standards. She positioned herself as a figure capable of rhetorically rearticulating "the master's tools" to new ends via this mechanism of reinforcing historical regulatory norms. Not only did this rearticulating mechanism sustain Kelsey's epistemological filibuster, analysis of her approach shows that discourse of the past can guide the future and that scholars should conceive of how this argumentative strategy realistically operates in the present moment.

Kelsey thus used the existing standards to challenge Richardson-Merrell, disassociating the regulations from their original intent and reshaping them to aid her narrative of rejecting the Kevadon application. These appeals provided Kelsey with the means to sustain an epistemological filibuster in the pseudotechnical/public sphere. In fact, Kelsey drew from the FDA norms set in place during the opening of the 1960s both to bolster her resistant position for productive postponement and also to provide material barriers that would prevent the possibility of the drug application being passed without review or approval by a medical officer like herself.

Establishing a Public Advocacy Persona: Risk Considerations for Two

As a final strategy in Kelsey's epistemological filibuster, she positioned herself as both a scientist and a public advocate who challenged the safety of Kevadon and put the interests and health of the US population first. In her correspondence with Richardson-Merrell throughout the almost two-year period, she revealed the extent of her knowledge dealing with drugs that caused developmental deformities as well as her ongoing efforts to prioritize the safety of the public, including the unborn children of pregnant women.

As an MD/PhD student in pharmacology at the University of Chicago, Kelsey worked with Dr. E. M. K. Geiling, one of the founders of pharmacology in the United States.[53] Kelsey worked with Dr. Geiling's research team on sulfanilamide and its problematic, poisonous properties that led to the aforementioned 1938 law enforced by the FDA. Later in her career, she utilized this experience with pharmacological poisoning during research she conducted with her husband for a government project on malaria. The two researched quinine's effects on pregnant rabbits. They learned that while mother rabbits break down the drug quinine quickly, their fetuses are unable to do the same—making the drug safe for the mother rabbit but toxic for the unborn rabbit fetus.[54] Although Kelsey primarily centered her concerns about incidents of peripheral neuritis in patients who had consumed thalidomide abroad, her understanding of the effects that drugs could have on unborn children but not their mothers became paramount in her eventual questioning of the safety of thalidomide for pregnant women.

Evidence of her insightfulness regarding the public on both accounts appears in her original November 10, 1960, response to the Kevadon application. In that reply, Kelsey noted that "in several instances the reports do not represent detailed studies to determine the safety of the drug." The *Sunday Times* in London praised not only her blanket desire for more representative data affirming the drug's general safety but also her concerns for thalidomide's possible effects on pregnant mothers. As they noted, "There were not data to support the claim advanced in a report by one Dr. Ray Nulsen that expectant mothers suffering from nocturia (excessive passing of urine in the night) had no difficulty arising or returning to sleep after taking thalidomide."[55] From the onset, Kelsey presented her concerns about the safety of thalidomide, prioritizing the need for more clinical tests that accounted for pregnant mothers. Her remarks signal her use of experiential knowledge to prevent possible threats to the greater public health.

In several of Kelsey's subsequent discursive engagements between November 1960 and March 1962, she diligently inquired about the drug's safety for human consumption. In a May 1961 communication with a physician who had written her at Richardson-Merrell's request, she wrote, "We do not as yet have sufficient information with respect to this toxic effect to permit a complete evaluation of its safety."[56] Between

May 5, 1961, and September 7, 1961, she reiterated her concerns, as in an FDA meeting where she noted that in addition to the evidence she already required, she also needed evidence that thalidomide was safe for pregnant women due to, as her original memo reads, "peripheral neuritis symptoms in adults."[57] She had other concerns for the safety of the US population that developed in alternative meetings with Richardson-Merrell, which were also carefully documented. A "chronology of transactions with the William S. Merrell Company regarding 'Kevadon' (thalidomide)" that I uncovered in the Frances Oldham Kelsey Papers at the Library of Congress exemplifies this documentation. The chronology, written by John D. Archer, MD, identified a conference held on May 11, 1961, as the first time the FDA "specified a need for evidence that this drug would be safe during pregnancy."[58] The concern at the conference among Kelsey, Murray, and Dr. Smith (Kelsey's superior) was based exclusively on theoretical grounds. Regarding May 31, 1961, Archer wrote: "Dr. Murray submitted an amendment to Dr. Kelsey personally containing clinical data. A long explanatory covering letter included, among other things, reference to data in the amendment and previous submissions demonstrating that Kevadon was safe for the fetus when administered to pregnant women. (These studies generally were conducted late in pregnancy; I have not determined in this review whether all involved only late pregnancy.)"[59]

Taking the connection between the sedative and the public's health one step further, in the same rough draft of that May 11, 1961, meeting, Kelsey asked "Is there any dependence?" for thalidomide users, and "Why do patients wish to continue with the drug?" She asked whether those who had used thalidomide reported hypotension and requested more details concerning "the possible hazards of combining Kevadon with barbituates [sic] or alcohol." She also requested from the pharmaceutical company "more details concerning the total dosage taken by . . . would-be suicides. Present data is not too convincing since dosages reported were for the most part in range of fatal dosage for barbituates [sic] and much below fatal doses for Doriden."[60] Identifying Kelsey's questions from this illustrates an important point about Kelsey's concerns for the greater public: she believed the drug had wide-ranging consequences for pregnant women, yes, but for other individuals as well. Kelsey established that Kevadon could (1) be addictive, (2) have harmful outcomes when mixed with alcohol and other barbiturates, and (3) be used by individuals who wanted to end their lives by suicide. Her reference to Doriden (glutethimide), another sedative, evinces this communication as another instance where her working knowledge of pharmacology prompted important questions about the safety of the drug for public audiences. Kelsey required more information on these points because she recognized the widespread consequences of the drug going to market and its possible impact on several groups throughout the United States.

Not surprisingly, her concluding question asked, "Is the drug safe during pregnancy?" Aligned with her overarching concern for the population at large, this question later earned her fame for diverting a thalidomide catastrophe in the United States. Kelsey's questioning of the many ways in which thalidomide had still not been proven as safe for humans helped her block the drug application's movement forward. Kelsey clearly acted as a public official doing her job within the technical sphere to advocate for the safety of the public and their future families; her questioning and prioritizing of the population at the general level and at the fetal level allowed her to further sustain the epistemological filibuster that would prevent Richardson-Merrell from introducing Kevadon to US markets.

Up until the end of the controversy, even with the knowledge that thalidomide caused developmental malformations in fetuses, Kelsey maintained a professional stance to put the safety of the public first. In a memo of a telephone interview from November 30, 1961, Kelsey noted that "a recent study by a Dr. Lenz of Hamburg indicated that in 20 cases of malformed infants, 14 of the mothers were taking contergan [thalidomide] during pregnancy"; further, Kelsey was concerned "at recent reports that the incidence of peripheral neuritis was now reported to be in the range of 1:250." After noting additional connections to peripheral neuritis, Kelsey concluded by observing that "under such circumstances we continue to question the safety of this drug when used as a simple sedative or hypnotic."[61] She used her regulatory position to reason on behalf of the health and well-being of the general public, despite withstanding a "withering siege of professional aggravation, provocation, and intimidation" at the hands of Richardson-Merrell.[62] Kelsey reaffirmed the importance of safety by putting the dangerous factual and theoretical links first before saying she needed more evidence to prove that the sedative should continue being considered by the FDA. Her vigilance in prioritizing public safety and considering broader implications of the drug worked as a powerful rhetorical mechanism for enacting and reinforcing her epistemological filibuster. It also unquestionably warrants Kelsey's eventual heroic status and personification of what the FDA represented when it came to patient protection.[63]

Deciphering the Communication of an Epistemological Filibuster

On August 2, 1962, Pres. John F. Kennedy awarded Kelsey the President's

Medal for Distinguished Service for her exceptional judgment in evaluating thalidomide and preventing a domestic thalidomide crisis.[64] In this analysis, I delineate three rhetorical mechanisms enacted across what I identify as a public scientific regulatory controversy that helped sustain an epistemological filibuster by Dr. Frances Oldham Kelsey against the pharmaceutical company Richardson-Merrell. I demonstrate that the Kevadon application correspondence between Kelsey and Richardson-Merrell represents not just a science-based controversy that might be seen as a regulatory controversy but also as a public scientific regulatory controversy. In such a controversy, Kelsey supported her interests in both the public and technical spheres by effectively deploying rhetorical mechanisms that resulted not only in an averted public health catastrophe but also in amendments to federal regulatory law and policy implementation in the United States. As such, I extend the work of Boyd and Keränen, who have both offered engaging insights into the ways in which technical and public concerns and arguments are often altered and their boundaries challenged within a science-based controversy.[65]

By outlining the rhetorical tactics of the epistemological filibuster sustained within Kelsey's efforts to withhold approval against Kevadon, I open new avenues for thinking about the regulatory role of an impassioned employee concerned with the public's overall health to reveal significant aspects about the overlapping nature of the public and technical spheres in a historical public scientific regulatory controversy. Furthermore, I verify how engaging with a history of rhetoric can both connect to issues of the moment *and* engage theory that "transcends the particular case" (i.e., the thalidomide catastrophe) to participate "in a larger scholarly conversation" that in this case surrounded scientific controversies and the interpolation of the technical and public spheres for rhetoricians of health and science.[66]

Boyd notes that "regulatory decisions made in a very limited, technical arena generally go on to affect broader publics," and as such, "it is the nature of regulatory controversy, then, that technical discourses become part of public appeals and public concerns drive technical investigations."[67] Kelsey invited the public into the technical sphere by continuously demanding scientific proof that the drug thalidomide was safe for public consumption. Although her work initially focused on the issue of thalidomide's approval, as a fighting member of a regulatory body Kelsey effectually catalyzed the movement that would result in the FDA's widespread overhaul of drug regulation and produce regulatory change. Thus, this episode serves as both a *scientific* controversy where uncertainty is centered and a *regulatory* controversy in which she used the limited regulations in ways that allowed her to further sustain the epistemological filibuster to prevent the thalidomide catastrophe.

By implementing and sustaining an epistemological filibuster, Kelsey transitioned from being a working official for a regulatory body in the technical sphere with little authority to a member of the public advocating for the safety and well-being of the population of the United States and, more specifically, pregnant women who might find their children the victims of the deformities linked to thalidomide. The analysis of the correspondence between Kelsey and Richardson-Merrell serves as a model for future work on the rhetoric of science and history to build on because it reflects something that differs from a science-based controversy overlapping a regulatory controversy. Rather, this rhetorical history exemplifies a public-centered scientific controversy occurring in tandem with a public regulatory controversy in the technical sphere wherein one medical officer's agency and courage mitigated the massive catastrophe that would have occurred with the marketing of thalidomide to the US public.

All in all, the lifesaving outcomes of Dr. Frances O. Kelsey's epistemological filibuster with the pharmaceutical company may not be well known, but its historical and rhetorical importance should not be overlooked. And, as offered by this analysis, her rhetorical history surrounding the two-year engagement with Richardson-Merrell opens up new avenues for considering the strengthened utility of the epistemological filibuster as a productive delaying tactic. The case study encourages scholars of rhetoric of science to more closely define what they mean by a scientific controversy and a regulatory controversy, as the nuances developed by my analysis must be considered in order to effectively advance scholarship in this area.

Fortunately, even outside of academia, the heroic efforts of Dr. Frances Oldham Kelsey have not been lost to time, although these efforts may not be directly present in US public memory. She was inducted into the National Women's Hall of Fame in 2000, and in 2010, at one hundred years old, her long-time workplace awarded Dr. Kelsey herself with the FDA's first ever Dr. Frances O. Kelsey Award for Excellence and Courage in Protecting Public Health.[68] Later in the same year, Pres. Barack Obama wrote a personalized message to her: "Our country relies on dedicated public servants like Dr. Kelsey to create a better, healthier future for our children and grandchildren."[69] That Kelsey was recognized in this way so much later in her life showcases the importance of this overlooked heroine and the true impact of her epistemological filibuster on the United States, not only in preventing thalidomide-affected births but also in producing the vital drug regulation that we all depend on for our health and safety in our modern society.

Notes

1. George J. Annas and Sherman Elias, "Thalidomide and the *Titanic*: Reconstructing the Technology Tragedies of the Twentieth Century," *American Journal of Public Health* 89, no. 1 (1999): 98–101.

2. Martin Johnson, Raymond G. Stokes, and Tobias Arndt, *The Thalidomide Catastrophe: How It Happened, Who Was Responsible, and Why the Search for Justice Continues after More Than Six Decades* (Exeter, UK: Onwards and Upwards Publishers, 2018), 31.

3. Philip Knightly, Harold Evans, Elaine Potter, and Marjorie Wallace, *Suffer the Children: The Story of Thalidomide* (New York: Viking Press, 1979), 1.

4. Johnson, Stokes, and Arndt, *Thalidomide Catastrophe*, 24.

5. Frances Oldham Kelsey, *Autobiographical Reflections*, FDA Media Site, https://www.fda.gov, 54.

6. Rock Brynner and Trent Stephens, *Dark Remedy: The Impact of Thalidomide and Its Revival as a Vital Medicine* (Cambridge, MA: Perseus Publishing, 2001), 50–53.

7. Marcus Paroske, "Deliberating International Science Policy Controversies: Uncertainty and AIDS in South Africa," *Quarterly Journal of Speech* 95, no. 2 (2009): 151.

8. Leah Ceccarelli, "Controversy over Uncertainty: Argumentation Scholarship and Public Debate about Science," *ISSA Proceedings* (2010).

9. Nathan Crick and Joseph Gabriel, "The Conduit between Lifeworld and System: Habermas and the Rhetoric of Public Scientific Controversies," *Rhetoric Society Quarterly* 40, no. 3 (2010): 203.

10. Celeste M. Condit, John Lynch, and Emily Winderman, "Recent Rhetorical Studies in Public Understanding of Science: Multiple Purposes and Strengths," *Public Understanding of Science*, 21, no. 4 (2012): 386–400.

11. John Lyne and Henry F. Howe, "'Punctuated Equilibria': Rhetorical Dynamics of a Scientific Controversy," *Quarterly Journal of Speech* 72, no. 2 (1986): 132–47.

12. Crick and Gabriel, "Conduit between Lifeworld and System," 204.

13. Lawrence Prelli, "The Rhetorical Construction of Scientific Ethos," in *Landmark Essays on the Rhetoric of Science: Case Studies*, ed. Randy Allen Harris (Mahwah, NJ: Lawrence Erlbaum, 1997), 87–104.

14. Ron Von Burg, "Decades Away or *The Day After Tomorrow*? Rhetoric, Film, and the Global Warming Debate," *Critical Studies in Media Communication* 29, no. 1 (2012): 10.

15. Ceccarelli, "Controversy over Uncertainty."

16. Leah Ceccarelli, "Manufactured Scientific Controversy: Science, Rhetoric, and Public Debate," *Rhetoric & Public Affairs* 14, no. 2 (2011), 195–228.

17. Ceccarelli, "Controversy over Uncertainty," para. 4.

18. Marlia E. Banning, "When Poststructural Theory and Contemporary Politics Collide—The Vexed Case of Global Warming," *Communication and Critical/Cultural Studies* 6, no. 3 (2009): 285–304; Paroske, "Deliberating International Science Policy Controversies"; Rachel Avon Whidden, "The Manufacturing of Controversy: Debating Intelligent Design in Public," in *Critical Problems in Argumentation: Selected Papers from the Thirteenth NCA/AFA Conference on Argumentation*, ed. Charles Willard (Washington, DC: National Communication Association, 2005), 705–10.

19. Josh Boyd, "Public and Technical Interdependence: Regulatory Controversy, Out-Law Discourse, and the Messy Case of Olestra," *Argumentation & Advocacy*, 39, no. 2 (2002): 92 (emphasis added).

20. Lisa B. Keränen, "Mapping Misconduct: Demarcating Legitimate Science from 'Fraud' in the B-06 Lumpectomy Controversy," *Argumentation and Advocacy* 42, no. 2 (2005): 94.

21. Paroske, "Deliberating International Science Policy Controversies," 151.

22. John Rountree, "Legislation as a Site of Contested Meaning in United States Congressional Debates," master's thesis, Georgia State University, 2015.

23. Jeanette L. Drake, Yekaterina Y. Kontar, John C. Eichelberger, Scott T. Rupp, and Karen M. Taylor, eds., *Communicating Climate-Change and Natural Hazard Risk and Cultivating Resilience: Case Studies for a Multi-Disciplinary Approach* (New York: Springer, 2015), 45.

24. John Alexander Lynch, *What Are Stem Cells? Definitions at the Intersection of Science and Politics* (Tuscaloosa: University of Alabama Press, 2011).

25. Josh Compton and Brian Kaylor, "Inoculating for Small Pox Inoculation Objections in Reverend Cooper's *Letter to a Friend in the Country*," *Journal of Communication and Religion*, 36, no. 1 (2013): 92–107.

26. Kenneth C. Walker, "Mapping the Contours of Translation: Visualized Un/Certainties in the Ozone Hole Controversy," *Technical Communication Quarterly* 25, no. 2 (2016): 104–20.

27. John Joseph Rief, "Bioethics and Lifestyle Management: The Theory and Praxis of Personal Responsibility," master's thesis, University of Pittsburgh, 2013.

28. Kenny Walker and Lynda Walsh, "'No One Yet Knows What the Ultimate Consequences May Be': How Rachel Carson Transformed Scientific Uncertainty into a Site for Public Participation in *Silent Spring*," *Journal of Business and Technical Communication* 26, no. 1 (2012): 3–34.

29. Mollie K. Murphy, "Scientific Argument Without a Scientific Consensus: Rachel Carson's Rhetorical Strategies in the Silent Spring Debates," *Argumentation and Advocacy* 55, no. 3 (2018): 1–17.

30. Glory Tobiason, "Countering Expert Uncertainty: Rhetorical Strategies from the Case of Value-Added Modeling in Teacher Evaluation," *Minerva*, 57 (2019): 109–26.

31. Boyd, "Public and Technical Interdependence," 94.

32. David Zarefsky, "Four Senses of Rhetorical History," in Turner, *Doing Rhetorical History*, 32.

33. Paroske, "Deliberating International Science Policy," 151–152

34. Brynner and Stephens, *Dark Remedy*, 41.

35. "Well-paid hacks . . .": Brynner and Stephens, *Dark Remedy*, 35. The number fifty-one comes from the notes section for Brynner and Stephens's chapter 3; the citation is written as follows: **"fifty-one exchanges with the company**, CR, Senate, vol. 108, pt. 12, August 8, 1962, pp. 15932–34."

36. Brynner and Stephens, *Dark Remedy*, 49.

37. Thomas F. Gieryn, *Cultural Boundaries of Science: Credibility on the Line* (Chicago: University of Chicago Press, 1999).

38. Gieryn, *Cultural Boundaries of Science*, 21.

39. Brynner and Stephens, *Dark Remedy*, 49.

40. Morton Mintz, *The Therapeutic Nightmare* (Boston: Houghton Mifflin, 1965).

41. Knightly et al., *Suffer the Children*, 79.

42. Roger A. Pielke, *The Honest Broker: Making Sense of Science in Policy and Politics* (Cambridge: Cambridge University Press, 2007); Walker and Walsh, "'No One Yet Knows,'" 27.

43. Rough Draft Meeting between Dr. Jos. Murray and Drs. R.G. Smith, J. Archer, and F. Kelsey, May 11, 1961, Box II: 201, Folder 4, Frances Oldham Kelsey, Papers, Manuscript Division, Library of Congress, Washington, DC.

44. Arthur Daemmrich, "A Tale of Two Experts: Thalidomide and Political Engagement in the United States and West Germany," *Social History of Medicine* 15, no. 1 (2002): 152.

45. Daemmrich, "Tale of Two Experts," 153.

46. Scott P. Glauberman and Peter Barton Hutt, "The Real Thalidomide Baby: The Evolution of the FDA in the Shadow of Thalidomide, 1960–1997," *Food and Drug Law* (1997): 6.

47. Brynner and Stephens, *Dark Remedy*, 49.

48. Daemmrich, "Tale of Two Experts," 153.

49. Frances Oldham Kelsey, quoted in Knightly et al., *Suffer the Children*, 79.

50. Daemmrich, "Tale of Two Experts," 154.

51. Von Burg, "Decades Away?," 10.

52. Brynner and Stephens, *Dark Remedy*, 49.

53. Brynner and Stephens, *Dark Remedy*, 44.

54. Brynner and Stephens, *Dark Remedy*, 44–45.

55. Knightly et al., *Suffer the Children*, 74.

56. Knightly et al., *Suffer the Children*, 78.

57. Knightly et al., *Suffer the Children*, 79.

58. John D. Archer to Geo. P. Larrick and W. B. Rankin, April 17, 1962, Box II: 201, Folder 5, Kelsey Papers.

59. Archer to Larrick and Rankin, April 17, 1962, Kelsey Papers.

60. Rough Draft Meeting between Dr. Jos. Murray and Drs. R. G. Smith, J. Archer, and F. Kelsey, May 11, 1961, Kelsey Papers.

61. Memo of (Telephone) Interview Participants Dr. J. F. Murray of William S. Merrell Co. and Dr. F. O. Kelsey, Bureau of Medicine, FDA, November 30, 1961, Box II: 201, Folder 4, Kelsey Papers.

62. Brynner and Stephens, *Dark Remedy*, 50.

63. Geoff Watts, "Obituary: Frances Oldham Kelsey," *Lancet*, 386 (October 3, 2015): 1334.

64. National Women's Hall of Fame, "Frances Oldham Kelsey," accessed April 13, 2019, https://www.womenofthehall.org.

65. Lisa B. Keränen, "Public Engagements with Health and Medicine," *Journal of Medical Humanities* 35, no. 2 (2014): 103–9.

66. Zarefsky, "Four Senses of Rhetorical History," 27.

67. Boyd, "Public and Technical Interdependence," 104, 107.

68. US Food and Drug Administration, "Frances Oldham Kelsey: Medical Reviewer Famous for Averting a Public Health Tragedy," updated February 1, 2018, https://www.fda.gov.

69. Michelle Siu, "Canadian Doctor Averted Disaster by Keeping Thalidomide out of the US," *Globe and Mail*, November 24, 2014, https://www.theglobeandmail .com.

7

"To Wake Up the Latent Powers"

The Rhetoric of Henry McNeal Turner and the Legacy of the Israel AME Lyceum

Andre E. Johnson

On the evening of Monday, October 6, 1862, one year after the start of the Civil War, Rev. Henry McNeal Turner called together a group of friends to help found the Israel African Methodist Episcopal Church (AME) Lyceum. The purpose of lyceums, or to use Shirley Wilson Logan's phrase "literary societies,"[1] was "to wake up the latent powers of all the minds of all identified with it."[2] Turner saw it as a place and space where African Americans could not only come to learn about relevant topics and issues but also as an opportunity for orators to become better speakers and debaters. The society elected Turner as president; Thomas H. C. Hinton as vice president; J. B. Cross as secretary; William Tenny as treasurer; and J. T. Castin, McGill Pearce, and Win. Brown as managers. About a month after the Israel AME Church Lyceum's debut, Turner reported that the lyceum "was prospering flatteringly." He wrote that the "genius displayed by some young men that might have been considered raw material is astounding. It bids fair to be one of the noblest institutions ever connected with that church."[3]

In this essay, I bring attention to this particular institution—the Israel AME Lyceum—and its founder, Henry McNeal Turner. Instead of a traditional rhetorical history where I "offer insights that are central to the study of communication and unavailable through other approaches," this is more of a recovery project of a rhetorical institution.[4] While I engage in this recovery project, I do it with the understanding that I have limited access to the history of this institution. For example, there is no written history of the Israel AME Lyceum. Therefore, there are no significant studies about the institution, and thus what was said or how it was said; full extant speeches and debates are lost to history. I find myself echoing Melbourne Cummings as she notes in her essay on the problems of researching Black rhetoric: "Some of the greatest and most representative speeches were made without even a partial manuscript that could attest to the speaker's subject, the speech's motivational appeal, [and] what part it or the speaker played in influencing action or other people."[5] While sources for the study of African American rhetoric and public address have become more available since Cummings's writing in 1972, a recovery project like this one reminds us that there is still much discovery left to do.

This is not to say, however, that we do not know anything about the lyceum. For example, historian John W. Cromwell wrote that the Israel AME Lyceum "drew the most intellectual men to listen to lectures, participate in discussions, and read dissertations on timely topics."[6] Historian Kate Masur, in her study of African American life and leisure in Washington, DC, during the Civil War, wrote that one of the goals of the lyceum was to provide civic education for its participants.[7] The lyceum became known as "an institution renowned for its brilliant performance of debates, addresses, essays, and similar demonstrations of mind and matter."[8]

However, history left us with scattered scraps of analyses and reflections on the events that happened at the lyceum. Here, I argue that while I do not construct a traditional rhetorical history by excavating these scraps, I *do* attempt to create a rhetorical account by engaging in a recovery project. In short, drawing from Angela Ray's use of the phrase "cultural making rhetorical practice,"[9] I examine the rhetoric from not only some of the public addresses and debates delivered by Turner and others as part of the lyceum but also the rhetoric that describes the lyceum. In so doing, I argue not only that participants wanted to display their artistry in public address or debate but that writers who reported on the lyceum had as their aim a pedagogical function that helped shape their primarily African American audience into informed citizens. Finally, in the conclusion of this chapter, I offer some suggestions for further research concerning the case and rhetorical history overall.

Israel AME Church and Henry McNeal Turner

Israel AME Church was at the core of African American life in Washington, DC. Founded around 1820, the beginnings of Israel AME Church "centered around the evangelical activity" of Baltimore minister David Smith. After securing an old schoolhouse for $300, the church began to thrive. It quickly became a member of the Baltimore Conference of the AME Church and had the distinction of holding the first African American church conference in Washington, DC. The rapid growth of the church "caused a sensation and gave the church and the denomination a standing" that surpassed any other African American church in the area.[10] However, during the Civil War the influence of the Israel AME Church reached its height. During this time, Turner served as pastor. Although not formally educated, Turner, in many ways, was uniquely qualified to found the lyceum.

Turner was born a free Black man in Newberry Courthouse, South Carolina, on February 1, 1834. Dreams shaped Turner's young life. One dream, of Turner standing in front of a large crowd of both Black and white people looking to him for instruction, led Turner to believe that God had great things in store for him. These types of dreams also motivated his desire to receive a formal education to complement his providential visions. However, at the time, South Carolina did not allow African Americans to receive a formal education. According to legend, Turner acquired a spelling book and began to teach himself in earnest. Through the help of a divine "dream angel," who Turner believed appeared to him in his dreams to help him learn, he taught himself how to read and write. Further, by the time he was fifteen, he had read the entire Bible five times and memorized lengthy passages of Scripture.[11]

In 1853, at the age of nineteen, the Southern Methodist Church licensed Turner to preach, and he quickly gained fame as a dynamic preacher and orator. Despite his successes, however, Turner became disillusioned with the Southern Methodist Church because of their policy of not ordaining African Americans. During a visit to New Orleans for a preaching assignment, Turner met Willis Revels, pastor of the St. James AME Church. Revels introduced Turner to the AME Church and its traditions of Black empowerment. The story of the church's beginnings; the genesis story of its first bishop, Richard Allen; and the history of the denomination impressed Turner, as he had heard of neither the church nor the church's Black bishops and pastors.[12]

After joining the AME Church and moving to Baltimore in 1860, Turner's career rocketed. While there, he served two churches and took advantage of "some educational opportunities by studying grammar, Latin, Greek, theology, and the classics." In procuring an education, one biographer wrote, "whatever subject he undertook to study, he went to the heart of it."[13] Two years later, in 1862, Turner moved to Washington, DC, to serve as pastor of the large and influential Israel AME Church. Turner invited leading citizens of the city and powerful politicians to speak to the Black citizens in DC. While serving at Israel Church, Turner would spend hours in the Capitol listening to debates and arguments on the floor of the House of Representatives and in the Senate chamber. Watching politicians debate offered lessons in politics and deliberative oratory that would serve him well throughout his career.[14]

African American Lyceum Movement

Lyceums were ubiquitous in the nineteenth century, and anyone could start one with few resources. All one needed were a physical place and people willing to express their ideas and thoughts. According to Ray, in the nineteenth century, the word *lyceum* had come to mean "education" and "referred to any one of thousands of local societies that promoted learning." Lyceums typically met weekly and offered "members the opportunity to learn and practice skills in essay writing, debating, and public speaking."[15] While Ray contends that lyceums did not start as arenas for social reformers or radical politics, this aim changed when educational reformer Josiah Holbrook founded a mutual-improvement association in 1826 in Millbury, Massachusetts, that emerged as a "social institution."[16] Promoters and directors of lyceums turned to newspapers and other means of advertisement to promote lyceum activities that, in turn, led others to start their own. The rhetoric associated with the lyceum movement tended to blend the "themes of education and entertainment."[17]

In Ray's book *The Lyceum and Public Culture in the Nineteenth-Century United States*, she calls lyceums a "cultural making rhetorical practice that mixed the functions of public education and public entertainment." They were sites where "public selves and public cultures were constituted through the repetition of behavioral patterns, through recurrent rhetorical acts."[18] One of those recurrent rhetorical acts was to form and fashion what it meant to be an "American." As a culture-making rhetorical practice, lyceums helped constitute not only what it meant to be an American but what it meant to be a particular type of American. Typically, lyceum rhetoric and the culture surrounding it produced people who identified as white, male, cishet, middle class, and Protestant.

As lyceums became popular, however, Americans with identities outside of those hegemonic standards began to participate in the creation and promotion of lyceums. For instance, many lyceums early on did not admit women, but after the Civil War, the participation of women lecturers and debaters increased significantly.[19] For African Americans, invitations to speak at white-run lyceums were almost nonexistent. Outside of the much-heralded Black abolitionist Frederick Douglass, who became the first African American to lecture regularly in white-sponsored lyceums, many other active and qualified speakers did not receive invitations to speak or debate. Therefore, African Americans needed to found and promote their own lyceums and circuits to express their unique agency.[20]

In *Liberating Language*, Shirley Wilson Logan notes that African American lyceums in the nineteenth century "functioned as sites of rhetorical education for black Americans."[21] She argues that African Americans established their lyceums and literary societies not because of rejection from white lyceums but because of their strong desire for both economic and intellectual self-improvement. These lyceums gave space and place for African Americans to voice concerns and problems germane to them, while at the same time informing each other on subjects ranging from education and science to mathematics and economics. Moreover, the lyceums were a place where inexperienced speakers could learn how to present ideas publicly. As a site for rhetorical education, these lyceums taught students oratory and typically sponsored public speaking contests. A passel of these societies established libraries for public use, offered peer-review help in each other's speech making, taught essential principles in "elocutionary excellence," and, in some cases, published a weekly paper, such as the Demosthenian Institute's *Demosthenian Shield*.[22]

Logan argues that lyceums and literary societies "played an important role in the development of the rhetorical abilities of nineteenth-century African Americans" in four distinct ways. First, lyceums brought people together for "moral and mental improvement." Participants "performed and judged their own work and the works of others to build their confidence." Second, these societies helped to build a sense of equality among African Americans by allowing them to create and shape their rhetorical abilities. Third, these associations generated revenue that helped maintain other Black educational institutions. Finally, the lyceums permitted women to speak publicly and develop their rhetorical abilities.[23]

However, despite works by Logan and Ray, the scholarship that focuses on African American lyceums and the broader African American literary society movements in the nineteenth century is scant. I attempt to address this by examining the "history" we have on the Israel AME Lyceum, much of it written by Henry McNeal Turner.

Israel AME Church Lyceum

PUBLIC ADDRESSES

On November 24, 1862, a month after the founding of the Israel AME Lyceum, the lyceum welcomed AME bishop Daniel Payne to give a lecture. Payne was an AME legend. Consecrated as the sixth bishop of the AME Church in 1852, Payne would go on to found Wilberforce University and to become the first African American president of a college or university in America. He would later publish his autobiography that also doubled as one of the early works of AME history, titled *Recollections of Seventy Years*.[24]

Payne had a reputation as a good orator and preacher. Born on February 24, 1811, to "free" parents in Charleston, South Carolina, Payne had an opportunity early in his childhood to receive formal education from the Minor's Moralist Society. In his autobiography, he wrote fondly of his three years studying under "Thomas S. Bonneau, the most popular schoolmaster in the city."[25] There, Payne learned not only to read, write, and "cipher," but he also learned oratory from reading the *Columbian Orator*.

The day before his presentation at the lyceum, Bishop Payne graced the pulpit at Israel AME Church, and because the press announced that he would preach on that day, both Black and white people attended. On that day, however, Turner found Payne to have preached an unimpressive, lackluster "missionary sermon." Moreover, although Payne's "reasoning was masterly," Turner believed he "did not carry upon it that fervid pathos, which often distinguishes his able efforts."[26]

Fortunately, when Payne offered his lecture to the lyceum the next evening, he was in rare form. According to Turner, the bishop "so far surpassed the most sanguine expectations, that one could hardly value the lecture for admiring the man." Further, Turner added: "Those who heard it will never forget it. The papers spoke of him the next day, as being acquainted with the encyclopedia of science, and an oriental and modern linguist; as the conclusion of which, he paid a glowing tribute to the industry of the pastor and congregation of Israel Church, for the improvements lately made thereon."[27]

Lyceums served as sites where African Americans learned about history, politics, law, and other subjects, including geology. A month after Bishop Payne's presentations, Professor Solomon G. Brown of the Smithsonian Institute lectured on geology before the lyceum on Monday evening, December 22, 1862. Turner wrote that "I do not believe that I cross the bounds of truth when I say that I never heard or read an abler lecture on that subject in my life, though I have devoted more time to the study of that science, than any other in the range of my knowledge, and I am confident that I have read the ablest works on geology, that have ever come from the pen of man."[28]

Turner then admired the broad sweep of the lecture's content:

> Commencing at the Azoic age, he reviewed in the most magnificent style the development of the vegetable kingdom, passing through the various strata belonging to the period, he came to the Palegoic age, the age of mollusks, or Silurian period. Here he commented upon the fishes, shells, both of marine and freshwater, and the carboniferous

deposits of the ancient date. . . . Thus he went on treating most scientifically, the philosophy of Artesian wells, coal beds, coal oil, mineral ores, salts &c. He described the ratio of heat, in the descent into the heart of the earth, stating that though on the surface of the earth, the thermometer might stand at zero, in a depth of eighteen hundred feet, it would rise to 80 degrees Fahrenheit. And that since the days of Adam, the incessant fall of the atomic particles of matter had increased the present forming geological strata to the thickness of eight feet.[29]

He closed his praise for Professor Brown by writing, "The lecture was nothing more than an introduction to a course which he is to deliver before the said Lyceum. I regard Professor S. G. Brown as a geologist, and Rev. George T. Watkins is an ethnologist, two of our most scientific men."[30] As Turner's reporting of Brown's lecture demonstrates, the lyceum featured not only lectures that one may interpret as those that entertained, but it also featured those that informed.

The lecture at the Israel Lyceum must have been effective because, after that, Professor Brown's speaking engagements became plentiful. In a letter published in the *Christian Recorder* on March 7, 1863, Turner wrote, "Prof. S. G. Brown is increasing in popularity so rapidly, that he cannot comply with near all the applications he has for lectures. He lectured last Monday evening before the *Dumas Association* and has now before him application from four different quarters."[31]

The lyceum was also home for lectures concerning national matters. One such event found 2,500 in attendance, including about 500 white people, who experienced addresses from several orators. One address, delivered by Gen. David Bell Birney of the Union Army, gave in detail the views of President Lincoln regarding "Colored Troops" and the design of the government in forming a "board of examination" to assess officers to fill for the time being the most "responsible positions in these new organizations."[32] Turner found this talk hopeful, suggesting that there was no better opportunity for African Americans to get what they wanted. In a correspondence published on June 20, 1863, Turner wrote, "Suppose 500,000 colored men were under arms would not the nation really be under our arms too? Would the nation refuse us our rights in such a condition? Would it refuse us our vote? Would it deny us anything when its salvation was hanging upon us? No! Never!"[33]

The invitation of General Birney also served another purpose. About this time, Turner joined the efforts of other African Americans in insisting that the Union deploy Black soldiers. He also had another aim: joining the war effort himself by becoming a chaplain to those Black would-be enlisted people. His effort did not go unnoticed. After a series of defeats at the hands of the Confederacy and after the lobbying efforts of Black leaders, the Union enlisted African Americans, and President Lincoln rewarded Turner with a commission, making him the first African American chaplain in the armed forces.[34]

In addition to Turner's updates in the *Christian Recorder*, notices for upcoming lyceum events ran in other newspapers. For example, the *Daily National Republican* on January 9, 1863, published a "special notice" of the lecture that the lyceum scheduled for three days later. The paper reported, in part, that "Mr. William J. Watkins, the distinguished colored orator, will lecture on Monday evening, the 12th instant, in Israel Bethel (Capitol Hill), before the Israel Lyceum." His subject for the evening was "The Duties, and Probable Destinies of the Colored People," and admittance was ten cents. The notice went on to warn readers that a "very large audience may be expected" owing to Mr. Watkins being a "very popular lecturer and one of the most eloquent men in the country."[35]

While attending the Baltimore Annual Conference Missionary Society in November 1862, Turner saw Watkins and probably offered an invitation for Watkins to lecture at the Israel Lyceum. In a correspondence published on November 15, 1862, Turner remarked that "no man ever experiences from his friends a more cordial reception." He wrote that Watkins spoke to "crowded houses" despite the fee that he charged and that "no lectures among our people have been so well attended." In describing Watkins's oratory, Turner opined that Watkins had "surpassed the expectations of all by his splendid elocution, his inimitable power of description, his bold and vivid imagery, his burning satire, and his glowing eloquence."[36]

While Watkins was in Baltimore, the Galbraith Lyceum invited him to lecture. Organizers planned to hold the lecture at Saratoga Street African Baptist Church, where the Rev. Noah Davis served as pastor. However, at the last minute, due to Watkins's "abolition notoriety," Davis refused to house the lecture. In short, many were afraid of the repercussions that might come to the church and its pastor by allowing Watkins to speak there. Instead, Hiram Revels, an AME minister who was then the pastor of Madison Street Presbyterian Church in Baltimore and who would become the first African American US senator from the state of Mississippi in 1870, agreed to have the lecture at his church. Due to the notoriety of Watkins, even at the last minute, word spread enough that when it was time for the talk, the church was "crowded to overflowing."

Turner, for one, did not appreciate Davis's nervousness and timidity. He also sensed there was a tinge of jealousy from Davis because of Watkins's reputation as well. Instead, for Turner, the people "rebuked the needless timidity, the suicidal jealousy of old decrepit fogyism." He reasoned, "A man of Mr. Watkins' caliber cannot be suppressed, and I am glad to know that no man among us has more ardent friends than he." Turner closed his admiration of Watkins by writing, "May the Lord prosper him in his efforts to instruct and to elevate those who so much need his counsels."[37]

When the time came for Watkins to lecture at the Israel Lyceum, Turner, who was known to give glowing reviews of people he respected, surprisingly offered only a one-sentence response to Watkins's lecture. Published in the *Christian Recorder* on January 24, 1863, Turner expressed that "the lecture displayed the character of its author, who is known only to be admired."[38] One can only guess at the reason why Turner did not feel compelled to write more about the lecture, especially coming when it did: Only twelve days earlier, the Emancipation Proclamation took full effect, and many African Americans were still celebrating its passage. Although Turner did not see a need to address the speech adequately, however, another newspaper offered a review.

According to the January 15, 1863 edition of the Washington *Evening Star*, Turner opened with prayer and introduced the lecturer for the evening. Watkins started the lecture by "remarking on the revolutionary nature of the times." He argued that since "slavery [was] rushing down the dark abyss of ruin, amid hosannas of angels," African Americans should "rush out into the highway of human effort and responsibility" and ask God, "What must we do to be saved?" Here, according to the *Star*, Watkins called attention to "defects" within the African American community.[39]

First, Watkins argued that there was a "lack of unity" among African Americans. He reminded African Americans that "death and hell were summoning all of their forces to crush out their manhood" and that the "Southern Confederacy" did not hesitate to say, "Slavery is the normal condition of the colored race." Moreover, he reminded his audience that Alexander H. Stephens, vice president of the Confederate States of America (CSA), boasted that the CSA was the "first government built" on the belief that slavery was the "normal condition" of African Americans.[40]

Second, Watkins suggested that African Americans were not "sensitive enough to the indignities cast upon them on account of color." Watkins argued that if African Americans "possessed one-fourth of the sensitiveness of the Indian, they would not have submitted to slavery so long as they had." Part of the reason why enslaved people did not cry out, as Watkins suggested, "give me liberty or give me death" was because of the preaching and religious teaching that the enslaved people heard. Watkins "despised" the type of preaching he used to hear on the Eastern Shore: "Keep close to the side of Jesus, you have good masters; wait a little while, and you will see the new Jerusalem." Watkins not only rejected that theology, but he also dismissed what that theology apparently had done to African Americans. "It is useless to prate of equality with the white man," he argued, and then "lower [your] necks to receive the yoke." He counseled his readers to "by your actions" prove to the "white man" that you are men.[41]

Third, he suggested that African Americans did not "possess sufficiently elevated aspirations." He argued that African Americans should "elevate themselves" and not be "satisfied as they had been heretofore in the so-called menial positions." Watkins reasoned that if Black people continued to "monopolize those positions, every white man would have the right to look upon them as menials." While nothing was wrong with these jobs in and of themselves, Watkins did balk at these being the only jobs open to African Americans. Thus, he called for African Americans to leave those (menial) "occupations behind and look for something better."[42]

Fourth, Watkins suggested that African Americans were not appreciative of the "sign of the times" nor were they appreciative of their own condition. Therefore, he called on them to "let the world; and especially Jefferson Davis know that they were determined to be free." He also called upon African Americans to appreciate the efforts of their Republican friends and reminded them that it was their duty to "help them" as much as they could.

Further, he called on African Americans to "educate themselves to a higher development," for he reasoned that they could not "compete with the white man unless they become a comparatively educated people." He then closed his lecture by saying that while slavery was about to "breathe its last," if African Americans "did not do their duty," their "posterity would be enslaved."[43]

Watkins's rhetoric serves as an early example of what scholars would later call "rhetoric of uplift," "racial uplift," or "uplift rhetoric." This rhetoric seemly emphasized the role that African Americans must play in their own freedom or survival. Focused on agency, this type of rhetoric located itself within a collective possibility—that if all would do their part, good things could happen. Thus, when Watkins called on his audience to demand their freedom, to help their Republican friends, and to educate themselves because they will not be able to compete with white people unless they become an "educated people," he aimed to constitute an active, not passive, audience that would stake claim to their destiny.[44]

While some white-centered and Black-sponsored lyceums discriminated against women and did not allow them to participate, the Israel AME Lyceum seemed not to have any restrictions on women giving addresses to its members.[45] This fact was an emblem of Turner's progressive stance (at least by nineteenth-century standards as a minister) toward women's place in the US public sphere.[46] In one such case, on March 23, 1862, a group of (presumably African American) women from Baltimore came to acknowledge publicly the excellent work that the lyceum had done and to present them a Bible. Vice President Thomas H. C. Hinton offered a keynote address and delivered a "panegyric on the Lyceum and its illustrious founder, Rev. H. M. Turner." The writer, who went by the initials W.H.M., noted that Hinton paid a "high and glowing tribute" to Turner's "eminent abilities and indomitable energy and finished his excellent peroration with the sublime assertion that Turner was nearer the vicegerent of Washington than any man he knew."[47]

After Hinton's speech, the lyceum introduced "Mrs. Lydia Maddon," and she proceeded to deliver her address, which the writer characterized as being "performed in a calm and dignified manner." W.H.M. did not give the title of Maddon's address but noted the speech was "replete with all that was good and appropriate and was delivered with the best elocution." Maddon concluded her speech by saying that she hoped that "love, purity, and truth would be ever the motto of the Israel Lyceum." She went to her seat amid a rousing round of applause and praises.[48]

The following month, on April 20, 1863, a group of women from Washington, DC, presented the lyceum with a collection of books that compiled "some of the popular works of the day." The committee consisted of Mrs. Emeline Hillary, Mrs. Ann M. Madison, Mrs. Elizabeth Hicks, Mrs. Margaret Douglass, Mrs. Rosetta Forrest, and Mrs. Eleanor Barton. The exercises of the event consisted of "addresses and essays interspersed with music."[49]

Women also helped with the financial efforts of the lyceum. On July 30, 1863, a group of women from Washington, DC, started a series of fundraisers for the lyceum to retire a fifty-dollar debt the Lyceum incurred to make improvements to the hall. In writing the correspondence for the *Recorder*, Hinton noted that some of the same women who presented the books for the lyceum also participated in the fundraising efforts.[50]

Debates

The lyceum was also the home for rousing debates, and Turner would promote such discussions in the columns of the *Christian Recorder*. In an editorial published March 7, 1863, Turner incisively promoted one such debate: "Rev. W. A. Hughes, a minister of the A. M. E. Church and John Crew, Esq. of Baltimore City, are to debate a heavy question before the Israel Lyceum, on next Monday evening. Rev. Mr. Hughes, though 56 years of age, is as an expert upon his feet, and as sanguine for knowledge as a man at twenty. If some of our bull heads, claiming to be young ministers, were half as anxious for information as Rev. Hughes, who is old enough to be the father of many of them, they would find something to talk about, instead of blabbing out such consummate foolishness."[51]

The following week, in his coverage of the debate, he called the disputants "more than ordinarily eloquent." He also noted that "Mr. Crew handles the English language with great precision" and reasoned that Mr. Crew was able to do so because he was the student of the "venerable Rev. William Watkins." Mr. Hughes, on the other hand, "exhibited an acquaintance with science, art, and history, which so astonished the people of Washington, who have for many years been listening to his preaching, that they could hardly realize him as the same man." While the audience interrupted with loud shouts and applause for both, the consensus was that Mr. Hughes won the debate. "The house was crowded to the overflowing," Turner wrote, and "upon the whole, it was a literary treat."[52]

During the early part of 1863, the lyceum held a series of mock trials, and according to Turner, they attracted large audiences. While the law did not ban African Americans from attending court trials, apparently the opportunity to see Black people in the roles of attorneys and judges may have attracted attendance. One staged case involved someone stealing an apple from Turner, and when Turner discovered the apple missing, he called the sergeant at arms to "search the house." After an examination and searching for evidence, they charged Mr. Sidney W. Hubert with the crime. Turner then appointed four "lawyers"—Rev. William A. Hughes and Thomas H. C. Hinton as prosecuting attorneys and Mr. E. T. Crew and Rev. McGill Pearce as the defense. Turner also selected twelve people to serve on the jury, and Mr. J. F. N. Wilkinson acted as judge.[53]

According to Turner, "the audience sat apparently entranced at the maneuverings and scheming of the lawyers every night until it closed." The last night, he continued, "we could not find room for the people, and several well experienced gentlemen remarked that they never had been a better conducted suit, nor heard better law in any courthouse in their lives."[54] He continued: "They had law books, records, &c., and demanded as much respect from the audience as if it were a reality, and the witnesses declared they never felt more curious when in a courthouse than they did there. It was certainly productive of good, and materially enlightened the minds of our people, for many had never engaged in a lawsuit, nor seen one conducted. Judge Wilkinson occupied the chair with as much gravity and looked so austere and stern that no one dared to address his honor without almost feeling a corresponding submission."[55] After some serious debate among the jurors, they decided to acquit the prisoner.

Turner was not the only one to write about the lyceum for the *Christian Recorder*. When Turner traveled away on church business or promoting the war effort, such correspondents as Thomas H. C. Hinton filled the void. In a letter published on July 4, 1863, Hinton wrote that the "Israel Lyceum [was] flourishing." Hinton wrote about a "grand debate" on the subject, "Was There a War in Heaven or Not?" Participating in the debate taking the "negative" position on the question, Hinton was disappointed with the decision of the three judges. Instead of analyzing the arguments on the question, the presiding judge, Rev. David Smith, rendered the verdict: "The Bible says there was a war in heaven and it had nothing to do with how many heavens there were." The decision led Hinton to write, "This is the age of progress with some and it [is] certainly [one of] retrogression with others; but the Lord giveth and the Lord taketh it away, blessed be the name of the Lord."[56]

On July 23, 1863, the lyceum sponsored a debate that would have prompted some interest only because the topic had been the talk around Washington, DC, for some time. John Costin, David Dixon, Sydney Hubert, and Thomas H. C. Hinton debated on the subject, "Should the Colored Men of This Country Participate in the Present War?" The participants discussed the issue at great length, and the debate ended in a tie because the "gentlemen selected to decide the question according to the arguments addressed were unable to agree."[57]

Another lyceum event was a much-anticipated debate between Turner, Hinton, and Rev. William Hughes, who considered the question, "Has Not a Lady Equally a Right to Court a Gentleman as a Gentleman Has to Court a Lady?" An overflow crowd packed the church. Hinton called it a "gala night" because the audience included all the "fashionable ladies and gentlemen assembled from all over the city."[58]

Although Hinton participated in the debate and took the negative position, he had high praise for Turner, who was the only one to take the affirmative. According to Hinton, Turner and his arguments were "beyond description." Turner argued forcibly that a lady had equally the right to court a gentleman. This debate was also unique because of the five judges one was a woman. After the arguments, the judges deliberated for twenty-five minutes and came with the verdict declaring Turner the winner. Although Hinton did not describe the arguments used by Turner or what exactly he said, he believed that this decision (unlike that of the one on war in heaven) was fair and that Turner did make the strongest arguments of the three.[59]

THE CHANGING OF THE GUARD

Nearing the lyceum's first anniversary, it held elections for its officers, and to no one's surprise, the society elected Turner as president and Hinton as vice president for a second term. R. J. Collins replaced J. B. Cross as secretary, William Tunion replaced William Tunney as treasurer, and George W. Brown became chair of the committee of managers. Probably due to the collection of books donated to the lyceum from the women of Washington, DC, the lyceum named Samuel S. Savoy in the new position of librarian. Hinton had high regard for the lyceum's new manager, George W. Brown. He wrote that Brown was destined to step forth clothed with useful knowledge and had just recently participated in a debate at the lyceum on the question, "Was Brutus Justified in Taking Part against the Life of Julius Caesar?" He argued in the negative and "holding his position," Hinton wrote that he "came off a victoriously eloquent conqueror."[60]

Turner's involvement with the lyceum produced a series of rumors that he was about to establish a school in the Georgetown area. The rumors remained so persistent that the Washington, DC, *Evening Star* printed a story supporting the rumor. Turner, in turn, penned a correction to the story. "As for me, establishing a school in Georgetown or anywhere else," he wrote, "is more than I have any knowledge of at this time." He reminded his audience that he currently held the "pastoral charge" of Israel Church, a congregation of nearly one thousand people. He felt at the time that the people's "spiritual demands" were "so great" that his most "assiduous labor" was "inadequate to them." In short, Turner had no time to start a school.[61]

He did, however, offer a reason for the rumor. He believed the rumor started when someone surmised from cards found in Turner's church office that had "technological and scientific terms" written on them that Turner was planning to teach and thus establish a school. The cards, Turner wrote, were for "special use in the Israel Lyceum." He told readers that the lyceum was a "literary organization formed by several young men for the express purpose of establishing a literary nucleus, advancing the cause of general education, and for the improvement of their intellects."[62]

Nearing the end of 1863 and after his appointment as a chaplain, Turner resigned from Israel AME Church and his position in the lyceum. Writing about his departure, a correspondent for the *Recorder* known as L.H. noted Turner's influence in the city. "For the last eighteen months of the Rev. Turner's presence in Washington," wrote the correspondent, "through his instrumental and energetic powers, [he] established two noble Literary Institutions, namely—The Israel Lyceum and the Teachers' Sabbath Association. Said institutions have borne out of the quarry of ignorance, young ladies and young gentlemen who now stand up— advocating the elevation of their race."[63]

Conclusion

From establishing the lyceum through fulfilling his duties as chaplain, Turner by all accounts had a successful career. While serving in the Union Army, he continued to write for the *Christian Recorder* as a war correspondent. As one historian notes of his work, Turner's letters had a "distinctive writing style" and "a vigorous, clear prose." Many others, however, note Turner's use of "polysyllabic words, Latin quotations, convoluted sentences, opaque paragraphs, purple prose, and outright bombast."[64] Even when he wrote under the pseudonym "Uncle Sam," readers could identify his style.

In reading some of Turner's correspondence, English professor Jean Lee Cole notes that his style was "boisterous" and at times "bombastic." For her, Turner was a "lover of syllables and lists, hyperbole and excess; his sentences spill over the rules." At the same time, she continues, "the phrasing is rhythmic and almost musical." While Cole credits Turner's writing to his "unconventional education" and the "Methodist Divines" whom Turner heard preach, I contend that the lyceum influenced his rhetoric as well.[65] In short, agreeing with Cole, if Turner *wrote as he spoke*, much of Turner's writing grounds itself in the Black oratorical tradition—a tradition created, in part, by Black lyceums and literary societies.

At the end of the war, Turner moved to Georgia and started work on building the AME Church in that state. Moreover, he also found time for political ambitions. He became a member of the Georgia State Convention; after that, Bibb County, Georgia, elected him as its state representative in 1868 during the years of Reconstruction. After white conservatives took back the statehouse with voter intimidation and suppression tactics, Turner turned his attention back to the church. He served as the presiding elder and superintendent of missions for the state of Georgia, and under his leadership, the church grew exponentially.

After serving in these positions, Turner later became the publications manager of the church in 1876 and bishop in 1880. His career as bishop is worthy of a full-length study by itself: Outside of maybe Frederick Douglass, who died in 1895, and Booker T. Washington, who would not come to national prominence until 1895, Turner stood alone as the leading rhetorical figure in Black America between 1880 and his death in 1915. One could rightfully argue that Turner, along with Douglass, was one of the first African American public intellectuals whose influence extended beyond African Americans. As bishop, Turner was invited to speak all over the country. Even when Turner became a wholesale emigrationist, he could still command an audience.

After Turner's departure in 1863, the Israel Lyceum continued under the leadership of Thomas H. C. Hinton. On January 1, 1864, the lyceum held a "Freedom Jubilee" in commemoration of the Emancipation Proclamation, which had gone into effect a year earlier. On January 21, 1864, a group of speakers that included AME minister Richard Cain, who would later become bishop along with Turner in 1880, addressed the question of "Free Schools" in the district at the lyceum. Then on the next night, the lyceum hosted a lecture that presented the "claims in full of the African Civilization Society."[66] So the lyceum stayed busy with meetings that centered on lectures, debates, presentations, and essay readings.[67]

The lyceum probably continued until Israel's merger with Union Bethel AME in 1870. Two years later, the general conference of the church granted the name Metropolitan AME Church to the new church body. Metropolitan AME Church continued the liberating work that distinguished both Israel and Union Bethel, and it created the Bethel Literary and Historical Society in 1881.

Although my attention here focuses on a specific lyceum and a particular period in history, African American lyceums continued well into the twentieth century.[68] Many of these newer lyceums found homes at Black colleges and universities. Such schools as Fisk, Lemoyne Normal Institute (now Lemoyne Owen College in Memphis, Tennessee), Atlanta University, and a host of other institutions had lyceums, literary societies, and debating societies.[69]

With such a rich treasure trove to study, I suggest that students and scholars of rhetorical history would do well to focus their research energy on the African American lyceum movements. First, we would gain not only a better understanding of African American rhetoric generally but also more on the role of rhetorical training and pedagogy, particularly of marginalized communities in the nineteenth century. Second, we would also discover what topics the participants discussed beyond the typical issues of abolitionism and enfranchisement. These lyceums inserted Black voices into issues in the Black experience beyond slavery and the vote, allowing Black rhetors to explore broader topics pertinent to social, cultural, and political aspects of US citizenship. Finally, as I have done with Turner, a study of African American lyceums in this or any other period would produce other figures worthy of study. For instance, in my research for this essay, I discovered other names, some I had heard of and some I had not.

Those names include Josephine Ernestine Hughes Wyatt, who was known for her dramatic reading of the works of Paul Lawrence Dunbar; William E. Matthews, who was a prominent member of the Gailbraith Lyceum in Baltimore; the self-taught elocutionist and teacher Frances E. Preston; Rev. J. C. Price, known as the "Lion of the Lyceum" because of his strong oratorical skills, who would later become president of Livingstone College in Salisbury, North Carolina; and the great orator, elocutionist, and author Hattie Quinn Brown, who would become the first woman to run for elected office in the AME Church. Others include newspaper correspondent Lillian Parker Thomas, Rev. J. J. Durham, Victoria Clay Haley, Rev. William Bishop Johnson, and Maritcha Redmond Lyons of Brooklyn, New York, all of whom participated in African American lyceums. They spoke, they debated, they were there listening, and they were learning, as well. What were their stories? What about their careers? How did they help shape the African American rhetorical tradition? Rhetorical scholars may be able to answer these questions and to provide a more extensive understanding of the African American rhetorical tradition. This, in part, is the power of actuating rhetorical recovery as a part of rhetorical history.

Notes

1. Shirley Wilson Logan, *Liberating Language: Sites of Rhetorical Education in Nineteenth-Century Black America* (Carbondale: Southern Illinois University Press, 2008).

2. Henry McNeal Turner, "For Christian Recorder," *Christian Recorder*, October 18, 1862, Henry McNeal Turner Project, https://www.thehenrymcneal turnerproject.org.

3. Henry McNeal Turner, "Washington Correspondence," *Christian Recorder*, November 8, 1862, Henry McNeal Turner Project, https://www.thehenry mcnealturnerproject.org, paragraph 4.

4. Kathleen J. Turner, "Introduction: Rhetorical History as Social Construction," in Turner, *Doing Rhetoric History*, 2.

5. Melbourne Cummings, "Review: Problems of Researching Black Rhetoric," *Journal of Black Studies* 2, no. 4 (1972): 504.

6. John W. Cromwell, "The First Negro Churches in the District of Columbia," *Journal of Negro History* 7, no 1 (1922): 70.

7. Kate Masur, *An Example for All the Land: Emancipation and the Struggle for Equality in Washington, DC* (Durham: University of North Carolina Press, 2010), 33.

8. Melanee C. Harvey, "'Upon this Rock': Architectural, Material, and Visual Histories of Two Black Protestant Churches, 1881–1969," PhD diss., Boston University, 2017, 63, https://open.bu.edu/handle/2144/27076.

9. Angela G. Ray, *The Lyceum and Public Culture in the Nineteenth-Century United States* (Lansing: Michigan State University Press, 2005), 6.

10. Cromwell, "First Negro Churches," 69.

11. Andre E. Johnson. *The Forgotten Prophet: Bishop Henry McNeal Turner and the African American Prophetic Tradition* (Lanham, MD: Lexington Books, 2012), 17–18; Andre E. Johnson, "'Fighting the Devil with Fire': The Political Rhetoric of Henry McNeal Turner during Reconstruction," in *Handbook of Research on Black Males: Quantitative, Qualitative, and Multidisplinary*, ed. Theodore S. Ransaw, C. P. Gause, and Richard Majors (East Lansing: Michigan State University Press, 2019), 27–28.

12. Johnson, *Forgotten Prophet*, 19; Johnson, "'Fighting the Devil with Fire,'" 27–28.

13. Mungo Ponton, quoted in Johnson, *Forgotten Prophet*, 19.

14. Johnson, *Forgotten Prophet*, 19, 26; Johnson, "'Fighting the Devil with Fire,'" 28.

15. Angela G. Ray, "Learning Leadership: Lincoln at the Lyceum, 1838," *Rhetoric & Public Affairs* 13, no. 3 (2010): 357–58.

16. Angela G. Ray, "What Hath She Wrought? Women's Rights and the Nineteenth-Century Lyceum," *Rhetoric & Public Affairs* 9, no. 2 (2006): 187.

17. Angela G. Ray, "Frederick Douglass on the Lyceum Circuit: Social Assimilation, Social Transformation," *Rhetoric & Public Affairs* 5, no. 4 (2002): 627.

18. Ray, *Lyceum and Public Culture*, 6–7.

19. See Logan's *Liberating Language* and Ray's *Lyceum and Public Culture*, especially chapter 5.

20. Throughout this essay, I use the term African American and Black interchangeably.

21. Logan, *Liberating Language*, 59.

22. Logan, *Liberating Language*, 62.

23. Logan, *Liberating Language*, 94–95.

24. Daniel Alexander Payne, *Recollections of Seventy Years* (Nashville, TN:

AME Sunday School Union, 1888), Documenting the American South, 2001, https://docsouth.unc.edu/index.html.

25. Payne, *Recollections of Seventy Years*.

26. Henry McNeal Turner, "Washington Correspondence," *Christian Recorder*, December 6, 1862, Henry McNeal Turner Project, https://www.thehenrymcneal-turnerproject.org, paragraph 5.

27. Turner, "Washington Correspondence," December 6, 1862, paragraph 5.

28. Henry McNeal Turner, "Washington Correspondence," *Christian Recorder*, January 3, 1863, Henry McNeal Turner Project, https://www.thehenrymcnealturn-erproject.org, paragraph 4.

29. Turner, "Washington Correspondence," January 3, 1863, paragraph 5.

30. Turner, "Washington Correspondence," *Christian Recorder*, January 3, 1863, paragraph 6.

31. Turner, "Washington Correspondence," *Christian Recorder*, March 7, 1863, Henry McNeal Turner Project, https://www.thehenrymcnealturnerproject.org, paragraph 13.

32. Henry McNeal Turner (under the pseudonym "Uncle Sam"), "Washington Correspondence," *Christian Recorder*, June 20,1863, Henry McNeal Turner Project, https://www.thehenrymcnealturnerproject.org, paragraph 4.

33. Turner ("Uncle Sam"), "Washington Correspondence," June 20, 1863, paragraph 5.

34. For more on Turner and the Civil War see Stephen W. Angell's *Bishop Henry McNeal Turner and African-American Religion in the South* (Knoxville: University of Tennessee Press, 1992), chapter 2; and Johnson's *Forgotten Prophet*, chapter 1; as well as Andre E. Johnson, *No Future for the Negro: The Prophetic Pessimism of Bishop Henry McNeal Turner* (Jackson: University Press of Mississippi, 2020), chapter 3.

35. Special Notices, "Lecture," *Daily National Republican* (Washington, DC), January 9, 1863, Chronicling America: Historic American Newspapers, Library of Congress, http://chroniclingamerica.loc.gov/lccn/sn86053570/1863–01–09/ed-1/seq-3/, paragraph 4.

36. Henry McNeal Turner, "Washington Correspondence," *Christian Recorder*, November 15, 1862, Henry McNeal Turner Project, https://www.thehenry-mcnealturnerproject.org, paragraphs 8–9.

37. Turner, "Washington Correspondence," November 15, 1862, paragraphs 9–11.

38. Henry McNeal Turner, "Washington Correspondence," *Christian Recorder*, January 24, 1863, Henry McNeal Turner Project, https://www.thehenry-mcnealturnerproject.org, paragraph 14.

39. "The Destiny of the Colored Race, as Depicted by One of Themselves," *Evening Star* (Washington, DC), January 15, 1863, Chronicling America: Historic

American Newspapers, Library of Congress, http://chroniclingamerica.loc.gov/ lccn/sn83045462/1863–01–15/ed-1/seq-1/, paragraphs 2–3.

40. "Destiny of the Colored Race," paragraph 4.

41. "Destiny of the Colored Race," paragraph 5.

42. "Destiny of the Colored Race," paragraph 6.

43. "Destiny of the Colored Race," paragraph 7.

44. Uplift rhetoric is not, however, without its own problems. For one, the focus on agency typically comes at the expense of negating other factors, such as white supremacy. Second, many orators grounded it in the belief that if Black people acted a certain way or gained the right education, then white people would respect them. For more on the ideology of uplift rhetoric, see Kevin K. Gaines, *Uplifting the Race: Black Leadership, Politics, and Culture in the Twentieth Century* (Durham: University of North Carolina Press, 1996).

45. Logan, *Liberating Language*, 67–68.

46. As bishop, Turner would later ordain the first woman, Sarah Hughes, as elder in the AME Church in 1885. The other bishops rescinded the ordination and forbade Turner from doing it again. See Angell's *Bishop Henry McNeal Turner*, especially chapter 9.

47. W.H.M., "Washington Correspondence," *Christian Recorder,* April 4, 1863.

48. W.H.M., "Washington Correspondence."

49. R.J.C. and L.C., "Letter from Washington," *Christian Recorder*, May 2, 1863.

50. T. H. C. Hinton, "Washington Correspondence," *Christian Recorder*, August 1, 1863.

51. Turner, "Washington Correspondence," March 7, 1863, paragraph 7.

52. Henry McNeal Turner, "Washington Correspondence," *Christian Recorder*, March 14, 1863, Henry McNeal Turner Project, https://www.thehenrymcneal turnerproject.org, paragraph 5.

53. Henry McNeal Turner, "Washington Correspondence," *Christian Recorder*, April 11, 1863, Henry McNeal Turner Project, https://www.thehenrymcnealturnerproject.org/2017, paragraph 2.

54. Turner, "Washington Correspondence," April 11, 1863, paragraph 3.

55. Turner, "Washington Correspondence," April 11, 1863, paragraph 4.

56. T. H. C. Hinton, "From Washington," *Christian Recorder*, July 4, 1863.

57. T. H. C. Hinton, "Washington Correspondence," August 1, 1863.

58. T. H. C. Hinton, "Washington Correspondence," *Christian Recorder*, August 8, 1863.

59. T. H. C. Hinton, "Washington Correspondence," August 8, 1863.

60. T. H. C. Hinton, "Washington Correspondence," *Christian Recorder,* September 9, 1863.

61. *Evening Star* (Washington, DC), December 20, 1862, Chronicling America: Historic American Newspapers, Library of Congress, http://chronicling america.loc.gov/lccn/sn83045462/1862-12-20/ed-1/seq-3/.

62. *Evening Star*, December 20, 1862.

63. L.H., "Departure of the Rev. Henry M. Turner," *Christian Recorder*, November 28, 1863.

64. Andre E. Johnson, ed., *An African American Pastor before and during the American Civil War* (New York: Edwin Mellen Press, 2012), iii.

65. Jean Lee Cole, ed., *Freedom's Witness: The Civil War Correspondence of Henry McNeal Turner* (Morgantown: West Virginia Press, 2013), 18–19.

66. The African Civilization Society (not to be confused with the African Colonization Society) was founded by Henry Highland Garnett in 1858. The organization's goals were to get educated Black Americans to emigrate to Africa. It ceased operations in 1869 due to a lack of finances.

67. T. H. C. Hinton, "Washington Correspondence," *Christian Recorder*, January 16, 1864; "Washington Correspondence," *Christian Recorder*, January 30, 1864.

68. Logan, *Liberating Language*, 91.

69. Logan, *Liberating Language*, 91–93.

8

Crucial Intersections

Public Memories and/as Rhetorical History

Roseann M. Mandziuk

Since the publication of *Doing Rhetorical History* in 1998, rhetorical scholarship about the theory and practice of "public memory" has flourished. In profound ways, this research addresses one of the central questions posed in Kathleen J. Turner's introduction to *Doing Rhetorical History*: How can we understand history as a rhetorical construction? Focusing both upon such discursive forms as speeches and such material forms as statues, public memory studies exist at the crucial intersections among rhetorical appeals, historical representations, and public audiences. As such, inquiry into public memory exemplifies Turner's characterization of rhetorical history: "Our social construction of the past, then, is guided by and contained in the symbols and systems of symbols that give currency to our attitudes, values, beliefs, and actions."[1] Indeed, the processes of public memory mediate, reinforce, and constitute what a community acknowledges that it "knows" about history as this knowledge is expressed through rhetorical depictions and embodied in symbolic representations of the past.

Public memory inquiry in the rhetorical studies discipline often examines physical objects in view, such as memorials and monuments and particularly how their materiality makes claims upon those who interact with them.[2] Yet, often lost in public memory studies is the rhetorical history that grounds this materiality, precisely the other central dimension that Turner describes in her introductory essay to the original volume. The practice of doing rhetorical history is an endeavor to understand patterns of interaction and mine historical contexts in the act of creating meaning, a process that she describes as "selecting and molding various pieces of a massive historical jigsaw puzzle."[3] At the intersection of public memory with rhetoric, scholars often fail to explore the historical paths through which a monument, memorial, or museum first enters into the public realm and comes to occupy space in the material landscape. Discovering these undergirding patterns and piecing together the puzzle in historical narratives can illuminate ideological intersections previously hidden and enrich our understanding of contemporary public memory controversies.

The persistence of Confederate memorials, as well as opposition to them, provides a significant illustration of the missing dimension of rhetorical history in public memory studies. Many of these monuments have become the center of controversy, but few studies have considered their specific rhetorical history and the circumstances of their placement in seeking to understand contemporary clashes. Instead, demonstrations, protests, and even violence take center stage while the significant backstory of such monuments often remains untold. Only occasionally do accounts of these conflicts note that a great majority of the Confederate memorials remaining in public squares and near courthouses were placed there in the early twentieth century by a women's organization, the United Daughters of the Confederacy.

Far from a minor detail, this origin story is a provocative intersection of gender politics, ideology, and rhetorical history that goes far beyond the materiality of any single disputed memorial. An exploration of how the United Daughters of the Confederacy (UDC) came to prominence and ingrained its memorializing practices into the national landscape is an essential dimension for understanding the contemporary presences and absences of these monuments in public memory. As Carole Blair, Greg Dickinson, and Brian Ott remind us, memory sites do not just represent the past, they accrete their own pasts, such that rhetorical invention in memory places is ongoing: "We must attend as well to the intervening uses, deployments, circulations, and rearticulations in the time between the establishment of a place and our current practices in and of the place."[4] Consequently, a public memory study of Confederate memorials must push further than the contemporary headlines to examine the cultural and ideological intersections that constitute particular histories, as well as interrogate how memory is socially constructed and rendered into symbolic and material forms.

Here, I explore the intersection of gender and power that the UDC represents, specifically the role of these women in establishing Confederate memory sites and serving as their protectors. As historian Karen Cox argues, because the women in this organization were chiefly responsible for the movement to honor the Confederacy, "their role as shapers of public memory cannot be overemphasized."[5] A 2019 report by the Southern Poverty Law Center indicates that there are 780 Confederate monuments at county courthouses, town squares, state capitols, and other public venues other than cemeteries. Significantly, 604 of these were dedicated prior to 1950, and of the monuments at courthouses and "other conspicuous locations," the UDC funded and placed 411 of them.[6] As these Confederate monuments engender increased scrutiny following notorious acts of white supremacist violence, the UDC has reasserted its conservancy through statements and legal actions that challenge the removal of their memorials. This analysis of the UDC explores the rhetorical history, and the history of the rhetoric, of the women who largely created our contemporary terrain of Confederate monuments.

Devoted Daughters of the Lost Cause

The UDC's origins and a description of its major monument siting activities during the early twentieth century provide a crucial perspective for the current rhetorical battles over our Confederate past; yet the role of women in its commemoration and the sustenance of white supremacy receives little attention. Instead, accounts of public conflicts over Confederate monuments prominently feature dramatic depictions of angry torch-carrying white men, marching and chanting racist slogans. As Elizabeth Gillespie McRae notes, "Outrage over the violence and rhetoric of these men buries an equally important and certainly more intransigent story of longstanding grass-roots and national campaigns populated partly by white women who aim to maintain racial and economic inequities on the American landscape."[7] Contemporary cultural analyses and historical narratives often reproduce assumptions about traditional roles for women by casting them into supporting roles. Kelly McMichael observes this bias in her survey of Confederate monuments in Texas, noting that "historians assumed women to have had only a cursory role in the myth creation, usually mentioning how ladies passed out cookies at the old soldiers' meetings."[8] Indeed, far from recognizing their central role, "an element of surprise still animates discussions about white women supporting white supremacist politics."[9] Uncovering the intersection among myth, gender, and commemoration in the memorializing activities of the UDC reveals significant insights regarding the persistence of Confederate monuments in the US landscape and the interplay between women and white supremacy.

Founded in 1894 in Nashville, Tennessee, the UDC provided a social and political outlet for elite white women who had direct hereditary links to the Confederacy. Even now, UDC members must prove that they "are lineal or collateral blood descendants of men and women who served honorably in the Army, Navy, or Civil Service of the Confederate States of America, or who gave Material Aid to the Cause."[10] The UDC initiated five primary memorial, historical, benevolent, educational, and social aims, "but they directed most of their efforts toward raising funds for Confederate monuments, sponsoring Memorial Day parades and activities, and maintaining Confederate museums and relic collections."[11] Historian Gaines Foster argues that the organization had wide appeal for different types of women because under its auspices they "found a forum in which to vent their persisting hostilities and to voice their continuing admiration for the men of the Confederacy."[12] After its creation, the UDC's membership grew rapidly: Twenty chapters were chartered during its first year; by 1900, there were forty-two with nearly twenty thousand members;[13] and by 1912, eighty chapters boasted forty-five thousand members.[14]

The rhetorical legacy of the UDC strategically combines traditional gender ideologies with the constructed memory of a mythic South in defense of their commemorative practices. First, perhaps not surprisingly, it adroitly mined the limited cultural prescriptions for women's activities and political influence. In a study of the UDC's "Children's Catechism," Amy Heyse examines how the UDC successfully drew upon traditional gender roles, including republican motherhood and the cult of true womanhood, to establish their authority to undertake Confederate commemoration work in the years between the group's founding in 1894 through the 1920s.[15] The UDC justified its memorializing within a framework that defined commemoration as an essential part of women's work, strategically translating the traditionally feminine activity of caretaking to the public realm. In seeking to preserve the South's heritage, the UDC essentially extended "the vestal flame of piety, lighted up by Heaven in the breast of woman" to become devout beacons of public remembrance.[16]

The UDC engaged in an extraordinary dance among the competing expectations for the domestic and genteel southern lady and the necessarily public nature of their memorializing pursuits. As its members become prominent public advocates, the UDC still strove to preserve the image that it did not challenge traditional feminine dictates. Margaret Rutherford, the president of the Georgia UDC chapter who became historian general for the national organization in 1905, admonished that women should "'turn backward in loving emulation to the ideals set by the mothers and grandmothers of yesterday.'"[17] Although their commemoration activities necessarily moved them into the public eye, the UDC women remained steadfastly, and strategically, devoted to traditional womanhood. As Heyse concludes, "What is remarkable about the UDC is that the women achieved sustained success as agents of collective memory at a time when women attempting to participate in the public sphere often met with societal resistance."[18] Their proclaimed status as mothers, wives, and daughters who only were performing their familial and civic duty served as the primary source of ethos at the group's inception; it continues to undergird their rhetorical practices when their monument siting activities come into question.

The UDC assumed a leading role in promoting and substantiating the particular mythic ideology of the Lost Cause through commemoration. Following the Civil War, Confederate defenders and sympathetic historians articulated a comprehensive narrative of the South's rebellion "that encapsulated the longing and morose feelings of people in a defeated region by promoting a belief that, despite failures on the battlefield, the South was somehow redeemed because it was a place where old times and cherished ways of home, duty, family, and patriotism were not forgotten."[19] The reaffirmation of the admirable character of the South served to correct what Edward A. Pollard, in his 1866 book *The Lost Cause,* refers to as the "cloud of prejudice" in Northern accounts.[20] As the foundation for the shared identity and specific character of the South, this myth increasingly reified central tenets of religion and patriotism that were employed to forestall advocates for social diversity in the 1890s and beyond.[21]

The symbols of the Confederate past became sacred as expressions of Lost Cause ideology, and at its heart was the memory of the Confederate soldiers placed in service of white supremacy. These men were rendered into heroes "who came to embody transcendent truths about the redemptive power of Southern society" because they were impelled by "noble principles" to gallantry.[22] Monuments that commemorated both common soldiers and Confederate leaders thereby functioned "not just as symbols of grief and mourning, but also as defiant public symbols of the Lost Cause and the glorious 'Old South.'"[23] Sustaining this tale of abstract glory and moral supremacy required the explicit renunciation of slavery as the cause of the South's rebellion, even while race and difference remained a central tenet of the region's identity.[24] The historical convergence of reconciliation with segregation in the early twentieth century further contributed to the drive for monumentalizing, as even Northern states tolerated the commemoration of Confederate sites and in some cases even assisted in their establishment.[25] This historical confluence of unification fantasies and racist realities illuminates the inherent bond between Confederate commemoration and white supremacy.

The drive to promote the memory of the gallant Confederate soldier and thereby uphold white supremacy presented a perfect opportunity for white southern women to adopt the memorialization cause as their own project and to take a leadership role. Ironically, the commercialization of the monument manufacturing industry in Northern cities aided the prolific commemorative efforts by offering standard statue designs, usually the soldier at "parade rest" cast in inexpensive zinc, that could be quickly obtained via mail order catalogues.[26] Even with transient material construction that evoked past criticism for poor taste[27] and denigration as "bargain-bin racist tchotchkes,"[28] these monuments continue to exert ideological force.

Significantly, women's commemorative activities provided a potent protection that instantiated racism in the mask of a genteel southern lady. The commemoration of the soldiers' past valor melded seamlessly with the belief held by many that public life should be conducted according to moral convictions,[29] and, as H. E. Gully observes, the activities of women who joined Confederate commemoration organizations "strengthened the traditional white patriarchy and retarded the process of social integration, thereby stabilizing white southern society,"[30] thereby "shrouding racism in sepia romance."[31] The UDC, in particular, succeeded in rooting a "vision of the Lost Cause deeper into the nation's historical imagination than perhaps any other association,"[32] embodying the feminine role of honoring family heritage as it sought to shape public memory by establishing prominent monuments to white supremacy.

Dutiful Descendants: Rhetorics of Vindication and Victimage

In adopting the role of conservator of the ideology of the Lost Cause, the UDC was dedicated to promoting the moral values of its members and specifically to countering what they perceived as a false history of the South. The case for memorializing offered by the UDC has remained relatively stable since its founding: "'A people who have no monuments erected to perpetuate heroism and virtue have no history, and we must have our shining shafts of marble pointing to the fadeless stars, fit emblems of their lofty aspirations.'"[33] White women from varied backgrounds especially could unite around the cause of commemoration, and they undertook their task with zeal because they "understood the potential power in memory construction and used it to project the morals they valued, such morals as honor, sacrifice, and patriotism."[34] The UDC embraced commemoration to instantiate what it believed to be the correct version of southern history, and it justified these public pursuits by summoning the rhetorical resources of traditional femininity. The rhetoric that the UDC employed in defense of its memorializing encompassed two interrelated appeals: an expressed motive of vindication of their heritage and the justification of the persistence of their monuments within the rhetorical frame of victimage.

The UDC sought to ensure that the Confederacy would attain a revered place in the national memory and adroitly understood how erecting statues could serve as material proof to authenticate their honorable and blameless heritage. In its evangelism of southern ascendancy, Karen Cox argues that the UDC not only sought to instantiate its vision of morality, but it "raised the stakes of the Lost Cause by making it a movement about vindication as well as memorialization."[35] Central to a definition of vindication is the concept of avenging a perceived wrong, what B. L. Ware and Wil A. Linkugel recognize in defining the "vindicative" posture of apologia as the employment of appeals to transcendence, such that the rhetoric "aims not only at the preservation of the accused's reputation but also the recognition of his greater worth as a human being relative to that of his accusers."[36] The UDC understood that the physical placement of Confederate monuments would convey powerfully both a sense of moral elevation and a commanding message of legitimacy. As UDC member and spokeswoman Mary Poppenheim stated, "They knew monuments would speak more quickly, impressively, and lastingly to the eye than the written or printed word."[37]

The identification of vindication as the UDC's central motivation also reveals a deep connection between its memorializing activities and the legitimization of white supremacy. As Elizabeth Gillespie McRae argues, because the term *segregationist* is overcoded with masculine meanings, these rural and retrograde associations disguise "both the sophistication and breadth of white southern women's political work and by consequence the connections they cultivated with white supremacists nationwide."[38] Indeed, the UDC advantageously cloaked its memorializing in femininity and thereby thrived in the South "because it actively supported the racial status quo. . . . The [UDC's] activities were a natural complement to Jim Crow politics."[39] Placing commemoration in the conservancy of women "reduced the political or ideological implications of the memorial movement,"[40] and under this guise of doing "women's work," the UDC gained an extraordinary degree of freedom to exert its influence in the public realm. Essentially, the members constituted an apolitical identity as avenging angels who were compelled by their moral duty to guard the Confederate heritage and confirm its rightful place in the national historical narrative.

The physical location of the monuments placed in public spaces contributes significantly to their rhetorical power to signify the legitimacy of white supremacy. Rather than placing memorials in cemeteries, the UDC shifted its commemorations to public spaces as its membership grew. Fully 93 percent of Confederate monuments in courthouse squares were placed there after 1895, and more than half of these appeared between 1903 and 1912.[41] The UDC's focus on erecting permanent structures in public essentially strengthened the claims its monuments make on visitors. As Catherine W. Bishir notes, "The location of monuments in the state's principal civic places lent authority to the version of history they represented, while at the same time the monuments claimed those public spaces and thereby defined the setting for public life."[42] Locating monuments in public locales lends legitimacy to the commemoration because the community has designated these spaces as sacred sites in civic life. Hence, the memorials exhibit the rhetorical force of permanence even when disputed or defaced. Their public siting also powerfully links the material representation of Confederate memory to the practice of lynching that was an integral part of public life in the South, as each monument to a soldier serves "as a reminder of a regime formed to preserve slavery, enforce white supremacy, and impose racially motivated violence on black southerners."[43] Placing these monuments adjacent to courthouses or in central public squares reifies the racist violence sanctioned there, providing a direct ideological path from the commemorated soldier to the celebratory white crowds that surrounded lynched Black bodies.

The UDC had twenty-five thousand members with eight hundred chapters by 2000, and the website currently lists thirty-three states with chapters and divisions.[44] When contemporary clashes over its legacy of Confederate memorials arose, however, the UDC initially hesitated to actively defend their public monuments. After the 2015 killing of nine African American churchgoers by a white supremacist in Charleston, South Carolina, the UDC maintained a "curious silence" despite calls for the association to comment,[45] and following the 2017 violence in Charlottesville and the death of protestor Heather Heyer, the organization again remained "stunningly silent" and unresponsive to media inquiries.[46] A *Newsweek* reporter noted, "The UDC does not seem too eager to rescue its monuments,"[47] while the past president of the Kentucky division described the UDC as "reeling" from sadness and disbelief at the removals of its monuments.[48] Then, in a subsequent swift departure from its ostensible reticence to engage the monument controversies publicly, the UDC quickly launched a set of rhetorical strategies in late 2017.[49] It filed two lawsuits that illustrate how the contemporary UDC establishes its defense of past activities and seeks vindication for the legitimacy of its monuments upon the rhetorical edifice of victimage.

Posted on September 21, 2017, the UDC issued a statement on their website under the signature of Pres. Gen. Patricia M. Bryson that acknowledged "the feelings of citizens across the country currently being expressed concerning Confederate memorial statues and monuments that were erected by our members in decades past."[50] The statement also included several paragraphs in defense of the organization and its monuments. This post is one of the rare public comments issued by the UDC since it passed a resolution at its 1948 convention decrying the use of the Confederate battle flag as a political logo for southern Dixiecrats.[51] Next, the UDC filed two civil lawsuits. In the first case, following a decision in Louisiana by the Caddo Parish commissioners to remove the UDC monument that had stood before the courthouse since 1906, the Shreveport Chapter #237 filed suit on October 19, 2017, to block this action. In the second case, the Albert Sydney Johnston Chapter #2060 of Texas initiated its suit against the San Antonio mayor and city council members on October 23, 2017, after the city removed the monument that the UDC had placed in 1900 in the downtown Travis Park.

The 2017 website statement and the complaint documents filed in the two civil suits demonstrate how the UDC accomplishes its rhetorical construction of victimage by combining the traditional feminine character and democratic ideology. In *The Philosophy of Literary Form*, Kenneth Burke describes the rhetorical process of victimage, the human need for purification that arises when a social ill or accusation creates guilt that consequentially must be purged to achieve redemption. The identification of a scapegoat serves a "curative" function, providing "purification by dissociation."[52] The ritual cycle from guilt through purification to redemption occurs when a social body suffers; hence, the rhetoric of victimage is melodramatic "in the sense that it differentiates the field of actors into heroes and villains, enemies and allies, proponents and opponents."[53] Because the villain must be rejected and scorned for violating the legal or social order, the moral outrage at the offender in turn constitutes the wronged party as a moral agent.[54] Further, in analysis of how victimage functioned in two well-known race trials from the 1930s, William W. Lewis and John L. Lucaites argue that innocence is a necessary element of establishing the victimage to legitimate legal protection.[55] The UDC's identity of female conservatorship and true womanhood defined the purity and innocence of its members as those who had dutifully placed these monuments—in contrast to identifying those who sought to remove their monuments as their villainous and immoral scapegoat. This traditional femininity powerfully connected their rhetoric of vindication to the frame of victimage.

The UDC also framed the attacks upon its monuments as an outrage that continually would plague it in its determined and pious quest to protect the values represented by its Confederate heroes. This stance reflects Jeremy Engels's extension of Burke's description of victimage, a shift in its praxis that seeks to perpetuate, rather than to cure, the resentments felt by those who perceive that they are under siege.[56] This rhetoric of victimage construed as resentment is fueled by the identification of a tyrannizing minority that renders the defenders of morality into victims. While Engels argues that this idea of a moral majority besieged by a lesser tyrannizing force "has given birth to new values and new rhetorics of the Republican Right,"[57] the concept also illuminates the rhetorical themes characteristic of white supremacists who believe in the myth of the Lost Cause. Notably, research examining resentment largely has explored its integration with the masculinist rhetorics of such subjects as Neo-Nazi extremist groups or such conservative male politicians as Richard Nixon and Donald Trump,[58] to the exclusion of women's rhetorical uses.

In the discourse of the United Daughters of the Confederacy, the intersection of resentment with the politics of race and gender becomes a different and more insidious source of rhetorical power. In contrast to extremist white men, the white women of the UDC do not engage the angry rhetoric in response to perceived discrimination or any explicit racist tactics in the identification of their scapegoat. Rather, the members of the UDC consistently position themselves as apolitical traditional women who do the spiritually guided and femininely appropriate work of preserving Confederate memory, and as such they emphasize that they are not motivated by a desire for social transformation despite their agency and influence. The evocation of traditional feminine character allows the UDC to depict its members as women who are merely moral agents on a spiritually guided mission to preserve the patriotic and heroic history of the Confederacy. As UDC cofounder Anna Raines stated in 1897, "We are not a body of discontented suffragists thirsting for oratorical honors, but a sisterhood of earnest, womanly women, striving to fulfill the teaching of God's work in honor of our fathers."[59] This evocation of traditional feminine ideologies provides the narrative grounds for the UDC's articulation of a rhetorical drama that situates its members as innocent victims of a tyrannical minority who seek to destroy the sacrosanct Confederate monuments that these women have so lovingly established.

The UDC expresses its politics of resentment by depicting this tyrannical minority as an evil force that is irreconcilable with the principles of deference, respect, and fairness to which the UDC ascribes. It constructs the victimage around the reaffirmation of hegemonic gender ideologies and the appropriation of democratic principles in a rhetorical drama that opposes their actions and attitudes, as well as those that the Confederate monuments represent, against the aggressive revisionism of those who advocate for the removal of the memorials. This contrast echoes the ideology of the Lost Cause and the mythic depiction of the Confederate heroes whom the monuments commemorate as patriots representing transcendent values, while it also heightens the gender politics by placing these traditional, genteel women as victims of unwarranted and vicious attacks.

The UDC members advance a striking opposition between their respectful silence and the impudent speech of others, depicting themselves as steadfast servants who, as women, properly have not sought notoriety. In their website statement, the UDC proclaimed that it promotes "patriotism and good citizenship" and insisted that it has practiced proper female decorum and deference because "our members are the ones who, like our statues, have stayed quietly in the background, never engaging in public controversy."[60] By implication, those who "find anything connected to the Confederacy to be offensive" are ignorant and unpatriotic because "our Confederate ancestors were and are Americans." The UDC employed the language of pluralist ideology in its representation of the Confederate soldier as a national symbol while the members represent themselves as the champions of egalitarian values: "Indeed, we urge all Americans to honor their ancestors' contributions to our country as well. This diversity is what makes our nation stronger."[61] In honoring the brave Confederate soldiers, they construct for themselves an identity as the *true* protectors of diversity who must fight a constant battle to protect their values.

Within this narrative of victimage, the reluctant and heretofore passive UDC members therefore had no choice but to step forward and defend their legal rights to freedom of expression and due process in response to the assault they experienced at the hands of belligerent protestors and overreaching local governments. In the Caddo Parish complaint, the UDC claimed that its ability to exercise its first amendment right to free expression had been violated because the Confederate monument was its personal property and also sat on land that was given to the local UDC chapter in 1903. Consequently, the UDC argued that the parish did not have a "rational" basis for its prohibition and that its policies "have a chilling effect which potentially prohibits other individuals from exercising their rights to free speech such as displays of the American Flag on their private property."[62] The UDC's rhetoric neutralizes the racist meanings of the Confederate monuments by conflating its memorial with other patriotic symbols. The elevated status of its Lost Cause values also echoes in the additional contention that the Caddo Parish policies potentially "prohibit significant participation of religious groups because the defendants have exercised authority which can be used to regulate persons from displaying symbols of faith on their private property."[63] The UDC certifies its moral authority and role as victim by equating its persecution with the suppression of speech and religious freedoms.

To further articulate their victimage, the devoted women of the UDC depicted how they had been violated, silenced, and suppressed. In concert with their enactment of their proper role as the female guardians of Confederate memory, the UDC purported to have been bullied by forces that denied them their due process and the full participation that their status as devout women should ensure. In the Caddo Parish complaint, the UDC implicitly equated their ill treatment with that of the monument itself: "Furthermore, the plaintiff shows that the said monument is over one hundred (100) years old and sporadically vandalized by opponents of the Confederate Monument. Therefore, it is in a condition whereby its removal would cause much irreparable damage to it."[64] The continual victimization described in this statement has been perpetrated upon the sacred memory site as well as upon its devoted attendants who seek only to do their duty in preserving it.

In the San Antonio complaint, the UDC expressed its commitment to the preservation of Confederate memory as a communal bond between the female members, describing how the members "feel an emotional connection to the monument" and that "from woman to woman for 118 years, they have passed down stories and memories of the monument and the patriotic values it represents."[65] A double victimization of UDC members and their monuments rhetorically depicts violence done both to the community forged by the women and to the memories they sought to preserve.

Ultimately, the rhetoric of vindication aligns with the politics of resentment as it argues that there is no possible route for resolution with the inferior values and treasonous behaviors of those who persecute its members. The assault on the Confederate monuments is transmogrified into a violation of these innocent female conservators who believe these statues merely speak the truth of history and model transcendent principles to all. Correspondingly, those who seek to remove them are ignoble, unpatriotic, and dangerous. In the drama enacted by the UDC, the members' confirmed status as true women necessarily conveys to them an unquestionable authority both to locate and to defend the legitimacy of their monuments to the Confederate cause in public spaces.

Conclusion

The UDC holds itself up as the only true conservators of southern American values and as the authentic guardians of diversity in the public memory. Within its rhetorical frame, the traditional feminine values of sacrifice, devotion, and community that have marked the mission of the UDC from its beginnings both verify its authority and serve as the only legitimate values that should guide decisions about the place of Confederate monuments. The UDC's rhetoric of vindication and victimage thereby depicts the forces that seek to destroy the Confederate monuments as effectively undermining all that is patriotic and sacred in their transient pursuit of a sham politically correct sense of justice. In this drama, there is no possibility of resolution or redemption until the American historical narrative fully recognizes and gives an honored place in the national memory for the Confederate past and the Lost Cause. Yet it also recognizes this as the perpetual struggle visited upon all true women whose responsibility it is to champion morality and triumph over evil. Consequently, the brand of resentment that the UDC weaves in its tale of victimage necessarily sustains the pollution and guilt caused by any proponents who seek to remove the products of the UDC's legitimate feminine labor.

Forever altering the material landscape of the South, the United Daughters of the Confederacy achieved the rhetorical instantiation of the kind of Confederate history that Adelia A. Dunovant promoted in her speech to the UDC's 1901 general meeting in Wilmington, North Carolina: "It seems to me that our error lies in embalming, as it were, historic truths and putting them away in the tomb of the Confederacy—making them as devoid of energizing influence as an Egyptian mummy—instead of bringing them and keeping them ever before us in the vital, living present. Memory is not a passivity, but an ever-active faculty—History should be made to serve its true purpose by bringing its lessons into the present and using them as a guide to the future."[66]

Dunovant's comments strikingly illustrate how history is used to justify present actions, one of the four senses of rhetorical history identified by David Zarefsky in his chapter in *Doing Rhetorical History*.[67] Moreover, her admonition that memory is an active faculty serves as a potent reminder that in the rhetorical construction of public memory, as E. Culpepper Clark and Raymie E. McKerrow note, histories constructed from invented accounts of the past serve as argumentative resources in the present.[68]

The Confederate monuments that still stand throughout the United States continue to impose their rhetorical force in every one of the communities in which they were erected. These artifacts simultaneously signal the legitimacy of white supremacy to supporters and the illegitimate historical lessons to detractors. By drawing upon the ideologies of traditional femininity in defense of the Lost Cause, the UDC's memorializing creates a "landscape of permanent symbols that could not simply be lowered as with the battle flag."[69] More significantly, understanding the rhetoric of victimage utilized by the UDC illuminates the significant role of women in perpetuating white supremacy. Just as the monuments it placed in public squares inherently are linked to the legacy of lynching, so the victimage of white women in the face of protests often initiated from diverse communities and people of color harkens to the white supremacist image of the rape of white, female innocents by dark and evil others.

From its founding statements in 1894, the United Daughters of the Confederacy has asserted significant influence upon the commemorative landscape. Long after the intensive periods of monumentalizing that marked the early period of the twentieth century and the midcentury massive resistance to the civil rights cause, "white women had succeeded in their goal of filling the civic spaces of the South with monuments glorifying the Confederacy for 'unborn generations.'"[70] This analysis of the UDC provides a different and quite sobering vantage point into the persistent legacies of white supremacy in the United States. Recognition of the substantial role played by women in the instantiation of the Lost Cause mythology and the maintenance of racism forces consideration of rhetorical constructions far removed from the angry violence of the extremist young male who openly drapes himself in the Confederate flag. When we center our inquiries on how the rhetoric of women, like the members of the UDC, uses discursive protections that cloak racism in contemporary debates, the ways in which the UDC appropriates both traditional feminine ideologies and the rhetoric of democracy reveal a significant confluence with great explanatory power. Rendering conservation as a feminine activity motivated by deference provides a rhetorical mask that obscures the complex and objectionable realities of racist oppression that the monuments materially evoke. Moreover, the evocation of traditional feminine roles in concert with the politics of resentment yields a potent rhetorical reservoir that continues to be accessed by women who participate in the maintenance of white supremacy.

Notes

1. Kathleen J. Turner, "Introduction: Rhetorical History as Social Construction," in Turner, *Doing Rhetorical History*, 10.

2. See, for example, the contributions of Carole Blair, "Contemporary U.S. Memorial Sites as Exemplars of Rhetoric's Materiality," in *Rhetorical Bodies*, ed. Jack Selzer and S. Crowley (Madison: University of Wisconsin Press, 1999),

16–57; Nicole Maurantonio, "Material Rhetoric, Public Memory, and the Post It Note," *Southern Communication Journal* 80, no. 2 (2015): 83–101; and Kenneth S. Zagacki and Victoria J. Gallagher, "Rhetoric and Materiality in the Museum Park at the North Carolina Museum of Art," *Quarterly Journal of Speech* 95, no. 2 (2009): 171–91.

3. Turner, "Introduction," 12.

4. Carole Blair, Greg Dickinson, and Brian Ott, "Introduction: Rhetoric/ Memory/Place," in *Places of Public Memory: The Rhetoric of Museums and Memorials*, ed. Greg Dickinson, Carole Blair, and Brian L. Ott (Tuscaloosa: University of Alabama Press, 2010), 30–31.

5. Karen L. Cox, *Dixie's Daughters: The United Daughters of the Confederacy and the Preservation of Confederate Culture* (Gainesville: University Press of Florida, 2003), 72.

6. Southern Poverty Law Center, "Whose Heritage? Public Symbols of the Confederacy," February 1, 2019, https://www.splcenter.org/20180604/whose -heritage-public-symbols-confederacy.

7. Elizabeth Gillespie McRae, "The Women Behind White Power," *New York Times*, February 2, 2018, https://www.nytimes.com/2018/02/02/opinion/sunday /white-supremacy-forgot-women.html.

8. Kelly McMichael, "'Memories Are Short but Monuments Lengthen Remembrances': The United Daughters of the Confederacy and the Power of Civil War Memory," in *Lone Star Pasts: Memory and History in Texas*, ed. Elizabeth Hayes Turner, W. Fitzhugh Brundage, and Gregg Cantrell (College Station: Texas A&M University Press, 2006), 99.

9. McRae, "Women Behind White Power."

10. United Daughters of the Confederacy, Membership, https://www.hqudc .org.

11. Caroline E. Janney, *Burying the Dead but Not the Past: Ladies' Memorial Associations and the Lost Cause* (Chapel Hill: University of North Carolina Press, 2012), 168.

12. Gaines Foster, *Ghosts of the Confederacy: Defeat, the Lost Cause, and the Emergence of the New South 1865–1913* (New York: Oxford University Press, 1987), 174.

13. Janney, *Burying the Dead*,169.

14. Foster, *Ghosts of the Confederacy*, 72.

15. Amy Heyse, "The Rhetoric of Memory-Making: Lessons from the UDC's Catechisms for Children," *Rhetoric Society Quarterly* 38, no. 4 (2008): 408–32.

16. *The Young Ladies' Class Book: A Selection of Lessons for Reading in Prose and Verse*, quoted in Barbara Welter, "The Cult of True Womanhood," *American Quarterly* 18, no. 2 (1966): 152.

17. Quoted in Cox, *Dixie's Daughters*, 41.

18. Amy Heyse, "Women's Rhetorical Authority and Collective Memory: The United Daughters of the Confederacy Remember the South," *Women & Language* 33, no. 2 (2010): 31.

19. W. Stuart Towns, *Enduring Legacy: Rhetoric and Ritual of the Lost Cause* (Tuscaloosa: University of Alabama Press, 2012), 6–7; J. Michael Martinez, William D. Richardson, and Ron McNinch-Su, "Introduction: Understanding the Debate over Confederate Symbols," in *Confederate Symbols in the Contemporary South*, ed. J. Michael Martinez, William. D. Richardson, and Ron McNinch-Su (Gainesville: University Press of Florida, 2000), 14.

20. Edward A. Pollard, *The Lost Cause: A New Southern History of the War of the Confederates* (New York: E. B. Treat, 1868), 44.

21. David W. Blight, *Race and Reunion: The Civil War in American Memory* (Cambridge, MA: Harvard University Press, 2001).

22. Stephen Davis, "Empty Eyes, Marble Hand," *Journal of Popular Culture* 20, no.1 (1982): 8; Charles Reagan Wilson, *Baptized in Blood: The Religion of the Lost Cause, 1865–1920* (Athens: University of Georgia Press, 1980), 11.

23. Towns, *Enduring Legacy,* 34.

24. Keith Savage, *Standing Soldiers, Kneeling Slaves: Race, War, and Monument in Nineteenth-Century America* (Princeton, NJ: Princeton University Press, 1970), 130.

25. This confluence explains the seeming anachronisms of a Confederate memorial fountain in Montana, which was not dismantled until 2017, and the still existent markers denoting the Jefferson Davis Highway in the state of Washington. See "Protestors Arrested as City of Helena Removes Confederate Fountain," *Billings Gazette*, August 18, 2017, https://billingsgazette.com/news/state-and-regional/protesters-arrested-as-city-of-helena-removes-confederate-fountain/article_8e724ab3-b982–559e-a21a-8201c860c706.html; and Euan Hague and Edward H. Sebesta, "The Jefferson Davis Highway: Contesting the Confederacy in the Pacific Northwest," *Journal of American Studies* 45, no. 2 (2011): 281–301.

26. Sarah Beetham, "From Spray Cans to Minivans: Contesting the Legacy of Confederate Soldier Monuments in the Era of 'Black Lives Matter,'" *Public Art Dialogue* 6, no. 1 (2016): 9–33.

27. Davis, "Empty Eyes, Marble Hand," 2–21.

28. Katy Waldman, "Rotten Monuments: Donald Trump Has a Lot in Common with the Antiquated, Racist Confederate Statues He Defends," *Slate Magazine*, August 15, 2017, http://www.slate.com.

29. W. Fitzhugh Brundage, "'Woman's Hand and Heart and Deathless Love': White Women and the Commemorative Impulse in the New South," in *Monuments to the Lost Cause: Women, Art, and the Landscapes of Southern Memory*, ed. Cynthia Mills and Pamela H. Simpson (Knoxville: University of Tennessee Press, 2003), 73.

30. H. E. Gulley, "Women and the Lost Cause: Preserving a Confederate Identity in the American Deep South," *Journal of Historical Geography* 19, no. 2 (1993): 129.

31. Katy Waldman, "Guardians of White Innocence," *Slate Magazine.* September 25, 2017, https://slate.com.

32. Blight, *Race and Reunion*, 273.

33. Quoted in McMichael, "Memories Are Short," 95–96.

34. McMichael, "Memories Are Short," 96–97.

35. Cox, *Dixie's Daughters*, 1.

36. B. L. Ware and Wil A. Linkugel, "They Spoke in Defense of Themselves: On the Generic Criticism of Apologia," *Quarterly Journal of Speech* 59, no. 3 (1973): 283.

37. Mary B. Poppenheim, *History of the United Daughters of the Confederacy* (Richmond, Virginia: Garrett and Massie, 1938), 21.

38. Elizabeth Gillespie McRae, *Mothers of Massive Resistance: White Women and the Politics of White Supremacy* (New York: Oxford University Press, 2018), 9.

39. Cox, *Dixie's Daughters*, 160; Janney, *Burying the Dead*, 173.

40. J. Michael Martinez and Robert M. Harris, "Graves, Worms, and Epitaphs: Confederate Monuments in the Southern Landscape," in *Confederate Symbols in the Contemporary South*, ed. J. Michael Martinez, William D. Richardson, and Ron McNinch-Su (Gainesville: University Press of Florida, 2000), 136–37.

41. John J. Winberry, "'Lest We Forget': The Confederate Monument and the Southern Townscape," *Southeastern Geographer* 23, no. 2 (1983): 107–21.

42. Catherine W. Bishir, "Landmarks of Power: Building a Southern Past, 1885–1915," *Southern Cultures* 1, no. 1 (1993): 6.

43. Beetham, "From Spray Cans to Minivans," 19.

44. Allen G. Breed, "Women's Group Behind Rebel Memorials Quietly Battles On," *U.S. News & World Report*, August 10, 2018, https://www.usnews.com/news/best-states/virginia/articles/2018–08–10/womens-group-behind-rebel-memorials-quietly-battles-on. The current UDC website only includes information about states and divisions or chapters but does not explain that difference, making it challenging to get an accurate count of its membership.

45. Kevin Levin, "The United Daughters of the Confederacy's Curious Silence on the Confederate Flag Debate," *Civil War Memory* (blog), June 30, 2015, http://cwmemory.com/2015/06/30/the-united-daughters-of-the-confederacys-curious-silence-on-the-confederate-flag-debate/.

46. Peter Galuszka, "The Women Who Erected Confederate Statues Are Stunningly Silent," *Washington Post*, October 13, 2017, https://www.washingtonpost.com.

47. Max Kutner, "As Confederate Statues Fall, the Group Behind Most of

Them Stays Quiet," *Newsweek*, August 25, 2017, http://www.newsweek.com/united-daughters-confederacy-statues-monuments-udc-653103.

48. Jennifer Levitz, "Daughters of Confederacy 'Reeling' from Memorial Removals," *Wall Street Journal,* August 21, 2017, https://www.wsj.com/articles/daughters-of-confederacy-reeling-from-memorial-removals-1503307806.

49. The UDC also garnered attention when its Tennessee division sued a private entity, Vanderbilt University, over its plans to remove the word *Confederate* from a residence hall that had been funded with a $50,000 donation from the UDC in 1933. The UDC eventually won the lawsuit in 2016 and subsequently were compensated $1.2 million, the contemporary equivalent to the original donation.

50. United Daughters of the Confederacy, "Statement from the President General," https://hqudc.org/. This post originally appeared on the UDC website under Bryson's authorship and most recently appears under the signature of the president general for 2020–22, Linda Edwards.

51. Kutner, "As Confederate Statues Fall."

52. Kenneth Burke, *The Philosophy of Literary Form: Studies in Symbolic Action*, 3rd ed. (Berkeley: University of California Press, 1973), 202.

53. Michael Blain, "The Politics of Victimage: Power and Subjection in a U.S. Anti-Gay Campaign," *Critical Discourse Studies* 2, no. 1 (2005): 34.

54. Burke, *Philosophy of Literary Form*, 39–40.

55. William W. Lewis and John L. Lucaites, "Race Trials: The Rhetoric of Victimage in the Racial Consciousness of 1930s America," in *Argument in a Time of Change*, ed. James F. Klumpp (Annandale, VA: National Communication Association, 1998), 269–74.

56. Jeremy Engels, "The Politics of Resentment and the Tyranny of the Minority: Rethinking Victimage for Resentful Times," *Rhetoric Society Quarterly* 40, no. 4 (2010): 303–25.

57. Engels, "Politics of Resentment," 306.

58. Mitch Berbrier, "The Victim Ideology of White Supremacists and White Separatists in the United States," *Sociological Focus* 33, no. 2 (2000): 175–91; Rebecca Townsend, "Trump's Warsaw Address, or How the 'West' Was Widened," *Journal of Contemporary Rhetoric* 8, no. 1/2 (2018): 84–106; Engels, "Politics of Resentment."

59. Cox, *Dixie's Daughters*, xx.

60. UDC, "Statement from the President General."

61. UDC, "Statement from the President General."

62. Shreveport Chapter #237 of the United Daughters of the Confederacy v. The Caddo Parish Commission, Western District Court of Louisiana, Case 5:17-cv-01346, October 19, 2017, 12, https://www.courtlistener.com/recap/gov.uscourts.lawd.159604/gov.uscourts.lawd.159604.1.

63. *Shreveport Chapter*, 12.

64. *Shreveport Chapter*, 12.

65. Albert Sidney Johnston Chapter #2060, United Daughters of the Confederacy v. Ron Nirenberg, et.al. and the City of San Antonio, US District Court, Western District of Texas, Case 5:17-cv-01072-DAE, October 23, 2017, 6, https://www.scribd.com/document/363277016/United-Daughters-of-the-Confederacy-lawsuit-against-the-City-of-San-Antonio.

66. Quoted in Heyse, "Women's Rhetorical Authority," 408.

67. David Zarefsky, "Four Senses of Rhetorical History," in Turner, *Doing Rhetorical History*, 28.

68. E. Culpepper Clark and Raymie E. McKerrow, "The Rhetorical Construction of History," in Turner, *Doing Rhetorical History*, 33–35.

69. Janney, *Burying the Dead*, 199.

70. Brundage, "'Woman's Hand and Heart,'" 78.

III
APPROACHES TO NATIONALISM AND TRANSNATIONALISM

9

Decolonizing Rhetorical History

Matthew deTar

Over the past two decades, rhetorical studies scholarship has global-ized. Special journal issues have challenged the singular unity of an idea of "América," refined methods of comparative analysis for global rhetorical study, and questioned the hegemony of a global human rights regime; and individual essays on global topics have expanded in many directions beyond US cases, Western paradigms, and/or attendant he-gemonic analytic constructs.[1] These projects move rhetorical studies away from a singular focus on US history and politics and toward global cases, diverse forms of rhetorical practice, and non-Greek and -Roman traditions of persuasion. Although this disciplinary shift has been crit-ical of some of the more traditional and even recently innovative meth-ods and concepts that structure scholarship in rhetorical studies, it is only just beginning to address large-scale questions about the status and foundations of disciplinary knowledge in a global context. In many ways, contemporary rhetorical studies scholarship is beginning to ex-plore the questions that animated postcolonial scholarship in a number of disciplines in the 1980s and 1990s. This recalibration toward global commitments has led to increasing explorations of decolonial politics in rhetorical studies.

Drawing from this disciplinary trajectory, this essay asks: How does rhetorical history change when it is attuned to the colonialism of knowl-edge production? As scholars in rhetorical studies explore difference, race, non-Western cases, and transnational movements, it is imperative to be critical of the form this expansion takes, since expansion—as both a metaphor and a material emblem for physical and symbolic terrain—is now nearly synonymous with colonialism. An important and well-analyzed feature of expansion is the kind of historical teleology that ac-companies and makes possible this expansion. In the nineteenth- and twentieth-century United States, expansion was founded on and left in its wake a teleology of progress of the European Enlightenment that jus-tified slavery, settler colonialism, genocide against Indigenous peoples, and whole populations figured as prehistoric relics, backward, and thus

nonbeings. One of the primary projects of colonialism (beyond exploitation) is, as Dipesh Chakrabarty argues, to universalize European history as global History (capitalization intended), a project that institutes a
global perspectival hegemony that always orients in relation to Europe.[2]
This hegemony is insidious and powerful, and rhetorical history interested in advancing decolonial politics must first and foremost contend
with H/history as a way of knowing the world.

In order to outline the necessary attunements of a decolonial rhetorical history, I explore the phrase "the minority question" in Turkey, testing theoretical concepts and methods of analysis that might help rhetorical historians make sense of the phrase. The minority question has a
long history of use in Turkish politics from the beginning of the Turkish
Republic (1923) to the present, and Turkish national identity and public
discourse is deftly aware of Turkey's own Orientalization and marginality from the perspective of European history.[3] This makes the minority
question in Turkey a complexly layered historical phenomenon that also
employs history in its construction of knowledge.[4] In its individual instances, the phrase can reference a range of marginalized populations
in Turkey, from ethnic groups such as Armenians, Greeks, or Kurds to
Muslim religious minorities like Alevis and Sufis. The range of populations addressed by the phrase means that the phrase appears consistently
over the century of the Turkish Republic's history, emerging as a kind of
uniform, ahistorical category that nevertheless folds a variety of historical particularities into its purview.

Rhetorical analysis of the minority question might make use of a
number of classical rhetorical concepts that have gained new life in contemporary political theory, most prominently metonymy. For political
theorists such as Ernesto Laclau, metonymy creates "relations of equivalence" between differently situated Others and the state, making it a
useful tool for constructing the people of contemporary populism.[5] But
metonymy, like the phrase "the minority question" itself, harbors its own
commitments to specific forms of history, and metonymy as an abstract
theoretical figure assumes a suspect relationship to temporality generally. As with any theoretical concept, metonymy is a historical construction that appears in the guise of the universal in the realm of abstract
theory, thus eliding its own historical construction. Showing the metonymic function of the phrase "the minority question" serves to doubly
displace historical consideration of the phrase, substituting metonymy's
elisions of history for those that constitute the minority question.

In this essay, I specify metonymy's historical forms vis-à-vis
the minority question. Beginning with an outline of the theoretical

commitments of a decolonial rhetorical history, I then consider some of the historical particularities of the minority question in Turkey. The figural dynamics of this phrase indicate some of the tangled layers of historical thinking that produce knowledge within academic disciplines, knowledge about Europe's Others and knowledge about the Others of the Turkish state. The schematic analysis of the minority question in Turkey included here gestures to the possibilities of decolonial rhetorical histories, where historical investigations ask questions of history itself rather than taking historical forms of knowing for granted. I then conclude with a sketch of the comparative possibilities and analytic processes of a decolonial rhetorical history.

Commitments of a Decolonial Rhetorical History

Critiques of rhetorical methods are neither new in rhetorical studies nor unique to decolonial approaches to rhetorical history. As Lisa A. Flores argues, in the mid-1990s a number of rhetorical scholars began to advocate for very different critical approaches to rhetorical methods, especially as these methods attempted to make sense of race and cultural difference. A fundamental argument of the work of these critical scholars contended that the analytic tools of rhetorical criticism cannot be implemented uncritically to make sense of race and cultural difference.[6] Eric King Watts similarly contends that "voice" in rhetorical scholarship became a re/presentation (perhaps almost a euphemism) of the marginalized speaker and that the concept helped eliminate the possibility of actually hearing the marginalized by speaking over them.[7] Because voice comes to rhetorical scholarship in this already reordered, interpreted, and recognizable form, the tools of rhetorical analysis would perform a second-order violence of misrecognition as they interpret a marginalized other already rearranged by norms of recognition. Along with Raka Shome's outline of a postcolonial critique of the rhetorical canon and its methods in her widely cited "Postcolonial Interventions in the Rhetorical Canon,"[8] numerous scholars around the discipline began articulating necessary fundamental revisions to rhetorical critical methods and questioning the applicability of a rhetorical canon that privileges the United States, Europe, and ancient Greece.

Many of these concerns remain paramount in contemporary critical approaches to rhetorical criticism. Karma R. Chávez interrogates some of the discipline's foundational concepts, like citizenship and public, that smuggle normative "ways of knowing and being" into the structure of analysis.[9] Jessica Enoch and many others argue against the "additive" model of diversifying the discipline, which substitutes a proliferation of different cases (more genders, more races, more places) for a meaning-ful critique of the methods and theoretical foundations of rhetorical criti-cism.[10] Extending this argument, Sara Baugh-Harris and Darrel Wanzer-Serrano critique projects of canonization writ large because these must always revert to logics of universalization that have been the mechanism for reproducing white normativity.[11] Issues of method and canon also an-imate Charles Morris's broad critique of public address and historiogra-phy, both of which operate as "regime[s] of the normal" that structure recognition of/in the past through lenses of "sexual normalcy."[12] These articulations make clear the complicity of disciplinary structures and presumptions in the logics of colonialism, white supremacy, sexual and gender normativity, and other forms of oppression. Among their brutali-ties and violence, colonialism and white supremacy have built epistemic orders and disciplines of knowledge to sustain and justify their activity, and contemporary rhetorical studies scholarship is no exception to this heritage.

These critical approaches to rhetorical theory and method also ani-mate studies of rhetorical history. In an essay in this volume's predeces-sor, *Doing Rhetorical History*, E. Culpepper Clark and Raymie E. McKer-row argue that history is a "selective remembering to validate thought and action," and as such, it should be treated as a form of argumenta-tion.[13] Their perspective recognizes that elements like narrative form structure the legitimacy and recognizability of a collection of events as history, but Clark and McKerrow also insist that history is "incapable of being de-rhetoricized," as history has no existence outside its argumen-tative form.[14] For Michelle Ballif, history's rhetorical character means that "to write *any history* (of rhetoric) demands 'systematic exclusions' of figures, of events, of artifacts, of whatever cannot be accounted for or synthesized by the historical narrative."[15] The aspiration to ever-larger and more complete historical totality is therefore a chimera, and the rhe-torical historian's task is to think beyond the "values of re/presentation and rules of cognition that govern our historiographical practices."[16] This "thinking beyond" does not attempt to "say the unsayable, but says that it cannot say."[17] The limits of representation in historiography, the neces-sary constitution of power and authority in historical thinking, and the normative effect of historical methods all occupy critical studies of rhe-torical history.[18]

Postcolonial and decolonial theory offer an avenue for simultane-ously addressing (1) issues of method with regard to the objects of rhe-torical theory and (2) the issue of the nature and function of history. Geoff Bennington and Robert Young say of the project of structuralism that it "addressed questions *to* history even as it tended to repress the question *of* history."[19] If rhetorical scholars are interested in the problems of method, theory, concepts, canon, tradition, and historical writing as outlined above, I think it is imperative to avoid making these problems into questions addressed "*to* history" and rather to attach these problems to "the question *of* history" in rhetorical history. That is, we should not only ask what representational, narrative, or rhetorical form gives authority *to* "history" but also what "forms of sequence and succession" are inherent in history as a concept.[20] The question *of* history foregrounds the way that chronology transforms into teleology; it attends to presumptions of continuity and causation, and it requires attention to the conditions in the present by which we *recognize* both subjects and objects of historical investigation. The question *of* history dwells on the idea that a concept of history is itself historical and simultaneously foundational to our perception of time. Finally, the question *of* history attends to the way forms of historical thinking are imported in a variety of analytic concepts.

Much of my articulation of "the question *of* history" here develops from Foucault's language in *The Archaeology of Knowledge*. As Robert J. C. Young argues in *White Mythologies*, Foucault's critical account of history and knowledge was always specifically a critical account of the hegemony of Western European history and knowledge, and Foucault should therefore be read in connection with the critical goals of decolonial scholarship.[21] I take up Foucault's critical account of history as I hear it resonating with the demands of theorists like Chakrabarty and Gayatri Spivak, even when Foucault himself is the direct target of criticism for Spivak. For Chakrabarty, "reason colludes with the logic of historicist thought" to produce modernity's "others"—gendered, raced, marginalized, and oppressed in the present.[22] Against this collusion, Chakrabarty asks us "to seek out relentlessly this connection between violence and idealism that lies at the heart of the process by which narratives of citizenship and modernity come to find a natural home in 'history.'"[23] Where Foucault's focus at the time of *The Archaeology of Knowledge* was to redirect historical investigation toward the discontinuities and shifting epistemic structures that produce different disciplines of knowledge—like history—in modernity, Foucault's project shifted toward the intimate connection of disciplines of knowledge with power in a way that seems to reflect Chakrabarty's concerns with history and modernity. "The question *of* history" posed in this chapter reflects the imperatives circulating in both Chakrabarty and Foucault.

Insofar as I link Foucault's critique of history to a decolonial project, this must also be a Foucault filtered through Spivak's masterful critique in "Can the Subaltern Speak?" Spivak's primary criticism of Foucault is that he uncritically blends together two senses of representation in his historical studies, "representation as 'speaking for,' as in politics, and representation as 're-presentation,' as in art or philosophy."[24] Foucault's histories primarily focus on radical historical breaks in epistemes or discursive forms, requiring him to talk about forms of knowledge radically other to modern Europe. By conflating two senses of representation in his work, he constitutes this Other while presuming it speaks transparently through his work in its own voice, rather than recognizing that he is "speaking for." For Spivak, the authority of Foucault's work is built on this slippage between "speaking for" and "letting speak" that can perform the colonial silencing of the Other that his work seeks to challenge. Foucault refuses to entertain a "constitutive contradiction" between these two forms of representation in the institutions he analyzes and in which he is situated, making him likely to reproduce the "epistemic violence" he so critically maps in his histories.[25] A decolonial rhetorical history building on Foucault must attend to the representational practices structuring rhetorical history because colonialism was always a project of representation in addition to exploitation.[26]

Decolonial methods in rhetorical history promise an acknowledgment that historical writing is nontotalizable. The struggle is not for better totalization, as critiques of "hearing more voices" and additive models of canons and disciplinary methods have shown. But acknowledging that our histories are partial too often reproduces problematic theories of history rather than achieving a nontotalizing historical writing. Rhetorical historians must attend to the mechanisms where distinctions between the historical and the Other of history are maintained, *both* in historical artifacts *and* in the methodological and theoretical tools of academics. Chávez's critique of citizenship as a disciplinary concept discussed above can point the way to this decolonial rhetorical history: The citizen is a historical being that constitutes ahistorical others in vernacular use, *and* it is a critical concept that imports its vernacular ahistorical exclusions into scholarship. Furthermore, decolonial rhetorical history, whether focused on a particular case as a partial history or on a longer historical scope of analysis as Hawhee and Olson advocate, must remember that history frequently presumes a continuity that quickly becomes teleology and substitutes out the nuance of the particular for the familiar of universal History.[27] History operates hegemonically, and decolonial rhetorical history must sift through its myriad articulations of knowledge.

The Minority Question and History in Turkey

In modern Turkish history, since the end of World War I, the term *minority* has encapsulated a variety of legal, political, and social connotations. After World War I, the League of Nations attempted to protect minority rights globally through frameworks known as "The Minority Treaties." In Turkey, these treaties specified groups whose rights would be guaranteed by separate Western European countries or the United States, primarily defining these groups by religious difference—Jews and Christians, for instance, would be guaranteed rights in the new post-Ottoman state. This grouping consolidated numerous ethnic groups into single minority units defined by religious categories—Armenians, Greeks, and Russian Orthodox Christians, for example, all became "Christians"—and completely ignored some ethnic minority groups such as Kurds and Alevis by lumping all Muslims together under the Sunni state. In contemporary Turkey, the term *minority* continues to circulate as a kind of metonymy for myriad ethnic and religious groups, such that contemporary Turkish newspapers continue to refer to "the minority question" in discussing Kurds (primarily now conceived as an ethnic group), Alevi Turks (primarily conceived as a Muslim religious group distinct from Sunni Islam), and Armenians (a religious and ethnic group). All of these groups pose distinct minority questions, but "the minority question" circulates in Turkey as an interchangeable reference to all of these groups.[28]

One way to begin to understand the function of "the minority question" as a phrase in Turkey is to locate the way in which the minority in the question operates as a metonymy. In the lexicon of classical rhetoric, metonymy is a substitution of one concept for a related concept, such as the substitution of heart for emotions.[29] In Turkey, the concept minority operates as a metonymy because it situates all possible ethnic, religious, and other marginalized groups as equivalent to one another in some way (and thus substitutable for one another). Following Laclau's work, "the minority" as metonymy creates a chain of equivalence between various Others by positioning them in a stable relationship to the Turkish state.[30] When speaking of a specific ethnic or religious group, use of such phrases as "the minority question" or "the minority problem" or "the minority issue" in newspaper headlines and public speeches creates a substitution of a single Other for any one of the equivalent Others in their shared relationship to the Turkish state. The classical lexicon as filtered through contemporary political theory offers a compelling (and recognizable) account of this question in Turkish history.

But there is more to "the minority question" as a phrase that the formal structure of minority-as-metonymy leaves out. In the nineteenth century, the Ottoman Empire faced increasing foreign debts, lost a number of wars of national independence that reduced its territory, and began to be thought of as "the sick man of Europe."[31] In this context, European powers began to debate an issue euphemistically referred to as the Eastern question or the Eastern problem, which designated at least two major political issues: first, the European countries sought to profit and gain territory and resources from the vulnerable Ottoman Empire without creating a major war; and second, in the twentieth century the phrases referred to the Armenian genocide after World War I. In this sense, the Ottoman Empire was Europe's Eastern problem, and the Armenian genocide was the Ottoman Empire's (and Europe's) Eastern problem. Apart from these varied definitions of the Eastern problem in relation to the Ottoman Empire, however, the most acute Eastern problem of twentieth century Europe was "the Jewish question," ostensibly beginning as a question of assimilation and ending in the Holocaust. To speak of the minority question in contemporary Turkey implies this varied history as well, and all that goes with it—the continued denial of the Armenian genocide by the Turkish state, comparisons between the Armenian genocide and the Holocaust, a continued antipathy to European opportunism at Turkey's expense, and an ongoing anxiety about the Europeanness of Turkey. The minority question, the Eastern question, and the Jewish question bear a colloquial resemblance to one another that contains and recirculates this historical knowledge in a way that exceeds the formal structure of metonymy.

In this case, applying metonymy as an analytic concept to explain the phrase "the minority question" in Turkey flattens the historical depth contained in the phrase, even as it articulates part of the phrase's function. This flattening results from the relationship between figure forms, language, and history. As Paul de Man argues, rhetorical studies in the eighteenth and nineteenth centuries increasingly emphasized the activities of cataloguing tropes and naming devices, constituting the whole of rhetoric as "ornament" subjugated to the truth of the symbol.[32] For de Man, this history described language as inherently literal and situated figures as strategies for deviating from the norm. Departing from de Man, we can also think of this history of rhetoric as partly responsible for our ability to imagine rhetorical figures as transportable across unrelated and grammatically diverse languages (like Turkish, English, or ancient Greek). When figures become separated from language, they also become ahistorical, theoretical universals, forms with names like metaphor, metonymy, and synecdoche. As theoretical universals, classical rhetorical figures reside outside of temporality and secure for themselves a position of static objectivity. Although a figure form such as metonymy may be able to generate productive analyses of political phenomena like the minority question, these analyses will be partial, necessarily obfuscating historical particularity and depth that does not fit the objective perspective and universal form of the figure.

To be skeptical of metonymy's normative function in analysis does not necessarily demonstrate identifiable cultural values transported by metonymy into analysis. In this case, however, the ahistorical *status* presumed by metonymy that flattens the historical depth of the minority question mirrors Spivak's concerns about representing the Other as well as Chakrabarty's explanation of how European history becomes universal. Here, metonymy masquerades as a *universal* theoretical form to be applied in analysis of language use, when it actually includes a *particular* conception of history as tracing contiguity between elements. The relatedness of different marginalized populations in Turkey is a function of their unique constitution as Other by the Turkish state and its definition of citizenship, and the metonymic connection of different marginalized populations therefore reinforces that Turkish state discourse at the expense of any historical variation between those populations. The historical variation is especially palpable when comparing Alevi Turks, who have periodically been the target of mob violence in major cities like Istanbul, and Kurds, who have been targeted by the Turkish military itself in massive attacks (e.g., aerial bombardment, razing villages, and conventional warfare) in rural areas and even some cities in the southeast of the country. The minority question consistently names an unmoving, ahistorical constitutive paradox of the Turkish state, and the contiguity presumed by metonymy does not admit historical variation across populations, making the phrase operate as a silencing of the Other that substitutes state-centered history for difference.

Although a history of the minority question in Turkey needs to attend to the question's differential material effects, it must also account for specific ways of policing the form of the phrase that reinforces Turkish state discourse. One instance of this policing appeared in 2005 in the wake of an interview given to the German-language Swiss periodical *Das Magazin* by Orhan Pamuk, one of Turkey's most well-known and best-selling novelists. The interview primarily focused on political symbolism in Pamuk's 2002 novel, *Snow*, on its reception in Turkey, and on the challenges of Turkey's accession to the European Union.[33] Turkish media outlets circulated the interview as a single brief statement, however: "30,000

Kurds were killed here. And a million Armenians. And almost no one dares mention it. So I do."[34] Reaction to this statement was broadly critical, ranging from university professors denouncing the statement as "a great falsehood" to municipally organized book burnings to death threats sent to Pamuk.[35] Six months after the interview, prosecutors in Istanbul indicted Pamuk for his remarks under the ambiguous charges of "denigrating Turkishness" and insulting the Turkish military.[36] Although the charges were dropped on (very political) technical grounds shortly after the trial began, this variety of critical reactions to Pamuk's interview outlines broad policing and disciplinary mechanisms circulating around the minority question.[37]

Many of the policing mechanisms mobilized after Pamuk's statement reinforce both the Turkish state as the subject of historical teleology and the minority as its ahistorical, nonmodern Other. Despite the ambiguous language of Pamuk's statement, his connection of the death totals from the Armenian genocide in 1915 to the numbers of Kurds killed during the civil war in Turkey in the 1990s implies Turkish state culpability for both atrocities, narratives insistently challenged by the Turkish state. In the case of the Armenian genocide, Turkish official history understates the number of Armenian deaths by as much as a factor of ten, juxtaposing Armenian deaths after World War I to supposedly comparable numbers of Muslim deaths and framing the bloodshed as localized intercommunal violence.[38] In the case of Kurds killed in the 1990s in Turkey, Pamuk referenced official statistics from the Turkish state that are widely known within Turkey but that are widely understood to refer to a campaign of terror waged by the Kurdistan Workers' Party (PKK) against Turks and Kurds unsympathetic to the PKK.[39] In both cases, then, Turkish official history has segregated these episodes of Turkish state violence away from the continuity of the Turkish state, as this violence is not attributed to the state but instead to its Others. Pamuk's simple statement disrupts a historical teleology widely presumed in Turkey to be true.

In a number of reactions to Pamuk's statement, it is precisely the hierarchical order of Turkish official history in relation to its Others that is defended. For instance, one editorialist coined the term *black writer* (*kara yazar*) to describe Pamuk's moral character after the *Das Magazin* interview, arguing that Pamuk had "put his interior blackness (*karalık*) in the title of a book," referring to Pamuk's 1990 novel *The Black Book* (*Kara Kitap*).[40] The idea of Pamuk as a "black writer" is more than a pun on one of his book's titles, however. The term also references the concept of the black Turk (*kara Türk*), an epithet for poor, uneducated, religious, rural Turks, who are out of step with modern Turkey.[41] The black Turk concept also implies affinity with the 1920s euphemism for Kurds, who were known as "mountain Turks," a phrase that constituted the Kurdish population as future Turks plagued by the cultural backwardness and reactionary politics associated with religion.[42] If Pamuk's statement disrupts Turkish official history, it is possible to come to this history's defense by locating Pamuk as reactionary, out of step with modern Turkey, backward, a criminal, and a minority himself, or—at the opposite end of the spectrum—a European agent.[43] All of these positions exist apart from the chronology and teleology of the Turkish state, and they serve to defend a form of historical development as well as the narrative layered on top of that notion of history.

Thinking about the minority question in this way helps articulate how the minority marks a static conceptual position in Turkish republican nationalist ideology, but also how supposedly neutral theoretical concepts can reinforce this ideology. The minority certainly works as a formal metonymy: it creates relationships of equivalence between different ethnic and religious groups so that they can be substituted for one another in their subordinate relationship to the Turkish state. But the figural qualities of the minority question do not stop at the formal limits of metonymy. The term also performs and reproduces historical social norms by paralleling the structure of well-known phrases in Turkish history. At the analytic and vernacular levels, metonymy and the phrase "the minority question" traffic in historical commitments that must be interrogated in analysis. It is perhaps more productive to think of both the minority and the minority question as figures or tropes in their own right, figures that are socially and historically contingent, circulate norms of understanding in their performance, and uniquely mobilize and combine the representational maneuvers documented in the classical lexicon.[44] Treating these phrases as figures in their own right foregrounds the question *of* history and associated representational dynamics by avoiding the presumption that metonymy is the best name for the figural operation of these phrases. By attending to the possibility that metonymy and other theoretical universals enable the importation of universal conceptions of history, rhetorical historians can destabilize history's colonial impetus and map the layered different locations where theories of history appear and prestructure knowledge of the past.

Conclusion: Listening for Ahistorical Echoes

The preceding exploration of the minority question in Turkey begins from a desire to present the question *of* history within rhetorical analyses of past events, objects, and phenomena. Posing this question is intended to build new methodologies and make visible the limitations and commitments imposed on scholarly work by the practice of history itself. To push against these limitations and commitments even further, we might ask what comparisons are possible outside of the time *and geography* of history. As discussed above, one critical way that historical practice imposes limits on imagination is through presumptions about causation, contiguity, and teleology, but these presumptions also register limited geographies where causation, contiguity, or teleology could possibly be located. Tracing causation within Europe, for instance, might be easier than tracing transatlantic or global causation because the contiguity of geography within Europe aids the presumption of relation and causation between events. Historical causation can imply and be supported by geographical proximity, and the presumed relationship between geographical contiguity and historical causation can make global comparison difficult if not impossible.[45] Proceeding with an attention to the question *of* history, perhaps we should ask whether the preceding exploration of the minority question has any *ahistorical* echoes.

For well over a century in the United States, philosophers, politicians, civil leaders, and others debated a massive range of issues known as "the Negro question." In the late 1840s, the phrase referenced the mechanics of the end of slavery in the British Empire, especially in arguments between Thomas Carlyle and John Stuart Mill that were widely republished in the United States.[46] But the phrase also circulated through the Harlem Renaissance and in the civil rights movement, where it could reference anything from Reconstruction and reparations to American Marxism. In 1903, W. E. B. Du Bois simultaneously described and challenged the phrase's status as an independent rhetorical entity with his question: "How does it feel to be a problem?"[47] But the "Negro" question remained a powerful euphemism for the litany of manifestations of anti-Black racism, until, perhaps, the colorblind racism of the 1970s made the term "Negro" in the language of the question itself uncouth.[48]

The phrase "the Negro question" has a long historical life, but the phrase also demonstrates how history itself maintains status quo white supremacy. As Frank B. Wilderson III argues, following Frantz Fanon and others, the violence directed at Black bodies in history has no analog among living beings, and this violence "continually repositions the Black as a void of historical movement" by turning "the African into a thing."[49] For Calvin L. Warren, the ahistorical nonbeing of Blackness makes the "Negro" question into an unresolvable and foundational ontological question rather than a kind of policy query.[50] The internal contradiction of the question is embodied by the concept of the "free Black," since "['Black'] has something like existence but no recourse to the unfolding of Being or the revelation of its withdrawal" and therefore stands in stark tension with the idea of freedom of beings.[51] In the phrase "the Negro question," then, history itself is constitutive of white supremacy as Black people are figured in the question as nonhistorical objects, unchanging phenomena, the kind of "problem" Du Bois asked about. The question *of* history emerges in the "Negro" question as the constitutive function of anti-Black racism and white supremacy.

The nonhistorical form of Blackness produced by the "Negro" question also results from a range of simultaneous rhetorical operations including euphemism, synecdoche, and perhaps even polyptoton, a form of repetition that produces "the impression that a consistent phenomenon is being discussed consistently."[52] The euphemistic character of the phrase is clear from the simple juxtaposition of the neutral word *question* with the brutalities that it references. This euphemism separates the recurring, constant violence of anti-Black racism from the arena of political debate in which the phrase circulates. From there, the question also operates as a synecdoche in any specific instance by focusing on a single issue (economic equality in the 1960s, for instance) as a part of the whole—a whole that might be variously labeled "the legacy of slavery" or "foundational and recurrent antiblack racism," but the naming of this "whole" is partly foreclosed by the euphemism. The synecdoche is perhaps only possible after the repetitive operation of polyptoton. In this case, the existence of the "Negro" question as a consistent whole over more than a century might be the simple product of repetition across time but without historical development (polyptoton), and therefore, the possibility of synecdoche depends on this previous figural operation. Each of these figural operations reproduces the nonhistorical nature of Blackness: euphemism writes over dehistoricizing violence, and synecdoche emerges from an ahistorical repetition (polyptoton) to recirculate the question *inside* history but disconnected from its previous instances. The question operates beyond the formal contours of a single figure.

In many ways, then, the figural mechanics of the phrase "the Negro question" in the United States resemble the layered figuration within the minority question in Turkey, despite their very different locations in time and geography. The minority question marks an ahistorical position within the Republican nationalist frame in Turkey, and the "Negro" question marks a similar position within the American white supremacist frame. These historical frames produce their Others located outside of the particularities of each history (nonmodern, backward, and inhuman are only some variations on the nonhistorical Other), and comparing across histories can help destabilize the presumed universality of history. If we hear the echoes of these questions in one another, might we infer that something comparable has happened across similar governmental forms differently located in time, geography, and global power? The parallel linguistic/figural form of these questions speaks to the possibilities of comparative rhetorical work that takes on history as it is constituted by colonial violence, racism, and erasures of being.

The task of newly theorizing history itself is a requisite of decolonial rhetorical history. We must begin from the presumption that theories of history are constituted in practice, that rhetorical phenomena themselves simultaneously constitute and rely on forms of sequence, succession, continuity, contiguity, causation, and teleology. A specific—rather than universal—combination of these interrelated temporal concepts grounds rhetorical action, theories of history that are already presumed and ground in rhetorical action. As this chapter indicates, different concepts of history produce and rely on different *ahistorical* Others, whether that is the ambiguous and flexible minority in Turkey or Black in the United States. As such, presumptions about what moves through time and how are at the very heart of the circulation of power. Finally, presumptions of historical form may attend the theoretical concepts we bring to analysis, as the ahistorical vacuum of theory is a space of post-Enlightenment Europe. A decolonial rhetorical history must investigate the theories of history presumed in rhetorical action, the ahistorical Others presumed in these forms of history, and the structure of history that can be layered on top of rhetorical action in the application of theoretical concepts. These questions *of* history must be asked anew in each instance, as a uniform answer only emerges when history is imagined as total.

Notes

1. See, for instance, Christa J. Olson and René Agustín De los Santos, eds., "La Idea de la Retórica Americana/The Idea of American Rhetoric," *Rhetoric Society Quarterly* 45, no. 3 (2015): 193–277; LuMing Mao, ed., "Comparative Rhetoric," *Rhetoric Society Quarterly* 43, no. 3 (2013): 209–309; and Arabella Lyon and Lester C. Olson, eds., "Human Rights Rhetoric: Traditions of Testifying and Witnessing," *Rhetoric Society Quarterly* 41, no. 3 (2011): 203–93.

2. Dipesh Chakrabarty, *Provincializing Europe: Postcolonial Thought and Historical Difference* (Princeton, NJ: Princeton University Press, 2008), 29–30.

3. Orientalism refers to a Western style of thought and representation of the Middle East, Near East, and Far East that reflects and reproduces European stereotypes, constructing the "Orient" as an object of knowledge that the West can dominate, restructure, and have authority over. For Edward Said, the Orient is

"almost a European invention" that helps to define Europe by standing in as Europe's contrasting image. See Said, *Orientalism* (New York: Vintage Books, 1994), 1. Turkey and the Ottoman Empire have historically had acute critical awareness of these European representations, developing policies and strategies to explicitly combat them since at least the invention of photography. Meltem Ahıska outlines a kind of historical anxiety of (mis)representation in Turkey through which Turkey develops counterrepresentations of the West from a perspective of "having been Orientalized," a process she calls "Occidentalism." See Ahıska, "Occidentalism: The Historical Fantasy of the Modern," *South Atlantic Quarterly* 102, no. 2–3 (2003): 351–79.

4. The minority question resembles a historical phenomenon that itself "argues from history," in Zarefsky's sense. See David Zarefsky, "Four Senses of Rhetorical History," in Turner, *Doing Rhetorical History*, 28.

5. Ernesto Laclau, *On Populist Reason* (New York: Verso, 2005), 73–74, 109–10.

6. Lisa A. Flores, "Between Abundance and Marginalization: The Imperative of Racial Rhetorical Criticism," *Review of Communication* 16, no. 1 (2016): 9–10. Among the essays she mentions as "turning point" pieces in this critique of methods are Kent A. Ono and John M. Sloop, "The Critique of Vernacular Discourse," *Communication Monographs* 62, no. 1 (1995): 19–46; and Thomas K. Nakayama, "Show/Down Time: 'Race,' Gender, Sexuality, and Popular Culture," *Critical Studies in Mass Communication* 11, no. 2 (1994): 162–79.

7. Eric King Watts, "'Voice' and 'Voicelessness' in Rhetorical Studies," *Quarterly Journal of Speech* 87, no. 2 (2001): 182–83.

8. Raka Shome, "Postcolonial Interventions in the Rhetorical Canon: An 'Other' View," *Communication Theory* 6, no. 1 (1996): 40–59.

9. Karma R. Chávez, "Beyond Inclusion: Rethinking Rhetoric's Historical Narrative," *Quarterly Journal of Speech* 101, no. 1 (2015): 163.

10. Jessica Enoch, "Releasing Hold: Feminist Historiography without the Tradition," in *Theorizing Histories of Rhetoric*, ed. Michelle Ballif (Carbondale: Southern Illinois University Press, 2013), 58–73. See also Karrieann Soto Vega and Karma R. Chávez, "Latinx Rhetoric and Intersectionality in Racial Rhetorical Criticism," *Communication and Critical/Cultural Studies* 15, no. 4 (2018): 319–25; Martin Law and Lisa M. Corrigan, "On White-Speak and Gatekeeping: or, What Good Are the Greeks?" *Communication and Critical/Cultural Studies*, 15, no. 4 (2018): 326–30; and Shome, "Postcolonial Interventions."

11. Sara Baugh-Harris and Darrel Wanzer-Serrano, "Against Canon: Engaging the Imperative of Race in Rhetoric," *Communication and Critical/Cultural Studies* 15, no. 4 (2018), 337.

12. Charles E. Morris III, "Introduction: Portrait of a Queer Rhetorical/ Historical Critic," in *Queering Public Address: Sexualities in American Historical*

Discourse, ed. Charles E. Morris III (Columbia: University of South Carolina Press, 2007), 7, 12.

13. E. Culpepper Clark and Raymie E. McKerrow, "The Rhetorical Construction of History," in Turner, *Doing Rhetorical History*, 35.

14. Clark and McKerrow, "Rhetorical Construction," 39. See also Hayden White, "The Value of Narrativity in the Representation of Reality," *Critical Inquiry* 7, no. 1 (1980): 5–27; and Hayden White, *Metahistory: The Historical Imagination in Nineteenth-Century Europe* (Baltimore: Johns Hopkins University Press, 1973), 1–42.

15. Michelle Ballif, "Introduction," in Ballif, *Theorizing Histories of Rhetoric*, 3 (original emphasis).

16. Ballif, "Introduction," 6.

17. Ballif, "Introduction," 7 (quoting Lyotard).

18. See also LuMing Mao, "Writing the Other into Histories of Rhetorics: Theorizing the Art of Recontextualization," in Ballif, *Theorizing Histories of Rhetoric*, 41–57. Many of the "Octolog" roundtables held decennially at the Conference on College Composition and Communication and reprinted in *Rhetoric Review* survey similar themes. See, for instance, Lois Agnew et al., "Octolog III: The Politics of Historiography in 2010," *Rhetoric Review* 30, no. 2 (2011): 109–54.

19. Geoff Bennington and Robert Young, "Introduction: Posing the Question," in *Post-Structuralism and the Question of History*, ed. Derek Attridge, Geoff Bennington, and Robert Young (New York: Cambridge University Press, 1987), 3.

20. Michel Foucault, *The Archaeology of Knowledge and The Discourse on Language*, trans. A. M. Sheridan Smith (New York: Harper Colophon, 1976), 169.

21. Robert J. C. Young, *White Mythologies: Writing History and the West*, 2nd ed. (New York: Routledge, 2004), 49–50.

22. Chakrabarty, *Provincializing Europe*, 238. Throughout this essay I primarily use the term *decolonial* rather than the term *postcolonial* to denote a swath of intellectual and political commitments. Darrel Allan Wanzer, following Walter Mignolo, argues that rhetorical scholars should pursue decolonial as opposed to postcolonial rhetorics since the former aim at delinking thought from modernity and its epistemological frameworks, specifically capitalism. See Wanzer, "Delinking Rhetoric, or Revisiting McGee's Fragmentation Thesis through Decoloniality," *Rhetoric & Public Affairs* 15, no. 4 (2012): 647–58; and Mignolo, *The Darker Side of Western Modernity: Global Futures, Decolonial Options* (Durham, NC: Duke University Press, 2011). Yet a primary argument of Chakrabarty's essay in *Provincializing Europe*, "Postcoloniality and the Artifice of History," is that Marx yokes the universal concept of "capital" to the concept of "history" in a way that makes history "theoretically knowable" and universalizes European history worldwide (Chakrabarty, *Provincializing Europe*, 30). Chakrabarty's purpose is to critique this epistemological proposition in a way that seems to me consonant

with the commitments that Wanzer outlines. I use the term *decolonial* to follow a growing convention in rhetorical studies as well as to emphasize a politics associated with that term, even though I am less convinced of a significant difference between postcolonial and decolonial projects.

23. Chakrabarty, *Provincializing Europe*, 45.

24. Gayatri Spivak, "Can the Subaltern Speak?" in *Marxism and the Interpretation of Culture*, ed. Cary Nelson and Lawrence Grossberg (Champaign: University of Illinois Press, 1988), 275.

25. Spivak, "Can the Subaltern Speak?," 274, 281.

26. A decolonial analysis of history that references Foucault's critiques of history must read Foucault through these criticisms that rightly undermine his authority in academic work. My references here to Foucault attempt to build on Chakrabarty's argument that "provincializing Europe cannot ever be a project of shunning European thought" (Chakrabarty, *Provincializing Europe*, 255).

27. Chakrabarty, *Provincializing Europe*, 30. See also Etienne Balibar, "Ideas of Europe: Civilization and Constitution," *Iris: European Journal of Philosophy & Public Debate* 1, no. 1 (2009): 3–17. Debra Hawhee and Christa J. Olson advocate a return to broader historical investigation that combines synchronic and diachronic approaches to history but that appears at times to presume continuity as an organizing principle. See Debra Hawhee and Christa J. Olson, "Pan-Historiography: The Challenges of Writing History across Time and Space," in Ballif, *Theorizing Histories of Rhetoric*, 93, 96.

28. This consideration of the phrase "the minority question" in Turkey is schematic for the purpose of focusing more on the concept of history rather than elaborating a complete case study. For further analysis of the idea of the minority in Turkey, see Matthew deTar, *Figures That Speak: The Vocabulary of Turkish Nationalism* (Syracuse, NY: Syracuse University Press, 2021).

29. For this example, see Kenneth Burke, "Four Master Tropes," in *A Grammar of Motives* (Berkeley: University of California Press, 1969), 506. Burke also describes metonymy as a substitution by reduction (the abstract emotions are reduced to the material heart). Political theories of metonymy do not widely emphasize the reductive function of metonymy, and Laclau's primary emphasis is on metonymy as "contiguity."

30. Laclau, *On Populist Reason*, 73–74, 77–83.

31. For more on the history of this phrase, see Dimitris Livanios, "The 'Sick Man' Paradox: History, Rhetoric, and the 'European Character' of Turkey," *Journal of Southern Europe and the Balkans*, vol. 8, no. 3 (December 2006): 299–300.

32. Paul de Man, *The Rhetoric of Romanticism* (New York: Columbia University Press, 1984). For a longer view of this argument about figures in the history of rhetoric, see Jeanne Fahnestock, *Rhetorical Figures in Science* (New York: Oxford University Press, 1999).

33. Peer Teuwsen, "'Der meistgehasste Türke'" (The most hated Turk), *Das Magazin*, February 5, 2005. *Das Magazin* is a weekly insert in three high-circulation newspapers in Switzerland and is somewhat similar in content and aesthetic to the *New York Times Magazine*.

34. İsmail Erel, "'Kimse söylemiyor, bari ben söyleyeyim'" (Nobody says it, at least I say it), *Hürriyet*, February 9, 2005, http://webarsiv.hurriyet.com.tr/2005/02/09/596844.asp. This article is a Turkish translation of excerpts of the interview. Translations of this brief statement varied in important ways in newspapers in Turkey, and this translation is my own, based on this *Hürriyet* translation of the excerpted interview.

35. Alper Uruş, "1 milyon Ermeni'yi ve 30 bin Kürt'ü kestik mi?" (Did we slaughter 1 million Armenians and 30 thousand Kurds?), *Vatan*, February 9, 2005, http://haber.gazetevatan.com/Haber/46650/1/Gundem; Murat Belge, "'Love Me, or Leave Me?': The Strange Case of Orhan Pamuk," October 17, 2005, https://www.opendemocracy.net; Murat İri and H. Esra Arcan, "The Orhan Pamuk Case: How Mainstream Turkish Media Framed His Freedom of Speech," *Sosyal Bilimler Dergisi* 18 (2007): 17–24.

36. Maureen Freely, "Why They Killed Hrant Dink," *Index on Censorship* 36, no. 2 (2007): 16. Freely (17) states that in 2005–6, there were nearly eighty prosecutions under Article 301. Other prominent figures indicted under the article include Elif Şafak (author), Hrant Dink (Turkish-Armenian scholar), Perihan Mağden (Turkish columnist for the *Taraf* daily), and most surprisingly, Joost Lagendijk, the Dutch chairman of the EU-Turkey Joint Parliamentary Committee. See Bülent Algan, "The Brand New Version of Article 301 of Turkish Penal Code and the Future of Freedom of Expression Cases in Turkey," *German Law Journal* 9, no. 12 (2008): 2238.

37. In December 2005, the court suspended proceedings due to constitutional changes implemented in June 2005, which was between the time of Pamuk's statement (February) and the time of his indictment (August). The law required Turkey's minister of justice to approve proceedings under the old law. The minister denied this approval in the run-up to an EU review of Turkey's entire justice system as part of EU Accession negotiations. See Sebnem Arsu, "Court Drops Charges against Author for 'Insulting' Turkey," *New York Times*, January 23, 2006, https://www.nytimes.com.

38. This narrative is on gruesome display in the Armenian Question room of the Istanbul Military Museum. Muslim civilians suffered approximately 5 percent of the casualties of Armenians in Anatolia during 1915 to 1920. See Ronald Grigor Suny and Fatma Müge Göçek, "Introduction: Leaving It to the Historians," in *A Question of Genocide: Armenians and Turks at the End of the Ottoman Empire*, ed. Ronald Grigor Suny, Fatma Müge Göçek, and Norman Naimark (New York: Oxford University Press, 2011).

39. Belge, "'Love Me, or Leave Me?'"

40. Fatih Altaylı, "Kara yazar" (Black writer), *Hürriyet*, February 11, 2005.

41. M. Hakan Yavuz, "Cleansing Islam from the Public Sphere," *Journal of International Affairs* 54, no. 1 (2000): 22; Mücahit Bilici, "Black Turks, White Turks: On the Three Requirements of Turkish Citizenship," *Insight Turkey* 11, no. 3 (2009): 23.

42. E. Fuat Keyman, "Articulating Citizenship and Identity: The 'Kurdish Question' in Turkey," in *Citizenship in a Global World: European Questions and Turkish Experiences*, ed. E. Fuat Keyman and Ahmet İçduygu (New York: Routledge, 2005), 277; Mesut Yeğen, "The Kurdish Question in Turkey: Denial to Recognition," in *Nationalisms and Politics in Turkey: Political Islam, Kemalism and the Kurdish Issue*, ed. Marlies Casier and Joost Jongerden (New York: Routledge, 2011), 71; Bilici, "Black Turks, White Turks," 30.

43. "Ermeniler kahraman ilan etti" (Armenians declare a hero), *Hürriyet*, February 27, 2005; Ardıç Aytalar, "Sözlerine öfke" (His words of rage), *Hürriyet*, February 15, 2005, http://hurarsiv.hurriyet.com.tr/goster/ShowNew. aspx?id=296710. Although this essay focuses on the Turkish state's power over history, Turkey is also constituted as the Other to Europe in ways that leave it outside European history, a fact that is the topic of public discourse in Turkey (including in this criticism of Pamuk). See Matthew deTar, "A Confluence of Margins," *Departures in Critical Qualitative Research* 8, no. 2 (2019): 1–7.

44. The circulation of social norms in performance is theorized in Judith Butler, *Frames of War: When Is Life Grievable?* (New York: Verso, 2010), 3–4; and Judith Butler, *Undoing Gender* (New York: Routledge, 2004), 40–56.

45. A notable exception might be the tricontinental movement. Anne Garland Mahler, *From the Tricontinental to the Global South: Race, Radicalism, and Transnational Solidarity* (Durham, NC: Duke University Press, 2018).

46. David Theo Goldberg, "Liberalisms's Limits: Carlyle and Mill on 'The Negro Question,'" in *Philosophers on Race: Critical Essays*, ed. Julie K. Ward and Tommy L. Lott (Malden, MA: Blackwell Publishers, 2002), 145–66. As Goldberg notes, Mill's writing on "the woman question" also marks and reproduces limits to egalitarianism in liberalism (166).

47. W. E. B. Du Bois, *The Souls of Black Folk*, ed. Henry Louis Gates Jr. (New York: Oxford University Press, 2007), 2.

48. See Eduardo Bonilla-Silva, *Racism without Racists: Colorblind Racism and the Persistence of Racial Inequality in America*, 5th ed. (New York: Rowman & Littlefield, 2018).

49. Frank B. Wilderson III, *Red, White, & Black: Cinema and the Structure of U.S. Antagonisms* (Durham, NC: Duke University Press, 2010), 38.

50. Calvin L. Warren, *Ontological Terror: Blackness, Nihilism, and Emancipation* (Durham, NC: Duke University Press, 2018), 16. See also Lisa M. Corrigan,

"Decolonizing Philosophy and Rhetoric: Dispatches from the Undercommons," *Philosophy and Rhetoric* 52, no. 2 (2019): 181.

51. Warren, *Ontological Terror*, 15.

52. This somewhat idiosyncratic definition of polyptoton belongs to Fahnestock, *Rhetorical Figures in Science*, x.

10

Forgetting or Remembering the Nation?

Amnesic Rhetoric and Circulation of the Past

Chandra A. Maldonado

At a 2018 academic conference I met a man who loved Theodore Roosevelt and was an avid collector of Roosevelt political memorabilia. Very excited about my work on Roosevelt, he proceeded to tell me about his collection as he reminisced about old newspaper stories he had gathered in his personal archive. He was particularly taken by the well-known story about Roosevelt getting shot during a campaign trail address during his third presidential term and refusing to go to the hospital until after he had finished his speech. As legend has it, Roosevelt's life was saved due to the lodging of the bullet, just mere inches away from his heart, in his folded-up speech and his eyeglass case. Soon after the end of the conference, I received an email from my new colleague with a few links to images of his massive collection as well as contact information for one of his colleagues, a local memorabilia collector. This connection would lead me to other Roosevelt enthusiasts in a social media group where members post photos of the latest additions to their collections. Here, many artifacts visually represent a multitude of decades in US politics, including the rise of the resulting Bull Moose Party after the failed assassination attempt on Roosevelt and his unsuccessful run for the Republican nomination in the 1912 presidential election.

As we see in this example, memory circulates not only through various forms of material visual culture but also through the stories shared among people such as that of the failed assassination attempt. Such narratives tend to frame and contextualize people's experiences within a rhetorical continuum referencing common touchstones and dominant stories within the shared memories. Looking back on my brief encounter with this fellow Roosevelt enthusiast, it is clear to me that even outside of the typical (material) structures of public commemorative spaces, the narratives of people and everyday chance encounters facilitate the *flow of memory* within the networks of public dialogue.[1] These networks of communication determine how and to what extent we embrace (or confront) our nation's past. I identify this flow as a rhetorical act of continuity because the recalling of a past event, or in this case collectively remembering the very masculine persona of a well-known public figure in our nation's political history, relies on the interconnections among a material culture and the narratives that help us remember.

In the case of reframing rhetorical history, this act of continuity manifests within a nexus of experiences that rhetorically invoke, reclaim, and restore a past. To a certain extent, these experiences can affect the ways in which we embrace or reject identity—regardless of the origins of the narratives or the context in which we recall them. For example, if we consider the term "progressivism" in our contemporary political moment, its current usage stresses a force to promote political reform. Yet the original (and populist) context can be traced back to Roosevelt, who was considered to be the first progressive in American politics because of his stance against corruption in business and politics, attention to environmental sustainability, and support for the woman's suffrage movement. The point here is that a century later the once Rooseveltian notion of "progressive" politics manages to circulate back for contemporary purposes, in this case connecting with citizens. Such memories situate the past being invoked as a scaffolded path toward a better future or new vision, rather than as a point of departure.

As a rhetorical historian, understanding the process by which commemorative discourse constitutes a state of continuity is essential because historical contextualizations inform analyses about how language or symbolism participates in the social construction of individual and collective identities on multiple levels. Memory is a process situated within a social contextualization of meaning making, one that continuously flows through multiple channels of communication. It is not just a manifestation of a singular text, artifact, site, or, in some cases, place. Rather, the process emerges through all of these elements. Thus, understanding the process that illustrates the emergence of public memory through the discourse or text and how multiple generations have engaged that memory is vital to understanding the extent to which its presence stabilizes our lives in the contemporary moment. This is where the rhetorical function of circulation becomes fundamental to understanding the process of public commemoration.

In general, in this chapter I focus on the relationship between material institutional structures (e.g., memorials and monuments) and the visitors in those spaces who, by recalling the perceived ideal, co-construct their experience through the circulation of memory. Here, I introduce the rhetoric of amnesia to illustrate the distinction from the rhetoric of forgetting in commemorative practice, as these terms are defined differently through the presence or absence of choices. As a rhetorical lens for understanding memory and commemorative practice in public culture, *amnesic rhetoric* emerges from a lack of choice in commemorative display for visitors; on the other hand, *forgetting* results from a range of choices in institutional commemorative practice.[2] Thus, the theoretical concept of *circulation as amnesia* points to a state of rhetorical agency produced by the actions of visitors as an extension of the agency produced through the materiality of the memorial. Such a focus can increase our understandings of the impact of multiple publics circulating through these spaces and their efforts to continually invoke historical narratives through their experiences, whether consciously or not. I do so to argue for the need to move away from analyzing the static features of popular public displays by showcasing the benefits of methodologies that foreground the relationality between visitors and such displays. As such, while this chapter focuses on the circulation of memory between institutional and individual commemoration, amnesia functions in part as a relationship of power.

Specifically, this chapter explores the extent to which cultural circulation has preserved the "ideal" characteristics of "American exceptionalism"—a cultural sensibility mainly defined through hegemonic masculinity. Here, I identify exceptionalism through the commonly circulated notion of masculinity that has been historically defined through the toxic hegemonic framework associated with the characteristics of white, American, cis-gendered, and heterosexual men.[3] Thus, this project traces the circulation of exceptionalism that has been performed and embodied by celebrated men (like Roosevelt) in dominant culture as exemplars of American superiority. As such, I argue that the embodiment of this conqueror role functions as a rhetorical process that promotes identification with an exclusive notion of American exceptionalism. Moreover, the re-circulation of this aspect of the exceptional American identity performs a symbolic function of continuity, often working against the promotion of inclusivity of citizenship and nationhood.

In the last part of this chapter, I illustrate this argument through a rhetorical analysis of the Theodore Roosevelt Memorial on Theodore Roosevelt Island in Washington, DC, in order to explicate how and to what extent these practices work together. Here, I argue that the reiterations of visitors emerge and persist as a unified understanding of national character in various ways (actions/performances) within the memorial space. Therefore, in this case study, visitors act as the main force in the circulation of the narrative of "Rooseveltian" white masculinity as exceptional Americanism.[4] As part of the concluding section, I suggest ways that scholars interested in studying the rhetorics of memory and commemorative practice can utilize *circulation as amnesia* to highlight the embodiment of such narratives as significant aspects of rhetorical agency.[5] The embodiment of the visitors circulating through commemorative spaces is important to consider because of the material imprint visitors leave on the space for others through their movement and actions. The critical application of amnesic rhetoric as a framing for circulation methodology contributes to understanding the rhetorical force behind the "life" of an artifact. Importantly, it also enables a better understanding of how and to what extent specific historical narratives take shape and circulate as part of both individual and collective identity formation in relation to the political undertones of commemorative practice.[6]

Amnesic Circulation and Rhetorical Agency in Commemorative Practice

Barbara Biesecker contends that the notion of Americanness might be achieved through the representation of community and togetherness as a unified collective.[7] Here, the methodological framework of rhetorical circulation is typically used to explore the ways in which various texts, artifacts, and discourses evolve through movement within a historical or a contemporary context.[8] Through an exploration of a variety of rhetorical artifacts she argues that as a response to the current status of national character these artifacts show how to be good American citizens by emphasizing certain narratives while neglecting others.

Other scholars, such as Charles E. Morris III in "My Old Kentucky Homo: Lincoln and the Politics of Queer Public Memory," focus on the circulation of specific narratives that play a vital role in how history may be repressed. Morris looks at the discontent among Lincoln historians when the work of Larry Kramer presented material evidence, in the form of letters, that documented Lincoln's possible homosexuality, contradicting their work. This resulted in the public's response of a "homosexual panic" that acts as an extension of Lincoln's memory (an alternate history) but also questions our own national heritage and the dominant heterosexual narratives with which our collective identity, presidential identity, and nation are built.[9] Although contesting dominant American national identities is significant in Morris's essay, his most compelling point is about the place of the rhetorical historian as an ideological component (participant) when constructing history.

Many scholars who utilize historical research as part of their scholarship find this methodological framework to be useful. For example, recalling David Zarefsky's four senses of rhetorical history, Cara Finnegan claims that analyzing the visual through circulation may help critics to better understand the history "in and around" images.[10] Much like Michael Calvin McGee's work on fragmentation, historical circulation can also shed light on the rhetorical choices involved in a contemporary repurposing of a text or artifact.[11] Such a process can also help critics understand how and to what extent communities emerge from the multiple reiterations and flow of the process.[12] Those who are concerned with the formation and impact of commemorative work have also noted that circulation plays an important part in understanding the material circumstances of historical artifacts and their role in the making of memory.[13]

Returning to the earlier example of progressivism, when contemporary politics embrace Roosevelt to exert a progressive agenda, politicians use the iconic Roosevelt not to represent the evolved version of progressivism today but instead to anchor public perceptions in a version of the old-time Progressive Era. Thus, this connection through the circulation process becomes an effective determinant for how others may see progressive ideology in the present moment. In this sense, social constructs and the icons that represent them are continuously reiterated and managed, even in the absence of the icon, in a process I call cocreation. Through this process, particularly the reiteration of narratives that promote a sense of identity, rhetors are able to manipulate the process to fit their political agendas.

In some form or another, the exploration of the cocreation experience has already been utilized through commemorative practices that promote a lack of materiality. V. William Balthrop, Carole Blair, and Neil Michel interrogate other World War II commemorative scholarship by asking the question that I have contemplated myself: "Can memorials be faceless in terms of representing a past?" While the World War II Memorial in Washington, DC, openly invites interpretations of a past, it also speaks to the present moment through such gestures as George W. Bush's name on the memorial (since he was the president in office when the memorial was dedicated) and the parallel of such fictional veterans as Tom Hanks.[14] Blair, Balthrop, and Michel point to similar claims in their analysis of France's Fleury-devant-Douaumont.[15] Here, after examining the material features of the site, the authors conclude that through the site's material absence Fleury-devant-Douaumont invites visitors to imagine the destruction of war, as it also invites visitors to visualize the peacefulness of the village before the war as if the war never took place. This observation may invite visitors to assume an alternative position, one that can either cause the visitors to imagine the worst situation possible or cleanse the narratives of violence—the latter an even more dangerous view as it acts as a silencer of war. While these authors centralize their arguments around the memorials themselves, I am more concerned with how our cultural logics about identity and difference are affected in the presence of absence and how our own actions become a replacement in the absence of those histories. Participatory critical rhetoric provides a chance for the critic/participant to experience how memory still flows through the actions of the visitors who circulate and act upon that space, while still taking into account the materialization of the site of commemoration. This necessary flow results in the experience of "spontaneous and strategic (inter)actions of material bodies as rhetoric unfolds."[16]

As mentioned above, while some memory and commemorative scholarship utilizes the focus of co-creator collaboration in public memory, most commemorative scholarship has yet to focus on the importance of the cocreator as a central rhetorical agent. What I argue as part of this circulation process is that the fit and public reception of the text/artifact with the cocreator process acts as a lens for understanding how some of these structural systems work toward anchoring the receiver of the message in the past (nostalgic reception) or in the present (transformative reception). This is not to say that the cocreator possesses full rhetorical authority during this circulation process. Rather, their actions perpetuate a specific flow that can play a part in how the receiver identifies with and embodies the message.

To demonstrate this idea, I use the case study of the Roosevelt Memorial on Theodore Roosevelt Island in Washington, DC, to illustrate the extent to which the site's unconventional commemorative characteristics still continue to circulate the theme of conquest, one of the primary tropes of American exceptionalism. This analysis explicates how the space's agency exhibits power (or not) by including the experience of the critic/visitor as a material/affective component in the circulation process. This exploration is necessary because memory and commemorative discourse are labeled and organized through the material composition of the space.

A Walk through the Theodore Roosevelt Memorial

According to Steve Markos's *National Park Planner*, the history of Theodore Roosevelt Island and the Roosevelt Memorial does not follow the progression of other commemorative sites that typically boast strong public support, sustainable funding, and the expediency to move forward with construction.[17] Unlike the positive support for the building of the Roosevelt memorial in the American Museum of Natural History (AMNH) in New York, the Washington, DC, memorial struggled.

According to the US Department of the Interior's National Park Service registry, shortly after Congress approved the Tidal Basin in DC as the initial location for the commemoration of Roosevelt in the 1920s, Congress reversed the decision due to public disapproval. The report claims that the Theodore Roosevelt Association (TRA) and the general public had an aggressive debate about the memorial's installation. The public saw the association's approach to the matter to be uninviting primarily because TRA bypassed the Commission of Fine Arts to speak to Congress directly, asserting their "uncritical belief in Roosevelt's greatness." Congress debated the matter from 1923 to 1926 before rejecting the project, citing reservations about memorializing Roosevelt so soon after his death and before such other historical figures as Thomas Jefferson.[18]

What is interesting about the ways in which this document describes the original plans for the memorial at the Tidal Basin is the magnitude with which the TRA exhibited its own sense of his superiority through these plans. Designed by John Russell Pope, the same architect who imagined the Roosevelt commemorative site in New York, the project would have transformed the location into a "vast memorial precinct, stretching over a third of a mile from east to west." Beyond the reflecting pool and enormous Doric peristyle columns, according to the Park Service description,

> Roosevelt appeared in the abstract, as a 200-foot jet of water representing his vital spirit . . . surged from a raised basin in the topmost island. The linking of the colonnades by a central fountain symbolized the president, with his Yankee father and Confederate mother, as the leader who embodied a final unification of North and South; the memorial thus advanced the notion that Roosevelt had completed the work of nation building begun by Washington and Lincoln, the major theme embodied by the Washington Mall. Four barges, each carrying winged victories and groups of men, women, and children, projected from the top island, "symbolical ships [that] carry the message of Roosevelt's life to the four points of the compass." The monument's vast size and sense of continuous outward expansion were meant to suggest endless national growth and unlimited glory.[19]

The self-imposed importance and privilege exhibited in the description of the original memorial plans is indicative of Roosevelt's rebranding of himself in response to public critiques during his early career. Despite his political victories as a state assemblyman in New York (1881–83) and his larger-than-life persona that overflowed with a sense of self-importance, Roosevelt believed many did not take him seriously in the political arena. From degrading comments by his political opponents to newspaper coverage characterizing Roosevelt's high-pitched voice and fancy clothes as "delicate," Roosevelt had been publicly cast as "effeminate."[20] Of course, such an image posed a danger to his political ambitions and his desire for power. In Roosevelt's eyes the only way to achieve success was through rebranding himself. He utilized larger-than-life imagery, echoed in the proposed memorial, to become what we know today as the embodiment of powerful and exceptional American masculinity.[21]

Even though there were significant delays in obtaining approval for the memorial after the vote against its initial location, in 1931 the TRA moved to purchase Anacostia Island from the Washington Gas Light Company in the hope of finding a new home. After the end of World War II, the funds for the memorial finally came through; the National Park Service made the island available to the public for the first time in the early 1950s. In 1956, the TRA commissioned Eric Gugler and Paul Manship to redesign Pope's plans for the memorial in time for the centennial commemoration of Roosevelt; again, due to debates over the design, funding of nearly $2.5 million fell through, which resulted in the dedication of the island without a memorial.[22] In 1960, the National Capital Planning Commission approved the memorial, but the Senate vetoed the bill until it gained the approval of the Roosevelt family.

Problematically, the original design by Gugler and Manship, like Pope's earlier design, faced broad public ridicule. Roosevelt's daughter Alice Roosevelt Longworth called the design "a 'globular jungle gym' which 'would desecrate the memory of anyone.'" Conservationists across the nation criticized the design of the armillary sphere as being "a 'bulging excrescence,' 'an onion ring fried in molten bronze,' and 'doughnuts in limbo.'" Conservationists also worried that the design would "destroy an enduring, living and meaningful memorial," even though the association promised that the island would maintain its natural surroundings.[23] Finally, the Roosevelt family approved a "down-sized" version of Gugler and Manship's original design because of its "less invasive" overturn of the natural landscape. Even Roosevelt's daughter could not find anything wrong with the finished memorial: "I like it enormously. I think I have a rather mean disposition, but I can find nothing critical to say about it."[24] After a seven-year building process, the memorial concluded construction in 1967 to be dedicated by Pres. Lyndon B. Johnson on Roosevelt's 106th birthday.

Although gaining public support for the landscaping on Roosevelt Island and the creation of the memorial constituted nothing short of a struggle, even more problematic is the erasure of visible prehistory associated with the island before the construction of the memorial. The amnesic visibility of the island's history is multilayered, working through erasures—a form of conquering nonexceptional Americanness. These erasures include the island's early Indigenous history as a site occupied by Native peoples, shown in the discovery of pottery fragments dating back to the early colonial era when the land was still named Anacostia Island. Additional erasures include the island's history of slavery and postwar use. Between 1717 and 1833, the John Mason family occupied the island. Mason, an American merchant and son of founding father George Mason, turned the island into a plantation estate maintained by the labor of enslaved people. Archeological surveys show some of the remnants of the Mason House and buildings thought to be quarters for those enslaved from the period. Later, the island became a training ground for the First United States Colored Troops during the American Civil War. Moreover, between the 1860s and the 1930s when the Theodore Roosevelt Association purchased the island, various people used the land as a popular resort and even a "cultivated commercial garden."[25] In spite of these findings, during the island's initial landscaping project commissioned by the Olmsted brothers in the 1930s, the landscaping team removed, destroyed, or disguised the artifacts from prior eras. In addition, the landscaping team also moved the intact artifacts from the site to another part of the island, disregarding public disapproval.[26]

I am troubled by my experiences on Roosevelt Island because of the extent to which the absence of such artifacts acknowledging Indigenous people, enslaved people, and African American troops constructs a specific story around forgetting or absence. The result, what I have referred to as an amnesic experience, still manages to circulate residues that may trigger embedded ideological traces. To an extent, the historical linkages with the island's past have problematic characteristics that symbolically invoke colonial sensibilities. For example, from the National Park Service's efforts to "enhance its character as a 'native' forest" to the two extended bridges over the moat that surround the 1967 "open-air" monument, the site's design and large statue of Roosevelt together visually represent a sturdy fortress and the connotations of a powerful emperor.[27] At least, this was the experience for me the first time that I visited the site in November 2017.

However, the overwhelming feeling I experienced after locking eyes with the monumental Roosevelt statue faded after I entered the plaza.

The generic codes of commemorative practice (in the visual material sense) tend to show some sort of unification in location and structure, not to mention care and upkeep of the site. These characteristics have invoked the same sense of Americanism within the processes of that institutionalized rhetoric, the sense of pride. The conditions of the plaza were unmanaged and therefore not as pristine as I had imagined, and to an extent, the memorial failed to meet my expectations of commemorative practices. For example, although the footbridges located on the opposite ends of the space seemed grand in their size and form, they appeared to be worn down and discolored from natural corrosion and weathering. The same description applies to the extravagant but waterless moat surrounding the perimeter of the memorial. The once imagined water-filled moat was at the time of my visit only partially filled, containing dead leaves and standing water as brown as sewage. The moat resembled the foot bridges in its discoloration; various shades of brown and green were found along the edges as if algae had grown there for years. The fountains in the center of the plaza did not function and were discolored from the spreading algae and cracked so deeply that it would be surprising if they could hold water. It is obvious that the upkeep of the plaza is not a prime concern, especially compared to the upkeep of memorials on the National Mall and the Tidal Basin.

The two main paths that lead visitors out of the plaza split into multiple hiking trails, with posts marking the number of each trail. Logically, I started walking on trail number one with the expectation that I would be led to trail number two and so on, but instead, the path led to a new trail and a new number that was out of order. I also did not have a sense of direction leading back to the plaza; I had to trust that one of these trails would take me there. While navigating the trails that would eventually lead back to Memorial Plaza, being in an unfamiliar and secluded environment invoked fears of being lost, or perhaps forgotten. I was very concerned about getting back to Memorial Plaza before the sun went down because at that time I knew of only one area that would lead me to an exit off the island. This lack of order invoked an uncertainty that made me question the point of this path in general. Roosevelt had once commented about the value of exploring and finding himself in nature; was I too supposed to get lost and see who emerged on the other side, once I found my way back?[28] This would give the visitor (in this case myself) significant rhetorical agency, but on the other hand, it would also reinforce one of Roosevelt's national ideals: exceptionalism emerges from our relation to nature.

Stories about the harsh unsettled wilderness—where one can

re-create one's own identity—are central to many myths regarding American national identity and to an extent the creation of the ideal American who is physically strong, determined, and masculine.[29] Such narratives in American popular culture have always been connected to the "Great Outdoors." While the memorial is only one part of the island, the island itself is about two miles long, with multiple trails and paths leading visitors to different areas of the island. On my way back to Memorial Plaza, I started to notice a significant change in my surroundings: many trees had fallen over or were cut down. The noticeable change went from apparent uniformity to unpredictability and chaos.

Many of the trees still standing within the area exhibited an imprint or trace of past visitors. For instance, as I proceeded down one of the paths, I noticed carvings all over the trunks of large trees. Some engravings were simple initials, while others had symbols such as "person x + person y = ♥" or the usual initials and "wuz here," markers for moments within visitors' experiences that they wanted to document in a way that others would find. The act of tree carving is not necessarily linked to Roosevelt, the memorial, or Theodore Roosevelt Island; however, the action may be interpreted as a form of conquering. To be clear, as a way of commemorating one's presence during a significant period, "tagging" would be considered a marker for that experience to claim or show "proof" of one's presence within that place or in that moment. Here, I am not just commenting on everyday tagging but also of how explorers on expeditions have documented new territories and lands that have been "discovered." Famed explorers Lewis and Clark, for example, frequently documented their experiences by leaving traces of their discoveries. While some historians have concluded that there is no evidence of instruction from the government that directed the Lewis and Clark expedition to do so, there is speculation that they were advised by other expedition parties to "mark their trail on behalf of the United States government as 'unquestionable proof of the journey.'"[30] Thus, through these material changes, the island is transformed into a living space that collects, performs, and shifts one's memory space—a result of visitors manipulating their individual experiences as collective cocreators.

Once I arrived back at Memorial Plaza, a young Black mother noticed my failed attempts to take a selfie with the large Roosevelt statue and offered to help me document my own memory. We quickly struck up a conversation, sharing why we were visiting the island. The mother wanted a local outing with her sons to commemorate her successful completion of her masters of education degree, which then led to our conversation about graduate school life and the struggles associated with balancing family and work life. Her two young sons were off in the distance, throwing stones and play-fighting with two large sticks as if they were swords. After the mother yelled for the boys to drop the stones, they met her in front of the Roosevelt statue. She began to direct the two boys to stand still while she took a photo to create and document their own memory on the island. The mother wanted a memory of their family visit because the last time they visited the island five years ago, the boys were about three inches shorter with a lot less energy. As the younger son grew impatient with his mother's photographic activities, the mother reminded him that taking that photo was extremely important because it was going in the family album. With that, the younger son raised his other arm with the large stick he had picked up from the trails, mimicking the Roosevelt statue behind him for the documentation of their experience and for the family photo. His mother turned to me and commented, "He is the comedian in the family." This child's interaction within the amnesic state of the memorial space, specifically his imitation of Teddy Roosevelt, rhetorically suggests a transformation of his individual (Black) identity into an exceptional American (white) one. Such an embodiment of Roosevelt by this Black child unconsciously embraced a whitewashed circulation of American exceptionalism, both through his performance of self-conquering and through the performance's rhetorical continuance of the erasure of Indigenous roots of the land's history.

For myself, during the exchange I had with the young mother I identified with the work/life struggles of everyday life and even the typical narrative of the Protestant work ethic, a staple of the "American dream." To be clear, as a working-class woman myself, I related to some of the hardships associated with the mother's narrative, especially the financial struggles of full-time graduate work (I was writing my dissertation at the time). Yet, as this visitor reminded me during that moment, hard work pays off. Thus, her access to the American Dream was attainable through hard work, while I, even within an amnesic state, unconsciously exhibited my own privilege. Not only was I on a funded research trip (while my partner waited in the car with our socially anxious and terrified thirteen-year-old dog), but I was a white woman exploring a site whose history once spoke of Indigenous tribes that settled on the land, once spoke of the slave plantation of a DC socialite, and once spoke of the training grounds of many Black soldiers who fought in the American Civil War, before the land became a racialized and gendered marker for American exceptionalism.

On a separate visit the following year in October 2018, the state of the Roosevelt Memorial had not changed. Leaves still filled the surrounding dirty moat that framed the magnitude of Roosevelt's visual presence within the space of Memorial Plaza, and visitors still went about their day. Some talked in groups, while others jogged on the trails. Much like the young boys and their mother the year earlier, during this visit I observed an interesting conversation. From a stone bench across Memorial Plaza, I observed a young white family walking toward the Roosevelt statue. A woman pushed a baby stroller and kept to herself, while a father and son walked hand and hand a short distance behind her. As they walked toward the Roosevelt statue the young boy turned to his father and asked, "Dad, who is Teddy Roosevelt?" With that question the father responded happily from the beginning, with a narrativized account of Roosevelt's life starting with "Teddy Roosevelt was president when they first invented cars."[31] "Cool, dad!" the little boy replied. The exchange between the son and father invoked a common characteristic of the exceptional ideal—conquering "uncivilized" territory through the act of invention. Here, the narrative about the origination of cars being connected to the US presidency, and especially Theodore Roosevelt, signals a point of power, particularly one that includes the domination (or conquering) of nature through ingenuity and machinery. Here, the exchange between the father and son not only circulated the theme of conquest, it also invoked the power relationship associated with it and the passing down of that "privilege" to the younger (white) male generation.

To be sure, Roosevelt's ascension as the ideal American was not a result of his political achievements; rather, it was due to "his masterful use of the discourse of civilization," capitalizing on his persona as a willful "civilized white man"—a collective national identity he thought to be in crisis.[32] Resisting this crisis of identity, Roosevelt fashioned himself as a symbol for the American people, and especially American men, constantly projecting these traits into public affairs, "equating his own early struggles with physical debility with his country's rise to power" and from global insignificance to power across sectors.[33] In Roosevelt's mind, the United States would only be able to exhibit power and dominance over other nations through "imperialistic control over races of inferior manhood."[34] This sense of superiority was only claimed through the willingness and ability to live the "strenuous life," a connection to fictional narratives that demonstrated that the nation's "strength" was determined by young men killing large deadly animals or fighting Indigenous people.[35] For the observation of the father and son, I was led to a point of exclusion, even from a place of privilege. Much like the identity role performed by the wife/mother pushing the baby stroller, excluded from the conversation of the father/son duo to complete the ideal of the family unit, I, too, was excluded from the exceptionalist narrative as a middle-aged and childless woman.

From what I observed and experienced those days, the *flow* of the American exceptionalism ideal continues to function in part because of the circulation of visitors and their experiences within that space. The point here is not so much about displaying the extent to which these families communicated Roosevelt's memory but instead to illustrate how and to what extent beyond the material components of a static site, visitors (and even critics) participate within and become part of the site's production and circulation of discourse. My own experience in the circulation of American exceptionalism through Roosevelt's memory is situated within concerns related to the production of (un)conscious identities and how they are performed, as well as the racial implications associated with those distinctions in our current political moment. Not only are the histories of Indigenous tribes, enslaved people, and African American soldiers not circulated amongst the visitors who presently visit the site but moreover the creators of the memorial had removed the only remnants of these histories—a move that in essence replaced one act of colonialism with another. Thus, the exceptional narrative continues to circulate as commonplace, within an amnesic state of historical circulation.

Both my passive and my interactive experiences with both of these families on different occasions showed the extent to which masculine identities circulate through the rhetorical transference of embodiment and the oral transmission of certain national mythologies within the traditional family unit.[36] These various interactions with the memorial and embodiments of Roosevelt show multiple ways that people collapse their individual identities in favor of the national collective through expression of rhetorical continuity with such dominant civic narratives as American exceptionalism. In each case, this amnesic state rhetorically manipulates the experience of the visitors into their acceptance of histories and circumstances without necessarily being aware of them.

Furthermore, my concerns in this case study lie with the ethical ramifications associated with not only what or whom hierarchies choose to memorialize or commemorate but also how the effects of these power structures continue to impact public consciousness and dialogue even with the emergence of an erasure (or closure) of memory within an amnesic state. In the case of the little boys and their mother on a family outing, the father and son teaching lessons of a past American president, and even the couples who carved their initials to commemorate the memories of their love and time spent on Roosevelt Island, we still emulate a rhetorical past, and conquer it because of how we perform those identities in relation to others within the space and at times beyond it. This is because we function with an additional layer, one that constantly changes as a product of our being in the world and participating within the flow of memory. In this case, the significant role of conquering circulates within an amnesic state because the interactions of visitors within the site actively bridge the gap between the institutional histories that are both remembered and forgotten discourses of American exceptionalism.

Regardless of the circumstances, these parallel narratives operate as scapegoats whereby those in power can justify their actions in the present.[37] While I cannot speak for the active and passive exchanges of each family within their unit or how they experienced the memorial and the island, I can speak about the extent to which their actions affected my own understanding of the site: the more important rhetorical lesson here comes from the uptake of these narratives by visitors who perform and narrate those roles through embodied performance and traditional storytelling of nationhood as a form of circulation. Here, I echo Morris with my own concerns extending to the ways in which rhetoricians approach the study of memory as mere sites or artifacts of representation rather than focusing on the processes by which such narratives are produced and circulated, without the consideration of themselves or others as participants within that flow. The point here is to illustrate that regardless of the presence or absence of the site's history, the visitors, including myself, entered a state of amnesia that reinforced the continuum of the island's exceptional rhetoric, thus circulating regardless of the state of its (visual) presence.

Where We Go from Here: Amnesic Circulation and Public Memory

The amnesic state of memory jars the experience of the visitor because it continues to flow and change. As Vivian puts it, "memory is unavoidably, and sometimes maddeningly, inconstant"; indeed, a causality of this disruption is the permanence that facilitates safety, certainty, and comfort, especially when it comes to identity formation.[38] If there is no past to anchor, then there is no foundation to build upon. Yet, with absence there is still a form of continuity. I have worked to underscore that within a state of amnesia, the unified discourse, in this case as exhibited through the role/theme of conquering, acts as a trope for a multifaceted master narrative of exceptionalism. I have also worked to illustrate that what emerges is not dependent solely on the material displays of memory (or their absence) but on the circulation of that trope through the people who embrace it.

Thus, using amnesia as a rhetorical framework for circulation helps to highlight the ambiguity that the material features of the memorial produce. Instead of forgetting, or at least offering clear indicators of how visitors may read and interact within the memorial, it becomes a place where runners get to partake in their daily exercising routine, individuals sit with one another to talk about life while creating their own memories, families pass down stories about America to the next generation, and even dogs get to run and play as members of the Ruff Riders Club.[39] The mixture of individual (personalized) and collective (institutionalized) memories becomes problematic because it assembles into a natural rhetorical erasure.

Of course, memorials and other commemorative displays do not physically circulate like that of an image or photograph in a newspaper, magazine, or other visual platforms where public discourse may be articulated, rearticulated, and, indeed, reimagined. However, this case shows that circulation is not dependent on material form. In fact, circulation at the Roosevelt Memorial occurs through the interactions of visitors with the site and each other. To be clear, circulation in this view is both emplaced and embodied as it works through the centralization of visitors as rhetorical agents who preserve, rearticulate, and thus circulate such common ideological ideals of American exceptionalism. This includes their experience of material changes to the site, their physical circulation through the memorial, and conversations between visitors, especially the stories they share. I find this approach to be liberating for scholars who focus not on the impact of public memory but the extent to which the production of public memory generates patterns of specific commemorative practices that form social and political structures over periods of time, space, and material (even digital) realities. Thus, the circulation of historical memory within an amnesic state is an extension of Finnegan and Kang's contributions to historical work and visual discourse. In this way, I apply circulation as a network of texts that circulate unified narratives (such as people, places, experiences, contemporary narratives, and historical narratives) to illustrate the extent to which commemoration goes beyond the text (or site) itself, including multiple points of connection.

This case study highlights the need for further investigation using the lenses of circulation and amnesic rhetoric to better understand how and to what extent discourse circulation is interactive. Moreover, this method offers rhetorical scholars a view of how (1) memory and commemoration practices are multidimensional, (2) visitors and their circulation work as multifunctional networks, and finally (3) multiple narratives circulate throughout time and space in relation to each other. To be clear, understanding commemorative displays distinctly or the extent to which they "move" on their own terms is not necessary for us to identify their significance in producing/circulating/reiterating public discourse. From my view, that places too much significance on the material nature of the display instead of its function within a larger network of circulation.

The larger body of research from which this case is drawn shows that amnesic rhetoric is a small node within a larger system of circulation. As such, from a methodological standpoint this chapter sets the groundwork necessary to explore the circulation of amnesia through a commemorative site that is seen as static and thus largely ignored.[40] As rhetoricians we should not hinder ourselves by becoming fixated on the rhetorical significance of specific commemorative displays but instead work more closely to understand how and to what extent a specific discourse emerges and circulates over a period of time as a "master" narrative. As rhetorical historians, we should critically engage how this narrative survives through us based on our own lived experiences and on the buried narratives of yesteryears. By evoking these networks of memory, social implications emerge that affect the ways in which we identify with our present and understand possibly the problematics of our past. Reframing rhetorical history means being attentive to absences in history as they affect absences in the present. This highlights larger questions about the impact of memory and commemorative practices as a prime concern of rhetorical investigation.

Notes

1. Here, I define networks as a multidimensional mode of commemorative practice. See Chandra A. Maldonado, "Remembering Roosevelt: Arguing for Memory through Public and Private Networks," in *Networking Argument*, ed. Carol Winkler (New York: Routledge, 2020).

2. For more on forgetting see Bradford Vivian, *Public Forgetting: The Rhetoric and Politics of Beginning Again* (University Park: Pennsylvania State University Press, 2010).

3. For the purposes of this essay, I refer to hegemonic masculinity in the US culture not situated in gender studies, but instead how and to what extent toxic white masculinity continues to maintain a foothold in American politics and public culture, in order to situate myself within a conversation about American national character and public memory. See Michael Kimmel, *Angry White Men* (New York: Nation Books, 2013); Chauncey Devega, "Toxic White Masculinity: The Killer That Haunts American Life," *Salon*, February 15, 2018, https://www.salon.com/2018/02/15/toxic-white-masculinity-the-killer-that-haunts-american-life/; Amanda Pickett, "Questioning White Masculinity in the U.S," Words in the Bucket, December 28, 2016, https://www.wordsinthebucket.com.

4. In a recent publication, I define manifest masculinity (manifest destiny)

through specific characteristics (masculinity as conquest, masculinity as innovative, and masculinity in the form of a savior) that are performed within and throughout commemorative practices in visual culture. See Chandra A. Maldonado, "Recovering Teddy, Recovering Trump: The Rhetoric of Manifest-Masculinity in a Drunk and Rap Battle Generation," in *Gender, Race, and Social Identity in American Politics: The Past and Future of Political Access*, ed. Lori L. Montalbano (Lanham, MD: Lexington Books, 2019), 237–54.

5. I utilize Michael Kammen's notion of historical amnesia. Kammen notes that historical amnesia, or what he calls "amnesia and historical ignorance," has been used to bolster our desires to be anchored in a perceived past that we can identify with and capitalize on. See Michael Kammen, *Mystic Chords of Memory* (New York: Vintage, 1993), 12.

6. Alon Confino, "Collective Memory and Cultural History: Problems of Method," *American Historical Review* 102, no. 5 (1997): 1386–1403. One might see a logical comparison here to Phaedra Pezzullo's concept of enshrinement. Interestingly, enshrinement from my perspective calls for a more public display of commemoration; however, the concept can also be applied to the circulation and embodiment of narratives. For more on the concept of enshrinement, see Phaedra Pezzullo, *Toxic Tourism* (Tuscaloosa: University of Alabama Press, 2009), 100.

7. Barbara Biesecker, "Remembering World War II: The Rhetoric and Politics of National Commemoration at the Turn of the 21st Century," *Quarterly Journal of Speech* 88, no.4 (2002): 393–409.

8. Laurie Gries, "Iconographic Tracking: A Digital Research Method for Visual Rhetoric and Circulation," *Computers and Composition* 30, no. 4 (2013): 332–48.

9. Charles E. Morris III, "My Old Kentucky Homo: Lincoln and the Politics of Queer Public Memory," in *Framing Public Memory*, ed. Kendall Phillips (Tuscaloosa: University of Alabama Press, 2004), 99.

10. David Zarefsky, "Four Senses of Rhetorical History," in Turner, *Doing Rhetorical History*, 19–32. See also Cara Finnegan, "Doing Rhetorical History of the Visual: The Photograph and the Archive," in *Defining Visual Rhetorics*, ed. Charles A. Hill and Marguerite Helmers (Mahwah, NJ: Lawrence Erlbaum Associates, 2004), 120–45.

11. Michael Calvin McGee, "Text, Context, and the Fragmentation of Contemporary Culture," *Western Journal of Communication* 54, no. 3 (Summer 1990): 274–89. See also Lester Olson and James J. Kimble, "Visual Rhetoric Representing Rosie the Riveter: Myth and Misconception in J. Howard Miller's 'We Can Do It!' Poster," *Rhetoric & Public Affairs* 9 no. 4, (2007): 533–69.

12. Michael Warner, "Publics and Counterpublics," *Public Culture* 14, no. 1 (2002): 49–90.

13. Carole Blair, "Contested Histories of Rhetoric: The Politics of Preser-

vation, Progress, and Change," *Quarterly Journal of Speech* 78, no. 4 (1992): 403–28; Kendall Phillips, "The Failure of Memory: Reflections on Rhetoric and Public Remembrance," *Western Journal of Communication* 74, no. 2 (2010): 208–23.

14. V. William Balthrop, Carole Blair, and Neil Michel, "The Presence of the Present: Hijacking 'The Good War'?," *Western Journal of Communication* 74, no. 2 (2010): 170–207.

15. Carole Blair, V. William Balthrop, and Neil Michel, "Mood of the Material War Memory and Imagining Otherwise," *Cultural Studies↔Critical Methodologies* 13, no. 1 (2013): 6–20.

16. Michael Middleton et al., *Participatory Critical Rhetoric: Theoretical and Methodological Foundations for Studying Rhetoric In Situ* (Lanham, MD: Lexington Books, 2015), 62.

17. Steve Markos, "Theodore Roosevelt Island—Roosevelt Memorial," National Park Planner last updated June 4, 2020, http://npplan.com.

18. US Department of the Interior, National Park Service, *National Register of Historic Places Registration Form* (Washington, DC: National Archives, 2001), Section 8, 44.

19. US Department of the Interior, National Park Service, *National Register of Historic Places*, 45.

20. Gail Bederman, *Manliness and Civilization: A Cultural History of Gender and Race in the United States 1880–1917* (Chicago: University of Chicago Press, 1996), 170.

21. Bederman, *Manliness and Civilization*, 170.

22. Eric Gugler was an American architect best known for his redesign of the White House's West Wing during FDR's presidency.

23. US Department of the Interior, National Park Service, *National Register of Historic Places*, Section 8, 60.

24. US Department of the Interior, National Park Service, *National Register of Historic Places*, 61.

25. US Department of the Interior, National Park Service, *National Register of Historic Places*, Section 7, 3.

26. Regarding the preservation debate over the Mason House, the Roosevelt Memorial Association director Hermann Hagedorn commented: "The Island could not be nine-tenths a memorial to Theodore Roosevelt and one-tenth a memorial to General John Mason or his son" (75). For more on the preservation debate, see US Department of the Interior, National Park Service, *Historic American Landscapes Survey* (Washington, DC: National Archives, 2007), 75–78.

27. US Department of the Interior, National Park Service, *National Register of Historic Places*, 2.

28. See Darrin Lunde, *The Naturalist: Theodore Roosevelt, a Lifetime of Exploration, and the Triumph of American Natural History* (New York: Broadway Books, 2016).

29. Gregory Dickinson, Brian L. Ott, and Eric Aoki, "Memory and Myth at the Buffalo Bill Museum," *Western Journal of Communication* 69, no. 2 (2005): 86. See also Eric Aoki, Gregory Dickinson, and Brian L. Ott, "The Master Naturalist Imagined: Directed Movement and Simulations at the Draper Museum of Natural History," in *Places of Public Memory: The Rhetoric of Museums and Memorials*, ed. Gregory Dickinson, Carole Blair, and Brian L. Ott (Tuscaloosa: University of Alabama Press, 2010), 238.

30. Robert A. Saindon, "They Left Their Mark: Tracing the Obscure Graffiti of the Lewis and Clark Expedition," in *Explorations: Into the World of Lewis & Clark*, ed. Robert A. Saindon (Great Falls, MT: Lewis and Clark Trail Heritage Foundation, 2003), 493.

31. He was likely referring to the start of the mass production of automobiles in the United States during the early twentieth century.

32. Bederman, *Manliness and Civilization*, 171.

33. Richard Slotkin, *Gunfighter Nation: The Myth of the Frontier in Twentieth-Century America* (New York: Macmillan, 1992), 37.

34. Bederman, *Manliness and Civilization*,171.

35. As part of the American exceptionalism narrative the conquest theme is used in contrast to "uncivilized" societies. Ironically, however, in 1899 Roosevelt spoke against the "over-civilized" man emerging in America at the turn of the century. See Theodore Roosevelt, "The Strenuous Life," April 10, 1899, Voices of Democracy, https://voicesofdemocracy.umd.edu.

36. See Patrizia Albenese, "Nationalism and Motherhood," in *Encyclopedia of Motherhood*, ed. Andrea O' Reilly (Los Angeles: Sage, 2010), 893–94; and Beth Baron, *Egypt as a Woman: Nationalism, Gender, and Politics* (Berkeley: University of California, 2010), 53–55.

37. Maldonado, "Recovering Teddy, Recovering Trump," 238–39.

38. Vivian, *Public Forgetting*, 1.

39. The Ruff Riders Membership Program was created by Friends of Roosevelt Island, in part to raise funds to help with the maintenance of the memorial. Please see https://theodorerooseveltisland.org/index.php/support-us/item/3 -ruff-rider-membership.

40. I also want to note that a single case study is a brief example for showcasing the implications of applying a framework of amnesic rhetoric. This chapter is part of a project with a larger set of case studies tracking the extent to which such forms of circulation rhetorically reinforce this dominant narrative, commonly related to the displacement of nondominant cultures in the United States in favor of the defined roles associated with the normative hegemonic white ideal.

11

The Greatest Hero of the Great War

Alvin C. York as a Rhetorical Construction

Daniel P. Overton

On April 26, 1919, the *Saturday Evening Post* positioned Alvin C. York to be considered the greatest hero of the Great War. Through George Pattullo's pen, the *Post* told of York's travails in the Argonne Forest, where he purportedly silenced 35 machine gun nests, killed 20 German infantrymen, and captured another 132 soldiers—including 4 officers—as prisoners of war. Impressive statistics for any soldier over the course of a long conflict, York purportedly accomplished all this by himself on a single October day in 1918. Following such remarkable achievements in France, his story initially remained untold in the United States, even in his native Tennessee. Yet after Pattullo's article, "The Second Elder Gives Battle," York would become "without a doubt, the most famous American soldier of the war,"[1] partially because the *Post* boasted a circulation of over two million people, the largest in the world.[2] For his bravery, Sergeant York received the nation's highest distinction, the Congressional Medal of Honor. He became a folk hero, the embodiment of American valor in World War I. Upon returning to American soil on May 22, 1919, York spent a five-day furlough in New York City and Washington, DC. He received a room in the Waldolf Astoria, a banquet in his honor, and a private audience with Sec. of War Newton D. Baker, having previously met with Pres. Woodrow Wilson in France.[3] In short, York was a star.

The First World War boasted many possible American stars, men and women of remarkable achievement and courage, heroic figures potentially worthy of national attention and praise. For instance, Harry J. Adams reportedly captured 300 prisoners with only a handgun, and the aptly named Hercules Korgia purportedly forced a group of 256 soldiers to surrender. Samuel Woodfill overcame 5 enemy machine gun nests on October 12, 1919, in the Argonne.[4] Actually, York's general, John J. Pershing, seemed to favor Woodfill over York, citing Woodfill's actions as "the highest type of heroism."[5] Why, then, did York become the singular hero of the war? I suggest York or, more precisely, Pattullo's textual rendering of York became the preferred image for Americans following the Great War due to Pattullo's careful construction of York as a heroic individual and as a hesitant warrior. In particular, Pattullo elided two key parts of York's story: the role of other soldiers aiding York in battle and the repeated attempts of York to achieve conscientious objector status. By exposing these omissions, it should become clear that Pattullo's York was a rhetorical creation, a historical fiction created to meet the ideological needs of the American public, one that illustrates particularly well history as an "indispensable" process involving "an unstable pattern of remembered things redesigned and newly colored to suit the convenience of those who make use of it."[6]

Specifically, through York Pattullo addressed two major tensions in the post–World War I period: the place or displacement of the individual in an increasingly industrialized system and the growing ambivalence concerning the compatibility of Wilsonian internationalism and Americanism. As such, he essentially answered two major questions. First, can the individual thrive in a mechanized world? Second, was the United States right to fight the war in Europe? As a single, simple, intuitive mountaineer, Pattullo's York achieved victory by his skill and his courage, proving man still mattered in the age of machines. Moreover, as an initially devout pacifist, Pattullo's York was also a reluctant soldier: he did not rush headlong into violence. In him, Americans could see themselves as earnest and cautious warriors, able to retain nationalistic righteousness. Americans did not want to fight, but necessity laid the battle upon them. Pattullo's York served as a narrative enactment of the commitment to make the world safe for democracy while maintaining American exceptionalism. If, as Lamay suggests, "York's story was tailor made for a quintessential American hero,"[7] it is largely because Pattullo proved a capable tailor, stitching together a version of Alvin York that best served his rhetorical purposes and the rhetorical and ideological needs of his audience.

My analysis proceeds in four sections. First, I provide brief theoretical reflections on the suasive power of selection and deflection in historical narratives. Second, I describe the *Saturday Evening Post* and its constituted readership. In the third section, I focus on the omission of other soldiers present during York's heroic acts, and in the fourth, I discuss the implications of omitting York's various attempts to gain conscientious objector status. Pattullo's York served as an effective rhetorical historical narrative, judged not simply by the fame it brought York but also by the role York's story played and continues to play in the larger collective memory.

Selection and Deflection in Historical Narratives

This study would not exist without the key theoretical insights provided in *Doing Rhetorical History*. Among those insights is E. Culpepper Clark and Raymie McKerrow's assertion that history principally explains "the present by connecting it to the past," specifically by representing a community's values in historical narrative form.[8] As such, rhetors can harness the emotional and cultural power of past figures or principles to endow their public address with credibility, creating narratives that are likely to be accepted by communities with vested interest in certain purportedly traditional value systems. By invoking past events, the rhetor can both "frame the present" and "conform that past to the present."[9] As Gronbeck notes, "Historians set brackets and articulate causal connections between contexts and events in order to naturalize or make coherent the stories and interpretations they are offering."[10] Consequently, the positing of "causal connections" can be understood as a rhetorical strategy to create a historical narrative that resonates inside a particular cultural milieu. If one considers "history as a series of rhetorical problems, situations that call for public persuasion to advance a cause or overcome an impasse,"[11] then significant public addresses often hinge on attempts to motivate a public to accept particular interpretations of present and past events. The stories that a people celebrate reveal the values of that people, not just due to patterns of articulation and circulation but also due to the rhetorical choices that rhetors make to invest their narratives with meaning in consideration of the delicate interplay between "text and context."[12]

In the Gospel of John, the gospel writer hyperbolically suggests that "the world itself could not contain" all the stories of Jesus's life,[13] so some disparate moments had to be chosen purposefully and formed into a coherent whole. In like manner, the historical facts that could comprise a narrative history of the First World War are too many to record in any single book. Which facts to collect, publish, and emphasize remain the purview of the rhetor. As David Zarefsky pithily puts it, "Facts do not speak; they must be spoken for."[14] The selection of Alvin York as a representative figure of the Great War has implications that might render his selection a desirable choice for a particular author, including a motivation toward a certain interpretation of historical or current events. The choice of particular facts and the accompanying process of speaking for such facts plays a key part in the process of mobilizing history for rhetorical purposes; the choice also serves as a clear example of the rhetorical process of constructing histories.

Concordantly, what historians select for inclusion in their narratives is clearly important in the construction of history, but perhaps more important is that which is deflected, those elements *not* selected for particular reasons. Pattullo focused on York's heroism in battle to the virtual exclusion of all other soldiers present, allowing him to portray a great individual hero. Similarly, he focused on York's initial pacifism without noting the extent of his repeated attempts to claim conscientious objector status, allowing him to portray an appropriately hesitant but overwhelmingly patriotic warrior. Pattullo elided or deflected key details of York's historical narrative, creating a particular version of York that is constituted through these voids. That is, "What gets 'left out' in a historical reconstruction, however precise the methods used in deriving the data on which interpretation rests, influences the final creation."[15] In what follows, I describe the circumstances in which George Pattullo left out the two above key details regarding Alvin York's story, noting the power of this selection and deflection to produce a rhetorical rendering of York designed to resonate with a particular constituted audience and with the American people generally. This study extends the theoretical legacy of *Doing Rhetorical History* by considering specifically the ways rhetors recreate historical figures and narratives to best serve the contemporary audiences at their disposal.

The *Post*-Reading Public

The publication of Pattullo's story in the *Saturday Evening Post* proved central to its success. Aside from boasting the largest subscriber base in the world at the time, the *Post* was a perfect place for Pattullo's piece as a source that boasted of its "frank Americanism."[16] The historian and journalist Frank Luther Mott describes the *Post* as an outfit that is "generally agreed" to have become "as American as public school, the big department store, the television network, the hot dog, and the ice cream cone."[17] When Cyrus Curtis purchased the *Post* in 1897 and hired George Lorimer in 1898, the pair made several significant adjustments to the declining weekly paper, and with surprisingly suddenness, these changes rebranded the *Post* as an indispensable repository of American history and patriotism. The *Saturday Evening Post* eventually billed itself as the "quintessentially American" magazine and became one of the most influential media outlets in American history.[18]

Struggling with only about two thousand subscribers, the *Post* had no distinctive voice or identity in 1897, but Curtis and Lorimer provided both in three principle ways: by creating a mythical history, by transforming the paper's aesthetic, and by constituting an audience of average Americans through specific editorial choices. First, they endowed the *Post* with a history, principally through a primarily fictional connection to Benjamin Franklin. About four months after Curtis purchased the *Post*, its masthead of January 29, 1898, claimed for the first time ever that Benjamin Franklin founded the *Post* as the *Pennsylvania Gazette* in 1728, aging the paper almost one hundred years in the space of a week.[19] Although any possible substantiation of this claim requires mental gymnastics and the acceptance of dubious linkages, Lorimer established the *Post* as an essential piece of Americana, anchored in the supposed connection to Franklin. The evocation of Franklin provided far more than an earlier founding date to the *Post*: it gave the paper a new "goal and a standard." As the paper developed under Lorimer, "the plain common sense, homely democracy, shrewd pragmatism, and faith in the recognized virtues which we think of as characteristic of Franklin have been consistently worked into the editorial pattern of the *Saturday Evening Post*."[20] Franklin's name gave the publication an ethos, heft, and direction it would not otherwise possess.

Curtis and Lorimer also significantly changed the *Post*'s nondescript aesthetic into an eventually iconic series of colorful covers and advertisements. They printed the first color cover in 1899, and by 1903, every cover was a lavishly colored image, notably featuring the work of J. C. Leyendecker and later Norman Rockwell, inviting readers to purchase the magazine through its deployment of attractive and vibrant Americana artwork.

Finally, Curtis and Lorimer shaped the content of the *Post* to reach a specific audience, the so-called average American. Lorimer "would, in fact, *invent* the average American—some compound of nineteenth-century values and twentieth-century opportunities."[21] The average American was a hard-working individual, likely a white male, intent on pulling himself up by his bootstraps all the way to success. Mott summarized the key editorial content pertinent to retaining this reader as "business, public affairs, and romance," and whether through fiction or nonfiction, the articles "emphasize[d] personalities to a remarkable degree."[22] Lorimer printed a description of his average reader as a "man of affairs who has had his own way to make, and has gained a fair degree of material success without having had the time or opportunity to gloss over his attainments with the 'rubbed finish' of bookishness and ripe culture. He is a product of the common schools, not of the college, and his special training has been picked up in the store, the shop, the office or the factory instead of in the classroom."[23] Articles published to reach this demographic include "Getting and Keeping a Business Position," "Why Young Men Fail," and "How I Made My First $1,000"—the last one by none other than steel magnate Andrew Carnegie.[24] The *Post* printed stories of young men who worked hard to earn fortunes, endorsing the rosy romantic ideals of capitalism in American popular life. The periodical was even delivered by a network of *"Post* boys," literal children who sold issues all around their neighborhoods for approximately one and a half cents profit per paper. The boys were even offered the opportunity to purchase an "exclusive agency" and build their own small franchise of *Post* deliverers. As such, "the *Post* subscribed fully to the nineteenth-century belief that boys who worked and saved their earnings were being properly trained for a life of diligence and thrift."[25] Despite a heavy new emphasis on men and boys, women continued to read the *Post* in large numbers, likely for its quality fiction and strong emphasis on a certain romantic image of the American dream.[26]

The result of these substantial changes to the history, aesthetic, and content of the *Post* invited readers to inhabit a "reconfigured subject position."[27] Essentially, the *Post* constituted its readers intentionally as "average Americans" by its articles and images and constituted its readers extensionally through patterns of circulation provided by *Post* boys and articulations regarding the latest colorful cover.[28] The *Post* hailed each reader as a "representative American," who was "a compendium of nineteenth-century values; he worked hard, saved money, and assumed the duties of citizenship responsibly. The American was pragmatic and self-reliant, dedicated to his own social and economic betterment."[29] The *Post* readers received weekly reminders about the sort of people they were, complete with catchy accompanying artwork and advertisements of respectable products. Armed with the ethos of Benjamin Franklin, the *Post* called its readers to attention and to action in the preservation of true American values, ones potentially under attack.

Jan Cohn described this particularly well: "Readers *became* a national community as they came to know, to share in, and to talk to one another about familiar stories by familiar writers about familiar characters. . . . The very appearance of another Rockwell or Leyendecker cover enriched and confirmed the culture of *Post* readership. To read the *Post* was to become American, to participate in the American experience."[30] Consequentially, Cohn argues, "Lorimer and the *Post* played their most significant role in the development of a mass national consciousness."[31] Lorimer and the editorial staff of the *Post* regularly provided their many readers with a romantic, personality-driven model of American history and governance; readers committed themselves to "getting ahead in a new world by respecting the values of the old."[32] As such, a narrative of the nearly incomprehensible First World War filtered through the experience of a single hardworking young frontiersman with old-fashioned values—a narrative that openly displayed the righteousness of the American cause—would resonate effectively with this constituted *Post* public. It was rhetorically crafted to do just that.

York as a Single-Handed Hero

Paul Fussell notes "the drift of modern history domesticates the fantastic and normalizes the unspeakable," suggesting this trend began with the "catastrophe" of the Great War.[33] It is worth noting that the warfare of the First World War proved unusually unspeakable. Fought in the otherworldly environment of the trenches, the war was, in the words of English soldier Siegfried Sassoon, "mainly a matter of holes and ditches."[34] Funneled like ants through muddy ruts, soldiers constantly faced death. The industrial technology of World War I allowed for more efficient weaponry, but the style of war remained quite archaic. This reality was nearly unimaginable to most across the ocean. At the onset of the war, French troops wore bright red and blue uniforms, and they rode on horses, mimicking battles of bygone years. Their horses met with barbed wire. Their bright clothing attracted rapid-fire machine gun rounds that riddled them to shreds. For the first time on a large scale, war was industrialized. One young American soldier wrote his pastor, "Don't think I am downhearted because I am writing you, but it's a queer thing I can't explain, that ever since I volunteered I've felt like a cog in a huge wheel. The cog may get smashed up, but the machine goes on."[35] Perhaps for this reason, George Pattullo never mentioned an active trench in his article. He wanted York to romantically stand out amid the machines, rather than fade into the unspeakable and unromantic trench warfare of the First World War.

Because machines controlled World War I, the mission of war seemed to depend on manufacturing and engineering, not on the warrior and his skill. Industrialization transformed the soldier into a depersonalized trigger finger, not a moral agent, so "the warrior was the passive operative doing a job that had to be done."[36] The incorporation of gas masks and complex drab uniforms in subterranean trenches further blurred the line between man and machine. Here, Pattullo's York provided a means to romanticize a thoroughly unromantic conflict. In York, Americans reaffirmed the individual and the hero. He represented a John Henry notion that an individual man of good moral cloth still had a place in an increasingly mechanized war and in an increasingly mechanized world.[37] Pattullo's York did not need any human or mechanical help nor explosive or automatic weapons; he simply required a couple of guns and his downhome intuition. Pattullo's York was a frontiersman after all, a "*real* American" who brought about victory through rudimentary skill,[38] suggesting the warrior had a place yet in modern warfare and life.

Nostalgia has the power to reaffirm "identities bruised by recent turmoil."[39] A wistfulness for a bygone era is the natural reaction to widespread systemic change, stemming from the established traditional "myth of a primitive happier state."[40] Citizens long for yesteryear as an indictment of the present milieu and as a method of constructing an idealized past. Thus, "York represented, to a world disillusioned by the rapacious efficiency of modern and total warfare, a simpler time."[41] Pattullo's portrayal of York as an individualist Appalachian frontiersman not only harkened to a less complicated bygone era, it tapped into the substantial desire of contemporary Americans for simplicity in the face of drastic change, both in terms of the war and of demographic shifts.

If anyone knew how to effectively mobilize frontier nostalgia, it was George Pattullo. Described by one source as "brash, urbane, charming, and manipulative,"[42] Pattullo made a career producing symbols of Americana through personality profiles and short fiction. After the Canadian American journalist achieved modest success as the Sunday editor of the Boston Herald, he left his desk job to partner with the famed Texan cowboy photographer Erwin E. Smith in 1908, eventually becoming his "closest friend."[43] Smith and Pattullo traveled widely in the southwestern states, particularly New Mexico, Texas, and Arizona. While Smith took photographs, Pattullo wrote fictional western pieces for several periodicals, largely for the Saturday Evening Post and McClure's Magazine, occasionally paired with Smith's pictures. As such, Pattullo's career depended upon an American infatuation with the frontier environment. Americans perceived cowboys and frontiersmen as honest hard workers who lived free from the shackles of society. Full of the distinctly American spirit of "individuality and opportunism,"[44] these heroes simultaneously embodied the distant other and "the last sentinel on the parapet of Americanism" for increasingly urbanized Americans.[45]

When the Post assigned Pattullo to France shortly after the armistice, he continued to write largely fictional stories of combat, until he came across Alvin York. Mostly ignoring the differences between western writing and war reportage, Pattullo described York in the language of his cowboy pieces. His stylistic influences are obvious, as he explicitly created York in the image of the frontier: "Have you ever seen a gunman of the old Southwest? A real gunman, not the loud, quarrelsome, spurious saloon hero? Well, that's York." York and the typical American cowboy shared "the same rather gentle voice in ordinary conversation, with a vibrant note when he is stirred that fairly trumpets danger, he has the same gray eyes, flecked with brown—eyes which can harden to pin points. And he has the same unhurried, half-indolent confidence of manner."[46] Pattullo knew well the American fascination with the western hero; it had paid his bills for several years prior to the war.

Additionally, Pattullo's York became an idealized version of the real deal, an otherworldly fantastical mountaineer. He was "a whale of a man," with an "absolute sureness of self." His red hair "flames like a headlight," and his eyes, though kind, had "the peculiar high and piercing quality of the hawk's." As a devout Christian, York refused to drink, gamble, or swear, and when asked if he ever swore in the heat of battle, York replied, "'Not a single cuss.'" Incredibly, "never once did he do the wrong thing" for "this Tennessee mountaineer seems to do everything correctly by intuition." Finally, "no amount of military training could have improved his tactics, yet with York it was entirely the working of instinct, for until November 14, 1917, he was living on a small farm on Wolf River."[47] This simple frontiersman just *knew* what to do; his intuition was perfect, superior even to the best of West Point. York's personality and skills were geographically endowed and internationally appreciated. Pattullo depicted Sergeant York as a lone ranger forced out of his mountains to be a hero. In him, *Post* readers remembered their idealized past and mitigated their complicated present, a present that included unprecedented and unforeseen carnage.

Although there is general consensus that York did the lion's share of the work on that October day, he was accompanied by a dwindling patrol of other American soldiers, and pertinently, his Medal of Honor citation commends him for "fearlessly leading 7 men" to charge occupied machine gun nests.[48] Indeed, Pattullo admits, "There were seven other Americans present at the fight," but even so, Pattullo insists, "It was York's battle and only York's."[49] Pattullo seemed to understand that the story carried more weight if York acted alone—particularly as the other seven soldiers heralded from urban areas, had roots in Eastern and Central Europe, and worshipped in non-Protestant churches or synagogues at a time when America "was suspicious of anything foreign."[50] Pattullo so emphasized York that the other seven soldiers at the battle and those who died getting the battalion into position vanished.[51] In doing so, Pattullo magnified York's bravery, emphasized his cunning, and legitimized his folksy wisdom as a rugged individual.

Pattullo wrote his entire story almost wholly ignoring the potential contributions of other soldiers, and later writers, even prominent popular and expert sources to this day, followed suit, especially in applying the adverb "singlehandedly" to York's conquests to underscore his heroic achievement.[52] In 1922, the *New York Times*, for example, credited York with "singlehandedly" killing 20 Germans, capturing 128 prisoners, and silencing 35 machine guns.[53] The Tennessee Historical Commission reiterated the adverb "singlehandedly" on its historical marker in York's memory. The excellent National World War I Museum and Memorial in Kansas City included just a couple sentences about Alvin York in its timeline exhibit, but in those few words, they managed to include the claim that York "singlehandedly" accomplished such incredible feats. The other soldiers present undoubtedly contributed their hands in service alongside York's "single" sharpshooting hand, but "singlehandedly" remains the most consistent descriptor of York's deeds that day. Pattullo's York continues to be a potent rhetorical force.

Pertinently, Janice Hocker Rushing postulates that the American "Western myth," the bread and butter of Pattullo's career, can be analyzed through the tension between two major values or obligations: individualism and community.[54] The cowboy or the frontiersman must act for the benefit of his community, but he must also be self-sufficient and independent. A cowboy cannot be a hero without both a rugged individualism and a concern for the needs of his community: "To cope with the harshness and savagery of the frontier environment, he must above all be a rugged individualist. However, in order to settle and civilize the frontier, he must continually face the demands of the community for cooperation and conformity."[55] Similarly, as a hero, Pattullo's mythic York brought about single-handed justice; in doing so, he protected his fellow soldiers and esteemed community. York's fellow patrol members, then, are absent in activity but present in motive.

Pattullo provided an identifiable hero, an individual to stand out among the relatively new machines of war, a nostalgic name to emerge out of the statistics. Pattullo's York functioned as an exemplar of what American citizens could accomplish through their naturally endowed intuition. Through his hard work and his instinct, Pattullo's York was able to stand up against the German army and to return victorious, a line of prisoners in tow. Pattullo constructed a herculean version of York, one who needed no help or assistance; he was a true individual, a self-sufficient American who knew his way around a set of bootstraps. Pattullo's York was literally an army of one. Accustomed to understanding abstract principles through celebrated individual personalities, the *Post* public appreciated precisely what Pattullo provided to them.

York as a Pacifist

Indubitably, York's conversion from pacifism to militarism continually received a prominent place in his story. Not simply a military hero, York served as the exemplar of an American with strong principled if uninformed reasons against war who changed his mind and adopted a nationalistic trust in the United States as an instrument of righteousness. In short, York was an unlikely soldier, coming from an isolated region and an isolating faith. Those from the Wolf River valley rarely left, and still reeling from the Civil War, most residents considered going "off to war in France virtually incomprehensible."[56] At the time, some suggested that drafted Appalachian mountain men occasionally believed America to be again at war again with England, and they were "deeply suspicious" to hear England was a close ally.[57] Thus, if York, a frontier pacifist—one born and raised in innocent isolation—fought in a foreign war, that war must be of grave importance. For such a good man to fight, the cause must be moral and just. It must be as President Wilson proclaimed: "We enter this war only where we are clearly forced into it because there are no other means of defending our rights."[58] Ultimately, York's abandoned pacifism, as presented by Pattullo, served to legitimize both the war and the authority of the state during a time of crisis.

The title of Pattullo's piece is telling.[59] "The Second Elder Gives Battle" locates York's positional authority within his local church. The term "second elder" indicates York was the second in command at his specific congregation, leading hymns, teaching Sunday school, and contributing to decisions made on behalf of the church. By pairing "Second Elder" with "Battle," Pattullo constructs an antithetical dichotomy, that a man of God would become a man of violence. Readers might infer that second elders typically do not "give battle," but rather, they adhere to the teachings of Jesus, turning the other cheek. Hence, before his readers ever processed a word in the body of his article, the title prepared them to engage with a story about both religion and violence, about a devout second elder and the circumstances through which he could heroically go to war.

Beyond the title, Pattullo references York's theological commitments throughout his article. At the start of the profile, he wrote that York's church "is opposed to any form of fighting; they are conscientious objectors."[60] For Pattullo, this detail was the key to York's narrative. His acts of purported redemptive violence were contextualized and effectually cleansed by his pacifism. He killed out of sheer necessity as a cautious soldier of the Lord, and as such, his violence and the violence of the allied forces generally arose from duty, both to God and to country and was thusly rendered just. Later, Pattullo states, "In my estimation, [York's action] stands out as the greatest individual feat of the war. Not only because of the amazing things he did that day [in battle] but *because of the man's deep religious convictions and scruples.*"[61] For Pattullo, York's "deep religious convictions" played a central role in his retelling. They framed and suffused all of York's actions, especially those actions fundamentally opposed to his prior nonviolent beliefs. Pattullo's York came to personify the general milieu surrounding the Great War in the United States. Just as York needed to be convinced to fight, America required compelling reasons to broach the international conflict. Just as York eventually saw the productive value of violence, specifically violence approved and sanctioned by God toward a noble cause, Americans generally believed their troops comprised divine instruments of righteousness. Actually, Pattullo informed his readers that York still struggled with his actions from time to time, but he was at peace because he fought in a "sanctified cause."[62]

In this way, Pattullo's York might be understood as something like an "ultimate definition" for Wilsonian internationalism. Robert C. Rowland and John M. Jones suggest, "An ultimate definition lies at the nexus of an operational definition within a coherent narrative, a connotative definition tied to key value terms, and an epistemic definition functioning as a worldview."[63] The epistemic argument that America as an emerging superpower must "make the world safe for democracy" receives a narrative enactment in York's story. Due to its exceptional nature, the nation could pursue a global interventionist presence to spread such an ideal form of governance *only* if forced to do so. This policy played out in York's aversion to violence alongside his willingness to kill for the greater good, the American way of life. Here, the definitional arguments about democracy, war, and internationalism are incarnated into a narrative about Alvin York, an ultimate definition for Wilsonian values and international priorities. Pertinently, Pattullo's York became convinced to fight by the exceptional nature of his country and by a confirmation of righteousness of the American war-making process.

Although many tried to dissuade Pattullo's York of his pacifism, Pattullo contended that Maj. Edward Buxton and Capt. Edward Danforth succeeded by finally citing a passage from the prophet Ezekiel: "But if the watchman see the sword come, and blow not the trumpet, and the people be not warned; if the sword come, and take any person from among them, he is taken away in his iniquity; but his blood will I require at the watchman's hands."[64] The captain and the major equated America with God's watchman of the world, so it was the US Army's destiny to mete out divine retribution. If America is God's nation, then no real criticism can be offered against her military endeavors. As Seymour Martin Lipset notes, "The United States primarily goes to war against evil, not, in its self perception, to defend material interests."[65] Holy war and crusade imagery abounded as Germany became other, totally separate, not quite human.[66] Journalist Mildred Aldrich referred to Germans as "the most absolute synonym of evil history has ever seen."[67] In his memoirs, York even said, "We were to be peacemakers. . . . We were to help make peace, the only way the Germans would understand."[68]

Although Pattullo portrayed York's conversion to militarism as the obvious Christian development, this decision represents a departure from standard Christian doctrines, essentially a heresy. Generally speaking, orthodox Christianity includes two robust traditions of accounting for the Christian's responsibility to the state with regard to violence.[69] The first is pacifism, that Christians must follow the example of Jesus and must not pursue the state's calls for violence. The second is just war theory, mediated through Augustine, that Christians may participate in conflicts that are deemed just through two multifaceted traditional criteria, *jus ad bellum* and *jus in bello*, the right to go to war and the right conduct during war. Pattullo's York was convinced to fight principally by an argument that represents neither Christian tradition; instead, it is something more akin to heterodox nationalism or civil religion, that whatever a select country chooses to do must be just or must be blessed by God by the simple virtue that such a godly country decided to do it. Note that the argument that convinced Pattullo's York could be used to justify the German war cause just as easily as it did for America.

During the World Wars in a time of surging patriotism, Americans developed a strong disdain for pacifists in general. Religious leaders would accuse conscientious objectors of "aiding the enemy," dubbing them "freak specimens of humanity" with "dwarfed conscience[s]."[70] Actually, York was just one of a large number of Christians in America who converted from pacifism to militarism in the midst of the "super-patriotism" of the First World War.[71] The US government routinely imprisoned conscientious objectors from unofficial peace churches with little available recourse, and the public vilified them. Pattullo noted that York "didn't suggest timber for a conscientious objector."[72] That is, he seemed to be made of better stuff than typical draft dodgers. York's difficult decision to bear the sword for his government was subtly characterized as a move away from his yokel religious philosophy toward a mature, realistic, and legitimate Christian faith. Pacifism was silly, and war required the death of such silliness. As mediated by Pattullo, York's story reinforced the idea "that conscientious objectors were simply unaware of the obligations of citizenship," lacking the basic truths about war and faith.[73] Americans associated pacifism with the intellectual backwoods, and in the military, Pattullo's York discovered the obviously better interpretation of Scripture. This perspective devalues the robust tradition of various religious pacifists during the war, in addition to those liberal intellectual pacifists.[74] Pattullo's York might seem to adjust to a more mature form of Christianity, but in assessing the biblical argument that convinced Pattullo's York, he appears to be worshipping at the altar of American civil religion, trusting that whatever America does must be divinely blessed.

Pattullo consistently emphasized the incompatibility of patriotic duty and principled nonviolence: "For though York joined the army when drafted he remained troubled for months, and it was only after his captain had laid his doubts by quoting biblical authority for taking up the sword that he saw his duty clearly."[75] Initially, York could not see his evident reasonable duty, primarily because he felt a moral obligation to abstain from killing. Friends and family also influenced him in this way. "The congregation were unanimous on the point: York must ask for exemption as a conscientious objector. Pastor R. C. Pile urged it long and eloquently. His mother, faced with the prospect of losing the head of the household at a time when her health was not robust, and with three children on her hands, backed up his arguments."[76] Regarding their advice and prohibitions, "York refused. He belonged to the Church of Christ in Christian Union and subscribed to its doctrines, but he was not going to back out of serving his country when it was drawn into war."[77] Duty, theological conviction, and family obligations collided in Pattullo's York, and for the author and his public, York proved he was a true American when, ignoring a host of distractions, he came to clearly see his supreme duty: obedience to the state. For Pattullo, York's willingness to break his second-order conviction, pacifism, for his first-order conviction, patriotism, defined his character and necessitated his honor. York's pacifism proved an asset insofar as it demonstrated him to be skeptical of violence, mirroring the American ideal, but it was a liability insofar as it kept him out of the war. Deliberate attempts to achieve conscientious objector status would be undesirable, as this might be evidence of a deficient nationalism or patriotism. Pattullo's York was emphatic: he "refused to ask for exemption" as a conscientious objector.[78]

Contrary to Pattullo's York, however, the historical York did apply for conscientious objector status, in accordance with the will of his pastor, his church, and his family. The last question, number twelve, on the draft registration card asked, "Do you claim exemption from draft (specify grounds)?" York carefully penned his answer, "Yes, don't want to fight."[79] Unfortunately, the draft board denied his application—but York went on to appeal the decision four separate times.[80] Pattullo's York was a lackluster pacifist, one who never actually filed for conscientious objection, but the actual York applied *five times*, his application denied due to the lack of a standard denominational peace creed for his Church of Christ in Christian Union. For Pattullo, it was important that York have his pacifist roots without ever actually following through on the requisite paperwork. If Pattullo had admitted to York's repeated conscientious objector filings, he would not be able to claim his "patriotism was stronger than any other impulse."[81] In truth, York's strongest impulse was for community and nonviolence. After the war, York resumed a pacifist stance, even occasionally questioning the involvement of the United States in the First World War.[82]

Pattullo's York embodied a morally rigorous, self-disciplined American, full of convictions. For this man, endowed with all the mystic intuition of an Appalachian frontiersman, to put down his Bible and pick up his rifle for war, that war must carry a truly great and righteous cause. Pattullo's York ignored the advice of his mother, ignored the advice of his pastor, ignored the advice of his church, and ignored even his own conscience to answer the highest call, the duty of citizenship. Americans in need of salve for their own consciences, or Americans in need of reassurance that the devastation had been unavoidable righteous retribution need only look to York to see the inherent goodness of the cause.

Conclusion

Alvin York served to embody American involvement in the war amid devastation, illustrating romantic individualism and hesitant heroism, traits that mirrored broader American identity markers. As the most famous American soldier of the Great War, his story entered American collective memory as a resource to be used during the next major war. As Gronbeck notes, "The collective memory is recalled, seemingly, so as to let the past guide the present, but it can do so only when the past itself is remade."[83] After twenty years of rejecting offers, York finally sold the rights to his life, and his story became a major motion picture in 1941, remaking the past once again. Originally, York only agreed to sign the contract if the movie would focus not on his exploits in war but on his work to bring education to his home region. After being convinced about the perils of the impending Second World War, however, York allowed for the film to portray his acts of heroism, and a large portion of the movie concerns the narrative of his religious conversion and his decision to leave pacifism behind. The film amassed a $2 million budget, the highest ever for a Warner Brothers production at that time, and it became a commercial and critical success.[84] The film earned Gary Cooper, who portrayed York, an Academy Award for best actor.

The movie served to motivate many to support the war effort. John Belton described how the film functioned to foster a certain interventionist logic prior to the Second World War, similar to the way the Pattullo piece provided a narrative enactment of such ideology after the first: "York (and America) can uphold, without rupturing them, the basic isolationist principles that underpin his (our) identity while realizing his (our) obligations to things outside of himself (ourselves). Retaining its inherent distaste for European entanglements and war, America could, at the same time, give itself over to the larger historical (and moral) necessity of fighting fascism."[85] York's story—the canonized version first drafted by Pattullo—pervasively informed both World Wars. He rendered each conflict legible, representing the heroism of the First World War and paving the way for the Second World War. Pattullo provided readers with an individual hero and a reluctant fighter, an important commemorative, rhetorical device. However, in so doing, he removed the community of soldiers surrounding York in battle and the peace witnesses surrounding York in Tennessee. The sum result was an effective rhetorical/historical personality capable of connecting deeply with readers of the *Post* and with average Americans generally during several decades of the twentieth century—even up to the present moment.

Notes

1. George Pattullo, "The Second Elder Gives Battle," *Saturday Evening Post*, April 26, 1919, 3–4; Kimberly J. Lamay, "The Creation of an American Collective Memory of the First World War; 1917–1941," PhD diss., State University of New York, Albany, 2013, 114.

2. Edward J. Klekowski and Libby Klekowski, *Eyewitnesses to the Great War: American Writers, Reporters, Volunteers and Soldiers in France, 1914–1918* (Jefferson, N.C.: McFarland, 2012), 203. Movie mogul Henry Aitken claimed in the *Post* that "two million people buy this publication; . . . [and] undoubtedly ten million see it." Henry E. Aitken, "With Odds of 100,000 to 1, Will You Take a Chance?," *Saturday Evening Post* 187, no. 43 (1915): 47.

3. David D. Lee, *Sergeant York: An American Hero* (Lexington: University Press of Kentucky, 1985), 59–61.

4. Lee, *Sergeant York*, 65.

5. Michael E. Birdwell, "Alvin Cullum York: The Myth, the Man, and the Legacy," *Tennessee Historical Quarterly* 71, no. 4 (2012): 324; quoted in Lee, *Sergeant York*, 52.

6. Carl L. Becker, "Everyman His Own Historian," in *The Vital Past: Writings on the Uses of History*, ed. Stephen Vaughn (Athens: University of Georgia, 1985), 35.

7. Lamay, "Creation of an American Collective Memory," 114.

8. E. Culpepper Clark and Raymie E. McKerrow, "The Rhetorical Construction of History," in Turner, *Doing Rhetorical History: Concepts and Cases*, 35.

9. Bruce E. Gronbeck, "The Rhetorics of the Past: History, Argument, and Collective Memory" in Turner, *Doing Rhetorical History*, 58.

10. Gronbeck, "Rhetorics of the Past," 59.

11. David Zarefsky, "Four Senses of Rhetorical History," in Turner, *Doing Rhetorical History*, 30.

12. Zarefsky, "Four Senses," 21.

13. John 21:25, English Standard Version.

14. Zarefsky, "Four Senses of Rhetorical History," 20.

15. Clark and McKerrow, "Rhetorical Construction of History," 36.

16. Isaac F. Marcosson, *Adventures in Interviewing* (New York: John Lane, 1919), 66.

17. Frank Luther Mott, *A History of American Magazines, 1741–1930*, vol. 4 (Cambridge, MA: Harvard Belknap Press, 1957), 716.

18. Jan Cohn, *Creating America: George Horace Lorimer and the "Saturday Evening Post"* (Pittsburgh, PA.: University of Pittsburgh Press, 1989), 83.

19. See Mott, *History of American Magazines*, 682–84, for a more thorough description of how the founding myth of the *Post* took shape. Mott describes the new founding date of 1728 as "the best-known date in the history of American periodicals."

20. Mott, *History of American Magazines*, 685.

21. Cohn, *Creating America*, 28.

22. Mott, *History of American Magazines*, 688.

23. Alexander Revell, "The Plain Business Man," *Saturday Evening Post*, September 1, 1900, 16–17.

24. Robert Ogden, "Getting and Keeping a Business Position," *Saturday Evening Post*, November 4, 1899, 345–46; Ogden, "Why Young Men Fail: A Clear Explanation by Shrewd Business Men," *Saturday Evening Post*, October 28, 1899, 327; Andrew Carnegie, "How I Made My First $1,000," *Saturday Evening Post*, February 11, 1899, 527.

25. Cohn, *Creating America*, 39.

26. Mott, *History of American Magazines*, 688.

27. Maurice Charland, "Constitutive Rhetoric: The Case of the *Peuple Québécois*," *Quarterly Journal of Speech* 73, no. 2 (1987): 142.

28. James Jasinski, "A Constitutive Framework for Rhetorical Historiography: Toward an Understanding of the Discursive (Re)Constitution of 'Constitution' in *The Federalist Papers*," in Turner, *Doing Rhetorical History*, 74.

29. Cohn, *Creating America*, 10.

30. Cohn, *Creating America*, 10.

31. Cohn, *Creating America*, 28.

32. Tom Pendergast, *Creating the Modern Man: American Magazines and Consumer Culture, 1900–1950* (Columbia: University of Missouri Press, 2000), 55.

33. Paul Fussell, *The Great War and Modern Memory* (New York: Oxford University Press, 2013), 74.

34. Siegfried Sassoon, *Memoirs of an Infantry Officer* (New York: Coward, McCann, 1930), 228.

35. Walter T. Bromwich, "Private Walter Bromwich Questions God's Purpose in Time of War," in *Grace under Fire: Letters of Faith in Times of War*, ed. Andrew Carroll (New York: Doubleday, 2007), 23.

36. Edward Linenthal, *Changing Images of the Warrior Hero in America: A History of Popular Symbolism* (New York: E. Mellen, 1982), 111. Linenthal suggests two major themes, the soldier as romantic hero and the soldier as nameless victim, met in the commemoration of unknown soldiers, a phenomenon in many countries after World War I. The Unknown Soldier serves both as a faceless cog of war and as a self-sacrificing, devoted individual warrior.

37. The subject of an important piece of American folklore, John Henry was reputedly an African American railroad laborer who challenged the new steam-powered drill with only his hammer and his grit. See John Douglas, "John Henry: 'Take This Hammer, It Won't Kill You,'" *Southern Cultures* 10, no. 2 (2004): 73–86. Patullo's York could be considered something of a John Henry figure in the folklore of the First World War.

38. Mary F. Brewer, "Offerings on the Altar of National Pride: Pioneer Plays and American Identity," *Studies in Theatre and Performance* 31, no. 3 (2011): 249.

39. David Lowenthal, *The Past Is a Foreign Country* (New York: Cambridge University Press, 1985), 13. See also Fred Davis, "Nostalgia, Identity and the Current Nostalgia Wave," *Journal of Popular Culture* 11, no. 2 (1977): 414–24.

40. Raymond Williams, *The Country and the City* (New York: Oxford University Press, 1973), 44.

41. Birdwell, "Alvin Cullum York," 324.

42. B. Byron Price, *Imagining the Open Range: Erwin E. Smith, Cowboy Photographer* (Fort Worth, TX: Amon Carter Museum, 1998), 49.

43. Eldon S. Branda, "Portrait of a Cowboy as a Young Man," *Southwestern Historical Quarterly* 71, no. 1 (1967): 69.

44. Ronald H. Carpenter, "Frederick Jackson Turner and the Rhetorical Impact of the Frontier Thesis," *Quarterly Journal of Speech* 63, no. 2 (1977): 125.

45. William W. Savage, *The Cowboy Hero: His Image in American History & Culture*, 1st ed. (Norman: University of Oklahoma Press, 1979), 15.

46. Pattullo, "Second Elder Gives Battle," 3.

47. Pattullo, "Second Elder Gives Battle," 3.

48. The French Croix de Guerre Medal citation is more explicit. York "with 7

men succeeded in . . . capturing several machine guns and 132 prisoners, including 4 officers." Quoted in John Perry, *Sgt. York: His Life, Legend & Legacy* (Nashville: Broadman & Holman, 1997), 97.

49. Pattullo, "Second Elder Gives Battle," 3.

50. Michael E. Birdwell, "Gobble Like a Turkey: Alvin C. York and American Popular Culture," in *Rural Life and Culture in the Upper Cumberland*, eds. Michael E. Birdwell and W. Calvin Dickinson (Lexington: University Press of Kentucky, 2004), 163.

51. Some have suggested that Bernard Early should be considered the real hero of the day. Early, York's commanding officer, was wounded immediately prior to York's heroism. York almost certainly would not have been in position to capture all those prisoners without Early's leadership. Some have even suggested that Early did most of the work, while York merely took the credit, but given significant testimony to the contrary, this position is minor and unlikely. Lee, *Sergeant York*, 44–45.

52. See Timothy M. La Goy, "Soldiers of Conscience: Conscription and Conscientious Objection in the United States and Britain During World War I," PhD diss., State University of New York at Albany, 2010, 258; Milton Bagby, "Time Capsule," *American History* 33, no. 5 (1998): 74.

53. "Tennessee's War Hero," *New York Times*, July 16, 1922, 1.

54. Janice Hocker Rushing, "The Rhetoric of the American Western Myth," *Communication Monographs* 50, no. 1 (1983): 17. See also Leroy G. Dorsey, *We Are All Americans, Pure and Simple: Theodore Roosevelt and the Myth of Americanism* (Tuscaloosa: University of Alabama Press, 2007), 5–6.

55. Rushing, "Rhetoric of the American Western Myth," 16.

56. Birdwell, "Gobble Like a Turkey," 160.

57. Theodore Roosevelt III, "The Sword of the Lord and of Gideon," in *Rank and File: True Stories of the Great War* (New York: Charles Scribner's Sons, 1928), 39.

58. Woodrow Wilson, "Necessity of War against Germany," in *Selected Addresses and Public Papers of Woodrow Wilson*, ed. Albert Bushnell Hart (New York: Boni & Liveright, 1917), 196.

59. Pattullo, "Second Elder Gives Battle."

60. Pattullo, "Second Elder Gives Battle," 3.

61. Pattullo, "Second Elder Gives Battle," 3.

62. Pattullo, "Second Elder Gives Battle," 3.

63. Robert C. Rowland and John M. Jones, *Reagan at Westminster: Foreshadowing the End of the Cold War* (College Station: Texas A&M University Press, 2010), 78.

64. Ezekiel 33:6, quoted in Pattullo, "Second Elder Gives Battle," 4.

65. Seymour Martin Lipset, *American Exceptionalism: A Double-Edged Sword* (New York: W. W. Norton, 1996), 20.

66. Linenthal, *Changing Images*, 98.

67. Mildred Aldrich, *On the Edge of the War Zone, from the Battle of the Marne to the Entrance of the Stars and Stripes* (Boston: Small, Maynard, 1917), 101. Bourne subverts this position by insisting that German ideology underlies most progress in Western thought, and by castigating Germany as other and evil, Americans destroy their own ideological platform, creating a vacuum that must be somehow ameliorated. Randolph S. Bourne, "American Use for German Ideals," in *War and the Intellectuals: Essays by Randolph S. Bourne, 1915–1919*, ed. Carl Resek (New York: Harper & Row, 1964), 48–52.

68. Alvin Cullum York and Thomas John Skeyhill, *Sergeant York, His Own Life Story and War Diary* (Garden City, NY: Doubleday, 1928), 178.

69. Paul Ramsey and Stanley Hauerwas, *Speak Up for Just War or Pacifism: A Critique of the United Methodist Bishops' Pastoral Letter "In Defense of Creation"* (University Park: Pennsylvania State University Press, 1988).

70. G. H. P. Showalter, "So-Called Conscientious Objectors," *Firm Foundation* (1919): 2; Foy E. Wallace, "The Christian and the Government," *Bible Banner* 4, no. 8 (1942): 6.

71. Michael W. Casey, "From Pacifism to Patriotism: The Emergence of Civil Religion in the Churches of Christ during World War I," *Mennonite Quarterly Review* 66, no. 3 (1992): 378.

72. Pattullo, "Second Elder Gives Battle," 3.

73. Christopher Joseph Nicodemus Capozzola, *Uncle Sam Wants You: World War I and the Making of the Modern American Citizen* (New York: Oxford University Press, 2008), 69.

74. With regard to the former, see Susan Schultz Huxman and Gerald Biesecker-Mast, "In the World but Not of It: Mennonite Traditions as Resources for Rhetorical Invention," *Rhetoric & Public Affairs* 7, no. 4 (2004): 539–54. As an example of the latter, see Randolph S. Bourne, *Untimely Papers* (New York: B. W. Huebsch, 1919), 164–72.

75. Pattullo, "Second Elder Gives Battle," 3.

76. Pattullo, "Second Elder Gives Battle," 4.

77. Pattullo, "Second Elder Gives Battle," 4.

78. Pattullo, "Second Elder Gives Battle," 3.

79. Reproduced in Capozzola, *Uncle Sam Wants You*, 68.

80. York and Skeyhill, *Sergeant York*, 157–63.

81. Pattullo, "Second Elder Gives Battle," 4.

82. Given the substantial costs of the First World War, about 60 percent of surveyed Americans expressed regret about American involvement by 1937. In the intervening years between World Wars, York consistently tried to direct attention away from his military career and toward his efforts to strengthen educational opportunities in Appalachia. Michael Birdwell, *Celluloid Soldiers:*

Warner Bros Campaign against Nazism, rev. ed. (New York: New York University Press, 2000), 89.

83. Gronbeck, "Rhetorics of the Past," 56.

84. Birdwell, "Alvin Cullum York," 327.

85. John Belton, *American Cinema/American Culture,* 4th ed. (New York: McGraw-Hill, 2008), 207.

12

Writing the Sovereign Citizen in Cold War Era Expatriation Law

A Rhetorical History of Yaser Hamdi's Settlement Agreement (2004)

Margaret Franz

What does it mean to be a US citizen? An enigmatic case, *Hamdi v. Rumsfeld* (2004) demonstrates that the question remains unsettled. Detained in Afghanistan at the very beginning of the War on Terror in 2001, Yaser Esam Hamdi found himself held incommunicado as an enemy combatant in Guantanamo Bay, Cuba, despite his status as a US citizen.[1] Even his father's numerous writ of habeas corpus petitions did not grant him the fundamental rights of a US citizen—a hearing to contest his detention—until the Supreme Court finally declared in 2004 that, although US citizens can be classified as enemy combatants, they must be granted habeas hearings.[2] Nevertheless, the US government did not give Hamdi a hearing. Instead, it released him from detention under the condition that he reside in Saudi Arabia, renounce his US citizenship, and foreswear his capacity to sue the US government.[3] In other words, Yaser Hamdi, a dual Saudi Arabian and US citizen, born in Baton Rouge, Louisiana, was expatriated in a way that seemed nonconsensual and thus illegal.

Although the United States has a long history of nonconsensually expatriating its citizens, the Warren Court (1953–69) ended the practice when *Afroyim v. Rusk* (1967) declared that only citizens can relinquish their citizenship status.[4] According to legal historian Patrick Weil, *Afroyim* held that the US citizen is essentially "sovereign," or outside the grasp of congressional power to judge who is and is not a citizen.[5] As Weil suggests, the Warren Court's construction of citizenship finally made the letter of the law square with the United States' history of liberal ideals about citizenship as an inherent right that is granted at birth and can only be modified through one's choice.[6]

Yet Hamdi's settlement agreement complicates this depiction of sovereign citizenship because many argue that he could not consent to expatriate himself while in indefinite detention.[7] Reflecting the case's incongruency with common understandings of US citizenship, David Dow, a law professor from the University of Houston, even wrote a letter to the *New York Times* correcting the newspaper's assertion that Hamdi was no longer a US citizen. Citing *Afroyim* and its follow-up *Vance v. Terrazas* (1980), he argued that "the United States government has no authority to compel such a renunciation, and Mr. Hamdi's proclamation that he is no longer an American is legally meaningless."[8] Dow was not alone in viewing the case as out of step with dominant understandings of citizenship. Already horrified by the executive power asserted in the Patriot Act and the detention of US citizens Jose Padilla and John Walker Lindh, legal commenters and journalists depicted Hamdi's detention and expatriation as signs that the understanding of "US citizen" articulated in *Afroyim* had been corrupted by the rampant xenophobic paranoia undergirding the War on Terror. Particularly, many wondered *why* Hamdi was expatriated without being granted a hearing. How was his expatriation authorized?[9]

Legal scholars have mainly answered this question by assessing whether Hamdi's expatriation violated the precedents set in *Afroyim* and *Vance*.[10] However, as I will show, the depictions in these cases of how citizens voluntarily expatriate themselves make this a question that is largely undecidable. This uncertainty stems in part from the indeterminacy of all legal texts.[11] It also, however, stems from a persistent ambiguity regarding the source of authority to make and unmake citizens that has been written into expatriation law. As Dow stated, according to *Afroyim* and *Vance*, only the citizen can relinquish their status. However, Hamdi reportedly "eagerly" signed the settlement agreement in order to get out of indefinite detention, and then, he explicitly renounced his US citizenship in Riyadh upon arriving in Saudi Arabia.[12] Did Hamdi expatriate himself, or was he coerced? If coerced, does that preclude the definition of US citizenship?

Because these questions do not have clear-cut answers, this chapter poses another line of questioning: Why did Hamdi's expatriation strike so many legal scholars as incongruent with US citizenship law? More importantly, how has expatriation law been written so as to allow for such contradictory understandings of citizenship? How have these contradictions affected understandings of US citizenship in public life? Answering these questions from the perspective of rhetorical history illuminates how US citizenship has been shaped in and through legal and rhetorical cultures that have obfuscated the source of authority to determine citizenship. That is, Hamdi's expatriation is only one case in a larger pool of contested denationalizations and nationalizations that gain the force of law through reference to disparate bodies of power (e.g., congressional plenary power and territorial jurisdiction).[13] Specifically, I argue that the rhetorical devices—mainly the inverted parallelism of chiasmus—used to describe citizenship during the Cold War equivocated the relationship between citizen and state, and thus widened a gap in how US citizenship is represented conceptually and how it has been written into law.

In exploring why Hamdi's expatriation seemed so out of step with norms of US citizenship, I begin by summarizing how the relationship between rhetorical history and legal studies illuminates the struggle between law, context, and history animating conceptual imaginations of citizenship. I then trace the legal-rhetorical context that purportedly authorized it: the Warren Court's expatriation decisions during the Cold War. Specifically, I focus on how the Court articulated the Fourteenth Amendment to expatriation law in a series of cases in 1958 and detail how chiasmus supported this reading of the Fourteenth Amendment in the landmark decision *Afroyim v. Rusk* (1967). Figuring the citizen-country relationship with chiasmus, *Afroyim* equivocated the source of authority to make and unmake citizens. Third, the essay turns to how the citizen in *Afroyim* is reconstituted in *Vance v. Terrazas* (1980), which holds that only a citizen's explicit renunciation counts as grounds for expatriation. However, in this case, the ambiguity of the citizen-country relationship is mitigated by substituting a citizen's assent for her intent. Last, returning to Hamdi's settlement agreement, I argue that because the *Vance* decision figured speech as the mediator between country and citizen, Hamdi's entrance into the liberal citizen subject identity—through the granting of habeas corpus by the majority opinion—is also the moment where he becomes "outlawed" through his own speech. The public discomfort concerning the decision signals our need to revisit the chiasmic relationship between citizen and country upheld in *Afroyim* and *Vance* and to think about the ethics of language as mediating our political relationship to the state.

Law as Rhetorical Historiography

As the tracing of symbolic constructions, rhetorical history is a method for understanding how such concepts as citizenship are shaped over time through their articulation in multiple domains of public life.[14] Specifically, James Jasinski's outline of constitutive rhetorical historiography in *Doing Rhetorical History* analyzes how political concepts are (re)constituted *rhetorically*, through textual practices that shape how ideas can be stated and made sense of, as well as *historically*, through everyday interaction and embodied performances.[15] Discursive practices, such as tropes, schemes, and patterns of usage, bear a constitutive relationship to the shaping of ideas throughout time, "creat[ing] what they describe as they simultaneously describe what they create."[16] Thus, the central project of a constitutive rhetorical historiography charts such alterations in "usages" in order to analyze how the "idioms of public life (e.g., liberalism, conservatism, free market capitalism, pro-choice or pro-life)" are reconstituted at particular historical moments.[17] Attending to "the integrity of the text as a field of discursive action" unveils "the ways specific discursive strategies and textual dynamics shape and reshape the contours of political concepts and ideas."[18]

Jasinski's constitutive rhetorical historiography offers particular insight into the social construction of such legal concepts as citizenship because reading and writing law requires reviewing centuries of precedent and legal doctrines to make judgments about the present.[19] That means that legal texts must be read against multiple historically situated "fields of discursive action" that no doubt influence how they are reconstituted in the particular instances in which they are interpreted and written. Jasinski's use of "historiography," as opposed to "history," also conveys how legal texts are not rhetorical simply because they are written in language and directed towards particular audiences.[20] The whole procedure of reading and writing law is also fundamentally rhetorical because it involves using practices of invention that assemble texts into a particular time and space in order to authorize a decision about the present.[21] That is, similar to how historiography focuses on *how* and *why* history is written as such, studying the development of legal concepts involves tracing how concepts are reviewed and rewritten throughout time. Timothy Barouch makes this point in his analysis of "late liberal jurisprudence," arguing that "when a judge authors an opinion, he or she is doing more than declaring a winner, articulating an ideology, and sending an opinion into circulation. He or she is performing the habits and practices of sound judgment through rhetorical choices."[22] These rhetorical choices have broader cultural effects not just in the sense that their hegemonic weight perpetuates and hardens ideologies. According to Barouch, the rhetorical choices of jurists "reshape forms of argument that construct judicial authority."[23] Thus, making law is both an inventive practice that requires the jurist to assemble arguments from prior case law and a practice in reconstituting the law's authority as such.

For this reason, reading and writing law is a practice in rhetorical historiography, wherein the jurist reconstructs, or reconstitutes, past texts in order to interpret and create new law from old as well as new ways of justifying itself. Importantly, however, Hamdi's settlement agreement shows that the process of rhetorical historiography can disrupt commonly held assumptions about what legal words mean. As legal historian Robert Gordon claims: "The historicized past poses a perpetual threat to the legal rationalizations of the present. Brought back to life, the past unsettles and destabilizes the stories we tell about law to make us feel comfortable with the way things are."[24] This is because the practice of history brings with it its own discursive patterns, figures, and, ultimately, "traces" that complicate how the past can be "tamed" for present use.[25] In analyzing the process of using the past to validate present notions of citizenship, this essay traces the fragments of legal history that were reviewed, put together, and disseminated in legal culture during the *Hamdi* case. For this reason, I begin my inquiry into *Hamdi* with the Warren Court's treatment of expatriation in the 1960s.

Writing the Sovereign Citizen during the Cold War

Chief Justice Earl Warren's expatriation jurisprudence is often seen as a quiet civil rights revolution because, while it ended a surge of nonconsensual expatriations during the twentieth century, it was not as publicized as *Brown v. Board of Education* or *Miranda v. Arizona*.[26] Nevertheless, the Court's intervention into expatriation law mitigated a practice that journalists and legal scholars increasingly described as unfair and illegal.[27] Indeed, between 1907 and the *Afroyim* decision in 1967, twenty-two thousand people were "consensually" expatriated by states attorneys.[28] Despite a consistent legal doctrine mandating that expatriation be voluntary,[29] during this time period an increasing number of expatriates appealed the supposedly voluntary process of expatriation. However, until the 1950s, the Supreme Court declined to intervene in the vast majority of these cases because the Nationalization Act of 1906 and the Expatriation Act of 1907 gave Congress the power to both define and judge "the outward and visible standards" of the "volition" to expatriate, in turn authorizing Congress to "compel the individual to accept the consequences of his freely willed decision."[30] "Voluntary" expatriating acts included marrying male foreigners, serving in a foreign military, and voting in a foreign election. Although the Cable Act of 1922 stopped the expatriation of women after marrying a foreigner,[31] the Nationality Act of 1940 added even more avenues for ostensibly voluntary expatriation. Now, citizens could be expatriated for demonstrating a "lack of attachment" to the Constitution during naturalization and for residing abroad for extended periods of time.[32] Because of these laws, most judicial reviews of expatriation law up until the 1950s dealt with how the

US government should prove which citizens committed predetermined expatriating acts willingly.

The actual congressional power to declare expatriating acts did not get contested until 1958, when Justices Earl Warren and Hugo Black began reading the Fourteenth Amendment of the Constitution as privileging the citizen's status as a legal subject over Congress's power to determine the criteria for citizenship.[33] In 1958, the Supreme Court reviewed three cases that highlighted the conflict between the Fourteenth Amendment's definition of citizenship and Congress's traditional power over naturalization and foreign affairs: *Perez v. Brownell* (1958), *Nishikawa v. Dulles* (1958), and *Trop v. Dulles* (1958).

Like most expatriation cases, all three involve the exclusion of people who did not fit the Cold War body politic due to their racial identity or their apparent lack of patriotism. For instance, Clemente Martinez Perez was born in El Paso, Texas, in 1909, but because he moved to Mexico at the age of ten or eleven, he did not become aware that he was a US citizen until 1928.[34] In the early 1940s, he took advantage of the alien railroad labor program and entered the United States as a Mexican laborer. In 1947, however, upon trying to enter the United States as a citizen, he was excluded on the grounds that he had expatriated himself by voting in a Mexican election and by not serving in the military during World War II. With the help of the ACLU, he sued US Attorney General Herbert Brownell in 1954, requesting that he be declared a US citizen because voting in a foreign election does not signal voluntary renunciation of US citizenship.[35] In a 5–4 vote, the Supreme Court ended up ruling against Perez, declaring that Congress had the authority to pass legislation that avoided "serious international embarrassment," potentially resulting from voting in foreign elections.[36]

Mitsugi Nishikawa was born in California in 1916. After he moved to Japan in 1939 to attend university, World War II began, and he was forced to join the Japanese Army. After the war ended, the US consulate in Japan denied his application for a passport to return to the United States on the grounds that he had expatriated himself for serving in a foreign army. With the help of the ACLU, he sued Dulles on the grounds that the Japanese government forced him to serve in their military, and thus, he had not voluntarily surrendered his US citizenship. In a 7 to 2 vote, the Court ruled in favor of Nishikawa because he served in a foreign military under duress.

Alfred Trop was born in Ohio. Although Trop was white and did not hold dual citizenship with another country, the US government deemed him unfit for citizenship because he demonstrated a lack of patriotism upon abandoning his post on May 22, 1944, when serving in the US military in Casablanca.[37] He was only AWOL for one day before surrendering to a US officer. However, he was convicted of desertion and sentenced to three years hard labor.[38] When he tried to apply for a passport in 1952, the US State Department denied his application on the grounds that he had expatriated himself according to the Nationality Act of 1940, which defined refusal to serve in the military during wartime as an expatriating act. With the help of the ACLU, he also sued Dulles on the grounds that expatriation should not be a punishment for military violations. As in *Nishikawa*, the Court agreed, and ruled in Trop's favor.

Together, these cases lay the discursive blueprint for *Afroyim*'s construction of what Weil calls "the sovereign citizen," or the citizen whose status emerges from and is sustained by birth or naturalization within US jurisdiction. As Weil argues, the sovereign citizen is sovereign precisely because his or her status precludes state recognition. Even though the most publicized phrase from Warren's *Perez* dissent was that citizenship is "nothing less than the right to have rights,"[39] Weil argues that Trop and Nishikawa establish that citizen sovereignty goes further than the articulation of citizenship with rights because it protects citizens from unwilling expatriation even if they also possess another nationality. In effect, sovereign citizenship redefines the concept as "both a club that limits entrance from outsiders and a public good that places no inherent limits to the secured rights of its members."[40] In other words, sovereignty's association with ultimate power secures the citizen against the state's declaration of laws that outlaw the citizen's identification with threatening associations. Even in the context of Cold War rhetoric of securitization, then, the figure of the sovereign citizen protects individual legal subjects from an overreach of state power.

Warren's early drafts in *Perez* reflect his belief in the necessity of a secure citizenship status that precedes congressional power. For instance, he described individual sovereignty as preceding the whims of Congress: "The people who created this government endowed it with broad powers. They created a sovereign state with power to function as sovereignty. But the citizens themselves are sovereign, and their citizenship is not subject to the general powers of their government."[41] Warren expanded on this concept in his majority opinion in *Trop*, which stated that "in our country the people are sovereign and the Government cannot sever its relationship to the people by taking away their citizenship."[42] Here, Warren used his characteristic precise and normative style to locate the citizen's status as negating the government's ability to alter the individual's legal status.

As mentioned above, Warren supported this novel view of citizenship by referring to the Fourteenth Amendment's citizenship clause. While Justice Felix Frankfurter did not see the relevance of the Fourteenth Amendment to expatriation laws because of Congress's traditional power over naturalization and foreign affairs, Black and Warren wrote in various memoranda, draft opinions, and correspondences that the citizenship clause invalidated congressional power to determine acts that constitute expatriation apart from the citizen's explicit renunciation.[43] Unlike the Fourteenth Amendment's due process clause, which permits the deprivation of life, liberty, or property as long as the government follows a certain set of procedures, Black and Warren expressed that the language of the citizenship clause gave absolute protection to the basic right of citizenship. For example, Warren corresponded with one of his law clerks about the notion of "sovereignty of the individual" and its relevance to expatriation law.[44] Moreover, in a memorandum regarding *Perez v. Brownell* (1957), Warren cited the monumental citizenship decision *United States v. Wong Kim Ark* (1898) as holding that "Congress is without power to alter the effect of birth in the United States."[45] Both Warren and Black viewed US citizenship as a one-way street where once individuals are "subject to jurisdiction" they cannot be expunged "because one branch of that government can be said to have a conceivably rational basis to do so" unless they choose to leave.[46] In this way, Warren and Black argued that once a citizen becomes a citizen—either through birth-on-soil or naturalization—she is the ultimate source of sustaining that status.

Even though Warren and Black did not manage to completely withdraw congressional authority to define a citizen's intent to expatriate by overturning *Perez*, *Afroyim v. Rusk* gave them another opportunity to do so in 1967.[47] In this case, Black authored the majority decision overturning *Perez* and, thus, congressional authority to expatriate citizens without their explicit renunciation. Here, then, the sovereign citizen became an official part of law.[48] It is no surprise then that, like *Perez*, *Afroyim*'s rhetoric was largely praised both in the mainstream press and in law journals. For example, the *Boston Globe* characterized the goal of the "liberal wing" of the Court as to "protect" and "guard" citizenship.[49] A few days later the *Globe* ran a story titled "No More Banishment," which lauded Black's statement that "citizenship should not be trifled with."[50] This phrase was quoted by a number of articles in the days following the publication of the opinion.[51] A *New York Times* article titled "Always a Citizen" claimed on June 1 that "Chief Justice Warren's magisterial dissent in the *Perez v. Brownell* denationalization case in 1958 is one of the most impressive opinions in his service on the Supreme Court. That opinion has now nine years later achieved vindication in the Court's ruling this week."[52]

One of the most highly circulated excerpts from *Afroyim* aptly captures the form of sovereign citizenship: "Citizenship in this Nation is a part of a co-operative affair. *Its citizenry is the country and the country is its citizenry.* The very nature of our free government makes it completely incongruous to have a rule of law under which a group of citizens temporarily in office can deprive another group of citizens of their citizenship."[53] Here, the citizen's intent to expatriate shifts from something that can be outwardly determined by policy to something that only the citizen herself determines. In doing so, Black's rhetoric finally embodies the kind of sovereign citizenship described in *Perez* and *Trop* by putting the citizen in an egalitarian relationship with the government, which is deemed incapable of erecting laws that undo one's citizenship status. This egalitarianism is formally expressed by the chiasmus or inverted parallelism, "its citizenry is the country, and the country is its citizenry," which is then reiterated by the use of citizens as a synecdoche for Congress. Both formal moves construct a congruency between citizen and state. Indeed, Thomas Alexander Aleinikoff argues that the celebrated phrasing turns on the "congruency thesis," which sees citizenship as the "meeting ground of sovereignty and democracy: sovereignty is located in the citizenry (the *demos*) that selects those who will captain the ship of the state."[54] Such a configuration exemplifies the ideal of liberal self-governance, where the citizen regulates his or her own will, in turn forming part of the larger body politic.

It is important that Black expressed the notion of sovereign citizenship via chiasmus, putting words and things into a congruent relationship by reversing their order. As Robert Hariman states, chiasmus is a seldom used yet often-quoted trope because most see it as overly ornamental and artificial.[55] Nevertheless, chiasmus has a long history of figuring relationships of power, such as the "king's two bodies" refrain: "The king is dead. Long live the king."[56] Chiasmus is frequently used to represent complex relationships of power perhaps because the instability and ambiguity among terms generates a third, often unstated, term that grounds an ontological claim concerning the relationship between objects as well as the relationship between word and world.[57] Chiasmus thereby generates an ambiguity about how objects are put into relation in the first place. For instance, the above refrain leaves unanswered the question of how the king lives on once he dies. Throughout history, the English parliament, monarchy, and common law courts struggled over precisely which part of the king's two bodies sustained sovereign power upon the death of a monarch.[58]

Justice John M. Harlan II attacked the chiasmic relationship between citizen and country in his dissent. He argued that, "finally, the Court declares that its result is bottomed upon the 'language and the purpose' of the Citizenship Clause of the Fourteenth Amendment; in explanation, the Court offers only the terms of the clause itself, the contention that any other result would be 'completely incongruous' and the *essentially arcane* observation that the 'citizenry is the country and the country is its citizenry.' I can find nothing in this extraordinary series of circumventions which permits, still less compels, the imposition of this constitutional constraint upon the authority of Congress."[59]

Harlan highlighted the ambiguity (i.e., the arcaneness) of the chiasmus while lamenting that the majority based its judgment on the "terms" present in the citizenship clause itself. Ironically, for Harlan the judicial branch of the state did not adequately judge why the citizenship clause's words remove the state from the position of ultimate judge. Justice Frankfurter's former law clerk Alexander Bickel expressed a similar condemnation of the opinion's ambiguity. In an article attacking the Warren Court's figuration of citizenship during this time period, Bickel wrote that the relationship expressed in the chiasmus was "regressive rhetoric."[60] Comparing the chiasmus to Justice Roger Taney's conflation of white people and the nation-state in *Dred Scott* (1857), Bickel argued that the phrase is overly ambiguous: "A relationship between government and the governed that turns on citizenship can always be dissolved or denied. . . . It is at best something that was given, and given to some and not others, and it can be taken away."[61]

Bickel and Harlan's critiques portend the problems with interpreting the citizen's intent to expatriate that the *Hamdi* case illuminates decades later. Although the expatriation cases from the 1940s and 1950s directed the US government to judge the citizen's will through establishing the facticity of predetermined expatriating acts, *Afroyim* deprived the government of its authority to determine what constituted the will to expatriate aside from explicit and formal renunciation. As sovereign, the citizen herself determined her will to expatriate. Because citizenship "sticks" to the body at birth or naturalization unless the citizen *intended* to detach from the country, Congress lost the power to determine at the onset what acts detach the *person* from the *citizen*. As will be evident in *Vance v. Terrazas* and later during Hamdi's settlement agreement, the citizen-country chiasmus opens questions about sovereignty posed by Harlan and Bickel. What mediates the relationship between citizen and country? Who decides when citizens expatriate themselves?

Reconstituting the Sovereign Citizen in *Vance v. Terrazas* (1980)

Weil suggests that *Afroyim* is the apotheosis of citizen sovereignty and that a subsequent expatriation decision, *Vance v. Terrazas* (1980), affirms the Warren Court's linking of the citizenship clause to the sovereign citizen.[62] In glowing praise of Warren Court liberalism, Weil states that "to the specter of expatriation that cast a tall shadow over a great many American citizens, the United States Supreme Court, under Warren's leadership, responded by embracing the innovative concept of citizenship sovereignty. Nowhere else in the democratic world has a court of law defined so smartly and with such novelty the complexity of the link between the individual and the nation-state."[63]

The discourse of expatriation in public culture supports Weil's arguments. After the 1980s, expatriation largely became associated with taxes and corporate interests in offshore banking as well as with wealthy retirees known as expats.[64] The privileged connotation of both of these associations signals that expatriation was no longer seen as something imposed on "undesirable" citizens by the government and was instead a voluntary choice carried out by wealthy individuals. Nevertheless, an attention to how *Vance* deals with *Afroyim*'s chiasmus foreshadows the problems with consent and sovereignty that arise during the settlement agreement's reliance on expatriation law.

In 1947, Laurence J. Terrazas was born in the United States to Mexican parents, acquiring dual citizenship at birth. In the fall of 1970, Terrazas filled out an application for a certificate of Mexican nationality in order to continue to study at a university in Monterrey, Mexico. In doing so, he swore "adherence, obedience, and submission to the laws and authorities of the Mexican republic" and "expressly renounce[d] United States citizenship, as well as any submission, obedience, and loyalty to any foreign government, especially to that of the United States of America."[65] After Terrazas revealed his activities to an officer in the US consulate, the US Department of State issued a certificate of loss of nationality. In response, Terrazas filed suit against Secretary of State Cyrus Vance. The District Court found in favor of Vance, claiming that Terrazas had acted "voluntarily in swearing allegiance to Mexico and renouncing allegiance to the United States."[66] However, the Court of Appeals reversed, finding that taking an oath to a foreign state was not "clear, convincing, and unequivocal evidence" of "intent on [the] appellee's part to renounce his United States citizenship."[67]

In both the district and appeals levels of *Vance*, justices struggled to square assent with intent in deciding whether Terrazas voluntarily relinquished his US citizenship upon uttering the words of the oath for Mexican nationality. While the District Court claimed that the court must read Terrazas's intent from his assent in the oath, the Court of Appeals claimed that the US government did not prove that upon speaking the oath Terrazas intended to renounce his US citizenship. In weighing these two holdings in the context of expatriation case law, Supreme Court Justice Byron White similarly struggled with intent and assent in reading the citizen's desire to expatriate oneself. He wrote that "in the last analysis [of *Afroyim*], expatriation depends on the will of the citizen rather than on the will of Congress and its assessment of his conduct."[68] White then argued that the Court, "in overruling *Perez*, 'reject[ed] the idea . . . that, aside from the Fourteenth Amendment, Congress has any general power, express or implied, to take away an American citizen's citizenship without his assent' and that 'assent should not therefore be read as a code word for intent to renounce.'"[69] In considering case law, White struggled with deciphering intent from assent. Conceding that it was impossible to know the mind of the individual, he wrote, "It is difficult to understand that assent to loss of citizenship would mean anything less than an intent to relinquish citizenship." This led to the conclusion that "an expatriation act and an intent to relinquish citizenship must be proved by a preponderance of the evidence. We also hold that when one of the statutory expatriating acts is proved, it is constitutional to presume it to have been a voluntary act until and unless proved otherwise by the actor."[70]

In this way, *Vance* maintained the integrity of the citizen-country chiasmus by defining the will of the citizen as legible through assent. Since there is no way to truly know the citizen's mind, the Court must judge intent only by what it can see and hear.

On one hand, this articulation of will represents the epitome of liberal notions of consent. For example, Western thought imagines the community of citizens as one in which speech substitutes for violence.[71] Legible speech is the medium par excellence by which the liberal subject exercises her will in the political sphere. On the other hand, by figuring speech as mediating between citizen and country, *Vance* continues to locate the power of interpretation in what Robert Cover calls the jurispathic principle, or the power of the courts and the state to decide what to make of a citizen's speech.[72] The jurispathic principle of legal interpretation privileges the state's authority over deciding legal meaning because of the law's association with the "state's imperfect monopoly over the domain of violence."[73]

If intent to expatriate arises from the citizen's speech, then both Terraza and Hamdi's renunciations are valid.[74] As mentioned above, Hamdi "eagerly" signed the settlement agreement.[75] Yet, as a number of legal scholars have stated, anyone who knows anything about consent would argue that Hamdi assented under extreme duress and coercion.[76] Moreover, Hamdi did not even receive his end of the deal; the Department of Justice never actually granted his habeas hearing. In the end, Hamdi's only words to the state were the words that expatriated him. Nevertheless, it is impossible to discern Hamdi's intention regarding expatriating himself given the relationship between citizen and country articulated in *Vance*. Because it is impossible to know the mind of the citizen, the state, with all its jurispathic power, has to decipher intent from his speech.

Conclusion: Hamdi's Settlement Agreement and the Enigma of US Citizenship

From the perspective of the state, Hamdi's intent to expatriate was readily apparent through his agreement to expatriate himself. Indeed, the agreement stipulated that "Hamdi agrees to appear before a diplomatic or consular officer of the United States at the United States Embassy in Riyadh, Saudi Arabia, formally to renounce any claim that he may have to United States nationality pursuant to Section 349(a)(5)."[77] Yet, from the beginning of his ordeal, the US government directed Hamdi's ability to communicate intent through channels it had predetermined. First, he could only speak through his father, who petitioned on his behalf. Then, his speech was filtered through his court-appointed lawyer Frank Dunham, whom the government denied access to his client and then censored. During oral arguments, Dunham indicated that he could not even represent Hamdi's speech: "Well, I've only recently been allowed to talk to my client, Your Honor, and everything he has told me they tell me is classified, so I'm not allowed to convey it to the Court this morning."[78] Finally, Justice Sandra Day O'Connor's plurality decision held that enemy combatants who are citizens must be granted a forum to contest their status.[79] In announcing her decision to the press, she reiterated that even when classified as enemy combatants, citizens must be given the opportunity to receive "notice of the factual basis for his classification and a fair opportunity to rebut the government's factual assertions before a neutral decision maker." Hamdi must be given the opportunity to tell "his side of the story."

However, despite O'Connor's lofty rhetoric, Hamdi never received the opportunity to break out of the sanctioned channels of communicating consent. After months of negotiation with Saudi Arabia, the US government released Hamdi from detention upon renouncing his US citizenship and agreeing to never step foot on US soil again—the soil upon which he was born. Once granted the chance to express his will as a citizen, Hamdi paradoxically outlawed himself in order to attain freedom. Necessarily mediated by the official channels of communication—the lawyer, the signature, the oath of renunciation—Hamdi's speech only mattered to the US government whence it fulfilled the mission of expunging him from citizenship. As Cover has claimed, the legal meanings of speech acts always occur in the shadow of violence and coercion.[80]

Set against the legal rhetoric making up the history of expatriation law, Hamdi's settlement agreement serves as an uneasy reminder that one's citizenship status is only as secure as the state's authorization to recognize it.[81] That such a conceptualization of citizenship feels so discomforting and foreign is, of course, not a novel phenomenon. For example, studying early American public culture, Jennifer Mercieca has shown how the stories we tell about citizenship have never quite matched up with the laws and policies used to define and regulate citizenship.[82] However, by tracing the rhetorical process of constituting and reconstituting the citizen within legal discourse, we can move closer to inventing new and different ways of figuring the citizen in law. Cover gestures towards this possibility in his discussion of the world of rules, narratives, and norms—the *nomos*—involved in making law meaningful to people. He states, "Legal meaning is a challenging enrichment of social life, a potential restraint on arbitrary power and violence. We ought to stop circumscribing the nomos; we ought to invite new worlds."[83] Rhetorical historiography is an apt method for figuring out how tracing the development of legal meaning as well as for conjuring up new worlds and new interpretations. Thinking back to Jasinski's method of tracing changes in political concepts as they manifest in historical texts, we can begin writing a new rhetorical historiography of citizenship by how we deliberate about what it means to belong to a country today.

Notes

1. Michael H. Mobbs, "Declaration of Michael H. Mobbs" (Virginia: Special Advisor to the Under Secretary of Defense for Policy, July 24, 2002). Importantly, according to Peter Nyers, "Yaser Hamdi" is actually spelled "Himdy." The discrepancy is the result of "improper translation from the Arabic to English on his Saudi passport and then on his American birth certificate." Citing Nyers, Jacqueline Stevens argues that the permanence of "Yaser Hamdi" in public and legal discourse, despite the error, encapsulates the instability of citizenship as a legal status. See Jacqueline Stevens, "The Alien Who Is a Citizen," in *Citizenship in*

Question: Evidentiary Birthright and Statelessness, ed. Benjamin N. Lawrance and Jacqueline Stevens, (Durham, NC: Duke University Press, 2017), 221.

2. Hamdi v. Rumsfeld, 542 US 507 (2004). For an overview of the development of habeas corpus as a check on government power, see Alan Clarke, "Habeas Corpus: The Historical Debate," *New York Law School Journal of Human Rights* 14 (1998): 375–434.

3. "Hamdi v. Rumsfeld Settlement Agreement," Washington, DC, September 24, 2004, http://news.findlaw.com/hdocs/docs/hamdi/91704stlagrmnt.html.

4. See Ben Herzog, *Revoking Citizenship: Expatriation in America from the Colonial Era to the War on Terror* (New York: New York University Press, 2017); and Patrick Weil, *The Sovereign Citizen: Denaturalization and the Origins of the American Republic* (Philadelphia: University of Pennsylvania Press, 2013). For an explanation of the history of deporting US citizens, see Kevin R. Johnson, "The Forgotten Repatriation of Persons of Mexican Ancestry and Lessons for the War on Terror," *Pace Law School Review* 26, no. 1 (2005): 1–26; and Johnson, "Race, the Immigration Laws, and Domestic Race Relations: A Magic Mirror into the Heart of Darkness," *Indiana Law Journal* 73 (1998): 1111–60.

5. Weil, *Sovereign Citizen.*

6. Weil, *Sovereign Citizen,* 260. Here, Weil draws on the legacy of Alexis de Toqueville who described US citizenship as fundamentally different from citizenship in Europe because it was based in consent and (supposedly) not ascription. For similar histories of the ideal of US citizenship in comparison to its legal evolution, see James H. Kettner, *The Development of American Citizenship, 1608–1870* (Chapel Hill: University of North Carolina Press, 2014); and Rogers M. Smith, *Civic Ideals: Conflicting Visions of Citizenship in US History* (New Haven, CT: Yale University Press, 1999).

7. Saad Gul, "Return of the Native—An Assessment of the Citizenship Renunciation Clause in Hamdi's Settlement Agreement in the Light of Citizenship Jurisprudence," *Northern Illinois University Law Review* 27 (2007): 131; Abigail D. Lauer, "The Easy Way Out? The Yaser Hamdi Release Agreement and the United States' Treatment of the Citizen Enemy Combatant Dilemma," *Cornell Law Review* 91 (2006): 927.

8. David R. Dow, "Opinion: Yaser Hamdi, US Citizen," *New York Times,* October 15, 2004, https://www.nytimes.com/2004/10/15/opinion/yaser-hamdi-us -citizen-312622.html#story-continues-1.

9. For examples of commentary from legal experts see: Michael Dorf, "Who Decides Whether Yaser Hamdi, or Any Other Citizen, Is an Enemy Combatant?," Findlaw, August 21, 2002, https://supreme.findlaw.com; Cass Sustein, "The Smallest Court in the Land," *New York Times,* July 4, 2004, https:// www.nytimes.com; Anita Ramasastry, "Do Hamdi And Padilla Need Company?," Findlaw, August 21, 2002, https://supreme.findlaw.com; and Stephen

I. Vladeck, "Enemy Aliens, Enemy Property, and Access to the Courts," *Lewis &Clark Law Review* 11, no. 4 (2007): 963–96. Importantly, Hamdi's depiction of citizenship continues to be controversial. See Mark Stern, "Stephen Breyer Is Worried about the Forever War's Permanent Prisoners. He's 15 Years Too Late," *Slate*, June 10, 2019, https://slate.com; Ian Zuckerman, "Hoda Muthana and Trump's Assault on Birthright Citizenship," *Guardian*, March 1, 2019, https://www.theguardian.com.

10. See for example, Gul, "Return of the Native"; Lauer, "Easy Way Out?"; Patti Tamara Lenard, "Democratic Citizenship and Denationalization," *American Political Science Review* 112, no. 1 (2018): 99–111; and Peter J. Spiro, "Expatriating Terrorists Symposium: Citizenship, Immigration, and National Security after 9/11," *Fordham Law Review* 82 (2014): 2169–88.

11. Legal indeterminacy is a core tenet of critical race theory, critical legal rhetoric, and critical legal studies. For representative examples, see Richard Delgado and Jean Stefancic, *Critical Race Theory* (New York: New York University Press, 2017); Marouf Hasian Jr., Celeste Condit, and John Lucaites, "The Rhetorical Boundaries of 'the Law': A Consideration of the Rhetorical Culture of Legal Practice and the Case of the 'Separate but Equal' Doctrine," *Quarterly Journal of Speech* 82, no. 4 (November 1996): 323–42; and Mark V. Tushnet, "Following the Rules Laid Down: A Critique of Interpretivism and Neutral Principles," *Harvard Law Review* 96, no. 4 (1983): 781–827.

12. Joel Brinkley and Eric Lightblau, "US Releases Saudi-American It Had Captured in Afghanistan," *New York Times*, October 12, 2004, sec. A.

13. See Herzog, *Revoking Citizenship*; Benjamin N. Lawrance and Jacqueline Stevens, *Citizenship in Question: Evidentiary Birthright and Statelessness* (Durham, NC: Duke University Press, 2019).

14. Kathleen J. Turner, "Introduction: Rhetorical History as Social Construction," in Turner, *Doing Rhetorical History*, 4.

15. James Jasinski, "A Constitutive Framework for Rhetorical Historiography: Toward an Understanding of the Discursive (Re)Constitution of 'Constitution' in *The Federalist Papers*," in Turner, *Doing Rhetorical History*, 74.

16. Jasinski, "Constitutive Framework," 74.

17. Jasinski, "Constitutive Framework," 78.

18. Jasinski, "Constitutive Framework," 74.

19. Frederick Schauer, "Why Precedent in Law (and Elsewhere) Is Not Totally (or Even Substantially) about Analogy," *Perspectives on Psychological Science* 3, no. 6 (2008): 454–60.

20. There are too many examples of scholarship that demonstrate the rhetoricity of law to cite here. However, two are especially influential in legal studies: Marianne Constable, *Our Word Is Our Bond: How Legal Speech Acts* (Stanford, CA: Stanford University Press, 2014), especially 35–40; and James Boyd White,

Heracles' Bow: Essays on the Rhetoric and Poetics of the Law (Madison: University of Wisconsin Press, 1989).

21. This is also Peter Odell Campbell's point in "The Procedural Queer: Substantive Due Process, *Lawrence v. Texas*, and Queer Rhetorical Futures," *Quarterly Journal of Speech* 98, no. 2 (May 2012): 203–29. Regarding Justice Kennedy's jurisprudence, Campbell argues that legal procedure and procedural arguments are rhetorical in that they "reveal the presence of a futuristic, always-open-to-change vision in Kennedy's framing of constitutional law" (204).

22. Timothy Barouch, "The Judicial Character of Late Liberal Prudence: Paul v. Davis," *Rhetoric & Public Affairs* 21, no. 3 (2018): 422; Hasian, Condit, and Lucaites, "Rhetorical Boundaries."

23. Barouch, "Judicial Character," 422.

24. Robert W. Gordon, *Taming the Past: Essays on Law in History and History in Law* (New York: Cambridge University Press, 2017), 5.

25. Gordon, *Taming the Past*, 5.

26. For an overview of Warren's judicial style and impact on liberal public culture, see Morton J. Horwitz, *The Warren Court and the Pursuit of Justice* (New York: Hill and Wang, 1999); Lucas A. Powe, *The Warren Court and American Politics* (Cambridge, MA: Harvard University Press, 2002); Michal R. Belknap, *The Supreme Court under Earl Warren, 1953–1969* (Columbia: University of South Carolina Press, 2005). For an analysis on Warren's rhetoric in *Brown v. Board of Education* as it relates to the evolution of "equality," see Hasian, Condit, and Lucaites, "Rhetorical Boundaries."

27. Mainstream journalistic opposition to expatriation is not represented in print until the late 1950s with Anthony Lewis's reporting for the *New York Times*. Legal scholarship began to criticize the naturalization acts and expatriation policy in 1925 (see Charles Cheney Hyde, "The Non-Recognition and Expatriation of Naturalized American Citizens," *The American Journal of International Law* 19, no. 4 [1925]: 742–44), but sustained criticism does not appear in legal journals until the 1950s.

28. Weil, *Sovereign Citizen*, 179. Importantly, this number does not include the roughly six hundred thousand US citizens of Mexican ancestry who were forcibly "patriated" to Mexico during the 1930s via deportation. See Johnson, "Forgotten Repatriation," and "Race, Immigration Laws."

29. Expatriation Act of 1868, 25 Stat § (1868); See Weil, *Sovereign Citizen*; Herzog, *Revoking Citizenship*.

30. John P. Roche, "The Expatriation Cases: Breathes There the Man, with Soul So Dead," *Supreme Court Review*, 1963, 331.

31. Leti Volpp, "Citizenship Undone," *Fordham Law Review* 75 (2007): 2579. Volpp highlights that Asian American women were still not eligible for citizenship during this time period.

32. Nationality Act of 1940, Pub. L. No. 801, 8 US (1940).

33. "14th Amendment of US Constitution," accessed September 9, 2018, https://www.law.cornell.edu/constitution/amendmentxiv. The citizenship clause states: "All persons born or naturalized in the United States and subject to the jurisdiction thereof, are citizens of the United States and of the State in which they reside." Warren explicitly stated the relevance of the Fourteenth Amendment to expatriation law in a memorandum regarding *Perez v. Brownell* in 1956 where he wrote: "A consideration of the power of Congress to declare American citizenship forfeit must begin with the first sentence of [section 1] of the Fourteenth Amendment." See Earl Warren, Papers, "Memorandum" on Perez v. Brownell, May 31, 1957, Box 150, no. 572, Library of Congress, Washington, DC, Manuscript/Mixed Material. https://lccn.loc.gov/mm82052258.

34. Perez v. Brownell, 356 US 44 (1957).

35. Weil, *Sovereign Citizen*, 163.

36. *Perez* at 43. In 1958, voting in a foreign election was seen as a potential cause of disastrous foreign relations because the Saar Plebiscite of 1935 was a relatively recent memory. In the plebiscite many German Americans voted in favor of reunification with Germany. This issue came up during *Perez*'s oral arguments.

37. Trop v. Dulles, 356 US 86 (1957) at 87.

38. Trop v. Dulles at 88

39. It is unclear whether Warren was citing Hannah Arendt's well-known definition of citizenship from *On the Origin of Totalitarianism*. See Stephanie DeGooyer et al., *The Right to Have Rights* (New York: Verso, 2018), 20–21.

40. Weil, *Sovereign Citizen*, 178.

41. Draft of *Perez,* March 25, 1958Warren Papers, Box 150.

42. *Trop v. Dulles.*

43. Frankfurter's opinions about the Fourteenth Amendment were well-known. In regards to expatriation law, during the time of the conference in 1958, he sent out memoranda to the justices, compiling his law clerk Alexander Bickel's research on the narrow scope of the amendment. Felix Frankfurter, Frank W. Buxton, and William H. Moody, in Felix Frankfurter, Papers, Library of Congress, Washington, DC, Manuscript/Mixed Material, https://lccn.loc.gov/mm73047571, box 25, 14.

44. Warren Papers, Correspondence, April 4, 1958, Box 150, 1.

45. Warren Papers, "Memorandum," 3.

46. Warren Papers, draft of Warren's *Perez* opinion, March 25, 1958, Box 150, 1.

47. *Afroyim v. Rusk,* 387 US. This case involved a naturalized US citizen who was expatriated after voting in an Israeli election.

48. Weil, *Sovereign Citizen*, 179.

49. "High Court Ruling Guards Citizenship," *Boston Globe*, May 30, 1967, 8.

50. "No More Banishment," *Boston Globe*, June 4, 1967, 4.

51. "Once a Citizen . . . ," *New York Times*, June 4, 1967, sec. The Week in Review.

52. "Always a Citizen," *New York Times*, June 4, 1967, 4.

53. *Afroyim* at 268.

54. Thomas Alexander Aleinikoff, *Semblances of Sovereignty: The Constitution, the State, and American Citizenship* (Cambridge, MA: Harvard University Press, 2009), 192.

55. Robert Hariman, "What Is a Chiasmus? Or, Why the Abyss Stares Back," in *Chiasmus and Culture*, ed. Anthony Paul and Boris Wiseman (New York: Berghahn Books, 2014), 46.

56. Ernst Kantorowicz, *The King's Two Bodies: A Study in Medieval Political Theology* (Princeton, NJ: Princeton University Press, 2016), 55.

57. Hariman, "What Is a Chiasmus?," 47.

58. See Victoria Kahn, *The Future of Illusion: Political Theology and Early Modern Texts* (Chicago: University of Chicago Press, 2014); and Kantorowicz, *King's Two Bodies*.

59. *Afroyim* at 269 (emphasis mine).

60. Alexander M. Bickel, "Citizenship in the American Constitution Symposium: Pivotal Decisions of the Supreme Court," *Arizona Law Review* 15 (1973): 387.

61. Bickel, "Citizenship."

62. Weil, *Sovereign Citizen*, 177.

63. Weil, *Sovereign Citizen*, 177.

64. I conducted a corpus analysis by using search terms (and variants) "denationalization," "denaturalization," and "expatriation," in Lexis Nexis, ProQuest Historical Newspaper, and Hein Online Law Journal databases from 1980 to 2018.

65. Vance v. Terrazas, 444 US 252 (1980).

66. *Vance* at 257.

67. *Vance* at 257–58.

68. *Vance* at 261.

69. *Vance* at 260–61.

70. *Vance* at 270.

71. J. G. A. Pocock, "The Ideal of Citizenship since Classical Times," in *The Citizenship Debates: A Reader*, ed. Gershon Shafir (Minneapolis: University of Minnesota Press, 1998).

72. Robert Cover, *Narrative, Violence, and the Law: The Essays of Robert Cover*, ed. Martha Minow, Michael Ryan, and Austin Sarat (Ann Arbor: University of Michigan Press, 1995), 139.

73. Cover, *Narrative, Violence, and the Law*, 153.

74. Jonathan David Shaub, "Expatriation Restored," *Harvard Journal on Legislation* 55, no. 2 (2018): 439.

75. Brinkley and Lightblau, "US Releases Saudi-American."

76. Gul, "Return of the Native"; Lauer, "Easy Way Out?"

77. "Hamdi v. Rumsfeld Settlement Agreement," 2.

78. "Hamdi v. Rumsfeld Settlement Agreement," 22–23.

79. *Hamdi v. Rumsfeld*, 542 US 507 (2004).

80. Cover, *Narrative, Violence, and the Law*, 145.

81. This is Stevens's broader point in "Alien Who Is a Citizen."

82. Jennifer Mercieca, *Founding Fictions* (Tuscaloosa: University of Alabama Press, 2010).

83. Cover, *Narrative, Violence, and the Law*, 172.

13

The Frankfurt Anecdote and Rhetorical History

Toward a Method for Reading National Security Archives

Andrew D. Barnes

A paradox of the vast and profitable exercise of presidential rhetorical history is the scholar's reliance on access to archival holdings despite the elusive nature of archival research methods. A pattern often emerges where the acknowledgments section mentions presidential libraries or specific archivists who aided in research yet contains no account of how the researcher gathered data. Peer-reviewed journal manuscripts tend to sketch the quantity of research (e.g., how many archives were visited), and sometimes they proffer a page or document count. Questions abound: How does the scholar know what to look for? When is the search complete? And how can the problem of cherry-picked data be avoided?

A typical graduate seminar trains students in the following sequence: learn as much as possible through secondary scholarly research, engage in an immersive archival process (i.e., read everything), and keep detailed notes of records pulled in addition to notes and observations on materials reviewed. Once complete, the researcher uses the gathered materials to support scholarly argument. Two presumptions may prevail: The scholar's authority based on credentials and preceding reputation leads to the assumption that they were careful, meticulous, and honest in their presentation of data; and/or the quality of argument will help demonstrate how veracity emerged from sufficient archival research methods. In either case, methods used by the scholar to navigate presidential archives are often invisible. I draw attention to this phenomenon to demonstrate the utility of an explicit and prescriptive approach for archival research.

In this chapter, I argue that national security archives are a unique site for rhetorical inquiry. They differ from their domestic counterparts in at least three ways: the expansive and diffuse nature of textual production and storage across multiple agencies, a culture that features different ideological drivers of policy, and secrecy. As such, we need a new method for reading this specific type of archive. This method is underpinned by a rhetorical theory of circulation and my own rhetorical analysis of strategic studies literature, a subset of international relations theory. Grounding method in a theory of circulation draws attention to the relationship among power, influence, and communicative flows across the various participants inside the presidency. Attention to security studies as a rhetorical culture allows for a reconstruction of the symbolic system that informs the policy-making process. All historical work is a reconstruction; reconstructing communicative flows within national security archives reveals deeper connections between public and private texts and their material consequence.

The case proceeds in three parts. First, I review the literature on presidential organizational practices to reveal how the agency of staff can be wielded to impel textual production and circulation. Second, I argue that national security archives require additional hierarchical analysis. Operatives within the presidency create texts that collectively constitute an archive. Yet long before individuals are appointed, they receive both educational and formal job training that inculcates them into a rhetorical culture. I read strategic studies as a rhetorical culture to reveal the first principles of national security and draw on these insights to fashion a method for reading archives. Third, my engagement with national security archives to study President Kennedy's speech in June 1963 in Frankfurt serves as a representative anecdote for the utility of this rhetorical approach to archival research.

Recovering Text(s): National Security Archives and the Frankfurt Anecdote

The significance of presidential public address is built into situations such as the inaugural, the State of the Union, or the need to address a national crisis. In each instance, the president is positioned as leader of the nation. Response to this exigency in the form of public address performs a ritual for an audience that exists in a moment of importance. A case of significance is harder to make when a president speaks on foreign soil, to a foreign audience, and on issues that are of more importance to that foreign audience than that to an American audience. In these moments it is difficult to assess significance precisely because it is difficult to assess relations among rhetor, text, context, and audience.

In June 1963, President Kennedy traveled to the Federal Republic of Germany (West Germany; hereafter FRG) and delivered three prominent addresses: one in Frankfurt and two in Berlin. The speeches in

Berlin have been studied and rightfully so.[1] Yet, attention to the Frankfurt speech remains slight despite its place in the historical record and accessibility through the American Presidency Project.[2] Perhaps the absence of critical attention is the result of the speeches in Berlin acquiring a dramatic place in collective memory, thereby overshadowing the Frankfurt address. However, this explanation is unsatisfying. Kennedy's speechwriter and the principle architect of the address, Theodore Sorensen, recalled that the Frankfurt address was "one of the most carefully reworked speeches of his Presidency";[3] the administration also carefully selected the prose, the place, and the invited audience of the address.[4] By declaring that we are "partners for peace—not in a narrow bilateral context but in a framework of Atlantic partnership," Kennedy spoke clearly and artfully, opening possible lines for identification between his foreign and domestic audiences by stressing common values and purpose.[5] However, I recognized that staff attention on its own does not advance a case of significance for public speech. I needed stronger evidence.

Recovering the context of a speech is a quintessential element of rhetorical history. The Frankfurt address seemingly had no direct situational exigence or antecedent, compounding the problem of building a case for significance. Although the Soviet Union presented challenges early in the Kennedy presidency, his visit to the FRG occurred ten months after the Cuban Missile Crisis and nearly two years after the armed standoff at Checkpoint Charlie. Neither the Soviet Union nor the German Democratic Republic (hereafter GDR) threatened the territorial integrity of the FRG, including Berlin, or allied access routes through the GDR to Berlin. Domestic politics in Europe were also stable. The chancellor of the FRG, Konrad Adenauer, was aging but had survived the most recent election and was planning his transition and the rise of his successors. Stasis in transnational relations suggests that care in a public speech would only be necessary so as to avoid disruption. Working in the knowledge that rhetoric is often temporary, limited, and disposable—even for presidents—the Frankfurt address could have been simply a perfunctory execution of presidential decorum. I sought evidence to demonstrate otherwise, searching for contextual evidence outside of the historical record.

Kathleen J. Turner characterizes rhetorical history as socially constructed where rhetorical processes construct particular social realities in a specific context. Turner observes that rhetoric as process requires an understanding of the potential and effect of symbols within systems. As a result, to study history as process is to treat history as "an essentially rhetorical process."[6] For Turner, doing rhetorical history requires a rhetorical critic's "message-centered" focus and "rhetorical history's contextual construction."[7] However, organizing potential, effect, symbols, and systems—a coherent packaging indeed—only seems possible if these elements are knowable to the rhetorician. I sought evidence from the Kennedy Presidential Library and Museum archives to build a case for significance and to reconstruct the political context of the speech so that I could make sense of its symbolic operation. My research experiences demonstrated the need for a new method for reading national security archives. To substantiate this claim, I first demonstrate the limitations of common approaches to presidential archival research.

Stabilizing Conditions for Archival Research Methods in Presidential Libraries

Three practices stabilize the traditional immersive or "read everything" approaches to research in presidential archives (particularly studies of domestic policy): the production and circulation of texts, organizational hierarchy, and the law. The presidency operates as a rhetorical institution.[8] By this, I mean that rhetorical practice is central to internal policy-making practices as well as to publicizing and defending these decisions to an audience in service of the democratic ideal. This practice of circulating texts—anything from newspaper clips to policy briefs or memorandum—establishes what is included and excluded from the policy-making process. Thus, attention to the production of a text, as well as who creates them and where those texts circulate, forms the backbone of historical research in the archive. Knowledge of organizational structure allows a scholar to predict the location of these texts within a given archive.

The personal prerogatives of the president inform organizational hierarchy and deliberative practice. To this end, how the president wants to manage and be managed matters. As Bruce Buchanan notes, "each new president literally starts over, *tabula rasa*, imposing new procedures, new assumptions, and a new atmosphere or culture."[9] Constructing the executive branch is the first task of the president-elect; although executive reorganization can happen during a president's tenure, it is often limited. Two competing models emerge from the cottage industry on "best practices" for forming a presidency. In the first, the metaphor of the wagon wheel prevails.[10] The president operates at the center (hub) of the decision making while advisors (spokes) provide information and opinion. This model is associated with Franklin D. Roosevelt, John F. Kennedy, Jimmy Carter, and early iterations of the Lyndon B. Johnson and William Jefferson Clinton administrations.[11] In the second, the metaphor of dam or breakwater dominates. Here, a chief of staff is the conduit from a president to his staff as well as the reverse: the strong chief of staff model controls the flow of information and access to the president.[12] The Dwight D. Eisenhower, Ronald Reagan, George H. W. Bush, and Barack Obama presidencies are exemplars of this model.[13] Outliers aside, initial hierarchical organization of the presidency can stabilize the larger bureaucracy given cabinet-level and senior staff appointments.[14] Each model, in its own way, provides direction for queries that will return archival materials relevant to the research question.

Organizational practice is also stabilized by the permanent existence of such White House departments as the Domestic Policy Council, the National Economic Council, the Office of Legislative Affairs, the National Security Council, and the Office of White House Counsel. The staffing of these existing structures also matters. However, presidencies are idiosyncratic in that job titles and descriptions are continually in flux given staffing instability: individuals regularly join and leave the administration. To that end, organizational charts, titles, and job descriptions allow the critic to ascertain institutional power and agency of individuals within these structures. Although it may seem mechanistic, I draw attention to these organizational practices because they inform compliance with the Presidential Records Act of 1978. The legal responsibility to preserve records typically falls to individual advisors or the staff secretaries of councils and other operating groups within the administration. Research guides are frequently constructed from these files and not reorganized. Unlike libraries that can rely on the Dewey Decimal or Library of Congress Classification system, no such organizational method exists for presidential archives. As a result, scholars can generate meaningful insights by mapping the rhetorical processes of an institution over time through an archival review of councils and individuals relevant to a research question.[15]

Resolving a Problem Inherent to National Security Archives: The Need for New Methods

The responsibility for national security policy is diffuse: fiefdoms of power and expertise exist across the various intelligence agencies, the Department of State, the Department of Defense, and White House staff appointed to the National Security Council. As a result, the immersive or read everything method of archival research can lead to frustration. Those engaged in historical work understand that the archives of the Department of State are voluminous, as are presidential materials in such libraries as those for Eisenhower, Kennedy, Nixon, Ford, and Carter, where most documents have been fully declassified. An appropriately structured research question can narrow the scope of research, thereby making navigation in the archives manageable. Yet a narrow question does not always produce textual results that allow for a critical reading of the relationship between text and context. The Frankfurt anecdote illustrates the problem.

President Kennedy's speaking situation suggested a claim of significance could be built around four facts: Frankfurt was (1) the first address of three nationally televised speeches, (2) in a culturally symbolic location, (3) to an audience of political elites for an extended amount of time (thirty-three minutes and twenty-four seconds), and (4) with potential ramifications for the transatlantic alliance consisting of France, Germany, the United Kingdom, and the United States. Unfortunately, initial archival research did not substantiate this case. The speech files on the Frankfurt address are thin; they contain three of the four speech drafts and two memoranda providing direction to Sorensen.[16] Additionally, the speech files contain assessments from the US Information Agency concluding that the West German people did not require a psychological boost that a state visit could provide.[17] A narrow research question allowed me to read everything in the speech files; yet I was left with little insight into the purposes, prospects, potential, or effect of the address.[18]

Undeterred, I expanded my scope of inquiry. A reformulated research question led me to expand my date range and data set, necessitating a visit to the US Federal Archives II.[19] A kind archivist informed me that my inquiry concerning three months in 1963 would return more than forty boxes and ten thousand pages. The enormity of textual production at the institutional level makes it exceedingly difficult for a single scholar to reestablish relations among context, institutional process, and the production of public address given an expansive method for archival engagement. My narrow question produced too few results while my expanded question produced far too many. How, then, might the scope of research be expanded to sufficiently wield productive results while avoiding the tsunami of documents that results from the read everything approach? I contend that a rhetorical and cultural method for reading national security archives offers scholars a method for bringing narrative coherence to an extensive set of texts and actors scattered across the executive branch—for developing a rhetorical history.

All nations are in the security business to some degree; citizens must be protected from external threats, and that requires a state to construct and implement policies that afford protection. Andrew M. Johnston argues that national security policy is the product of a preexisting culture, a culture he labels strategic studies.[20] A cultural lens reveals how strategic culture is "made by political entrepreneurs from the materials of national memory (or its inverse, national amnesia) to serve specific interests." The experiences and knowledge of individual actors inform the construction of a "social fact" that in turn "determines the contours of 'appropriate' behavior."[21] These "social facts," or what John Gaddis labels operational codes, entail assumptions about how the world works that correspond with an ideological worldview and set of policy preferences.[22] Facts and behavior are not edicts implemented through fiat; rhetoric underwrites the explanatory power of facts and the justificatory power for action. Although neither Johnston nor Gaddis feature rhetoric, the case can plainly be made that strategic studies is a rhetorical culture.

To establish strategic studies as a rhetorical culture, I follow the work of Benjamin Lee and Edward LiPuma.[23] For them, a rhetorical culture exists if it satisfies three conditions. First, texts (demonstrating abstraction, interpretation, evaluation, and the deployment of agency) must be constructed and circulated among members of the culture. Second, rhetorical forms (narrative, tropes, and the like) or conventions (style) must be present. And third, a culture must reconstitute itself through textual production and circulation. Recent communication scholarship demonstrates that the presidency satisfies these conditions as a rhetorical culture.[24] These three conditions also characterize our national security culture. For example, diplomatic cables frequently deploy an informative form of thick description when relaying current events (style). Policy papers from the Department of State often enumerate lessons from the past; for these texts, historical argument informs the process of constructing policy (interpretation and evaluation). National Security directives, on the other hand, are decrees that circulate and are followed given the power inherent within the military chain of command (reconstitution).

A culture of security exists both inside and outside of a given administration due to the fact that inhabitants of this culture are students in training, professors tasked with student development and security research, government operatives, and political appointees, often with significant overlap among them.[25] I turn to the extant international relations literature on strategic studies, a subarea of political science as a discipline, that tends to the production of security for the nation-state. Concepts of grand strategy, strategy, and tactics are particularly important to the operational codes of strategic studies as a culture.[26] These concepts afford a hierarchical structure of decision making, beginning with abstract ideals and concluding with specific and narrow actions. Terry Deibel labels this hierarchy the "logic of statecraft."[27] Grand strategy, strategy, and tactics also provide a kind of cardinal direction for vertical and horizontal communication flows within the executive branch. Although context shifts over time (for example, the move from a centralized focus on the Soviet Union during the Cold War to a more recent turn to terrorism or to China), strategic thinkers will continue to develop policy on these three levels of analysis. Explicating these levels through a case study of the process that led to Kennedy's public address in Frankfurt demonstrates the rhetorical and cultural method for reading national security archives.

Grand Strategy

Stephen Walt argues that grand strategy "identifies the objectives that must be achieved to produce security, and describes the political and military actions that are believed to lead to this goal."[28] This definition alone propositionally requires a state to understand itself (values, strengths, weaknesses, and assets) and the international political environment (what constitutes a threat to national security broadly construed), and to put in place policies over time that provide security (what is required to protect the populace from identified threats to a nation-state). These propositions of grand strategy require deliberation, given that none are the result of natural conditions, axiomatically true, agreed upon by presidential advisors, or in some cases even knowable.[29]

The deliberative process to establish a grand strategy often occurs during meetings of the National Security Council (NSC) early in the tenure of an administration. Given the United States is not a dictatorship, and given that most presidents value advisors who share the objective of establishing a grand strategy that hews towards the operational codes of a president, viewpoints will generally coalesce toward consensus. Deliberation within the council typically produces three results. First, the group will establish a hierarchical order of the needs and wants an administration might have, given an accounting of the United States' place in global politics. Second, grand strategy is limited for all administrations by time and resources; therefore, the group will rank responses to international challenges based on perceived importance. Third, deliberation produces a central text articulating the grand strategy and then a series of related texts for specific individuals or departments that circulate horizontally for edits and final approval. Once approved, these documents travel vertically through the administration to provide guidance for those tasked with implementation.[30] For our purposes, identifying the grand strategy of an administration allows the critic to map foreign policy logics as they circulate through the administration.

President Kennedy inherited a grand strategy all too reliant on nuclear deterrence. The Basic National Security Policy (BNSP) of the United States in 1959 declared, "A central aim of US policy must be to deter the Communists from use of their military power" due to the "disastrous character of general nuclear war, the danger of local conflicts developing into general war, and the serious effect of further Communist aggression."[31] The consensus of Kennedy and his advisors was that this policy was problematic. Reliance on mutually assured destruction afforded no flexibility in response to minor military incursions, let alone the case of an accident or an accidental launch within the chain of command. As Carl Kaysen, special assistant for National Security Affairs, argued, "current war plans from the SIOP [Single Integrated Operational Plan for general nuclear war] and JSCP [Joint Strategic Capabilities Plan] down to the operational orders of the striking elements are such that once the signal for general war is given, we react in a pre-determined way."[32] An organizational imperative for Kennedy was control over the chain of command with respect to nuclear war: he, and he alone, could give the strike order. Over the course of the next two years, Walter Rostow, deputy special assistant to the president, revised the BNSP; NSC Action Memorandum 37 codified a section of this document mandating presidential approval for nuclear launch.[33] The rest of the draft BNSP document was not codified into policy, but its circulation throughout the bureaucracy nevertheless made it an influential document.[34]

The last draft is of interest because it articulated the fundamental precepts of Kennedy's grand strategy. The draft argued that "the long term goal" is to "foster and develop an evolving international community" that would (among other aims) "settle their differences by political means or legal processes rather than by armed conflict."[35] The BNSP further specified that it was "the interest of the US to achieve its wartime objective while limiting the destructiveness of warfare; in this sense, it is the goal of US policy that any war be a limited war."[36] This policy of "strategic flexibility" sought to keep any war a limited war and, therefore, was an attempt to move away from a policy of mutually assured destruction. The objectives outlined in this document suggest a need for increased diplomacy and flexibility in war fighting. By examining grand strategy, we can observe how Kennedy adhered to the established ideological binaries of the Cold War (the struggle between Communism and capitalism) while attempting to defuse the dangers inherent to this binary logic (eradication of evil in practical terms meant war). These documents then specify a worldview of competitive coexistence where the United States and its allies must continually work anew to maintain the alliance, preserve the status of Western territory, and deter Communist aggression.[37] A grand strategy of strategic flexibility produced unintended consequences in transatlantic relations.

Strategy

Strategy is the operationalization of grand strategy; it establishes objectives and courses of action that achieve the long-term goals and outcomes sought by grand strategy. For Gaddis, strategy establishes the relations between ends and means, intentions and capability, or objectives and resources.[38] Given regional and country-specific challenges, strategy is unlikely to be universal. And because geopolitics is unstable, strategy must be consistently reviewed and adapted to shifting conditions and circumstances when necessary. For this reason, Barry Posen encourages us to think about strategy as a process of establishing "an interlinked chain of problems that must be solved."[39] European security strategy required preserving the territorial integrity of Berlin by deterring Soviet aggression, which would aid the long-term project of European unity. And European unity would provide a geopolitical space for democratic capitalism. These interlinked policy goals (ends) were stabilized in the Eisenhower administration by the concept of mutually assured destruction (means): it was assumed that if the consequences of nuclear war were unthinkable then war itself became an impossibility. Under these conditions, a stalemate would ensure that ideological competitors could survive and thrive. Kennedy's grand strategy of "strategic flexibility" destabilized the conditions for existing European strategy precisely because it called into question American retaliation to Communist aggression. France and Germany also had a hand in destabilizing US security policy. US attempts at forging commitments that would create the conditions of economic interdependence in Europe stumbled. A European common market had been established, but France worked diligently to exclude the United Kingdom. It succeeded, with the aid of Germany. Additionally, the Franco-German treaty was signed and celebrated; this particular policy advanced the hegemonic ambitions of France. If these two nations were no longer enemies, they could become military partners. France worked to develop its own nuclear deterrent that could be used to deter Soviet aggression against Germany. As a result, the Kennedy administration worried that Pres. Charles de Gaulle of France might draw Pres. Konrad Adenauer of Germany away from the United States.[40] Adenauer and de Gaulle deeply distrusted negotiations with the Soviet Union and fretted Kennedy would misstep.[41] Both were concerned that abandoning mutually assured destruction opened the possibility for a conventional war that would destroy

Europe while leaving the superpowers relatively unscathed. These shifting conditions led President Kennedy to bemoan during a NSC meeting, "Do not expect that the Europeans will do anything for us even though we have done a lot for them."[42] Tension threatened a rift in the transatlantic alliance.

On January 22, 1963, President de Gaulle called into question whether Europe should rely on the mutual defense commitments enshrined by the North Atlantic Treaty Organization (NATO).[43] For de Gaulle, the United States's response to the Soviet Union supplying Cuba with missiles and warheads had not taken into consideration the concerns of European allies; attacking the Soviet Union to ensure the security of the United States could have meant the annihilation of Europe. This was no small charge. First, this line of reasoning could be used to justify the creation of a French deterrent, which would threaten command and control of nuclear weapons through NATO and justify reactionary proliferation across Eastern Europe. The ability of the French to spark mutually assured destruction also posed a threat to American security. Second, it served as a direct and personal challenge to President Kennedy. By suggesting that when pushed, Kennedy might not defend Europe, de Gaulle cast doubt on the validity of strategic flexibility as a policy and US commitments to all European countries. This doubt carried particular resonance in West Berlin, which depended completely on the US military to provide territorial integrity and security.

Despite the gravity of de Gaulle's posturing, Kennedy's public response was muted.[44] However, the archives reveal feverish textual production and circulation of secret documents related to de Gaulle and the implications of his press conference. Cables from Western Europe covered both the press conference and press response, starting the gears moving within intelligence agencies. The Bureau of Intelligence and Research, housed within the Department of State, altered its assessment of European policy. Previously, it had read European relations as constantly in flux, which offered certain advantages to the United States (e.g., one moves away, another moves closer).[45] A month later, the bureau argued that European preferences were shifting toward de Gaulle, which would increase the "difficulties the United States confronts in persuading the Allies to implement its current strategic doctrine."[46]

To investigate the de Gaulle problem, the NSC established a secret study group consisting of top advisors with the purpose of reconsidering European policy.[47] David Bruce, ambassador to the FRG under Eisenhower and ambassador to the United Kingdom for Kennedy, argued that de Gaulle's policy ran contrary to US grand strategy, which had always been to "deny Europe to communist control," and that the United States should "mobilize our resources in combination with Europe to serve the whole free world."[48] In a memo to McGeorge Bundy, the secretary of state, Asst. Sec. of Defense Robert Neumann expressed the problem in starker terms: "These papers proceed from the assumption that the press conference of General de Gaulle . . . has brought into the open the basic incompatibility between French and US policies and objectives, and that this disagreement is fundamental[ly] . . . destructive to our long-standing policy. . . . It is therefore imperative to prevent de Gaulle's policy from infecting other European powers."[49] If strategy is the suturing together of means and ends, the archival record demonstrates a shift from engagement to containment. And although President Kennedy decided to seek the political means to contain France, military force was considered an option in January.[50]

Containment of de Gaulle's hegemonic ambitions required a specific type of rhetorical performance. In response to the GDR's provocative move to divide Berlin in 1961, President Kennedy asked Dean Acheson to analyze events and propose possible responses for the National Security Council. In Acheson's archival papers, an unattributed paper from the Department of State argued: "Berlin's importance for the US is largely intangible but nonetheless undeniable. The current significance of the city for our foreign policy can scarcely be exaggerated. Since 1948 we have, by our own choice, made Berlin the example and the symbol of our determination and our ability to defend the free parts of the world against communist aggression. . . . US prestige is totally committed. . . . Abandonment of Berlin . . . would have a shattering effect on NATO and our other alliances."[51]

The choice of Berlin as a symbol of freedom and US prestige was just as apt in 1963 as it had been two years earlier. De Gaulle's press conference publicized the possibility of a crisis of commitment within the alliance. The Cold War was a rhetorical war precisely because words constituted policy; Kennedy's unequivocal declaration of intent to guarantee the security of West Berlin would demonstrate the commitment. However, the grand strategy of strategic flexibility in conjunction with de Gaulle's strategic maneuvering opened a rift in the alliance on the question of US security commitments to Berlin specifically and Europe generally.

Cognizant of the need to exert leadership on a personal and public level, the Kennedy administration designed an "informal working visit" to West Germany as a direct response to the challenge posed by de Gaulle.[52] Undersecretary of State George Ball argued that a trip to

West Germany was essential to maintaining any semblance of European strategy. He wrote to the president: "Never, at any time since the war . . . has Europe been in graver danger of back-sliding into the old destructive habits—the old fragmentation and national rivalries that have twice brought the world to disaster in the past. Your trip must be planned in cold-blooded recognition of these lamentable facts."[53] This war was a distinct possibility because "a Germany not tied closely and institutionally to the West can be a source of great hazard."[54] By May 1963, the administration concluded that a state visit was worthwhile if it could achieve the strategic objective of containing French ambitions by drawing German elites away from de Gaulle and toward Kennedy.[55] The administration recognized that this required German politicians, however uncomfortable, to "choose the Atlantic partnership over a narrow relation to de Gaulle and that this choice is visible."[56]

Continued attention to strategic studies as a culture puts on display an additional problem for the Kennedy administration. It is one thing to forge consensus on the need for policy change within the administration. It is a different problem entirely for foreign security cultures to align their security objectives and policies with those of the United States. To this end, tactics were needed to sway political opinion.

Tactics

If strategy is the formation of objectives or apprehending an interlinked series of problems to solve, tactics are actions that bring a state closer to achieving that stated objective or solving a given problem. Cases examined by strategic studies literature typically focus on war fighting;[57] as a result, it is common for tactics to be considered maneuvers on the battlefield or improvisations during combat that lead to success or failure. However, other facets of state influence can operate at the tactical level. William Martel posits that tactics are those actions that "signify or symbolize the extent to which smaller-scale actions or developments align with and thus support the larger purposes articulated in the state's grand strategy."[58] He continues, "The tactical level embraces the unique context of the 'human dimension' and the role of 'chance and probability.'"[59] These elements—generating support for larger communal identifications, the use of symbols as action, and polysemic response—suggest that, in some situations, presidential public address operates as a tactic to achieve strategic objectives.

In public or private, presidential speech deploys a system of shared symbols to constitute meaning for an audience. In the case of a presidential speech to a foreign audience, on foreign land, with a different native language and culture, lines of identification can be limited. This is particularly true in the realm of national security. Strategic studies, as previously noted, operates as a system of signification. As articulated by the Kennedy administration, the precepts at the core of strategic flexibility at once demonstrated the value of Germany (its essential role in preventing Communist expansion) while denying the sacrosanct value of Berlin (a limited war might be fought over Berlin, so long as that war did not go nuclear).

Locating Germany as the crux of US security policy afforded equal significance to Konrad Adenauer as president of the FRG. Given the generational differences between the two leaders, Kennedy's personal performance was essential to tactical success. In a direct memorandum to the president, McGeorge Bundy argued that "if he trusts us, he will do nearly anything," and that "he is more interested in your state of mind and will."[60] Walter Rostow concurred: "I am convinced that we are on the right track; that the political majority in Europe is with us; and that if we do not break our stride or project uncertainty, the Atlantic relationship will fall into place."[61] Private speech, in this case personal diplomacy, can reveal the thinking of a president; it displays logic, presents evidence, and gives reasons. On questions of foreign policy, the performance of private speech can work tactically to advance strategic policy, particularly if the president's interlocutor is in agreement. Public speech can work in a similar manner, particularly if that speech operates as a tactic to build support for a series of actions that a foreign political audience can take to support US strategic policy. The administration conceived of the trip for a particular strategic purpose (i.e., bringing Germany closer to the United States and further from an alliance with de Gaulle), and the three speeches, along with personal diplomacy with Adenauer, functioned tactically to achieve those strategic aims.

Various entities within the administration took great care in crafting Kennedy's specific address to Frankfurt. As is often the case, the State Department prepared speech drafts that they then circulated to White House communication staff. Arthur Schlesinger, special assistant to the president, derisively described his impression of these drafts as one of "predominant banality and vapidity" for they "fail to convey any sense of a fresh American voice or distinctive Kennedy approach."[62] Schlesinger well understood the essential role of presidential ethos for performative success; the absence of a distinct approach or voice risked a mediocre performance that could invite questions about the president's personal commitment. Therefore, the address required a symbolic concept that could credibly substantiate US security commitments while transcending differences between the United States and West Germany.[63]

The planning process for the working state visit evidences the rhetorical culture. Dean Rusk, the secretary of state, played a central role. On May 1, 1963, a cable from the Berlin consulate confirmed their understanding of the importance of the upcoming visit. The purpose of the visit was to "demonstrate a new and unmistakable breadth and depth of US-Berlin solidarity."[64] The consulate argued that the itinerary would achieve established objectives through the "impressive and personalized form" of President Kennedy at "important symbolic sites."[65] As a result, the consulate was tasked with ensuring "maximum (preferably record) public attendance" when the president was in public.[66] The American vantage point assigned particular symbolic importance to Berlin generally, and the Berlin Wall specifically, during the Cold War. For West German citizens, however, political and cultural symbols existed beyond Berlin; the Paulskirche (St. Paul's Church) in Frankfurt was one. In 1848, the Frankfurt Assembly convened in the Paulskirche to create a new democratic nation by unifying disparate states. Although that political effort was ultimately unsuccessful, as were most of the liberal offshoots of the 1848 German Revolution, the drafted constitution codified such democratic ideals as universal suffrage. As such, the assembly and the symbolic quality of the Paulskirche was chosen as the site for Kennedy's speech because it afforded lines of identification premised on a shared political tradition that transcended national borders and oceans.

President Kennedy deployed analogy to emphasize the democratic quality that informed US-German relations.[67] Leaders of the American Revolution convened in Faneuil Hall in Boston much like leaders of the liberal revolution convened in the Paulskirche in Frankfurt. These respective sites underwrite identification along parallel political traditions. This political tradition, argued the president, entailed responsibility: "Unless liberty flourishes in all lands, it cannot flourish in one. . . . The spirit of the Frankfurt Assembly, like the spirit of Faneuil Hall, must live in many hearts and nations if it is to live at all."[68] Emphasizing fidelity to democracy, Kennedy contended, "In our commitment we can and must speak and act with but one voice. Our roles are distinct but complementary—and our goals are the same: peace and freedom for all men, for all time, in a world of abundance, in a world of justice."[69] Applied to the geopolitics of the moment, Kennedy constructed a shared political tradition and then appropriated this tradition to service US strategic interests. If Germany and the United States shared a unified purpose, the alliance could not be divided.

At Bundy's direction, two other sections of the address received heavy editing: US commitments to Europe and a model for alliance participation predicated on equality among nations. Of interest, surveys administered by the US Information Agency found that "Atlantic community" operated as an identificatory symbol that tested well with the German public.[70] Making his case to President Kennedy, Bundy observed, "It is our hope that . . . by what you say there, you will be able to emphasize the enduring commitment of the United States to peace and progress through the Atlantic partnership."[71] Unsurprisingly, both sections, commitment and participation, attempted to give meaning to the concept of Atlantic community along the lines articulated by Bundy.

Recall the crisis de Gaulle sparked by publicly questioning US resolve to defend Europe. Although Kennedy did not mention de Gaulle by name in the address, the section on US security commitments to Europe operated enthymematically as a direct refutation to his assertions. "Some say that the United States will neither hold to these purposes nor abide by its pledges," argued President Kennedy, "but such doubts fly in the face of history."[72] He continued, "For 18 years the United States has stood its watch for freedom all around the globe, . . . above all, here in Europe."[73] The president posited a self-evident reason to accept the fidelity of US commitments: "The United States will risk its cities to defend yours because we need your freedom to protect ours."[74] The president performed as though personally affronted by the notion that America was not a reliable ally. He then outlined US commitments as evidence for why de Gaulle's assertions should be rejected. His discourse on division positioned de Gaulle as a threat from within. Kennedy contended, "Those who would doubt our pledge or deny this indivisibility—those who would separate Europe from America or split one ally from another—would only give aid and comfort to the men who make themselves our adversaries and welcome any Western disarray."[75] The only response in this scenario, where military strength depended on unity, was to contain the ambitions of de Gaulle.

President Kennedy's discussion of partnership prioritized containment of de Gaulle. He argued, "The first task of the Atlantic Community was to assure its common defense," which "was and still is indivisible."[76] The problem for the Kennedy administration was not the attainment of a collective good through an alliance but preservation of that collective good. To avoid backsliding into "narrow nationalism," the president relied on lessons from Greek history. The partnership section of the speech specifically referenced Thucydides's account of the Peloponnesian security arrangements for its lessons on the dangers of relaxation and complacency that lead to disunity. This reading is complemented by a rhetorical question that bridged time and context to position German political elites as similar to the Peloponnesians: "Is this also to be the story of the Grand Alliance?" asked Kennedy; "Welded in a moment of imminent danger, will it disintegrate into complacency, with each member pressing its own ends to the neglect of the common cause?"[77] He concluded this section by articulating, in practical terms, the responsibilities that partnership required from his German audience. "Let us go on, from words to actions, to intensify our efforts for still greater unity among us, to build new associations and institutions on those already established," commanded Kennedy, for "it is only a fully cohesive Europe that can protect us all against the fragmentation of our alliance."[78]

Combined, the symbolic location of the Paulskirche and the concept of "Atlantic partnership" operated to yoke German national interest to US policy. Limited evidence from the archives suggests the speech achieved its tactical goal. A local news telecast claimed that the president's speech deserved particular attention as a "grandiose demonstration of the German-American community of destiny."[79] The *New York Times* reprinted a caption from the *Deutsche Zeitung* of Cologne, observing: "President Kennedy's symbolic words 'Ich bin ein Berliner' opened a new chapter of German-American relations. . . . But the contents of the new chapter will be written in sober language. It will follow the principles outlined by Kennedy in his Paulskirche speech."[80] In this case, public address operated tactically to advance US European security policy.

Conclusion

Rhetorical methods for reading presidential foreign policy address abound. Following the tradition of Michael Leff, a close reading of the logic and artistry of the Frankfurt address is possible.[81] Given other established rhetorical theories, a critic could read the Frankfurt speech generically,[82] for its prophetic dualism,[83] for its construction of enemies,[84] or as a form of ideological world making.[85] The problem addressed by this chapter is not a method for reading foreign policy address: rather, the Frankfurt address puts on display the struggle to establish the relations between context and text that Turner argues is necessary for doing the work of rhetorical history.

From the hindsight that our contemporary perspective affords, it is tempting to overlook the importance of the Frankfurt address. As John Murphy notes, "if the United States did not craft an Atlantic community, the opportunity would be missed and the alliance lost."[86] True enough, but why? And how might the symbolic construction of an Atlantic community solidify the transatlantic alliance between the United States, Germany, and France? I argue that the scholarly process of situating a single speech within the broader context of national security policy is necessary to answer these types of research questions. What I label the Frankfurt anecdote stands in for this process. As the analysis demonstrates, immersion in national security archives might be insufficient for generating narrative clarity out of archival materials, an essential task for rhetorical history. Attention to the organization of personnel is a starting point for a rhetorical reading of the archive. After all, influence often impels the production and circulation of texts within the presidency. However, an initial foray into the national security archives of President Kennedy, with a focus on established leaders with power inside the administration, provided scant evidence for the significance of this particular speech. Worse, expanding the research question produced an overwhelming amount of material given an immersive, read everything approach. As a result, a method predicated on reading strategic studies as a rhetorical culture brought coherence to a diffuse set of archival materials.

The critical value of this approach is best demonstrated by Erin Rand, who reminds us that rhetorical cultures constitute a system of signification that, when studied, can reveal the "matrices of power" that affect our material world.[87] A rhetorical and cultural approach to national security allows the critic to map power and consequence as demonstrated by the analysis of the Frankfurt address and its context. First, the method allowed for a reconstruction of a national security context, substantiating a case for significance for public address. Second, the method established clear linkages between Kennedy grand strategy, strategic policy for Europe, and tactical political maneuvering in the form of public address. It is my hope that the method articulated herein provides the means and confidence to spur future scholarship.

Notes

1. See, for example, Michael S. Bruner, "Symbolic Uses of the Berlin Wall, 1961–1989," *Communication Quarterly* 37, no. 4 (Fall 1989): 319–28; Noel D. Cary, "Kennedy in Berlin," *Central European History* 42, no. 1 (March 2009): 188–91; Frank Costigliola, "The Pursuit of Atlantic Community: Nuclear Arms, Dollars, and Berlin," in *Kennedy's Quest for Victory: American Foreign Policy, 1961–1963*, edited by Thomas G. Paterson, 24–56 (New York: Oxford University Press, 1989); Campbell Craig, "Kennedy's International Legacy, Fifty Years On," *International Affairs* 89, no. 6 (November 2013): 1367–78; Isabel Fay and Jim Kuypers, "Transcending Mysticism and Building Identification through Empowerment of the Rhetorical Agent: John F. Kennedy's Berlin Speeches on June 26, 1963," *Southern Communication Journal* 77, no. 3 (May 2012): 198–215; David Clay Large, *Berlin* (New York: Basic Books, 2000); W. R. Smyser, *Kennedy and the Berlin Wall: "A*

Hell of a Lot Better than a War" (Lanham, MD: Rowman & Littlefield Publishers, 2009).

2. To my knowledge, no journal articles exist that analyze the Frankfurt address. Where Frankfurt appears in print, it is frequently as a passing observation overshadowed by Berlin. John Murphy conducted a short analysis of the Frankfurt address; yet, he too concluded—without the support of archival research—that the address was relatively insignificant, particularly in comparison to the address from the Rathaus Schöneberg in Berlin. See John M. Murphy, *John F. Kennedy and the Liberal Persuasion* (East Lansing: Michigan State University Press, 2019), 189–94. Previously, the public papers of presidents would be published in a multivolume bound set. Those efforts continue; yet most scholars rely on the digitization efforts of the American Presidency Project to access the public papers of US presidents.

3. Theodore C. Sorensen, *Kennedy* (New York: Harper Perennial Political Classics, 2009), 581.

4. The audience was composed of political leaders from the FRG. For example, Kennedy's introduction recognized members of the Bundestag in general. He addressed members in the political line of succession, such as Vice Chancellor Ludwig Erhard specifically. Erhard succeeded Konrad Adenauer four months after the address. Kennedy also mentioned Kurt Kiesinger, who was president of Baden-Württemberg (a state within the FRG) at the time. Kiesinger would assume the chancellery from Erhard in 1966.

5. John F. Kennedy, "Address in the Assembly Hall at the Paulskirche in Frankfurt, June 25, 1963," online by Gerhard Peters and John T. Woolley, The American Presidency Project, permanently available at: https://www.presidency.ucsb.edu.

6. Kathleen J. Turner, "Introduction: Rhetorical History as Social Construction," in Turner, *Doing Rhetorical History*, 2.

7. Turner, "Introduction," 2–3.

8. A narrow interdisciplinary consensus among communication and political science scholars has emerged on the relationship between rhetoric and the presidency. Each recognizes that the institution of the presidency relies on communication and that these communicative practices are rhetorical. The possibilities and limitations of rhetoric, rhetoric's relationship to the Constitution, and the impact of presidential speech on political deliberation are fiercely contested. For the contours of this controversy and the need for revision, see Mary E. Stuckey, "Rethinking the Rhetorical Presidency and Presidential Rhetoric," *Review of Communication* 10, no. 1 (January 2010): 38–52. Stephen Heidt pushes further, arguing that this "rethinking" should abandon metatheory about the presidency given changes in communication technology and practices. See Stephen J. Heidt, "The Study of Presidential Rhetoric in Uncertain Times: Thoughts on Theory and Praxis," in

Reading the Presidency: Advances in Presidential Rhetoric, ed. Stephen J. Heidt and Mary E. Stuckey (New York: Peter Lang, 2019), 1–25.

9. Bruce Buchanan, "Constrained Diversity: The Organizational Demands of the Presidency," *Presidential Studies Quarterly* 20, no. 4 (Fall 1990): 792.

10. Charles Walcott and Karen M. Hult, "White House Structure and Decision Making: Elaborating the Standard Model," *Presidential Studies Quarterly* 35, no 2 (June 2005): 303–18.

11. David B. Cohen and George A. Krause, "Presidents, Chiefs of Staff, and White House Organizational Behavior: Survey Evidence from the Reagan and Bush Administrations," *Presidential Studies Quarterly* 30, no 3 (September 2000): 421–42.

12. David B. Cohen and Charles E. Walcott, "The Office of the Chief of Staff," White House Transition Project, Rice University's Baker Institute for Public Policy, 2017, http://whitehousetransitionproject.org.

13. Cohen and Walcott, "Office of the Chief of Staff."

14. The presidency of George W. Bush operated as an outlier, as Vice President Cheney wielded unmatched influence. See James P. Pfiffner, "The Contemporary Presidency: Decision Making in the Bush White House," *Presidential Studies Quarterly* 39, no. 2 (June 2009): 363–85. The presidency of Donald J. Trump operated as another outlier. President Trump's management "differed significantly from his predecessors" and was characterized "by the lack of a coherent policy process, infighting among factions of his staff, and conflict between Trump and his national security cabinet." See James Pfiffner, "Organizing the Trump Presidency," *Presidential Studies Quarterly* 48, no. 1 (March 2008): 153–67.

15. A method for reading archives is necessary but not always sufficient for conducting research. Scholars can often face obstruction from individual archivists. See Charles E. Morris III, "Archival Queer," *Rhetoric & Public Affairs* 9, no. 1 (Spring 2006): 145–51. Presidential archives present their own set of problems. Classification schemes and discretionary privilege can sustain the withholding of documents from the public. See Shawn J. Parry-Giles, "Archival Research and the American Presidency: The Political and Rhetorical Complexities of Presidential Records," in Parry-Giles and Hogan, *Handbook of Rhetoric*, 157–83. And finally, President Obama's refusal to construct and maintain an archive sets a troubling precedent, certainly obstructing access to documents. See Mary E. Stuckey, "Presidential Secrecy: Keeping Archives Open." *Rhetoric & Public Affairs* 9, no. 1 (Spring 2006): 138–44. For additional issues related to public address and archival research, see the collected essays in "Forum: The Politics of Archival Research," *Rhetoric & Public Affairs* 9, no. 1 (Spring 2006): 113–52.

16. "Germany + Naples (NATO)—DRAFTS 6/22/63–7/2/63," Papers of Theodore C. Sorensen, JFK Speech Files 1961–1963, Box 74, John F. Kennedy, Papers, Kennedy Presidential Library and Museum, Boston.

17. "The Role and Trend of Public Opinion in Western Europe 1961," February 16, 1962, folder "Europe, General 1/61—9/62," Kennedy Papers, National Security Files, Regional Security, Box 212.

18. My initial research question was: How did the speechwriting staff approach the rhetorical invention of the Frankfurt address?

19. My second research question was: How did the circulation of documents within the national security apparatus of the presidency lead to and influence the invention of the Frankfurt address?

20. Andrew M. Johnston, *Hegemony and Culture in the Origins of NATO Nuclear First Use, 1945–1955* (New York: Palgrave Macmillan, 2005), 20.

21. Johnston, *Hegemony and Culture*, 20.

22. John Lewis Gaddis, *Strategies of Containment: A Critical Appraisal of American National Security Policy during the Cold War* (New York: Oxford University Press, 2005), viii–ix.

23. Benjamin Lee and Edward LiPuma, "Cultures of Circulation: The Imaginations of Modernity," *Public Culture* 14, no. 1 (2002): 191–213.

24. For a primer on the implications of rhetorical circulation for communication scholarship, see the forum edited by Mary E. Stuckey: "Forum on Rhetorical Circulation."

25. Zbigniew Brzezinski, in Burkean terms, serves as a representative anecdote: he completed his doctoral degree at Harvard University School of Government and then served as a professor at Harvard and later Columbia University. He was the principal foreign policy advisor to the Humphrey and Carter campaigns and elevated to National Security Advisor after Carter's election. Both prior to and after his government service, Brzezinski authored prominent journal articles and books. And he demonstrated that bipartisan consensus on strategic thinking was possible. See Zbigniew Brzezinski and Brent Scowcroft, *America and the World: Conversations on the Future of American Foreign Policy* (New York: Basic Books, 2008).

26. Strategic studies as a field of inquiry solidified in the aftermath of the shared trauma of World War II, in particular its conclusion through the use of nuclear weapons. Nuclear weapons revealed the inherent truth to Ivan Bloch's observation that industrial innovations make it impossible to imagine surviving modern warfare. See I. S. Bloch, *The Future of War in Its Technical, Economic and Political Relations: Is War Now Impossible?*, trans. R. C. Long (New York: Garland Publishing, 1923). Yet it was also obvious that nation-states would continue to challenge competitors, press advantages, and generally work to increase and use their power. As a result, strategic studies sought to understand the use of state power through historical case studies for the purposes of providing logics that would establish an international order. For a brief history on this field, see Constantinos Koliopoulos, "Historical Approaches to Security/Strategic Studies,"

in *Oxford Research Encyclopedia of International Studies* (New York: Oxford University Press, 2010), np, and available online at https://oxfordre.com/internationalstudies. My reading of security studies as a rhetorical culture is indebted to previous efforts to situate the study and production of international relations as a distinctly rhetorical process. See Francis A. Beer and Robert Hariman, *Post-Realism: The Rhetorical Turn in International Relations* (East Lansing: Michigan State University Press, 1996). I have excluded specific debates emerging from and between different schools of thought within international relations for the simple reason that the concepts of grand strategy, strategy, and tactics persist despite the ideology of a particular school. That is, the methodology articulated herein allows for a mapping of the archive and its ideology.

27. Terry L. Deibel, "Grand Strategy Lessons for the Bush Administration," *Washington Quarterly* 12, no. 3 (1989): 127.

28. Stephen N. Walt, "The Case for Finite Containment. Analyzing US Grand Strategy," *International Security* 14, no. 1 (Summer 1989): 6.

29. William C. Martel, *Grand Strategy in Theory and Practice: The Need for an Effective American Foreign Policy* (New York: Cambridge University Press, 2015).

30. Pres. Dwight Eisenhower formalized the process for national security, culminating in a Basic National Security Policy (BNSP). Presidents Kennedy, Johnson, Nixon, Ford, and Carter each constructed and edited his own BNSP. Section 603 of the Goldwater-Nichols Department of Defense Reorganization Act of 1986 required presidents to produce and distribute to Congress a National Security Strategy of the United States (in two versions: public and secret), the first of which replaced the BNSP in 1987.

31. "Basic National Security Policy, NSC 59061," August 5, 1959, collection, "Presidential Directives on National Security. Part I. From Truman to Clinton," Accession Number PD00583, *Digital National Security Archive*, accessed on November 23, 2017.

32. Carl Kaysen to McGeorge Bundy, "Comments on Draft Proposed 'Military and Related Aspects of Basic National Security Policy,'" June 8, 1961, folder "Staff memoranda: Kaysen, Carl, September 1961: 1–6," Kennedy Papers, National Security Files, Meetings and Memoranda, Box 320.

33. McGeorge Bundy to Robert McNamara, "National Security Action Memorandum N. 37: SACEUR Procedures for Ordering Use of Nuclear Weapons," April 6, 1961, folder "National Security Action Memoranda [NSAM]: NSAM 37, SACEUR Procedures for Ordering Use of Nuclear Weapons," Kennedy Papers, National Security Files, National Security Action Memoranda, Box 329.

34. Gaddis, *Strategies of Containment*, 199.

35. Walter Rostow to President Kennedy, "Basic National Security Policy Short Version," August 2, 1962, folder "Basic National Security Policy, July 1962—February 1963," Kennedy Papers, National Security Files, Subjects, Box 294.

36. Rostow to Kennedy, August 2, 1962, Kennedy Papers.

37. Theodore Sorensen remarked in his biography that President Kennedy understood the improbability in his time of winning the Cold War: Kennedy "sought to halt the external expansion of the Soviet regime, not its internal philosophy and development. He regarded Communist aggression and subversion as intolerable, but not Communism itself." See Sorensen, *Kennedy*, 514.

38. Gaddis, *Strategies of Containment*, viii.

39. Barry R. Posen, "The Struggle against Terrorism: Grand Strategy, Strategy, and Tactics," *International Security* 26, no. 3 (Winter 2001–2): 42.

40. George Ball to President Kennedy, June 20, 1963, "The Mess in Europe and the Meaning of Your Trip," folder, "President's Trip. Europe, 6/63–7/63; General; [Folder 3 of 4]," Kennedy Papers, National Security Files, Trips and Conferences, Box 239.

41. "Meeting with Chancellor Adenauer," May 17, 1963, folder, "Staff Memoranda, Henry Kissinger, 3/63–5/63," Kennedy Papers, National Security Files, Meetings and Memoranda, Box 321.

42. "Notes on Remarks by President Kennedy before the National Security Council," January 22, 1963, collection, "The Berlin Crisis, 1958–1962," Accession Number: CC02869, *Digital National Security Archive*, accessed on November 23, 2017, ProQuest.

43. I relied on the transcript prepared by the Division of Language Services in the Department of State that was circulated as part of the Policy Review Group. See "General de Gaulle's Press Conference," January 14, 1963, folder, Europe Subjects, PR Group, Unnumbered Series, 1963 [Folder 1 of 2]," Kennedy Papers, National Security Files, Regional Security, Box 214.

44. By my count, the president did not produce an immediate address to this exigency. On six separate occasions, Kennedy did receive questions from the press about de Gaulle or nuclear weapons; in each case, the president deftly framed French proliferation as a matter of national sovereignty and expressed confidence that de Gaulle would cooperate with NATO. See the American Presidency Project, Documents, News Conference, January 24, 1963; February 7, 1963; February 14, 1963; February 21, 1963; April 3, 1963; April 24, 1963, available at https://www.presidency.ucsb.edu.

45. Thomas L. Hughes to McGeorge Bundy, April 6, 1963, "Possibilities and Limitations in Dealing with de Gaulle (REU-31)," folder, "Europe, General 4/63–11/63 [Folder 2 of 2]," Kennedy Papers, National Security Files, Regional Security, Box 214.

46. Thomas L. Hughes to McGeorge Bundy, June 19, 1963, "France, Europe and the United States: Five Months Later (REU-46)," folder, "Europe, General 4/63–11/63 [Folder 2 of 2]," Kennedy Papers, National Security Files, Regional Security, Box 214. Ray Cline, deputy director of intelligence at the Central

Intelligence Agency, worried that publics would be "susceptible to sentimentality about their national pride and traditions, and de Gaulle's appeal to this sentiment strikes responsive chords in most of Western Europe." See Ray Cline to McGeorge Bundy, "Europe in the 60s," May 27, 1963, folder, "Europe General 4/63–11/63 [Folder 2 of 2]," Kennedy Papers, National Security Files, Regional Security, Box 214.

47. George Ball chaired the European Policy Review Group. For additional information on group participants and committee assignments see "Organization of the European Policy Review Group," January 29, 1963, folder, "Europe Subjects, PR Group, Unnumbered Series, 1963 [Folder 1 of 2]," Kennedy Papers, National Security Files, Regional Security, Box 214.

48. Untitled Paper, February 9, 1963, folder, "US Policy Towards Europe," Kennedy Papers, National Security Files, Regional Security, Box 214.

49. "The Impact of Domestic Politics in Foreign Policy in Germany, France and Italy," folder, "Europe Subjects, PR Group, Numbered Series [1963]," Kennedy Papers, National Security Files, Regional Security, Box 214.

50. "Comments on US Policy Vis-a-Vis de Gaulle," folder, "Europe Subjects, PR Group, Numbered Series [1963]," Kennedy Papers, National Security Files, Regional Security, Box 214. See also "Possible US Military Action Toward Other Continental NATO Nations to Generate Pressures by Them against France," folder, "Europe Subjects, PR Group, Numbered Series [1963]," Kennedy Papers, National Security Files, Regional Security, Box 214.

51. "The Importance of Berlin," undated and attached to memorandum, Foy D. Kohler to Dean Acheson, June 22, 1961, "Transmitting Two Papers Requested by You," collection, "The Berlin Crisis, 1958–1962," Accession Number: BC02105, *Digital National Security Archive*, accessed on November 23, 2017.

52. President Kennedy's itinerary included stops in Berlin. The division and occupation of the city by multiple nations meant that diplomatic protocol prevented a state level visit. Furthermore, the administration sought to downplay the geopolitical implications beyond NATO allies. President Kennedy was the second American president to visit the FRG since the Potsdam Conference in 1945, and the administration wanted to communicate clearly to Khrushchev that the diplomatic status of both Berlin and the FRG had not changed. Hence, the administration cast this as an informal working visit rather than an official state visit.

53. George Ball to President Kennedy, "The Mess in Europe and the Meaning of Your Trip," June 20, 1963, folder, "President's Trip, Europe, 6/63–7/63, General [Folder 3 of 4]," Kennedy Papers, National Security Files, Trips and Conferences, Box 239.

54. Ball to Kennedy, "The Mess in in Europe," Kennedy Papers.

55. Thomas Sorensen, deputy director of policy and plans in the

Department of State, summarized the administration's position: "It [a visit] needs to be done now; the President is the only one who can do it, and he can do it more effectively in Europe than here." Thomas C. Sorenson to McGeorge Bundy, June 14, 1963, "Memorandum on Reasons for the President's Trip to Europe," folder, "President's Trip. Europe, 6/63–7/63; General; [Folder 2 of 4]," Kennedy Papers, National Security Files, Trips and Conferences, Box 239.

56. "Planning Memorandum on Future Policy for Europe," February 2, 1963, folder, "Europe Subjects, PR Group, Unnumbered Series, 1963 [Folder 2 of 2]," Kennedy Papers, National Security Files, Regional Security, Box 214.

57. For example, see Edward Luttwak, *Strategy: The Logic of War and Peace* (Cambridge, MA: Belknap Press of Harvard University Press, 2001). War fighting has a specific meaning in the realm of strategic studies: it includes planning and preparation in addition to the specifics for carrying out a hostile military campaign.

58. Martel, *Grand Strategy*, 28.

59. Martel, *Grand Strategy*, 29.

60. McGeorge Bundy to President Kennedy, "The MLF and Adenauer," June 20, 1963, folder, "Memos to the President 6/63—8/63," Kennedy Papers, National Security Files, McGeorge Bundy Correspondence, Box 405.

61. Walter Rostow to President Kennedy, "'The European Trip and 'Greatness in the 1960s,'" June 19, 1963, folder, "President's Trip. Europe, 6/63–7/63; General; [Folder 2 of 4]," . Kennedy Papers, National Security Files, Trips and Conferences, Box 239.

62. Arthur Schlesinger to President Kennedy, "The European Tour," June 8, 1963, folder, "President's Trip. Europe, 6/63–7/63; General; [Folder 2 of 4]," Kennedy Papers, National Security Files, Trips and Conferences, Box 239.

63. Schlesinger to Kennedy, June 8, 1963, Kennedy Papers.

64. Untitled Cable from Berlin Consulate to Secretary of State, No. 1122, May 1, 1963, folder, "Germany Security 4/63–11/63," Kennedy Papers, President's Office Files, Countries, Box 117 A.

65. Untitled Cable, May 1, 1963, Kennedy Papers.

66. Untitled Cable, May 1, 1963, Kennedy Papers.

67. Official White House transcripts of public address exist in the public papers of a president. In this case, I have used Remarks of the President in the Assembly Hall of Paulskirche, Frankfurt, Germany, June 25, 1963, folder, "Address in the Assembly Hall at the Paulskirche, Frankfurt, 25 June 1963," Kennedy Papers, President's Office Files, Speech Files, Box 45. I used an audio recording to authenticate the transcript of the address. See "Remarks in the Assembly Hall at the Paulskirche in Frankfurt, 25 June 1963," Kennedy Papers, digital archives, accessed at https://www.jfklibrary.org/asset-viewer/archives/JFKWHA /1963/JFKWHA-199/JFKWHA-199. Presidents are unique rhetors. It is important

to recognize that textual authentication can produce negative outcomes for critics and studied communities alike. See Jason Edward Black, "Native Authenticity, Rhetorical Circulation, and Neocolonial Decay: The Case of Chief Seattle's Controversial Speech," *Rhetoric & Public Affairs* 15, no. 4 (Winter 2012): 635–45.

68. Remarks of the President, lines 12–24, Kennedy Papers.

69. Remarks of the President, lines 39–43, Kennedy Papers.

70. "The Role and Trend of Public Opinion in Western Europe 1961," February 16, 1962, folder, "Europe, General 1/61–9/62," Kennedy Papers, National Security Files, Regional Security, Box 212.

71. McGeorge Bundy to President Kennedy, May 22, 1963, "Why are we going to Europe?," folder, "Memos to the President 5/63," Kennedy Papers, National Security Files, Correspondence, Box 405.

72. Remarks of the President, lines 68–69, Kennedy Papers.

73. Remarks of the President, lines 71–72, Kennedy Papers.

74. Remarks of the President, lines 93–94, Kennedy Papers.

75. Remarks of the President, lines 95–98, Kennedy Papers.

76. Remarks of the President, lines 91–92, Kennedy Papers.

77. Remarks of the President, lines 160–70, Kennedy Papers.

78. Remarks of the President, lines 182–86, Kennedy Papers.

79. "Foreign Radio and Press Assessment of President Kennedy's Visit to West Europe from 22 June to 2 July 1963 Daily Report, Foreign Broadcast Information Service," July 2, 1963, folder "President's Trip. Europe, 6/63–7/63 General [Folder 1 of 4]," Kennedy Papers, Trips and Conferences, Box 239.

80. "As Germans See Him." *New York Times*, June 30, 1963.

81. Michael C. Leff, "Interpretation and the Art of the Rhetorical Critic," *Western Journal of Speech Communication* 44, no. 4 (1980): 337–49.

82. Karlyn Kohrs Campbell and Kathleen Hall Jamieson, "Presidential War Rhetoric," in *Presidents Creating the Presidency: Deeds Done in Words* (Chicago: The University of Chicago Press, 2008).

83. Philip Wander, "The Rhetoric of American Foreign Policy," *Quarterly Journal of Speech* 70, no. 4 (1984): 339–61.

84. Robert L. Ivie, "Metaphor and the Rhetorical Invention of Cold War 'Idealists,'" *Communication Monographs* 54, no. 2 (1987): 165.

85. Raymie E. McKerrow, "Critical Rhetoric: Theory and Praxis," *Communication Monographs* 56, no. 2 (1989): 91.

86. Murphy, *John F. Kennedy*, 189–94.

87. Erin J. Rand, "An Inflammatory Fag and a Queer Form: Larry Kramer, Polemics, and Rhetorical Agency," *Quarterly Journal of Speech* 94, no. 3 (August 2008): 297–319.

IV
METAHISTORIES AND PEDAGOGIES

14

Reading the Logos in Hebrew

A Provocation for Rethinking through Rhetorical History

Lisbeth A. Lipari

In the history of rhetoric, few terms command as much respect, intrigue, and confusion as the Greek term *logos*. It appears as a theme with countless variations in scholarly books and journals across a wide range of disciplines, from rhetoric to classics and from philosophy to theology. Similarly, in the rhetoric of history the concept of logos takes a seat at the high table of philosophy, where it has been investigated through the millennia by countless philosophers who debate its meaning, purpose, and history. Ultimately, there is still little consensus as to what it meant to its earliest progenitors: the sixth century BCE pre-Socratics of eastern-most Greece.

Here, I respond to Turner's invitation to understand history as an essentially rhetorical practice and process.[1] By taking an interdisciplinary rhetorical historical approach, I work against the standard narrative tradition that historicizes the ancient Greeks as somehow sealed off from surrounding cultures. After all, hybridity, intertextuality, cultural appropriation, and colonization are hardly new historical phenomena; yet, the received histories, those conventional and generally accepted as "true" historical narratives of "revolutionary" ancient Greek rhetoric and philosophy, tend to emphasize its originality and innovation without reference to surrounding cultures. Such readings come at the expense of the kinds of cultural dispersion, interconnection, and circulation that were so characteristic of the eastern Mediterranean region in the archaic preclassical age.[2] I read the innovations of the sixth-century pre-Socratics not through the lens of later Greek and German thought as Martin Heidegger does, nor through the received narrative of classical Greece as Jonathan Barnes does, nor through the lens of Christianity and the Johannine word as Hippolytus has, but instead through the lens of the ancient Hebrew scriptures, some of which predate the pre-Socratics by centuries.[3] In what follows, I examine ideas and texts attributed to the sixth-century BCE Ionians (Thales, Xenophanes, Anaximander, Anaximenes, and Heraclitus) with several texts from the early Hebrew Prophets (commonly dated from the eighth to the seventh centuries BCE), as well as several early books of the Torah (sixth and seventh centuries BCE). But first, I offer a few notes about rhetorical history.

The Challenges of Ancient Rhetorical History

Given the inevitably rhetorical nature of history (i.e., *which* stories we tell and *how* we tell them), how should a rhetorical historian to proceed? Humbly, it turns out. As Bruce E. Gronbeck notes in *Doing Rhetorical History*, "the past is inaccessible, even unknowable."[4] By virtue of our awareness of rhetoric and the unremitting nature of hermeneutics that continually forestalls complete understanding, we cannot imagine a past as some kind of buried treasure that, properly resurrected and reconstructed, will reveal capital T Truths as they were known.[5] Just as the past both engendered and shaped the present, so the present will inevitably reconfigure the future and the past. Moreover, as David Zarefsky notes, "historians not only argue *about* history; they also argue *from* it, using historical premises to justify current actions and beliefs."[6] Thus, as with any rhetorical history, scholarship about the pre-Socratics poses a series of theoretical problems involving (1) questions of what and how evidence is selected, distilled, and interpreted and (2) which narratives, temporal periodization, punctuation, and interpretive frameworks are chosen to render the historical account coherent.

In the case of ancient rhetorical history, scholars must grapple with evidential questions of amazing complexity: What documents exist; who wrote them; how, to whom, and for what purpose were they written? In terms of the pre-Socratics, there simply are no surviving intact original texts. Moreover, most scholarship on this period depends on subsequent interpretations by much later philosophers who "have their own philosophies to advance."[7] As E. Culpepper Clark and Raymie McKerrow note, history is always "partial and interested, never complete or indifferent."[8] The time elapsed between the composition of the original texts and the later recounting of those texts can be immense—from several centuries to a millennium or more—further complicating questions about a given text's credibility and interpretation.[9] For example, a text attributed to Anaximander, who is said to have died around 540 BCE, was recounted by Simplicius, a thousand years later in 534 CE.

A second set of questions relate to issues of periodization, temporal punctuation, and cultural scale: When and where does the story begin and end, and what is its range and scope?[10] Which actors and actions are included in the narrative and which excluded? What unstated assumptions about cultural exchange, material and symbolic flows, and contrasting time periods govern the narrative? And perhaps foremost, how do scholars accurately, coherently, and responsibly distill innumerable actions, actors, and settings into a single coherent narrative? How do scholars account for the unfathomably complex interactions of human beings and events that arise not from rational steps in a causal chain but from the concatenation of random synchronicities and turbulent contestations that characterize historical actualities?

In terms of evidence, the original and most referenced collection of pre-Socratic ideas—the evidentiary basis for most research in the area—was compiled by the German scholar Hermann Diels in 1903 and revised by Walther Kranz in 1952.[11] In this widely accepted system, Diels and Kranz gave every ancient thinker an identifying number and every fragment of text both a letter and number. The letter A reflects what they considered testimony (accounts, paraphrases, allusions, or assessments) of the original author's thought, and the letter B indicates fragments presumed to be *ipsissima verba*—the precise words of the original author. Complicating these seemingly simple categories is the fact that while some accounts of pre-Socratic thought are from scholars who had direct access to original primary texts, many more are from secondary and even tertiary sources. According to Barnes, "Not all purported quotations are actual quotations. (And not all actual quotations are purported citations). . . . The counterfeiting of early texts was a popular pastime in the ancient world."[12] And just as worrisome: some quoted texts may have been misremembered or mistranslated, and some may simply have chosen different words for the translation.

For an example of this evidential difficulty, the text of Hippolytus of Rome (a bishop in second century CE and the source for many Heraclitus fragments) attributes some passages to Heraclitus with quotation marks and some without. Diels and Kranz catalogue passages with quotation marks as B fragments (ipsissima verba), and those without as A fragments (testimony). In the context of rhetorical history, where careful attention to language is paramount, how much credence should a contemporary rhetorical scholar place on these differences in punctuation? F. Legge, an early twentieth-century English translator of Hippolytus, urges caution: "In his account of the tenets of the philosophers, he [Hippolytus] repeatedly alters or misunderstands his authorities. . . . Some of this inaccuracy may possibly be due to mistakes in copying and re-copying by scribes who did not understand what they were writing; but when all is said there is left a sum of blunders which can only be attributed to great carelessness on the part of the author."[13] Another more recent example is found in Donald L. Ross, who critiques Hippolytus's account of Brahmanic theology. According to Ross, Hippolytus's rendering is likely derived from third-century BCE ethnographic descriptions by members of the Alexandrian expeditions to India. He finds the text laden with Platonic metaphors, as well as allusions to the *Phaedo*, suggesting that either Hippolytus or his sources relied on Plato extensively as an interpretive framework for representing Indian philosophy.[14]

For the most part, rhetorical scholars are particularly careful when it comes to questions of evidentiary fidelity. In the influential studies of the pre-Socratic logos, both Christopher Lyle Johnstone and Edward Schiappa employ the hermeneutic principle of triangulation using a variety of Greek literature. Johnstone's sources include Aristophanes, Xenophon, Plato, Aristotle, and Diogenes Laertius, while Schiappa uses "pre-Protagorean sources of Homer and Heraclitus on one side and the post-Protagorean writings of Plato and Aristotle [because] Greek philosophical language underwent considerable change during the sixth, fifth, and fourth centuries BCE."[15] Like Eric Alfred Havelock, these authors attribute much rhetorical and linguistic invention to the pre-Socratics, arguing that they built new philosophical and rhetorical ground by "stretching" older words into newer meanings. As Johnstone contends, "thought precedes and instigates the development of terminology precisely because there are ideas—not yet formed into concepts—for the expression of which no terms exist."[16] He points to how the pre-Socratics repurposed such archaic terms as *genesis, logos, theos, kosmos,* and *arche* figuratively, in order "to express new ways of perceiving the causes of events and the relations among them."[17] Similarly, Havelock says the use of the word *logos* by sophists was driven by the growing importance of democratic deliberation wherein "the advance of theory has outstripped the capacity of vocabulary. . . . *Logos* and *legein* were called on to carry this impossible burden."[18] These rhetorical histories thus emphasize the role of the pre-Socratics in generating seemingly revolutionary advancements in forms of thought and understanding: not only distinct from their predecessors but unique to the world.

Thus, the predominant received narratives of rhetorical history and Western philosophy depict the pre-Socratics as the first philosophers, who collectively introduced a uniquely systematic, rational, and scientific kind of thought into a world infused with mythical, and presumably irrational and supernatural, ways of thinking.[19] Barnes holds that the pre-Socratics initiated the birth of science and philosophy, while Charles H. Kahn contends that "what the system of Anaximander represents to us is nothing less than the advent, in the west at any rate, of a rational outlook on the natural world."[20] Some scholars even classify the fragments of pre-Socratic thought under such contemporary scientific categories as astronomy, meteorology, geology, oceanography, biology, and psychology.[21] And some scholars downplay or deny any relationship between Greek thinking and the thought of far more ancient civilizations in Egypt, Mesopotamia, and the greater eastern Mediterranean region. Barnes asserts that "the most characteristic and significant features of early Greek thought have no known parallels in Egypt or in Babylon or in Lydia."[22] Moreover, he stresses that "it is difficult to find a single clear case of influence."[23]

Other contemporary scholars demonstrate a curious ambivalence about the impact of surrounding cultures on the development of early Greek thought. They seem to follow the received narrative while nodding cautiously and equivocally to suggestions of contact with what they often term "the orient."[24] While Daniel W. Graham notes that Thales's Phoenician roots "are downplayed by Kirk,"[25] he himself doubles back by saying, "Thales's cosmological view may originate with Egyptian and Near Eastern conceptions. Nevertheless, Thales goes beyond myth in sketching a cosmology in which natural replaces supernatural explanation."[26] Similarly, although Robin Osborne questions "just how evolutionary the Greeks were," he then quickly asserts that "what happened in Greece was really new."[27] Many scholars thus tentatively acknowledge the far older cultural matrix surrounding Greece and then promptly minimize or effectively erase it.

A minority of both ancient and modern scholars, however, do attest to contact and exchange between Greece and other cultures in the region.[28] After all, the notion that the Greeks inherited little other than the Phoenician alphabet and a little Babylonian astronomy stretches plausibility perhaps a bit too far. For example, Philip L. Kohl and Bertille Lyonnet explore how cultural "evolution and dispersion are not opposed, but complementary concepts."[29] They found evidence of a vast network of interregional exchanges of Bronze Age materials and people that spans from the Indus Valley, through the Middle East and Transcaucasia, to the eastern Mediterranean. These networks demonstrate how historical perspectives on internal cultural development often miss the rhythms of interconnection and the "circulation of materials, peoples, and ideas over long distances."[30] Cyrus Gordon, the great mid-twentieth-century scholar of linguistics and Semitic languages, dismisses the received narrative that opposes Greece and Israel: "Suffice it to say that the prevailing attitude may be described as the tacit assumption that ancient Israel and Greece are two water-tight compartments, totally different from each other. One is said to be sacred; the other, profane; one, Semitic; the other, Indo-European. One, Asiatic and Oriental; the other, European and

Occidental. But the fact is that both flourished during the same centuries, in the same East Mediterranean corner of the globe, with both ethnic groups in contact with each other from the start."[31]

As a matter of fact, most of the earliest pre-Socratics were Ionian Greeks: they clustered along the Lydian coast of the Aegean Sea, the easternmost region of Greece closest to Asia Minor (now Turkey), near the ancient Anatolian kingdoms and along the same shoreline as key Phoenician cities, not far from the nearby kingdoms of Israel and Judah. Anaximenes, Anaximander, and Thales (whose father was Phoenician) all lived in the Ionian city of Miletus, with Xenophanes and Heraclitus from the neighboring cities of Colophon and Ephesus respectively. At the time, the city of Miletus was a center of both material and intellectual exchange with important trade routes linking Babylon, Egypt, Lydia, and Phoenicia. As Robin Waterfield notes, "ideas always travel with trade."[32] In fact, Thales is said to have based his prediction of an eclipse around 580 BCE on Babylonian astronomical tables. Although scholars such as Kathleen Freeman acknowledge this, and also speculate that Thales learned geometry from the Egyptians, they quickly qualify that information: "The question is was the material collected by the Babylonians and Egyptians in any way scientifically arranged or analyzed already; or was it a record of data and practical rules only?"[33] Consistent with received "revolutionary" narratives these scholars assume that although Thales may have acquired data from the elder civilizations, it only became science when investigated by the Ionians and other Greeks.

Regardless of how it is glossed, transfers of knowledge both east and west accompanied the trade of materials. In particular, this knowledge included the substantial ancient Egyptian literature, written in hieroglyphics, and the detailed and extensive ancient Babylonian and Assyrian records and literature, written in cuneiform. Both of these systems were "the result of a process of continual transmission of themes and forms between cultures of vastly different origins and modes of life."[34] With the approximately tenth-century BCE innovation of the Phoenician "phonetic" alphabetic script used for Hebrew and later Greek, it became possible to write anything with only a few dozen symbols, as compared to the thousands needed to write in cuneiform and hieroglyphics.[35] Given this rich historical and rhetorical background, it seems only reasonable to extend the study of pre-Socratic rhetoric beyond the Greek world to an enriched historical interanimation with surrounding civilizations.

The Rhetorical History of Logos: A Case Study

Somewhere in the third and second centuries BCE, when the Hellenized

Jews translated the Hebrew Bible from Hebrew into Greek (known by its Latin title as the Septuagint, or LXX [seventy], or the number of translators), they translated the Hebrew verbal root רבד (dabar/dvar) as *logos*.[36] The root, dabar, plays a key role in the Hebrew scriptures; and depending on prefixes, suffixes, vowels, and other inflections, it has several derivatives and meanings related to utterance, words, and speaking. Dabar may thus mean words (Bereshit/Gen. 11:1), things (Gen. 15:1), or matters (Shemot/Ex. 18:19). It is the first word of the first sentence in the book we call Bamidbar/Numbers רבדיו הוהי (va'dabar Hashem), "and he said"; and it is the title of the fifth book, Devarim/Deuteronomy םירבד, "the words." Also worth noting is the fact that four of the five books of the Torah (Pentatuch) are titled in Hebrew with language directly pertaining to words, speech, and speaking. In addition to those mentioned above, the book the Greeks entitled Leviticus is in Hebrew ארקיו (v'yakra), "he called," and the book the Greeks entitled Exodus is in Hebrew תומש (Shemot, the names). The *LXX* frequently uses the Greek word λογος (logos) to translate the Hebrew word dabar in both Exodus and Deuteronomy, especially when used to convey the idea of God's words.[37] How did the Greek word logos, a relatively rare word during the time of Homer in the eighth century BCE meaning reckoning or speaker, come to mean God's words by the time of the Septuagint, completed five or six centuries later in the third century BCE?

According to Francis E. Peters's historical lexicon of Greek philosophical terms, "the word itself [logos/λογοσ] is not strongly attested until the time of Heraclitus" in the sixth century BCE. Only then does the word logos come to be used with regard to "a peculiar doctrine that centers around *logos* in a more technical sense: for him *logos* is an underlying organizational principle of the universe, related to the common meaning of *logos* as proportion."[38] Prior to that, the word logos is found only three times in Homer's *Iliad* and three times in Homer's *Odyssey*.[39] Contemporary scholars in both philosophy and rhetoric have spilled much ink over the meanings of logos among the pre-Socratics, especially as found in the work of Heraclitus.[40] As Barnes notes, "every interpretation of Heraclitus' thought is controversial."[41]

Of the many fragments attributed to Heraclitus (circa 500 BCE), three make use of the word logos in a seemingly new way: as an allusion to an overarching power or phenomena that governs all things. Some scholars interpret this as a "technical" use of logos as a law or principle, some as an overarching form of reason, some more theologically oriented as divine speech, and some simply as an account or recounting. Not surprisingly, the Greek word logos translates into

English differently by different classical scholars. Waterfield uses the word "principle," Barnes "account" (the rarely used but more traditional rendering, e.g., from Homer), Graham "word," and Kirk, Raven, and Schofield "logos."

Two primary themes govern the interpretation of logos, one a more logical, rational, and scientific rendering and the second with a more theological reading. The first theme is illustrated by the oft-repeated phrase "from mythos to logos," which, as previously mentioned, is said to describe the transition from a supernatural mythos to a more rational logos. Johnstone contends that the latter worldview emerged in Greece during the sixth century BCE, beginning with the Ionian thinkers—Thales, Anaximander, Anaximenes, Xenophanes, and Heraclitus. He maintains that this conceptual and linguistic revolution arose from a combination of factors, including the invention of alphabetic writing, the appearance of prose, the creation of philosophical vocabulary and syntax, and the use of argument and abstraction of thought. From a slightly different rhetorical perspective, Reames argues for a materialist conception of logos: "Language, in this case, is not above or outside the volatile flux of phusis—language, logos, is inextricable from and implicated in the very matter it describes."[42] Schiappa, too, downplays the metaphysical or divine aspects of speech by emphasizing the more rational and logical aspects of argument. He sees the sophistic sense of logos as a much more expansive term than what would later be called rhetoric and holds that "Protagoras seems to have been the first Sophist to privilege logos over the mytho-poetic tradition."[43] In concert with Havelock, Schiappa attributes the rise of logos over mythos to the new and emerging Greek rationalism that required argument rather than poetry or epic.

In contrast to this more rationalist rendering of logos, the classical scholars G. S. Kirk, J. E. Raven, and Malcolm Schofield define logos as a kind of divine knowledge: "God cannot here be essentially different from Logos; and the Logos is, among other things, the constituent of things."[44] Even Waterfield, who translates logos as principle, also says "the logos is divine."[45] Similarly, Johnstone references the divine aspect of the logos: "Heraclitus, then, can be read as holding that wisdom is a matter of understanding the plan or design, the intelligence or purpose 'in accordance with which all things come to pass' (DK 1). This plan, moreover, is comprehended by the term logos, which, although it is accessible to the human mind, is not easily understood"[46] Significantly, this more theological rendering of logos is consonant with the surprising allusions to monotheism said to occur in early pre-Socratic thought, most significantly with the elder Ionians Xenophanes and (to a lesser degree) Thales.

The seemingly earliest allusion to Greek monotheism is attributed to Thales, who is said to have maintained a conception of an imminent God who is present everywhere.[47] The earliest reporter on Thales is Aristotle (circa 350 BCE), who observed, "Some say that the [soul] is mixed in the totality; this is perhaps the reasons Thales thought all things are full of gods."[48] Aristotle also asserted that ancient people gave "an account of the gods. . . . Thales, however, is said to have made this explicit statement about the first cause."[49] Over eight hundred years later, Diogenes Laertius (approximately 250 CE) tributes to Thales "of existing things, god is the oldest, for he is ungenerated."[50] In Freeman's rendering, Thales was a pupil of the Egyptians and the Chaldeans (Babylonians), and was one of the first Greek thinkers to "philosophize about things heavenly and divine."[51] While not interpreted as monotheists in quite the same way, Anaximenes and Anaximander are both said to have held a conception of an infinite source of all things that was intelligent, eternal, deathless, and all knowing. Neither Anaximander or Anaximenes specifically called this source of all things God, rather, they described it as an unmoving mind substance—either air or akin to air, fire, or water in combination.

Following these three earlier Ionians, Xenophanes (circa 530 BCE) is widely held to have been "the first critical theologian" who argued "for what would to the Greeks have been the extraordinary concept of monotheism."[52] Graham says Xenophanes "at least adumbrates the concept of monotheism for the first time in the Greek tradition,"[53] holding that "if God is the mightiest being of all, he says, it is fitting for him to be one. For if there were two or more, he would no longer be mightiest and best of all. . . . Since there is one God he is alike everywhere, seeing and hearing and having the other senses throughout."[54] In the second century CE, Sextus Empiricus attributed to Xenophanes the idea that "if the divine exists, it is a living thing; if it is a living thing, it sees—for he sees as a whole, he thinks as a whole, he hears as a whole."[55] Similarly, over one thousand years later in the fifth century CE, Simplicius draws on Aristotle's pupil Theophrastus to contend that Xenophanes "supposed that there is one principle, that what exists is one and all, and neither limited nor limitless, neither moving nor motionless. He [Theophrastus] agrees that an account of his views belongs to a different inquiry from the study of nature; for Xenophanes said that this 'one and all' is god. He shows that god is one from the fact that he is the most powerful of all things."[56]

In addition, Simplicius says that Xenophanes advanced the idea that this single God was ungenerated, neither limited nor limitless; that he "always reposes in the same state, not moving at all, nor is it fitting for him to come and go now here and there"; and that "far from toil he governs everything by thought."[57] Johnstone finds this account particularly important as it expresses "the idea that the 'one god,' unmoved and in no way similar to mortals, generates movement in the world by thinking. It is mind that permeates and moves all things."[58] As Johnstone reads it, "what is certain is that, beginning early in the sixth century B.C.E. along the western coast of Asia Minor, there emerged a way of understanding and being-in-the-world that in some respects constituted a radical departure from the mythopoetic mindset that preceded it. . . . The pursuit of wisdom aimed finally at being 'touched' by a god, and wise speech is *entheos logos*—filled with the divine."[59]

Curiously, in spite of the fact that the world's first monotheistic religion had emerged nearby and several centuries earlier, there have been few investigations into thematic, conceptual, or discursive parallels between the monotheism of Xenophanes and the Hebrew scriptures.[60] Consider, however, the following phrases from Xenophanes (circa 530 BCE) in comparison to passages from the eighth-century Hebrew Prophet Isaiah (circa 740 BCE). Xenophanes's fragment describing God's limitlessness, "complete he sees, complete he thinks, complete he hears,"[61] is quite reminiscent of how a number of Hebrew prophets, including Isaiah and Jeremiah (circa 627 BCE), repeatedly describe the Hebrew God's all-knowing, all-hearing, all-seeing powers: "Before they call I will answer; while they are yet speaking I will hear" (Isa. 65:24). Similarly, Jeremiah (33:3) tells the people "call to me and I will answer you, and will tell you great and hidden things that you have not known." This idea of a hidden all-knowing God recurs throughout the books of the prophets Isaiah and Jeremiah.[62] Similarly, where Xenophanes characterizes God as an unmoving effortless mind—"He remains forever in the same place, entirely motionless, Nor is it proper for him to move from one place to another. But effortlessly he shakes all things by thinking with his mind"[63]—Isaiah's God states, "I am the Lord, who made all things, who alone stretched out the heavens, who spread out the earth by myself" (Isa. 44:24), as well as "behold, I am the Lord, the God of all flesh. Is there anything too hard for me?" (Isa. 32:27). Even Xenophanes's claim that "for all things are from earth and in earth all things end"[64] resonates with the angry God of Genesis who scolds Adam and Eve, saying, "Until you return to the ground—For from it you were taken. For dust you are, and to dust you shall return" (Gen. 3:19).

Consider now the more theological rendering of logos found in two fragments from Heraclitus, one attested by Sextus and Hippolytus (both from the second century CE), and one solely by Hippolytus. Kirk, Raven, and Schofield translate the first fragment, numbered 22B1 by Diels and

Kranz, as "of the Logos which is as I describe it men always prove to be uncomprehending, both before they have heard it and when once they have heard it. For although all things happen according to this Logos men are like people of no experience, even when they experience such words and deeds as I explain."[65] If the more theological reading of logos is also correct, how might the theological thought of Heraclitus and the earlier pre-Socratics relate to ancient Mesopotamian and Egyptian literature in general and Hebrew scripture in particular? Here I would point to the strong resonances between the logos of this fragment and divine words spoken by the Hebrew prophets Isaiah and Jeremiah, both of whom wandered the city of Jerusalem imploring audiences to listen to the word of God and chastising people for their refusal to comprehend what they hear. When Isaiah (6:9) hears the voice of God say, "Go, say to the people, hear indeed but do not understand, See, indeed but do not grasp." And when Jeremiah (5:21) is instructed to speak to the House of Jacob in Judah, he is instructed to announce, "Hear this, O foolish people, Devoid of intelligence, That have eyes that can't see, that have ears but can't hear!" Again and again, these two prophets beg the people of Jerusalem to listen to the divine word, and again and again, the people fail. Once again Jeremiah (6:12) asks, "To whom shall I speak, Give warning that they may hear? Their ears are blocked And they cannot listen. See the word of the Lord has become for them, An object of scorn; they will have none of it."

These are not, however, the only similarities between Hebrew scripture and the Heraclitus logos fragments. Consider the Heraclitus fragment B50, which is translated by Kirk, Raven, and Schofield as "listening not to me but to the Logos, it is wise to agree that all things are one."[66] The phrasing bears an uncanny resemblance to the Shema, one of the oldest, holiest, and most-frequently recited prayers in Hebrew, chanted at least twice daily, morning and evening.[67] The Shema prayer, named after its first word, שְׁמַע, first appears in the book of Devarim/Deuteronomy, where it is delivered by Moses after he recounts the story of the Israelites' forty-year exodus through the desert. In Deuteronomy (6:4), the Shema begins: "Listen, Israel, the Lord, our God, the Lord is one."[68] Like the Heraclitan imperative in fragment B50, the Shema constitutes a self-standing aphoristic whole. Moreover, it has three clauses, the first of which begins with an imperative to listen, the second of which invokes the divine, and the third and final of which ends in an assertion of unity and singularity ("all things are one" versus "God is one"). Unlike Heraclitus's fragment B50, however, there is no need for the Hebrew prophet to remind the audience to listen to the divine word rather than himself because it is understood that Hebrew prophets are speaking not their own words but the divine words of God. In the Shema, the divine word and God are one and the same.[69] The parallels between the Hebrew Shema and the B50 fragment from Heraclitus are striking.

From a rhetorical historical perspective then, the regions, timelines, periods, and scale used to chronicle history are always understood to be constructions that are shaped by, with, and for a given narrative rather than as actual boundaries of time and space. Thus, the apparent isolation of ancient Greece from other East Mediterranean cultures should give rhetorical scholars pause. Moreover, the close geographical and temporal proximity of the Ionians to the Hebrews, who theorized both a monotheistic God and divine speech some centuries before the Ionian Greeks, gives rise to reasonable questions about contact and exchange. But in spite of these considerations, there has been a puzzling disinterest in the way both Xenophanes's monotheism and Heraclitus's logos bear an uncanny resemblance to Hebrew thought.

Conclusion

Schiappa echoes Havelock's contention that "for over 2000 years our understanding of who the sophists were has been dominated by Plato's writing, [and] Aristotle's treatment of the Sophists paralleled Plato's." Schiappa argues that "so powerful was the combined indictment by Plato and Aristotle that their judgments concerning the Sophists remained the standard view in most modern histories of ancient Greece. Plato's and Aristotle's respective rhetorical definitions became accepted as accurate *descriptions* of the Sophists."[70] Might we not change these terms to identify a similar problem with our understandings of the pre-Socratics? For even while Schiappa acknowledges that "most ancient and classical texts have been interpreted through unstated assumptions,"[71] a long-standing yet seemingly unchallenged assumption continues to be that the pre-Socratics emerge sui generis in sixth century BCE Ionia.

But while questions about the relationship between East Mediterranean civilizations and the earliest pre-Socratics are clearly issues of rhetorical history, they are at the same time extremely difficult questions to answer. As Clark and McKerrow note, history is best understood as a process of understanding, never its object.[72] The further we get from the original texts the dimmer the sounds of the historical voice and the louder the shouts of subsequent ideas, debates, ideologies, and frameworks. But as Momigliano reminds us, often the questions are more important than the answers, regardless of our ability to answer them. And there are contemporary as well as ancient reasons why relationships between ancient Greece and ancient East Mediterranean civilizations have been neglected or erased, and those reasons need to be raised from the depths and examined afresh.

But perhaps the idea of influence is itself the wrong approach to describe the complex interpenetrating and fluid processes of cultural flow. For the word *influence* connotes a linear process of cause and effect, imposing a forced coherence that neglects the interrelated cultural matrices into which new ideas are adapted, absorbed, and adopted. Further, the idea of influence can tend to reinforce teleological and developmental notions of history that impose contemporary categories and conceptions where they may not belong. While revolution makes for a good story line, it seems to run counter to well-documented forms of cultural exchange that have long characterized the East Mediterranean region. For example, in addition to providing confirmation for events recounted in the Hebrew bible, Egyptian texts and records from Assyria and Babylon also illuminate an underlying shared cultural milieu in relation to law, mythology, scribal culture, prophecy, poetry, ritual, and narrative form.[73] And as with each eastern Mediterranean culture, the Hebrew scriptures reflect that shared historic cultural milieu while also bespeaking ideas and forms that are distinct. Further, given that the regional divisions were continually interpenetrated and overlapped due to the ceaseless wars of empire, colonization, and forced exile, as well as the fact that elite populations from conquered cities were routinely deported to the ruling cities, there is a good case to be made for cultural diffusions far and wide.[74]

A related problem pertains to the scale and scope of the narrative of rhetoric's history, in particular, the delimited centrality of Greek thought in relation to ancient rhetoric. Two collections of thoughtful rhetorical scholarship bear witness to this problem. Both collections, which investigate rhetoric of cultures as richly diverse as ancient Assyrian, Chinese, Egyptian, Indian, Irish, Japanese, Hebrew, and Mesopotamian, are gathered together and positioned with respect to Greece (i.e., as non-Greek)—even though Greek rhetoric is not a subject of these collections.[75] It is as if Greece is the unmarked standard against which all else must be measured. And when this received narrative of ancient Greece persists as inseparable from our notions of "ancient rhetoric," it is seemingly impossible to render anything outside of its terms. But as Walter Benjamin so hopefully notes, "nothing that has ever happened should be regarded as lost for history"[76]

Thus, beyond interpreting texts, cataloging evidence, and searching for cause and effect, good rhetorical scholarship must also tangle with the doing, undoing, and redoing of contested interpretive frameworks that forever confront us with the challenge of how to plausibly tell a singular and apparently coherent story that could be conveyed in myriad ways from any number of contradictory perspectives. History is always rhetorical in the sense that evidence and interpretation are always contextual, situated, partial—always grounded in a set of shared narrative practices and understandings, and the layerings of language caked with time.

Notes

1. Kathleen J. Turner, "Introduction: Rhetorical History as Social Construction," in Turner, *Doing Rhetorical History*, 1–15.

2. See, for example, Walter Burkert, *The Orientalizing Revolution: Near Eastern Influence on Greek Culture in the Early Archaic Age* (Cambridge, MA: Harvard University Press, 1992); Martin L. West, *The East Face of Helicon: West Asiatic Elements in Greek Poetry and Myth* (New York: Clarendon Press, 1997); Martin Bernal, *Black Athena: The Afroasiatic Roots of Classical Civilization* (New Brunswick, NJ Rutgers University Press, 1987).

3. Jonathan Barnes, ed., *Early Greek Philosophy* (New York: Penguin Classics, 1987); Jonathan Barnes, *The Presocratic Philosophers*, rev. ed. (Boston: Routledge & Kegan Paul, 1982); Martin Heidegger, *Early Greek Thinking*, trans. David Farrell Krell and Frank Capuzzi (New York: Harper & Row, 1984); Hippolytus, *Refutation of All Heresies*, trans. M. David Litwa (Williston, VT: Society of Biblical Literature, 2015).

4. Bruce E. Gronbeck, "The Rhetorics of the Past: History, Argument, and Collective Memory," in Turner, *Doing Rhetorical History*, 48.

5. As Gadamer explains, events of understanding always occur in a historical context, which "is why understanding is not merely a reproductive but always a productive activity as well." Hans-Georg Gadamer, *Truth and Method*, trans. Joel Weinsheimer and Donald G. Marshall, 2nd rev. ed. (New York: Continuum, 2003), 296.

6. David Zarefsky, "Four Senses of Rhetorical History," in Turner, *Doing Rhetorical History*, 19–32.

7. Daniel W. Graham, ed., *The Texts of Early Greek Philosophy: The Complete Fragments and Selected Testimonies of the Major Presocratics* (New York: Cambridge University Press, 2010), 7.

8. E. Culpepper Clark and Raymie E. McKerrow, "The Rhetorical Construction of History," in Turner, *Doing Rhetorical History*, 46.

9. For example, Aristotle and his pupil Theophrasus wrote about the pre-Socratics in the fourth century BCE, while Sextus Empiricus wrote in the second century CE, and Simplicius wrote in the sixth century CE.

10. Gronbeck refers to such questions as "bracketing" in "Rhetorics of the Past," 51.

11. Hermann Diels and Walther Kranz, *Die Fragmente der Vorsokratiker, griechisch und deutsch*, 6 (Berlin: Weidmann, 1951). The English translation of Diel's German translation from the Greek is found in Kathleen Freeman and Hermann Diels, *Ancilla to the Pre-Socratic Philosophers: A Complete Translation of the Fragments in Diels, Fragmente Der Vorsokratiker* (Cambridge, MA: Harvard University Press, 1971). Freeman's companion volume is also very useful. Kathleen Freeman and Hermann Diels, *The Pre-Socratic Philosophers: A Companion to Diels, Fragmente Der Vorsokratiker*, 2nd ed. (Oxford: B. Blackwell, 1949).

12. Barnes, *Early Greek Philosophy*, xxix.

13. Hippolytus, *Philosophumena, or, The Refutation of All Heresies*, trans. Francis Legge, vol. 1 (New York: Macmillan, 1921), 10.

14. Donald L. Ross, "Platonist Brahmans? Platonic Metaphors in Refutation of All Heresies 1.24," *Hermathena* Summer, no. 198 (2015): 35–51.

15. Edward Schiappa, *Protagoras and Logos: A Study in Greek Philosophy and Rhetoric* (Columbia: University of South Carolina Press, 1991), 34.

16. Christopher Lyle Johnstone, *Listening to the Logos: Speech and the Coming of Wisdom in Ancient Greece* (Columbia: University of South Carolina Press, 2012), 9.

17. Johnstone, *Listening to the Logos*, 9.

18. Eric Alfred Havelock, *The Liberal Temper in Greek Politics* (London: J. Cape, 1957), 192. The ancient Greek *legein* (λεγειν) is the present active indicative of the verbal root *lego* (λεγω)—to pick out, gather, count, tell, say, or speak. It is the same root from which *logos* derives.

19. But, of course, none of these categories existed until later philosophers assigned them.

20. Charles H. Kahn, *Anaximander and the Origins of Greek Cosmology* (New York: Columbia University Press, 1960), 7.

21. See, for example, John Mansley Robinson, *An Introduction to Early Greek Philosophy: The Chief Fragments and Ancient Testimony, with Connecting Commentary* (Boston: Houghton Mifflin, 1968), and Graham, *Texts of Early Greek Philosophy*.

22. Barnes, *Presocratic Philosophers*, xvii.

23. Barnes, *Presocratic Philosophers*, xvii.

24. Postcolonial and critical scholarship have revealed many problematically Eurocentric and Orientalist patterns in Western scholarship of non-European cultures, one of which involves the question of naming. In response to these concerns, I will use either the geographical term eastern Mediterranean or civilizational names such as Mesopotamia, Egypt, Hebrew, Hittite. However, some quotations contain such problematic regional names as "Near East" or "Orient."

25. Graham, *Texts of Early Greek Philosophy*, 38. The reference is to Heraclitus and G. S. Kirk, *The Cosmic Fragments* (Cambridge: Cambridge University Press, 1954).

26. Graham, *Texts of Early Greek Philosophy*, 40.

27. Simon Goldhill and Robin Osborne, eds., *Rethinking Revolutions through Ancient Greece* (Cambridge: Cambridge University Press, 2006), 6.

28. From the ancients, see, for example, Herodotus, *The Histories*, trans. Aubrey De Selincourt (New York: Penguin Books, 1954); and Flavius Josephus and Steve Mason, *Flavius Josephus: Translation and Commentary, Life of Josephus 9* (Boston: Brill Academic Publishers, 2001). For more mid-twentieth-century treatments, see Michael C. Astour, *Hellenosemitica: An Ethnic and Cultural Study in West Semitic Impact on Mycenaean Greece* (Leiden, Netherlands: E. J. Brill, 1967); Francis Macdonald Cornford, *From Religion to Philosophy: A Study in the Origins of Western Speculation* (New York: Harper, 1957); and Cyrus H. Gordon, *Homer and Bible: The Origin and Character of East Mediterranean Literature* (Ventnor, NJ: Ventnor Publishers, 1967).

29. Philip L. Kohl and Bertille Lyonnet, "By Land and By Sea: The Circulation of Materials and Peoples, ca. 3500–1800 B.C.," in *Intercultural Relations between South and Southwest Asia: Studies in Commemoration of E.C.L. during Caspers (1934–1996)*, ed. Eric Olijdam and Richard H. Spoor (Oxford: Archaeopress, 2008), 29.

30. Kohl and Lyonnet, "By Land and Sea," 29.

31. Cyrus H. Gordon, *Before the Bible: The Common Background of Greek and Hebrew Civilizations* (New York: Harper & Row, 1962), 11.

32. Robin Waterfield, *The First Philosophers* (Oxford: Oxford University Press, 2000), 3.

33. Freeman and Diels, *Pre-Socratic Philosophers*, 50. See also Freeman and Diels. *Ancilla to the Pre-Socratic Philosophers*.

34. Louis L. Orlin, *Life and Thought in the Ancient Near East* (Ann Arbor: University of Michigan Press, 2010), 186.

35. Phoenician and Hebrew were mutually intelligible dialects of the same shared language. Quinn argues that Phoenicians were not a singular national or ethnic identity but a diverse collection of peoples whose identities were based on geographical, family, and colonial ties as well as religious practices. There is some debate about whether proto-Sinatic, proto-Hebrew, or proto-Phoenician was the underlying language. See, for example, Josephine Crawley Quinn, *In Search of the Phoenicians* (Princeton, NJ: Princeton University Press, 2018); Geoffrey Khan, ed., *Encyclopedia of Hebrew Language and Linguistics* (Boston: Brill, 2013).

36. According to the Talmud, "when the Torah was translated into Greek, three days of darkness enveloped the world" (Megillah Ta'anit, Tractate Megillah, Kelman 2014).

37. See, for example, Exod. 4:28, 20:1, 34:27–28, 35:1; and Deut. 3:26, 9:10, 12:28, 27:26, and 28:14.

38. Francis E. Peters, *Greek Philosophical Terms: A Historical Lexicon* (New York: New York University Press, 1967), 111.

39. Gregory R. Crane, ed., Perseus Digital Library, University, accessed April 17, 2012, http://www.perseus.tufts.edu.

40. Scholars in both philosophy and rhetoric have written a great deal interpreting the ideas of Heraclitus, in part because the fragments attested to him are the most numerous and also because they comprise some of the longest fragments from the earliest Ionian pre-Socratics.

41. Barnes, *Early Greek Philosophy*, 48.

42. Robin Reames, "The Logos Paradox: Heraclitus, Material Language, and Rhetoric," *Philosophy and Rhetoric* 46, no. 3 (2013): 329. *Phusis* is typically translated as nature and is often opposed to *nomos*, law.

43. Schiappa, *Protagoras and Logos*, 57.

44. G. S. Kirk, J. E. Raven, and Malcolm Schofield, *The Presocratic Philosophers: A Critical History with a Selection of Texts*, 2nd ed (New York: Cambridge University Press, 2007), 191.

45. Waterfield, *First Philosophers*, 37.

46. Johnstone, *Listening to the Logos*, 55.

47. That is, worshipping a singular God rather than the pantheon of Greek gods and goddesses said to characterize mythos.

48. Aristotle, *The Basic Works of Aristotle*, ed. Richard McKeon (New York: Random House, 1941), 411a7–8 A22. See also Graham, *The Texts of Early*, 35.

49. Graham, *Texts of Early Greek Philosophy*, 38.

50. Barnes, *Early Greek Philosophy*, 16–17. This is quoted from Diogenes Laertius, "Lives of Eminent Philosophers, Book VIII, Chapter 4. Archytas (Fourth Century B.C.)," trans. Robert Drew Hicks, 1925, a woefully inaccurate work that Freeman labels "full of blunders" (Freeman and Diels, *Pre-Socratic Philosophers*).

51. Freeman and Diels, *Pre-Socratic Philosophers*, 50.

52. Waterfield, *First Philosophers*, 22 and 23.

53. Graham, *Texts of Early Greek Philosophy*, 131.

54. Graham, *Texts of Early Greek Philosophy*, 113.

55. Barnes, *Early Greek Philosophy*, 4.

56. Simplicius, in Barnes, *Early Greek Philosophy*, 44.

57. Simplicius, in Barnes, *Early Greek Philosophy*, 44.

58. Johnstone, *Listening to the Logos*, 52.

59. Johnstone, *Listening to the Logos*, 35.

60. For example, "I am the first and I am the last, And there is no god but me" (Isa. 44:6) and "it has been clearly demonstrated to you that the Lord alone is God; there is none beside Him" (Deut. 4:35).

61. Sextus, in Waterfield, *First Philosophers*, 26.

62. Although debates of course ensue, most scholars believe that the earliest portions of Isaiah were written during or close to the Assyrian assault on Jerusalem in the eighth century, around 740 BCE, with the last part possibly written about one hundred years later during the Babylonian captivity of the Jews (after about 600 BCE), obviously by a different author. See Walter Brueggemann and Patrick D. Miller, *Old Testament Theology: Essays on Structure, Theme, and Text* (Minneapolis, MN: Fortress Press, 1992).

63. Simplicius, in Waterfield, *First Philosophers*, 27.

64. Barnes, *Early Greek Philosophy*, 45.

65. Kirk, Raven, and Schofield, *Presocratic Philosophers*, 187. For comparison, Barnes translates this as: "Of this account which holds forever men prove uncomprehending, both before hearing it and when first they have heard it. For although all things come about in accordance with this account, they are like Tiros as they try words and deeds of the sort which I expound." See Barnes, *Early Greek Philosophy*, 49.

66. Kirk, Raven, and Schofield, *Presocratic Philosophers*, 187.

67. Ben Zion Bokser and Baruch M. Bokser, eds., *The Talmud: Selected Writings* (New York: Paulist Press, 1989), 59.

68. The prayer continues with the instructions to "love your God with all your heart, with all your soul and with all your resources" and to pass on the instructions to one's children, to write them on one's doorpost, and so forth. The Shema is never to be forgotten; it is to be continually spoken, listened to, and heard.

69. Even Barnes references the word logos with the "Greek Bible, where it is customarily translated as "'the Word (of God).'" Barnes, *Early Greek Philosophy*, 49–50.

70. Schiappa, *Protagoras and Logos*, 7.

71. Schiappa, *Protagoras and Logos*, 21.

72. Clark and McKerrow, "Rhetorical Construction of History," 38.

73. See for example, K. D. Irani and Morris Silver, *Social Justice in the Ancient World*, (Westport, CT: Greenwood Publishing Group, 1995); James B. Pritchard, *The Ancient Near East: An Anthology of Texts and Pictures* (Princeton, NJ: Princeton University Press, 2011); Raik Heckl, "'Deep Is the Well of the Past': Reconsidering the Origins of the Exodus Motif in Its Cultural Context," *Verbum et Ecclesia* 34, no. 2 (May 2013): 1–6; Matthijs J. de Jong, *Isaiah among the Ancient Near Eastern Prophets: A Comparative Study of the Earliest Stages of the Isaiah Tradition and the Neo-Assyrian Prophecies* (Boston: Brill, 2007); David B. Weisberg, *Leaders and Legacies in Assyriology and Bible: The Collected Essays of David B. Weisberg* (Winona Lake, IN: Eisenbrauns, 2012); and J. J. M. Roberts, *The Bible and the Ancient Near East: Collected Essays* (Winona Lake, IN: Eisenbrauns, 2002).

74. For example, there was a robust and educated Jewish community held in

captivity in Babylon for around seventy years between roughly 608 and 538 BCE. By no means all but many of the exiles stayed for generations compiling, among other things, the Babylonian Talmud.

75. Carol Lipson and Roberta A. Binkley, eds., *Ancient Non-Greek Rhetorics* (West Lafayette, IN: Parlor Press, 2009); and Carol Lipson and Roberta A. Binkley, eds., *Rhetoric before and beyond the Greeks* (Albany: State University of New York, 2004).

76. Walter Benjamin, *Illuminations*, 1st ed. (New York: Harcourt, Brace & World, 1968), 254.

15

A Rhetorical History of Southern Rhetoric

Christina L. Moss

S outhern rhetoric is arguably the first established regional rhetorical
study in the communication discipline.[1] When in 1947 Dallas Dickey
called for attention to southern oratory as an advancement to the teaching and research of American public address, he did so to both increase
the depth of public address scholarship and to put southern oratory on
the scholarship map: "The field of Southern oratory is almost completely
unworked, and offers great opportunities for the student of rhetorical history and criticism. If we are to have in our day a body of research on significant and influential speakers, we should not delay in our activities."[2]
With that Dickey delineated an area of study for students of rhetoric and
distinguished himself as a founder of southern rhetorical history and
criticism. In the decades that followed Dickey's call, the rhetorical history of southern rhetoric and public address has evolved in fits and starts.
Part of the inconsistency comes from, on the one hand, the origins and
mindset of southern oratorical analysis and, on the other, its reflection of
societal and disciplinary politics.

Here, I argue that the history of southern rhetorical critique navi-
gates a tension between southern mythology and southern regional identity. These tensions show up in odd and varied ways related to context,
cultural values, identity, disciplinary directions, and temporality. Southern mythology and southern regional identity cannot fully explain the
wholeness and complexity of the South; yet scholars have often relied
on them to analyze southern rhetoric, resulting in critiques not only incomplete but at times in conflict with other known aspects of southern
culture. Within these points of conflict southern rhetorical regional critiques develop. By offering a rhetorical history of southern rhetoric, I am-
plify Kathleen J. Turner's argument that "historical research provides an
understanding of rhetoric as a process rather than simply as a product."[3]
This rhetorical process weaves in and out of the social and cultural contexts in which it develops, and rhetorical analysts add to this process by
affecting, reflecting, and sometimes rejecting the social and cultural contexts in which they write. It is little wonder, then, that at times we should

be self-reflexive, turning our rhetorical, historical, critical, and theoretical eyes on ourselves.

To examine how the tensions have evolved in this rhetorical history of southern public address, I examine four major stages of southern rhetoric's rhetorical history: claiming southern regionalism, an emerging area of study, developing discussions, and challenges for future advancement.

The Conceptualization and Claiming of Southern Regional Rhetoric

The South and its oratory drew the attention of scholars early in the discipline's formation. In fact, one of the first essays published in the *Quarterly Journal of Speech* in 1920 critiqued the oratory of Henry Grady.[4] Although author Charles F. Lindsley does not call for criticism of "southern oratory," Lindsley identifies Grady as a southerner, commenting on his attitudes and their roots in southern culture. Two years later, in his ambitious essay tracing major periods of the history of oratory, Charles A. Fritz recognizes several southerners as great American orators: Patrick Henry, Richard Henry Lee, John Rutledge, John Calhoun, Henry Clay, and Charles Sumner.[5] Robert Oliver's "Studies in Political and Social Views of the Slave-Struggle Orators" in 1937 focuses on Henry Clay's speeches and influence.[6] These early examples of southern rhetorical critique primarily focus on the speaker's general oratorical and historical qualities, with only a secondary nod to their regional status.

African American speakers, including some who were either born in the South or had southern roots of some kind, received a bit of recognition during this period. The 1926 book review of *Negro Orators and Their Orations* by Carter G. Woodson—the first time the *Quarterly Journal of Speech Education* (*QJSE*) included any review or critique of African American public address—indicates a growing awareness of the role of African Americans in both the nation's history and America's oratorical development.[7] Naming such speakers as Booker T. Washington and Frederick Douglass as examples of excellent orators, the volume includes numerous quotations of many speakers against slavery who described their own experiences as evidence of the brutal realities.[8]

Although scholars knew of southern orators and readily included white male orators in the canon, these early discussions assessed their subjects as *American* orators, not necessarily *southern*. At this time, the *QJSE* board and its publisher, the National Association of Academic Teachers of Public Speech, consisted primarily of faculty from northeastern and Big Ten schools. The authors of the articles mentioned here taught at institutions in Minnesota, Massachusetts, and New York—northerners in the

1920s at the emergence of a cultural war over southern identity that would greatly shape not only how southerners viewed themselves but also how the rest of the nation regarded them. Consequently, southern rhetorical scholars became aware of an identity based on cultural differences, separate from the rest of the nation. The major move into southern rhetoric would not occur until two decades later.

Dallas Dickey

It is little surprise that, coming from Louisiana State University, Professor Dallas C. Dickey would define the beginnings of southern oratory and later southern rhetoric.[9] His interests developed through several influences. Although Dickey spent his precollege days in Indiana, his graduate studies resulted in the first public address dissertation at LSU, "Seargent S. Prentiss, Whig Orator of the Old South," completed in 1938.[10] He credited southern historians at LSU, specifically Wendell Holmes Stephenson, for his interest in southern oratory and history.[11] Moreover, Dickey's southern oratorical work developed after critical reporting of the 1925 Scopes trial by northern journalists, such as H. L. Mencken's condescending description of the South as the "Sahara of the Bozarts," and the spirited rebuttal in 1930 by a group of southerners in history, English, and economics in *I'll Take My Stand: The South and the Agrarian Tradition*.[12]

Dickey's official call for southern oratory as a field of study appeared in 1947 in "Southern Oratory: A Field for Research."[13] He outlines many of the speakers deserving academic and critical attention, organizing them into such categories as historical leaders, "Negro speaking," and "contemporary" southern speakers.[14] His striking list named Jefferson Davis, Huey Long, and Booker T. Washington, as well as thirty-one other men of political or religious distinction.[15] The term "men" is intentional: Dickey mentions no women orators, even though such speakers as the Grimke sisters from South Carolina, or Memphians Mary Church Terrell and Ida B. Wells, would easily fit some of the categorical requirements. He does, however, note that "a field completely unstudied in American Public Address and one of specific interest in the South is that of Negro Speaking." African American preaching and education particularly interested Dickey: "Every Southern city, hamlet, or rural community has had Negro preaching of every denomination." Furthermore, he extends interest to Black educators who "have spoken on all phases of reform and on matters of intimate concern to their race."[16]

Additionally, Dickey's contribution consisted of calling attention to the people and subjects of the South mostly ignored in oratorical studies.

In his 1943 *Quarterly Journal of Speech* article, "What Directions Should Future Research in American Public Address Take?," Dickey critiques a collection edited by W. Norwood Brigance over nine years, *A History and Criticism of American Public Address.* Acknowledging that the volumes could only undertake the initial stages of oratorical study, he identifies areas for additional investigation. Although he does not begin with the premise that Brigance's compilation ignores southern orators, his articulation of speakers who needed to be studied emphasizes southerners, many of whom had connections to Lost Cause politics.[17]

Dickey not only names those orators suitable for research, he also asserts clear expectations as to how southern rhetorical research should be conducted. Dickey believed that the southern speaker must be understood as a part of history: "The demand which we must make on the oratorical critic is that he must know more of history than we expect the historian to know of oratory."[18] His concern over the quality of research on southern leaders reflects "the special mission" of his writings: "revealing the distinctiveness of the South—particularly the Old South—through critical examination of its oratory."[19] Several times in the 1947 article he notes his desire for the southern orator to deliver solutions to the "race problem." This hope emerges especially in his discussion of some southern preachers and contemporary speakers who were reformers, "seeking to direct the thinking of their hearers on such problems as race relations," an issue "which Southerners themselves must meet and solve."[20] Even as Dickey made the call for southern oratorical scholarship, then, he believed oratory had the power to change the attitudes of white southerners. Dickey had faith that not only southern orators but also southern oratorical critics could redeem the South as worthy of the attention of scholars as well as those outside the region.

Dissatisfied at the way historians had stereotyped southern orators, Dickey led the charge both to examine the distinctiveness of *southern* oratory and to defend the quality of southern orators. Taking issue, for example, with historian Merle Curti's claim that most Old South oratory was "as ephemeral as it was florid," Dickey characterizes Curti's comment as a sloppy generalization of southern public speaking style.[21] "How much more ephemeral," he asks, "were the Southern orators than those of New England or the Middle West? In a very real sense, any speech is likely to be ephemeral."[22] Dickey then speculates: "Possibly too, the fact that the South became the minority element preceding the Civil War, and then fought a losing civil conflict followed by years of the slowest rebuilding, has had something to do with the quality of the generalizations made concerning her people, manners, and attitudes."[23] After challenging

Curti's overarching claim, Dickey follows his own dictum that research must undergird any such generalizations: he enumerates southern orators who were varied in content and whose delivery was demonstrably neither florid nor ephemeral. He thus argues *from* history to dispute Curti's stereotypical assessment.[24] Dickey's defense of white male southern oratorical style constituted a significant moment for southern oratory in particular and public address studies in general.

Although historians had their place, Dickey demonstrated that southern oratorical scholars could add to historical understandings in ways historians were ill-equipped to accomplish. Using the standards and criteria of a historical rhetorical critic, Dickey emphasized the value of a rhetorical viewpoint on history, which framed the direction of southern oratorical studies from that point forward.

Dickey's Legacy

During the 1950s, numerous scholars published critiques focusing on southern speakers and/or issues particular to the South, especially the Confederacy and slavery, with varying signs of Dickey's impact.[25] Some scholars indicated a clear and direct influence from Dickey, citing his works in their scholarship. Coming from such schools as Northwestern, the University of Wisconsin, and the University of Iowa, others studied orators of history and politics who happened to be southern and in doing so, inadvertently furthered Dickey's call. Ernest Bormann, for example, published two articles on the demagoguery of Louisiana governor Huey Long, thus advancing the association of southern and demagogic rhetoric.[26] These efforts also offered an initial step to include southern (albeit white) women in southern oratory: Anthony Hillbruner's 1958 article, "Frances Wright: Egalitarian Reformer," examines the rhetoric of a white Tennessee woman who developed a community to help enslaved people make the transition into emancipation.[27]

Perhaps the most direct connections, however, came through the graduate students from Dickey's new institution, the University of Florida, including such apprentices as Wayne Eubank, Merrill Christophersen, Kevin Kearney, James Golden, and Ralph T. Eubanks. All of these scholars added to the knowledge and canon of southern oratory, including southern preachers, southern men of US history, and southern politicians, and they associated southern rhetoric with specific issues considered distinctive to the South.

The claiming of southern regional influence far surpassed the geographical boundaries of southern states or the scholars in southern universities. Two articles at this time by Charles Lomas and by

Donald Hargis, authors from UCLA, exhibit particular signs of an application of regionalism beyond geographical bounds, although neither cited Dickey.[28] Each deals with the state political influence of southerners who had migrated to the West: Lomas discusses the significant political impact of southerners who came to California to seek their fortune, and Hargis addresses how southerners' positions on states' rights and southern cultural values helped inform the California state constitution. Many of these were judges, former governors, lawyers, and statesmen from the South who "dominated the politics of the state during most of the period from its admission in 1850 until 1861," when Union sentiments surged.[29] Lomas argues that "energy, ruthlessness, native capacity, and superior political skill and experience" of southerners made them particularly effective in California politics,[30] while Hargis points to their characteristics as "indefatigable in daily routine," savvy in matters of political organization, and able to serve as "a leavening agent for the extremists from the North."[31] These studies of southern qualities outside of the South noted the interdependencies of regionalism.

Dallas Dickey and subsequent scholars marked the beginning of southern oratory and rhetorical scholarship. The criticism and awareness of southern rhetoric would become a significant factor in public address scholarship during the next four decades.

An Emerging Area of Study

When Dallas Dickey died in 1957, much remained to be accomplished in the area of southern oratory. While scholars continued analyses of southern speakers, anthologies, and definitions of southern rhetoric, new questions emerged: Is the South distinct from other regions? If so, is that distinction its rhetorical value? Despite its distinct history, is the South primarily a part of the United States, or more importantly a separate entity? Such questions forged the connection between southern identity and southern rhetoric, primarily through mythic analysis. As scholarship developed, both journals and anthologies reflected similar contributions.

Leading the charge was LSU professor Waldo Braden. A midwesterner by birth, Braden did not initially study southern oratory. When Dickey died, Braden's peers in the Speech Association of America approached him to edit Dickey's unfinished project on Old South oratory.[32] Braden cautiously accepted, turning the focus of his scholarship to southern rhetoric. He and those who worked with him developed the study of southern rhetorical and public address into a subarea of American public address.

The emergence of southern rhetoric and public address as an area of study required greater clarity on what constituted southern public address, who spoke it and to whom, and how to best understand it. In a 1961 essay, "The Emergence of the Concept of Southern Oratory," Braden struggled to develop a clear definition, concluding that those proposing distinctiveness in southern regionalism rendered it "myth-encrusted."[33] According to Braden, myths in southern oratory occurred on two levels: the mythological creation of southern orators (grandiloquent, ephemeral, and florid), and the myths referenced within the speeches themselves (such as the Lost Cause Myth or the Solid South Myth). As a result, Braden contended, these myths constrained scholarship and suggested generic and stylistic similarities that did not actually exist, qualities that deserved serious attention. Braden recognized that the southern oratorical canon failed to demonstrate "a dimension sufficiently broad to represent speaking in the South."[34] To his credit, Braden continued to advance the numbers of rhetorical critiques of southern oratory even as he refuted the myths surrounding white, male, Protestant politicians, preachers, and businessmen.

Despite Braden's description of southern oratory as myth encrusted and lacking distinctiveness, the notion of distinctiveness found reinforcement in the critiques published in both anthologies and journals. Former Dickey advisee Kevin Kearney, for example, argued in 1966 that the South *could* be defined as distinctive. Citing Dickey's call for southern oratorical research, Kearney asks, "What's Southern about Southern Oratory?"[35] Kearney's answer delineates such criteria as the speaker's motive and context, familiarity with southern culture, and place of residence, which he declares valid because they entailed a "Southern response to what was interpreted as a Southern problem by Southerners who were motivated to act in the best interest of the South."[36] Kearney offers the example of nullification as a uniquely "southern" context and motive that required such speakers as John C. Calhoun and Henry Clay to be familiar with southern culture. Kearney saw southern oratory as associated with southern speakers and audiences, tying it directly to the ways in which the South appeared distinctive or unique.

Although several scholars persisted in the now traditional focus on the South primarily as white male demagogues who championed the Lost Cause, Braden's advocacy for broadening the definition of southern oratory served as a springboard for rhetorical analysts to explore the social dynamics of the time. Racial violence, civil rights struggles, and controversies over desegregation took center stage in such articles as Kearney's "The 1960 Campaign Speaking of Orval Faubus," Wayne Flynt's "The Ethics of Democratic Persuasion and the Birmingham Crisis," and Harry Bowen's "Does Non-Violence Persuade?"[37]

This attention to contemporary issues included the increase in the regionally significant topics of southern preachers and religion.[38] Although Dickey had mentioned southern preachers and preaching in his 1947 call and rhetorical scholars in the past had analyzed them, this new turn moved from sermons to the broader cultural and social application of rhetoric, southern regionalism, and religion. For example, Beryl McClerren's "Southern Baptists and the Religious Issue during the Presidential Campaigns of 1928 and 1960" and Ray McCain's "Speaking on School Desegregation by Atlanta Ministers" deal with the contemporaneous political influence of religion. Going beyond analyses of speakers and speeches, these studies provide more detailed explorations of the role of southern religious rhetoric in society.

In addition to this move toward contemporary issues, scholarship evidenced the fluidity of southern regionalism as well as its connection to national identity and national awareness.[39] John Makay's "George C. Wallace: Southern Spokesman with a Northern Audience," for example, argues that Wallace gave his speech in Indiana during the Democratic primaries of 1964 because he related to the blue collar steel workers and "wanted to reinforce his identity as a man for the working class."[40] Cal Logue's work on Atlanta journalist Ralph McGill assesses McGill's editorial work as an antisegregationist during a peak time in the South's time of racial intolerance.[41] Such scholarship explored the complicated questions of how southern identity works rhetorically both inside and outside the South and the ability of southerners to influence audiences and people beyond geographical boundaries and assumed stereotypes. It would be some time, however, before the spoken words of the southern enslaved people, suffragists, southern African Americans, antisuffragists, and antilynching activists would be examined with reference to their southernness.

Developing Discussions

The clearest continuation of the earlier conversations came in the form of Braden's follow-up to *Oratory of the Old South*: the 1979 edited volume of *Oratory of the New South*.[42] Focusing on the rhetoric of accommodation in the post–Civil War years, the contributions in *Oratory of the New South* examine attempts to revitalize southern morale and confidence in the face of defeat. The sequel continues Braden's discussion of the limitations of southern mythology and his assumptions about southern oratory, including the lack of generic or stylistic similarities. Of the eight chapters, two offer greater inclusion: one compares the rhetoric of Booker T. Washington and W. E. B. Du Bois, while another provides a general critique of southern women's rhetoric between 1870 and 1920.

During this time, Braden furthered his goal to discredit the myths associated with southern rhetoric. In an investigation of southern oratory published in 1970, Braden studies C. Alphonso Smith's 1922 oration, "Southern Oratory before the War,"[43] to assess the English professor's contribution to the conceptualization of southern oratory. In it, Braden discovers a speech that stirred "Southern pride" and "establish[ed] the South has a distinctive culture," all while urging "a careful study of the genre."[44] In short, Braden argues that "the responsibility for developing the image [of mythologized Southern oratory] in some ways belongs to Smith,"[45] an image southern rhetorical scholars must evaluate and address.

While Dickey had focused on the historical validity of southern oratory, Braden utilized southern mythology to make the case that the South's presentation of itself and its oratory was not factual. Instead, southern rhetoric relied on a romanticized mythology that focused on the Lost Cause, the Old South, the New South, and the Solid South, and these perspectives seeped into the criticism. Braden claims such myths proved an "oversimplification of events, persons and relationships" that developed in the public imaginary over time and that "is more emotional than logical in substance."[46] Braden was right to question the regional mythology as both a romanticized view and a folklore that implicitly focused primarily on white southerners.[47]

Despite Braden's arguments, some studies continued the tradition of examining southern politicians and issues of secession, epideictic speeches surrounding Confederate ceremonies, and rhetoric during Reconstruction.[48] In a new move, however, John Saxon's "Contemporary Southern Oratory" reframes contemporary southern rhetoric as one of optimism in contrast to the despondency of the Old South.[49] Moving the focus from the Old South mythology and history to contemporary southern oratory, Saxon's focus on the "New" South finds that current speakers, politicians, and issues revealed an optimism, a "spirit of renewal, of change, of departure from the past, a recognition that the South will no longer frustrate itself with lost or negative causes." Saxon argues southern oratory seemed to be turning from "the rhetoric of racial prejudice" to "problem solving." In perhaps his most nuanced argument, Saxon observes that southern orators tended to "prophesy a death of sectionalism in its historical sense" but exhibit a retention of "regional identification and not sectional defiance."[50] Saxon begins by citing Dickey, Braden, and Kearney, but he ends by claiming new purpose for southern orators.

The 1970s also saw communication scholars publishing more work on African American rhetoric, some of which took place within southern contexts. Braden's interest in Booker T. Washington spread to others, with particular attention to his conciliatory rhetoric.[51] Scholars justified the study of Washington's speeches for its sheer quantity; for his ability to speak to Black, white, and mixed audiences; for his leadership; and for the controversies surrounding his philosophy. Using a different perspective, Philip Wander examined how the proslavery movement used their depiction of African American children as "savage" to defend the stance of southern white people, demonstrating the rhetorical construction of racism through physical subordination of description.[52] Critiques of civil rights rhetoric also began to emerge. However, white rhetorical scholars classified critiques of African American southerners as civil rights rhetoric, not southern oratory. For example, we still have no rhetorical study of how Martin Luther King Jr. was a *southerner* as well as a minister and a civil rights leader, and how those intersectional identities influenced each other and his rhetoric. Nor has there been a study on the southern identity of antilynching activist and journalist Ida B. Wells or of education leader and civil rights activist Mary McLeod Bethune.

Although the 1970s found somewhat greater expansion of the topic of southern rhetoric, the period also brought forth fewer articles overall focusing on southerners and southern rhetoric or oratory. A search in databases shows somewhat fewer journal articles used the word *southern* in the title: only five appeared in the 1970s, while eight appeared in the 1960s. Several explanations are possible. The discipline shifted away from historical and neo-Aristotelian analysis and toward more theoretical discussions of rhetoric. The attention of the national news media also changed during this decade, as the South's struggles during the civil rights movement gave way to stories on the more nationally focused issues of busing, the Vietnam War, women's rights, and Black power. The 1976 presidential election of Georgian Jimmy Carter offered only a brief recurrence of southern identity on the national stage.

The 1980s and 1990s

The influence of Dickey and Braden continued in the 1980s and 1990s. Cal Logue and Howard Dorgan, former students of Waldo Braden, published two major edited books: *Oratory of Southern Demagogues* in 1981 and *A New Diversity in Contemporary Southern Rhetoric* in 1987.[53] In the first volume, Logue and Dorgan examine the roots of demagoguery and its appeal to poor working-class white people as an introduction to chapters on nine southern demagogues, from Jefferson Davis to Gene Talmadge. In the second, they tackle the aftermath of the 1954 Supreme Court decision *Brown v. Board of Education*, to explicate the rhetorical responses of southern Black people, advocates of white supremacy and states' rights, and white moderates and liberals. Ranging from white Protestant ministers to Black activists, from Jimmy Carter to Sam Ervin, and from anti–Equal Rights Amendment advocates to white Citizens' Councils, the essays weave a rich examination of thirty years of public dialogue. By addressing more contemporary rhetoric, both books carry on Braden's mission to enlist and preserve southern rhetorical criticism as well as Dickey's call to add southern rhetorical critique to the discipline.

In these books and in journal articles, the more traditional focus on white male rhetoric in reference to the Civil War,[54] southern oratory on the New South or southern politics,[55] and white southern preaching predominate.[56] However, subject matter on the South expanded to include more analysis on African American southern rhetoric, including Donald Martin and Vicky Gordon Martin's appraisal of Barbara Jordan's use of language, Logue's assessment of the communicative strategies of Black slaves on antebellum plantations, and Cal Logue and Thurmon Garner's analysis of the shifts in the rhetorical status of enslaved Black people after achieving freedom.[57] Joining these new forays, William Strickland offers examples of Indigenous rhetoric in the South by exploring how Cherokees spoke against Andrew Jackson's Indian removal policy.[58]

As textualized southern rhetorical voices became more diverse, popular culture depictions of southern rhetoric gained attention. Several scholars took on such southern cultural texts and contexts as country music, journalism, film, and other rhetorical constructs.[59] Perhaps one of the most prolific during this period was Stephen A. Smith at the University of Arkansas. His 1985 work, *Myth, Media, and the Southern Mind,* introduces a contemporary rhetorical analysis of the century of myths that comprise southern culture.[60] While Smith concentrates on media over traditional oratory, his critique relies on mythological analysis in the same way that Braden's work does; also like Braden, Smith sees these myths as firmly entrenched in a primarily white southern past: the Old South, the Lost Cause, and the New South. For example, Smith's discussion of the transition of gender roles—from the "southern belle" myth to the "Good Ole Girl" myth and from the cavalier myth to the "Good Ole Boy" myth—all concentrate on white conceptions.

Smith posits three themes as emerging to replace white supremacy myths: equality (Black and white people can now move forward together), distinctiveness (the cultural characteristics of the South are both singular and valuable), and place and community (the South serves as a metaphor for home: "a place that possesses a peculiar, yet imperfect, integrity stemming from a rich history").[61]

At points, Smith's work seems to usher in a reformation. Unlike definitions of "southern" in previous scholarship that referred only to a white South, in several instances Smith claims these mythical themes are for Black *and* white people. Smith argues, for example, that "the mythic vision of equality and a biracial egalitarian South slowly emerged. For the first time in one hundred fifty years, the South had produced a new myth of its own identity which not only refused to recycle but completely rejected the tenets of the old mythology."[62] Similarly, Smith declares that "despite the suggestion by some scholars that the contemporary rhetoric of whites and Blacks reflects different value systems, the mythic theme of community and place . . . is one shared by both Blacks and whites in the contemporary Southern mythology."[63] Although current research would find this casting of mythic experience and identity as identical to be problematic, at least Smith's consideration of Black mythic engagement with the South offers a move (albeit a slow one) toward recognition of different experiences and identities of the South among white and Black populations.[64] Only later would white scholars appreciate that Black people, and others of color living in the South, created their own conceptions of the South, southern identity, and strategies used to disrupt white southern mythology.

In the last two decades of the twentieth century, then, the legacies of Dickey and Braden continued, even as new scholarly voices initiated an increase in interest and publications of southern rhetoric, southern rhetorical criticism, and analysis of southern culture beyond speeches and, in the process, bridged rhetorical criticism with media and popular culture and extended the concept of southern and southerner. Yet this research left much of what was considered southern about southern rhetoric and oratory defined through whiteness. The tensions resulting from this rhetorical history provide jumping off points for future discussions.

Challenges for Future Scholarship

As the work on southern rhetorical regionalism continues, the rhetorical history of the area leaves us with several challenges. Some of these challenges have been addressed with creativity and success, while others remain only superficially engaged, needing much more attention. To assess the status of these challenges, we may usefully turn to how the legacies of southern rhetoric entered into the millennium through the work of Stuart Towns.

Towns served as a significant bridge into the millennium because he struggled with the regional tensions of those who came before. Like fellow University of Arkansan Smith, Towns saw the need to go beyond what had been done before but remained limited by previous methodological constraints and the whiteness of southern rhetorical identity. These struggles show up in his two books focusing on southern rhetoric and oratory. In echoes of Smith, Towns's first volume, *Oratory and Rhetoric of the Nineteenth Century South*, ventures beyond the list of orators who are or are not southern to describe feelings associated with being southern, in particular the "intense ties to place," an overwhelming attachment to "home," and the defensiveness and paranoia that mark the memories and experiences of southerners in the South.[65] These memories contain the myths and legacies of the South both past and present, from reverence of "moonlight and magnolias" and the Lost Cause to conflicts over civil rights and Sunbelt prosperity.[66] Towns depicts a southern regionalism that seems familiar yet continually changing. Southerners, for example, come in a variety of occupations, locations, and characteristics: "Louisiana oilfield worker, Appalachian mill hand, Saturn car plant skilled technician, Nashville song writer, migrant farm worker, Orlando businesswoman, media evangelist, Gulf Coast shrimper, cotton farmer, urban professional, Ozark 'hillbilly.'"[67]

In *Public Address in the Twentieth-Century South*, Towns makes a solid effort to diversify those considered southern.[68] He still primarily features the generally included white male orators: George Wallace, Theodore Bilbo, Orval Faubus, Huey Long, and Jimmy Carter. Yet he also includes women's rights crusader Rebecca Felton, antilynching activist Jessie Daniel Ames, writer Lillian Smith, state senator Barbara Jordan, and civil rights activists Daisy Bates, Fannie Lou Hamer, and Diane Nash. In a section on the civil rights movement, Towns also features such African American men as Benjamin Mays, Marion Barry Jr., and Wyatt Tee Walker.

Towns's work, then, reflects the tensions over southern rhetoric and public address of the times: he wrestles with white southern mythology, past anthologies, and southern rhetorical critiques, even as he struggles to make southern regional definitions broader and more inclusive. Towns lays the groundwork for acknowledging a multiplicity of Souths and southern regional identities, reflecting the difficult challenges moving forward.

Thankfully, scholars are addressing some of these challenges. The very idea of who can be counted as a southerner, and by what criteria, remain points of the very tensions created by past scholarship and cultural norms.[69] Patricia Davis's work on African American southern identity, for example, pushes back against the well-established white southern regional identity to argue that African American southern identity demonstrates a disruption and defiance of white southern mythology and memory.[70] Scholars now extend arguments beyond the South as Black and white people to the inclusion of Latinx and Indigenous peoples.[71] Examinations of southern religion's rhetorical influence both for and against social justice have pushed beyond primarily white religions.[72] Other scholars continue to assess how popular culture such as film, music, television, commemoration, and foodways, among other examples, not only perpetuate white southern heteronormative myths but also push back and question white southern identities and memories.[73] And while studies continue to discuss the influence of southern political rhetoric and regional memory, they now do so beyond geographical boundaries to instead discuss how regional identity bobs and weaves within and outside of national identity.[74]

Dickey's call to study southern oratory reflected white regional ideals about the South of 1947. Truly exploring the rich complexity of the South, its rhetorics, its identities, and its influence requires crossing the boundaries set by previous scholarship. We need wider explorations of Latinx, Indigenous tribes, Vietnamese, Korean, and Chinese southerners. We need to push religious and southern regional identities beyond Christianity and into Judaism, Islam, and other religious beliefs. The ever-changing demands for and strategies of social justice and activism look nothing like the public memory of past civil rights activism.[75] Ongoing investigations into the ways in which popular culture meets, constrains, and denies multiple southern identities are required. Furthermore, the interrelationships between the American South and the Global South beg investigation.[76]

While Dallas Dickey and those who followed began with the goal to critique southern oratory and to increase the attention toward southern speakers, this legacy leaves us with a need to heed Bruce Gronbeck's admonition that "the past . . . is more than merely of historical interest; its importance to social, political, moral, and economic analyses or problems and their presumed alleviation is undeniable."[77] Moreover, as a result, "multiple rhetorics of the past have been practiced by various groups of advocates"—so even with "the form of traditions, the past appears to make direct demands on our hearts and minds, . . . [and] those same traditions can be sites of struggle for contemporary social-political supremacy."[78] This rhetorical history of southern rhetoric demonstrates what is at stake: we must understand how our framing, evaluating, and researching of regionalism awakens us to some possibilities while blinding us to others.

Notes

1. I am primarily basing this claim on two considerations: (1) The identification of southern oratory as a regional entity among the earliest publications in

the recognized speech discipline as discussed in this chapter, and (2) in 1968 the *Western Communication Journal* editor, Ernest Earl Ettlich, cited southern oratory as a reference for the identification of Western regional oratory. See Earl E. Ettlich, "Symposium: Western Oratory," *Western Speech* 32, no. 1 (1968): 2–4.

2. Dallas Dickey, "Southern Oratory: A Field for Research," *Quarterly Journal of Speech* 33, no. 4 (1947): 459.

3. Kathleen J Turner, "Introduction: Rhetorical History as Social Construction," in Turner, *Doing Rhetorical History*, 15.

4. Charles F. Lindsley, "Henry Woodfin Grady, Orator," *Quarterly Journal of Speech Education* 6, no. 2 (1920): 41.

5. Charles A. Fritz, "A Brief Review of the Chief Periods in the History of Oratory" *Quarterly Journal of Speech* 8, no. 1 (1922):48, https://doi.org/10.1080/00335632209379363.

6. Robert T. Oliver, "Studies in the Political and Social Views of the Slave-Struggle Orators," *Quarterly Journal of Speech* 23, no. 3 (1937): 409–17.

7. Russell H. Wagner, "Negro Orators and Their Orations," *Quarterly Journal of Speech Education* 12, no. 4 (1926): 379–82.

8. One logical conclusion is that some of these former enslaved people probably came from southern farms or plantations.

9. Waldo W Braden and Ralph T. Eubanks, "Dallas C. Dickey: Pioneer of the Critical Study of Southern Public Address," *Southern Speech Communication Journal* 44, no. 2 (1979): 119–46.

10. Braden and Eubanks, "Dallas C. Dickey," 125. Prentiss's first name is spelled variously, but Dickey used "Seargent" in his dissertation.

11. Braden and Eubanks, "Dallas C. Dickey,"123.

12. Twelve Southerners, *I'll Take My Stand: The South and the Agrarian Tradition* (Baton Rouge: Louisiana State University Press, 1978).

13. Dallas C. Dickey, "Southern Oratory," 463.

14. The whole list of categories includes historical leaders, obscure men of influence, "general and specific periods and special issues and events in southern history," the history of public speaking of a particular southern state, preaching, "Negro speaking," and "contemporary" southern speakers. See Dickey, "Southern Oratory," 462–64.

15. Other major speakers include James Madison, Sam Houston, Jefferson Davis, Huey Long, John Sharp Williams, George Poindexter, Henry S. Foote, James Henry Thornwell, Richard Menifee, Ben Tillman, Booker T. Washington, Eugene Talmadge, Theodore Bilbo, Ellis Arnall, and Claude Pepper. Dickey, "Southern Oratory," 462–64.

16. Dickey, "Southern Oratory," 462

17. A sampling of the speakers includes William C. Preston of South Carolina, L. Q. C. Lamar of Mississippi, Lamar Hamilton, Henry Washington

Hilliard of Alabama, Jefferson Davis, and John C. Calhoun. See Dallas Dickey, "What Direction Should Future Research in Public Address Take?" *Quarterly Journal of Speech* 29, no. 3 (1943): 300–304.

18. Dickey, "Southern Oratory," 459.

19. Braden and Eubanks, "Dallas C. Dickey," 129.

20. Dickey, "Southern Oratory," 463.

21. Dallas C. Dickey, "Were They Ephemeral and Florid?," *Quarterly Journal of Speech* 32, no. 1 (1946): 16.

22. Dickey, "Were They Ephemeral," 17

23. Dickey, "Were They Ephemeral," 17.

24. David Zarefsky, "Four Senses of Rhetorical History," in Turner, *Doing Rhetorical History*, 28.

25. Margaret Burr Des Champs, "Benjamin Morgan Palmer, Orator-Preacher of the Confederacy," *Southern Speech Journal* 19, no. 1 (September 19, 1953): 14–22; James Golden, "A Southern Unionist Speaks in the North on the Eve of the Civil War," *Southern Speech Journal* 20 (1954): 28–36; Merrill G. Christophersen, "The Charleston Conversationalists," *Southern Speech Journal* 20 (1954): 99–108; Ralph Richardson, "The Rhetorical Death Rattle of the Confederacy," *Southern Speech Journal* 20 (1954): 109–16; Glenn E. Reddick, "When the Southern Senators Said Farewell," *Southern Speech Journal* 15 (March 1950): 196–97; and William B. Hesseltine and Henry L. Eubank Jr., "Old Voices in the New South," *Quarterly Journal of Speech* 39, no. 4 (December 1953): 451.

26. Ernest G. Bormann, "Huey Long: Analysis of a Demagogue." *Today's Speech* 2, no. 3 (1953): 16–20; and Ernest G. Bormann, "A Rhetorical Analysis of the National Radio Broadcast of Senator Huey Pierce Long," *Speech Monographs* 24, no. 4 (1957): 244–58.

27. Anthony Hillbruner, "Frances Wright: Egalitarian Reformer," *Southern Speech Journal* 23, no. 3 (Summer 1958): 193–203.

28. Charles Lomas, "Southern Orators in California before 1861," *Southern Speech Journal* 15, no. 1 (September 1949): 21–37; and Donald E. Hargis, "Southerners in the California Constitutional Convention: 1849," *Southern Speech Journal* 19, no. 2 (March 1954): 193–204.

29. Lomas, "Southern Orators in California," 21.

30. Lomas. "Southern Orators in California," 21.

31. Hargis, "Southerners in the California Constitutional Convention," 204.

32. The Speech Association of America later became the National Communication Association.

33. Waldo W. Braden, "The Emergence of the Concept of Southern Oratory," *Southern Speech Journal* 26, no. 3 (1961): 183, https://doi.org/10.1080/10417946109371601.

34. Braden, "Emergence," 183.

35. Kevin Kearney, "What's Southern about Southern Oratory?" *Southern Speech Journal* 32, no. 1 (1966): 19–30.

36. Kearney, "What's Southern about Southern Oratory?" 25–26.

37. Kevin E. Kearney, "The 1960 Campaign Speaking of Orval Faubus," *Southern Speech Journal* 27, no. 2 (Winter 1961): 102–9; Wayne Flynt, "The Ethics of Democratic Persuasion and the Birmingham Crisis," *Southern Speech Journal* 35, no. 1 (1969): 40–53; and Harry W. Bowen, "Does Non-Violence Persuade?" *Today's Speech* 11, no. 2 (1963): 10–31, https://doi.org/10.1080/01463376309385325.

38. Jerry L. Tarver, "Baptist Preaching from Virginia Jails, 1768–1778," *Southern Speech Journal* 30, no. 2 (Winter 1964): 139–48; R. E. Davis, "Billy Sunday: Preacher-Showman," *Southern Speech Journal* 32 (Winter 1966): 83–97; Wayne C. Eubank, "Palmer's Century Sermon, New Orleans, January 1, 1901," *Southern Speech Journal* 35, no. 1 (Fall 1969): 28–39; William Banowsky and Wayne C. Eubank, "The Preaching of H. Leo Boles," *Southern Speech Journal* 28, no. 4 (Summer 1963): 318–29; and William E. Lampton, "Worldiness: Helmot Thielicke's Quest for Relevant Preaching," *Southern Speech Journal* 34 (Summer 1969): 245–55.

39. When I use the term *fluidity* in reference to southern regionalism, I refer to a critical regionalism designation that sees regionalism as flowing until verbally or symbolically manifested. This manifestation can vary in a multitude of ways as a regional identity is constituted. See Jenny Rice, "From Architectonic to Tectonics: Introducing Regional Rhetorics," *Rhetoric Society Quarterly* 42, no. 3 (2012): 201–13; and Douglas R. Powell, *Critical Regionalism: Connecting Politics and Culture in the American Landscape* (Chapel Hill: University of North Carolina Press, 2012).

40. John J. Makay, "George C. Wallace: Southern Spokesman with a Northern Audience," *Central States Speech Journal* 19 (Fall 1968): 202–8.

41. Cal M. Logue, "Ralph McGill: Convictions of a Southern Editor," *Journalism Quarterly* 45, no. 4 (Winter 1968): 647–52.

42. Waldo W. Braden, *Oratory in the New South* (Baton Rouge: Louisiana State University Press, 1979).

43. Waldo W. Braden, "C. Alphonso Smith on Southern Oratory before the War," *Southern Speech Journal* 36, no. 2 (Winter 1970): 127–38.

44. Braden, "C. Alphonso Smith," 131.

45. Braden, "C. Alphonso Smith," 137–38.

46. Waldo W. Braden, "Myths in Rhetorical Context," in *The Oral Tradition in the South* (Baton Rouge: Louisiana State University Press, 1983), 65–82. This essay was originally published in the *Southern Speech Communication Journal* in 1975.

47. Braden's use of mythology here was as a means to analyze rhetoric. While he remained consistent in his use of myth as a tool for analysis, the concept of southern mythology would undergo much evalutation and critique

influenced by southern literature, history, and cultural studies. Such an analysis, albeit interesting, is beyond the scope of this chapter.

48. Douglas P. Starr, "Secession Speeches of Four Deep South Governors Who Would Rather Fight than Switch," *Southern Speech Communication Journal* 38, no. 2 (Winter 1972): 131–41; Joseph J. Hemmer Jr., "The Charleston Platform Debate in Rhetorical-Historical Perspective," *Quarterly Journal of Speech* 56, no. 4 (December 1970): 406, https://doi.org/10.1080/00335637009383028; Howard Dorgan, "The Doctrine of Victorious Defeat in the Rhetoric of Confederate Veterans," *Southern Speech Communication Journal* 38, no. 2 (1972): 119–30; and Cal M. Logue, "The Rhetorical Appeals of Whites to Blacks during Reconstruction," *Communication Monographs* 44, no. 3 (1977): 241, https://doi .org/10.1080/03637757709390135.

49. John D. Saxon, "Contemporary Southern Oratory: A Rhetoric of Hope, Not Desperation," *Southern Speech Communication Journal* 40, no. 3 (1975): 262–74, https://doi.org/10.1080/10417947509372270.

50. Saxon, "Contemporary Southern Oratory," 268–70.

51. Andrew King, "Booker T. Washington and the Myth of Heroic Materialism," *Quarterly Journal of Speech* 60, no. 3 (1974): 323–28; Robert L. Heath, "A Time for Silence: Booker T. Washington in Atlanta," *Quarterly Journal of Speech* 64, no. 4 (December 1978): 385, https://doi.org/10.1080/00335637809383444; and Thomas E. Harris and Patrick C. Kennicott, "Booker T. Washington: A Study of Conciliatory Rhetoric," *Southern Speech Communication Journal* 37, no. 1 (Fall 1971): 47–59.

52. Philip C. Wander, "The Savage Child: The Image of the Negro in the Pro-Slavery Movement," *Southern Speech Communication Journal* 37, no. 4 (Summer 1972): 335–60.

53. Cal M. Logue and Howard Dorgan, ed., *Oratory of Southern Demagogues* (Baton Rouge: Louisiana State University Press, 1981); and Cal M. Logue and Howard Dorgan, ed., *A New Diversity in Contemporary Southern Rhetoric* (Baton Rouge: Louisiana State University Press, 1987).

54. Waldo W. Braden and Harold D. Mixon, "Epideictic Speaking in the Post–Civil War South and the Southern Experience," *Southern Communication Journal* 54, no. 1 (Fall 1988): 40–57, http://ezproxy.memphis.edu; Rebecca Drake Grade, "Origin of the Lost Cause Argument: Analysis of Civil War Letters," *Southern Speech Communication Journal* 49, no. 4 (Summer 1984): 420–30; Keith Griffin, "The Light That Failed: A Rhetorical Analysis of Walter Hines Page as a Ceremonial Orator," *Southern Speech Communication Journal* 46, no. 3 (Spring 1981): 228–50, http://ezproxy.memphis.edu; and Stanford P. Gwin, "Slavery and English Polarity: The Persuasive Campaign of John Bright against English Recognition of the Confederate States of America," *Southern Speech Communication Journal* 49, no. 4 (Summer 1984): 406–19.

55. J. Louis Campbell III, "In Search of the New South," *Southern Speech Communication Journal* 47, no. 4 (Summer 1982): 361–88; Waldo W. Braden, "The Rhetoric of a Closed Society," *Southern Speech Communication Journal* 45, no. 4 (Summer 1980): 333–51; J. Michael Hogan, "Wallace and the Wallacites: A Reexamination," *Southern Speech Communication Journal* 50, no. 1 (Fall 1984): 24–48; Ronald H. Carpenter, "On American History Textbooks and Integration in the South: Woodrow Wilson and the Rhetoric of Division and Reunion, 1829–1889," *Southern Speech Communication Journal* 51, no. 1 (Fall 1985): 1–23; and Campbell, "In Search of the New South," 361–88.

56. Howard Dorgan, "'Ol' Time Way' Exhortation: Preaching in the Old Regular Baptist Church," *Journal of Communication & Religion* 10, no. 2 (September 1987): 24–30; and Donald K. Enholm, David Curtis Skaggs, and W. Jeffrey Welsh, "Origins of the Southern Mind: The Parochial Sermons of Thomas Cradock of Maryland, 1744–1770," *Quarterly Journal of Speech* 73, no. 2 (May 1987): 200, https://doi.org/10.1080/00335638709383803.

57. Donald R. Martin and Vicky Gordon Martin, "Barbara Jordan's Symbolic Use of Language in the Keynote Address to the National Women's Conference," *Southern Speech Communication Journal* 49, no. 3 (Spring 1984): 319–30; Cal M. Logue, "Transcending Coercion: The Communicative Strategies of Black Slaves on Antebellum Plantations," *Quarterly Journal of Speech* 67, no. 1 (February 1981): 31–46, https://doi.org/10.1080/00335638109383549; and Cal M. Logue and Thurmon Garner, "Shifts in Rhetorical Status of Blacks after Freedom," *Southern Communication Journal* 54, no. 1 (Fall 1988): 1–39.

58. William M. Strickland, "The Rhetoric of Removal and the Trail of Tears: Cherokee Speaking against Jackson's Indian Removal Policy, 1828–1832," *Southern Speech Communication Journal* 47, no. 3 (Spring 1982): 292–309.

59. V. William Balthrop, "Culture, Myth, and Ideology as Public Argument: An Interpretation of the Ascent and Demise of 'Southern Culture,'" *Communication Monographs* 51, no. 4 (1984): 339, https://doi.org/10.1080/036377584093 90206; Carl Bryan Holmberg, "Toward the Rhetoric of Music: Dixie," *Southern Speech Communication Journal* 51, no. 1 (1985): 71–82; Stephen A. Smith, "Sounds of the South: The Rhetorical Saga of Country Music Lyrics," *Southern Speech Communication Journal* 45, no. 2 (1980): 164–72; E. Culpepper Clark, "Francis Warrington Dawson: The New South Revisited," *American Journalism* 3, no. 1 (1986): 5–23; Dennie Hall, review of Charles W. Eagles, "Jonathan Daniels and Race Relations: The Evolution of a Southern Liberal," American Journalism 1, no. 2 (1984): 88, https://www.tandfonline.com/doi/abs/10.1080/08821127.198 4.10731024; William A. Haskins, "Rhetorical Vision of Equality: Analysis of the Rhetoric of the Southern Black Press during Reconstruction," *Communication Quarterly* 29, no. 2 (1981): 116–22, https://doi.org/10.1080/01463378109369396; Leonard Ray Teel, "The Shaping of a Southern Opinion Leader: Ralph McGill

and Freedom of Information," *American Journalism* 5, no. 1 (1988): 14–27; and Kenneth P. O'Brien, "The Southern Heroine in the Films of the 1930s," *Journal of Popular Film & Television* 14, no. 1 (1986): 23–32, https://doi.org/10.1080/01956 051.1986.9944213.

60. Stephen A. Smith, *Myth, Media, and the Southern Mind* (Fayetteville: University of Arkansas Press, 1985).

61. Smith, *Myth*, 131.

62. Smith, *Myth*, 91.

63. Smith, *Myth*, 117.

64. Houston Baker, *Turning South Again: Re-thinking Modernism/Re-reading Booker T.* (Durham, NC: Duke University Press, 2001). Baker asks the very question of what it means to be a Black man and to call the South home. He concludes the tension is at the very core of Black *being*.

65. W. Stuart Towns, *Oratory and Rhetoric in the Nineteenth-Century South: A Rhetoric of Defense* (Westport, CT: Praeger, 2000), 3–4.

66. Towns, *Oratory and Rhetoric*, 4–5.

67. Towns, *Oratory and Rhetoric*, 2.

68. W. Stuart Towns, *Public Address in the Twentieth-Century South: The Evolution of a Region* (Westport, CT: Praeger, 2000).

69. Antonio De Valesco, "'I'm a Southerner, Too': Black Southern Counterpublics and Confederate Monuments in Memphis, Tennessee," *Southern Communication Journal* 84, no. 4 (2019): 233–45; Brandon Inabinet and Christina Moss, "Complicit in Victimage: Imagined Marginality in Southern Communication Criticism," *Rhetoric Review* 38, no. 2 (2019): 160–72, https://doi.org/10.1080/07350198.2019 .1582228; and Patricia Davis, *Laying Claim: African American Cultural Memory and Southern Identity* (Tuscaloosa: University of Alabama Press, 2016).

70. Davis, *Laying Claim*.

71. Jason Edward Black, "A Clash of Native Space and Institutional Place in Local Choctaw–Upper Creek Memory Site Decolonizing Critiques and Scholar-Activist Interventions," *American Indian Culture and Research Journal* 36, no. 3 (2012): 19–44; and Bernadette Marie Calafell, "Disrupting the Dichotomy: 'Yo Soy Chicana/o?' in the New Latina/o South," *Communication Review* 7, no. 2 (2004): 175–204, https://doi.org/10.1080/10714420490448705.

72. Andre E. Johnson and Earle J. Fisher, "'But, I Forgive You?': Mother Emanuel, Black Pain and the Rhetoric of Forgiveness," *Journal of Communication & Religion* 42, no. 2 (2019): 5–19; Christina L. Moss and Ronald Jackson, "Introduction to Special Issue: We March Lest We Forget," *Howard Journal of Communications* 289, no 2 (2017): 1–9, https://doi.org/10.1080/10646175.2017.1287611.

73. Examples include Ashli Quesinberry Stokes and Wendy Atkins-Sayre, *Consuming Identity: The Role of Food in Redefining the South* (Jackson: University Press of Mississippi, 2016); Jason Edward Black and Vernon Ray Harrison,

"Southern Paternal Generationalism and the Rhetoric of the Drive-By Truckers," *Western Communication Journal* 79, no. 3 (2015): 293–306; Joshua Daniel Phillips and Rachel Alicia Griffin, "Crystal Mangum as Hypervisible Object and Invisible Subject: Black Feminist Thought, Sexual Violence and the Pedagogical Repurcussions of the Duke Lacrosse Rape Case," *Women's Studies in Communication* 38, no. 1 (2015): 36–56, https://doi.org/10.1080/07491409.2014.964896; Patricia G. Davis, "The Other Southern Belles: Civil War Reenactment, African American Women, and the Performance of Idealized Femininity," *Text & Performance Quarterly* 32, no. 4 (October 2012): 308–31, https://doi.org/10.1080/10462937.2012 .707783; Rachel Alicia Griffin, "Problematic Representations of Strategic Whiteness and 'Post-Racial' Pedagogy: A Critical Intercultural Reading of *The Help*," *Journal of International & Intercultural Communication* 8, no. 2 (May 2015), 147– 66, https://doi.org/10.1080/17513057.2015.1025330; Christina L. Moss, "Reclaiming the Rural South: Queen Sugar and African-American Southern Identity," in Atkins-Sayre and Stokes, *City Places, Country Spaces*; Kristen E. Hoerl, "Burning Mississippi into Memory? Cinematic Amnesia as a Resource for Remembering Civil Rights," *Critical Studies in Media Communication* 26, no. 1 (2009), 54–79; Carole Blair and Neil Michel, "Reproducing Civil Rights Tactics: The Rhetorical Performances of the Civil Rights Memorial," *Rhetoric Society Quarterly* 30, no. 2 (2000): 31–55, https://doi.org/10.1080/02773940009391174; Victoria Gallagher, "Reconciliation and Amnesia in the Birmingham Civil Rights Institute," *Rhetoric and Public Affairs* 2, no. 2 (1999): 303–20; Rebecca Bridges Watts, *Contemporary Southern Identity: Community through Controversy* (Jackson: University Press of Mississippi, 2007); E. Patrick Johnson, *Honeypot: Black Southern Women Who Love Women* (Durham, NC: Duke University Press, 2019); and E. Patrick Johnson, *Sweet Tea: Black Gay Men of the South* (Chapel Hill: University of North Carolina Press, 2011).

74. Samuel Perry, "President Trump and Charlottesville: Uncivil Mourning and White Supremacy," *Journal of Contemporary Rhetoric* 8, no. 1 (2018): 57–71; Sean Patrick O'Rourke and Melody Lehn, *Rhetoric, Race, and Religion and the Charleston Shootings: Was Blind but Now I See* (Lanham, MD: Lexington Books, 2019); Ryan Neville-Shepard, "Rand Paul at Howard University and the Rhetoric of the New Southern Strategy," *Western Journal of Communication* 82, no. 1 (2018): 20–39, https://doi.org/10.1080/10570314.2017.1320809; and Christina L. Moss, "A Nation Divided: Regional Identity, National Narratives, and Senator Zell Miller in the 2004 Presidential Election," *Southern Communication Journal* 76, no. 1 (2011): 76–96.

75. Amanda Nell Edgar and Andre E. Johnson, *The Struggle over Black Lives Matter and All Lives Matter* (Lexington, MD: Lanham Books, 2018).

76. The term *Global South* here is used as a regional identity to explain divisions in the world based not on geography but instead on resources, economies,

and politics with the North having greater abundance and the South having far less. For more, see Martyn Bone's discussion of a transnational South in *The Postsouthern Sense of Place in Contemporary Fiction* (Baton Rouge: Louisiana State University Press, 2005); and Raka Shome, "Thinking Culture and Cultural Studies—from/of the Global South," *Communication and Critical/Cultural Studies* 16, no. 3 (2019): 196–218, https://doi.org/10.1080/14791420.2019.1648841.

77. Bruce Gronbeck, "The Rhetorics of the Past: History, Argument, and Collective Memory," in Turner, *Doing Rhetorical History*, 49.

78. Gronbeck, "Rhetorics of the Past," 49–50.

16

Knowledge, Rhetorical History, and Undergraduate Scholars

Reimagining Liberal Education

Sean Patrick O'Rourke and Melody Lehn

I n the mid-1990s, two seemingly disparate areas of active scholarship emerged in rhetoric. The first was the extension of an interest in undergraduate research from the sciences and social sciences to the humanities. Recognized early on by scholars in languages,[1] the understanding that undergraduate research in the humanities could produce excellent scholarship and deepen the traditional classroom experience spread quickly to rhetoricians in both writing and speaking.[2] The second was an outgrowth of, or perhaps more accurately a response to, the increased interest in textual criticism and close reading in public address studies. "Rhetorical history," as the new scholarship came to be called, sought to investigate "the study of rhetorical processes in historical contexts, a study making a distinct contribution to both rhetorical and historical knowledge."[3]

We suggest that these two areas—undergraduate research and rhetorical history—have for too long stood apart. Working from the assumption that undergraduate students can conduct original research and make significant contributions to humanities scholarship, we propose a way forward that joins the work of undergraduate scholars, archival research, and rhetorical history. After a brief discussion of the status of undergraduate research in rhetorical studies, we provide an overview of undergraduate research in the rhetoric curriculum at two liberal arts colleges. From this overview, we propose that undergraduate work in rhetoric is central to three knowledge-producing activities that can be developed and nurtured in an intentionally scaffolded curriculum. We conclude with final thoughts about the implications of having undergraduate researchers "do rhetorical history."

Undergraduate Research in Rhetoric Studies: An Emerging Conversation

Over the last quarter century, the most frequent commonplace in undergraduate research[4] conversations has been that the humanities came late—and reluctantly—to the party.[5] Once in, however, the humanities have demonstrated an adaptability and creativity few could have foreseen twenty-five years ago. The current state of undergraduate research in the humanities, and the scholarship about it, is better than it has ever been.

The many benefits of undergraduate research to students, faculty, and institutions are well-documented and familiar to those who have made undergraduate research a part of their scholarly and pedagogical activity.[6] Although rhetoricians have increasingly regarded undergraduate research as a core aspect of liberal learning, we have been slower to meaningfully engage rhetorical studies as a subfield and rhetorical history as an approach or method. And yet, in recent years we have seen limited progress in the discipline's journals on the topic of undergraduate research, particularly in rhetoric. Over a decade ago, Laurie Grobman argued "that undergraduate research production and authorship should be viewed along a continuum of scholarly authority."[7] In 2003, Grobman and Candace Spigelman (both at Penn State University—Berks) founded *Young Scholars in Writing: Undergraduate Research in Writing and Rhetoric (YSW)* as an international "refereed journal dedicated to publishing research articles written by undergraduates in a wide variety of disciplines associated with rhetoric and writing."[8] Committed to the belief "that research can and should be a crucial component of rhetorical education,"[9] editors of *YSW* have guided undergraduate research in rhetoric[10] (including first-year writing[11]) through a rigorous and inclusive peer-review process whereby other undergraduates serve as readers in concert with a faculty advising editor and the journal's editor. On rare occasions, state and regional publications in the field have also featured undergraduate research in rhetoric.[12] And, in some cases, campuses have founded their own undergraduate research publications and featured scholarship in rhetoric in those venues.[13] However, the fact remains that many of the most prominent rhetoric journals fail to adequately or regularly engage rhetorical pedagogy in general and research in rhetoric by and/or about undergraduates in particular.[14] The related associations, symposia, and gatherings—including those sponsored by the Rhetoric Society of America, the American Society for the History of Rhetoric, the International Society for the History of Rhetoric, the biennial Public Address Conference, and the Southern Colloquium on Rhetoric—do not, as a rule, program or support undergraduate research.

Whereas our publications in rhetoric have often fallen short, our professional organizations have created and sustained spaces for undergraduate research presentations. Several of our state and regional conferences accept, showcase, and reward exemplary undergraduate projects in rhetoric. For the past thirty years, the Southern States Communication Association (SSCA) has sponsored the Theodore Clevenger Undergraduate Honors Conference, one of the oldest and most prestigious undergraduate research forums in the field. Following SSCA's example, the other three regional conferences—hosted by the Eastern, Central, and Western States Communication Associations, respectively—all now boast their own undergraduate research conferences.[15] Some state conferences in communication also intentionally reserve space for undergraduate research in rhetoric.[16] In composition studies, the Conference on College Composition and Communication formed the Committee on Undergraduate Research in 2011 to develop and support undergraduate research activities, including an Undergraduate Research Poster Session, at its annual convention.[17] The conference's journal, *College Composition and Communication*, has in recent years increasingly reserved space for scholarship on undergraduate research as well.[18] Unfortunately, the sine qua non gathering for undergraduate research in rhetoric, the Hayward Conference on Rhetorical Criticism, is now defunct. For many years, teachers and students of rhetoric gathered at Hayward for "a dialogue on rhetorical practice and theory"[19] and benefited tremendously from the exchange. Despite—or perhaps because of—this somewhat checkered past, we see great potential for undergraduate research in rhetoric generally and in rhetorical history specifically.

Undergraduate Researchers Doing Rhetorical History

In the introduction to *Doing Rhetorical History: Concepts and Cases*, Kathleen J. Turner traces the disciplinary arguments and tensions between rhetorical critics and rhetorical historians, as well as rhetorical theorists and the rest of us. Writing at what she suggests was an opportune moment, Turner reassesses the importance of rhetorical history, alongside rhetorical criticism and rhetorical theory, an importance that was a given at the beginning of the modern discipline. Far from serving as "mere history" to our colleagues or replicating rhetorical criticism that "seeks to understand the message in context," rhetorical history, as Turner defines it, "seeks to understand the context through messages that reflect and construct that context."[20] That is, Turner argues, rhetorical history should reassert its rightful place among the field's approaches to rhetorical scholarship.

David Zarefsky expands Turner's definition in his own essay in *Doing Rhetorical History*. In his essay, Zarefsky defines four senses of rhetorical history: (1) the history of rhetoric, by which he means the "development, from classical times to the present, of principles of effective discourse"; (2) the rhetoric of history, by which he means the ways that rhetoric is essential to our understanding of how history is archived, recorded, written, and used persuasively; (3) the historical study of rhetorical practice, or the ways in which the historical record (and perhaps commentary about that record) illuminates our understanding of rhetorical events; and (4) the study of historical events from a rhetorical point of view, in which history is regarded and interpreted from a rhetorical perspective that accounts for how exigencies and their responses create and shape historical events.[21]

Rhetorical history, we argue, presents itself as an area of our field's scholarship open to, and ripe for, undergraduate engagement in all four of Zarefsky's senses of the term. Several characteristics of rhetorical history are important in this regard. First, rhetorical history, while not in any way averse to contributions from theory (rhetorical or otherwise), does not require theory for its scholarly fulfillment. By the time undergraduate students begin to work with us on rhetorical history, they typically have been introduced to, but only partially versed in, theory. Put another way, students are only beginning to work with theory. They are often daunted and sometimes turned off by it but are rarely saturated enough to produce engaged theoretical scholarship. Second, in our experience, undergraduate students in rhetoric tend to be drawn to the field by speeches, protests, debates, and arguments—and, most importantly, the controversies and contexts those discourses grow out of and in turn shape. That is, students gravitate toward rhetorical history. Third, rhetorical history as a guiding approach to public address helps students understand the multifaceted, multivocal character of our public life. Rhetorical history is distinctive in its commitment to exploring the many voices that create a controversy, the many sides that constitute a public debate, the vast number of positions and perspectives that citizens voice on the problems that confront them, and where and how we might encounter those voices.

Undergraduate Research in the Rhetoric Curriculum at Two Liberal Arts Colleges

For the past fifteen years, the two authors have—separately and together —been involved in integrating undergraduate research into the rhetoric curriculum at two liberal arts colleges, Furman University and Sewanee: The University of the South. In both programs we have worked to create an architecture of undergraduate research that integrates first-year programs and introductory rhetoric courses with upper-division classes in rhetorical history and public address, as well as study-away courses. Some students also participate in university-funded collaborative summer research projects with faculty, and this work produces significant scholarship too. The curricular architecture of the programs scaffolds undergraduate research experiences throughout a student's university-level education and, in so doing, seeks to cultivate a deep appreciation for research and scholarship over the course of a student's years in the university. That appreciation, in turn, fosters a "learning-through-inquiry" approach to liberal education,[22] and rhetorical history is central to this approach.

The rhetoric program at Furman has been a part of the college from its beginnings in 1826, first as an endowed chair of Sacred Rhetoric and later as a curriculum in speech and debate. It disappeared briefly and then reappeared in the early 2000s, when the university approved an interdisciplinary major in Communication Studies and then later a stand-alone discipline-based department of the same name. The rhetoric program at Sewanee is in its infancy, although it has the benefit of emerging from Sewanee's well-established English and creative writing programs, as well as the faculty's decision, in 2014, to make Speaking and Listening the centerpiece of the university's Quality Enhancement Plan for reaccreditation.[23]

Both institutions define themselves as national liberal arts colleges,[24] and both rhetoric programs have crafted historical, preceptual, and critical humanities-based programs. The curricula at both arose out of efforts to rethink course offerings and major requirements designed to engage students by "invigorating and stimulating . . . intellectual curiosity" and pursuing "knowledge, understanding, and wisdom" as well as "intellectual" growth.[25] One key component to that invigoration and stimulation is a more robust curriculum that invites students to engage in several different, graduated, research experiences.

The Rhetoric and Public Address Courses

In the two curricula, all students at the university take a first-year writing seminar and one additional upper-division course designated "Writing Intensive" in the university's general education requirements. Rhetoric faculty have offered several first-year writing seminars over the last ten years. These courses offer students the opportunity to research public discourses within a tightly delimited subject domain, learning the methods and techniques of rhetorical, historical, and text-critical research while also practicing good scholarly writing. Because they have limited enrollments, the first-year seminars allow for intensive one-on-one composing, editing, and revising sessions. Several students have presented and published their work at undergraduate honors conferences and in Young Scholars in Writing's "Spotlight on First-Year Writing" section.

Students entering the program must take two required rhetoric courses, RHET 101: Public Speaking and RHET 201: Introduction to Rhetoric.[26] The public speaking course requires students to engage in research or investigation of cross-disciplinary study that encounters not only scholarly literature but also journalism, government-sponsored research, and interest-group advocacy.[27] They then present arguments in the form of in-class public speeches and, occasionally, public commentary. The course helps students understand the many nuances of controversies, teaches them to eschew the simplistic either/or dichotomies so prevalent in our public discourse, and encourages them to be better thinkers, researchers, speakers, listeners, and critics.

Upper-division courses include such 300-level survey courses as a yearlong US Public Address sequence that runs from 1620 to the present, a yearlong History of Rhetoric sequence that covers rhetorical theory (and some practice) from antiquity to the present, and semester-long courses in Rhetorical Criticism, African American Protest, and Voices of American Women. The upper-division courses also include 400-level courses with a sharper focus, such as Rhetoric in the Age of Protest: 1948–1973, Speakers' Rights and Responsibilities, and the Rhetoric of Mass and Social Media. Finally, the upper-division offerings include study-away courses (e.g., Rhetorics of Social Activism, Rhetoric in the Scottish Enlightenment, and the Rhetoric of Irish Nationalism), as well as directed and independent study opportunities.

Refining, Recovering, and Generating Knowledge

Given this scaffolded curriculum, how and in what ways can undergraduates, working collaboratively with faculty or on their own under faculty direction, advance knowledge in rhetorical history and, at the same time, learn and grow as undergraduates should? In what follows, we turn to the three knowledge-producing activities noted above, and the forms or models of undergraduate research in rhetorical history related to each.

REFINING KNOWLEDGE AS DOING RHETORICAL HISTORY

In our scaffolded curriculum, *refining* knowledge is the activity most undergraduate rhetoric students engage first. Students refine knowledge when they read published scholarship (student and otherwise) and respond to that scholarship in "commentary and response" pieces and "letters to the dead" (and sometimes living) orators and rhetoricians. Refining knowledge gradually eases them into the field, orients them as early as possible to the scholarly demands and standards of the discipline, and invites them to continue to engage rhetorical artifacts in meaningful ways. Refining knowledge is, thus, an outcome of assignments and activities in the courses in which it occurs. Because refining knowledge provides students entrée to a wide range of literature and scholarship, they engage it early in their time with us. Accordingly, we design several of the activities in Public Speaking, Introduction to Rhetoric, and some upper-division courses as knowledge refining. Student scholars learn the aforementioned standards and norms and, over time, come to be more proficient at knowledge-refining activities that introduce them to rhetorical history.

The "Letter to a Dead/Living Rhetorician" assignment primarily correlates to Zarefsky's first and third senses of rhetorical history as the history of rhetoric and the historical study of rhetorical practice. This assignment requires students to address a letter to a dead or living rhetorician; that is, a key figure in the history of rhetoric or rhetorical practice (e.g., Isocrates, Cicero, or Sojourner Truth), someone who has written a history of rhetoric (e.g., Patricia Bizzell, Thomas Conley, or George Kennedy), or someone who has published a historical study of rhetorical practice (e.g., Martin Medhurst, Belinda A. Stillion Southard, or Susan Zaeske). Students address a central concern of the course that correlates to an issue that interests them. For instance, a student might raise the question of how ethics should be taught to young orators in a letter to Isocrates or suggest to Plato that the analogy between the teacher of rhetoric and the teacher of boxing has problems—and indicate to him what the student thinks those problems are. An exceptional letter to a dead or living rhetorician will demonstrate a deep understanding of the issues and nuances of the subject or problem, a knowledge of the addressee's work in the area, and an awareness of the rhetoric of the student's own effort.

The "Comment and Response" assignment embraces all four of Zarefsky's senses of rhetorical history, but particularly the second and fourth senses: the rhetoric of history and the study of historical events from a rhetorical point of view. This assignment requires students to select a full-length essay published in *Young Scholars in Writing* and craft a response—usually between 750 and 1,250 words—that provides a clear, concise, and accurate account of what the author does and constructively engages the author's argument. The best papers will participate with the author and others in a mutual quest for knowledge and understanding. While students may disagree (perhaps even vehemently) with the author, they should strive for a tone of intellectual curiosity, civil inquiry, and principled advocacy. Over the past ten years, twenty-eight students in our programs have published "Comment and Response" pieces in peer-reviewed journals and nearly as many have engaged published authors in our field in web-based exchanges fashioned in epistolary form.[28]

In both assignments, refining knowledge encourages students to engage in the ongoing conversation that rhetorical scholarship is or at least ought to be.[29] The activity not only mimics the ideal conversations that animate scholarship in the field of rhetorical history but also actually engages those conversations. Undergraduate scholars are not mere bystanders. They are active participants in the conversation and are therefore held to professional standards of evidence, argument, historical proof, and judgment, as well as collegial norms of civility, decorum, and generosity (although one wonders to what extent such norms still exist, given disputes by academics on various listservs and social media platforms[30]). Refining knowledge includes all aspects of critique: the fair and accurate summary of a scholarly position or claim, the generous "best-light" reading of another's work, the rigorous critique of that work (which may include an assessment of the assumptions and inferences made, evidence presented, contrary arguments and proof considered, and language deployed), the extension of the scholarship to related fields and subject domains, the presentation of alternative explanations and points of view, the ethical and moral implications of the study under review, and related activities and considerations. Refining knowledge places the field's received wisdom in the bright light of judicious scrutiny when the student responds to it. The desired outcome of such activity is the cultivation of knowledge—testing it, improving it, honing it, and sometimes debunking it—so that the conversation continues in constructive ways.

Recovering Knowledge as Doing Rhetorical History

Students' real engagement with rhetorical history, however, occurs as they work (in collaboration with faculty or, eventually for some, on their own) to *recover* knowledge from archives, living rhetors, and other sites of rhetorical activity and preservation. Recovering knowledge involves students in work that discovers, preserves, and provides general access to lost or corrupted rhetorical texts. Scholarship that recovers knowledge most typically occurs in Sewanee's Center for Speaking and Listening but may also occur in the context of study-away courses (such as our three-week spring course in California) or more traditional classrooms.[31] It may also take several forms.

For example, students have collaborated with faculty on speech discovery, transcription, and preservation projects. In one of our projects, we collaborated with the University of California at Berkeley's Social Activism Sound Recording Project, headquartered at the Bancroft Library. That project, spearheaded by Gary Handman, has archived and curated audio recordings of protest discourses of the 1960s and early 1970s in the antiwar, Free Speech, Black Panther, and LGBTQ movements, to name but a few. There are, however, no texts and few contexts. Working closely with faculty, tutors in our center painstakingly transcribe texts, reconstruct contexts, and recover and preserve key elements of the rhetorical history of these important movements. Our students and faculty also helped to recover knowledge crucial to the rhetorical history of the civil rights movement when we collaborated with researchers at Florida State University and St. Joseph's College on a project to reconstruct a history of *Women and the Civil Rights Movement, 1954–1965*, rooted in the Smithsonian Institution's Moses Moon recordings archive.[32] With our students, we have also engaged, as part of a study-away program on the rhetorics of social activism, in oral history projects with rhetorical activists as diverse as Phyllis Lyon, founder of the Daughters of Bilitis; Clarence Jones, Martin Luther King Jr.'s attorney; and Dorothy Cotton, the Southern Christian Leadership Conference's director of education. Most recently, three of our center tutors are assisting a visiting dean's Fellow in Rhetoric and Women's and Gender Studies, Professor Jamie Capuzza from the University of Mount Union, in a research project about male allyship in the early women's rights movement. Under Professor Capuzza's direction, the student researchers (Anna Day, Kathryn Hicks, and Kendall Stallings) are meticulously searching the six volumes of Elizabeth Cady Stanton, Susan B. Anthony, and Matilda Joslyn Gage's *History of Woman Suffrage*, identifying rhetorical artifacts by men who are mentioned across the volumes, tracking down those primary texts, and creating a searchable database that will be hosted on the center's website.[33] By mapping the rhetorical history of their contributions to suffrage efforts, this project both deepens and broadens our understanding of men's attempts to help women secure the ballot—in a way that is accessible for other rhetorical historians.

Scholarship that recovers knowledge also makes use of students' language and text-critical skills and facilities. Those engaged in recovery projects work collaboratively with participating faculty to discover lost oratorical (and other) texts, learn how to establish scholarly, critical editions of those texts, and provide public access to those texts by creating transcriptions, translations, and electronic versions of them, often with commentary. Translations offer rhetorical historians access to texts and contexts unavailable to them prior to the scholarship of the students.

Those students who offer translations will often work with two members of the faculty, one in rhetoric and rhetorical history and the other in the language of translation.[34] Those who create critical editions of rhetorical texts often delve deep into archives, online sources, audio and video recordings, and other primary texts to publish a scholarly edition that not only collates the various versions but also adds scholarly commentary and citations.[35] This work occurs in all study-away courses, as well as upper-division courses in US Public Address, Voices of American Women, the History of Rhetoric, and Rhetorics of Protest. Over the past ten years, more than one hundred students have participated in projects that recover knowledge.[36]

GENERATING KNOWLEDGE AS DOING RHETORICAL HISTORY

Generating knowledge, usually reserved for advanced students, involves investigating, writing, and publishing original studies of rhetorical history. Generating knowledge asks undergraduates to produce original advances on scholarship generally, not just other student scholarship, and requires them to do the kind of work we do. To make that possible, however, we must cultivate an understanding of the challenges, standards, norms, and practices of humanities scholarship over the entire three to four years they are with us. This work might take place in first-year seminars, but it is far more likely to bear fruit if nurtured in upper-division courses and senior seminars. In total, 106 students in our programs have published in peer-reviewed journals or presented competitively selected papers at scholarly conferences in the last ten years. Moreover, 78 of them have published full-blown scholarly essays (not the shorter "Comment and Responses" or "Letters to the Dead").[37]

For example, one of our best students investigated, as part of Sewanee's larger Roberson Project on Slavery, Race, and Reconciliation, the rhetorical history of the university's founding.[38] A main objective of the Roberson Project is "to conduct comprehensive research into the history of slavery, race, and racial injustice in connection with the University of the South and to publish its findings."[39] Scouring the university's archive, William Merriman uncovered William Giles Dix's speech advocating for a national-caliber, liberal-arts oriented university at Sewanee. Merriman masterfully traced the rhetorical history of liberal arts colleges in the antebellum period; the growing sectional rivalries that animated that history; the struggle for identity, control, and reach of educational institutions; and the controversy over church control of the institution's mission. A tutor in our Speaking and Listening Center, Merriman presented his essay, "Reconstituting a Transcendent University: Rhetorical

Criticism of William Giles Dix's *An Address,*" to the Clevenger Undergraduate Honors Conference at the 2018 Southern Communication Association Convention. Judges awarded Merriman the Franklin Shirley Award for the top undergraduate paper (out of 139 at the conference), and the essay is now under consideration for publication. Merriman's inquiry most closely aligns with Zarefsky's fourth sense of rhetoric and offers a template for how undergraduate researchers can examine historical events from a rhetorical perspective at their institutions.

Conclusion

In the tradition of Augustine, we intend this chapter to be a pointing essay, one that seeks to suggest what might be as much as it describes and explains what is or has been.[40] Accordingly, we end the discussion with some ideas about future research by undergraduates, in collaboration with or under the direction of faculty, in the broad area of rhetorical history.

One of the most promising approaches, limned in our essay, is to engage undergraduates in group projects devoted to excavating, preserving, and providing access to primary materials in digital humanities projects. As the collaborations with UC Berkeley's Social Activism Sound Recording project and the Moses Moon archive suggest, such endeavors allow students to work together in teams; to bounce interpretations, ideas, organizing structures, and problems off one another and faculty participants; and to work with primary rhetorical artifacts in careful, scholarly ways. The end results of such efforts are usually databases, typically critical editions of rhetorical artifacts curated for further scholarly work. Whether the materials are the songs of the Highlander Folk School, the audiofiles of 1960s student protests, the voices of abolitionist women gleaned from nineteenth-century newspapers and periodicals, or the more contemporary online rhetorical efforts of those fighting for marriage equality, the rhetorical material students find and preserve are essential primary sources for scholars doing rhetorical history.

A second and related area is to study the argumentation and rhetoric of emerging local controversies. Mining the "local" for rhetorical history allows students and faculty to conduct research without the expense of travel and the limits distance often places on access to materials. The local also encourages the study of emerging controversies, inviting students to investigate arguments, debates, and discussions about policies and values as they spread from their origins into the public sphere, animating publics and counterpublics across physical venues, traditional print and broadcast media, and social media. To capture these discourses and begin to study them in depth engages students in real-time scholarly work, fieldwork in rhetoric that recovers and assesses arguments in "real world" controversies. Two examples are Edward Schiappa's work with graduate students on the Minnesota Twins stadium controversy, research that resulted in a fascinating study,[41] and Sean O'Rourke's project on the Martin Luther King Jr. holiday controversy in Greenville, South Carolina.[42] In each case, students worked with a faculty director but did a significant amount of the research in teams, writing up their findings with the guidance of the faculty mentor. The benefits to the students of this kind of "learning while doing" is, we would suggest, obvious. The benefits to rhetorical history have yet to be fully realized. Given the enormous number of local controversies over, for example, neo-Confederate monuments,[43] environmental protection, law enforcement and implicit racial bias, and free speech issues on campus, the possibilities seem nearly endless.

A third area for undergraduate work in rhetorical history is in studies of social, political, and economic movements. Much of what makes movement studies rhetorically rich and robust is that the dynamics at play are often disparate, always multivocal, and invariably moving with the ebb and flow of forces not under their control. The gathering of the rhetorical artifacts of social movement protest provides, therefore, an effort well suited for undergraduate research teams. We are thinking here of studies of, for example, Me Too, Occupy Wall Street, Black Lives Matter, or the Tea Party, all movements that could benefit from concerted efforts by undergraduate and faculty collaborative teams.

These three suggestions for future research are by no means exhaustive. Indeed, they represent merely the most accessible approaches to rhetorical history—in all four of the senses David Zarefsky outlined and Kathleen J. Turner envisioned—by students and their faculty mentors. Our hope is that these and other areas of rhetorical history begin to see renewed interest and energy in the years ahead as we continue to reframe rhetorical history and reimagine liberal education in new and productive ways.

Notes

1. David Bost, "Seven Obstacles to Undergraduate Research in the Humanities (and Seven Solutions)," *CUR Newsletter* 13 (1992–93): 35–40.

2. Laurie Grobman and Joyce Kinkead, "Introduction: Illuminating Undergraduate Research in English," in *Undergraduate Research in English Studies*, ed. Laurie Grobman and Joyce Kinkead (Urbana, IL: NCTE, 2010): ix–xxxii; and Sean Patrick O'Rourke, Stephen Howard, and Andrianna Lee Lawrence, "*Respondeo etsi Mutabor*: The Comment and Response Assignment, Young Scholars, and the

Promise of Liberal Education," *Young Scholars in Writing: Undergraduate Research in Writing and Rhetoric* 10 (2013): 27–37.

3. Kathleen J. Turner, "Introduction: Rhetorical History as Social Construction," in Turner, *Doing Rhetorical History*, 8.

4. By "undergraduate research," we refer not only to research students conduct for graded written and/or oral course assignments but also to the co- and extracurricular opportunities that might grow out of (or happen in conjunction with) work completed in the classroom. We understand undergraduate research to include both presentations (on campus, in the community, and at disciplinary conferences) and publications (in academic books and journals, newspapers, online forums, and perhaps other venues). The research our students do includes archival work, oral histories, textual criticism, rhetorical criticism, and—the focus of this essay—rhetorical history.

5. See, e.g., Bost, "Seven Obstacles," 35–36; Grobman and Kinkead, "Introduction," ix–xii.

6. See Conference on College Composition and Communication, "CCCC Position Statement on Undergraduate Research in Writing: Principles and Best Practices," March 2017, https://cccc.ncte.org); Andrea J. Sell, Angela Naginey, and Cathy Alexander Stanton, "The Impact of Undergraduate Research on Academic Success," *Scholarship and Practice of Undergraduate Research* 1 (2018): 19–29. Of course, faculty can only guide undergraduate research well when they have access to interested and prepared students, adequate time and funding opportunities, department and institutional support, and a way for it to count positively in their personnel files. See further Janet A. Morrison et al., "Surveying Faculty Perspectives on Undergraduate Research, Scholarship, and Creative Activity: A Three-Institution Study," *Scholarship and Practice of Undergraduate Research* 2 (2018): 43–54.

7. Laurie Grobman, "The Student Scholar: (Re)Negotiating Authorship and Authority," *College Composition and Communication* 61 (2009): 177.

8. *Young Scholars in Writing*, "About the Journal," accessed September 4, 2020, https://youngscholarsinwriting.org.

9. *Young Scholars in Writing*, "About the Journal."

10. See, for example, undergraduate students directed by Sean O'Rourke and published in *YSW*: Susan West Heimburger, "Of Faith and Fact: Haywood N. Hill's 'This I Believe,'" *Young Scholars in Writing* 2 (2004): 29–37; Mary Virginia Tynan, "Cry Deception and Let Loose the Dogs of War: The Rhetorical Ethics of Colin Powell's 'Denial and Deception,'" *Young Scholars in Writing* 3 (2005): 30–37; Jennifer E. M. Hill, "Reframing the Victim: Rhetoric for Segregation in the *Greenville News*," *Young Scholars in Writing* 9 (2012): 45–57; Matthew Morris, "Rhetorical Analysis of 'The Drum Major Instinct' in Martin Luther King, Jr. on Leadership," *Young Scholars in Writing* 12 (2015): 4–14; Luke D. Christie,

"'America! America!': Vanishing Time and Space in Clarence Jordan's 'Things Needed for Our Peace,'" *Young Scholars in Writing* 13 (2016): 20–31.

11. See, for example, first-year writing projects directed by Sean O'Rourke and published in *YSW*: Angela Acampora, "SCUM Manifesto: The Argument for a 'Male Misogyny,'" *Young Scholars in Writing* 9 (2012): 137–44; Jordan Allums, "A Society for Brotherhood: Rhetoric for Resistance," *Young Scholars in Writing* 13 (2016): 125–36.

12. For example, the *Carolinas Communication Annual* featured a designated section for undergraduate and graduate research called "Spotlight on Debut Scholarship" under Melody Lehn's editorship (2016–2018). See especially Kate Stevens, "The Future That Could Have Been: Bayard Rustin, Civil Rights, and Coalition Politics," *Carolinas Communication Annual* 32 (2016): 30–42.

13. See, as just two examples, the *Vanderbilt Undergraduate Research Journal* (http://vurj.vanderbilt.edu/) and the *Furman Humanities Review* (https://scholar-exchange.furman.edu/). The Council on Undergraduate Research offers a more comprehensive list to its members at https://www.cur.org/resources/students/journals/. The British Conference of Undergraduate Research offers a somewhat different list, searchable by subject or title at https://www.bcur.org/undergraduate-journals/.

14. Among those we would mention here are the *Journal for the History of Rhetoric* (formerly *Advances in the History of Rhetoric*), *Rhetorica*, *Rhetoric & Public Affairs*, *Rhetoric Review*, and *Rhetoric Society Quarterly*.

15. These are ECA's James C. McCroskey and Virginia P. Richmond Undergraduate Scholars Conference, CSCA's Undergraduate Honors Conference, and WCA's Undergraduate Scholars Research Conference. In a related vein, we would also highlight the DePauw University Undergraduate Honors Conference in Communication and Theatre, a distinct and long-standing forum for exemplary undergraduate research. At this writing, the future of the annual DePauw conference is uncertain due to the COVID-19 pandemic. See further https://www.depauw.edu/academics/departments-programs/communication-theatre/undergraduate-honors-conferenc/.

16. Among them are the Alabama Communication Association, the Carolinas Communication Association, the Ohio Communication Association, and the Pennsylvania Communication Association. See further Jeff Tyus, "Untapped Potential: The Role of Faculty and State Associations in Developing the Undergraduate Researcher," *Ohio Communication Journal* 54 (2016): 11–17.

17. Conference on College Composition and Communication, "Committee on Undergraduate Research," Governance and Resolutions, Committees, updated March 2018, https://cccc.ncte.org.

18. See, for example, Grobman, "Student Scholar." Several essays focus attention on the rich possibilities for undergraduate research in archives. See

Wendy Hayden, "'Gifts' of the Archives: A Pedagogy for Undergraduate Research," *College Composition and Communication* 66 (2015): 402–26; Jessica Enoch and Pamela VanHaitsma, "Archival Literacy: Reading the Rhetoric of Digital Archives in the Undergraduate Classroom," *College Composition and Communication* 67 (2015): 216–42.

19. Harold Barrett, "A Conference in Rhetorical Criticism," *Speech Teacher* 16 (1967): 134–36.

20. Turner, "Introduction," 2–4.

21. David Zarefsky, "Four Senses of Rhetorical History," in Turner, *Doing Rhetorical History*, 19–32.

22. See Virginia S. Lee, "What Is Inquiry-Guided Learning?" *New Directions for Teaching and Learning* 129 (Spring 2012): 5–14; Beth Godbee, Katie Ellington, and Megan Knowles, "Why Inquiry Matters: An Argument and Model for Inquiry-Based Writing Courses," *Wisconsin English Journal* 58 (2016): 7–21.

23. See Sewanee: The University of the South, "Learning to Speak, Speaking to Learn: Quality Enhancement Plan," February 23–25, 2016, https://www.sewanee.edu/media/qep/QEP_Jan16_rev-(1).pdf.

24. In the Carnegie classification system, both schools are "highly residential," "more selective," "Baccalaureate Colleges [with an] Arts & Sciences Focus." Both can be found using Carnegie's "Lookup" key at http://carnegieclassifications.iu.edu/lookup/lookup.php. Both schools are also members of the Associated Colleges of the South, a consortium of sixteen liberal arts colleges (http://colleges.org/).

25. The *Furman Catalogue 2007–2008* used this language, at pages 5 and 6, to indicate the key goals of liberal education at that institution, http://www2.furman.edu/sites/hr/documents/2007–2008_catalog.pdf. At this writing, Furman's catalogue no longer includes this language. See also *Sewanee Catalogue 2019–2020* at http://e-catalog.sewanee.edu/university/purpose/.

26. The numbering system reflects Sewanee's current curriculum, although the numbers and course options resemble Furman's quite closely because O'Rourke was deeply involved in the creation of both curricula.

27. At both institutions, we have discovered that our colleagues limit the term *research* to discipline-specific scholarship and exclude wide-ranging investigations that cross disciplinary boundaries. We believe public speaking students need to do both discipline-specific research and cross-disciplinary investigation.

28. For the comment and response scholarship in just the last seven years, see, e.g., William James Rankin, "A Response to Caitlin Eha," *Young Scholars in Writing: Undergraduate Research in Writing and Rhetoric* 15 (2018): 124–27; Jennifer Bilton, "A Response to Aubrey Young," *Young Scholars in Writing: Undergraduate Research in Writing and Rhetoric* 12 (2015): 148–50; Luke D. Christie, "A Response to Ashley K. Allen," *Young Scholars in Writing: Undergraduate Research in*

Writing and Rhetoric 12 (2015): 151–52; Suzanne Burton, "A Response to Ashley K. Allen," *Young Scholars in Writing: Undergraduate Research in Writing and Rhetoric* 12 (2015): 153–54; Julia Cooper, "A Response to Michaela Cullington," *Young Scholars in Writing: Undergraduate Research in Writing and Rhetoric* 11 (2014): 91–93; Caroline Walters, "A Response to Sarah-Kate Magee," *Young Scholars in Writing: Undergraduate Research in Writing and Rhetoric* 11 (2014): 96–98; Jordan Delk, "A Response to Mark Ulrich," *Young Scholars in Writing: Undergraduate Research in Writing and Rhetoric* 10 (2013): 126–28; Evelyn Henson, "A Response to Zoë Snider," *Young Scholars in Writing: Undergraduate Research in Writing and Rhetoric* 10 (2013): 129–31. The letters to the dead and living are currently under negotiation. When we moved from Furman to Sewanee, we lost access to much of our web-based material, and we are in conversation now with Furman officials to make that material available on Sewanee's website.

29. We are thinking here, of course, of Kenneth Burke's now classic description of the "unending conversation" about rhetoric, sometimes referred to as the "Burkean Parlor." Burke writes,

> Imagine that you enter a parlor. You come late. When you arrive, others have long preceded you, and they are engaged in a heated discussion, a discussion too heated for them to pause and tell you exactly what it is about. In fact, the discussion had already begun long before any of them got there, so that no one present is qualified to retrace for you all the steps that had gone before. You listen for a while, until you decide that you have caught the tenor of the argument; then you put in your oar. Someone answers; you answer him; another comes to your defense; another aligns himself against you, to either the embarrassment or gratification of your opponent, depending upon the quality of your ally's assistance. However, the discussion is interminable. The hour grows late, you must depart. And you do depart, with the discussion still vigorously in progress.

See his *The Philosophy of Literary Form: Studies in Symbolic Action, 3rd ed* (Berkeley: University of California Press, 1973), 110–11.

30. Consider Collen Flaherty, "Difficult Conversations," *Inside Higher Ed*, September 26, 2019, https://www.insidehighered.com/news/2019/09/26/national-communication-association-suspends-discussion-listserv.

31. Sewanee's Center for Speaking and Listening (CS&L), which opened in the fall of 2017, is located in the university library's Learning Commons. Trained student tutors staff the CS&L, and we serve as the CS&L's directors. The CS&L offers assistance to members of the Sewanee community who seek help as they investigate, develop, refine, and practice oral presentations—speeches, addresses, arguments, debates, and dialogues—and as they seek to understand,

through listening, those spoken discourses. To learn more about the CS&L's mission, see Sean Patrick O'Rourke, "Wisdom and Eloquence," *Vital Speeches of the Day* 83 (2017): 344–45, and the CS&L website (https://new.sewanee.edu /academics/center-for-speaking-listening/).

32. Davis W. Houck and David E. Dixon, "Introduction: Recovering Women's Voices from the Civil Rights Movement," in *Women and the Civil Rights Movement, 1954–1965*, ed. Davis W. Houck and David E. Dixon (Waco, TX: Baylor University, 2006), ix–xxvii. See, in particular, xv.

33. See Elizabeth Cady Stanton, Susan B. Anthony, and Matilda Joslyn Gage, *History of Woman Suffrage*, 6 vols. (New York: Foster and Wells, 1881–1922). Many thanks to Dr. Capuzza for generously allowing us to include her project in this chapter.

34. One student edited and then published the first complete English translation of the speeches by the Commandancia of the Ejercito Zapatista de Liberacion Nacional. See Margaret-Elliotte Czentnar, ed. and trans., "'Comrades, Light Your Fires': English Translation," *Furman Humanities Review* 20 (2009): 159–85. Another student offered the first complete English translation of a speech by the martyred Salvadoran Jesuit Ignacio Ellacuria. See Tierney Short, ed. and trans., "1982 Commencement Address Delivered at Santa Clara University by Ignacio Ellacuria," *Furman Humanities Review* 18 (2007): 33–41.

35. See Ashley Hannifin, ed., "'Speech to the Control of Atomic Energy Commission,' by Bernard Baruch," *Furman Humanities Review* 15 (2004): 100–113 (a scholarly, critical edition of a speech that existed in only two printed copies, one in the United States and one in Australia, but that is essential to understanding the rhetorical history of the Cold War, antinuclear protest rhetoric, and American diplomacy of the day); and Todd Mayes, ed., "'Speech on the Bombings,' by Stanford Brookshire," *Furman Humanities Review* 16 (2005): 105–9 (a scholarly, critical edition of the Charlotte, North Carolina, mayor's speech after the first major anti–civil rights violence of the sixties, a speech central to understanding the rhetorical history of civil rights rhetoric).

36. We are now attempting to transfer the results of those projects from the Furman domain to Sewanee.

37. A good portion of these larger projects focus on rhetorical history. See, e.g., Stevens, "Future That Could Have Been"; Jordan Allums, "Society of Brotherhood"; Rachel Whitted, "The Sacred and the Profane: An Analysis of the Rhetoric in David Brower's Campaign to Save the Grand Canyon," *Young Scholars in Writing: Undergraduate Research in Writing and Rhetoric* 11 (2014): 73–79; Lindsay Harroff, "Reconciling through Truth: Reconciliation and the Rhetoric of Atonement and Official Apology," *Furman Humanities Review* 23 (2012): 67–89; Christine Hardman, "Building an Empire on Love: Martin Luther King, Jr., the Sit-In Movement, and the Rhetoric of the 'Durham Address,'" *Furman*

Humanities Review 22 (2011): 97–117; Emily Parsons, "Gloria Steinem and the Rhetoric of the Corporate Personality," *Furman Humanities Review* 19 (2008): 85–104; and Ashley Hannifin, "The Quick and the Dead: Bernard Baruch and Cold War Rhetoric," *Furman Humanities Review* 15 (2004): 79–99.

38. Sewanee: The University of the South, The Roberson Project on Slavery, Race, and Reconciliation, accessed September 4, 2020, https://new.sewanee.edu/.

39. Sewanee, Roberson Project, "Learn More."

40. As Augustine notes, "Although I can lift my finger to point something out, I cannot supply the vision by means of which either this gesture or what it indicates can be seen." *On Christian Doctrine*, trans. D. W. Robertson Jr. (Indianapolis, IN: Bobbs-Merrill, 1958), 4.

41. See Edward Schiappa, ed., *Squeeze Play: The Campaign for a New Twins Stadium* (Minneapolis: Minnesota Public Advocacy Research Report, 1998). It is available for download from the Minnesota Legislative Reference Library at https://www.leg.state.mn.us/docs/NonMNpub/oclc40058393.pdf. The study involved ten graduate students plus Professor Schiappa.

42. Sean Patrick O'Rourke, Susan West Heimburger, and Stephanie Kershner, "Argument in Local Controversy: The King Holiday Debate in Greenville County, South Carolina," paper presented to the National Communication Association, Chicago, IL, November 2004 (available from O'Rourke). The study involved eight students plus O'Rourke.

43. By "neo-Confederate monuments," we refer to the Southern Poverty Law Center's excellent description of "a reactionary, revisionist branch of American white nationalism typified by its predilection for symbols of the Confederate States of America, typically paired with a strong belief in the validity of the failed doctrines of nullification and secession—in the specific context of the antebellum South—that rose to prominence in the late 20th and early 21st centuries." See further Southern Poverty Law Center, "Neo-Confederate," accessed September 4, 2020, https://www.splcenter.org/fighting-hate/extremist-files/ideology/neo-confederate. See also Sean Patrick O'Rourke and Melody Lehn, eds., *Rhetoric, Race, Religion, and the Charleston Shootings: Was Blind but Now I See* (Lanham, MD: Lexington Books, 2020), especially chapters 9 and 10 by Camille K. Lewis and Patricia G. Davis, respectively.

Works Cited

Acampora, Angela. "SCUM Manifesto: The Argument for a 'Male Misogyny.'" *Young Scholars in Writing* 9 (2012): 137–44.

Ackerman, Robert. *The Myth and Ritual School: J. G. Frazer and the Cambridge Ritualists*. New York: Routledge, 2002.

Adams, Heather Brook. "Eleanor Roosevelt, 'Address by Mrs. Franklin D. Roosevelt—The Chicago Civil Liberties Committee,' March 14, 1940." *Voices of Democracy: The US Oratory Project* 4 (2009): 60–82. https://voicesofdemocracy.umd.edu.

Afroyim v. Rusk. 387 U.S. 253 (1967). Accessed June 18, 2017. https://www.loc.gov/item/usrep387253/.

Agnew, Lois, Laurie Gries, Zosha Stuckey, Vicki Tolar Burton, Jay Dolmage, Jessica Enoch, Ronald L. Jackson II, LuMing Mao, Arthur E. Walzer, Ralph Cintron, and Victor Vitanza. "Octolog III: The Politics of Historiography in 2010." *Rhetoric Review* 30, no. 2 (2011): 109–54.

Ahıska, Meltem. "Occidentalism: The Historical Fantasy of the Modern." *South Atlantic Quarterly* 102, no. 2–3 (2003): 351–79.

Ahmad, Asam. "Useful Martyrs and Invisible Deaths." *{Young}ist*, January 22, 2015. https://youngist.github.io/clean-blog/useful-martyrs-invisible-deaths#.XcMhW5NKhN0.

Ahmann, Matthew. *Race: Challenge to Religion*. Chicago: Henry Regnery, 1963.

Aitken, Henry E. "With Odds of 100,000 to 1, Will You Take a Chance?" *Saturday Evening Post* 187, no. 43 (1915): 47.

Albenese, Patrizia. "Nationalism and Motherhood." In *Encyclopedia of Motherhood*, edited by Andrea O' Reilly, 893–94. Los Angeles: Sage, 2010.

Albert Sidney Johnston Chapter #2060, United Daughters of the Confederacy v. Ron Nirenberg, et.al. and the City of San Antonio. US District Court, Western District of Texas, Case 5:17-cv-01072-DAE, October 23, 2017. https://www.scribd.com/document/363277016/United-Daughters-of-the-Confederacy-lawsuit-against-the-City-of-San-Antonio.

Aldrich, Mildred. *On the Edge of the War Zone, from the Battle of the Marne to the Entrance of the Stars and Stripes*. Boston: Small, Maynard, 1917.

Aleinikoff, Thomas Alexander. *Semblances of Sovereignty: The Constitution, the State, and American Citizenship*. Cambridge, MA: Harvard University Press, 2009.

Algan, Bülent. "The Brand New Version of Article 301 of Turkish Penal Code and the Future of Freedom of Expression Cases in Turkey." *German Law Journal* 9, no. 12 (2008): 2238–52.

Allums, Jordan. "A Society for Brotherhood: Rhetoric for Resistance." *Young Scholars in Writing* 13 (2016): 125–36.

Altaylı, Fatih. "Kara yazar" (Black writer). *Hürriyet*, February 11, 2005. https://www.hurriyet.com.tr/kara-yazar-295790.

"Always a Citizen." *New York Times*, June 4, 1967, 4.

The American Presidency Project. Documents, News Conferences, 1963. Accessed June 10, 2019. https://www.presidency.ucsb.edu.

Angell, Stephen W. *Bishop Henry McNeal Turner and the African-American Religion in the South.* Knoxville: University of Tennessee Press, 1992.

Annas, George J., and Sherman Elias. "Thalidomide and the *Titanic*: Reconstructing the Technology Tragedies of the Twentieth Century." *American Journal of Public Health* 89, no. 1 (1999): 98–101.

Aoki, Eric, Gregory Dickinson, and Brian L. Ott. "The Master Naturalist Imagined: Directed Movement and Simulations at the Draper Museum of Natural History." In *Places of Public Memory: The Rhetoric of Museums and Memorials*, edited by Gregory Dickinson, Carole Blair, and Brian L. Ott, 238–66. Tuscaloosa: University of Alabama Press, 2010.

Aristotle. *The Basic Works of Aristotle.* Edited by Richard McKeon. New York: Random House, 1941.

Arsu, Sebnem. "Court Drops Charges against Author for 'Insulting' Turkey." *New York Times*, January 23, 2006. https://www.nytimes.com.

"As Germans See Him." *New York Times*, June 30, 1963.

Astour, Michael C. *Hellenosemitica: An Ethnic and Cultural Study in West Semitic Impact on Mycenaean Greece.* Leiden, Netherlands: E. J. Brill, 1967.

Athearn, Robert G. *In Search of Canaan: Black Migration to Kansas, 1879–1880.* Lawrence: Regents Press of Kansas, 1978.

Atkins-Sayre, Wendy, and Ashli Quesinberry Stokes. *City Places, Country Spaces: Rhetorical Explorations of the Rural/Urban Divide.* New York: Peter Lang Publishers, 2019.

Atkinson, Bruce. "The Seven Solas: Toward Reconciling Evangelical and Anglo-Catholic Perspectives." *Virtue Online*, December 31, 2009. https://virtueonline.org/seven-solas-toward-reconciling-evangelical-and-anglo-catholic-perspectives.

Attia, Hagar. "Unit on Theodore Roosevelt, 'Law and Order in Egypt,' Cairo, Egypt, March 28, 1910." Recovering Democracy Archives: Speech Recovery Project. https://recoveringdemocracyarchives.umd.edu.

Augustine. *On Christian Doctrine.* Translated by D. W. Robertson Jr. Indianapolis: Bobbs-Merrill, 1958.

Aytalar, Ardıç. "'Sözlerine öfke'" (His words of rage). *Hürriyet*, February 15, 2005. https://www.hurriyet.com.tr/gundem/sozlerine-ofke-296710.

Bagby, Milton. "Time Capsule." *American History* 33, no. 5 (1998): 74.

Baker, Houston. *Turning South Again: Re-thinking Modernism/Re-reading Booker T.* Durham, NC: Duke University Press, 2001.

Balibar, Etienne. "Ideas of Europe: Civilization and Constitution." *Iris: European Journal of Philosophy & Public Debate* 1, no. 1 (2009): 3–17.

Ball, Moya Ann. "Theoretical Implications of Doing Rhetorical History." In Turner, *Doing Rhetorical History*, 61–71.

Ballif, Michelle. "Introduction." In *Theorizing Histories of Rhetoric*, edited by Michelle Ballif, 1–7. Carbondale: Southern Illinois University Press, 2013.

Balthrop, V. William. "Culture, Myth, and Ideology as Public Argument: An Interpretation of the Ascent and Demise of 'Southern Culture.'" *Communication Monographs* 51, no. 4 (1984): 339–52. https://doi.org/10.1080/03637758409390206.

Balthrop, V. William, Carole Blair, and Neil Michel. "The Presence of the Present: Hijacking 'The Good War'?." *Western Journal of Communication* 74, no. 2 (2010): 170–207.

Banks, William P., Matthew B. Cox, and Caroline Dadas, eds. *Re/Orienting Writing Studies: Queer Methods, Queer Projects.* Logan: Utah State University Press, 2019.

Banning, Marlia E. "When Poststructural Theory and Contemporary Politics Collide—The Vexed Case of Global Warming." *Communication and Critical/Cultural Studies* 6, no. 3 (2009): 285–304.

Banowsky, William, and Wayne C. Eubank. "The Preaching of H. Leo Boles." *Southern Speech Journal* 28, no. 4 (Summer 1963): 318–29.

Barnes, Jonathan. *Early Greek Philosophy.* New York: Penguin Classics, 1987.

———. *The Presocratic Philosophers.* Rev. ed. Boston: Routledge & Kegan Paul, 1982.

Baron, Beth. *Egypt as a Woman: Nationalism, Gender, and Politics.* Berkeley: University of California, 2010.

Barouch, Timothy. "The Judicial Character of Late Liberal Prudence: Paul v. Davis." *Rhetoric & Public Affairs* 21, no. 3 (2018): 417–66.

Barrett, Harold. "A Conference in Rhetorical Criticism." *Speech Teacher* 16 (1967): 134–36.

Barton, David. *Original Intent: The Courts, the Constitution & Religion.* Aledo, TX: WallBuilder Press, 2000.

Barton, Keith C., and Linda S. Levstik. *Teaching History for the Common Good.* New York: Routledge, 2013.

"Basic National Security Policy, NSC 59061." August 5, 1959. Collection, "Presidential Directives on National Security. Part I. From Truman to Clinton," Accession Number PD00583. Digital National Security Archive. ProQuest.

Bates, Beth Tompkins. *Pullman Porters and the Rise of Protest Politics in Black America, 1925–1945.* Chapel Hill: University of North Carolina Press, 2001.

Baugh-Harris, Sara, and Darrel Wanzer-Serrano. "Against Canon: Engaging the Imperative of Race in Rhetoric." *Communication and Critical/Cultural Studies* 15, no. 4 (2018): 337–42.

Baylor Religion Survey. "American Values, Mental Health, and Using Technology in the Age of Trump." September 2017. Waco, TX: Baylor University.

Becker, Carl L. "Everyman His Own Historian." In *The Vital Past: Writings on the Uses of History*, edited by Stephen Vaughn, 20–36. Athens: University of Georgia, 1985.

Bederman, Gail. *Manliness and Civilization: A Cultural History of Gender and Race in the United States, 1880–1917.* Chicago: University of Chicago Press, 1996.

Beer, Francis A., and Robert Hariman. *Post-Realism: The Rhetorical Turn in International Relations.* East Lansing: Michigan State University Press, 1996.

Beetham, Sarah. "From Spray Cans to Minivans: Contesting the Legacy of Confederate Soldier Monuments in the Era of 'Black Lives Matter.'" *Public Art Dialogue* 6, no. 1 (2016): 9–33.

Belge, Murat. "'Love Me, or Leave Me?': The Strange Case of Orhan Pamuk." Open Democracy, October 17, 2005. https://www.opendemocracy.net.

Belknap, Michal R. *The Supreme Court under Earl Warren, 1953–1969.* Columbia: University of South Carolina Press, 2005.

Belton, John. *American Cinema/American Culture.* 4th ed. New York: McGraw-Hill, 2008.

Benjamin, Walter. *Illuminations.* 1st ed. New York: Harcourt, Brace & World, 1968.

Bennington, Geoff, and Robert Young. "Introduction: Posing the Question." In *Post-Structuralism and the Question of History*, edited by Derek Attridge, Geoff Bennington, and Robert Young, 1–11. New York: Cambridge University Press, 1987.

Berbrier, Mitch. "The Victim Ideology of White Supremacists and White Separatists in the United States." *Sociological Focus* 33, no. 2 (2000): 175–91.

Bergstein, Avrohom. "Daniel the Prophet of the Bible, His Life and Accomplishments." Accessed September 18, 2019. https://www.chabad.org.

Bernal, Martin. *Black Athena: The Afroasiatic Roots of Classical Civilization.* New Brunswick, NJ: Rutgers University Press, 1987.

Bey, Marquis. "The Trans*-Ness of Blackness, the Blackness of Trans*-Ness." *TSQ: Transgender Studies Quarterly* 4, no. 2 (2017): 275–95.

Bickel, Alexander M. "Citizenship in the American Constitution Symposium: Pivotal Decisions of the Supreme Court." *Arizona Law Review* 15 (1973): 387.

Biesecker, Barbara. "Of Historicity, Rhetoric: The Archive as Scene of Invention." *Rhetoric & Public Affairs* 9, no. 1 (2006): 124–31.

———. "Remembering World War II: The Rhetoric and Politics of National Commemoration at the Turn of the 21st Century." *Quarterly Journal of Speech* 88, no. 4 (2002): 393–409.

Bilici, Mücahit. "Black Turks, White Turks: On the Three Requirements of Turkish Citizenship." *Insight Turkey* 11, no. 3 (2009): 23–35.

Bilton, Jennifer. "A Response to Aubrey Young." *Young Scholars in Writing: Undergraduate Research in Writing and Rhetoric* 12 (2015): 148–50.

Birdwell, Michael E. "Alvin Cullum York: The Myth, the Man, and the Legacy." *Tennessee Historical Quarterly* 71, no. 4 (2012): 318–39.

————. *Celluloid Soldiers: Warner Bros Campaign against Nazism*. Rev. ed. New York: New York University Press, 2000.

————. "Gobble Like a Turkey: Alvin C. York and American Popular Culture." In *Rural Life and Culture in the Upper Cumberland*, edited by Michael E. Birdwell and W. Calvin Dickinson, 159–77. Lexington: University Press of Kentucky, 2004.

Bishir, Catherine W. "Landmarks of Power: Building a Southern Past, 1885–1915." *Southern Cultures* 1, no. 1 (1993): 5–45.

Bizzell, Patricia. "Rabbi Abraham Joshua Heschel, 'Religion and Race' (14 January 1963)." *Voices of Democracy* 1 (2006): 1–14. https://voicesofdemocracy.umd.edu.

Black, Edwin. *Rhetorical Criticism: A Study in Method*. Madison: University of Wisconsin Press, 1965.

Black, Jason Edward. *American Indians and the Rhetoric of Removal and Allotment*. Jackson: University Press of Mississippi, 2015.

————. "A Clash of Native Space and Institutional Place in Local Choctaw–Upper Creek Memory Site Decolonizing Critiques and Scholar-Activist Interventions." *American Indian Culture and Research Journal* 36, no. 3 (2012): 19–44.

————. "Native Authenticity, Rhetorical Circulation, and Neocolonial Decay: The Case of Chief Seattle's Controversial Speech." *Rhetoric & Public Affairs* 15, no. 4 (Winter 2012): 635–45.

Black, Jason Edward, and Vernon Ray Harrison. "Southern Paternal Generationalism and the Rhetoric of the Drive-By Truckers." *Western Communication Journal* 79, no. 3 (2015): 293–306.

Black, Jason Edward, and Charles E. Morris III, eds. *An Archive of Hope: Harvey Milk's Speeches and Writings*. Berkeley: University of California Press, 2013.

Blackman, Lisa. *Haunted Data: Affect, Transmedia, Weird Science*. London: Bloomsbury, 2019.

Blain, Michael. "The Politics of Victimage: Power and Subjection in a U.S. Anti-Gay Campaign." *Critical Discourse Studies* 2, no. 1 (2005): 31–50.

Blair, Carole. "Contemporary U.S. Memorial Sites as Exemplars of Rhetoric's Materiality." In *Rhetorical Bodies*, edited by Jack Selzer and Sharon Crowley, 16–57. Madison: University of Wisconsin Press, 1999.

————. "Contested Histories of Rhetoric: The Politics of Preservation, Progress, and Change." *Quarterly Journal of Speech* 78, no. 4 (1992): 403–28.

————. "'We Are All Just Prisoners Here of Our Own Device': Rhetoric in Speech Communication after Wingspread." In *Making and Unmaking the Prospects of Rhetoric: Selected Papers from the 1996 Rhetoric Society of America Conference*, edited by Theresa Enos, 29–36. Mahwah, NJ: Lawrence Erlbaum Associates, 1997.

Blair, Carole, V. William Balthrop, and Neil Michel. "Mood of the Material War Memory and Imagining Otherwise." *Cultural Studies↔Critical Methodologies* 13, no. 1 (2013): 6–20.

Blair, Carole, Greg Dickinson, and Brian Ott. "Introduction: Rhetoric/Memory/Place." In *Places of Public Memory: The Rhetoric of Museums and Memorials*, edited by Greg Dickinson, Carole Blair, and Brian L. Ott, 1–35. Tuscaloosa: University of Alabama Press, 2010.

Blair, Carole, and Neil Michel. "Reproducing Civil Rights Tactics: The Rhetorical Performances of the Civil Rights Memorial." *Rhetoric Society Quarterly* 30, no. 2 (2000): 31–55. https://doi.org/10.1080/02773940009391174.

Blight, David W. *Race and Reunion: The Civil War in American Memory*. Cambridge, MA: Harvard University Press, 2001.

Bloch, I. S. *The Future of War in Its Technical, Economic, and Political Relations: Is War Now Impossible?* Translated by R. C. Long. New York: Garland Publishing, 1923.

Bobbitt, David, and Harold Mixon. "Prophecy and Apocalypse in the Rhetoric of Martin Luther King, Jr." *Journal of Communication & Religion* 17, no. 1 (1994): 27–38.

Bokser, Ben Zion, and Baruch M. Bokser, eds. *The Talmud: Selected Writings*. New York: Paulist Press, 1989.

Bone, Martyn. *The Postsouthern Sense of Place in Contemporary Fiction*. Baton Rouge: Louisiana State University Press, 2005.

Bonilla-Silva, Eduardo. *Racism without Racists: Colorblind Racism and the Persistence of Racial Inequality in America*. 5th ed. New York: Rowman & Littlefield, 2018.

Booth, Wayne C. *Modern Dogma and the Rhetoric of Assent*. Chicago: University of Chicago Press, 1974.

Bormann, Ernest G. "Huey Long: Analysis of a Demagogue." *Today's Speech* 2, no. 3 (1953): 16–20.

———. "A Rhetorical Analysis of the National Radio Broadcast of Senator Huey Pierce Long." *Speech Monographs* 24, no. 4 (1957): 244–58.

Bost, David. "Seven Obstacles to Undergraduate Research in the Humanities (and Seven Solutions)." *CUR Newsletter* 13 (1992–93): 35–40.

Bourne, Randolph S. *Untimely Papers*. New York: B. W. Huebsch, 1919.

———. "American Use for German Ideals." In *War and the Intellectuals: Essays by Randolph S. Bourne, 1915–1919*, edited by Carl Resek, 48–52. New York: Harper & Row, 1964.

Bowen, Harry W. "Does Non-Violence Persuade?" *Today's Speech* 11, no. 2 (1963): 10–31. https://doi.org/10.1080/01463376309385325.

Boyd, Gregory A. *The Myth of a Christian Nation: How the Quest for Political Power Is Destroying the Church*. Grand Rapids, MI: Zondervan, 2005.

Boyd, Josh. "Public and Technical Interdependence: Regulatory Controversy, Out-Law Discourse, and the Messy Case of Olestra." *Argumentation & Advocacy* 39, no. 2 (2002): 91–109.

Braden, Waldo W. "C. Alphonso Smith on Southern Oratory before the War." *Southern Speech Journal* 36, no. 2 (Winter 1970): 127–38.

———. "The Emergence of the Concept of Southern Oratory." *Southern Speech Journal* 26, no. 3 (1961): 173–83. https://doi.org/10.1080/10417946109371601.

———. "Myths in Rhetorical Context." In *The Oral Tradition in the South*. Baton Rouge: Louisiana State University Press, 1983. 65–82.

———. *Oratory of the New South*. Baton Rouge: Louisiana State University Press, 1979.

———. "The Rhetoric of a Closed Society." *Southern Speech Communication Journal* 45, no. 4 (Summer 1980): 333–51.

Braden, Waldo, and Ralph T. Eubanks. "Dallas C. Dickey: Pioneer of the Critical Study of Southern Public Address." *Southern Speech Communication Journal* 44, no. 2 (1979): 119–46.

Braden, Waldo W., and Harold D. Mixon. "Epideictic Speaking in the Post–Civil War South and the Southern Experience." *Southern Communication Journal* 54, no. 1 (Fall 1988): 40–57.

Bradley, Adam. *Ralph Ellison in Progress: From* Invisible Man *to* Three Days Before the Shooting. New Haven, CT: Yale University Press, 2010.

Branch, Taylor. *At Canaan's Edge*. New York: Simon & Schuster, 1998.

———. *Pillar of Fire*. New York: Simon & Schuster, 1998.

Branda, Eldon S. "Portrait of a Cowboy as a Young Man." *Southwestern Historical Quarterly* 71, no. 1 (1967): 69–71.

Breed, Allen G. "Women's Group Behind Rebel Memorials Quietly Battles On." *U.S. News & World Report*, August 10, 2018. https://www.usnews.com/news/best-states/virginia/articles/2018-08-10/womens-group-behind-rebel-memorials-quietly-battles-on.

Brewer, Mary F. "Offerings on the Altar of National Pride: Pioneer Plays and American Identity." *Studies in Theatre and Performance* 31, no. 3 (2011): 243–58.

Brigance, W. Norwood. "Whither Research?" *Quarterly Journal of Speech* 19, no. 4 (1933): 552–61.

Brinkley, Joel, and Eric Lightblau. "US Releases Saudi-American It Had Captured in Afghanistan." *New York Times*, October 12, 2004, section A.

Britton, Bianca. "Germany Marks 30 Years Since the Fall of the Berlin Wall." CNN, November 9, 2019. https://www.cnn.com.

Bromwich, Walter T. "Private Walter Bromwich Questions God's Purpose in Time of War." In *Grace under Fire: Letters of Faith in Times of War*, edited by Andrew Carroll, n.p. New York: Doubleday, 2007.

Brown v. Board of Educ., 347 U.S. 483 (1954).

Brown, Gillian. *The Consent of the Governed: The Lockean Legacy in Early American Culture*. Cambridge, MA: Harvard University Press, 2001.

Browne, Nick. "The Spectator-in-the-Text: The Rhetoric of *Stagecoach*." In *Film Theory and Criticism: Introductory Readings*, 7th ed., edited by Leo Braudy and Marshall Cohen, 125–40. New York: Oxford University Press, 2009.

Brueggemann, Walter, and Patrick D. Miller. *Old Testament Theology: Essays on Structure, Theme, and Text*. Minneapolis, MN: Fortress Press, 1992.

Brundage, W. Fitzhugh. "'Woman's Hand and Heart and Deathless Love': White Women and the Commemorative Impulse in the New South." In *Monuments to the Lost Cause: Women, Art, and the Landscapes of Southern Memory*, edited by Cynthia Mills and Pamela H. Simpson, 64–85. Knoxville: University of Tennessee Press, 2019.

Bruner, Michael S. "Symbolic Uses of the Berlin Wall, 1961–1989." *Communication Quarterly* 37, no. 4 (Fall 1989): 319–28.

Brynner, Rock, and Trent Stephens. *Dark Remedy: The Impact of Thalidomide and Its Revival as a Vital Medicine*. Cambridge, MA: Perseus Publishing, 2001.

Brzezinski, Zbigniew, and Brent Scowcroft. *America and the World: Conversations on the Future of American Foreign Policy*. New York: Basic Books, 2008.

Buchanan, Bruce. "Constrained Diversity: The Organizational Demands of the Presidency." *Presidential Studies Quarterly* 20, no. 4 (Fall 1990): 791–822.

Burdick, Anne, Johanna Drucker, Peter Lunenfeld, Todd Presner, and Jeffrey Schnapp. "Digital Humanities Fundamentals." In *Digital Humanities*, edited by Anne Burdick, Johanna Drucker, Peter Lunenfeld, Todd Presner, and Jeffrey Schnapp, 122–24. Cambridge, MA: Massachusetts Institute of Technology Press, 2016.

Burke, Kenneth. *A Grammar of Motives*. Berkeley: University of California Press, 1969.

———. *Language as Symbolic Action: Essays in Life, Literature, and Method*. Berkeley: University of California Press, 1966.

———. *The Philosophy of Literary Form: Studies in Symbolic Action*. 3rd ed. Berkeley: University of California Press, 1973.

———. *A Rhetoric of Motives*. Berkeley: University of California Press, 1969.

Burke, Peter. *Eyewitnessing: The Uses of Images as Historical Evidence*. Ithaca, NY: Cornell University Press, 2008.

Burkert, Walter. *The Orientalizing Revolution: Near Eastern Influence on Greek Culture in the Early Archaic Age*. Cambridge, MA: Harvard University Press, 1992.

Burton, Suzanne. "A Response to Ashley K. Allen." *Young Scholars in Writing: Undergraduate Research in Writing and Rhetoric* 12 (2015): 153–54.

Butler, Judith. *Frames of War: When Is Life Grievable?* New York: Verso, 2010.

———. *Undoing Gender*. New York: Routledge, 2004.

Byron, Paul. "'How Could You Write Your Name Below That?' The Queer Life and Death of Tumblr." *Porn Studies* 6, no. 3 (2019): 336–49.

Calafell, Bernadette Marie. "Disrupting the Dichotomy: 'Yo Soy Chicana/o?' in the New Latina/o South." *Communication Review* 7, no. 2 (2004): 175–204. https://doi.org/10.1080/10714420490448705.

———. *Monstrosity, Performance, and Race in Contemporary Culture*. New York: Peter Lang, 2015.

Calloway-Thomas, Carolyn, and John Louis Lucaites, eds. *Martin Luther King Jr. and the Sermonic Power of Public Discourse.* Tuscaloosa: University of Alabama Press, 1993.

Camp, Sherrita. *African American Topeka.* Charleston, SC: Arcadia Publishing, 2013.

Campbell, J. Louis, III. "In Search of the New South." *Southern Speech Communication Journal* 47, no. 4 (Summer 1982): 361–88.

Campbell, James M. "African Americans in Southern Cities." In *Reconstruction: People and Perspectives,* edited by James M. Campbell and Rebecca J. Fraser, 45–66. Santa Barbara, CA: ABC-CLIO, 2008.

Campbell, John Angus. "Special Issue on Rhetorical Criticism." *Western Journal of Communication* 54, no. 3 (1990): 249–376.

Campbell, Karlyn Kohrs. "'Conventional Wisdom'—'Traditional' Form: A Rejoinder." *Quarterly Journal of Speech* 58, no. 4 (1972): 451–54.

———. *Key Texts of the Early Feminists.* Vol. 2 of *Man Cannot Speak for Her.* Westport, CT: Praeger Press, 1989.

———. "The Rhetoric of Women's Liberation: An Oxymoron." *Quarterly Journal of Speech* 59, no. 1 (1973): 74–86.

———. "Rhetorical Criticism 2009: A Study in Method." In Parry-Giles and Hogan, *Handbook of Rhetoric and Public Address,* 86–107.

Campbell, Karlyn Kohrs, and Kathleen Hall Jamieson. *Presidents Creating the Presidency: Deeds Done in Words.* Chicago: University of Chicago Press, 2008.

Campbell, Peter Odell. "The Procedural Queer: Substantive Due Process, *Lawrence v. Texas,* and Queer Rhetorical Futures." *Quarterly Journal of Speech* 98, no. 2 (May 2012): 203–29.

Capozzola, Christopher Joseph Nicodemus. *Uncle Sam Wants You: World War I and the Making of the Modern American Citizen.* New York: Oxford University Press, 2008.

Carnegie, Andrew. "How I Made My First $1,000." *Saturday Evening Post,* February 11, 1899, 527.

Carpenter, Ronald H. "Frederick Jackson Turner and the Rhetorical Impact of the Frontier Thesis." *Quarterly Journal of Speech* 63, no. 2 (1977): 117–29.

———. "On American History Textbooks and Integration in the South: Woodrow Wilson and the Rhetoric of Division and Reunion, 1829–1889." *Southern Speech Communication Journal* 51, no. 1 (Fall 1985): 1–23.

Carr, Robert. *Black Nationalism in the New World: Reading the African-American and West Indian Experience.* Durham, NC: Duke University Press, 2002.

Carson, David L. "Ralph Ellison: Twenty Years After." In *Conversations with Ralph Ellison,* edited by Maryemma Graham and Amritjit Singh, 192–214. Jackson, MS: University Press of Mississippi, 1995.

Cary, Noel D. "Kennedy in Berlin." *Central European History* 42, no. 1 (March 2009): 188–91.

Casey, Michael W. "From Pacifism to Patriotism: The Emergence of Civil Religion in the Churches of Christ during World War I." *Mennonite Quarterly Review* 66, no. 3 (1992): 367–80.

Cathcart, Robert S. "Movements: Confrontation as Rhetorical Form." *Southern Speech Communication Journal* 43, no. 3 (1978): 233–47.

Ceccarelli, Leah. "Controversy over Uncertainty: Argumentation Scholarship and Public Debate about Science." *ISSA Proceedings* (2010): np.

———. "Manufactured Scientific Controversy: Science, Rhetoric, and Public Debate." *Rhetoric & Public Affairs* 14, no. 2 (2011): 195–228.

Chakrabarty, Dipesh. *Provincializing Europe: Postcolonial Thought and Historical Difference*. Princeton, NJ: Princeton University Press, 2008.

Charland, Maurice. "Constitutive Rhetoric: The Case of the *Peuple Québécois*." *Quarterly Journal of Speech* 73, no. 2 (1987): 133–50.

Chávez, Karma R. "Beyond Inclusion: Rethinking Rhetoric's Historical Narrative." *Quarterly Journal of Speech* 101, no. 1 (2015): 162–72.

Cheney, Lynne V. "The End of History." *Historian* 57, no. 2 (1995): 454–56.

———. "The End of History, Part II." *Wall Street Jounal*, April 1, 2015. http://www.wsj.com/articles/lynne-cheney-the-end-of-history-part-ii-1427929675.

Chesebrough, David B. *Frederick Douglass: Oratory from Slavery*. Westport, CT: Greenwood Press, 1998.

Chestnut, Trichita M. "'. . . There Is No East, No West . . .' Dr. Martin Luther King, Jr. Visits Cold War Berlin." October 7, 2014. https://rediscovering-black-history.blogs.archives.gov.

Christie, Luke D. "'America! America!': Vanishing Time and Space in Clarence Jordan's 'Things Needed for Our Peace.'" *Young Scholars in Writing* 13 (2016): 20–31.

———. "A Response to Ashley K. Allen." *Young Scholars in Writing: Undergraduate Research in Writing and Rhetoric* 12 (2015): 151–52.

Christophersen, Merrill G. "The Charleston Conversationalists." *Southern Speech Journal* 20, no. 1 (1954): 99–108.

Church, Michael. "Benjamin Singleton's Scrapbook." *Kansas Memory* (blog). March 20, 2009. https://www.kansasmemory.org/blog/post/63836394.

Cicero. *De Natura Deorum Libri Tres*. Edited by Joseph B. Mayor and J. H. Swainson. Cambridge: Cambridge University Press, 2010.

Clark, E. Culpepper. "Francis Warrington Dawson: The New South Revisited." *American Journalism* 3, no. 1 (1986): 5–23.

Clark, E. Culpepper, and Raymie E. McKerrow. "The Rhetorical Construction of History." In Turner, *Doing Rhetorical History*, 33–46.

Clarke, Alan. "Habeas Corpus: The Historical Debate." *New York Law School Journal of Human Rights* 14 (1998): 375–434.

Clary-Lemon, Jennifer. "Archival Research Processes: A Case for Material Methods." *Rhetoric Review* 33, no. 4 (2014): 381–402.

Cohen, David B., and George A. Krause. "Presidents, Chiefs of Staff, and White

House Organizational Behavior: Survey Evidence from the Reagan and Bush Administrations." *Presidential Studies Quarterly* 30, no 3 (September 2000): 421–42.

Cohen, David B., and Charles E. Walcott. "The Office of the Chief of Staff." White House Transition Project. Rice University's Baker Institute for Public Policy, 2017. http://whitehousetransitionproject.org.

Cohn, Jan. *Creating America: George Horace Lorimer and the "Saturday Evening Post."* Pittsburgh, PA: University of Pittsburgh Press, 1989.

Cole, Bruce. "Our American Amnesia." *Wall Street Journal,* June 11, 2002. https://www.wsj.com/articles/SB102375410062692040.

Cole, Jean Lee, ed. *Freedom's Witness: The Civil War Correspondence of Henry McNeal Turner.* Morgantown: West Virginia University Press, 2013.

Compton, John, and Brian Kaylor. "Inoculating for Small Pox: Inoculation Objections in Reverend Cooper's *Letter to a Friend in the Country.*" *Journal of Communication and Religion* 36, no. 1 (2013): 92–107.

Condit, Celeste M., John Lynch, and Emily Winderman. "Recent Rhetorical Studies in Public Understanding of Science: Multiple Purposes and Strengths." *Public Understanding of Science* 21, no. 4 (2012): 386–400.

Conference on College Composition and Communication. "CCCC Position Statement on Undergraduate Research in Writing: Principles and Best Practices." CCCC Position Statements, Professional Issues. March 2017. https://cccc.ncte.org.

———. "Committee on Undergraduate Research." Governance and Resolutions, Committees. Updated March 2018. https://cccc.ncte.org.

Confino, Alon. "Collective Memory and Cultural History: Problems of Method." *American Historical Review* 102, no. 5 (1997): 1386–1403.

Constable, Marianne. *Our Word Is Our Bond: How Legal Speech Acts.* Stanford, CA: Stanford University Press, 2014.

Cooper, Julia. "A Response to Michaela Cullington." *Young Scholars in Writing: Undergraduate Research in Writing and Rhetoric* 11 (2014): 91–93.

Cornford, Francis Macdonald. *From Religion to Philosophy: A Study in the Origins of Western Speculation.* New York: Harper, 1957.

Cornwell, Susan, and Imani Moise. "As Migrants Languish in Border Facilities, U.S. Congress Struggles to Finalize Military Aid." *Reuters,* June 26, 2019. https://www.reuters.com.

Corrigan, Lisa M. "Decolonizing Philosophy and Rhetoric: Dispatches from the Undercommons." *Philosophy and Rhetoric* 52, no. 2 (2019): 163–88.

Costello, Maureen. "Meet Mike Hucksterbee." HuffPost, May 14, 2011. https://www.huffpost.com/entry/meet-mike-hucksterbee_b_861905.

Costigliola, Frank. "The Pursuit of Atlantic Community: Nuclear Arms, Dollars, and Berlin." In *Kennedy's Quest for Victory: American Foreign Policy, 1961–1963,* edited by Thomas G. Paterson, 24–56. New York: Oxford University Press, 1989.

Cover, Robert. *Narrative, Violence, and the Law: The Essays of Robert Cover.* Edited by

Martha Minow, Michael Ryan, and Austin Sarat. Ann Arbor: University of Michigan Press, 1995.

Cox, Karen L. *Dixie's Daughters: The United Daughters of the Confederacy and the Preservation of Confederate Culture*. Gainesville: University Press of Florida, 2003.

Crable, Bryan. "From Sacrifice to Sacraments: Ralph Ellison's Appropriation of Jane Ellen Harrison's *Themis*." In *Global Ralph Ellison: Transnational Aesthetics and Politics*, edited by Tessa Roynon and Marc C. Conner, np. Oxford: Peter Lang Press, 2021.

———. *Ralph Ellison and Kenneth Burke: At the Roots of the Racial Divide*. Charlottesville: University of Virginia Press, 2012.

———. *White Sacraments: Race, Rhetoric, Blackness*. Columbus: Ohio State University Press, forthcoming.

———. "'Who Invents Rituals?': Ralph Ellison Reads Lord Raglan." *Literature of the Americas* 5 (2018): 27–42. https://doi.org/10.22455/2541–7894–2018–5-27 –42.

Craig, Campbell. "Kennedy's International Legacy, Fifty Years On." *International Affairs* 89, no. 6 (November 2013): 1367–78.

Cram, E. "Archival Ambience and Sensory Memory: Generating Queer Intimacies in the Settler Colonial Archive." *Communication and Critical/Cultural Studies* 13, no. 2 (2016): 109–29.

Crane, Gregory R., ed. Perseus Digital Library. Tufts University. Accessed April 17, 2012. http://www.perseus.tufts.edu.

Crick, Nathan, and Joseph Gabriel. "The Conduit between Lifeworld and System: Habermas and the Rhetoric of Public Scientific Controversies." *Rhetoric Society Quarterly* 40, no. 3 (2010): 201–23.

Cromwell, John W. "The First Negro Churches in the District of Columbia." *Journal of Negro History* 7, no 1 (1922): 64–106.

Crowley, Sharon. "Afterword: A Reminiscence." In *Theorizing Histories of Rhetoric*, edited by Michelle Ballif, 190–98. Carbondale: Southern Illinois University Press, 2013.

Cummings, Melbourne. "Review: Problems of Researching Black Rhetoric." *Journal of Black Studies* 2, no. 4 (1972): 503–10.

Czentnar, Margaret-Elliotte, ed. and trans. "'Comrades, Light Your Fires': English Translation." *Furman Humanities Review* 20 (2009): 159–85.

Daemmrich, Arthur. "A Tale of Two Experts: Thalidomide and Political Engagement in the United States and West Germany." *Social History of Medicine* 15, no. 1 (2002): 137–58.

Darsey, James. *The Prophetic Tradition and Radical Rhetoric in America*. New York: New York University Press, 1997.

Davis, Fred. "Nostalgia, Identity and the Current Nostalgia Wave." *Journal of Popular Culture* 11, no. 2 (1977): 414–24.

Davis, Patricia G. *Laying Claim: African American Cultural Memory and Southern Identity*. Tuscaloosa: University of Alabama Press, 2016.

———. "The Other Southern Belles: Civil War Reenactment, African American Women, and the Performance of Idealized Femininity." *Text & Performance Quarterly* 32, no. 4 (October 2012): 308–31. https://doi.org/10.1080/10462937.2012.707783.

Davis, R. E. "Billy Sunday: Preacher-Showman." *Southern Speech Journal* 32 (Winter 1966): 83–97.

Davis, Stephen. "Empty Eyes, Marble Hand." *Journal of Popular Culture* 20, no. 1 (1982): 2–21.

DeGooyer, Stephanie, Alastair Hunt, Lida Maxwell, and Samuel Moyn. *The Right to Have Rights.* New York: Verso, 2018.

Deibel, Terry L. "Grand Strategy Lessons for the Bush Administration." *Washington Quarterly* 12, no. 3 (1989): 127–38.

de Jong, Matthijs J. *Isaiah among the Ancient Near Eastern Prophets: A Comparative Study of the Earliest Stages of the Isaiah Tradition and the Neo-Assyrian Prophecies.* Boston: Brill, 2007.

Delany, Martin Robison. *The Condition, Elevation, Emigration, and Destiny of the Colored People of the United States: Politically Considered.* Philadelphia, PA: self-published, 1852. Accessed June 20, 2019. https://archive.org/details/conditionelevati00dela_0.

Delany, Samuel R. *Times Square Red, Times Square Blue.* New York: New York University Press, 1999.

Delgado, Richard, and Jean Stefancic. *Critical Race Theory.* New York: New York University Press, 2017.

Delk, Jordan. "A Response to Mark Ulrich." *Young Scholars in Writing: Undergraduate Research in Writing and Rhetoric* 10 (2013): 126–28.

de Man, Paul. *The Rhetoric of Romanticism.* New York: Columbia University Press, 1984.

Dennison, Nillin. "14-Year-Old Emmett Castle is 19th Reported Trans Death by Suicide This Year." Planet Transgender, October 9, 2015. https://planettransgender.com.

Derrida, Jacques. *Specters of Marx: The State of the Debt, the Work of Mourning, and the New International.* Translated by Peggy Kamuf. New York: Routledge, 1994.

de Saint Felix, Skye. "Unit on Marie Watson, 'A Voice from the Eastern Shore,' Hyattsville, MD, November 5, 1945." Recovering Democracy Archives: Speech Recovery Project. https://recoveringdemocracyarchives.umd.edu.

Des Champs, Margaret Burr. "Benjamin Morgan Palmer, Orator-Preacher of the Confederacy." *Southern Speech Journal* 19, no. 1 (1953): 14–22.

"The Destiny of the Colored Race, as Depicted by One of Themselves." *Evening Star* (Washington, DC), January 15, 1863. Chronicling America: Historic American Newspapers, Library of Congress. http://chroniclingamerica.loc.gov/lccn/sn83045462/1863–01–15/ed-1/seq-1/.

deTar, Matthew. "A Confluence of Margins." *Departures in Critical Qualitative Research* 8, no. 2 (2019): 1–7.

———. *Figures That Speak: The Vocabulary of Turkish Nationalism*. Syracuse, NY: Syracuse University Press, 2021.

Deutsche Welle (DW). "Remembering Martin Luther King's Visit to Berlin." November 9, 2014. https://www.dw.com/en/remembering-martin-luther-kings-visit-to-berlin/a-17907455.

Devega, Chauncey. "Toxic White Masculinity: The Killer That Haunts American Life." Salon, February 15, 2018. https://www.salon.com/2018/02/15/toxic-white-masculinity-the-killer-that-haunts-american-life/.

De Velasco, Antonio. "'I'm a Southerner, Too': Black Southern Counterpublics and Confederate Monuments in Memphis, Tennessee." *Southern Communication Journal* 84, no. 4 (2019): 233–45.

Dickey, Dallas. "Southern Oratory: A Field for Research." *Quarterly Journal of Speech* 33, no. 4 (1947): 458–63.

———. "Were They Ephemeral and Florid?" *Quarterly Journal of Speech* 32, no.1 (1946): 16–20.

———. "What Direction Should Future Research in Public Address Take?" *Quarterly Journal of Speech* 29, no. 3 (1943): 300–304.

Dickinson, Gregory, Brian. L. Ott, and Eric Aoki, "Memory and Myth at the Buffalo Bill Museum." *Western Journal of Communication* 69, no. 2 (2005): 85–108.

Diels, Hermann, and Walther Kranz. *Die Fragmente der Vorsokratiker, Griechisch und Deutsch, Erbesserte Auflage*. Berlin: Weidmann, 1951.

Dorf, Michael. "Who Decides Whether Yaser Hamdi, or Any Other Citizen, Is an Enemy Combatant?" Findlaw, August 21, 2002. https://supreme.findlaw.com.

Dorgan, Howard. "The Doctrine of Victorious Defeat in the Rhetoric of Confederate Veterans." *Southern Speech Communication Journal* 38, no. 2 (1972): 119–30.

———. "'Ol' Time Way' Exhortation: Preaching in the Old Regular Baptist Church." *Journal of Communication & Religion* 10, no. 2 (September 1987): 24–30.

Dorsey, Leroy G. *We Are All Americans, Pure and Simple: Theodore Roosevelt and the Myth of Americanism*. Tuscaloosa: University of Alabama Press, 2007.

Douglas, John. "John Henry: 'Take This Hammer, It Won't Kill You.'" *Southern Cultures* 10, no. 2 (2004): 73–86.

Douglass, Frederick. "Address of the Colored National Convention to the People of the United States." *Proceedings of the Colored National Convention*. Rochester: New York, July 6, 1853, 11.

———. "Fred. Douglass on Whites and Blacks: His Opposition to Colored Exodus from the South." *Baltimore Sun*, May 5, 1879, 1.

———. *The Frederick Douglass Papers, Series One: Speeches, Debates, and Interviews*. Vol. 4, 1864–1880. Edited by John W. Blassingame and John R. McKivigan. New Haven, CT: Yale University Press, 1991.

———. "The Southern Exodus." *Baltimore American*, May 5, 1879, 1.

———. "Southern Questions: The Negro Exodus from the Gulf States." American Social Science Association, Saratoga Springs, NY, September 12, 1879. *Journal of Social Science* 11 (May 1880): 1–21.

Dow, David R. "Opinion: Yaser Hamdi, US Citizen." *New York Times*, October 15, 2004. https://www.nytimes.com/2004/10/15/opinion/yaser-hamdi-us-citizen-312622.html#story-continues-1.

Downey, Matthew T. "Pictures as Teaching Aids: Using the Pictures in History Textbooks." *Social Education* 44, no. 2 (January 1980): 93–100.

Doxtader, Erik. "Making Rhetorical History in a Time of Transition: The Occasion, Constitution, and Representation of South African Reconciliation." *Rhetoric & Public Affairs* 4, no. 2 (2001): 223–60.

Drake, Jeanette L., Yekaterina Y. Kontar, John C. Eichelberger, Scott T. Rupp, and Karen M. Taylor, eds. *Communicating Climate-Change and Natural Hazard Risk and Cultivating Resilience: Case Studies for a Multi-Disciplinary Approach.* New York: Springer Press, 2015.

Drechsel, Benjamin. "The Berlin Wall from Visual Perspective: Comments on the Construction of a Political Media Icon." *Visual Communication* 9, no. 1 (2010): 3–24.

Du Bois, W. E. B. *The Souls of Black Folk.* Edited by Henry Louis Gates Jr. New York: Oxford University Press, 2007.

Earhart, Amy E. "The Digital Humanities as a Laboratory." In *Humanities and the Digital*, edited by David Theo Goldberg and Patrik Svensson, 391–400. Boston: Massachusetts Institute of Technology Press, 2015.

Edgar, Amanda Nell, and Andre E. Johnson. *The Struggle over Black Lives Matter and All Lives Matter.* Lanham, MD: Lexington Books, 2018.

EDSITEment! The Best of the Humanities on the Web. Accessed June 28, 2019. https://edsitement.neh.gov/.

Eichrodt, Walther. "Is Typology Exegesis an Appropriate Method?" Translated by James Barr. In *Essays on Old Testament Hermeneutics*, edited by Claus Westermann, 224–45. New York: John Knox, 1979.

Ellison, Ralph. *The Collected Essays of Ralph Ellison.* Edited by John F. Callahan. New York: Modern Library, 1995.

———. *Invisible Man.* New York: Vintage Books, 1980.

———. Papers. Manuscript Division, Library of Congress, Washington, DC.

Engelberg, Jacob, and Gary Needham. "Purging the Queer Archive: Tumblr's Counterhegemonic Pornographies." *Porn Studies* 6, no. 3 (2019): 350–54.

Engels, Jeremy. "The Politics of Resentment and the Tyranny of the Minority: Rethinking Victimage for Resentful Times." *Rhetoric Society Quarterly* 40, no. 4 (2010): 303–25.

Enholm, Donald K., David Curtis Skaggs, and W. Jeffrey Welsh. "Origins of the Southern Mind: The Parochial Sermons of Thomas Cradock of Maryland, 1744–1770." *Quarterly Journal of Speech* 73, no. 2 (May 1987): 200–218. https://doi.org/10.1080/00335638709383803.

Enoch, Jessica. "Releasing Hold: Feminist Historiography without the Tradition."

In *Theorizing Histories of Rhetoric*, edited by Michelle Ballif, 58–73. Carbondale: Southern Illinois University Press, 2013.

Enoch, Jessica, and David Gold. "Introduction: Seizing the Methodological Moment: The Digital Humanities and Historiography in Rhetoric and Composition." *College English* 76, no. 2 (2013): 105–14.

Enoch, Jessica, and Pamela Van Haitsma. "Archival Literacy: Reading the Rhetoric of Digital Archives in the Undergraduate Classroom." *College Composition and Communication* 67 (2015): 216–42.

Erel, İsmail. "'Kimse söylemiyor, bari ben söyleyeyim'" (Nobody says it, at least I say it). *Hürriyet*, February 9, 2005. http://webarsiv.hurriyet.com.tr/2005/02/09/596844.asp.

"'Ermeniler kahraman ilan etti'" (Armenians declare a hero). *Hürriyet*, February 27, 2005.

Ettlich, Earl E. "Symposium: Western Oratory." *Western Speech* 32, no. 1 (1968): 2–4.

Eubank, Wayne C. "Palmer's Century Sermon, New Orleans, January 1, 1901." *Southern Speech Journal* 35, no. 1 (Fall 1969): 28–39.

Eyman, Douglas. *Digital Rhetoric: Theory, Method, and Practice*. Ann Arbor: University of Michigan Press, 2015.

Fahnestock, Jeanne. *Rhetorical Figures in Science*. New York: Oxford University Press, 1999.

Fay, Isabel, and Jim Kuypers. "Transcending Mysticism and Building Identification through Empowerment of the Rhetorical Agent: John F. Kennedy's Berlin Speeches on June 26, 1963." *Southern Communication Journal* 77, no. 3 (May 2012): 198–215.

Fea, John. *Was America Founded as a Christian Nation? A Historical Introduction*. Louisville, KY: Westminster John Knox Press, 2011.

Finnegan, Cara A. "Doing Rhetorical History of the Visual: The Photograph and the Archive." In *Defining Visual Rhetorics*, edited by Charles A. Hill and Marguerite Helmers, 120–45. Mahwah, NJ: Lawrence Erlbaum Associates, 2004.

———. "What Is This a Picture Of? Some Thoughts on Images and Archives." *Rhetoric & Public Affairs* 9, no. 1 (2006): 116–23.

Flaherty, Colleen. "Difficult Conversations." *Inside Higher Education*, September 26, 2019. https://www.insidehighered.com/news/2019/09/26/national-communication-association-suspends-discussion-listserv.

Flores, Lisa A. "Between Abundance and Marginalization: The Imperative of Racial Rhetorical Criticism." *Review of Communication* 16, no. 1 (2016): 4–24.

———. "Towards an Insistent and Transformative Rhetorical Criticism." *Communication and Critical/Cultural Studies* 15, no. 4 (2018): 349–57.

Flynt, Wayne. "The Ethics of Democratic Persuasion and the Birmingham Crisis." *Southern Speech Journal* 35, no.1 (1969): 40–53.

Foley, Barbara. *Wrestling with the Left: The Making of Ralph Ellison's* Invisible Man. Durham, NC: Duke University Press, 2010.

Fontenrose, Joseph E. *The Ritual Theory of Myth*. Berkeley: University of California Press, 1966.

"Forum: The Politics of Archival Research." *Rhetoric & Public Affairs* 9, no. 1 (Spring 2006): 113–52.

Foster, Gaines. *Ghosts of the Confederacy: Defeat, the Lost Cause, and the Emergence of the New South, 1865–1913*. New York: Oxford University Press, 1987.

Foucault, Michel. *The Archaeology of Knowledge and the Discourse on Language*. Translated by A. M. Sheridan Smith. New York: Harper Colophon, 1976.

Fowler, Randall. "Unit on Paul Robeson, 'Forge Negro-Labor and Unity for Peace,' Chicago, IL, June 10, 1950." Recovering Democracy Archives: Speech Recovery Project. https://recoveringdemocracyarchives.umd.edu.

Frankfurter, Felix. Papers. Library of Congress, Washington, DC, Manuscript/Mixed Material. https://lccn.loc.gov/mm73047571.

Freely, Maureen. "Why They Killed Hrant Dink." *Index on Censorship* 36, no. 2 (2007): 15–29.

Freeman, Kathleen, and Hermann Diels. *Ancilla to the Pre-Socratic Philosophers: A Complete Translation of the Fragments in Diels, Fragmente Der Vorsokratiker*. Cambridge, MA: Harvard University Press, 1971.

———. *The Pre-Socratic Philosophers: A Companion to Diels, Fragmente Der Vorsokratiker*. 2nd ed. Oxford, UK: B. Blackwell, 1949.

Freeman, Tzvi. "What Is Emunah?" Accessed March 18, 2018. https://www.chabad.org.

Fritz, Charles A. "A Brief Review of the Chief Periods in the History of Oratory." *Quarterly Journal of Speech* 8, no. 1 (1922): 26–48. https://doi.org/10.1080/00335632209379363.

Frye, Northrop. *The Great Code: The Bible and Literature*. New York: Harcourt Brace Jovanovich, 1982.

Furman University. *Furman Catalogue 2007–2008*. http://www2.furman.edu/sites/hr/documents/2007–2008_catalog.pdf.

Fussell, Paul. *The Great War and Modern Memory*. New York: Oxford University Press, 2013.

Gadamer, Hans-Georg. *Truth and Method*. 2nd rev. ed. Translated by Joel Weinsheimer and Donald G. Marshall. New York: Continuum, 2003.

Gaddis, John Lewis. *Strategies of Containment: A Critical Appraisal of American National Security Policy during the Cold War*. New York: Oxford University Press, 2005.

Gaines, Kevin K. *Uplifting the Race: Black Leadership, Politics, and Culture in the Twentieth Century*. Durham: University of North Carolina Press, 1996.

Gaines, Robert N. "The Processes and Challenges of Textual Authentication." In Parry-Giles and Hogan, *Handbook of Rhetoric and Public Address*, 133–56

Gallagher, Victoria. "Reconciliation and Amnesia in the Birmingham Civil Rights Institute." *Rhetoric & Public Affairs* 2, no. 2 (1999): 303–20.

Galuszka, Peter. "The Women Who Erected Confederate Statues Are Stunningly Silent." *Washington Post*, October 13, 2017. https://www.washingtonpost.com.

Germana, Michael. *Ralph Ellison, Temporal Technologist*. New York: Oxford University Press, 2018.

(German) Federal Government. "Remembrance, Commemoration, Celebrations." November 9, 2019. https://www.bundesregierung.de/breg-en/news/30-jahre-mauerfall-1690550.

German Way and More. "Martin Luther King Jr. in Berlin." Notable People. Accessed June 20, 2019. https://www.german-way.com.

———. "MLK: 1964 Berlin Locations Tour." Accessed June 20, 2019. https://www.german-way.com/notable-people/featured-bios/martin-luther-king-jr-in-berlin/mlk-1964-berlin-locations-photo-tour/.

Ghaziani, Amin, and Matt Brim, eds. *Imagining Queer Methods*. New York: New York University Press, 2019.

Gieryn, Thomas F. *Cultural Boundaries of Science: Credibility on the Line*. Chicago: University of Chicago Press, 1999.

Glauberman, Scott P., and Peter Barton Hutt. "The Real Thalidomide Baby: The Evolution of the FDA in the Shadow of Thalidomide, 1960–1997." *Food and Drug Law* (1997): np.

Glaude, Eddie S., Jr. *Exodus! Religion, Race, and Nation in Early Nineteenth-Century Black America*. Chicago: University of Chicago Press, 2000.

Glenn, Cheryl, and Jessica Enoch. "Drama in the Archives: Rereading Methods, Rewriting History." *College Composition and Communication* 61, no. 2 (2009): 321–42.

Godbee, Beth, Katie Ellington, and Megan Knowles. "Why Inquiry Matters: An Argument and Model for Inquiry-Based Writing Courses." *Wisconsin English Journal* 58 (2016): 7–21.

Godfrey, Elaine, and Adam Harris. "The 10 Presidential Candidates Who Support Busing." *Atlantic*, July 10, 2019. https://www.theatlantic.com.

"Going Down." Topeka (Kansas) *Colored Citizen*, May 10, 1879.

"Going Public: Humanities Beyond the Classroom." MLA: Action Network, September 25, 2018. https://action.mla.org.

Goldberg, David Theo. "Liberalism's Limits: Carlyle and Mill on 'The Negro Question.'" In *Philosophers on Race: Critical Essays*, edited by Julie K. Ward and Tommy L. Lott, 145–66. Malden, MA: Blackwell Publishers, 2002.

Golden, James. "A Southern Unionist Speaks in the North on the Eve of the Civil War." *Southern Speech Journal* 20, no. 1 (1954): 28–36.

Goldhill, Simon, and Robin Osborne, eds. *Rethinking Revolutions through Ancient Greece*. Cambridge: Cambridge University Press, 2006.

Goldstein, Dana, and Anemona Hartocollis. "'Separatist Programs for Separate Communities': California School District Agrees to Desegregate." *New York Times*, August 9, 2019. https://www.nytimes.com/2019/08/09/us/sausalito-school-segregation.html.

Gombrich, E. H. *Art and Illusion: A Study in the Psychology of Pictorial Representation*. A. W. Mellon Lectures in the Fine Arts. Washington, D.C.: National Gallery of Art, 1956.

Goodman, Paul. *Of One Blood: Abolitionism and the Origins of Racial Equality.* Berkeley: University of California Press, 1998.

Good News Bible: Catholic Study Edition. New York: Sadlier, 1979.

Gordon, Avery. *Ghostly Matters: Haunting and the Sociological Imagination.* Minneapolis: University of Minnesota Press, 2008.

Gordon, Cyrus H. *Before the Bible: The Common Background of Greek and Hebrew Civilizations.* New York: Harper & Row, 1962.

———. *Homer and Bible: The Origin and Character of East Mediterranean Literature.* Ventnor, NJ: Ventnor Publishers, 1967.

Gordon, Dexter B. *Black Identity: Rhetoric, Ideology, and Nineteenth-Century Black Nationalism.* Carbondale: Southern Illinois University Press, 2003.

Gordon, Robert W. *Taming the Past: Essays on Law in History and History in Law.* New York: Cambridge University Press, 2017.

Grade, Rebecca Drake. "Origin of the Lost Cause Argument: Analysis of Civil War Letters." *Southern Speech Communication Journal* 49, no. 4 (Summer 1984): 420–30.

Graham, Daniel W., ed. *The Texts of Early Greek Philosophy: The Complete Fragments and Selected Testimonies of the Major Presocratics.* New York: Cambridge University Press, 2010.

Graham, Nathalie. "Tumblr Is Dead: The Internet Could Be Next." *Stranger,* December 17, 2018. https://www.thestranger.com.

Grattan, Laura. *Populism's Power: Radical Grassroots Democracy in America.* Oxford: Oxford University Press, 2016.

Green, Steven K. *Inventing a Christian America: The Myth of the Religious Founding.* New York: Oxford University Press, 2015.

Gries, Laurie. "Iconographic Tracking: A Digital Research Method for Visual Rhetoric and Circulation." *Computers and Composition* 30, no. 4 (2013): 332–48.

———. "Mapping Obama Hope: A Data Visualization Project for Visual Rhetorics." *Kairos: A Journal of Rhetoric, Technology, and Pedagogy* 21, no. 2 (2017). http://kairos.technorhetoric.net.

Griffin, Keith. "The Light That Failed: A Rhetorical Analysis of Walter Hines Page as a Ceremonial Orator." *Southern Speech Communication Journal* 46, no. 3 (Spring 1981): 228–50.

Griffin, Rachel Alicia. "Problematic Representations of Strategic Whiteness and 'Post-Racial' Pedagogy: A Critical Intercultural Reading of *The Help.*" *Journal of International & Intercultural Communication* 8, no. 2 (May 2015): 147–66. https://doi.org/10.1080/17513057.2015.1025330.

Grobman, Laurie. "The Student Scholar: (Re)Negotiating Authorship and Authority." *College Composition and Communication* 61 (2009): 175–96.

Grobman, Laurie, and Joyce Kinkead. "Introduction: Illuminating Undergraduate Research in English." In *Undergraduate Research in English Studies,* edited by Laurie Grobman and Joyce Kinkead, ix–xxxii. Urbana, IL: NCTE, 2010.

Gronbeck, Bruce E. "The Rhetorics of the Past: History, Argument, and Collective Memory." In Turner, *Doing Rhetorical History*, 47–60.

Gul, Saad. "Return of the Native—An Assessment of the Citizenship Renunciation Clause in Hamdi's Settlement Agreement in the Light of Citizenship Jurisprudence." *Northern Illinois University Law Review* 27 (2007): 131–67.

Gulley, H. E. "Women and the Lost Cause: Preserving a Confederate Identity in the American Deep South." *Journal of Historical Geography* 19, no. 2 (1993): 125–41.

Gwin, Stanford P. "Slavery and English Polarity: The Persuasive Campaign of John Bright against English Recognition of the Confederate States of America." *Southern Speech Communication Journal* 49, no. 4 (Summer 1984): 406–19.

Hague, Euan, and Edward H. Sebesta. "The Jefferson Davis Highway: Contesting the Confederacy in the Pacific Northwest." *Journal of American Studies* 45, no. 2 (2011): 281–301.

Hall, Dennie. Review of Charles W. Eagles, "Jonathan Daniels and Race Relations: The Evolution of a Southern Liberal." *American Journalism* 1, no. 2 (1984): 88, https://www.tandfonline.com/doi/abs/10.1080/08821127.1984.10731024.

Hamdi v. Rumsfeld. 542 US 507 (2004).

"Hamdi v. Rumsfeld Settlement Agreement." Washington, DC. 2004. http://news.findlaw.com/hdocs/docs/hamdi/91704stlagrmnt.html.

Hammerback, John C., and Richard J. Jensen. "History and Culture as Rhetorical Constraints: Cesar Chavez's Letter from Delano." In Turner, *Doing Rhetorical History*, 207–20.

Hannifin, Ashley. "The Quick and the Dead: Bernard Baruch and Cold War Rhetoric." *Furman Humanities Review* 15 (2004): 79–99.

———, ed. "'Speech to the Control of Atomic Energy Commission,' by Bernard Baruch." *Furman Humanities Review* 15 (2004): 100–113.

Haraway, Donna. "Situated Knowledges: The Science Question in Feminism and the Privilege of Partial Perspective." *Feminist Studies* 14, no. 3 (1988): 575–99.

Hardman, Christine. "Building an Empire on Love: Martin Luther King, Jr., the Sit-In Movement, and the Rhetoric of the 'Durham Address.'" *Furman Humanities Review* 22 (2011): 97–117.

Hargis, Donald E. "Southerners in the California Constitutional Convention: 1849." *Southern Speech Journal* 19, no. 2 (March 1954): 193–204.

Hariman, Robert. "What Is a Chiasmus? Or, Why the Abyss Stares Back." In *Chiasmus and Culture*, edited by Anthony Paul and Boris Wiseman, 45–68. New York: Berghahn Books, 2014.

Harris, Thomas E., and Patrick C. Kennicott. "Booker T. Washington: A Study of Conciliatory Rhetoric." *Southern Speech Communication Journal* 37, no. 1 (Fall 1971): 47–59.

Harrison, Jane Ellen. *Themis: A Study of the Social Origins of Greek Religion.* 2nd ed. Cambridge: Cambridge University Press, 1927.

Harroff, Lindsay. "Reconciling through Truth: Reconciliation and the Rhetoric of Atonement and Official Apology." *Furman Humanities Review* 23 (2012): 67–89.

Hartog, François. *Regimes of Historicity: Presentism and Experiences of Time*. Translated by Saskia Brown. New York: Columbia University Press, 2017.

Harvey, Melanee C. "'Upon this Rock': Architectural, Material, and Visual Histories of Two Black Protestant Churches, 1881–1969." PhD diss., Boston University, 2017. https://open.bu.edu/handle/2144/27076.

Hasian, Marouf, Jr., Celeste Condit, and John Lucaites. "The Rhetorical Boundaries of 'the Law': A Consideration of the Rhetorical Culture of Legal Practice and the Case of the 'Separate but Equal' Doctrine." *Quarterly Journal of Speech* 82, no. 4 (November 1996): 323–42.

Haskins, William A. "Rhetorical Vision of Equality: Analysis of the Rhetoric of the Southern Black Press during Reconstruction." *Communication Quarterly* 29, no. 2 (1981): 116–22. https://doi.org/10.1080/01463378109369396.

Hatfield, Joe Edward. "The Queer Kairotic: Digital Transgender Suicide Memories and Ecological Rhetorical Agency." *Rhetoric Society Quarterly* 49, no. 1 (2019): 25–48.

Hauser, Gerard A. "Rhetorical Democracy and Civic Engagement." In *Rhetorical Democracy: Discursive Practices of Civic Engagement*, edited by Gerard A. Hauser and Amy Grim, 1–14. New York: Routledge, 2004.

Havelock, Eric Alfred. *The Liberal Temper in Greek Politics*. London: J. Cape, 1957.

Hawhee, Debra, and Crista J. Olson. "Pan-Historiography: The Challenges of Writing History across Time and Space." In *Theorizing Histories of Rhetoric*, edited by Michelle Ballif, 98–101. Carbondale: Southern Illinois University Press, 2013.

Hayden, Wendy. "'Gifts' of the Archives: A Pedagogy for Undergraduate Research." *College Composition and Communication* 66 (2015): 402–26.

Heath, Robert L. "A Time for Silence: Booker T. Washington in Atlanta." *Quarterly Journal of Speech* 64, no. 4 (December 1978): 385–99. https://doi.org/10.1080/00335637809383444.

Heckl, Raik. "'Deep Is the Well of the Past': Reconsidering the Origins of the Exodus Motif in Its Cultural Context." *Verbum et Ecclesia* 34, no. 2 (May 2013): 1–6.

Heidegger, Martin. *Early Greek Thinking*. Translated by David Farrell Krell and Frank Capuzzi. New York: Harper & Row, 1984.

Heidt, Stephen J. "The Study of Presidential Rhetoric in Uncertain Times: Thoughts on Theory and Praxis." In *Reading the Presidency: Advances in Presidential Rhetoric*, edited by Stephen J. Heidt and Mary E. Stuckey, 1–25. New York: Peter Lang, 2019.

Heimburger, Susan West. "Of Faith and Fact: Haywood N. Hill's 'This I Believe.'" *Young Scholars in Writing* 2 (2004): 29–37.

Hemmer, Joseph J., Jr. "The Charleston Platform Debate in Rhetorical-Historical

Perspective." *Quarterly Journal of Speech* 56, no. 4 (December 1970): 406–14. https://doi.org/10.1080/00335637009383028.

Henson, Evelyn. "A Response to Zoë Snider." *Young Scholars in Writing: Undergraduate Research in Writing and Rhetoric* 10 (2013): 129–31.

Herodotus. *The Histories.* Translated by Aubrey De Selincourt. New York: Penguin Books, 1954.

Hertz, J. H., ed. *The Pentateuch and Haftorahs.* 2nd ed. London: Soncino Press, 1993.

Herzog, Ben. *Revoking Citizenship: Expatriation in America from the Colonial Era to the War on Terror.* New York: New York University Press, 2017.

Heschel, Abraham Joshua. *The Prophets.* Peabody, MA: Hendrickson Publishing, 2007.

Heschel, Susannah. "A Friendship in the Prophetic Tradition: Abraham Joshua Heschel and Martin Luther King, Jr." *Telos* 182 (2018): 67–84.

———. *Moral Grandeur and Spiritual Audacity.* New York: Farrar Straus Giroux, 1996.

———. "Theological Affinities in the Writings of Heschel and King." In *Black Zion: African American Religious Encounters with Judaism*, edited by Yvonne Chireau and Nathaniel Deutsch, 168–86. London: Oxford University Press, 2000.

Hesseltine, William B., and Henry L. Eubank Jr. "Old Voices in the New South." *Quarterly Journal of Speech* 39, no. 4 (December 1953): 451–61.

Heyse, Amy. "The Rhetoric of Memory-Making: Lessons from the UDC's Catechisms for Children." *Rhetoric Society Quarterly* 38, no. 4 (2008): 408–32.

———. "Women's Rhetorical Authority and Collective Memory: The United Daughters of the Confederacy Remember the South." *Women & Language* 33, no. 2 (2010): 31–53.

"High Court Ruling Guards Citizenship." *Boston Globe*, May 30, 1967, 8.

Hill, Jennifer E. M. "Reframing the Victim: Rhetoric for Segregation in the *Greenville News*." *Young Scholars in Writing* 9 (2012): 45–57.

Hillbruner, Anthony. "Frances Wright: Egalitarian Reformer." *Southern Speech Journal* 23, no. 3 (Summer 1958): 193–203.

Hinger, Charlotte. *Nicodemus: Post-Reconstruction Politics and Racial Justice in Western Kansas.* Norman: University of Oklahoma Press, 2016.

Hinton, T. H. C. "From Washington." *Christian Recorder*, July 4, 1863.

———. "Washington Correspondence." *Christian Recorder*, August 1, 1863.

———. "Washington Correspondence." *Christian Recorder*, August 8, 1863.

———. "Washington Correspondence." *Christian Recorder*, September 9, 1863.

———. "Washington Correspondence." *Christian Recorder*, January 16, 1864.

———. "Washington Correspondence." *Christian Recorder*, January 30, 1864.

Hippolytus. *Philosophumena, or, The Refutation of All Heresies.* Vol. 1. Translated by Francis Legge. New York: Macmillan, 1921.

———. *Refutation of All Heresies.* Translated by M. David Litwa. Williston, VT: Society of Biblical Literature, 2015.

Hoerl, Kristen E. "Burning Mississippi into Memory? Cinematic Amnesia as a

Resource for Remembering Civil Rights." *Critical Studies in Media Communication* 26, no. 1 (2009): 54–79.

Hogan, J. Michael. "Wallace and the Wallacites: A Reexamination." *Southern Speech Communication Journal* 50, no. 1 (Fall 1984): 24–48.

Hohn, Maria, and Martin Klimke. *A Breath of Freedom: The Civil Rights Struggle, African American GIs, and Germany.* New York: Palgrave, 2010.

Holmberg, Carl Bryan. "Toward the Rhetoric of Music: Dixie." *Southern Speech Communication Journal* 51, no. 1 (1985): 71–82.

Holzer, Harold, ed. *Lincoln as I Know Him.* Chapel Hill, NC: Algonquin Books, 2009.

Horwitz, Morton J. *The Warren Court and the Pursuit of Justice.* New York: Hill and Wang, 1999.

Houck, Davis W. "Textual Recovery, Textual Discovery: Returning to Our Past, Imagining Our Future." In Parry-Giles and Hogan, *Handbook of Rhetoric and Public Address*, 111–32.

Houck, Davis W., and David E. Dixon. "Introduction: Recovering Women's Voices from the Civil Rights Movement." In *Women and the Civil Rights Movement, 1954–1965*, edited by Davis W. Houck and David E. Dixon, xv–xxvii. Waco, TX: Baylor University, 2006.

———. *Women and the Civil Rights Movement, 1954–1965.* Jackson: University Press of Mississippi, 2009.

Houdek, Matthew. "The Imperative of Race for Rhetorical Studies: Toward Divesting from Disciplinary and Institutionalized Whiteness—Special Forum on Race and Rhetoric." *Communication and Critical/Cultural Studies* 15, no. 4 (2018): 292–99.

———. "The Rhetorical Force of 'Global Archival Memory': (Re)Situating Archives along the Global Memoryscape." *Journal of International and Intercultural Communication* 9, no. 3 (2016): 204–21.

Howell, William. "Unit on Harry T. Burn, 'The New Citizenship,' Knoxville, TN, September 20, 1921." Recovering Democracy Archives: Speech Recovery Project. https://recoveringdemocracyarchives.umd.edu.

Hulliung, Mark. *The Social Contract in America: From the Revolution to the Present Age.* Lawrence: University Press of Kansas, 2007.

Hunter, Lauren. "Abraham Lincoln, 'Speech of Hon. Abraham Lincoln at Cooper Institute,' New York City, New York, February 27, 1860." *Voices of Democracy: The US Oratory Project* 13 (2018): 1–12. http://voicesofdemocracy.umd.edu.

Hunter, Lauren, Saul Castillo, and Fielding Montgomery, "Unit on César Chávez, 'César Chávez at Graham Hall,' St. Louis, MO, February 1, 1973." In Recovering Democracy Archives. https://recoveringdemocracyarchives .umd.edu/rda-unit/speech-at-graham-memorial-chapel-washington -st-louis-university.

Hutton, Patrick H. *History as an Art of Memory.* Hanover, NH: University Press of New England, 1993.

Huxman, Susan Schultz, and Gerald Biesecker-Mast. "In the World but Not of It:

Mennonite Traditions as Resources for Rhetorical Invention." *Rhetoric & Public Affairs* 7, no. 4 (2004): 539–54.

Hyde, Charles Cheney. "The Non-Recognition and Expatriation of Naturalized American Citizens." *American Journal of International Law* 19, no. 4 (1925): 742–44.

Hyman, Stanley Edgar. "Myth, Ritual, and Nonsense." *Kenyon Review* 11, no. 3 (1949): 463–66.

———. Papers. Manuscript Division, Library of Congress, Washington, DC.

"The Importance of Berlin." Undated and attached to memorandum, Foy D. Kohler to Dean Acheson, June 22, 1961. "Transmitting Two Papers Requested by You." Collection, "The Berlin Crisis, 1958–1962," Accession Number: BC02105, Digital National Security Archive. ProQuest.

Inabinet, Brandon, and Christina Moss. "Complicit in Victimage: Imagined Marginality in Southern Communication Criticism." *Rhetoric Review* 38, no. 2 (2019): 160–72. https://doi.org/10.1080/07350198.2019.1582228.

Irani, K. D., and Morris Silver. *Social Justice in the Ancient World*. Westport, CT: Greenwood Publishing Group, 1995.

İri, Murat, and H. Esra Arcan. "The Orhan Pamuk Case: How Mainstream Turkish Media Framed His Freedom of Speech." *Sosyal Bilimler Dergisi* 18 (2007): 17–24.

Ivie, Robert L. "Metaphor and the Rhetorical Invention of Cold War 'Idealists.'" *Communication Monographs* 54, no. 2 (1987): 165–82.

Jack, Bryan M. *The St. Louis African American Community and the Exodusters*. Columbia: University of Missouri Press, 2007.

Janney, Caroline E. *Burying the Dead but Not the Past: Ladies' Memorial Associations and the Lost Cause*. Chapel Hill: University of North Carolina Press, 2012.

Jasinski, James. "A Constitutive Framework for Rhetorical Historiography: Toward an Understanding of the Discursive (Re)Constitution of 'Constitution' in *The Federalist Papers*." In Turner, *Doing Rhetorical History*, 72–92.

Jasinski, James, and Jennifer R. Mercieca. "Analyzing Constitutive Rhetorics: The Virginia and Kentucky Resolutions and the 'Principles of '98.'" In Parry-Giles and Hogan, *Handbook of Rhetoric and Public Address*, 313–41.

Jeffress, Robert. *America Is a Christian Nation*. DVD. Pathway to Victory. Virginia Beach, VA: CBN, 2019.

Jensen, J. Vernon. *Ethical Issues in the Communication Process*. Mahawah, NJ: Lawrence Erlbaum, 1997.

Jensen, Richard J., and John C. Hammerback. *The Words of César Chávez*. College Station: Texas A&M University Press, 2002.

Jensen, Robin E. "Sexual Polysemy: The Discursive Ground of Talk about Sex and Education in U.S. History." *Communication, Culture and Critique* 1, no. 4 (2008): 396–415. https://doi.org/10.1111/j.1753–9137.2008.00032.x.

Johnson, Andre E., ed. *An African American Pastor before and during the American Civil War*. New York: Edwin Mellen Press, 2012.

———. "'Fighting the Devil with Fire': The Political Rhetoric of Henry McNeal

Turner during Reconstruction." In *Handbook of Research on Black Males: Quantitative, Qualitative, and Multidisciplinary*, edited by Theodore S. Ransaw, C. P. Gause, and Richard Majors, 27–28. East Lansing: Michigan State University Press, 2019.

———. *The Forgotten Prophet: Bishop Henry McNeal Turner and the African American Prophetic Tradition*. Lanham, MD: Lexington Books, 2012.

———. *No Future for the Negro: The Prophetic Pessimism of Bishop Henry McNeal Turner*. Jackson: University Press of Mississippi, 2020.

Johnson, Andre E., and Earle J. Fisher. "'But, I Forgive You?': Mother Emanuel, Black Pain, and the Rhetoric of Forgiveness." *Journal of Communication & Religion* 42, no. 2 (2019): 5–19.

Johnson, Andre, and Anthony J. Stone Jr. "'The Most Dangerous Negro in America': Rhetoric, Race, and the Prophetic Pessimism of Martin Luther King Jr." *Journal of Communication & Religion* 41, no. 1 (2018): 8–22.

Johnson, E. Patrick. *Honeypot: Black Southern Women Who Love Women*. Durham, NC: Duke University Press, 2019.

———. *Sweet Tea: Black Gay Men of the South*. Chapel Hill: University of North Carolina Press, 2011.

Johnson, Kevin R. "The Forgotten Repatriation of Persons of Mexican Ancestry and Lessons for the War on Terror." *Pace Law School Review* 26, no. 1 (2005): 1–26.

———. "Race, the Immigration Laws, and Domestic Race Relations: A Magic Mirror into the Heart of Darkness." *Indiana Law Journal* 73 (1998): 1111–60.

Johnson, Martin, Raymond G. Stokes, and Tobias Arndt. *The Thalidomide Catastrophe: How It Happened, Who Was Responsible, and Why the Search for Justice Continues after More Than Six Decades*. Exeter, UK: Onwards and Upwards Publishers, 2018.

Johnston, Andrew M. *Hegemony and Culture in the Origins of NATO Nuclear First Use, 1945–1955*. New York: Palgrave Macmillan, 2005.

Johnstone, Christopher Lyle. *Listening to the Logos: Speech and the Coming of Wisdom in Ancient Greece*. Columbia: University of South Carolina Press, 2012.

Jones, Martha S. *Birthright Citizens: A History of Race and Rights in Antebellum America*. Cambridge: Cambridge University Press, 2018.

Jorgensen-Earp, Cheryl R. "Mable Vernon, 'The Picketing Campaign Nears Victory,' National Advisory Council Conference, December 7, 1917." *Voices of Democracy: The US Oratory Project* 2 (2007): 1–25. https://voicesofdemocracy.umd.edu.

Josephus, Flavius, and Steve Mason. *Flavius Josephus: Translation and Commentary, Life of Josephus 9*. Boston: Brill Academic Publishers, 2001.

Kahn, Charles H. *Anaximander and the Origins of Greek Cosmology*. New York: Columbia University Press, 1960.

Kahn, Victoria. *The Future of Illusion: Political Theology and Early Modern Texts*. Chicago: University of Chicago Press, 2014.

Kammen, Michael. *Mystic Chords of Memory*. New York: Vintage, 1993.

Kansas Historical Society. "Exodusters." Kansapedia, Topeka. https://www.kshs.
    org/kansapedia.

Kantorowicz, Ernst. *The King's Two Bodies: A Study in Medieval Political Theology.*
    Princeton, NJ: Princeton University Press, 2016.

Kaplan, Edward K. *Spiritual Radical: Abraham Joshua Heschel in America, 1940–*
    1972. New Haven, CT: Yale University Press, 2007.

Katz, William Loren. *The Black West: A Documentary and Pictorial History of the
    African American Role in the Westward Expansion of the United States.*
    New York: Touchstone Book, 1996.

Kearney, Kevin E. "The 1960 Campaign Speaking of Orval Faubus." *Southern
    Speech Journal* 27, no. 2 (Winter 1961): 102–9.

———. "What's Southern about Southern Oratory?" *Southern Speech Journal* 32,
    no. 1 (1966): 19–30.

Keil, Lars-Broder. "When Martin Luther King Jr. Spoke to East Berlin." *Daily Dose,*
    January 18, 2016. https://www.ozy.com.

Kelley, Blair L., ed. *Right to Ride: Streetcar Boycotts and African American Citizen-
    ship in the Era of Plessy v. Ferguson.* Chapel Hill: University of North
    Carolina Press, 2010.

Kelly, Edmund. *The Great Exodus of the Colored People from the South to the West.*
    American Broadsides and Ephemera, Series 1, no. 13897. Washington,
    DC: np, 1879, 1.

Kelsey, Frances Oldham. *Autobiographical Reflections.* FDA Media Site. Accessed
    May 12, 2019. https://www.fda.gov.

———. Papers. Manuscript Division, Library of Congress, Washington, DC.

Kengor, Paul. "Martin Luther King and the Berlin Wall." *Washington Post,* October
    30, 2014. https://www.washingtonpost.com/opinions/martin-luther-king-
    and-the-berlin-wall/2014/10/30/b72c90aa-48ad-11e4-b72e-d60a9229cc10_
    story.html?noredirect=on&utm_term=.34f2058a795a

Kennedy, John. "Address in the Assembly Hall at the Paulskirche in Frankfurt,
    June 25, 1963." The American Presidency Project. https://www.presi-
    dency.ucsb.edu.

———. Papers. Kennedy Presidential Library and Museum, Boston.

Keränen, Lisa B. "Mapping Misconduct: Demarcating Legitimate Science from
    'Fraud' in the B-06 Lumpectomy Controversy." *Argumentation and Advo-
    cacy* 42, no. 2 (2005): 94–113.

———. "Public Engagements with Health and Medicine." *Journal of Medical Hu-
    manities* 35, no. 2 (2014): 103–9.

Kettner, James H. *The Development of American Citizenship, 1608–1870.* Chapel
    Hill: University of North Carolina Press, 2014.

Keyman, E. Fuat. "Articulating Citizenship and Identity: The 'Kurdish Question' in
    Turkey." In *Citizenship in a Global World: European Questions and Turkish
    Experiences,* edited by E. Fuat Keyman and Ahmet İçduygu, 267–88. New
    York: Routledge, 2005.

Khan, Geoffrey, ed. *Encyclopedia of Hebrew Language and Linguistics*. Boston: Brill, 2013.

Kibbey, Ann. *The Interpretation of Material Shapes in Puritanism: A Study of Rhetoric, Prejudice, and Violence*. London: Cambridge University Press, 1986.

Kimmel, Michael. *Angry White Men*. New York: Nation Books, 2013.

King Institute. "Commemorating the 50th Anniversary of King's Berlin Trip." Martin Luther King, Jr. Research and Education Institute, Stanford University. October 6, 2014. https://kinginstitute.stanford.edu.

King, Andrew. "Booker T. Washington and the Myth of Heroic Materialism." *Quarterly Journal of Speech* 60, no. 3 (1974): 323–28.

King, Martin Luther, Jr. "A Challenge to the Churches and Synagogues." In *Race: Challenge to Religion*, edited by Mathew Ahmann, 155–69. Chicago: Henry Regnery, 1963.

———. "East or West, God's Children." September 13, 1964. Inside the Cold War, Kings Sermon in East Berlin. 2015. http://insidethecoldwar .org/.

Kirk, G. S. *The Cosmic Fragments*. Cambridge: Cambridge University Press, 1954.

Kirk, G. S., J. E. Raven, and Malcolm Schofield. *The Presocratic Philosophers: A Critical History with a Selection of Texts*. 2nd ed. New York: Cambridge University Press, 2007.

Klee, Miles. "A Note to Badly Drawn Webcomics Everywhere." *Bad Art* (blog), March 1, 2018. https://medium.com/s/bad-art/a-note-to-badly-drawn -webcomics-everywhere-533804510f67.

Klekowski, Edward J., and Libby Klekowski. *Eyewitnesses to the Great War: American Writers, Reporters, Volunteers and Soldiers in France, 1914–1918*. Jefferson, NC: McFarland, 2012.

Knightly, Philip, Harold Evans, Elaine Potter, and Marjorie Wallace. *Suffer the Children: The Story of Thalidomide*. New York: Viking Press, 1979.

Kohl, Philip L., and Bertille Lyonnet. "By Land and By Sea: The Circulation of Materials and Peoples, ca. 3500–1800 B.C." In *Intercultural Relations between South and Southwest Asia: Studies in Commemoration of E.C.L. during Caspers (1934–1996)*, edited by Eric Olijdam and Richard H. Spoor, 29–42. Oxford, UK: Archeaopress, 2008.

Koliopoulos, Constantinos. "Historical Approaches to Security/Strategic Studies" In *Oxford Research Encyclopedia of International Studies*, np. New York: Oxford University Press: 2010. https://oxfordre.com/internationalstudies.

Kutner, Max. "As Confederate Statues Fall, the Group Behind Most of Them Stays Quiet." *Newsweek*, August 25, 2017. http://www.newsweek.com/ united-daughters-confederacy-statues-monuments-udc-653103.

Laclau, Ernesto. *On Populist Reason*. New York: Verso, 2005.

LaCocque, Andre, and Paul Ricoeur. *Thinking Biblically: Exegetical and Hermeneutical Studies*. Translated by David Pellauer. Chicago: University of Chicago Press, 1998.

Laertius, Diogenes. *Lives of Eminent Philosophers, Book VIII*. Translated by Robert Drew Hicks. New York: Freeman, 1925.

La Goy, Timothy M. "Soldiers of Conscience: Conscription and Conscientious Objection in the United States and Britain during World War I." PhD diss., State University of New York at Albany, 2010.

Lamay, Kimberly J. "The Creation of an American Collective Memory of the First World War, 1917–1941." PhD diss., State University of New York at Albany, 2013.

Lampton, William E. "Worldiness: Helmot Thielicke's Quest for Relevant Preaching." *Southern Speech Journal* 34 (Summer 1969): 245–55.

Large, David Clay. *Berlin*. New York: Basic Books, 2000.

LaSpina, James A. *The Visual Turn and the Transformation of the Textbook*. Mahwah, NJ: Routledge, 1998.

Lassiter, Matthew D. *The Silent Majority: Suburban Politics in the Sunbelt South*. Princeton, NJ: Princeton University Press, 2006.

Lathem, Edward Connery, ed. *Bernard Bailyn on the Teaching and Writing of History*. Hanover, NH: University Press of New England, 1994.

Lauer, Abigail D. "The Easy Way Out? The Yaser Hamdi Release Agreement and the United States' Treatment of the Citizen Enemy Combatant Dilemma." *Cornell Law Review* 91 (2006): 927–56.

Law, Martin, and Lisa M. Corrigan. "On White-Speak and Gatekeeping: or, What Good Are the Greeks?" *Communication and Critical/Cultural Studies* 15, no. 4 (2018): 326–30.

Lawrance, Benjamin N., and Jacqueline Stevens. *Citizenship in Question: Evidentiary Birthright and Statelessness*. Durham, NC: Duke University Press, 2019.

Lawson, Richard. "Cannes Kicks Off with a Zombie Comedy for the Trump Age," review of *The Dead Don't Die*. *Vanity Fair*, May 15, 2019. https://www.vanityfair.com/hollywood/2019/05/the-dead-dont-die-movie-review-jim-jarmusch-cannes.

Learn Our History. About Us. https://learnourhistory.com.

———. *The Civil War: Brother against Brother*. DVD. Glendale Heights, IL, 2013.

———. *The Declaration of Independence*. DVD. Glendale Heights, IL, 2011.

———. *9/11 and the War on Terror*. DVD. Glendale Heights, IL, 2011.

———. *One Nation Under God*. DVD. Glendale Heights, IL, 2013.

———. Our Lessons. https://learnourhistory.com/our-lessons

Lee, Benjamin, and Edward LiPuma. "Cultures of Circulation: The Imaginations of Modernity." *Public Culture* 14, no. 1 (2002): 191–213.

Lee, David D. *Sergeant York: An American Hero*. Lexington: University Press of Kentucky, 1985.

Lee, Naette, and Lauren Hunter. "Unit on George Gillette, 'The Garrison Dam Agreement Signing,' Fort Berthold, ND, May 21, 1948." Recovering Democracy Archives: Speech Recovery Project. https://recoveringdemocracyarchives.umd.edu.

Lee, Richard, ed. *The American Patriot's Bible: The Word of God and the Shaping of America*. Nashville, TN: Thomas Nelson, 2011.

Lee, Virginia S. "What Is Inquiry-Guided Learning?" *New Directions for Teaching and Learning* 129 (Spring 2012): 5–14.

Leeman, Richard W. "Fighting for Freedom Again: African American Reform Rhetoric in the Late Nineteenth Century." In *The Rhetoric of Nineteenth-Century Reform*, vol. 5, edited by Martha S. Watson and Thomas R. Burkholder, 1–35. East Lansing: Michigan State University Press, 2008.

Leff, Michael C. "Interpretation and the Art of the Rhetorical Critic." *Western Journal of Speech Communication* 44, no. 4 (1980): 337–49.

Leith, James. "Ephemera: Civic Education through Images." In *Revolution in Print: The Press in France, 1775–1800*, edited by Robert Darnton and Daniel Roche, 270–89. Berkeley: University of California Press, 1989.

Lenard, Patti Tamara. "Democratic Citizenship and Denationalization." *American Political Science Review* 112, no. 1 (2018): 99–111.

Lerner, Robert, Althea K. Nagai, and Stanley Rothman. *Molding the Good Citizen: The Politics of High School History Texts*. Westport, CT: Praeger, 1995.

Levin, Kevin. "The United Daughters of the Confederacy's Curious Silence on the Confederate Flag Debate." *Civil War Memory* (blog), June 30, 2015. http://cwmemory.com/2015/06/30/the-united-daughters-of-the-confederacys-curious-silence-on-the-confederate-flag-debate/.

Levitz, Jennifer. "Daughters of Confederacy 'Reeling' from Memorial Removals." *Wall Street Journal*, August 21, 2017. https://www.wsj.com/articles/daughters-of-confederacy-reeling-from-memorial-removals-1503307806.

Lewis, William W., and John L. Lucaites. "Race Trials: The Rhetoric of Victimage in the Racial Consciousness of 1930s America." In *Argument in a Time of Change*, edited by James F. Klumpp, 269–74. Annandale, VA: National Communication Association, 1998.

L.H. "Departure of the Rev. Henry M. Turner." *Christian Recorder*, November 28, 1863.

Lindsley, Charles. F. "Henry Woodfin Grady, Orator." *Quarterly Journal of Speech Education* 6, no. 2 (1920): 35–56.

Linenthal, Edward. *Changing Images of the Warrior Hero in America: A History of Popular Symbolism*. New York: E. Mellen, 1982.

Lipson, Carol, and Roberta A. Binkley, eds. *Ancient Non-Greek Rhetorics*. West Lafayette, IN: Parlor Press, 2009.

———, eds. *Rhetoric before and beyond the Greeks*. Albany: State University of New York, 2004.

Lipset, Seymour Martin. *American Exceptionalism: A Double-Edged Sword*. New York: W. W. Norton, 1996.

Livanios, Dimitris. "The 'Sick Man' Paradox: History, Rhetoric, and the 'European Character' of Turkey." *Journal of Southern Europe and the Balkans* 8, no. 3 (December 2006): 299–311.

Lockhart, P. R. "At NAACP Convention, 2020 Democrats Criticize Trump's Record on Race." *Vox*, July 24, 2019. https://www.vox.com/identities/2019/7/24/20726568/naacp-democratic-primary-2020-donald-trump-racism.

Logan, Shirley Wilson. *Liberating Language: Sites of Rhetorical Education in Nineteenth-Century Black America*. Carbondale: Southern Illinois University Press, 2008.

Logue, Cal M. "Ralph McGill: Convictions of a Southern Editor." *Journalism Quarterly* 45, no. 4 (Winter 1968): 647–52.

———. "The Rhetorical Appeals of Whites to Blacks in Reconstruction." *Communication Monographs* 44, no. 3 (1977): 241–51. https://doi.org/10.1080/03637757709390135.

———. "Transcending Coercion: The Communicative Strategies of Black Slaves on Antebellum Plantations." *Quarterly Journal of Speech* 67, no. 1 (February 1981): 31–46. https://doi.org/10.1080/00335638109383549.

Logue, Cal M., and Howard Dorgan, eds. *A New Diversity in Contemporary Southern Rhetoric*. Baton Rouge: Louisiana State University Press, 1987.

———, eds. *Oratory of Southern Demagogues*. Baton Rouge: Louisiana State University Press, 1981.

Logue, Cal M., and Thurmon Garner, "Shifts in Rhetorical Status of Blacks after Freedom." *Southern Communication Journal* 54, no. 1 (Fall 1988): 1–39.

Lomas, Charles. "Southern Orators in California before 1861." *Southern Speech Journal* 15, no. 1 (September 1949): 21–37.

Lovell, John. *Black Song: The Forge and the Flame*. New York: Macmillan, 1972.

Lowenthal, David. *The Past Is a Foreign Country*. New York: Cambridge University Press, 1985.

Lucas, Stephen E. "The Renaissance of Public Address: Text and Context in Rhetorical Criticism." *Quarterly Journal of Speech* 74, no. 2 (1988): 241–60.

———. "The Schism in Rhetorical Scholarship." *Quarterly Journal of Speech* 67, no. 1 (1981): 1–20.

Lucas, Stephen E., and Martin J. Medhurst, eds. *Words of a Century: The Top 100 American Speeches, 1900–1999*. New York: Oxford University Press, 2009.

Lunde, Darrin. *The Naturalist: Theodore Roosevelt, a Lifetime of Exploration, and the Triumph of American Natural History*. New York: Broadway Books, 2016.

Luttwak, Edward. *Strategy: The Logic of War and Peace*. Cambridge, MA: Belknap Press of Harvard University Press, 2001.

Luxenberg, Steve. *Separate: The Story of Plessy v. Ferguson, and America's Journey from Slavery to Segregation*. New York: W. W. Norton, 2019.

Lynch, Christopher. "Reaffirmation of God's Anointed Prophet: The Chiasm in Martin Luther King's Mountaintop Speech." *Howard Journal of Communications* 6 (1995): 12–31.

Lynch, John Alexander. *What Are Stem Cells? Definitions at the Intersection of Science and Politics*. Tuscaloosa: University of Alabama Press, 2011.

Lyne, John, and Henry F. Howe. "'Punctuated Equilibria': Rhetorical Dynamics of a Scientific Controversy." *Quarterly Journal of Speech* 72, no. 2 (1986): 132–47.

Lyon, Arabella, and Lester C. Olson, eds. "Human Rights Rhetoric: Traditions of Testifying and Witnessing." *Rhetoric Society Quarterly* 41, no. 3 (2011): 203–93.

Magness, Phillip W., and Sebastian N. Page. *Colonization after Emancipation: Lincoln and the Movement for Black Resettlement.* Columbia: University of Missouri Press, 2011.

Mahler, Anne Garland. *From the Tricontinental to the Global South: Race, Radicalism, and Transnational Solidarity.* Durham, NC: Duke University Press, 2018.

Makay, John J. "George C. Wallace: Southern Spokesman with a Northern Audience." *Central States Speech Journal* 19 (Fall 1968): 202–8.

Maldonado, Chandra A. "Recovering Teddy, Recovering Trump: The Rhetoric of Manifest-Masculinity in a Drunk and Rap Battle Generation." In *Gender, Race, and Social Identity in American Politics: The Past and Future of Political Access*, edited by Lori L. Montalbano, 237–54. Lanham, MD: Lexington Books, 2019.

———. "Remembering Roosevelt: Arguing for Memory through Public and Private Networks." In *Networking Argument*, edited by Carol Winkler. New York: Routledge, 2020.

Manning, Chandra. *Troubled Refuge: Struggling for Freedom in the Civil War.* New York: Vintage Books, 2017.

Manovich, Lev. "Synthetic Realism and Its Discontents" In *Film Theory and Criticism: Introductory Readings*, 7th ed., edited by Leo Braudy and Marshall Cohen, 785–801. London: Oxford University Press, 2009.

Mao, LuMing, ed. "Comparative Rhetoric." *Rhetoric Society Quarterly* 43, no. 3 (2013): 209–309.

———. "Writing the Other into Histories of Rhetorics: Theorizing the Art of Recontextualization." In *Theorizing Writing Histories of Rhetoric*, edited by Michelle Baliff, 41–57. Carbondale: Southern Illinois Press, 2013.

Marcosson, Isaac F. *Adventures in Interviewing.* New York: John Lane, 1919.

Markos, Steve. "Theodore Roosevelt Island—Roosevelt Memorial." National Park Planner, last updated June 4, 2020. http://npplan.com.

Marsden, George M. *Fundamentalism and American Culture.* 2nd ed. New York: Oxford University Press, 2006.

Martel, William C. *Grand Strategy in Theory and Practice: The Need for an Effective American Foreign Policy.* New York: Cambridge University Press, 2015.

Martin, Donald R., and Vicky Gordon Martin. "Barbara Jordan's Symbolic Use of Language in the Keynote Address to the National Women's Conference." *Southern Speech Communication Journal* 49, no. 3 (Spring 1984): 319–30.

Martin, Waldo E., Jr. *The Mind of Frederick Douglass.* Chapel Hill: University of North Carolina Press, 1984.

Martinez, J. Michael, and Robert M. Harris. "Graves, Worms, and Epitaphs: Confederate Monuments in the Southern Landscape." In *Confederate Symbols in the Contemporary South*, edited by J. Michael Martinez, William D. Richardson, and Ron McNinch-Su, 136–37. Gainesville: University Press of Florida, 2000.

Martinez, J. Michael, William D. Richardson, and Ron McNinch-Su. "Introduction: Understanding the Debate over Confederate Symbols." In *Confederate Symbols in the Contemporary South*, edited by J. Michael Martinez, William D. Richardson, and Ron McNinch-Su, 1–14. Gainesville: University Press of Florida, 2000.

Masur, Kate. *An Example for All the Land: Emancipation and the Struggle for Equality in Washington, DC*. Durham: University of North Carolina Press, 2010.

Masur, Louis P. "'Pictures Have Now Become a Necessity': The Use of Images in American History Textbooks." *Journal of American History* 84, no. 4 (March 1, 1998): 1409–24.

Mattson, Kevin. *Creating a Democratic Public: The Struggle for Urban Participatory Democracy during the Progressive Era*. University Park: Pennsylvania State University Press, 1998.

Maurantonio, Nicole. "Material Rhetoric, Public Memory, and the Post It Note." *Southern Communication Journal* 80, no. 2 (2015): 83–101.

Mayer-Schönberger, Victor. *Delete: The Virtue of Forgetting in the Digital Age*. Princeton, NJ: Princeton University Press, 2009.

Mayes, Todd, ed. "'Speech on the Bombings,' by Stanford Brookshire." *Furman Humanities Review* 16 (2005): 105–9.

McCain, Ray. 1964. "Speaking on School Desegregation by Atlanta Ministers. *Southern Speech Journal* 29, n. 3 (1964): 256–62.

McClerren, Beryl F. "Southern Baptists and the Religious Issue during the Presidential Campaigns of 1928 and 1960." *Central States Speech Journal* 18, no. 2 (1967): 104–12.

McCloud, Scott. *Understanding Comics: The Invisible Art*. New York: HarperPerennial, 1994.

McConnell, Judith Lynne, and Blythe F. Hinitz. "In Their Words: A Living History of the Brown Decisions." *Educational Studies* 37, no. 1 (2005): 77–8.

McFeely, William S. *Frederick Douglass*. New York: W. W. Norton, 1991.

McGee, Michael Calvin. "The 'Ideograph': A Link between Rhetoric and Ideology." *Quarterly Journal of Speech* 66, no. 1 (1980): 1–16.

———. "'Social Movement': Phenomenon or Meaning?" *Central States Speech Journal* 31, no. 4 (1980): 233–44.

———. "Text, Context, and the Fragmentation of Contemporary Culture." *Western Journal of Communication* 54, no. 3 (Summer 1990): 274–89.

McKerrow, Raymie E. "Critical Rhetoric: Theory and Praxis." *Communication Monographs* 56, no. 2 (1989): 91.

McMichael, Kelly. "'Memories Are Short but Monuments Lengthen Remembrances': The United Daughters of the Confederacy and the Power of Civil War Memory." In *Lone Star Pasts: Memory and History in Texas*, edited by Elizabeth Hayes Turner, W. Fitzhugh Brundage, and Gregg Cantrell, 95–118. College Station: Texas A&M University Press, 2006.

McRae, Elizabeth Gillespie. *Mothers of Massive Resistance: White Women and the Politics of White Supremacy*. New York: Oxford University Press, 2018.

———. "The Women Behind White Power." *New York Times*, February 2, 2018. https://www.nytimes.com/2018/02/02/opinion/sunday/white-supremacy -forgot-women.html.

Medhurst, Martin J. "The History of Public Address as an Academic Study." In Parry-Giles and Hogan, *Handbook of Rhetoric and Public Address*, 19–66.

Mercieca, Jennifer. *Founding Fictions*. Tuscaloosa: University of Alabama Press, 2010.

Merkel, Angela. "Commencement Address, Harvard University, May 30, 2019." American Rhetoric Online Speech Bank, Speech Bank, https://american-rhetoric.com.

Meyrowitz, Joshua. *No Sense of Place: The Impact of Electronic Media on Social Behavior*. Oxford: Oxford University Press, 1985.

Michalski, Sergiusz. *Reformation and the Visual Arts: The Protestant Image Question in Western and Eastern Europe*. London: Routledge, 2013.

Middleton, Michael, Aaron Hess, Danielle Endres, and Samantha Senda-Cook. *Participatory Critical Rhetoric: Theoretical and Methodological Foundations for Studying Rhetoric In Situ*. Lanham, MD: Lexington Books, 2015.

Mignolo, Walter D. *The Darker Side of Western Modernity: Global Futures, Decolonial Options*. Durham, NC: Duke University Press, 2011.

Miller, Keith D. "Alabama as Egypt: Martin Luther King Jr. and the Religion of Slaves." In Calloway-Thomas and Lucaites, *Martin Luther King Jr.*, 18–32.

———. "Second Isaiah Lands in Washington, DC: Martin Luther King, Jr.'s 'I Have a Dream' as Biblical Narrative and Biblical Hermeneutic." *Rhetoric Review* 26, no. 4 (2007): 405–24.

———. *Voices of Deliverance: The Language of Martin Luther King, Jr., and Its Sources*. Athens: University of Georgia Press, 1998.

Minow, Martha. *Brown's Wake: Legacies of America's Educational Landmark*. New York: Oxford University Press, 2010.

Mintz, Morton. *The Therapeutic Nightmare*. Boston: Houghton Mifflin, 1965.

Mobbs, Michael H. "Declaration of Michael H. Mobbs." Virginia: Special Advisor to the Under Secretary of Defense for Policy, July 24, 2002. https://www.pbs.org/wgbh/pages/frontline/shows/sleeper/tools/mobbshamdi.html.

Momigliano, Arnaldo. *Essays in Ancient and Modern Historiography*, 1st US ed. Middleton, CT: Wesleyan University Press, 1977.

Mondin, Alessandra. "'Tumblr Mostly, Great Empowering Images:' Blogging, Reblogging, and Scrolling Feminist, Queer, and BDSM Desires." *Journal of Gender Studies* 26, no. 3 (2017): 282–92.

Moreno, Paul D. *Black Americans and Organized Labor: A New History*. Baton Rouge: Louisiana State University Press, 2006.

Morgan, David. *Protestants and Pictures: Religion, Visual Culture, and the Age of American Mass Production*. New York: Oxford University Press, 1999.

Morris, Charles E., III. "Archival Queer." *Rhetoric & Public Affairs* 9, no. 1 (Spring 2006): 145–51.

———. "The Archival Turn in Rhetorical Studies; or, The Archive's (Re)turn." *Rhetoric & Public Affairs* 9, no. 1 (2006): 113–15.

———. "Context's Critic, Invisible Traditions, and Queering Rhetorical History." *Quarterly Journal of Speech* 101, no. 1 (2015): 225–43. https://doi.org/10.10 80/00335630.2015.995926.

———. "Contextual Twilight/Critical Liminality: J. M. Barrie's Courage at St. Andrews, 1922." *Quarterly Journal of Speech* 82, no. 3 (1996): 207–27.

———. "Introduction: Portrait of a Queer Rhetorical/Historical Critic." In *Queering Public Address: Sexualities in American Historical Discourse*, edited by Charles E. Morris III, 1–19. Columbia: University of South Carolina Press, 2007.

———. "My Old Kentucky Homo: Lincoln and the Politics of Queer Public Memory." In *Framing Public Memory*, edited by Kendall Phillips, 89–114. Tuscaloosa: The University of Alabama Press, 2004.

Morris, Charles E., III, and Jeffrey Allen Bennett, eds. "Special Issue: Rhetorical Criticism's Multitudes." *Review of Communication* 16, no. 1 (2016): 1–107.

Morris, Charles E., III, and Stephen Howard Browne, eds. *Readings in the Rhetoric of Social Protest*. 3rd ed. State College, PA: Strata Publishing, 2013.

Morris, Matthew. "Rhetorical Analysis of 'The Drum Major Instinct' in Martin Luther King, Jr. on Leadership." *Young Scholars in Writing* 12 (2015): 4–14.

Morrison, Janet A., Nancy J. Berner, Jill M. Manske, Rebecca M. Jones, Shannon N. Davis, and Pamela W. Garner. "Surveying Faculty Perspectives on Undergraduate Research, Scholarship, and Creative Activity: A Three-Institution Study." *Scholarship and Practice of Undergraduate Research* 2 (2018): 43–54.

Moses, Wilson Jeremiah. *The Golden Age of Black Nationalism, 1850–1925*. New York: Oxford University Press, 1978.

Moss, Christina L. "A Nation Divided: Regional Identity, National Narratives, and Senator Zell Miller in the 2004 Presidential Election." *Southern Communication Journal* 76, no. 1 (2011): 76–96.

———. "Reclaiming the Rural South: Queen Sugar and African-American Southern Identity." In Atkins-Sayre and Stokes, *City Places, Country Spaces*, 125–48.

Moss, Christina L., and Ronald Jackson, "Introduction to Special Issue: We March Lest We Forget." *Howard Journal of Communications* 289, no 2 (2017): 1–9. https://doi.org/10.1080/10646175.2017.1287611.

Mott, Frank Luther. *A History of American Magazines, 1741–1930*. Vol. 4. Cambridge, MA: Harvard Belknap Press, 1957.

Moyer, William Andrew, III. "Battle for the City on the Hill: Evangelical Interpretations of American History 1960–1996." PhD diss., George Washington University, 1998.

Murphy, John M. "Barack Obama and Rhetorical History." *Quarterly Journal of Speech* 101, no. 1 (2015): 213–24. https://doi.org/10.1080/00335630.2015.995927.

———. *John F. Kennedy and the Liberal Persuasion*. East Lansing: Michigan State University Press, 2019.

Murphy, Mollie K. "Scientific Argument without a Scientific Consensus: Rachel Carson's Rhetorical Strategies in the Silent Spring Debates." *Argumentation and Advocacy* 55, no. 3 (2018): 1–17.

Nakayama, Thomas K. "Show/Down Time: 'Race,' Gender, Sexuality, and Popular Culture." *Critical Studies in Mass Communication* 11, no. 2 (1994): 162–79.

National Women's Hall of Fame. "Frances Oldham Kelsey." Accessed April 13, 2019. https://www.womenofthehall.org.

Nationality Act of 1940. Pub. L. No. 801, 8 US (1940).

Naturalization Act. US House of Representatives and Senate, 1st Congress, 2d sess., 1 stat 103, March 26, 1790. https://docs.google.com/viewer?a=v&pid=sites&srcid=ZGVmYXVsdGRvbWFpbnxyYW1pcmV6YXB1c2h8Z3g6NzVjMGVhMDIxOWQzZjcz.

"The Negro Exodus: The Old Style and the New." *Harper's Weekly*, May 1, 1880. Digital Public Library of America. https://dp.la.

Neville-Shepard, Ryan. "Rand Paul at Howard University and the Rhetoric of the New Southern Strategy." *Western Journal of Communication* 82, no. 1 (2018): 20–39. https://doi.org/10.1080/10570314.2017.1320809.

Nissenbaum, Helen. *Privacy in Context: Technology, Policy, and the Integrity of Social Life*. Stanford, CA: Stanford University Press, 2010.

Noll, Mark A., George M. Marsden, and Nathan O. Hatch. *The Search for Christian America*. Colorado Springs: Helmers & Howard, 1989.

"No More Banishment." *Boston Globe*, June 4, 1967, 4.

North Carolina State University. Virtual Martin Luther King, Jr. Project. Accessed June 20, 2019. https://vmlk.chass.ncsu.edu/.

"Notes on Remarks by President Kennedy before the National Security Council." January 22, 1963, collection, "The Berlin Crisis, 1958–1962," Accession Number: CC02869, Digital National Security Archive. ProQuest.

O'Brien, Kenneth P. "The Southern Heroine in the Films of the 1930s." *Journal of Popular Film & Television* 14, no. 1 (1986): 23–32. https://doi.org/10.1080/01956051.1986.9944213.

Ogden, Robert. "Getting and Keeping a Business Position." *Saturday Evening Post*, November 4, 1899, 345–46.

———. "Why Young Men Fail: A Clear Explanation by Shrewd Business Men." *Saturday Evening Post*, October 28, 1899, 327.

Oliver, Robert T. "Studies in the Political and Social Views of the Slave-Struggle Orators." *Quarterly Journal of Speech* 23, no. 3 (1937): 409–17.

Olson, Christa J., and René Agustín De los Santos, eds. "La Idea de la Retórica Americana/The Idea of American Rhetoric." *Rhetoric Society Quarterly* 45, no. 3 (2015): 193–277.

Olson, Lester C. *Emblems of American Community in the Revolutionary Era: A Study in Rhetorical Iconology*. Washington, DC: Smithsonian Institution Press, 1991.

Olson, Lester, and James J. Kimble. "Visual Rhetoric Representing Rosie the Riveter: Myth and Misconception in J. Howard Miller's 'We Can Do It!' Poster." *Rhetoric & Public Affairs* 9, no. 4 (2007): 533–69.

"Once a Citizen." *New York Times*, June 4, 1967, section The Week in Review.

Ono, Kent A. and John M. Sloop. "The Critique of Vernacular Discourse." *Communication Monographs* 62, no. 1 (1995): 19–46.

Organization of American Historians. "History, Democracy, and Citizenship: The Debate over History's Role in Teaching Citizenship and Patriotism." April 1, 2004. http://www.oah.org .

Orlin, Louis L. *Life and Thought in the Ancient Near East*. Ann Arbor: University of Michigan Press, 2010.

O'Rourke, Sean Patrick. "Wisdom and Eloquence." *Vital Speeches of the Day* 83 (2017): 344–45.

O'Rourke, Sean Patrick, Susan West Heimburger, and Stephanie Kershner. "Argument in Local Controversy: The King Holiday Debate in Greenville County, South Carolina." Paper presented to the National Communication Association, Chicago, IL, November 2004.

O'Rourke, Sean Patrick, Stephen Howard, and Andrianna Lee Lawrence. "*Respondeo etsi Mutabor*: The Comment and Response Assignment, Young Scholars, and the Promise of Liberal Education." *Young Scholars in Writing: Undergraduate Research in Writing and Rhetoric* 10 (2013): 27–37.

O'Rourke, Sean Patrick, and Melody Lehn. *Rhetoric, Race, and Religion and the Charleston Shootings: Was Blind but Now I See*. Lanham, MD: Lexington Books, 2019.

Orth, Nikki. "Ella Baker, 'Address at the Hattiesburg Freedom Day Rally,' January 12, 1964." *Voices of Democracy: The US Oratory Project* 11 (2016): 25–43. http://voicesofdemocracy.umd.edu.

Osborn, Michael. "The Last Mountaintop of Martin Luther King, Jr." In Calloway-Thomas and Lucaites, *Martin Luther King Jr.*, 147–61.

———. *Michael Osborn on Metaphor and Style*. East Lansing: Michigan State University Press, 2018.

Painter, Nell Irvin. *Exodusters: Black Migration to Kansas after Reconstruction*. New York: W. W. Norton, 1986.

"Pap Singleton: To Kansas." PBS Learning Media, 2002. https://mpt.pbslearning-media.org.

Paroske, Marcus. "Deliberating International Science Policy Controversies: Uncertainty and AIDS in South Africa." *Quarterly Journal of Speech* 95, no. 2 (2009): 148–70.

Parrish, Timothy. *Ralph Ellison and the Genius of America*. Amherst: University of Massachusetts Press, 2012.

Parry-Giles, Shawn J. "Archival Research and the American Presidency: The Political and Rhetorical Complexities of Presidential Records," In Parry-Giles and Hogan, *Handbook of Rhetoric and Public Address*, 157–83.

———. "Unit on Frederick Douglass, 'The Southern Exodus,' May 4, 1879, Baltimore, MD." Recovering Democracy Archives: Speech Recovery Project. https://recoveringdemocracyarchives.umd.edu/rda-unit/the-southern-exodus.

Parry-Giles, Shawn, and J. Michael Hogan. "Introduction: The Study of Rhetoric and Public Address." In Parry-Giles and Hogan, *Handbook of Rhetoric and Public Address*, 1–16.

———, eds. *Handbook of Rhetoric and Public Address*. Malden, MA: Blackwell Publishing, 2010.

Parsons, Emily. "Gloria Steinem and the Rhetoric of the Corporate Personality." *Furman Humanities Review* 19 (2008): 85–104.

Patterson, GPat, and Leland G. Spencer. "Toward Trans Rhetorical Agency: A Critical Analysis of Trans Topics in Rhetoric and Composition and Communication Scholarship." *Peitho: Journal of the Coalition of Feminist Scholars in the History of Rhetoric & Composition* 22, no. 4 (2020): 1–24. https://cfshrc .org.

Pattullo, George. "The Second Elder Gives Battle." *Saturday Evening Post*, April 26, 1919, 3–4, 71–74.

Payne, Daniel Alexander. *Recollections of Seventy Years*. Nashville, TN: AME Sunday School Union, 1888. Documenting the American South, 2001, https:// docsouth.unc.edu/index.html.

Pendergast, Tom. *Creating the Modern Man: American Magazines and Consumer Culture, 1900–1950*. Columbia: University of Missouri Press, 2000.

Perelman, Chaïm. "Rhetoric and Philosophy." *Philosophy and Rhetoric* 1, no. 1 (1968): 15–24.

Peritz, Ingrid. "Canadian Doctor Averted Disaster by Keeping Thalidomide out of the US." *Globe and Mail*, November 24, 2014.

Perry, John. *Sgt. York: His Life, Legend & Legacy*. Nashville, TN: Broadman & Holman, 1997.

Perry, Samuel. "President Trump and Charlottesville: Uncivil Mourning and White Supremacy." *Journal of Contemporary Rhetoric* 8, no. 1 (2018): 57–71.

Peters, Francis E. *Greek Philosophical Terms: A Historical Lexicon*. New York: New York University Press, 1967.

Pezzullo, Phaedra. *Toxic Tourism*. Tuscaloosa: University of Alabama Press, 2009.

Pfiffner, James P. "The Contemporary Presidency: Decision Making in the Bush White House." *Presidential Studies Quarterly* 39, no. 2 (June 2009): 363–85.

———. "Organizing the Trump Presidency." *Presidential Studies Quarterly* 48, no. 1 (March 2008): 153–67.

Pfitzer, Gregory M. *Picturing the Past: Illustrated Histories and the American Imagination, 1840–1900*. Washington, DC: Smithsonian Institution Press, 2002.

Phillips, Joshua Daniel, and Rachel Alicia Griffin. "Crystal Mangum as Hypervisible Object and Invisible Subject: Black Feminist Thought, Sexual Violence and the Pedagogical Repercussions of the Duke Lacrosse Rape Case." *Women's Studies in Communication* 38, no. 1 (2015): 36–56. https:// doi.org/10.1080/07491409.2014.964896.

Philipsen, Gerry. "Speech Codes." In *Developing Communication Theories*, edited by

Gerry Philipsen and Terrance L. Albrecht, 119–56. Albany: State University of New York, 1977.

Phillips, Alyson Farzad. "Unit on Gloria Steinem and Dorothy Pitman Hughes, 'Speech to Naval Academy,' Annapolis, MD, May 4, 1972." Recovering Democracy Archives: Speech Recovery Project. https://recoveringdemocracyarchives.umd.edu.

Phillips, Kendall. "The Failure of Memory: Reflections on Rhetoric and Public Remembrance." *Western Journal of Communication* 74, no. 2 (2010): 208–23.

Pickett, Amanda. "Questioning White Masculinity in the U.S." Words in the Bucket, December 28, 2016. https://www.wordsinthebucket.com.

Pielke, Roger A. *The Honest Broker: Making Sense of Science in Policy and Politics.* Cambridge: Cambridge University Press, 2007.

Plessy v. Ferguson, 163 US 537 (1896).

Pocock, J. G. A. "The Ideal of Citizenship since Classical Times." In *The Citizenship Debates: A Reader*, edited by Gershon Shafir, 29–52. Minneapolis: University of Minnesota Press, 1998.

Pollard, Edward A. *The Lost Cause: A New Southern History of the War of the Confederates.* New York: E. B. Treat, 1868.

Poppenheim, Mary B. *History of the United Daughters of the Confederacy.* Richmond, VA: Garrett and Massie, 1938.

Posen, Barry R. "The Struggle against Terrorism: Grand Strategy, Strategy, and Tactics." *International Security* 26, no. 3 (Winter 2001–2): 39–55.

Posner, Miriam. "Creating a Network Graph with Gephi." Accessed August 20, 2019. http://miriamposner.com/dh101f15/index.php/creating-a-network-graph-with-gephi/.

Powe, Lucas A. *The Warren Court and American Politics.* Cambridge, MA: Harvard University Press, 2002.

Powell, Douglas R. *Critical Regionalism: Connecting Politics and Culture in the American Landscape.* Chapel Hill: University of North Carolina Press, 2012.

Prelli, Lawrence. "The Rhetorical Construction of Scientific Ethos." In *Landmark Essays on the Rhetoric of Science: Case Studies*, edited by Randy Allen Harris, 87–104. Mahwah, NJ: Lawrence Erlbaum, 1997.

Price, B. Byron. *Imagining the Open Range: Erwin E. Smith, Cowboy Photographer.* Fort Worth, TX: Amon Carter Museum, 1998.

Price, Melanye T. *Dreaming Blackness: Black Nationalism and African American Public Opinion.* New York: New York University Press, 2009.

Pritchard, James B. *The Ancient Near East: An Anthology of Texts and Pictures.* Princeton, NJ: Princeton University Press, 2011.

"Protestors Arrested as City of Helena Removes Confederate Fountain." *Billings Gazette*, August 18, 2017. https://billingsgazette.com/news/state-and-regional/protesters-arrested-as-city-of-helena-removes-confederate-fountain/article_8e724ab3-b982-559e-a21a-8201c860c706.html.

Quinn, Josephine Crawley. *In Search of the Phoenicians.* Princeton, NJ: Princeton University Press, 2018.

Raboteau, Albert J. *Slave Religion: The 'Invisible Institution' in the Antebellum South.* New York: Oxford University Press, 1978.

Raglan, Lord. *The Hero: A Study in Tradition, Myth, and Drama.* London: Methuen, 1936.

Ramasastry, Anita. "Do Hamdi And Padilla Need Company?" *Findlaw,* August 21, 2002. https://supreme.findlaw.com.

Rampersad, Arnold. *Ralph Ellison: A Biography.* New York: Vintage, 2008.

Ramsey, Paul, and Stanley Hauerwas. *Speak Up for Just War or Pacifism: A Critique of the United Methodist Bishops' Pastoral Letter "In Defense of Creation."* University Park: Pennsylvania State University Press, 1988.

Rand, Erin J. "An Inflammatory Fag and a Queer Form: Larry Kramer, Polemics, and Rhetorical Agency." *Quarterly Journal of Speech* 94, no. 3 (August 2008): 297–319.

Rankin, William James. "A Response to Caitlin Eha." *Young Scholars in Writing: Undergraduate Research in Writing and Rhetoric* 15 (2018): 124–27.

Rawson, K. J. "The Rhetorical Power of Archival Description: Classifying Images of Gender Transgression." *Rhetoric Society Quarterly* 48, no. 4 (2018): 327–51.

Ray, Angela G. "Frederick Douglass on the Lyceum Circuit: Social Assimilation, Social Transformation." *Rhetoric & Public Affairs* 5 no. 4 (2002): 625–48.

———. "Learning Leadership: Lincoln at the Lyceum, 1838." *Rhetoric & Public Affairs* 13, no. 3 (2010): 349–87.

———. *The Lyceum and Public Culture in the Nineteenth-Century United States.* Lansing: Michigan State University Press, 2005.

———. "What Hath She Wrought? Women's Rights and the Nineteenth-Century Lyceum." *Rhetoric & Public Affairs* 9 no. 2 (2006): 183–214.

Reames, Robin. "The Logos Paradox: Heraclitus, Material Language, and Rhetoric." *Philosophy and Rhetoric* 46, no. 3 (2013): 328–50.

Reddick, Glenn E. "When the Southern Senators Said Farewell." *Southern Speech Journal* 15, no. 3 (1950): 196–97.

"Report of the Minority." *Report and Testimony of the Select Committee of the United States Senate to Investigate the Causes of the Removal of the Negroes from the Southern States to the Northern States.* Part 1. Washington, DC: Government Printing Office, 1880, ix.

Revell, Alexander. "The Plain Business Man." *Saturday Evening Post,* September 1, 1900, 16–17.

Rice, Jenny. "From Architectonic to Tectonics: Introducing Regional Rhetorics." *Rhetoric Society Quarterly* 42, no. 3 (2012): 201–13.

Richardson, Heather Cox. *West from Appomattox: The Reconstruction of America after the Civil War.* New Haven, CT: Yale University Press, 2007.

Richardson, Ralph. "The Rhetorical Death Rattle of the Confederacy." *Southern Speech Journal* 20, no. 2 (1954): 109–16.

Richter, Andreas Kuno, dir. *Der King-Code: Martin Luther King Jr. in Berlin.* English version DVD. Hamburg, Ger.: Eikon Nord, 2014.

Rief, John Joseph. "Bioethics and Lifestyle Management: The Theory and Praxis of Personal Responsibility." Master's thesis, University of Pittsburgh, 2013.

R.J.C. and L.C. "Letter from Washington." *Christian Recorder*, May 2, 1863.

Roberts, J. J. M. *The Bible and the Ancient Near East: Collected Essays*. Winona Lake, IN: Eisenbrauns, 2002.

Robinson, Cedric J. *Forgeries of Memory and Meaning: Blacks and the Regimes of Race in American Theater and Film before World War II*. Chapel Hill: University of North Carolina Press, 2007.

Robinson, Dean E. *Black Nationalism in American Politics and Thought*. Cambridge: Cambridge University Press, 2001.

Robinson, John Mansley. *An Introduction to Early Greek Philosophy: The Chief Fragments and Ancient Testimony, with Connecting Commentary*. Boston: Houghton Mifflin, 1968.

Roche, John P. "The Expatriation Cases: Breathes There the Man, with Soul So Dead." *Supreme Court Review*, 1963, 325–56.

Roosevelt, Theodore Roosevelt. "The Strenuous Life." April 10, 1899. Voices of Democracy. https://voicesofdemocracy.umd.edu.

Roosevelt, Theodore, III. *Rank and File: True Stories of the Great War*. New York: Charles Scribner's Sons, 1928.

Ross, Donald L. "Platonist Brahmans? Platonic Metaphors in Refutation of All Heresies 1.24." *Hermathena* Summer, no. 198 (2015): 35–51.

Rosteck, Thomas. "Narrative in Martin Luther King's 'I've Been to the Mountaintop.'" *Southern Communication Journal* 58, no. 1 (1992): 22–32.

Rothstein, Richard. *The Color of Law: A Forgotten History of How Our Government Segregated America*. New York: Liveright Publishing, 2017.

Rountree, John. "Legislation as a Site of Contested Meaning in United States Congressional Debates." Master's thesis, Georgia State University, 2015.

Rowland, Robert C., and John M. Jones. *Reagan at Westminster: Foreshadowing the End of the Cold War*. College Station: Texas A&M University Press, 2010.

Ruberg, Bonnie, Jason Boyd, and James Howe. "Toward a Queer Digital Humanities." In *Bodies of Information: Intersectional Feminism and the Digital Humanities*, edited by Elizabeth Losh and Jacqueline Wernimont, 108–28. Minneapolis: University of Minnesota Press, 2018.

Rushing, Janice Hocker. "The Rhetoric of the American Western Myth." *Communication Monographs* 50, no. 1 (1983): 14–22.

Said, Edward W. *Orientalism*. New York: Vintage Books, 1994.

Saindon, Robert A., ed. *Explorations: Into the World of Lewis & Clark*. Great Falls, MT: Lewis and Clark Trail Heritage Foundation, 2003.

Salafia, Matthew. *Slavery's Borderland: Freedom and Bondage along the Ohio River*. Philadelphia: University of Pennsylvania Press, 2013.

Sanchez, John, and Mary E. Stuckey. "The Rhetoric of American Indian Activism in the 1960s and 1970s." *Communication Quarterly* 48, no. 2 (2000): 120–36. https://doi.org/10.1080/01463370009385586.

Sassoon, Siegfried. *Memoirs of an Infantry Officer*. New York: Coward, McCann, 1930.

Savage, Keith. *Standing Soldiers, Kneeling Slaves: Race, War, and Monument in Nineteenth-Century America*. Princeton, NJ: Princeton University Press, 1970.

Savage, William W. *The Cowboy Hero: His Image in American History & Culture*. 1st ed. Norman: University of Oklahoma Press, 1979.

Saxon, John D. "Contemporary Southern Oratory: A Rhetoric of Hope, Not Desperation," *Southern Speech Communication Journal* 40, no. 3 (1975): 262–74. https://doi.org/10.1080/10417947509372270.

Schares, Evan Mitchell. "The Suicide of Leelah Alcorn: Whiteness in the Cultural Wake of Dying Queers." *QED: A Journal in GLBTQ Worldmaking* 6, no. 1 (2019): 1–25.

Schauer, Frederick. "Why Precedent in Law (and Elsewhere) Is Not Totally (or Even Substantially) about Analogy." *Perspectives on Psychological Science* 3, no. 6 (2008): 454–60.

Schiappa, Edward. *Protagoras and Logos: A Study in Greek Philosophy and Rhetoric.* Columbia: University of South Carolina Press, 1991.

———. *Squeeze Play: The Campaign for a New Twins Stadium*. Minneapolis: Minnesota Public Advocacy Research Report, 1998. https://www.leg.state.mn.us/docs/NonMNpub/oclc40058393.pdf.

Schmöcker, Daniel, and Saraya Gomis. "King-Code ein multimediales Schul-Jugendprojekt." King-Code. Accessed October 9, 2019. https://king-code.de/homeen.htm.

Scott, Robert L., and Donald K. Smith. "The Rhetoric of Confrontation." *Quarterly Journal of Speech* 55, no. 1 (1969): 1–8.

Selby, Gary S. "Framing Social Protest: The Exodus Narrative in Martin Luther King's Montgomery Bus Boycott Rhetoric." *Journal of Communication and Religion* 24, no. 1 (2001): 68–93.

———. *Martin Luther King and the Rhetoric of Freedom: The Exodus Narrative in America's Struggle for Civil Rights*. Waco, TX: Baylor University Press, 2008.

Sell, Andrea J., Angela Naginey, and Cathy Alexander Stanton. "The Impact of Undergraduate Research on Academic Success." *Scholarship and Practice of Undergraduate Research* 1 (2018): 19–29.

Sewanee: The University of the South. Center for Speaking and Listening site. https://new.sewanee.edu/academics/center-for-speaking-listening/.

———. "Learning to Speak, Speaking to Learn: Quality Enhancement Plan." February 23–25, 2016. https://www.sewanee.edu/media/qep/QEP_Jan16_rev-(1).pdf.

———. The Roberson Project on Slavery, Race, and Reconciliation. Accessed September 4, 2020. https://new.sewanee.edu.

———. *Sewanee Catalogue 2019–2020.* http://e-catalog.sewanee.edu/university/purpose/.

Shaub, Jonathan David. "Expatriation Restored." *Harvard Journal on Legislation* 55, no. 2 (2018): 439.

Sheridan, Richard. "From Slavery in Missouri to Freedom in Kansas: The Influx of Black Fugitives and Contrabands into Kansas, 1854–1865." In *Kansas and the West: New Perspectives*, edited by Rita Napier, 164–68. Lawrence: University Press of Kansas, 2003.

Shome, Raka. "Postcolonial Interventions in the Rhetorical Canon: An 'Other' View." *Communication Theory* 6, no. 1 (1996): 40–59.

———. "Thinking Culture and Cultural Studies—from/of the Global South." *Communication and Critical/Cultural Studies* 16, no. 3 (2019): 196–218. https://doi.org/10.1080/14791420.2019.1648841.

Short, Tierney, ed. and trans. "1982 Commencement Address Delivered at Santa Clara University by Ignacio Ellacuria." *Furman Humanities Review* 18 (2007): 33–41.

Showalter, G. H. P. "So-Called Conscientious Objectors." *Firm Foundation*, 1919, 1–6.

Shreveport Chapter #237 of the United Daughters of the Confederacy v. The Caddo Parish Commission. Western District Court of Louisiana. Case 5:17-cv-01346. October 19, 2017. https://www.courtlistener.com/recap/gov.uscourts.lawd.159604/gov.uscourts.lawd.159604.1.

Sillars, Malcolm O. "Defining Movements Rhetorically: Casting the Widest Net." *Southern Speech Communication Journal* 46, no. 1 (1980): 17–32.

Simons, Herbert W. "Requirements, Problems, and Strategies: A Theory of Persuasion for Social Movements." *Quarterly Journal of Speech* 56, no. 1 (1970): 1–11.

Simpkins, Scott. *Literary Semiotics: A Critical Approach*. Lanham, MD: Lexington Books, 2001.

Singleton, Benjamin. Benjamin "Pap" Singleton Scrapbook. Kansas Historical Society. Accessed June 9, 2017. http://www.kansasmemory.org.

Sloane, Thomas O., ed. *Encyclopedia of Rhetoric*. New York: Oxford University Press, 2001.

Slotkin, Richard. *Gunfighter Nation: The Myth of the Frontier in Twentieth-Century America*. New York: Macmillan, 1992.

Smith, Rogers M. *Civic Ideals: Conflicting Visions of Citizenship in US History*. New Haven, CT: Yale University Press, 1997.

———. *Political Peoplehood: The Roles of Values, Interests, and Identities*. Chicago: University of Chicago Press, 2015.

Smith, Stephen A. *Myth, Media, and the Southern Mind*. Fayetteville: University of Arkansas Press, 1985.

———. "Sounds of the South: The Rhetorical Saga of Country Music Lyrics." *Southern Speech Communication Journal* 45, no. 2 (1980): 164–72.

Smylie, James H. "On Jesus, Pharaohs, and the Chosen People: Martin Luther King as Biblical Interpreter and Humanist." *Interpretation* 24, no. 1 (1970): 74–91.

Smyser, W. R. *Kennedy and the Berlin Wall: "A Hell of a Lot Better than a War."* Lanham, MD: Rowman & Littlefield Publishers, 2009.

Snorton, C. Riley, and Jin Haritaworn. "Trans Necropolitics: A Transnational

Reflection on Violence, Death, and the Trans of Color Afterlife." In *Transgender Studies Reader 2*, edited by Susan Stryker and Aren Z. Aizura, 66–76. New York: Routledge, 2013.

Snow, Malinda. "Martin Luther King's 'Letter from Birmingham Jail' as Pauline Epistle." *Quarterly Journal of Speech* 71, no. 3 (1985): 318–34.

Sokol, Jason. *The Heavens Might Crack*. New York: Basic Books, 2018.

Sorensen, Theodore C. *Kennedy*. New York: Harper Perennial Political Classics, 2009.

Soto Vega, Karrieann, and Karma R. Chávez. "Latinx Rhetoric and Intersectionality in Racial Rhetorical Criticism." *Communication and Critical/Cultural Studies* 15, no. 4 (2018): 319–25.

Southern Poverty Law Center. "Neo-Confederate." Accessed September 4, 2020. https://www.splcenter.org/fighting-hate/extremist-files/ideology/neo-confederate.

———. "Whose Heritage? Public Symbols of the Confederacy." February 1, 2019. https://www.splcenter.org/20180604/whose-heritage-public-symbols-confederacy.

"Special Issue: #RhetoricSoWhite." *Quarterly Journal of Speech* 105, no. 4 (2019): 465–507.

Special Notices. "Lecture." *Daily National Republican* (Washington, DC), January 9, 1863. Chronicling America: Historic American Newspapers, Library of Congress. http://chroniclingamerica.loc.gov/lccn/sn86053570/1863-01-09/ed-1/seq-3/.

Spiro, Peter J. "Expatriating Terrorists Symposium: Citizenship, Immigration, and National Security after 9/11." *Fordham Law Review* 82 (2014): 2169–88.

Spivak, Gayatri. "Can the Subaltern Speak?" In *Marxism and the Interpretation of Culture*, edited by Cary Nelson and Lawrence Grossberg, 271–313. Champaign: University of Illinois Press, 1988.

Stam, Robert. *Film Theory: An Introduction*. Malden, MA: Blackwell, 2000.

Stanton, Elizabeth Cady, Susan B. Anthony, and Matilda Joslyn Gage. *History of Woman Suffrage*. 6 vols. New York: Foster and Wells, 1881–1922.

Starr, Douglas P. "Secession Speeches of Four Deep South Governors Who Would Rather Fight than Switch." *Southern Speech Communication Journal* 38, no. 2 (Winter 1972): 131–41.

Steinke, Darcey. *The Gospel According to John*. New York: Grove Press, 1999.

Stephens, Randall J., and Karl Giberson. *The Anointed: Evangelical Truth in a Secular Age*. Cambridge, MA: Belknap Press of Harvard University Press, 2011.

Stern, Mark. "Stephen Breyer Is Worried about the Forever War's Permanent Prisoners. He's 15 Years Too Late." *Slate*, June 10, 2019. https://slate.com.

Stevens, Jacqueline. "The Alien Who Is a Citizen." In *Citizenship in Question: Evidentiary Birthright and Statelessness*, edited by Benjamin N. Lawrance and Jacqueline Stevens, 217–39. Durham, NC: Duke University Press, 2017.

Stevens, Kate. "The Future That Could Have Been: Bayard Rustin, Civil Rights, and Coalition Politics." *Carolinas Communication Annual* 32 (2016): 30–42.

Stillion Southard, Bjørn F. *Peculiar Rhetoric: Slavery, Freedom, and the African Colonization Movement.* Jackson: University Press of Mississippi, 2019.

Stokes, Ashli Quesinberry, and Wendy Atkins-Sayre. *Consuming Identity: The Role of Food in Redefining the South.* Jackson: University Press of Mississippi, 2016.

Stone, Allucquére Rosanne (Sandy). *The War of Desire and Technology at the Close of the Mechanical Age.* Cambridge: Massachusetts Institute of Technology Press, 1995.

Strickland, William M. "The Rhetoric of Removal and the Trail of Tears: Cherokee Speaking against Jackson's Indian Removal Policy, 1828–1832." *Southern Speech Communication Journal* 47, no. 3 (Spring 1982): 292–309.

Stryker, Susan. "My Words to Victor Frankenstein above the Village of Chamounix: Performing Transgender Rage." *GLQ: A Journal of Lesbian and Gay Studies* 1, no. 3 (1994): 227–54.

———. *Transgender History: The Roots of Today's Revolution.* 2nd ed. New York: Seal Press, 2017.

Stryker, Susan, Paisley Currah, and Lisa Jean Moore. "Introduction: Trans-, Trans, or Transgender?" *Women's Studies Quarterly* 36, no. 4 (2008): 11–22.

Stuckey, Mary E., ed. "Forum on Rhetorical Circulation." *Rhetoric & Public Affairs* 15, no. 4 (Winter 2012): 609–94.

———. "Presidential Secrecy: Keeping Archives Open." *Rhetoric & Public Affairs* 9, no. 1 (Spring 2006): 138–44.

———. "Rethinking the Rhetorical Presidency and Presidential Rhetoric." *Review of Communication* 10, no. 1 (January 2010): 38–52.

Suny, Ronald Grigor, and Fatma Müge Göçek. "Introduction: Leaving It to the Historians." In *A Question of Genocide: Armenians and Turks at the End of the Ottoman Empire*, edited by Ronald Grigor Suny, Fatma Müge Göçek, and Norman Naimark, 1–14. New York: Oxford University Press, 2011.

Sustein, Cass. "The Smallest Court in the Land." *New York Times*, July 4, 2004. https://www.nytimes.com.

Swisher, Kara. "Who Killed Tumblr? We All Did." *New York Times*, August 14, 2019. https://www.nytimes.com.

Tarver, Jerry L. "Baptist Preaching from Virginia Jails, 1768–1778." *Southern Speech Journal* 30, no. 2 (Winter 1964): 139–48.

Taylor, Diana. *The Archive and the Repertoire: Performing Cultural Memory in the Americas.* Durham, NC: Duke University Press, 2003.

Taylor, Quintard. *In Search of the Racial Frontier: African Americans in the American West: 1528–1990.* New York: W. W. Norton, 1998.

Teel, Leonard Ray. "The Shaping of a Southern Opinion Leader: Ralph McGill and Freedom of Information." *American Journalism* 5, no. 1 (1988): 14–27.

"Tennessee Town History: From Freedom to the Future." Tennessee Town Neighborhood Improvement Association, History. Updated March 14, 2019. https://tenntownnia.weebly.com.

"Tennessee's War Hero." *New York Times*, July 16, 1922, 1.

Terrill, Robert E. "Ways of Rhetorical History." *Review of Communication* 3, no. 3 (July 2003): 297–300.

Teuwsen, Peer. "'Der meistgehasste Türke'" (The most hated Turk). *Das Magazin*, February 5, 2005. https://web.archive.org/web/20090116123035/http://sc.tagesanzeiger.ch/dyn/news/kultur/560264.html.

Thurman, Scott, dir. *The Revisionaries*. DVD. New York: Kino International, 2012.

Tobiason, Glory. "Countering Expert Uncertainty: Rhetorical Strategies from the Case of Value-Added Modeling in Teacher Evaluation." *Minerva* 57, no. 1 (2019): 109–26.

Toomey, Russell B., Amy K. Syvertson, and Maura Shramko. "Transgender Adolescent Behavior." *Pediatrics* 142, no. 4 (2018): 1–8.

"To the Colored Citizens of the United States." Nicodemus, Graham County, KS, July 2, 1877, Kansas Memory, Kansas Historical Society. https://www.kansasmemory.org/item/208456.

Towns, W. Stuart. *Enduring Legacy: Rhetoric and Ritual of the Lost Cause*. Tuscaloosa: University of Alabama Press, 2012.

———. *Public Address in the Twentieth-Century South: The Evolution of a Region*. Westport, CT: Praeger, 2000.

Townsend, Rebecca. "Trump's Warsaw Address, or How the 'West' Was Widened." *Journal of Contemporary Rhetoric* 8, no. 1/2 (2018): 84–106.

Trop v. Dulles, 356 US 86 (1957).

Turner, Henry McNeal. "For Christian Recorder." *Christian Recorder*, October 18, 1862. Henry McNeal Turner Project, The Writings. https://www.thehenrymcnealturnerproject.org.

———. "Washington Correspondence." *Christian Recorder*, 1862–63. Henry McNeal Turner Project, The Writings. https://www.thehenrymcnealturnerproject.org.

———. (Under the pseudonym "Uncle Sam"). "Washington Correspondence." *Christian Recorder*, June 20, 1863, Henry McNeal Turner Project, The Writings. https://www.thehenrymcnealturnerproject.org.

Turner, Kathleen J., ed. *Doing Rhetorical History: Concepts and Cases*. Tuscaloosa: University of Alabama Press, 1998.

———. "Introduction: Rhetorical History as Social Construction." In Turner, *Doing Rhetorical History*, 1–15.

Tushnet, Mark V. "Following the Rules Laid Down: A Critique of Interpretivism and Neutral Principles." *Harvard Law Review* 96, no. 4 (1983): 781–827.

Twelve Southerners. *I'll Take My Stand: The South and the Agrarian Tradition*. Baton Rouge: Louisiana State University Press, 1978.

Tynan, Mary Virginia. "Cry Deception and Let Loose the Dogs of War: The Rhetorical Ethics of Colin Powell's 'Denial and Deception.'" *Young Scholars in Writing* 3 (2005): 30–37.

Tyus, Jeff. "Untapped Potential: The Role of Faculty and State Associations in

Developing the Undergraduate Researcher." *Ohio Communication Journal* 54 (2016): 11–17.

United Daughters of the Confederacy. Membership. Accessed June 15, 2018. https://www.hqudc.org.

———. "Statement from the President General." Accessed June 7, 2018. https://hqudc.org/.

University of Kansas. The Emmett Till Memory Project, Humanities for All, 2015. https://humanitiesforall.org.

University of Maryland. African American History, Culture and Digital Humanities, About. 2017. https://aadhum.umd.edu/asante/.

———. George Meany Memorial AFL-CIO Archives. Updated July 2021. https://www.lib.umd.edu.

———. Recovering Democracy Archives: Speech Recovery Project. https://recoveringdemocracyarchives.umd.edu/.

Uruş, Alper. "1 milyon Ermeni'yi ve 30 bin Kürt'ü kestik mi?" (Did we slaughter 1 million Armenians and 30 thousand Kurds?). *Vatan*, February 9, 2005. http://haber.gazetevatan.com/Haber/46650/1/Gundem.

US Department of the Interior. National Park Service. *Historic American Landscapes Survey.* Washington, DC: National Archives, 2007, 75–78.

———. *National Register of Historic Places Registration Form.* Section 8, 44. Washington, DC: National Archives, 2001.

———. *National Register of Historic Places Registration Form.* Section 8, 60. Washington, DC: National Archives, 2001.

US Food and Drug Administration. "Frances Oldham Kelsey: Medical Reviewer Famous for Averting a Public Health Tragedy." Updated February 1, 2018. https://www.fda.gov.

Vail, Mark. "The 'Integrative' Rhetoric of Martin Luther King Jr.'s 'I Have a Dream' Speech." *Rhetoric & Public Affairs* 9, no. 1 (2006): 53–55.

van Leeuwen, Theo. "Rhetoric and Semiotics." In *Oxford Handbook of Rhetorical Studies,* edited by Michael J. MacDonald, 673–82. Oxford: Oxford University Press, 2017. https://www.oxfordhandbooks.com.

———. "The Schoolbook as a Multimodal Text." *Internationale Schulbuchforschung* 14, no. 1 (1992): 35–58.

Vance v. Terrazas, 444 US 252 (1980).

Virginia Center for Digital History, Miller Center of Public Affairs. Reshaping the Nation and the Emergence of Modern America: 1877 to 1930s. University of Virginia, Charlottesville, 2005. http://www.vcdh.virginia.edu/solguide/VUS08/vus08a01.html.

Vivian, Bradford. *Public Forgetting: The Rhetoric and Politics of Beginning Again.* University Park: Pennsylvania State University Press, 2010.

Vladeck, Stephen I. "Enemy Aliens, Enemy Property, and Access to the Courts." *Lewis & Clark Law Review* 11, no. 4 (2007): 963–96.

Voices of Democracy: The US Oratory Project. https://voicesofdemocracy.umd.edu/.

Volpp, Leti. "Citizenship Undone." *Fordham Law Review* 75 (2007): 2579.

Von Berg, Ron. "Decades Away or *The Day After Tomorrow?* Rhetoric, Film, and the Global Warming Debate." *Critical Studies in Media Communication* 29, no. 1 (2012): 7–26.

Wagner, Russell H. "Negro Orators and Their Orations." *Quarterly Journal of Speech Education* 12, no. 4 (1926): 379–82.

Walcott, Charles, and Karen M. Hult. "White House Structure and Decision Making: Elaborating the Standard Model." *Presidential Studies Quarterly* 35, no 2 (June 2005): 303–18.

Waldman, Katy. "Guardians of White Innocence." *Slate Magazine*, September 25, 2017. https://slate.com.

———. "Rotten Monuments: Donald Trump Has a Lot in Common with the Antiquated, Racist Confederate Statues He Defends." *Slate Magazine*, August 15, 2017. http://www.slate.com/.

Walker, David. *David Walker's Appeal to the Coloured Citizens of the World.* Edited by Peter P. Hinks. University Park: Pennsylvania State University Press, 2002.

Walker, Kenneth C. "Mapping the Contours of Translation: Visualized Un/Certainties in the Ozone Hole Controversy." *Technical Communication Quarterly* 25, no. 2 (2016): 104–20.

Walker, Kenny, and Lynda Walsh. "'No One Yet Knows What the Ultimate Consequences May Be': How Rachel Carson Transformed Scientific Uncertainty into a Site for Public Participation in *Silent Spring.*" *Journal of Business and Technical Communication* 26, no. 1 (2012): 3–34.

Wallace, Foy E. "The Christian and the Government." *Bible Banner* 4, no. 8 (1942): 6.

Walt, Stephen N. "The Case for Finite Containment: Analyzing US Grand Strategy." *International Security* 14, no. 1 (Summer 1989): 5–49.

Walters, Caroline. "A Response to Sarah-Kate Magee." *Young Scholars in Writing: Undergraduate Research in Writing and Rhetoric* 11 (2014): 96–98.

Walzer, Michael. *Exodus and Revolution.* New York: Basic Books, 1985.

Wander, Philip C. "The Rhetoric of American Foreign Policy." *Quarterly Journal of Speech* 70, no. 4 (1984): 339–61.

———. "The Savage Child: The Image of the Negro in the Pro-Slavery Movement." *Southern Speech Communication Journal* 37 (Summer 1972): 335–60.

Wanzer, Darrel Allan. "Delinking Rhetoric, or Revisiting McGee's Fragmentation Thesis through Decoloniality." *Rhetoric & Public Affairs* 15, no. 4 (2012): 647–58.

Wanzer-Serrano, Darrel. "Rhetoric's Race/ist Problems." *Quarterly Journal of Speech* 105, no. 4 (2019): 465–76.

Ware, B. L., and Wil A. Linkugel. "They Spoke in Defense of Themselves: On the Generic Criticism of Apologia." *Quarterly Journal of Speech* 59, no. 3 (1973): 273–83.

Warner, Michael. "Publics and Counterpublics." *Public Culture* 14, no. 1 (2002): 49–90.

Warren, Calvin L. *Ontological Terror: Blackness, Nihilism, and Emancipation.* Durham, NC: Duke University Press, 2018.

Warren, Earl. Papers. Library of Congress, Washington DC Manuscript/Mixed Material. https://lccn.loc.gov/mm82052258

Washington, Booker T. "Address by Booker T. Washington, Principal Tuskegee Normal and Industrial Institute, Tuskegee, Alabama, at Opening of Atlanta Exposition." September 18, 1895. Library of Congress. https://memory.loc.gov/mss/mssmisc/ody/ody0605/0605001v.jpg.

Waterfield, Robin. *The First Philosophers*. Oxford: Oxford University Press, 2000.

Watts, Eric King. "'Voice' and 'Voicelessness' in Rhetorical Studies." *Quarterly Journal of Speech* 87, no. 2 (2001): 179–96.

Watts, Geoff. "Obituary: Frances Oldham Kelsey." *Lancet* 386 (October 3, 2015): 1334.

Watts, Rebecca Bridges. *Contemporary Southern Identity: Community through Controversy*. Jackson: University Press of Mississippi, 2007.

Waxman, Olivia B. "What Martin Luther King Jr. Said about Walls during His 1964 Visit to Berlin." *Time*, January 28, 2019. https://time.com.

Weaver, Richard. "Language Is Sermonic." In *Language Is Sermonic*, edited by Richard L. Johannesen, Rennard Strickland, and Ralph T. Eubanks, 201–25. Baton Rouge: Louisiana State University Press, 1970.

Weblowsky, R. J. Zwi, and Geoffrey Wigoder, eds. *The Oxford Dictionary of the Jewish Religion*. Oxford: Oxford University Press, 1997.

Weil, Patrick. *The Sovereign Citizen: Denaturalization and the Origins of the American Republic*. Philadelphia: University of Pennsylvania Press, 2013.

Weisberg, David B. *Leaders and Legacies in Assyriology and Bible: The Collected Essays of David B. Weisberg*. Winona Lake, IN: Eisenbrauns, 2012.

Welter, Barbara. "The Cult of True Womanhood." *American Quarterly* 18, no. 2 (1966): 151–74.

West, Martin L. *The East Face of Helicon: West Asiatic Elements in Greek Poetry and Myth*. New York: Clarendon Press, 1997.

Whidden, Rachel Avon. "The Manufacturing of Controversy: Debating Intelligent Design in Public." In *Critical Problems in Argumentation: Selected Papers from the Thirteenth NCA/AFA Conference on Argumentation*, edited by Charles Willard, 705–10. Washington, DC: National Communication Association, 2005.

White, Armond. "*The Dead Don't Die*: Climate-Change Comedy for the Alexandria Ocasio-Cortez Era." Review of *The Dead Don't Die*. *National Review*, June 14, 2019. https://www.nationalreview.com.

White, Hayden. *Metahistory: The Historical Imagination in Nineteenth-Century Europe*. Baltimore: Johns Hopkins University Press, 1973.

———. "The Value of Narrativity in the Representation of Reality." *Critical Inquiry* 7, no. 1 (1980): 5–27.

White, James Boyd. *Heracles' Bow: Essays on the Rhetoric and Poetics of the Law*. Madison: University of Wisconsin Press, 1989.

Whitehead, Andrew L., Samuel L. Perry, and Joseph O. Baker. "Make America Christian Again: Christian Nationalism and Voting for Donald Trump in the 2016 Presidential Election." *Sociology of Religion* 79, no. 2 (2018): 147–71.

Whitted, Rachel. "The Sacred and the Profane: An Analysis of the Rhetoric in David Brower's Campaign to Save the Grand Canyon." *Young Scholars in Writing: Undergraduate Research in Writing and Rhetoric* 11 (2014): 73–79.

W.H.M. "Washington Correspondence." *Christian Recorder,* April 4, 1863.

Wilderson, Frank B., III. *Red, White, and Black: Cinema and the Structure of U.S. Antagonisms.* Durham, NC: Duke University Press, 2010.

Williams, Raymond. *The Country and the City.* New York: Oxford University Press, 1973.

Wilsey, John D. *One Nation under God? An Evangelical Critique of Christian America.* Eugene, OR: Pickwick Publications, 2011.

Wilson, Charles Reagan. *Baptized in Blood: The Religion of the Lost Cause, 1865– 1920.* Athens: University of Georgia Press, 1980.

Wilson, Woodrow. "Necessity of War against Germany." In *Selected Addresses and Public Papers of Woodrow Wilson.* Edited by Albert Bushnell Hart, 196. New York: Boni & Liveright, 1917.

Winberry, John J. "'Lest We Forget': The Confederate Monument and the Southern Townscape." *Southeastern Geographer* 23, no. 2 (1983): 107–21.

Wrage, Ernest J. "Public Address: A Study in Social and Intellectual History." *Quarterly Journal of Speech* 33, no. 4 (1947): 451–57.

Yavuz, M. Hakan. "Cleansing Islam from the Public Sphere." *Journal of International Affairs* 54, no. 1 (2000): 21–42.

Yeğen, Mesut. "The Kurdish Question in Turkey: Denial to Recognition." In *Nationalisms and Politics in Turkey: Political Islam, Kemalism, and the Kurdish Issue,* edited by Marlies Casier and Joost Jongerden, 67–84. New York: Routledge, 2011.

York, Alvin Cullum, and Thomas John Skeyhill. *Sergeant York, His Own Life Story and War Diary.* Garden City, NY: Doubleday, 1928.

Young, Robert J. C. *White Mythologies: Writing History and the West.* 2nd ed. New York: Routledge, 2004.

Young Scholars in Writing. "About the Journal." Accessed September 4, 2020. https://youngscholarsinwriting.org.

Zagacki, Kenneth S., and Victoria J. Gallagher. "Rhetoric and Materiality in the Museum Park at the North Carolina Museum of Art." *Quarterly Journal of Speech* 95 no. 2 (2009): 171–91.

Zarefsky, David. "Four Senses of Rhetorical History." In Turner, *Doing Rhetorical History,* 19–32.

Zuckerman, Ian. "Hoda Muthana and Trump's Assault on Birthright Citizenship." *Guardian,* March 1, 2019. https://www.theguardian.com/commentisfree /2019/mar/01/hoda-muthana-trump-birthright-citizenship-isis.

Contributors

Andrew D. Barnes is instructor of advocacy studies in the School of Communication at James Madison University. His scholarship is situated at the intersection of presidential rhetoric, diplomacy, and rhetorical history. He is interested in how cosmopolitan appeals facilitate cross-cultural bonds with US presidents. In previous work, he has examined presidential speech at the United Nations General Assembly.

Jason Edward Black is professor of communication studies at the University of North Carolina, Charlotte. His research centers on rhetoric and social change, with an emphasis on Indigenous justice, LGBTQIA2S activism, and Black liberation. He is the coauthor of *Mascot Nation: The Controversy over Native American Representations in Sports* (University of Illinois Press, 2018) and the author of *American Indians and the Rhetoric of Removal and Allotment* (University Press of Mississippi, 2015). He is also coeditor of *Decolonizing Native American Rhetoric: Communicating Self-Determination* (Peter Lang, 2018), *An Archive of Hope: Harvey Milk's Speeches and Writings* (University of California Press, 2013), and *Arguments about Animal Ethics* (Lexington Books, 2010). His work has appeared in *American Indian Quarterly, American Indian Culture & Research Journal, Quarterly Journal of Speech, Rhetoric & Public Affairs,* and *Argumentation & Advocacy,* among other outlets. Black served as the 2020 Fulbright Research Chair in Transnational Studies at Brock University's Centre for Canadian Studies.

Bryan Crable is professor of communication/rhetorical studies and founding director of the Waterhouse Family Institute for the Study of Communication and Society at Villanova University. In addition to numerous articles and chapters on rhetorical theory and rhetorics of race, Dr. Crable is the author of *Ralph Ellison and Kenneth Burke: At the Roots of the Racial Divide* (University of Virginia Press, 2012) and the editor of *Transcendence by Perspective: Meditations on and with Kenneth Burke* (Parlor Press, 2014). His scholarship has twice earned the Charles Kneupper Award from the Rhetoric Society of America, as well as a Lifetime Achievement Award from the Kenneth Burke Society. His current book project, *White Sacraments* (forthcoming with Ohio State

University Press), demonstrates the theoretical and critical potential of rhetorical history. Drawing upon archival materials from both Ralph Ellison and Jane Ellen Harrison, he recasts American white supremacy as a sacramental ritual structure and practice.

Adrienne E. Hacker Daniels is the A. Boyd Pixley Professor of Humanities and professor of communication and rhetorical studies at Illinois College. Her research includes the study of the relationship between rhetorical and poetic theory with an emphasis on the rhetorical dimensions of more aesthetically grounded artifacts. She has published essays on Thornton Wilder, Gertrude Stein, W. H. Auden, Maurice Schwartz, and Hallie Flanagan. Her book chapters include an essay on WikiLeaks in *Regulating Social Media: Legal and Ethical Considerations* (Peter Lang, 2013) and an essay on interfaith dialogue in *A Communication Perspective on Interfaith Dialogue: Living within the Abrahamic Traditions* (Lexington Books, 2013). In 2016, she published an edited volume, *Communication and the Global Landscape of Faith* (Lexington Books). Her work on the First Amendment is represented in *First Amendment Studies* and book chapters in *Urban Communication Reader IV: Cities as Communicative Change Agents* (Peter Lang, 2021) and *Equal Protection v. Religious Freedom: Clashing American Rights* (Peter Lang, 2022). She is currently working on an essay about the American playwright Thornton Wilder.

Matthew deTar is assistant professor of rhetoric and culture at Ohio University. He is the author of *Figures That Speak: The Vocabulary of Turkish Nationalism* (Syracuse University Press, 2021). His work has appeared in *Communication and Critical/Cultural Studies*, *Rhetoric & Public Affairs*, *Journal of Contemporary Thought*, *Advances in the History of Rhetoric*, and *Departures in Critical Qualitative Inquiry*. His research has been supported by the Center for Religion, Law, and Democracy at Willamette University, the Institute for Turkish Studies at Georgetown University, and the Buffett Institute for Global Affairs at Northwestern University.

Margaret Franz is assistant professor of communication, media, and culture at the University of Tampa. She researches legal communication as it relates to race, coloniality, and national belonging. Her current project investigates the evolution of citizenship status in the United States by analyzing how official methods of interpretation coevolve with and respond to vernacular legal cultures that challenge state authority to define and enforce citizenship status. Her scholarship has appeared in *Social Identities*, *First Amendment Studies*, *Advances in the History of Rhetoric*, and *Communication and Critical/Cultural Studies*. With Kumarini Silva she edited the anthology *Migration, Identity, and Belonging: Borders and Boundaries of the Homeland* (Routledge, 2020).

Joe Edward Hatfield is assistant professor in the Department of Communication at the University of Arkansas. Hatfield studies the rhetoric of gender and sexuality, with a focus on how these markers of identity are culturally and technologically mediated in public. Hatfield's scholarship is published in *Communication, Culture & Critique*; *Rhetoric Society Quarterly*; *Text and Performance Quarterly*; and the edited collection *Queering the South on Screen* (University of Georgia Press, 2020). Hatfield is the recipient of the 2020 Charles Kneupper Award, an annual honor recognizing the most significant contribution to scholarship in rhetoric published in the latest volume of *Rhetoric Society Quarterly*.

J. Michael Hogan is the Edwin Erle Sparks Professor Emeritus of Rhetoric and the founding director of the Center for Democratic Deliberation at the Pennsylvania State University. He has served as a scholarly advisor to the National Constitution Center and is codirector of Voices of Democracy, an NEH-funded educational website. Hogan is the author, coauthor, or editor of eight books and more than seventy articles, book chapters, and reviews. He has won a number of scholarly awards, including the National Communication Association's Distinguished Scholar Award. Before moving to Penn State in 1997, he taught at the University of Virginia, Indiana University, and the University of Wisconsin-Madison.

Andre E. Johnson is associate professor of communication and the Scholar in Residence at the Benjamin L. Hooks Institute for Social Change at the University of Memphis. His scholarship focuses on the intersection of rhetoric, race, and religion, African American rhetoric and public address, social movements, and rhetorical history. Dr. Johnson is the author of *The Forgotten Prophet: Bishop Henry McNeal Turner and the African American Prophetic Tradition* (Lexington Books, 2012), the coauthor (with Amanda Nell Edgar, PhD) of *The Struggle over Black Lives Matter and All Lives Matter* (Lexington Books, 2018), and the author of *No Future in this Country: The Prophetic Pessimism of Bishop Henry McNeal Turner* (University Press of Mississippi, 2020).

Madison A. Krall is a PhD candidate in the Department of Communication at the University of Utah. Her scholarship explores how rhetorical norms and practices are related to public perceptions of science, health, and the body. Her coauthored chapter titled "The Zika Virus, Ebola Contagion Narratives and US Obsessions with Securitizing Neglected Infectious Diseases" is part of the edited collection *Embodying Contagion* (University of Wales Press, 2021), and she has coauthored articles appearing in journals such as *Quarterly Journal of Speech* and *Health Communication*. Krall teaches rhetoric and health communication courses and is currently completing a major project on the rhetoric surrounding the thalidomide disaster.

Melody Lehn is assistant professor of rhetoric and women's and gender studies at Sewanee: The University of the South, where she is also assistant director of the Center for Speaking and Listening. She writes at the intersection of rhetoric, politics, gender, and religion and has coedited two books: *Rhetoric: Concord and Controversy* with Antonio de Velasco (Waveland Press, 2012) and *Rhetoric, Race, Religion, and the Charleston Shootings: Was Blind but Now I See* with Sean Patrick O'Rourke (Lexington Books, 2020). Her articles and reviews have appeared in *Rhetoric & Public Affairs*, *Women & Language*, the *Carolinas Communication Annual*, and several edited collections. An award-winning teacher, she has most recently received the Dwight L. Freshley Award for Excellence in Early Career Teaching from the Southern States Communication Association in 2018 and the College Excellence in Teaching Award at Sewanee in 2019.

Lisbeth A. Lipari is professor in the Department of Communication at Denison University. With over thirty-five publications, Lipari's work explores dialogical, ethical, and rhetorical dimensions of language from historical and philosophical perspectives. Her book *Listening, Thinking, Being: Toward an Ethics of Attunement* (Pennsylvania State University Press, 2014) received the top book award from NCA's Ethics Division in 2015 and the Philosophy of Communication Division in 2016. She is currently at work on a prequel to this book tentatively titled *The Hidden Word*.

Chandra A. Maldonado is adjunct assistant professor at Saint Augustine's University, where she enjoys teaching communication and media studies courses. Her primary research focuses on methodological approaches to memory and commemorative practices and visual rhetoric. This work has been published in multiple peer-reviewed venues such as *Rhetoric & Public Affairs*, *Trespassing Journal*, and *Rhetoric Society Quarterly*. Her most recent work focuses on the rhetoric of new age spirituality. She is also a certified shaman, reiki master teacher, and hypnotherapist.

Roseann M. Mandziuk is University Distinguished Professor in the Department of Communication Studies at Texas State University. Her research focuses upon images of women, the rhetorical uses of history, and the construction of public memory. She is coauthor of *Sojourner Truth: Wit, Story, and Song* (Greenwood Press, 1997), has published essays and book chapters examining historical and contemporary rhetoric, and served as editor of *Women's Studies in Communication*. A recipient of two Fulbright Scholar Awards, in India and in Poland, she also is a past president of the Southern States Communication Association and part of the presidential rotation of the National Communication Association. Her contributions have been recognized with national and regional professional association awards including the Michael M. Osborn Teacher-Scholar Award and the Francine Merritt Award for Contributions to Women in Communication.

Christina L. Moss is assistant professor of rhetoric at the University of Memphis. She teaches courses in rhetorical criticism, gender, and commemoration. Her research interests include southern rhetoric, public memory, southern culture, visual rhetoric, gender, and race. She has published in *Rhetoric Review, Howard Journal of Communications*, and *Southern Communication Journal*. She is coeditor with Brandon Inabinet of *Reconstructing Southern Rhetoric* (University Press of Mississippi, 2021) and is currently working on a book, also for the University Press of Mississippi, about the commemoration of the role of Selma, Alabama, in the freedom rights movement.

Christopher J. Oldenburg (PhD, University of Memphis) is associate professor of communication and rhetorical studies at Illinois College. His research interests include the rhetoric of the Catholic Church, Pope Francis, social justice, and American political discourse. Oldenburg's work has appeared in the *KB Journal* (Kenneth Burke Journal), *Communication Studies, Southern Communication Journal, Presidential Studies Quarterly*, and *Advances in the History of Rhetoric*. His book chapters include essays on the rhetoric of Pope Francis in *Communication and the Global Landscape of Faith* (Lexington Books, 2016) and in *Water, Rhetoric, and Social Justice* (Lexington Books, 2020). He is the author of *The Rhetoric of Pope Francis: Critical Mercy and Conversion for the Twenty-First Century* (Lexington Books, 2018) for which he was the recipient of the Religious Communication Association Book of the Year Award in 2019. He is currently working on an essay about Pope Francis, immigration, and the stylistic synthesis of the theological and rhetorical pastoral.

Sean Patrick O'Rourke is professor of rhetoric and American studies at Sewanee: The University of the South, where he also serves as chair of the Rhetoric Department and director of the Center for Speaking and Listening. He writes on rhetoric, rights, and protest, with a special interest in the period between 1948 and 1973. He is coeditor of three books: *Rhetoric, Race, Religion, and the Charleston Shootings: Was Blind but Now I See* (with Melody Lehn, Lexington Press, 2020); *Like Wildfire: The Rhetoric of the Civil Rights Sit-Ins* (with Lesli K. Pace, University of South Carolina Press, 2020); and *On Fire: Five Civil Rights Sit-Ins and the Rhetoric of Protest* (with Lesli K. Pace, University of South Carolina Press, 2021). A former president of the American Society for the History of Rhetoric, O'Rourke has held NEH, Lilly, Cothran, Brown, and Piper fellowships and has won awards for his teaching, scholarship, service, and mentoring.

Daniel P. Overton is assistant professor of communication in Seaver College at Pepperdine University. His research often considers issues of rhetorical history, particularly surrounding religion, nonviolence, and/or socialism. His work has been published in *Rhetorica* and the *Journal of Communication and Religion*, among other places, and he was previously awarded the Southern States Robert N. Bostrom Young Scholar Award. He considers the predecessor to this volume a major academic influence and, as such, is particularly grateful to be included in this one.

Shawn J. Parry-Giles is professor of the Department of Communication at the University of Maryland, College Park. She is also the director of the Rosenker Center for Political Communication and Civic Leadership at the University of Maryland. She studies rhetoric and politics with a focus on the presidency and the first lady. She is the author, coauthor, or coeditor of seven books, including *Memories of Lincoln and the Splintering of American Political Thought* (Pennsylvania State University Press, 2017); *Hillary Clinton in the News: Gender and Authenticity in American Politics* (University of Illinois Press, 2014); and *The Rhetorical Presidency, Propaganda, and the Cold War, 1945–1955* (Praeger, 2002). She also is coeditor of the NEH-funded Voices of Democracy: The U.S. Oratory Project and Recovering Democracy Archives: Speech Recovery Project. She teaches classes in US public address, presidential rhetoric, politics and media, and deliberative democracy.

Philip Perdue is assistant professor of English and communication studies, and director of communication studies at Presbyterian College. His scholarship addresses the relationship between Christian nationalism, rhetoric, and visual pedagogy. He is editor and contributing writer at Reading the Pictures, a nonprofit media organization focused on the analysis of news images and political narratives.

Kathleen J. Turner is professor emerita of communication studies at Davidson College. Her scholarship focuses on communication as a process of social influence, particularly in the areas of media, politics, popular culture, and women's issues. She edited this volume's predecessor, *Doing Rhetorical History: Concepts and Cases* (University of Alabama Press, 1998). Author of *Lyndon Johnson's Dual War: Vietnam and the Press*, the first book in communication to be published by the University of Chicago Press (1985), and coauthor of both *Public Speaking: Finding Your Voice* (Pearson, 2014) and *Communication Centers: A Theory-Based Guide to Training and Management* (Lexington Books, 2015), she has also written numerous articles, chapters, reviews, and monographs. Former president of the National Communication Association, she prizes her NCA Eckroyd Award for Outstanding Teaching in Higher Education, her Michael Osborn Teacher-Scholar Award from the Southern States Communication Association, and her three times as Scholar in Residence for the Hope Conference, also known as the NCA Institute for Faculty Development.

Index

Page numbers in italics refer to figures and tables.